Sister Marjorie,

We're so happy to be able
to celebrate with you the
25ᵀʰ anniversary of your
Profession of vows.

With Love,
Theresa, Joe, John

The
INSPIRATIONAL
WRITINGS of
C. S. LEWIS

Surprised by Joy

Reflections on the Psalms

The Four Loves

The Business of Heaven

The
INSPIRATIONAL
WRITINGS of
C.S. LEWIS

Surprised by Joy

Reflections on the Psalms

The Four Loves

The Business of Heaven

Published in 1991 by

Inspirational Press
A division of LDAP, Inc.
386 Park Avenue South
New York, NY 10016

Inspirational Press is a registered trademark of LDAP, Inc.
By arrangement with Harcourt Brace Jovanovich Inc.

Library of Congress Catalog Card Number: 87-81312
ISBN: 0-88486-047-7

Printed in the United States of America

CONTENTS

The INSPIRATIONAL WRITINGS of C.S. LEWIS

Surprised by Joy

Reflections on the Psalms

The Four Loves

The Business of Heaven

Surprised By Joy
The Shape of My Early Life

Surprised by joy — impatient as the wind
— WORDSWORTH

PREFACE

This book is written partly in answer to requests that I would tell how I passed from Atheism to Christianity and partly to correct one or two false notions that seem to have got about. How far the story matters to anyone but myself depends on the degree to which others have experienced what I call "joy." If it is at all common, a more detailed treatment of it than has (I believe) been attempted before may be of some use. I have been emboldened to write of it because I notice that a man seldom mentions what he had supposed to be his own most idiosyncratic sensations without receiving from at least one (often more) of those present the reply, "What! Have *you* felt that too? I always thought I was the only one."

The book aims at telling the story of my conversion and is not a general autobiography, still less "Confessions" like those of St. Augustine or Rousseau. This means in practice that it gets less like a general autobiography as it goes on. In the earlier chapters the net has to be spread pretty wide in order that, when the explicitly spiritual crisis arrives, the reader may understand what sort of person my childhood and adolescence had made me. When the "build-up" is complete, I confine myself strictly to business and omit everything (however important by ordinary biographical standards) which seems, at that stage, irrelevant. I do not think there is much loss; I never read an autobiography in which the parts devoted to the earlier years were not far the most interesting.

The story is, I fear, suffocatingly subjective; the kind of thing I have never written before and shall probably never write again. I have tried so to write the first chapter that those who can't bear such a story will see at once what they are in for and close the book with the least waste of time.

I

THE FIRST YEARS

Happy, but for so happy ill secured.
MILTON

I was born in the winter of 1898 at Belfast, the son of a solicitor and of a clergyman's daughter. My parents had only two children, both sons, and I was the younger by about three years. Two very different strains had gone to our making. My father belonged to the first generation of his family that reached professional station. His grandfather had been a Welsh farmer; his father, a self-made man, had begun life as a workman, emigrated to Ireland, and ended as a partner in the firm of Macilwaine and Lewis, "Boiler-makers, Engineers, and Iron Ship Builders." My mother was a Hamilton with many generations of clergymen, lawyers, sailors, and the like behind her; on her mother's side, through the Warrens, the blood went back to a Norman knight whose bones lie at Battle Abbey. The two families from which I spring were as different in temperament as in origin. My father's people were true Welshmen, sentimental, passionate, and rhetorical, easily moved both to anger and to tenderness; men who laughed and cried a great deal and who had not much of the talent for happiness. The Hamiltons were a cooler race. Their minds were critical and ironic and they had the talent for happiness in a high degree — went straight for it as experienced travelers go for the best seat in a train. From my earliest years I was aware of the vivid contrast between my mother's cheerful and tranquil affection and the ups and downs of my father's emotional life, and this bred in me long before I was old enough to give it a name a certain distrust or dislike of emotion as something uncomfortable and embarrassing and even dangerous.

Both my parents, by the standards of that time and place, were bookish or "clever" people. My mother had been a promising mathematician in her youth and a B.A. of Queen's College, Belfast, and before her death was able to start me both in French and Latin. She was a voracious reader of good novels, and I think the Merediths and Tolstoys which I have inherited were bought for her. My father's tastes were quite different. He was fond of oratory and had himself spoken on political platforms in England as a young man; if he had had independent means he would certainly have aimed

4

at a political career. In this, unless his sense of honor, which was fine to the point of being Quixotic, had made him unmanageable, he might well have succeeded, for he had many of the gifts once needed by a Parliamentarian — a fine presence, a resonant voice, great quickness of mind, eloquence, and memory. Trollope's political novels were very dear to him; in following the career of Phineas Finn he was, as I now suppose, vicariously gratifying his own desires. He was fond of poetry provided it had elements of rhetoric or pathos, or both; I think *Othello* was his favorite Shakespearean play. He greatly enjoyed nearly all humorous authors, from Dickens to W. W. Jacobs, and was himself, almost without rival, the best *raconteur* I have ever heard; the best, that is, of his own type, the type that acts all the characters in turn with a free use of grimace, gesture, and pantomime. He was never happier than when closeted for an hour or so with one or two of my uncles exchanging "wheezes" (as anecdotes were oddly called in our family). What neither he nor my mother had the least taste for was that kind of literature to which my allegiance was given the moment I could choose books for myself. Neither had ever listened for the horns of elfland. There was no copy either of Keats or Shelley in the house, and the copy of Coleridge was never (to my knowledge) opened. If I am a romantic my parents bear no responsibility for it. Tennyson, indeed, my father liked, but it was the Tennyson of *In Memoriam* and *Locksley Hall*. I never heard from him of the *Lotus Eaters* or the *Morte d'Arthur*. My mother, I have been told, cared for no poetry at all.

In addition to good parents, good food, and a garden (which then seemed large) to play in, I began life with two other blessings. One was our nurse, Lizzie Endicott, in whom even the exacting memory of childhood can discover no flaw — nothing but kindness, gaiety, and good sense. There was no nonsense about "lady nurses" in those days. Through Lizzie we struck our roots into the peasantry of County Down. We were thus free of two very different social worlds. To this I owe my lifelong immunity from the false identification which some people make of refinement with virtue. From before I can remember I had understood that certain jokes could be shared with Lizzie which were impossible in the drawing room; and also that Lizzie was, as nearly as a human can be, simply good.

The other blessing was my brother. Though three years my senior, he never seemed to be an elder brother: we were allies, not to say confederates, from the first. Yet we were very different. Our earliest pictures (and I can remember no time when we were not incessantly drawing) reveal it. His were of ships and trains and battles; mine, when not imitated from his, were of what we both called "dressed animals" — the anthropomorphized beasts of nursery literature. His earliest story — as my elder he preceded me in the transition from drawing to writing — was called *The Young Rajah*. He had already made India "his country"; Animal-Land was mine. I do not think any of the surviving drawings date from the first six years of my life which I am now describing, but I have plenty of them that cannot be much later. From them it appears to me that I had the better talent. From a very early age I could draw movement — figures that looked as if they were really running or fighting — and the perspective is good. But nowhere, either in my brother's work or my own, is there a single line drawn in obedience to an idea, however crude, of beauty. There is action, comedy, invention; but there is not even the germ of a feeling for design, and there is a shocking ignorance of natural form. Trees appear as balls of cotton wool stuck on posts, and there is nothing to show that either of us knew the shape of any leaf in the garden where we played almost daily. This absence of beauty, now that I come to think of it, is characteristic of our childhood. No picture on the walls of my father's house ever attracted — and indeed none deserved — our attention. We never saw a beautiful building nor imagined that a building could be beautiful. My earliest aesthetic experiences, if indeed they were aesthetic, were not of that kind; they were already incurably romantic, not formal. Once in those very early days my brother brought into the nursery the lid of a biscuit tin which he had covered with moss and garnished with twigs and flowers so as to make it a toy garden or a toy forest. That was the first beauty I ever knew. What the real garden had failed to do, the toy garden did. It made me aware of nature — not, indeed, as a storehouse of forms and colors but as something cool, dewy, fresh, exuberant. I do not think the impression was very important at the moment, but it soon became important in memory. As long as I live my imagination of Paradise will retain something of my brother's toy garden. And every day there were what we called "the Green Hills"; that is, the low line of the Castlereagh Hills which we saw from the nursery windows. They were not very far off but they were, to children, quite unattainable. They taught me longing — *Sehnsucht*; made me for good or ill, and before I was six years old, a votary of the Blue Flower.

If aesthetic experiences were rare, religious experiences did not occur at all. Some people have got the impression from my books that I was brought up in strict and vivid Puritanism, but this is quite untrue. I was taught the usual things and made to say my prayers and in due time taken to church. I naturally accepted what I was told but I cannot remember feeling much interest in it. My father, far from being specially Puritanical, was, by nineteenth-century and Church of Ireland standards, rather "high," and his approach to religion, as to literature, was at the opposite pole from what later became my own. The charm of tradition and the verbal beauty of Bible and Prayer Book (all of them for me late and acquired tastes) were his natural delight, and it would have been hard to find an equally intelligent man who cared so little for metaphysics. Of my mother's religion I can say almost nothing from my own memory. My childhood, at all events, was not in the least other-worldly. Except for the toy garden and the Green Hills it was not even imaginative; it lives in my memory mainly as a period of humdrum, prosaic happiness and awakes none of the poignant nostalgia with which I look back on my much less happy boyhood. It is not settled happiness but momentary joy that glorifies the past.

To this general happiness there was one exception. I remember nothing earlier than the terror of certain dreams. It is a very common trouble at that age, yet it still seems to me odd that petted and guarded childhood should so often have in it a window opening on what is hardly less than Hell. My bad dreams were of two kinds, those about specters and those about insects. The second were, beyond comparison, the worse; to this day I would rather meet a ghost than a tarantula. And to this day I could almost find it in my heart to rationalize and justify my phobia. As Owen Barfield once said to me. "The trouble about insects is that they are like French locomotives – they have all the works on the outside." *The works* – that is the trouble. Their angular limbs, their jerky movements, their dry, metallic noises, all suggest either machines that have come to life or life degenerating into mechanism. You may add that in the hive and the anthill we see fully realized the two things that some of us most dread for our own species – the dominance of the female and the dominance of the collective. One fact about the history of this phobia is perhaps worth recording. Much later, in my teens, from reading Lubbock's *Ants, Bees and Wasps,* I developed for a short time a genuinely scientific interest in insects. Other studies soon crowded it out; but while my entomological period lasted my fear almost vanished, and I am inclined to think a real objective curiosity will usually have this cleansing effect.

I am afraid the psychologists will not be content to explain my insect fears by what a simpler generation would diagnose as their cause – a certain detestable picture in one of my nursery books. In it a midget child, a sort of Tom Thumb, stood on a toadstool and was threatened from below by a stag beetle very much larger than himself. This was bad enough; but there is worse to come. The horns of the beetle were strips of cardboard separate from the plate and working on a pivot. By moving a devilish contraption on the *verso* you could make them open and shut like pincers: snip-snap – snip-snap – I can see it while I write. How a woman ordinarily so wise as my mother could have allowed this abomination into the nursery is difficult to understand. Unless, indeed (for now a doubt assails me), unless that picture itself is a product of nightmare. But I think not.

In 1905, my seventh year, the first great change in my life took place. We moved house. My father, growing, I suppose, in prosperity, decided to leave the semidetached villa in which I had been born and build himself a much larger house, further out into what was then the country. The "New House," as we continued for years to call it, was a large one even by my present standards; to a child it seemed less like a house than a city. My father, who had more capacity for being cheated than any man I have ever known, was badly cheated by his builders; the drains were wrong, the chimneys were wrong, and there was a draft in every room. None of this, however, mattered to a child. To me, the important thing about the move was that the background of my life became larger. The New House is almost a major character in my story. I am a product of long corridors, empty sunlit rooms, upstairs indoor silences, attics explored in solitude, distant noises of gurgling cisterns and pipes, and the noise of wind under the tiles. Also, of endless books. My father bought all the books he read and never got rid of any of them. There were books in the study, books in the drawing room, books in the cloakroom, books (two deep) in the great bookcase on the landing, books in a bedroom, books piled as high as my shoulder in the cistern attic, books of all kinds reflecting every transient stage of my parents' interest, books readable and unreadable, books suitable for a child and books most emphatically not. Nothing was forbidden me. In the seemingly endless rainy afternoons I took volume after volume from the shelves. I had always the same certainty of finding a book that was new to me as a man who walks into a field has of finding a new blade of grass. Where all these books had been before we came to the New House is a problem that never occurred to me until I began writing this paragraph. I have no idea of the answer.

Out of doors was "the view" for which, no doubt, the site had principally been chosen. From our front door we looked down over wide fields to Belfast Lough and across it to the long mountain line of Antrim shore—Divis, Colin, Cave Hill. This was in the far-off days when Britain was the world's carrier and the Lough was full of shipping; a delight to both us boys, but most to my brother. The sound of a steamer's horn at night still conjures up my whole boyhood. Behind the house, greener, lower, and nearer than the Antrim mountains, were the Holywood Hills, but it was not till much later that they won my attention. The northwestern prospect was what mattered at first; the interminable summer sunsets behind the blue ridges, and the rooks flying home. In these surroundings the blows of change began to fall.

First of all, my brother was packed off to an English boarding school and thus removed from my life for the greater part of every year. I remember well the rapture of his homecomings for the holidays but have no recollection of any corresponding anguish at his departures. His new life made no difference to the relations between us. I, meanwhile, was going on with my education at home; French and Latin from my mother and everything else from an excellent governess, Annie Harper. I made rather a bugbear of this mild and modest little lady at the time, but all that I can remember assures me that I was unjust. She was a Presbyterian; and a longish lecture which she once interpolated between sums and copies is the first thing I can remember that brought the other world to my mind with any sense of reality. But there were many things that I thought about more. My real life—or what memory reports as my real life—was increasingly one of solitude. I had indeed plenty of people to talk to: my parents, my grandfather Lewis, prematurely old and deaf, who lived with us; the maids; and a somewhat bibulous old gardener. I was, I believe, an intolerable chatterbox. But solitude was nearly always at my command, somewhere in the garden or somewhere in the house. I had now learned both to read and to write; I had a dozen things to do.

What drove me to write was the extreme manual clumsiness from which I have always suffered. I attribute it to a physical defect which my brother and I both inherit from our father; we have only one joint in the thumb. The upper joint (that furthest from the nail) is visible, but it is a mere sham; we cannot bend it. But whatever the cause, nature laid on me from birth an utter incapacity to make anything. With pencil and pen I was handy enough, and I can still tie as good a bow as ever lay on a man's collar; but with a tool or a bat or a gun, a sleeve link or a corkscrew, I have always been unteachable. It was this that forced me to write. I longed to make things, ships, houses, engines. Many sheets of cardboard and pairs of scissors I spoiled, only to turn from my hopeless failures in tears. As a last resource, as a *pis aller,* I was driven to write stories instead; little dreaming to what a world of happiness I was being admitted. You can do more with a castle in a story than with the best cardboard castle that ever stood on a nursery table.

I soon staked out a claim to one of the attics and made it "my study." Pictures, of my own making or cut from the brightly colored Christmas numbers of magazines, were nailed on the walls. There I kept my pen and inkpot and writing books and paintbox; and there

> *What more felicity can fall to creature*
> *Than to enjoy delight with liberty?*

Here my first stories were written, and illustrated, with enormous satisfaction. They were an attempt to combine my two chief literary pleasures — "dressed animals" and "knights in armor." As a result, I wrote about chivalrous mice and rabbits who rode out in complete mail to kill not giants but cats. But already the mood of the systematizer was strong in me; the mood which led Trollope so endlessly to elaborate his Barsetshire. The Animal-Land which came into action in the holidays when my brother was at home was a modern Animal-Land; it had to have trains and steamships if it was to be a country shared with him. It followed, of course, that the medieval Animal-Land about which I wrote my stories must be the same country at an earlier period; and of course the two periods must be properly connected. This led me from romancing to historiography; I set about writing a full history of Animal-Land. Though more than one version of this instructive work is extant, I never succeeded in bringing it down to modern times; centuries take a deal of filling when all the events have to come out of the historian's head. But there is one touch in the *History* that I still recall with some pride. The chivalric adventures which filled my stories were in it alluded to very lightly and the reader was warned that they might be "only legends." Somehow — but heaven knows how — I realized even then that a historian should adopt a critical attitude toward epic material. From history it was only a step to geography. There was soon a map of Animal-Land — several maps, all tolerably consistent. Then Animal-Land had to be geographically related to my brother's India, and India consequently lifted out of its place in the real world. We made it an island, with its north coast running along the back of the Himalayas; between it and Animal-Land my brother rapidly invented the principal steamship routes. Soon there was a whole world and a map of that world which used every color in my paintbox. And those parts of that world which we regarded as our own — Animal-Land and India — were increasingly peopled with consistent characters.

Of the books that I read at this time very few have quite faded from memory, but not all have retained my love. Conan Doyle's *Sir Nigel,* which first set my mind upon "knights in armor," I have never felt inclined to reread. Still less would I now read

Mark Twain's *A Connecticut Yankee in King Arthur's Court,* which was then my only source for the Arthurian story, blissfully read for the sake of the romantic clements that came through and with total disregard of the vulgar ridicule directed against them. Much better than either of these was E. Nesbit's trilogy, *Five Children and It, The Phoenix and the Wishing Carpet,* and *The Amulet.* The last did most for me. It first opened my eyes to antiquity, the "dark backward and abysm of time." I can still reread it with delight. *Gulliver* in an unexpurgated and lavishly illustrated edition was one of my favorites, and I pored endlessly over an almost complete set of old *Punches* which stood in my father's study. Tenniel gratified my passion for "dressed animals" with his Russian Bear, British Lion, Egyptian Crocodile and the rest, while his slovenly and perfunctory treatment of vegetation confirmed my own deficiencies. Then came the Beatrix Potter books, and here at last beauty.

I will be clear that at this time — at the age of six, seven and eight — I was living almost entirely in my imagination; or at least that the imaginative experience of those years now seems to me more important than anything else. Thus I pass over a holiday in Normandy (of which, nevertheless, I retain very clear memories) as a thing of no account; if it could be cut out of my past I should still be almost exactly the man I am. But imagination is a vague word and I must make some distinctions. It may mean the world of reverie, daydream, wishfulfilling fantasy. Of that I knew more than enough. I often pictured myself cutting a fine figure. But I must insist that this was a totally different activity from the invention of Animal-Land. Animal-Land was not (in that sense) a fantasy at all. I was not one of the characters it contained. I was its creator, not a candidate for admission to it. Invention is essentially different from reverie; if some fail to recognize the difference that is because they have not themselves experienced both. Anyone who has will understand me. In my daydreams I was training myself to be a fool; in mapping and chronicling Animal-Land I was training myself to be a novelist. Note well, a novelist; not a poet. My invented world was full (for me) of interest, bustle, humor, and character; but there was no poetry, even no romance, in it. It was almost astonishingly prosaic.[1] Thus if we use the word imagination in a third sense, and the highest sense of all, this invented world was not imaginative. But certain other experiences were, and I will now try to record them. The thing has been much better done by Traherne and Wordsworth, but every man must tell his own tale.

The first is itself the memory of a memory. As I stood beside a flowering currant bush on a summer day there suddenly arose in me without warning, and as if from a depth not of years but of centuries, the memory of that earlier morning at the Old House when my brother had brought his toy garden into the nursery. It is difficult to find words strong enough for the sensation which came over me; Milton's "enormous bliss" of Eden (giving the full, ancient meaning to "enormous") comes somewhere near it. It was a sensation of course, of desire, but desire for what? not, certainly, for a biscuit tin filled with moss, nor even (though that came into it) for my own past.

---

[1] For readers of my children's books, the best way of putting this would be to say that Animal-Land had nothing whatever in common with Narnia except the anthropomorphic beasts. Animal-Land, by its whole quality, excluded the least hint of wonder.

'Ιουλίανποθῶ [2] — and before I knew what I desired, the desire itself was gone, the whole glimpse withdrawn, the world turned commonplace again, or only stirred by a longing for the longing that had just ceased. It had taken only a moment of time; and in a certain sense everything else that had ever happened to me was insignificant in comparison.

The second glimpse came through *Squirrel Nutkin;* through it only, though I loved all the Beatrix Potter books. But the rest of them were merely entertaining; it administered the shock, it was a trouble. It troubled me with what I can only describe as the Idea of Autumn. It sounds fantastic to say that one can be enamored of a season, but that is something like what happened; and, as before, the experience was one of intense desire. And one went back to the book, not to gratify the desire (that was impossible — how can one *possess* Autumn?) but to reawake it. And in this experience also there was the same surprise and the same sense of incalculable importance. It was something quite different from ordinary life and even from ordinary pleasure; something, as they would now say, "in another dimension."

The third glimpse came through poetry. I had become fond of Longfellow's *Saga of King Olaf*: fond of it in a casual, shallow way for its story and its vigorous rhythms. But then, and quite different from such pleasures, and like a voice from far more distant regions, there came a moment when I idly turned the pages of the book and found the unrhymed translation of *Tegner's Drapa* and read

> *I heard a voice that cried,*
> *Balder the beautiful*
> *Is dead, is dead ——*

I knew nothing about Balder; but instantly I was uplifted into huge regions of northern sky. I desired with almost sickening intensity something never to be described (except that it is cold, spacious, severe, pale, and remote) and then, as in the other examples, found myself at the very same moment already falling out of that desire and wishing I were back in it.

The reader who finds these three episodes of no interest need read this book no further, for in a sense the central story of my life is about nothing else. For those who are still disposed to proceed I will only underline the quality common to the three experiences; it is that of an unsatisfied desire which is itself more desirable than any other satisfaction. I call it Joy, which is here a technical term and must be sharply distinguished both from Happiness and from Pleasure. Joy (in my sense) has indeed one characteristic, and one only, in common with them; the fact that anyone who has experienced it will want it again. Apart from that, and considered only in its quality, it might almost equally well be called a particular kind of unhappiness or grief. But then it is a kind we want. I doubt whether anyone who has tasted it would ever, if both were in his power, exchange it for all the pleasures in the world. But then Joy is never in our power and pleasure often is.

---

[2]Oh, I desire too much.

I cannot be absolutely sure whether the things I have just been speaking of happened before or after the great loss which befell our family and to which I must now turn. There came a night when I was ill and crying both with headache and toothache and distressed because my mother did not come to me. That was because she was ill too; and what was odd was that there were several doctors in her room, and voices and comings and goings all over the house and doors shutting and opening. It seemed to last for hours. And then my father, in tears, came into my room and began to try to convey to my terrified mind things it had never conceived before. It was in fact cancer and followed the usual course; an operation (they operated in the patient's house in those days), an apparent convalescence, a return of the disease, increasing pain, and death. My father never fully recovered from this loss.

Children suffer not (I think) less than their elders, but differently. For us boys the real bereavement had happened before our mother died. We lost her gradually as she was gradually withdrawn from our life into the hands of nurses and delirium and morphia, and as our whole existence changed into something alien and menacing, as the house became full of strange smells and midnight noises and sinister whispered conversations. This had two further results, one very evil and one very good. It divided us from our father as well as our mother. They say that a shared sorrow draws people closer together; I can hardly believe that it often has that effect when those who share it are of widely different ages. If I may trust my own experience, the sight of adult misery and adult terror has an effect on children which is merely paralyzing and alienating. Perhaps it was our fault. Perhaps if we had been better children we might have lightened our father's sufferings at this time. We certainly did not. His nerves had never been of the steadiest and his emotions had always been uncontrolled. Under the pressure of anxiety his temper became incalculable; he spoke wildly and acted unjustly. Thus by a peculiar cruelty of fate, during those months the unfortunate man, had he but known it, was really losing his sons as well as his wife. We were coming, my brother and I, to rely more and more exclusively on each other for all that made life bearable; to have confidence only in each other. I expect that we (or at any rate I) were already learning to lie to him. Everything that had made the house a home had failed us; everything except one another. We drew daily closer together (that was the good result) — two frightened urchins huddled for warmth in a bleak world.

Grief in childhood is complicated with many other miseries. I was taken into the bedroom where my mother lay dead; as they said, "to see her," in reality, as I at once knew, "to see it." There was nothing that a grown-up would call disfigurement — except for that total disfigurement which is death itself. Grief was overwhelmed in terror. To this day I do not know what they mean when they call dead bodies beautiful. The ugliest man alive is an angel of beauty compared with the loveliest of the dead. Against all the subsequent paraphernalia of coffin, flowers, hearse, and funeral I reacted with horror. I even lectured one of my aunts on the absurdity of mourning clothes in a style which would have seemed to most adults both heartless and precocious; but this was our dear Aunt Annie, my maternal uncle's Canadian wife, a woman almost as sensible and sunny as my mother herself. To my hatred for what I already felt to be all the fuss and flummery of the funeral I may perhaps trace something in me which I now recognize as a defect but which I have never fully overcome – a distaste for all that is public, all that belongs to the collective; a boorish inaptitude for formality.

My mother's death was the occasion of what some (but not I) might regard as my first religious experience. When her case was pronounced hopeless I remembered what I had been taught; that prayers offered in faith would be granted. I accordingly set myself to produce by will power a firm belief that my prayers for her recovery would be successful; and as I thought, I achieved it. When nevertheless she died I shifted my ground and worked myself into a belief that there was to be a miracle. The interesting thing is that my disappointment produced no results beyond itself. The thing hadn't worked, but I was used to things not working, and I thought no more about it. I think the truth is that the belief into which I had hypnotized myself was itself too irreligious for its failure to cause any religious revolution. I had approached God, or my idea of God, without love, without awe, even without fear. He was, in my mental picture of this miracle, to appear neither as Savior nor as Judge, but merely as a magician; and when He had done what was required of Him I supposed He would simply – well, go away. It never crossed my mind that the tremendous contact which I solicited should have any consequences beyond restoring the *status quo*. I imagine that a "faith" of this kind is often generated in children and that its disappointment is of no religious importance; just as the things believed in, if they could happen and be only as the child pictures them, would be of no religious importance either.

With my mother's death all settled happiness, all that was tranquil and reliable, disappeared from my life. There was to be much fun, many pleasures, many stabs of Joy; but no more of the old security. It was sea and islands now; the great continent had sunk like Atlantis.

II

CONCENTRATION CAMP

Arithmetic with Coloured Rods.
TIMES EDUCATIONAL SUPPLEMENT, NOV. 19, 1954

Clop-clop-clop-clop...we are in a four-wheeler rattling over the uneven squaresets of the Belfast streets through the damp twilight of a September evening, 1908; my father, my brother, and I. I am going to school for the first time. We are in low spirits. My brother, who has most reason to be so, for he alone knows what we are going to, shows his feelings least. He is already a veteran. I perhaps am buoyed up by a little excitement, but very little. The most important fact at the moment is the horrible clothes I have been made to put on. Only this morning — only two hours ago — I was running wild in shorts and blazer and sand shoes. Now I am choking and sweating, itching too, in thick dark stuff, throttled by an Eton collar, my feet already aching with unaccustomed boots. I am wearing knickerbockers that button at the knee. Every night for some forty weeks of every year and for many a year I am to see the red, smarting imprint of those buttons in my flesh when I undress. Worst of all is the bowler hat, apparently made of iron, which grasps my head. I have read of boys in the same predicament who welcomed such things as signs of growing up; I had no such feeling. Nothing in my experience had ever suggested to me that it was nicer to be a schoolboy than a child or nicer to be a man than a schoolboy. My brother never talked much about school in the holidays. My father, whom I implicitly believed, re-presented adult life as one of incessant drudgery under the continual threat of financial ruin. In this he did not mean to deceive us. Such was his temperament that when he exclaimed, as he frequently did, "There'll soon be nothing for it but the work-house," he momentarily believed, or at least felt, what he said. I took it all literally and had the gloomiest anticipation of adult life. In the meantime, the putting on of the school clothes was, I well knew, the assumption of a prison uniform.

We reach the quay and go on board the old "Fleetwood boat"; after some miser-able strolling about the deck my father bids us good-by. He is deeply moved; I, alas, am mainly embarrassed and self-conscious. When he has gone ashore we almost, by comparison, cheer up. My brother begins to show me over the ship and tell me about all the other shipping in sight. He is an experienced traveler and a complete man of the world. A certain agreeable excitement steals over me. I like the reflected port and starboard lights on the oily water, the rattle of winches, the warm smell from the engine-room skylight. We cast off. The black space widens between us and the quay; I feel the throb of screws underneath me. Soon we are dropping down the Lough and there is a taste of salt on one's lips, and that cluster of lights astern, receding from us, is everything I have known. Later, when we have gone to our bunks, it begins to blow. It is a rough night and my brother is seasick. I absurdly envy him this accomplishment. He is behaving as experienced travelers should. By great efforts I succeed in vomiting; but it is a poor affair — I was, and am, an obstinately good sailor.

No Englishman will be able to understand my first impressions of England. When we disembarked, I suppose at about six next morning (but it seemed to be midnight) I found myself in a world to which I reacted with immediate hatred. The flats of Lancashire in the early morning are in reality a dismal sight; to me they were like the banks of Styx. The strange English accents with which I was surrounded seemed like the voices of demons. But what was worst was the English landscape from Fleetwood to Euston. Even to my adult eye that main line still appears to run through the dullest and most unfriendly strip in the island. But to a child who had always lived near the sea and in sight of high ridges it appeared as I suppose Russia might appear to an English boy. The flatness! The interminableness! The miles and miles of featureless land, shutting one in from the sea, imprisoning, suffocating! Everything was wrong; wooden fences instead of stone walls and hedges, red brick farmhouses instead of white cottages, the fields too big, haystacks the wrong shape. Well does the *Kalevala* say that in the stranger's house the floor is full of knots. I have made up the quarrel since; but at that moment I conceived a hatred for England which took many years to heal.

Our destination was the little town of — let us call it Belsen — in Hertfordshire. "Green Hertfordshire," Lamb calls it; but it was not green to a boy bred in County Down. It was flat Hertfordshire, flinty Hertfordshire, Hertfordshire of the yellow soil. There is the same difference between the climate of Ireland and of England as between that of England and the Continent. There was far more weather at Belsen than I had ever met before; there I first knew bitter frost and stinging fog, sweltering heat and thunderstorms on the great scale. There, through the curtainless dormitory windows, I first came to know the ghastly beauty of the full moon.

The school, as I first knew it, consisted of some eight or nine boarders and about as many day boys. Organized games, except for endless rounders in the flinty playground, had long been moribund and were finally abandoned not very long after my arrival. There was no bathing except one's weekly bath in the bathroom. I was already doing Latin exercises (as taught by my mother) when I went there in 1908, and I was still doing Latin exercises when I left there in 1910; I had never got in sight of a Roman author. The only stimulating element in the teaching consisted of a few well-used canes which hung on the green iron chimney piece of the single schoolroom. The teaching staff consisted of the headmaster and proprietor (we called him Oldie), his grown-up son (Wee Wee), and an usher. The ushers succeeded one another with great rapidity; one lasted for less than a week. Another was dismissed in the presence of the boys, with a rider from Oldie to the effect that if he were not in Holy Orders he would kick him downstairs. This curious scene took place in the dormitory, though I cannot remember why. All these ushers (except the one who stayed less than a week) were obviously as much in awe of Oldie as we. But there came a time when there were no more ushers, and Oldie's youngest daughter taught the junior pupils. By that time there were only five boarders, and Oldie finally gave up his school and sought a cure of souls. I was one of the last survivors, and left the ship only when she went down under us.

Oldie lived in a solitude of power, like a sea captain in the days of sail. No man or woman in this house spoke to him as an equal. No one except Wee Wee initiated conversation with him at all. At meal times we boys had a glimpse of his family life. His son sat on his right hand; they two had separate food. His wife and three grown-up daughters (silent), the usher (silent), and the boys (silent) munched their inferior messes. His wife, though I think she never addressed Oldie, was allowed to make something of a reply to him; the girls — three tragic figures, dressed summer and winter in the same shabby black — never went beyond an almost whispered "Yes Papa," or "No Papa," on the rare occasions when they were addressed. Few visitors entered the house. Beer, which Oldie and Wee Wee drank regularly at dinner, was offered to the usher but he was expected to refuse; the one who accepted got his pint, but was taught his place by being asked a few moments later in a voice of thunderous irony, "Perhaps you would like a little more beer, Mr. N.?" Mr. N., a man of spirit, replied casually, "Well thank you, Mr. C., I think I would." He was the one who did not stay till the end of his first week; and the rest of that day was a black one for us boys.

I myself was rather a pet or mascot of Oldie's — a position which I swear I never sought and of which the advantages were purely negative. Even my brother was not one of his favorite victims. For he had his favorite victims, boys who could do nothing right. I have known Oldie enter the schoolroom after breakfast, cast his eyes round, and remark, "Oh, there you are, Rees, you horrid boy. If I'm not too tired I shall give you a good drubbing this afternoon." He was not angry, nor was he joking. He was a big, bearded man with full lips like an Assyrian king on a monument, immensely strong, physically dirty. Everyone talks of sadism nowadays but I question whether his cruelty had any erotic element in it. I half divined then, and seem to see clearly now, what all his whipping boys had in common. They were the boys who fell below a certain social status, the boys with vulgar accents. Poor P. — dear, honest, hard-working, friendly, healthy pious P. — was flogged incessantly, I now think, for one offense only; he was the son of a dentist. I have seen Oldie make that child bend down at one end of the schoolroom and then take a run of the room's length at each stroke; but

P. was the trained sufferer of countless thrashings and no sound escaped him until, toward the end of the torture, there came a noise quite unlike a human utterance. That peculiar croaking or rattling cry, that, and the gray faces of all the other boys, and their deathlike stillness, are among the memories I could willingly dispense with.[1]

The curious thing is that despite all this cruelty we did surprisingly little work. This may have been partly because the cruelty was irrational and unpredictable; but it was partly because of the curious methods employed. Except at geometry (which he really liked) it might be said that Oldie did not teach at all. He called his class up and asked questions. When the replies were unsatisfactory he said in a low, calm voice, "Bring me my cane. I see I shall need it." If a boy became confused Oldie flogged the desk, shouting in a crescendo, "Think — Think — THINK!!" Then, as the prelude to execution, he muttered, "Come out, come out, come out." When really angry he proceeded to antics; worming for wax in his ear with his little finger and babbling, "Aye, aye, aye, aye..." I have seen him leap up and dance round and round like a performing bear. Meanwhile, almost in whispers, Wee Wee or the usher, or (later) Oldie's youngest daughter, was questioning us juniors at another desk. "Lessons" of this sort did not take very long; what was to be done with the boys for the rest of the time? Oldie had decided that they could, with least trouble to himself, be made to do arithmetic. Accordingly, when you entered school at nine o'clock you took your slate and began doing sums. Presently you were called up to "say a lesson." When that was finished you went back to your place and did more sums — and so forever. All the other arts and sciences thus appeared as islands (mostly rocky and dangerous islands)

Which like to rich and various gems inlaid
The unadorned bosom of the deep

— the deep being a shoreless ocean of arithmetic. At the end of the morning you had to say how many sums you had done; and it was not quite safe to lie. But supervision was slack and very little assistance was given. My brother — I have told you that he was already a man of the world — soon found the proper solution. He announced every morning with perfect truth that he had done five sums; he did not add that they were the same five every day. It would be interesting to know how many thousand times he did them.

I must restrain myself. I could continue to describe Oldie for many pages; some of the worst is unsaid. But perhaps it would be wicked, and it is certainly not obligatory, to do so. One good thing I can tell of him. Impelled by conscience, a boy once confessed to him an otherwise undetectable lie. The ogre was touched; he only patted the terrified boy's back and said, "Always stick to the truth." I can also say that though he taught geometry cruelly, he taught it well. He forced us to reason, and I have been the better for those geometry lessons all my life. For the rest, there is a possible explanation of his behavior which renders it more forgivable. Years after, my brother met a man who had grown up in the house next door to Oldie's school. That man and his family, and (I think) the neighbors in general, believed Oldie to be insane. Perhaps

[1]This punishment was for a mistake in a geometrical proof.

they were right. And if he had fairly recently become so, it would explain a thing which puzzles me. At that school as I knew it most boys learned nothing and no boy learned much. But Oldie could boast an impressive record of scholarships in the past. His school cannot always have been the swindle it was in our time.

You may ask how our father came to send us there. Certainly not because he made a careless choice. The surviving correspondence shows that he had considered many other schools before fixing on Oldie's; and I know him well enough to be sure that in such a matter he would never have been guided by his first thoughts (which would probably have been right) nor even by his twenty-first (which would at least have been explicable). Beyond doubt he would have prolonged deliberation till his hundred-and-first; and they would be infallibly and invincibly wrong. That is what always happens to the deliberations of a simple man who thinks he is a subtle one. Like Earle's *Scepticke in Religion* he "is always too hard for himself." My father piqued himself on what he called "reading between the lines." The obvious meaning of any fact or document was always suspect: the true and inner meaning, invisible to all eyes except his own, was unconsciously created by the restless fertility of his imagination. While he thought he was interpreting Oldie's prospectus, he was really composing a school story in his own mind. And all this, I doubt not, with extreme conscientiousness and even some anguish. It might, perhaps, have been expected that this story of his would presently be blown away by the real story which we had to tell after we had gone to Belsen. But this did not happen. I believe it rarely happens. If the parents in each generation always or often knew what really goes on at their sons' schools, the history of education would be very different. At any rate, my brother and I certainly did not succeed in impressing the truth on our father's mind. For one thing (and this will become clearer in the sequel) he was a man not easily informed. His mind was too active to be an accurate receiver. What he thought he had heard was never exactly what you had said. We did not even try very hard. Like other children, we had no standard of comparison; we supposed the miseries of Belsen to be the common and unavoidable miseries of all schools. Vanity helped to tie our tongues. A boy home from school (especially during that first week when the holidays seem eternal) likes to cut a dash. He would rather represent his master as a buffoon than an ogre. He would hate to be thought a coward and a crybaby, and he cannot paint the true picture of his concentration camp without admitting himself to have been for the last thirteen weeks a pale, quivering, tear-stained, obsequious slave. We all like showing scars received in battle; the wounds of the *ergastulum,* less. My father must not bear the blame for our wasted and miserable years at Oldie's; and now, in Dante's words, "to treat of the good that I found there."

First, I learned, if not friendship, at least gregariousness. There had been bullying at the school when my brother first went there. I had my brother's protection for my first few terms (after which he left to go to a school we may call Wyvern) but I doubt if it was necessary. During those last declining years of the school we boarders were too few and too badly treated to do or suffer much in that way. Also, after a certain time, there were no new boys. We had our quarrels, which seemed serious enough at the time; but long before the end we had known one another too long and suffered too much together not to be, at the least, very old acquaintance. That, I think, is why Belsen did me, in the long run, so little harm. Hardly any amount of oppression from above takes the heart out of a boy like oppression from his fellows. We had many pleasant hours alone together, we five remaining boarders. The abandonment of organized games, though a wretched preparation for the public-school life to which most of us were destined, was at the time a great blessing. We were sent out for walks alone on half holidays. We did not do much walking. We bought sweets in drowsy village shops and pottered about on the canal bank or sat at the brow of a railway cutting watching a tunnel mouth for trains. Hertfordshire came to look less hostile. Our talk was not bound down to the narrow interests which satisfy public-school boys; we still had the curiosity of children. I can even remember from those days what must have been the first metaphysical argument I ever took part in. We debated whether the future was like a line you can't see or like a line that is not yet drawn. I have forgotten which side I took though I know that I took it with great zeal. And always there was what Chesterton calls "the slow maturing of old jokes."

The reader will notice that school was thus coming to reflect a pattern I had already encountered in my home life. At home, the bad times had drawn my brother and me closer together; here, where the times were always bad, the fear and hatred of Oldie had something the same effect upon us all. His school was in some ways very like Dr. Grimstone's school in *Vice Versa;* but unlike Dr. Grimstone's it contained no informer. We stood foursquare against the common enemy. I suspect that this pattern, occurring twice and so early in my life, has unduly biased my whole outlook. To this day the vision of the world which comes most naturally to me is one in which "we two" or "we few" (and in a sense "we happy few") stand together against something stronger and larger. England's position in 1940 was to me no surprise; it was the sort of thing that I always expect. Hence while friendship has been by far the chief source of my happiness, acquaintance or general society has always meant little to me, and I cannot quite understand why a man should wish to know more people than he can make real friends of. Hence, too, a very defective, perhaps culpably defective, interest in large impersonal movements, causes and the like. The concern aroused in me by a battle (whether in story or in reality) is almost in an inverse ratio to the number of the combatants.

In another way too Oldie's school presently repeated my home experience. Oldie's wife died; and in term time. He reacted to bereavement by becoming more violent than before; so much so that Wee Wee made a kind of apology for him to the boys. You will remember that I had already learned to fear and hate emotion; here was a fresh reason to do so.

But I have not yet mentioned the most important thing that befell me at Oldie's. There first I became an effective believer. As far as I know, the instrument was the church to which we were taken twice every Sunday. This was high "Anglo-Catholic."

On the conscious level I reacted strongly against its peculiarities — was I not an Ulster Protestant, and were not these unfamiliar rituals an essential part of the hated English atmosphere? Unconsciously, I suspect, the candles and incense, the vestments and the hymns sung on our knees, may have had a considerable, and opposite, effect on me. But I do not think they were the important thing. What really mattered was that I here heard the doctrines of Christianity (as distinct from general "uplift") taught by men who obviously believed them. As I had no skepticism, the effect was to bring to life what I would already have said that I believed. In this experience there was a great deal of fear. I do not think there was more than was wholesome or even necessary; but if in my books I have spoken too much of Hell, and if critics want a historical explanation of the fact, they must seek it not in the supposed Puritanism of my Ulster childhood but in the Anglo-Catholicism of the church at Belsen. I feared for my soul; especially on certain blazing moonlit nights in that curtainless dormitory — how the sound of other boys breathing in their sleep comes back! The effect, so far as I can judge, was entirely good. I began seriously to pray and to read my Bible and to attempt to obey my conscience. Religion was among the subjects which we often discussed; discussed, if my memory serves me, in an entirely healthy and profitable way, with great gravity and without hysteria, and without the shamefacedness of older boys. How I went back from this beginning you shall hear later.

Intellectually, the time I spent at Oldie's was almost entirely wasted; if the school had not died, and if I had been left there two years more, it would probably have sealed my fate as a scholar for good. Geometry and some pages in West's *English Grammar* (but even those I think I found for myself) are the only items on the credit side. For the rest, all that rises out of the sea of arithmetic is a jungle of dates, battles, exports, imports and the like, forgotten as soon as learned and perfectly useless had they been remembered. There was also a great decline in my imaginative life. For many years Joy (as I have defined it) was not only absent but forgotten. My reading was now mainly rubbish; but as there was no library at the school we must not make Oldie responsible for that. I read twaddling school stories in *The Captain*. The pleasure here was, in the proper sense, mere wish fulfillment and fantasy; one enjoyed vicariously the triumphs of the hero. When the boy passes from nursery literature to school stories he is going down, not up. *Peter Rabbit* pleases a disinterested imagination, for the child does not want to be a rabbit, though he may like pretending to be a rabbit as he may later like acting Hamlet; but the story of the unpromising boy who became captain of the First Eleven exists precisely to feed his real ambitions. I also developed a great taste for all the fiction I could get about the ancient world: *Quo Vadis, Darkness and Dawn, The Gladiators, Ben Hur*. It might be expected that this arose out of my new concern for my religion, but I think not. Early Christians came into many of these stories, but they were not what I was after. I simply wanted sandals, temples, togas, slaves, emperors, galleys, amphitheaters; the attraction, as I now see, was erotic, and erotic in rather a morbid way. And they were mostly, as literature, rather bad books. What has worn better, and what I took to at the same time, is the work of Rider Haggard; and also the "scientifiction" of H. G. Wells. The idea of other planets exercised upon me then a peculiar, heady attraction, which was quite different from any other of my literary interests. Most emphatically it was not the romantic spell of *Das Ferne*. "Joy" (in my technical sense) never darted from Mars or the Moon. This was something coarser and stronger. The interest, when the fit was upon me, was ravenous, like a lust. This particular coarse strength I have come to accept as a mark that the interest which has it is psychological, not spiritual; behind such a fierce tang there lurks, I suspect, a psychoanalytical explanation. I may perhaps add that my own planetary romances have been not so much the gratification of that fierce curiosity as its exorcism. The exorcism worked by reconciling it with, or subjecting it to, the other, the more elusive, and genuinely imaginative, impulse. That the ordinary interest in scientifiction is an affair for psychoanalysts is borne out by the fact that all who like it, like it thus ravenously, and equally by the fact that those who do not, are often nauseated by it. The repulsion of the one sort has the same coarse strength as the fascinated interest of the other and is equally a telltale.

So much for Oldie's; but the year was not all term. Life at a vile boarding school is in this way a good preparation for the Christian life, that it teaches one to live by hope. Even in a sense, by faith; for at the beginning of each term, home and the holidays are so far off that it is as hard to realize them as to realize heaven. They have the same pitiful unreality when confronted with immediate horrors. Tomorrow's geometry blots out the distant end of term as tomorrow's operation may blot out the hope of Paradise. And yet, term after term, the unbelievable happened. Fantastical and astronomical figures like "this time six weeks" shrank into practicable figures like "this time next week," and then "this time tomorrow," and the almost supernatural bliss of the Last Day punctually appeared. It was a delight that almost demanded to be stayed with flagons and comforted with apples; a delight that tingled down the spine and troubled the belly and at moments went near to stopping the breath. Of course this had a terrible and equally relevant reverse side. In the first week of the holidays we might acknowledge that term would come again—as a young man, in peacetime, in full health, acknowledges that he will one day die. But like him we could not even by the grimmest *memento mori* be brought to realize it. And there too, each time, the unbelievable happened. The grinning skull finally peered through all disguises; the last hour, held at bay by every device our will and imaginations knew, came in the end, and once more it was the bowler hat, the Eton collar, the knickerbockers, and (clop-clop-clop-clop) the evening drive to the quay. In all seriousness I think that the life of faith is easier to me because of these memories. To think, in sunny and confident times, that I shall die and rot, or to think that one day all this universe will slip away and become memory (as Oldie slipped away into memory three times a year, and with him the canes and the disgusting food, the stinking sanitation and the cold beds)—this is easier to us if we have seen just that sort of thing happening before. We have learned not to take present things at their face value.

In attempting to give an account of our home life at this time I am troubled by doubts about chronology. School affairs can to some extent be dated by surviving records, but the slow, continuous unfolding of family life escapes them. Our slight alienation from our father imperceptibly increased. In part no one was to blame; in a very great part we were to blame. A temperamental widower, still prostrated by the loss of his wife, must be a very good and wise man indeed if he makes no mistakes in bringing up two noisy and mischievous schoolboys who reserve their confidence wholly for each other. And my father's good qualities as well as his weaknesses incapacitated him for the task. He was far too manly and generous to strike a child for the gratification of his anger; and he was too impulsive ever to punish a child in cold blood and on principle. He therefore relied wholly on his tongue as the instrument of domestic discipline. And here that fatal bent toward dramatization and rhetoric (I speak of it the more freely since I inherit it) produced a pathetic yet comic result. When he opened his mouth to reprove us he no doubt intended a short well-chosen appeal to our common sense and conscience. But alas, he had been a public speaker long before he became a father. He had for many years been a public prosecutor. Words came to him and intoxicated him as they came. What actually happened was that a small boy who had walked on damp grass in his slippers or left a bathroom in a pickle found himself attacked with something like Cicero on Catiline, or Burke on Warren Hastings; simile piled on simile, rhetorical question on rhetorical question, the flash of an orator's eye and the thundercloud of an orator's brow, the gestures, the cadences and the pauses. The pauses might be the chief danger. One was so long that my brother, quite innocently supposing the denunciation to have ended, humbly took up his book and resumed his reading; a gesture which my father (who had after all only made a rhetorical miscalculation of about a second and a half) not unnaturally took for "cool, premeditated insolence." The ludicrous disproportion between such harangues and their occasions puts me in mind of the advocate in Martial who thunders about all the villains of Roman history while meantime *lis est de tribus capellis* —

> *This case, I beg the court to note,*
> *Concerns a trespass by a goat.*

My poor father, while he spoke, forgot not only the offense, but the capacities, of his audience. All the resources of his immense vocabulary were poured forth. I can still remember such words as "abominable," "sophisticated," and "surreptitious." You will not get the full flavor unless you know an angry Irishman's energy in explosive consonants and the rich growl of his r's. A worse treatment could hardly have been applied. Up to a certain age these invectives filled me with boundless terror and dismay. From the wilderness of the adjectives and the welter of the unintelligible, emerged ideas which I thought I understood only too well, as I heard with implicit and literal belief that our Father's ruin was approaching, that we should all soon beg our bread in the streets, that he would shut up the house and keep us at school all the year round, that we should be sent to the colonies and there end in misery the career of crime on which we had, it seemed, already embarked. All security seemed to be taken from me; there was no solid ground beneath my feet. It is significant that at this time if I woke in the night and did not immediately hear my brother's breathing from the neighboring bed, I often suspected that my father and he had secretly risen while I slept and gone off to America – that I was finally abandoned. Such was the effect of my father's rhetoric up to a certain age; then, quite suddenly, it became ridiculous. I can even remember the moment of the change, and the story well illustrates both the justice of my father's anger and the unhappy way in which he expressed it. One day my brother decided it would be a good thing to make a tent. Accordingly we procured a dust sheet from one of the attics. The next step was to find uprights; the stepladder and the wash house suggested itself. For a boy with a hatchet it was the work of a moment to reduce this to a number of disconnected poles. Four of these were then planted in the earth and the sheet draped over them. To make sure that the whole structure was really reliable my brother then tried sitting on top of it. We remembered to put away the ragged remains of the sheet but quite forgot about the uprights. That evening, when my father had come home from work and dined, he went for a stroll in the garden, accompanied by us. The sight of four slender wooden posts rising from the grass moved in him a pardonable curiosity. Interrogation followed; on this occasion we told the truth. Then the lightnings flashed and the thunder roared; and all would have gone now as it had gone on a dozen previous occasions, but for the climax – "Instead of which I find you have cut up the stepladder. And what for, forsooth? To make a thing like an abortive Punch-and-Judy show." At that moment we both hid our faces; not alas, to cry.

As will be seen from this anecdote one dominant factor in our life at home was the daily absence of our father from about nine in the morning till six at night. For the rest of the day we had the house to ourselves, except for the cook and housemaid with whom we were sometimes at war and sometimes in alliance. Everything invited us to develop a life that had no connection with our father. The most important of our activities was the endless drama of Animal-Land and India, and this of itself isolated us from him.

But I must not leave the reader under the impression that all the happy hours of the holidays occurred during our father's absence. His temperament was mercurial, his spirits rose as easily as they fell, and his forgiveness was as thorough-going as his displeasure. He was often the most jovial and companionable of parents. He could "play the fool" as well as any of us, and had no regard for his own dignity, "conned no state." I could not, of course, at that age see what good company (by adult standards) he was, his humor being of the sort that requires at least some knowledge of life for its full appreciation; I merely basked in it as in fine weather. And all the time there was the sensuous delight of being at home, the delight of luxury – "civilization," as we called it. I spoke just now of *Vice Versa*. Its popularity was surely due to something more than farce. It is the only truthful school story in existence. The machinery of the Garuda Stone really serves to bring out in their true colors (which would otherwise seem exaggerated) the sensations which every boy had on passing from the warmth and softness and dignity of his home life to the privations, the raw and sordid ugliness, of school. I say "had" not "has"; for perhaps homes have gone down in the world and schools gone up since then.

It will be asked whether we had no friends, no neighbors, no relatives. We had. To one family in particular our debt is so great that it had better be left, with some other matters, to the next chapter.

III

MOUNTBRACKEN AND CAMPBELL

For all these fair people in hall were in their first age; none happier under the heaven; their king, the man of noblest temper. It would be a hard task to-day to find so brave a fellowship in any castle.

GAWAIN AND THE GREEN KNIGHT

To speak of my nearer relatives is to remind myself how the contrast of Lewis and Hamilton dominated my whole early life. It began, for me, with the grandparents. Grandfather Lewis, deaf, slow-moving, humming his psalm chants, much concerned for his health and prone to remind the family that he would not be with them long, is contrasted with Grandmother Hamilton, the sharp-tongued, sharp-witted widow, full of heterodox opinions (even, to the scandal of the whole connection, a Home Ruler), every inch a Warren, indifferent to convention as only an old Southern Irish aristocrat could be, living alone in a large tumble-down house with half a hundred cats for company. To how many an innocent conversational gambit did she reply, "You're talking great nonsense"? Born a little later, she would, I think, have been a Fabian. She met vague small talk with ruthless statements of ascertainable fact and well-worn maxims with a tart demand for evidence. Naturally, people called her eccentric. Coming down a generation I find the same opposition. My father's elder brother "Uncle Joe," with his family of two boys and three girls, lived very close to us while we were at the Old House. His younger son was my earliest friend, but we drifted apart as we grew older. Uncle Joe was both a clever man and a kind, and especially fond of me. But I remember nothing that was said by our elders in that house; it was simply "grown-up" conversation — about people, business, politics, and health, I suppose. But "Uncle Gussie" — my mother's brother, A. W. Hamilton — talked to me as if we were of an age. That is, he talked about Things. He told me all the science I could then take in, clearly, eagerly, without silly jokes and condescensions, obviously liking it as much as I did. He thus provided the intellectual background for my reading of H. G. Wells. I do not suppose he cared for me as a person half so much as Uncle Joe did; and that (call it an injustice or not) was what I liked. During these talks our attention was fixed not on one another but on the subject. His Canadian wife I have already mentioned. In her also I found what I liked best – an unfailing, kindly welcome without a hint of sentimentality, unruffled good sense, the unobtrusive talent for making all things at all times as cheerful and comfortable as circumstances allowed. What one could not have one did without and made the best of it. The tendency of the Lewises to reopen old wounds and to rouse sleeping dogs was unknown to her as to her husband.

But we had other kin who mattered to us far more than our aunts and uncles. Less than a mile from our home stood the largest house I then knew, which I will here call Mountbracken, and there lived Sir W. E. Lady E. was my mother's first cousin and perhaps my mother's dearest friend, and it was no doubt for my mother's sake that she took upon herself the heroic work of civilizing my brother and me. We had a standing invitation to lunch at Mountbracken whenever we were at home; to this, almost entirely, we owe it that we did not grow up savages. The debt is not only to Lady E. ("Cousin Mary") but to her whole family; walks, motor drives (in those days an exciting novelty), picnics, and invitations to the theater were showered on us, year after year, with a kindness which our rawness, our noise, and our unpunctuality never seemed to weary. We were at home there almost as much as in our own house, but with this great difference, that a certain standard of manners had to be kept up. Whatever I know (it is not much) of courtesy and *savoir faire* I learned at Mountbracken.

Sir W. ("Cousin Quartus") was the eldest of several brothers who owned between them one of the most important industrial concerns in Belfast. He belonged in fact to just that class and generation of which the modern man gets his impressions through Galsworthy's Forsytes. Unless Cousin Quartus was very untrue to type (as he may well have been) that impression is grossly unjust. No one less a Galsworthian character ever existed. He was gracious, childlike, deeply and religiously humble, and abounding in charity. No man could feel more fully his responsibility to dependents. He had a good deal of boyish gaiety about him; at the same time I always felt that the conception of duty dominated his life. His stately figure, his gray beard, and his strikingly handsome profile make up one of the most venerable images in my memory. Physical beauty was indeed common to most of the family. Cousin Mary was the very type of beautiful old lady, with her silver hair and her sweet Southern Irish voice; foreigners must be warned that this resembles what they call a "brogue" about as little as the speech of a Highland gentleman resembles the jargon of the Glasgow slums. But it was the three daughters whom we knew best. All three were "grown up" but in fact much nearer to us in age than any other grown-ups we knew, and all three were strikingly handsome. H., the eldest and the gravest, was a Juno, a dark queen who at certain moments looked like a Jewess. K. was more like a Valkyrie (though all, I think, were good horsewomen) with her father's profile. There was in her face something of the delicate fierceness of a thoroughbred horse, an indignant fineness of nostril, the possibility of an excellent disdain. She had what the vanity of my own sex calls a "masculine" honesty; no man ever was a truer friend. As for the youngest, G., I can only say that she was the most beautiful woman I have ever seen, perfect in shape and color and voice and every movement — but who can describe beauty? The reader may smile at this as the far-off echo of a precocious calf love, but he will be wrong. There are beauties so unambiguous that they need no lens of that kind to reveal them; they are visible even to the careless and objective eyes of a child. (The first woman who ever spoke to my blood was a dancing mistress at a school that will come in a later chapter.)

In some ways Mountbracken was like our father's house. There too we found the attics, the indoor silences, the endless bookshelves. In the early days, when we were still only a quarter tamed, we often neglected our hostesses and rummaged on our own; it was there that I found Lubbock's *Ants, Bees and Wasps.* But it was also very different. Life there was more spacious and considered than with us, glided like a barge where ours bumped like a cart.

Friends of our own age — boy and girl friends — we had none. In part this is a natural result of boarding school; children grow up strangers to their next-door neighbors. But much more it was the result of our own obstinate choice. One boy who lived near us attempted every now and then to get to know us. We avoided him by every means in our power. Our lives were already full, and the holidays too short for all the reading, writing, playing, cycling, and talking that we wanted to get through. We resented the appearance of any third party as an infuriating interruption. We resented even more bitterly all attempts (excepting the great and successful attempt made by Mountbracken) to show us hospitality. At the period that I am now speaking of this had not yet become a serious nuisance, but as it became gradually and steadily more serious throughout our schooldays I may be allowed to say a word about it here and to get the subject out of our way. It was the custom of the neighborhood to give parties which were really dances for adults but to which, none the less, mere schoolboys and schoolgirls were asked. One sees the advantages of this arrangement from the hostess's point of view; and when the junior guests know each other well and are free from self-consciousness perhaps they enjoy themselves. To me these dances were a torment — of which ordinary shyness made only a part. It was the false position (which I was well able to realize) that tormented me; to know that one was regarded as a child and yet be forced to take part in an essentially grown-up function, to feel that all the adults present were being half-mockingly kind and pretending to treat you as what you were not. Add to this the discomfort of one's Eton suit and stiff shirt, the aching feet and burning head, and the mere weariness of being kept up so many hours after one's usual bedtime. Even adults, I fancy, would not find an evening party very endurable without the attraction of sex and the attraction of alcohol; and how a small boy who can neither flirt nor drink should be expected to enjoy prancing about on a polished floor till the small hours of the morning, is beyond my conception. I had of course no notion of the social nexus. I never realized that certain people were in civility obliged to ask me because they knew my father or had known my mother. To me it was all inexplicable, unprovoked persecution; and when, as often happened, such engagements fell in the last week of the holidays and wrested from us a huge cantle of hours in which every minute was worth gold, I positively felt that I could have torn my hostess limb from limb. Why should she thus pester me? I had never done her any harm, never asked *her* to a party.

My discomforts were aggravated by the totally unnatural behavior which I thought it my duty to adopt at a dance; and that had come about in a sufficiently amusing way. Reading much and mixing little with children of my own age, I had, before I went to school, developed a vocabulary which must (I now see) have sounded very funny from the lips of a chubby urchin in an Eton jacket. When I brought out my "long words" adults not unnaturally thought I was showing off. In this they were quite mistaken. I used the only words I knew. The position was indeed the exact reverse of what they supposed; my pride would have been gratified by using such schoolboy slang as I possessed, not at all by using the bookish language which (inevitably in my circumstances) came naturally to my tongue. And there were not lacking adults who would egg me on with feigned interest and feigned seriousness—on and on till the moment at which I suddenly knew I was being laughed at. Then, of course, my mortification was intense; and after one or two such experiences I made it a rigid rule that at "social functions" (as I secretly called them) I must never on any account speak of any subject in which I felt the slightest interest nor in any words that naturally occurred to me. And I kept my rule only too well; a giggling and gurgling imitation of the vapidest grown-up chatter, a deliberate concealment of all that I really thought and felt under a sort of feeble jocularity and enthusiasm, was henceforth my party manner, assumed as consciously as an actor assumes his role, sustained with unspeakable weariness, and dropped with a groan of relief the moment my brother and I at last tumbled into our cab and the drive home (the only pleasure of the evening) began. It took me years to make the discovery that any real human intercourse could take place at a mixed assembly of people in their good clothes.

I am here struck by the curious mixture of justice and injustice in our lives. We are blamed for our real faults but usually not on the right occasions. I was, no doubt, and was blamed for being, a conceited boy; but the blame was usually attached to something in which no conceit was present. Adults often accuse a child of vanity without pausing to discover on what points children in general, or that child in particular, are likely to be vain. Thus it was for years a complete mystery to me that my father should stigmatize as "affectation" my complaints about the itching and tickling of new underclothes. I see it all now; he had in mind a social legend associating delicacy of skin with refinement and supposed that I was claiming to be unusually refined. In reality I was in simple ignorance of that social legend, and if vanity had come into the matter would have been much prouder of having a skin like a sailor. I was being accused of an offense which I lacked resources to commit. I was on another occasion called "affected" for asking what "stirabout" was. It is, in fact, a "low" Irish word for porridge. To certain adults it seems obvious that he who claims not to know the Low must be pretending to be High. Yet the real reason why I asked was that I had never happened to hear the word; had I done so I should have piqued myself on using it.

Oldie's school you will remember, sank unlamented in summer 1910; new arrangements had to be made for my education. My father now hit upon a plan which filled me with delight. About a mile from the New House rose the large red-brick walls and towers of Campbell College, which had been founded for the express purpose of giving Ulster boys all the advantages of a public-school education without the trouble of crossing the Irish Sea. My clever cousin, Uncle Joe's boy, was already there and doing well. It was decided that I should go as a boarder, but I could get an *exeat* to come home every Sunday. I was enchanted. I did not believe that anything Irish, even a school, could be bad; certainly not so bad as all I yet knew of England. To "Campbell" I accordingly went.

I was at this school for so short a time that I shall attempt no criticism of it. It was very unlike any English public school that I have ever heard of. It had indeed prefects, but the prefects were of no importance. It was nominally divided into "houses" on the English pattern, but they were mere legal fictions; except for purposes of games (which were not compulsory) no one took any notice of them. The population was socially much more "mixed" than at most English schools; I rubbed shoulders there with farmers' sons. The boy I most nearly made a friend of was the son of a tradesman who had recently been going the rounds with his father's van because the driver was illiterate and could not keep "the books." I much envied him this pleasant occupation, and he, poor fellow, looked back on it as a golden age. "This time last month, Lewis," he used to say, "I wouldn't have been going in to Preparation. I'd have been coming home from my rounds and a wee tea cloth laid for me at one end of the table and sausages to my tea."

I am always glad, as a historian, to have known Campbell, for I think it was very much what the great English schools had been before Arnold. There were real fights at Campbell, with seconds, and (I think) betting, and a hundred or more roaring spectators. There was bullying, too, though no serious share of it came my way, and there was no trace of the rigid hierarchy which governs a modern English school; every boy held just the place which his fists and mother wit could win for him. From my point of view the great drawback was that one had, so to speak, no home. Only a few very senior boys had studies. The rest of us, except when seated at table for meals or in a huge "preparation room" for evening "Prep," belonged nowhere. In out-of-school hours one spent one's time either evading or conforming to all those inexplicable movements which a crowd exhibits as it thins here and thickens there, now slackens its pace and now sets like a tide in one particular direction, now seems about to disperse and then clots again. The bare brick passages echoed to a continual tramp of feet, punctuated with catcalls, scrimmages, gusty laughter. One was always "moving on" or "hanging about" — in lavatories, in storerooms, in the great hall. It was very like living permanently in a large railway station.

The bullying had this negative merit that it was honest bullying; not bullying con-science-salved and authorized in the *maison tolére* of the prefectorial system. It was done mainly by gangs; parties of eight or ten boys each who scoured those interminable corridors for prey. Their sorties, though like a whirlwind, were not perceived by the victim till too late; the general, endless confusion and clamor, I suppose, masked them. Sometimes capture involved serious consequences; two boys whom I knew were carried off and flogged in some backwater – flogged in the most disinterested fashion, for their captors had no personal acquaintance with them; art for art's sake. But on the only occasion when I was caught myself my fate was much milder and perhaps odd enough to be worth recording. When I had come to myself after being dragged at headlong speed through a labyrinth of passages which took me beyond all usual landmarks, I found that I was one of several prisoners in a low, bare room, half-lit (I think) by a single gas jet. After a pause to recover their breath two of the brigands led out the first captive. I now noticed that a horizontal row of pipes ran along the opposite wall, about three feet from the floor. I was alarmed but not surprised when the prisoner was forced into a bending position under the lowest pipe, in the very posture for execution. But I was very much surprised a moment later. You will remember that the room was half dark. The two gangsters gave their victim a shove; and instantly no victim was there. He vanished; without trace, without sound. It appeared to be sheer black magic. Another victim was led out; again the posture for a flogging was assumed; again, instead of flogging – dissolution, atomization, annihilation. At last my own turn came. I too received the shove from behind, and found myself falling through a hole or hatch in the wall into what turned out to be a coal cellar. Another small boy came hurtling in after me, the door was slammed and bolted behind us, and our captors with a joyous whoop rushed away for more booty. They were, no doubt, playing against a rival gang with whom they would presently compare "bags." We were let out again presently, very dirty and rather cramped, but otherwise none the worse.

Much the most important thing that happened to me at Campbell was that I there read *Sohrab and Rustum* in form under an excellent master whom we called Octie. I loved the poem at first sight and have loved it ever since. As the wet fog, in the first line, rose out of the Oxus stream, so out of the whole poem there rose and wrapped me round an exquisite, silvery coolness, a delightful quality of distance and calm, a grave melancholy. I hardly appreciated then, as I have since learned to do, the central tragedy; what enchanted me was the artist in Pekin with his ivory forehead and pale hands, the cypress in the queen's garden, the backward glance at Rustum's youth, the pedlars from Khabul, the hushed Chorasmian waste. Arnold gave me at once (and the best of Arnold gives me still) a sense, not indeed of passionless vision, but of a passionate, silent gazing at things a long way off. And here observe how literature actually works. Parrot critics say that *Sohrab* is a poem for classicists, to be enjoyed only by those who recognize the Homeric echoes. But I, in Octie's form room (and on Octie be peace) knew nothing of Homer. For me the relation between Arnold and

Homer worked the other way; when I came, years later, to read the *Iliad* I liked it partly because it was for me reminiscent of *Sohrab*. Plainly, it does not matter at which point you first break into the system of European poetry. Only keep your ears open and your mouth shut and everything will lead you to everything else in the end — *ogni parte ad ogni parte splende*.

About halfway through my first and only term at Campbell I fell ill and was taken home. My father, for reasons I do not quite know, had become dissatisfied with the school. He had also been attracted by accounts of a preparatory school in the town of Wyvern, though quite unconnected with Wyvern College; especially by the convenience that if I went there my brother and I could still do the journey together. Accordingly I had a blessed six weeks at home, with the Christmas holidays to look forward to at the end and, after that, a new adventure. In a surviving letter my father writes to my brother that I think myself lucky but he "fears I shall be very lonely before the end of the week." It is strange that having known me all my life he should have known me so little. During these weeks I slept in his room and was thus freed from solitude during most of those dark hours in which alone solitude was dreadful to me. My brother being absent, he and I could not lead one another into mischief; there was therefore no friction between my father and myself. I remember no other time in my life of such untroubled affection; we were famously snug together. And in the days, when he was out, I entered with complete satisfaction into a deeper solitude than I had ever known. The empty house, the empty, silent rooms, were like a refreshing bath after the crowded noise of Campbell. I could read, write, and draw to my heart's content. Curiously enough it is at this time, not in earlier childhood, that I chiefly remember delighting in fairy tales. I fell deeply under the spell of Dwarfs — the old bright-hooded, snowy-bearded dwarfs we had in those days before Arthur Rackham sublimed, or Walt Disney vulgarized, the earthmen. I visualized them so intensely that I came to the very frontiers of hallucination; once, walking in the garden, I was for a second not quite sure that a little man had not run past me into the shrubbery. I was faintly alarmed, but it was not like my night fears. A fear that guarded the road to Faerie was one I could face. No one is a coward at all points.

IV

I BROADEN MY MIND

I struck the board, and cry'd, 'No more;
I will abroad,'
What? shall I ever sigh and pine?
My lines and life are free: free as the rode,
Loose as the winde, as large as store.

HERBERT

In January, 1911, just turned thirteen, I set out with my brother to Wyvern, he for the College and I for a preparatory school which we will call Chartres. Thus began what may be called the classic period of our schooldays, the thing we both think of first when boyhood is mentioned. The joint journeys back to school with a reluctant parting at Wyvern station, the hilarious reunion at the same station for the joint journey home, were now the great structural pillars of each year. Growing maturity is marked by the increasing liberties we take with our traveling. At first, on being landed early in the morning at Liverpool, we took the next train south; soon we learned that it was pleasanter to spend the whole morning in the lounge of the Lime Street Hotel with our magazines and cigarettes and to proceed to Wyvern by an afternoon train which brought us there at the latest permitted moment. Soon too we gave up the magazines; we made the discovery (some people never make it) that real books can be taken on a journey and that hours of golden reading can so be added to its other delights. (It is important to acquire early in life the power of reading sense wherever you happen to be. I first read *Tamburlaine* while traveling from Larne to Belfast in a thunderstorm, and first read Browning's *Paracelsus* by a candle which went out and had to be relit whenever a big battery fired in a pit below me, which I think it did every four minutes all that night.) The homeward journey was even more festal. It had an invariable routine: first the supper at a restaurant — it was merely poached eggs and tea but to us the tables of the gods — then the visit to the old Empire (there were still music halls in those days) — and after that the journey to the Landing Stage, the sight of great and famous ships, the departure, and once more the blessed salt on our lips.

32

The smoking was of course, as my father would have said, "surreptitious"; not so the visit to the Empire. He was no Puritan about such matters, and often of a Saturday night would take us to the Belfast Hippodrome. I recognize now that I never had the taste for vaudeville which he shared with my brother. At the time I supposed myself to be enjoying the show, but I was mistaken. All those antics lie dead in my memory and are incapable of rousing the least vibration even of reminiscent pleasure; whereas the pain of sympathy and vicarious humiliation which I felt when a "turn" failed is still vivid. What I enjoyed was merely the et cetera of the show, the bustle and lights, the sense of having a night out, the good spirits of my father in his holiday mood, and — above all — the admirable cold supper to which we came back at about ten o'clock. For this was also the classical age of our domestic cookery, the age of one Annie Strahan. There were certain "raised pies" set on that table of which a modern English boy has no conception, and which even then would have astonished those who knew only the poor counterfeits sold in shops.

Chartres, a tall, white building further up the hill than the College, was a smallish school with less than twenty boarders; but it was quite unlike Oldie's. Here indeed my education really began. The Headmaster, whom we called Tubbs, was a clever and patient teacher; under him I rapidly found my feet in Latin and English and even began to be looked on as a promising candidate for a scholarship at the College. The food was good (though of course we grumbled at it) and we were well cared for. On the whole I got on well with my school fellows, though we had our full share of those lifelong friendships and irreconcilable factions and deadly quarrels and final settlements and glorious revolutions which made up so much of the life of a small boy, and in which I came out sometimes at the bottom and sometimes at the top.

Wyvern itself healed my quarrel with England. The great blue plain below us and, behind, those green, peaked hills, so mountainous in form and yet so manageably small in size, became almost at once my delight. And Wyvern Priory was the first building that I ever peceived to be beautiful. And at Chartres I made my first real friends. But there, too, something far more important happened to me: I ceased to be a Christian.

The chronology of this disaster is a little vague, but I know for certain that it had not begun when I went there and that the process was complete very shortly after I left. I will try to set down what I know of the conscious causes and what I suspect of the unconscious.

Most reluctantly, venturing no blame, and as tenderly as I would at need reveal some error in my own mother, I must begin with dear Miss C., the Matron. No school ever had a better Matron, more skilled and comforting to boys in sickness, or more cheery and companionable to boys in health. She was one of the most selfless people I have ever known. We all loved her; I, the orphan, especially. Now it so happened that Miss C., who seemed old to me, was still in her spiritual immaturity, still hunting, with the eagerness of a soul that had a touch of angelic quality in it, for a truth and a way of life. Guides were even rarer then than now. She was (as I should now put it) floundering in the mazes of Theosophy, Rosicrucianism, Spiritualism; the whole Anglo-American Occultist tradition. Nothing was further from her intention than to destroy my faith; she could not tell that the room into which she brought this candle was full of gun-powder. I had never heard of such things before; never, except in a nightmare or a fairy tale, conceived of spirits other than God and men. I had loved to read of strange sights and other worlds and unknown modes of being, but never with the slightest belief; even the phantom dwarf had only flashed on my mind for a moment. It is a great mistake to suppose that children believe the things they imagine; and I, long familiar with the whole imaginary world of Animal-Land and India (which I could not possibly believe in since I knew I was one of its creators) was as little likely as any child to make that mistake. But now, for the first time, there burst upon me the idea that there might be real marvels all about us, that the visible world might be only a curtain to conceal huge realms uncharted by my very simple theology. And that started in me something with which, on and off, I have had plenty of trouble since – the desire for the preternatural, simply as such, the passion for the Occult. Not everyone has this disease; those who have will know what I mean. I once tried to describe it in a novel. It is a spiritual lust; and like the lust of the body it has the fatal power of making everything else in the world seem uninteresting while it lasts. It is probably this passion, more even than the desire for power, which makes magicians. But the result of Miss C.'s conversation did not stop there. Little by little, unconsciously, unintentionally, she loosened the whole framework, blunted all the sharp edges, of my belief. The vagueness, the merely speculative character, of all this Occultism began to spread – yes, and to spread *deliciously* – to the stern truths of the creed. The whole thing became a matter of speculation: I was soon (in the famous words) "altering 'I believe' to 'one does feel.' " And oh, the relief of it! Those moonlit nights in the dormitory at Belsen faded far away. From the tyrannous noon of revelation I passed into the cool evening of Higher Thought, where there was nothing to be obeyed, and nothing to be believed except what was either comforting or exciting. I do not mean that Miss C. did this; better say that the Enemy did this in me, taking occasion from things she innocently said.

One reason why the Enemy found this so easy was that, without knowing it, I was already desperately anxious to get rid of my religion; and that for a reason worth recording. By a sheer mistake – and I still believe it to have been an honest mistake – in spiritual technique I had rendered my private practice of that religion a quite intolerable burden. It came about in this way. Like everyone else I had been told as a child that one must not only say one's prayers but think about what one was saying. Accordingly, when (at Oldie's) I came to a serious belief, I tried to put this into practice. At first it seemed plain sailing. But soon the false conscience (St. Paul's "Law," Herbert's "prattler") came into play. One had no sooner reached "Amen" than it whispered, "Yes. But are you sure you were really thinking about what you said?"; then, more subtly, "Were you, for example, thinking about it as well as you did last night?" The answer, for reasons I did not then understand, was nearly always No. "Very well," said the voice, "hadn't you, then, better try it over again?" And one obeyed; but of course with no assurance that the second attempt would be any better.

To these nagging suggestions my reaction was, on the whole, the most foolish I could have adopted. I set myself a standard. No clause of my prayer was to be allowed to pass muster unless it was accompanied by what I called a "realization," by which I meant a certain vividness of the imagination and the affections. My nightly task was to produce by sheer will power a phenomenon which will power could never produce, which was so ill-defined that I could never say with absolute confidence whether it had occurred, and which, even when it did occur, was of very mediocre spiritual value. If only someone had read to me old Walter Hilton's warning that we must never in prayer strive to extort "by maistry" what God does not give! But no one did; and night after night, dizzy with desire for sleep and often in a kind of despair, I endeavored to pump up my "realizations." The thing threatened to become an infinite regress. One began of course by praying for good "realizations." But had that preliminary prayer itself been "realized"? This question I think I still had enough sense to dismiss; otherwise it might have been as difficult to begin my prayers as to end them. How it all comes back! The cold oilcloth, the quarters chiming, the night slipping past, the sickening, hopeless weariness. This was the burden from which I longed with soul and body to escape. It had already brought me to such a pass that the nightly torment projected its gloom over the whole evening, and I dreaded bedtime as if I were a chronic sufferer from insomnia. Had I pursued the same road much further I think I should have gone mad.

This ludicrous burden of false duties in prayer provided, of course, an unconscious motive for wishing to shuffle off the Christian faith; but about the same time, or a little later, conscious causes of doubt arose. One came from reading the classics. Here, especially in Virgil, one was presented with a mass of religious ideas; and all teachers and editors took it for granted from the outset that these religious ideas were sheer illusion. No one ever attempted to show in what sense Christianity fulfilled Paganism or Paganism prefigured Christianity. The accepted position seemed to be that religions were normally a mere farrago of nonsense, though our own, by a fortunate exception, was exactly true. The other religions were not even explained, in the earlier Christian fashion, as the work of devils. That I might, conceivably, have been brought to believe. But the impression I got was that religion in general, though utterly false, was a natural growth, a kind of endemic nonsense into which humanity tended to blunder. In the midst of a thousand such religions stood our own, the thousand and first, labeled True. But on what grounds could I believe in this exception? It obviously was in some general sense the same kind of thing as all the rest. Why was it so differently treated? Need I, at any rate, continue to treat it differently? I was very anxious not to.

In addition to this, and equally working against my faith, there was in me a deeply ingrained pessimism; a pessimism, by that time, much more of intellect than of temper. I was now by no means unhappy; but I had very definitely formed the opinion that the universe was, in the main, a rather regrettable insititution. I am well aware that some will feel disgust and some will laugh, at the idea of a loutish, well-fed boy in an Eton collar, passing an unfavorable judgment on the cosmos. They may be right in either reaction, but no more right because I wore an Eton collar. They are forgetting what boyhood felt like from within. Dates are not so important as people believe. I fancy that most of those who think at all have done a great deal of their thinking in the first fourteen years. As to the sources of my pessimism, the reader will remember that, though in many ways most fortunate, yet I had very early in life met a great dismay. But I am now inclined to think that the seeds of pessimism were sown before my mother's death. Ridiculous as it may sound, I believe that the clumsiness of my hands was at the root of the matter. How could this be? Not, certainly, that a child says, "I can't cut a straight line with a pair of scissors, therefore the universe is evil." Childhood has no such power of generalization and is not (to do it justice) so silly. Nor did my clumsiness produce what is ordinarily called an Inferiority Complex. I was not comparing myself with other boys; my defeats occurred in solitude. What they really bred in me was a deep (and, of course, inarticulate) sense of resistance or opposition on the part of inanimate things. Even that makes it too abstract and adult. Perhaps I had better call it a settled expectation that everything would do what you did not want it to do. Whatever you wanted to remain straight, would bend; whatever you tried to bend would fly back to the straight; all knots which you wished to be firm would come untied; all knots you wanted to untie would remain firm. It is not possible to put it into language without making it comic, and I have indeed no wish to see it (now) except as something comic. But it is perhaps just these early experiences which are so fugitive and, to an adult, so grotesque, that give the mind its earliest bias, its habitual sense of what is or is not plausible.

There was another predisposing factor. Though the son of a prosperous man — a man by our present tax-ridden standards almost incredibly comfortable and secure — I had heard ever since I could remember, and believed, that adult life was to be an unremitting struggle in which the best I could hope for was to avoid the workhouse by extreme exertion. My father's highly colored statements on such matters had sunk deeply into my mind; and I never thought to check them by the very obvious fact that most of the adults I actually knew seemed to be living very comfortable lives. I remember summing up what I took to be our destiny, in conversation with my best friend at Chartres, by the formula, "Term, holidays, term, holidays, till we leave school, and then work, work, work till we die." Even if I had been free from this delusion, I think I should still have seen grounds for pessimism. One's views, even at that age, are not wholly determined by one's own momentary situation; even a boy can recognize that there is desert all round him though he, for the nonce, sits in an oasis. I was, in my ineffective way, a tenderhearted creature; perhaps the most murderous feelings I ever entertained were toward an under master at Chartres who forbade me to give to a beggar at the school gate. Add to this that my early reading — not only Wells but Sir Robert Ball — had lodged very firmly in my imagination the vastness and cold of space, the littleness of Man. It is not strange that I should feel the universe to be a menacing and unfriendly place. Several years before I read Lucretius I felt the force of his argument (and it is surely the strongest of all) for atheism —

> *Nequaquam nobis divinitus esse paratam*
> *Naturam rerum; tanta stat praedita culpa*
> *Had God designed the world, it would not be*
> *A World so frail and faulty as we see.*

You may ask how I combined this directly Atheistical thought, this great "Argument from Undesign" with my Occultist fancies. I do not think I achieved any logical connection between them. They swayed me in different moods, and had only this in common, that both made against Christianity. And so, little by little, with fluctuations which I cannot now trace, I became an apostate, dropping my faith with no sense of loss but with the greatest relief.

My stay at Chartres lasted from the spring term of 1911 till the end of the summer term 1913, and, as I have said, I cannot give an accurate chronology, between those dates, of my slow apostasy. In other respects the period is divided into two; about halfway through it a much loved under master, and the even more loved Matron, left at the same time. From that day onward there was a sharp decline; not, indeed, in apparent happiness but in solid good. Dear Miss C. had been the occasion of much good in me as well as of evil. For one thing, by awakening my affections, she had done something to defeat that antisentimental inhibition which my early experience had bred in me. Nor would I deny that in all her "Higher Thought," disastrous though its main effect on me was, there were elements of real and disinterested spirituality by which I benefited. Unfortunately, once her presence was withdrawn, the good effects withered and the bad ones remained. The change of masters was even more obviously for the worse. "Sirrah," as we called him, had been an admirable influence. He was what I would now describe as a wise madcap: a boisterous, boyish, hearty man, well able to keep his authority while yet mixing with us almost as one of ourselves, an untidy, rollicking man without a particle of affectation. He communicated (what I very much needed) a sense of the gusto with which life ought, whereever possible, to be taken. I fancy it was on a run with him in the sleet that I first discovered how bad weather is to be treated — as a rough joke, a romp. He was succeeded by a young gentleman just down from the University whom we may call Pogo. Pogo was a very minor edition of a Saki, perhaps even a Wodehouse, hero. Pogo was a wit, Pogo was a dressy man, Pogo was a man about town, Pogo was even a lad. After a week or so of hesitation (for his temper was uncertain) we fell at his feet and adored. Here was sophistication, glossy all over, and (dared one believe it?) ready to impart sophistication to us.

We became — at least I became — dressy. It was the age of the "knut": of "spread" ties with pins in them, of very low cut coats and trousers worn very high to show startling socks, and brogue shoes with immensely wide laces. Something of all this had already trickled to me from the College through my brother, who was now becoming sufficiently senior to aspire to knuttery. Pogo completed the process. A more pitiful ambition for a lout of an overgrown fourteen-year-old with a shilling a week pocket money could hardly be imagined; the more so since I am one of those on whom Nature has laid the doom that whatever they buy and whatever they wear they will always look as if they had come out of an old clothes shop. I cannot even now remember without embarrassment the concern that I then felt about pressing my trousers and (filthy habit) plastering my hair with oil. A new element had entered my life: Vulgarity. Up till now I had committed nearly every other sin and folly within my power, but I had not yet been flashy.

These hobbledehoy fineries were, however, only a small part of our new sophistication. Pogo was a great theatrical authority. We soon knew all the latest songs. We soon knew all about the famous actresses of that age — Lily Elsie, Gertie Millar, Zena Dare. Pogo was a fund of information about their private lives. We learned from him all the latest jokes; where we did not understand he was ready to give us help. He explained many things. After a term of Pogo's society one had the feeling of being not twelve weeks but twelve years older.

How gratifying, and how edifying, it would be if I could trace to Pogo all my slips from virtue and wind up by pointing the moral; how much harm a loose-talking young man can do to innocent boys! Unfortunately this would be false. It is quite true that at this time I underwent a violent, and wholly successful, assault of sexual temptation. But this is amply accounted for by the age I had then reached and by my recent, in a sense my deliberate, withdrawal of myself from Divine protection. I do not believe Pogo had anything to do with it. The mere facts of generation I had learned long ago, from another boy, when I was too young to feel much more than a scientific interest in them. What attacked me through Pogo was not the Flesh (I had that of my own) but the World: the desire for glitter, swagger, distinction, the desire to be in the know. He gave little help, if any, in destroying my chastity, but he made sad work of certain humble and childlike and self-forgetful qualities which (I think) had remained with me till that moment. I began to labor very hard to make myself into a fop, a cad, and a snob.

Pogo's communications, however much they helped to vulgarize my mind, had no such electric effect on my senses as the dancing mistress, nor as Bekker's *Charicles,* which was given me for a prize. I never thought that dancing mistress as beautiful as my cousin G., but she was the first woman I ever "looked upon to lust after her"; assuredly through no fault of her own. A gesture, a tone of the voice, may in these matters have unpredictable results. When the schoolroom on the last night of the winter term was decorated for a dance, she paused, lifted a flag, and, remarking, "I love the smell of bunting," pressed it to her face — and I was undone.

You must not suppose that this was a romantic passion. The passion of my life, as the next chapter will show, belonged to a wholly different region. What I felt for the dancing mistress was sheer appetite; the prose and not the poetry of the Flesh. I did not feel at all like a knight devoting himself to a lady; I was much more like a Turk looking at a Circassian whom he could not afford to buy. I knew quite well what I wanted. It is common, by the way, to assume that such an experience produces a feeling of guilt, but it did not do so in me. And I may as well say here that the feeling of guilt, save where a moral offense happened also to break the code of honor or had consequences which excited my pity, was a thing which at that time I hardly knew. It took me as long to acquire inhibitions as others (they say) have taken to get rid of them. That is why I often find myself at such cross-purposes with the modern world: I have been a converted Pagan living among apostate Puritans.

I would be sorry if the reader passed too harsh a judgment on Pogo. As I now see it, he was not too old to have charge of boys but too young. He was only an adolescent himself, still immature enough to be delightedly "grown up" and naïve enough to enjoy our greater naïveté. And there was a real friendliness in him. He was moved partly by that to tell us all he knew or thought he knew. And now, As Herodotus would say, "Good-by to Pogo."

Meanwhile, side by side with my loss of faith, of virtue, and of simplicity, something quite different was going on. It will demand a new chapter.

V

RENAISSANCE

*So is there in us a world of love to somewhat, though we
know not what in the world that should be.*

TRAHERNE

I do not much believe in the Renaissance as generally described by historians. The more I look into the evidence the less trace I find of that vernal rapture which is supposed to have swept Europe in the fifteenth century. I half suspect that the glow in the historians' pages has a different source, that each is remembering, and projecting, his own personal Renaissance; that wonderful reawakening which comes to most of us when puberty is complete. It is properly called a rebirth not a birth, a reawakening not a wakening, because in many of us, besides being a new thing, it is also the recovery of things we had in childhood and lost when we became boys. For boyhood is very like the "dark ages" not as they were but as they are represented in bad, short histories. The dreams of childhood and those of adolescence may have much in common; between them, often, boyhood stretches like an alien territory in which everything (ourselves included) has been greedy, cruel, noisy, and prosaic, in which the imagination has slept and the most unideal senses and ambitions have been restlessly, even maniacally, awake.

In my own life it was certainly so. My childhood is at unity with the rest of my life; my boyhood not so. Many of the books that pleased me as a child, please me still; nothing but necessity would make me reread most of the books that I read at Oldie's or at Campbell. From that point of view it is all a sandy desert. The authentic "Joy" (as I tried to describe it in an earlier chapter) had vanished from my life: so completely that not even the memory or the desire of it remained. The reading of *Sohrab* had not given it to me. Joy is distinct not only from pleasure in general but even from aesthetic pleasure. It must have the stab, the pang, the inconsolable longing.

This long winter broke up in a single moment, fairly early in my time at Chartres. Spring is the inevitable image, but this was not gradual like Nature's springs. It was as if the Arctic itself, all the deep layers of secular ice, should change not in a week nor in an hour, but instantly, into a landscape of grass and primroses and orchards in bloom, deafened with bird songs and astir with running water. I can lay my hand on the very moment; there is hardly any fact I know so well, though I cannot date it. Someone must have left in the schoolroom a literary periodical: *The Bookman,* perhaps, or the *Times Literary Supplement.* My eye fell upon a headline and a picture, carelessly, expecting nothing. A moment later, as the poet says, "The sky had turned round."

What I had read was the words *Siegfried and the Twilight of the Gods.* What I had seen was one of Arthur Rackham's illustrations to that volume. I had never heard of Wagner, nor of Siegfried. I thought the Twilight of the Gods meant the twilight in which the gods lived. How did I know, at once and beyond question, that this was no Celtic, or silvan, or terrestrial twilight? But so it was. Pure "Northernness" engulfed me: a vision of huge, clear spaces hanging above the Atlantic in the endless twilight of Northern summer, remoteness, severity . . . and almost at the same moment I knew that I had met this before, long, long ago (it hardly seems longer now) in *Tegner's Drapa,* that Siegfried (whatever it might be) belonged to the same world as Balder and the sunward-sailing cranes. And with that plunge back into my own past there arose at once, almost like heartbreak, the memory of Joy itself, the knowledge that I had once had what I had now lacked for years, that I was returning at last from exile and desert lands to my own country; and the distance of the Twilight of the Gods and the distance of my own past Joy, both unattainable, flowed together into a single, unendurable sense of desire and loss, which suddenly became one with the loss of the whole experience, which, as I now stared round that dusty schoolroom like a man recovering from unconsciousness, had already vanished, had eluded me at the very moment when I could first say *It is.* And at once I knew (with fatal knowledge) that to "have it again" was the supreme and only important object of desire.

After this everything played into my hands. One of my father's many presents to us boys had been a gramophone. Thus at the moment when my eyes fell on the words *Siegfried and the Twilight of the Gods,* gramophone catalogues were already one of my favorite forms of reading; but I had never remotely dreamed that the records from Grand Opera with their queer German or Italian names could have anything to do with me. Nor did I for a week or two think so now. But then I was assailed from a new quarter. A magazine called *The Soundbox* was doing synopses of great operas week by week, and it now did the whole *Ring.* I read in a rapture and discovered who Siegfried was and what was the "twilight" of the gods. I could contain myself no longer — I began a poem, a heroic poem on the Wagnerian version of the Niblung story. My only source was the abstracts in *The Soundbox,* and I was so ignorant that I made Alberich rhyme with *ditch* and Mime with *time.* My model was Pope's *Odyssey* and the poem began (with some mixture of mythologies)

> *Descend to earth, descend, celestial Nine*
> *And chant the ancient legends of the Rhine. . . .*

Since the fourth book had carried me only as far as the last scene of *The Rheingold,* the reader will not be surprised to hear that the poem was never finished. But it was not a waste of time, and I can still see just what it did for me and where it began to do it. The first three books (I may, perhaps, at this distance of time, say it without vanity) are really not at all bad for a boy. At the beginning of the unfinished fourth it goes all to pieces; and that is exactly the point at which I really began to try to make poetry. Up to then, if my lines rhymed and scanned and got on with the story I asked no more. Now, at the beginning of the fourth, I began to try to convey some of the intense excitement I was feeling, to look for expressions which would not merely state but suggest. Of course I failed, lost my prosaic clarity, spluttered, gasped, and presently fell silent; but I had learned what writing means.

All this time I had still not heard a note of Wagner's music, though the very shape of the printed letters of his name had become to me a magical symbol. Next holidays, in the dark, crowded shop of T. Edens Osborne (on whom be peace), I first heard a record of the *Ride of the Valkyries.* They laugh at it nowadays, and, indeed, wrenched from its context to make a concert piece, it may be a poor thing. But I had this in common with Wagner, that I was thinking not of concert pieces but of heroic drama. To a boy already crazed with "the Northernness," whose highest musical experience had been Sullivan, the *Ride* came like a thunderbolt. From that moment Wagnerian records (principally from the *Ring,* but also from *Lohengrin* and *Parsifal*) became the chief drain on my pocket money and the presents I invariably asked for. My general appreciation of music was not, at first, much altered. "Music" was one thing, "Wagnerian music" quite another, and there was no common measure between them; it was not a new pleasure but a new kind of pleasure, if indeed "pleasure" is the right word, rather than trouble, ecstasy, astonishment, "a conflict of sensations without name."

That summer our cousin H. (you remember, I hope, Cousin Quartus's eldest daughter, the dark Juno, the queen of Olympus), who was now married, asked us to spend some weeks with her on the outskirts of Dublin, in Dundrum. There, on her drawing-room table, I found the very book which had started the whole affair and which I had never dared to hope I should see, *Siegfried and the Twilight of the Gods* illustrated by Arthur Rackham. His pictures, which seemed to me then to be the very music made visible, plunged me a few fathoms deeper into my delight. I have seldom coveted anything as I coveted that book; and when I heard that there was a cheaper edition at fifteen shillings (though the sum was to me almost mythological) I knew I could never rest till it was mine. I got it in the end, largely because my brother went shares with me, purely through kindness, as I now see and then more than half suspected, for he was not enslaved by the Northernness. With a generosity which I was even then half ashamed to accept, he sank in what must have seemed to him a mere picture book seven and sixpence for which he knew a dozen better uses.

Although this affair will already seem to some readers undeserving of the space I have given it, I cannot continue my story at all without noting some of its bearings on the rest of my life.

First, you will misunderstand everything unless you realize that, at the time, Asgard and the Valkyries seemed to me incomparably more important than anything else in my experience — than the Matron Miss C., or the dancing mistress, or my chances of a scholarship. More shockingly, they seemed much more important than my steadily growing doubts about Christianity. This may have been — in part, no doubt was — penal blindness; yet that might not be the whole story. If the Northernness seemed then a bigger thing than my religion, that may partly have been because my attitude toward it contained elements which my religion ought to have contained and did not. It was not itself a new religion, for it contained no trace of belief and imposed no duties. Yet unless I am greatly mistaken there was in it something very like adoration, some kind of quite disinterested self-abandonment to an object which securely claimed this by simply being the object it was. We are taught in the Prayer Book to "give thanks to God for His great glory," as if we owed Him more thanks for being what He necessarily is than for any particular benefit He confers upon us; and so indeed we do and to know God is to know this. But I had been far from any such experience; I came far nearer to feeling this about the Norse gods whom I disbelieved in than I had ever done about the true God while I believed. Sometimes I can almost think that I was sent back to the false gods there to acquire some capacity for worship against the day when the true God should recall me to Himself. Not that I might not have learned this sooner and more safely, in ways I shall now never know, without apostasy, but that Divine punishments are also mercies, and particular good is worked out of particular evil, and the penal blindness made sanative.

Secondly, this imaginative Renaissance almost at once produced a new appreciation of external nature. At first, I think, this was parasitic on the literary and musical experiences. On that holiday at Dundrum, cycling among the Wicklow mountains, I was always involuntarily looking for scenes that might belong to the Wagnerian world, here a steep hillside covered with firs where Mime might meet Sieglinde, there a sunny glade where Siegfried might listen to the bird, or presently a dry valley of rocks where the lithe scaly body of Fafner might emerge from its cave. But soon (I cannot say how soon) nature ceased to be a mere reminder of the books, became herself the medium of the real joy. I do not say she ceased to be a reminder. All Joy reminds. It is never a possession, always a desire for something longer ago or further away or still "about to be." But Nature and the books now become equal reminders, joint reminders, of — well, of whatever it is. I came no nearer to what some would regard as the only genuine love of nature, the studious love which will make a man a botanist or an ornithologist. It was the mood of a scene that mattered to me; and in tasting that mood my skin and nose were as busy as my eyes.

Thirdly, I passed on from Wagner to everything else I could get hold of about Norse mythology, *Myths of the Norsemen, Myths and Legends of the Teutonic Race,* Mallet's *Northern Antiquities.* I became knowledgeable. From these books again and again I received the stab of Joy. I did not yet notice that it was, very gradually, becoming rarer. I did not yet reflect on the difference between it and the merely intellectual satisfaction of getting to know the Eddaic universe. If I could at this time have found anyone to teach me Old Norse I believe I would have worked at it hard.

And finally, the change I had undergone introduces a new difficulty into the writing of this present book. From that first moment in the schoolroom at Chartres my secret, imaginative life began to be so important and so distinct from my outer life that I almost have to tell two separate stories. The two lives do not seem to influence each other at all. Where there are hungry wastes, starving for Joy, in the one, the other may be full of cheerful bustle and success; or again, where the outer life is miserable, the other may be brimming over with ecstasy. By the imaginative life I here mean only my life as concerned with Joy — including in the outer life much that would ordinarily be called imagination, as, for example, much of my reading, and all my erotic or ambitious fantasies; for these are self-regarding. Even Animal-Land and India belong to the "Outer."

But they were no longer Animal-Land and India; some time in the late eighteenth century (their eighteenth century, not ours) they had been united into the single state of Boxen, which yields, oddly, an adjective *Boxonian,* not *Boxenian* as you might expect. By a wise provision they retained their separate kings but had a common legislative assembly, the Damerfesk. The electoral system was democratic, but this mattered very much less than in England, for the Damerfesk was never doomed to one fixed meeting place. The joint sovereigns could summon it anywhere, say at the tiny fishing village of Danphabel (the Clovelly of Northern Animal-Land, nestling at the foot of the mountains) or in the island of Piscia; and since the Court knew the sovereigns' choice earlier than anyone else, all local accommodation would be booked before a private member got wind of the matter, nor, if he reached the session, had he the least assurance that it would not be moved elsewhere as soon as he arrived. Hence we hear of a certain member who had never actually sat in the Damerfesk at all except on one fortunate occasion when it met in his home town. The records sometimes call this assembly the Parliament, but that is misleading. It had only a single chamber, and the kings presided. At the period which I know best the effective control, however, was not in their hands but in those of an all-important functionary known as the Littlemaster (you must pronounce this all as one word with the accent on the first syllable — like *Jerrybuilder*). The Littlemaster was a Prime Minister, a judge, and if not always Commander in Chief (the records waver on this point) certainly always a member of the General Staff. Such at least were the powers he wielded when I last visited Boxen. They may have been encroachments, for the office was held at that time by a man — or to speak more accurately, a Frog — of powerful personality. Lord Big brought to his task one rather unfair advantage; he had been the tutor of the two young kings and continued to hold over them a quasi-parental authority. Their spasmodic efforts to break his yoke were, unhappily, more directed to the evasion of his inquiry into their private pleasures than to any serious political end. As a result Lord Big, immense in size, resonant of voice, chivalrous (he was the hero of innumerable duels), stormy, eloquent, and impulsive, almost was the state. The reader will divine a certain resemblance between the life of the two kings under Lord

Big and our own life under our father. He will be right. But Big was not, in origin, simply our father first batrachised and then caricatured in some directions and glorified in others. He was in many ways a prophetic portrait of Sir Winston Churchill as Sir Winston Churchill came to be during the last war; I have indeed seen photographs of that great statesman in which, to anyone who has known Boxen, the frog element was unmistakable. This was not our only anticipation of the real world. Lord Big's most consistent opponent, the gadfly that always got inside his armor, was a certain small brown bear, a lieutenant in the Navy; and believe me or believe me not, Lieutenant James Bar was almost exactly like Mr. John Betjeman, whose acquaintance I could not then have made. Ever since I have done so, I have been playing Lord Big to his James Bar.

The interesting thing about the resemblance between Lord Big and my father is that such reflections of the real world had not been the germ out of which Boxen grew. They were more numerous as it drew nearer to its end, a sign of over-ripeness or even the beginning of decay. Go back a little and you will not find them. The two sovereigns who allowed themselves to be dominated by Lord Big were King Benjamin VIII of Animal-Land and Rajah Hawki (I think, VI) of India. They had much in common with my brother and myself. But their fathers, the elder Benjamin and the elder Hawki, had not. The Fifth Hawki is a shadowy figure; but the Seventh Benjamin (a rabbit, as you will have guessed) is a rounded character. I can see him still — the heaviest-jowled and squarest-built of all rabbits, very fat in his later years, most shabbily and unroyally clad in his loose brown coat and baggy checked trousers, yet not without a certain dignity which could, on occasion, take disconcerting forms. His earlier life had been dominated by the belief that he could be both a king and an amateur detective. He never succeeded in the latter role, partly because the chief enemy whom he was pursuing (Mr. Baddlesmere) was not really a criminal at all but a lunatic — a complication which would have thrown out the plans of Sherlock Holmes himself. But he very often got himself kidnaped, sometimes for longish periods, and caused great anxiety to his court (we do not learn that his colleague, Hawki V, shared this). Once, on his return from such a misadventure, he had great difficulty in establishing his identity; Baddlesmere had dyed him and the familiar brown figure reappeared as a piebald rabbit. Finally (what will not boys think of?) he was a very early experimenter with what has since been called artificial insemination. The judgement of history cannot pronounce him either a good rabbit or a good King; but he was not a nonentity. He ate prodigiously.

And now that I have opened the gate, all the Boxonians, like the ghosts in Homer, come clamoring for mention. But they must be denied it. Readers who have built a world would rather tell of their own than hear of mine; those who have not would perhaps be bewildered and repelled. Nor had Boxen any connection with Joy. I have mentioned it at all only because to omit it would have been to misrepresent this period of my life.

One caution must here be repeated. I have been describing a life in which, plainly, imagination of one sort or another played the dominant part. Remember that it never involved the least grain of belief; I never mistook imagination for reality. About the Northernness no such question could arise: it was essentially a desire and implied the absence of its object. And Boxen we never could believe in, for we had made it. No novelist (in that sense) believes in his own characters.

At the end of the Summer Term 1913 I won a classical entrance scholarship to Wyvern College.

VI

BLOODERY

Any way for Heaven sake
So I were out of your whispering.
WEBSTER

Now that we have done with Chartres we may call Wyvern College simply Wyvern, or more simply still, as Wyvernians themselves call it, the Coll.

Going to the Coll was the most exciting thing that had yet happened in my outer life. At Chartres we had lived under the shadow of the Coll. We were often taken there to see matches or sports or the finish of the great Goldbury Run. These visits turned our heads. The crowd of boys older than oneself, their dazzling air of sophistication, scraps of their esoteric talk overheard, were like Park Lane in the old "Season" to a girl who is to be a debutante next year. Above all, the Bloods, the adored athletes and prefects, were an embodiment of all worldly pomp, power, and glory. Beside them Pogo shrank into insignificance; what is a Master compared with a Blood? The whole school was a great temple for the worship of these mortal gods; and no boy ever went there more prepared to worship them than I.

If you have not been at such a school as Wyvern, you may ask what a *Blood* is. He is a member of the school aristocracy. Foreign readers must clearly understand that this aristocracy has nothing whatever to do with the social position of the boys in the outer world. Boys of good, or wealthy, family are no more likely to be in it than anyone else; the only nobleman in my House at Wyvern never became a Blood. Shortly before my time there the son of a very queer customer had been at least on the fringe of Bloodery. The qualifying condition for Bloodery is that one should have been at the school for a considerable time. This by itself will not get you in, but newness will certainly exclude you. The most important qualification is athletic prowess. Indeed if this is sufficiently brilliant it makes you a Blood automatically. If it is a little less brilliant, then good looks and personality will help. So, of course, will fashion, as fashion is understood at your school. A wise candidate for Bloodery

47

will wear the right clothes, use the right slang, admire the right things, laugh at the right jokes. And of course, as in the outer world, those on the fringes of the privileged class can, and do, try to worm their way into it by all the usual arts of pleasing.

At some schools, I am told, there is a sort of dyarchy. An aristocracy of Bloods, supported or at least tolerated by popular sentiment, stands over against an official ruling class of prefects appointed by the Masters. I believe they usually appoint it from the highest form, so that it has some claim to be an intelligentsia. It was not so at the Coll. Those who were made prefects were nearly all Bloods and they did not have to be in any particular form. Theoretically (though I do not suppose this would ever happen) the dunce at the bottom of the lowest form could have been made the captain — in our language, the Head — of the Coll. We thus had only a single governing class, in whom every kind of power, privilege, and prestige were united. Those to whom the hero worship of their juniors would in any case have gone, and those whose astuteness and ambition would under any system have enabled them to rise, were the same whom the official power of the Masters supported. Their position was emphasized by special liberties, clothes, priorities, and dignities which affected every side of school life. This, you will see, makes a pretty strong class. But it was strengthened still further by a factor which distinguishes school from ordinary life. In a country governed by an oligarchy, huge numbers of people, and among them some very stirring spirits, know they can never hope to get into that oligarchy; it may therefore be worth their while to attempt a revolution. At the Coll the lowest social class of all were too young, therefore too weak, to dream of revolt. In the middle class — boys who were no longer fags but not yet Bloods — those who alone had physical strength and popularity enough to qualify them as leaders of a revolution were already beginning to hope for Bloodery themselves. It suited them better to accelerate their social progress by courting the existing Bloods than to risk a revolt which, in the unlikely event of its succeding, would destroy the very prize they were longing to share. And if at last they despaired of ever doing so — why, by that time their school-days were nearly over. Hence the Wyvernian constitution was unbreakable. Schoolboys have often risen against their Masters; I doubt if there has ever been or ever can be a revolt against Bloods.

It is not, then, surprising if I went to the Coll prepared to worship. Can any adult aristocracy present the World to us in quite such an alluring form as the hierarchy of a public school? Every motive for prostration is brought to bear at once on the mind of the New Boy when he sees a Blood; the natural respect of the thirteen-year-old for the nineteen-year-old, the fan's feeling for a film star, the suburban woman's feeling for a duchess, the newcomer's awe in the presence of the Old Hand, the street urchin's dread of the police.

One's first hours at a public school are unforgettable. Our House was a tall, narrow stone building (and, by the way, the only house in the place which was not an architectural nightmare) rather like a ship. The deck on which we chiefly lived consisted of two very dark stone corridors at right angles to one another. The doors off

them opened into the studies — little rooms about six feet square, each shared by two
or three boys. The very sight of them was ravishing to a boy from a Prep school who
had never before had a *pied-à-terre* of his own. As we were still living (culturally) in
the Edwardian period, each study imitated as closely as possible the cluttered appearance of an Edwardian drawing room; the aim was to fill the tiny cell as full as it
could hold with bookcases, corner cupboards, knickknacks, and pictures. There were
two larger rooms on the same floor; one the "Pres' Room," the synod of Olympus, and
the other the New Boys' Study. It was not like a study at all. It was larger, darker, and
undecorated; an immovable bench ran round a clamped table. But we knew, we ten or
twelve recruits, that not all of us would be left in the New Boys' Study. Some of us
would be given "real" studies; the residue would occupy the opprobrious place for a
term or so. That was the great hazard of our first evening; one was to be taken and
another left.

As we sat round our clamped table, silent for the most part and speaking in whispers when we spoke, the door would be opened at intervals; a boy would look in,
smile (not at us but to himself) and withdraw. Once, over the shoulder of the smiler
there came another face, and a chuckling voice said, "Ho-ho! I know what *you're*
looking for." Only I knew what it was all about, for my brother had played
Chesterfield to my Stanhope and instructed me in the manners of the Coll. None of
the boys who looked in and smiled was a Blood; they were all quite young and there
was something common to the faces of them all. They were, in fact, the reigning or
fading Tarts of the House, trying to guess which of us were their destined rivals or
successors.

It is possible that some readers will not know what a House Tart was. First, as to
the adjective. All life at Wyvern was lived, so to speak, in the two concentric circles of
Coll and House. You could be a Coll pre or merely a House pre. You could be a Coll
Blood or merely a House Blood, a Coll Punt (*i.e.*, a pariah, an unpopular person) or
merely a House Punt; and of course a Coll Tart or merely a House Tart. A Tart is[1] a
pretty and effeminate-looking small boy who acts as a catamite to one or more of his
seniors, usually Bloods. Usually, not always. Though our oligarchy kept most of the
amenities of life to themselves, they were, on this point, liberal; they did not impose
chastity on the middle-class boy in addition to all his other disabilities. Pederasty
among the lower classes was not "side," or at least not serious side; not like putting
one's hands in one's pockets or wearing one's coat unbuttoned. The gods had a sense of
proportion.

The Tarts had an important function to play in making school (what it was advertised to be) a preparation for a public life. They were not like slaves, for their favors
were (nearly always) solicited, not compelled. Nor were they exactly like prostitutes,
for the liaison often had some permanence and, far from being merely sensual, was
highly sentimentalized. Nor were they paid (in hard cash, I mean) for their services;

[1]Here, and throughout this account, I sometimes use the "historic present." Heaven forfend I should be
taken to mean that Wyvern is the same today.

though of course they had all the flattery, unofficial influence, favor, and privileges which the mistresses of the great have always enjoyed in adult society. That was where the Preparation for Public Life came in. It would appear from Mr. Arnold Lunn's *Harrovians* that the Tarts at his school acted as informers. None of ours did. I ought to know, for one of my friends shared a study with a minor Tart; and except that he was sometimes turned out of the study when one of the Tart's lovers came in (and that, after all, was only natural) he had nothing to complain of. I was not shocked by these things. For me, at that age, the chief drawback to the whole system was that it bored me considerably. For you will have missed the atmosphere of our House unless you picture the whole place from week's end to week's end buzzing, tittering, hinting, whispering about this subject. After games, gallantry was the principal topic of polite conversation; who had "a case with" whom, whose star was in the ascendant, who had whose photo, who and when and how often and what night and where. . . . I suppose it might be called the Greek Tradition. But the vice in question is one to which I had never been tempted, and which, indeed, I still find opaque to the imagination. Possibly, if I had only stayed longer at the Coll, I might, in this respect as in others, have been turned into a Normal Boy, as the system promises. As things were, I was bored.

Those first days, like your first days in the army, were spent in a frantic endeavor to find out what you had to do. One of my first duties was to find out what "Club" I was in. Clubs were the units to which we were assigned for compulsory games; they belonged to the Coll organization, not the House organization, so I had to go to a notice board "Up Coll" to get my facts. And first to find the place – and then to dare to squeeze oneself into the crowd of more important boys around the notice board – and then to begin reading through five hundred names, but always with one eye on your watch, for of course there is something else to be done within ten minutes. I was forced away from the board before I had found my name, and so, sweating, back to the House, in a flurry of anxiety, wondering how I could find time to do the job tomorrow and what unheard-of disaster might follow if I could not. (Why, by the way, do some writers talk as if care and worry were the special characteristics of adult life? It appears to me that there is more *atra cura* in an average schoolboy's week than in a grown man's average year.)

When I reached the House something gloriously unexpected happened. At the door of the Pres' Room stood one Fribble; a mere House Blood, it is true, even a minor House Blood, but to me a sufficiently exalted figure; a youth of the lean, laughing type. I could hardly believe it when he actually addressed me. "Oh, I say, Lewis," he bawled, "I can tell you your Club. You're in the same one as me, B6." What a transition from all but despair to elation I underwent! All my anxiety was laid to rest. And then the graciousness of Fribble, the condescension! If a reigning monarch had asked me to dine, I could hardly have been more flattered. But there was better to follow. On every half-holiday I went dutifully to the B6 notice board to see whether my name was down to play that afternoon or not. And it never was. This was pure joy, for of course I hated games. My native clumsiness, combined with the lack of early training for which Belsen was responsible, had ruled out all possibility of my ever playing well enough to amuse myself, let alone to satisfy other players. I accepted games (quite a number of boys do) as one of the necessary evils of life, comparable to Income Tax or the Dentist. And so, for a week or two, I was in clover.

Then the blow fell. Fribble had lied. I was in a totally different Club. My name had more than once appeared on a notice board I had never seen. I had committed the serious crime of "Skipping Clubs." The punishment was a flogging administered by the Head of the Coll in the presence of the assembled Coll Pres. To the Head of the Coll himself — a red-headed, pimply boy with a name like Borage or Porridge — I can bear no grudge; it was to him a routine matter. But I must give him a name because the real point of the story requires it. The emissary (some Blood a little lower than the Head himself) who summoned me to execution attempted to reveal to me the heinousness of my crime by the words, "Who are you? Nobody. Who is Porridge? THE MOST IMPORTANT PERSON THERE IS."

I thought then, and I still think, that this rather missed the point. There were two perfectly good morals he could have drawn. He might have said, "We are going to teach you never to rely on secondhand information when firsthand is available" — a very profitable lesson. Or he might have said, "What made you think that a Blood could not be a liar?" But, "Who are you? Nobody," however just, seems hardly relevant. The implication is that I have skipped Club in arrogance or defiance. And I puzzle endlessly over the question whether the speaker really believed that. Did he really think it likely that an utterly helpless stranger in a new society, a society governed by an irresistible class on whose favor all his hopes of happiness depended, had set himself in the first week to pull the nose of The Most Important Person There Is? It is a problem which has met me many times in later life. What does a certain type of examiner mean when he says, "To show up work like this is an insult to the examiners"? Does he really think that the plowed candidate has insulted him?

Another problem is Fribble's share in my little catastrophe. Was his lie to me a hoax, a practical joke? Was he paying off some old score against my brother? Or was he (as I now think most likely) simply what our ancestors called a Rattle, a man from whose mouth information, true and false, flows out all day long without consideration, almost without volition? Some might think that, whatever his motive had originally been, he might have come forward and confessed his part when he saw what I was in for. But that, you know, was hardly to be expected. He was a very minor Blood, still climbing up the social stair; Burradge was almost as far above Fribble as Fribble was above me. By coming forward he would have imperiled his social position, in a community where social advancement was the one thing that mattered; school is a preparation for public life.

In justice to Wyvern, I must add that Fribble was not, by our standards, quite a fair representative of Bloodery. He had offended against the rules of gallantry in a manner which (my brother tells me) would have been impossible in his day. I said just now that the Tarts were solicited, not compelled. But Fribble did use all his prefectorial powers for a whole term to persecute a boy called, let us say, Parsley, who had refused his suit. This was quite easy for Fribble to do. The innumerable small regulations which a junior boy could break almost unawares enabled a prefect to make sure that a given boy was nearly always in trouble, while the fagging system made it easy to see that he had no leisure at all at any hour of any day. So Parsley learned what it was to refuse even a minor Blood. The story would be more impressive if Parsley had been a virtuous boy and had refused on moral grounds. Unfortunately he was "as common as a barber's chair," had been a reigning toast in my brother's day, and was now almost past his bloom. He drew the line at Fribble. But Fribble's attempt at coercion was the only instance of its kind I ever knew.

Indeed, taking them by and large, and considering the temptations of adolescents, so privileged, so flattered, our Bloods were not a bad lot. The Count was even kindly. The Parrot was nothing worse than a grave fool: "Yards-of-Face" they called him. Stopfish, whom some thought cruel, even had moral principles; in his younger days many (I'm told) had desired him as a Tart, but he had kept his virtue. "Pretty, but no good to anyone; he's *pie*," would be the Wyvernian comment. The hardest to defend, perhaps, is Tennyson. We did not much mind his being a shoplifter; some people thought it rather clever of him to come back from a tour of the town with more ties and socks than he had paid for. We minded more his favorite punishment for us rabble, "a clip." Yet he could truly have pleaded to the authorities that it meant merely a box on the ear. He would not have added that the patient was made to stand with his left ear, temple and cheek almost, but not quite, touching the jamb of a doorway, and then struck with full force on the right. We also grumbled a little in secret when we got up a tournament (either explicitly or virtually compulsory, I think) in a game called Yard Cricket, collected subscriptions, and neither held the tournament nor returned the cash. But you will remember that this happened in the Marconi period, and to be a prefect is a Preparation for Public Life. And for all of them, even Tennyson, one thing can be said; they were never drunk. I was told that their predecessors, a year before I came, were sometimes very drunk indeed in the House corridor at midday. In fact, odd as it would have sounded to an adult, I joined the House when it was in a stern mood of moral rearmament. That was the point of a series of speeches which the prefects addressed to us all in the House Library during my first week. It was explained with a wealth of threatenings that we were to be pulled Up or Together or wherever decadents are pulled by moral reformers. Tennyson was very great on that occasion. He had a fine bass voice and sang solos in the choir. I knew one of his Tarts.

Peace to them all. A worse fate awaited them than the most vindictive fag among us could have wished. Ypres and the Somme ate up most of them. They were happy while their good days lasted.

My flogging by pimply old Ullage was no unmerciful affair in itself. The real trouble was that I think I now became, thanks to Fribble, a marked man; the sort of dangerous New Boy who skips Clubs. At least I think that must have been the main reason why I was an object of dislike to Tennyson. There were probably others. I was big for my age, a great lout of a boy, and that sets one's seniors against one. I was also useless at games. Worst of all, there was my face. I am the kind of person who gets told, "And take that look off your face too." Notice, once more, the mingled justice and injustice of our lives. No doubt in conceit or ill temper I have often intended to look insolent or truculent; but on those occasions people don't appear to notice it. On the other hand, the moments at which I was told to "take that look off" were usually those when I intended to be most abject. Can there have been a freeman somewhere among my ancestors whose expression, against my will, looked out?

As I have hinted before, the fagging system is the chief medium by which the Bloods, without breaking any rule, can make a junior boy's life a weariness to him. Different schools have different kinds of fagging. At some of them, individual Bloods have individual fags. This is the system most often depicted in school stories; it is sometimes represented as — and, for all I know, sometimes really is — a fruitful relation as of knight and squire, in which service on the one part is rewarded with some degree of countenance and protection on the other. But whatever its merits may be, we never experienced them at Wyvern. Fagging with us was as impersonal as the labor market in Victorian England; in that way, too, the Coll was a preparation for public life. All boys under a certain seniority constituted a labor pool, the common property of all the Bloods. When a Blood wanted his O.T.C. kit brushed and polished, or his boots cleaned, or his study "done out," or his tea made, he shouted. We all came running, and of course the Blood gave the work to the boy he most disliked. The kit cleaning — it took hours, and then, when you had finished it, your own kit was still to do — was the most detested *corvée*. Shoe cleaning was a nuisance not so much in itself as in its attendant circumstances. It came at an hour which was vital for a boy like me who, having won a scholarship, had been placed in a high form and could hardly, by all his best efforts, keep up with the work. Hence the success of one's whole day in Form might depend on the precious forty minutes between breakfast and Morning School, when one went over the set passages of translation with other boys in the same Form. This could be done only if one escaped being fagged as a shoeblack. Not, of course, that it takes forty minutes to clean a pair of shoes. What takes the time is waiting in the queue of other fags in the "boot-hole" to get your turn at the brushes and blacking. The whole look of that cellar, the darkness, the smell, and (for most of the year) the freezing cold, are a vivid memory. You must not of course suppose that, in those spacious days, we lacked servants. There were two official "bootboys" paid by the Housemaster for cleaning all boots and shoes, and everyone, including us fags who had cleaned both our own shoes and the Blood's shoes daily, tipped the bootboys at the end of each term for their services.

For a reason which all English readers will understand (others will hear something of it in the next chapter) I am humiliated and embarrassed at having to record that as time went on I came to dislike the fagging system. No true defender of the Public Schools will believe me if I say that I was tired. But I was — dog tired, cab-horse tired, tired (almost) like a child in a factory. Many things besides fagging contributed to it. I was big and had possibly outgrown my strength. My work in Form was almost beyond me. I was having a good deal of dental trouble at the time, and many nights of clamorous pain. Never, except in the front-line trenches (and not always there) do I remember such aching and continuous weariness as at Wyvern. Oh, the implacable day, the horror of waking, the endless desert of hours that separated one from bedtime! And remember that, even without fagging, a school day contains hardly any leisure for a boy who does not like games. For him, to pass from the form room to the playing field is simply to exchange work in which he can take some interest for work in which he can take none, in which failure is more severely punished, and in which (worst of all) he must feign an interest.

I think that this feigning, this ceaseless pretense of interest in matters to me supremely boring, was what wore me out more than anything else. If the reader will picture himself, unarmed, shut up for thirteen weeks on end, night and day, in a society of fanatical golfers – or, if he is a golfer himself, let him substitute fishermen, theosophists, bimetalists, Baconians, or German undergraduates with a taste for autobiography – who all carry revolvers and will probably shoot him if he ever seems to lose interest in their conversation, he will have an idea of my school life. Even the hardy Chowbok (in *Erewhon*) quailed at such a destiny. For games (and gallantry) were the only subjects, and I cared for neither. But I must seem to care for both, for a boy goes to a Public School precisely to be made a normal, sensible boy – a good mixer – to be taken out of himself; and eccentricity is severely penalized.

You must not, from this, hastily conclude that most boys liked *playing* games any better than I did. To escape Clubs was considered by dozens of boys an obvious good. Leave off Clubs required the Housemaster's signature, and that harmless Merovingian's signature was imitable. A competent forger (I knew one member of the profession) by manufacturing and selling forged signatures could make a steady addition to his pocket money. The perpetual talk about games depended on three things. First, on the same sort of genuine (though hardly practical) enthusiasm which sends the crowds to the League Football Matches. Few wanted to play, but many wanted to watch, to participate vicariously in the triumphs of the Coll, or the House, team. Secondly, this natural feeling had the vigilant backing of all the Bloods and nearly all the Masters. To be lukewarm on such matters was the supreme sin. Hence enthusiasm had to be exaggerated where it existed and simulated where it did not. At cricket matches minor Bloods patrolled the crowd of spectators to detect and punish any "slackness' in the applause; it reminds one of the precautions taken when Nero sang. For of course the whole structure of Bloodery would collapse if the Bloods played in the spirit of play, for their recreation; there must be audience and limelight. And this brings us to the third reason. For boys who were not yet Bloods but who had some athletic promise, Games were essentially a *moyen de parvenir*. There was nothing recreational about Clubs for them any more than for me. They went to the playing fields not as men go to the tennis club but as stagestruck girls go to an Audition; tense and anxious, racked with dazzling hopes and sickening fears, never in peace of mind till they had won some notice which would set their feet on the first rung of the social ladder. And not then at peace either; for not to advance is to fall back.

The truth is that organized and compulsory games had, in my day, banished the element of play from school life almost entirely. There was no time to play (in the proper sense of the word). The rivalry was too fierce, the prizes too glittering, the "hell of failure" too severe.

The only boy, almost, who "played" (but not at games) was our Irish earl. But then he was an exception to all rules; not because of his earldom but because he was an untamable Irishman, anarch in grain, whom no society could iron out. He smoked a pipe in his first term. He went off by night on strange expeditions to a neighboring city; not, I believe, for women, but for harmless rowdyism, low life, and adventure. He always carried a revolver. I remember it well, for he had a habit of loading one chamber only, rushing into your study, and then firing off (if that is the right word) all the others at you, so that your life depended on his counting accurately. I felt at the time, and I feel still, that this (unlike the fagging) was the sort of thing no sensible boy could object to. It was done in defiance both of masters and Bloods, it was wholly useless, and there was no malice in it. I liked Ballygunnian; he, too, was killed in France. I do not think he ever became a Blood; if he had, he wouldn't have noticed it. He cared nothing for the limelight or for social success. He passed through the Coll without paying it any attention.

I suppose Popsy — the pretty redhead who was housemaid on "the Private Side" — might also rank as an element making for "play." Popsy, when caught and carried bodily into our part of the House (I think by the Count), was all giggles and screams. She was too sensible a girl to surrender her "virtue" to any Blood; but it was rumored that those who found her in the right time and place might induce her to give certain lessons in anatomy. Perhaps they lied.

I have hardly mentioned a Master yet. One master, dearly loved and reverenced, will appear in the next chapter. But other masters are hardly worth speaking of. It is difficult for parents (and more difficult, perhaps, for schoolmasters) to realize the unimportance of most masters in the life of a school. Of the good and evil which is done to a schoolboy masters, in general, do little, and know less. Our own House-master must have been an upright man, for he fed us excellently. For the rest, he treated his House in a very gentlemanly, uninquisitive way. He sometimes walked round the dormitories of a night, but he always wore boots, trod heavily and coughed at the door. He was no spy and no kill-joy, honest man. Live and let live.

As I grew more and more tired, both in body and mind, I came to hate Wyvern. I did not notice the real harm it was doing to me. It was gradually teaching me to be a prig; that is, an intellectual prig or (in the bad sense) a Highbrow. But that subject must wait for another chapter. At the tail end of this I must repeat (for this is the overall impression left by Wyvern) that I was tired. Consciousness itself was becoming the supreme evil; sleep, the prime good. To lie down, to be out of the sound of voices, to pretend and grimace and evade and slink no more, that was the object of all desire — if only there were not another morning ahead — if only sleep could last for ever!

VII

LIGHT AND SHADE

No situation, however wretched it seems, but has some
sort of comfort attending it.

GOLDSMITH

Here's a fellow, you say, who used to come before us as a moral and religious writer, and now, if you please, he's written a whole chapter describing his old school as a very furnace of impure loves without one word on the heinousness of the sin. But there are two reasons. One you shall hear before this chapter ends. The other is that, as I have said, the sin in question is one of the two (gambling is the other) which I have never been tempted to commit. I will not indulge in futile philippics against enemies I never met in battle.

("This means, then, that all the other vices you have so largely written about..." Well, yes, it does, and more's the pity; but it's nothing to our purpose at the moment.)

I have now to tell you how Wyvern made me a prig. When I went there, nothing was further from my mind than the idea that my private taste for fairly good books, for Wagner, for mythology, gave me any sort of superiority to those who read nothing but magazines and listened to nothing but the (then fashionable) Ragtime. The claim might seem unbelievable if I did not add that I had been protected from this sort of conceit by downright ignorance. Mr. Ian Hay somewhere draws a picture of the reading minority at a Public School in his day as boys who talked about "G. B. S. and G. K. C." in the same spirit in which other boys secretly smoked; both sets were inspired by the same craving for forbidden fruit and the same desire to be grown up. And I suppose boys such as he describes might come from Chelsea or Oxford or Cambridge homes where they heard things about contemporary literature. But my position was wholly different. I was, for example, a great reader of Shaw about the time I went to Wyvern, but I had never dreamed that reading Shaw was anything to be proud of. Shaw was an author on my father's shelves like any other author. I began reading him because his *Dramatic Opinions* contained a good deal about Wagner and

57

Wagner's very name was then a lure to me. Thence I went on to read most of the other Shaws we had. But how his reputation stood in the literary world I neither knew or cared; I didn't know there was "a literary world." My father told me Shaw was "a mountebank" but that there were some laughs in *John Bull's Other Island.* It was the same with all my other reading; no one (thank God) had ever admired or encouraged it. (William Morris, for some unfathomable reason, my father always referred to as "that whistlepainter.") I might be — no doubt I was — conceited at Chartres for being good at my Latin; this was something recognized as meritorious. But "Eng. Lit." was blessedly absent from the official syllabus, so I was saved from any possibility of conceit about it. Never in my life had I read a work of fiction, poetry, or criticism in my own language except because, after trying the first few pages, I liked the taste of it. I could not help knowing that most other people, boys and grown-ups alike, did not care for the books I read. A very few tastes I could share with my father, a few more with my brother; apart from that, there was no point of contact, and this I accepted as a sort of natural law. If I reflected on it at all, it would have given me, I think, a slight feeling, not of superiority, but of inferiority. The latest popular novel was so obviously a more adult, a more normal, a more sophisticated taste than any of mine. A certain shame or bashfulness attached itself to whatever one deeply and privately enjoyed. I went to the Coll far more disposed to excuse my literary tastes than to plume myself on them.

But this innocence did not last. It was, from the first, a little shaken by all that I soon began to learn from my form master about the glories of literature. I was at last made free of the dangerous secret that others had, like me, found there "enormous bliss" and been maddened by beauty. Among the other New Bugs of my year, too, I met a pair of boys who came from the Dragon School at Oxford (where Naomi Mitchison in her teens had just produced her first play) and from them also I got the dim impression that there was a world I had never dreamed of, a world in which poetry, say, was a thing public and accepted, just as Games and Gallantry were accepted at Wyvern; nay, a world in which a taste for such things was almost meritorious. I felt as Siegfried felt when it first dawned on him that he was not Mime's son. What had been "my" taste was apparently "our" taste (if only I could ever meet the "we" to whom that "our" belonged). And if "our" taste, then — by a perilous transition — perhaps "good" taste or "the right taste." For that transition involves a kind of Fall. The moment good taste knows itself, some if its goodness is lost. Even then, however, it is not necessary to take the further downward step of despising the "philistines" who do not share it. Unfortunately I took it. Hitherto, though increasingly miserable at Wyvern, I had been half ashamed of my own misery, still ready (if I were only allowed) to admire the Olympians, still a little over-awed, cowed rather than resentful. I had, you see, no standing place against the Wyvernian *ethos,* no side for which I could play against it; it was a bare "I" against what seemed simply the world. But the moment that "I" became, however vaguely, a *we* — and Wyvern not *the* world but *a* world — the whole thing changed. It was now possible, at least in thought, to retaliate. I can remember what may well have been the precise moment of this transition. A prefect called Blugg or Glubb or some such name stood opposite me, belching in my face, giving me some order. The belching was not intended as an insult. You can't "insult" a fag any more than an animal. If Bulb had thought of my reactions at all, he would have expected me to find his eructations funny. What pushed me over the edge into pure priggery was his face – the puffy bloated cheeks, the thick, moist, sagging lower lip, the yokel blend of drowsiness and cunning. "The lout!" I thought. "The clod! The dull, crass clown! For all his powers and privileges, I would not be he." I had become a Prig, a Highbrow.

The interesting thing is that the public-school system had thus produced the very thing which it was advertised to prevent or cure. For you must understand (if you have not been dipped in that tradition yourself) that the whole thing was devised to "knock the nonsense" out of the smaller boys and "put them in their place." "If the junior boys weren't fagged," as my brother once said, "they would become insufferable." That is why I felt so embarrassed, a few pages ago, when I had to confess that I got rather tired of perpetual fagging. If you say this, every true defender of the system will diagnose your case at once, and they will all diagnose it in the same way. "Ho-ho!" they will cry, "so *that's* the trouble! Thought yourself too good to black your betters' boots, did you? That just shows how badly you needed to be fagged. It's to cure young prigs like you that the system exists." That any cause except "thinking yourself too good for it" might awaken discontent with a fag's lot will not be admitted. You have only to transfer the thing to adult life and you will, apparently, see the full logic of the position. If some neighboring V.I.P. had irresistible authority to call on you for any service he pleased at any hour when you were not in the office – if, when you came home on a summer evening, tired from work and with more work to prepare against the morrow, he could drag you to the links and make you his caddy till the light failed – if at last he dismissed you unthanked with a suitcase full of his clothes to brush and clean and return to him before breakfast, and a hamper full of his foul linen for your wife to wash and mend – and if, under this regime, you were not always perfectly happy and contented; where could the cause lie except in your own vanity? What else, after all, could it be? For, almost by definition, every offense a junior boy commits must be due to "cheek" or "side"; and to be miserable, even to fall short of rapturous enthusiasm, is an offense.

Obviously a certain grave danger was ever present to the minds of those who built up the Wyvernian hierarchy. It seemed to them self-evident that, if you left things to themselves, boys of nineteen who played rugger for the county and boxed for the school would everywhere be knocked down and sat on by boys of thirteen. And that, you know, would be a very shocking spectacle. The most elaborate mechanism, therefore, had to be devised for protecting the strong against the weak, the close corporation of Old Hands against the parcel of newcomers who were strangers to one another and to everyone in the place, the poor, trembling lions against the furious and ravening sheep.

There is, of course, some truth in it. Small boys can be cheeky; and half an hour in the society of a French thirteen-year-old makes most of us feel that there is something to be said for fagging after all. Yet I cannot help thinking that the bigger boys would have been able to hold their own without all the complicated assurances, pattings on the back, and encouragement which the authorities gave them. For, of course, these authorities, not content with knocking the "nonsense" out of the sheep, were always coaxing and petting an at least equal quantity of "nonsense" into the lions; power and privilege and an applauding audience for the games they play. Might not the mere nature of boys have done all, and rather more than all, that needed doing in this direction without assistance?

But whatever the rationality of the design, I contend that it did not achieve its object. For the last thirty years or so England has been filled with a bitter, truculent, skeptical debunking, and cynical *intelligentsia*. A great many of them were at public schools, and I believe very few of them liked it. Those who defend the schools will, of course, say that these Prigs are the cases which the system failed to cure; they were not kicked, mocked, fagged, flogged, and humiliated enough. But surely it is equally possible that they are the products of the system? that they were not Prigs at all when they came to their schools but were made Prigs by their first year, as I was? For, really, that would be a very natural result. Where oppression does not completely and permanently break the spirit, has it not a natural tendency to produce retaliatory pride and contempt? We reimburse ourselves for cuffs and toil by a double dose of self-esteem. No one is more likely to be arrogant than a lately freed slave.

I write, of course, only to neutral readers. With the wholehearted adherents of the system there is no arguing, for, as we have already seen, they have maxims and logic which the lay mind cannot apprehend. I have even heard them defend compulsory games on the ground that all boys "except a few rotters" like the games; they have to be compulsory because no compulsion is needed. (I wish I had never heard chaplains in the armed forces produce a similar argument in defense of the wicked institution of Church Parades.)

But the essential evil of public-school life, as I see it, did not lie either in the sufferings of the fags or in the privileged arrogance of the Bloods. These were symptoms of something more all-pervasive, something which, in the long run, did most harm to the boys who succeeded best at school and were happiest there. Spiritually speaking, the deadly thing was that school life was a life almost wholly dominated by the social struggle; to get on, to arrive, or, having reached the top, to remain there, was the absorbing preoccupation. It is often, of course, the preoccupation of adult life as well; but I have not yet seen any adult society in which the surrender to this impulse was so total. And from it, at school as in the world, all sorts of meanness flow; the sycophancy that courts those higher in the scale, the cultivation of those whom it is well to know, the speedy abandonment of friendships that will not help on the upward path, the readiness to join the cry against the unpopular, the secret motive in almost every action. The Wyvernians seem to me in retrospect to have been the least spontaneous, in that sense the least boyish, society I have ever known. It would perhaps not be too much to say that in some boys' lives everything was calculated to the great end of advancement. For this games were played; for this clothes, friends, amusements, and vices were chosen.

And that is why I cannot give pederasty anything like a first place among the evils of the Coll. There is much hypocrisy on this theme. People commonly talk as if every other evil were more tolerable than this. But why? Because those of us who do not share the vice feel for it a certain nausea, as we do, say, for necrophily? I think that of very little relevance to moral judgment. Because it produces permanent perversion? But there is very little evidence that it does. The Bloods would have preferred girls to boys if they could have come by them; when, at a later age, girls were obtainable, they probably took them. Is it then on Christian grounds? But how many of those who fulminate on the matter are in fact Christians? And what Christian, in a society so worldly and cruel as that of Wyvern, would pick out the carnal sins for special reprobation? Cruelty is surely more evil than lust and the World at least as dangerous as the Flesh. The real reason for all the pother is, in my opinion, neither Christian nor ethical. We attack this vice not because it is the worst but because it is, by adult standards, the most disreputable and unmentionable, and happens also to be a crime in English law. The World will lead you only to Hell; but sodomy may lead you to jail and create a scandal, and lose you your job. The World, to do it justice, seldom does that.

If those of us who have known a school like Wyvern dared to speak the truth, we should have to say that pederasty, however great an evil in itself, was, in that time and place, the only foothold or cranny left for certain good things. It was the only counterpoise to the social struggle; the one oasis (though green only with weeds and moist only with fetid water) in the burning desert of competitive ambition. In his unnatural love affairs, and perhaps only there, the Blood went a little out of himself, forgot for a few hours that he was One of the Most Important People There Are. It softens the picture. A perversion was the only chink left through which something spontaneous and uncalculating could creep in. Plato was right after all. Eros, turned upside down, blackened, distorted, and filthy, still bore the traces of his divinity.

What an answer, by the by, Wyvern was to those who derive all the ills of society from economics! For money had nothing to do with its class system. It was not (thank Heaven) the boys with threadbare coats who became Punts, nor the boys with plenty of pocket money who became Bloods. According to some theorists, therefore, it ought to have been entirely free from bourgeois vulgarities and iniquities. Yet I have never seen a community so competitive, so full of snobbery and flunkeyism, a ruling class so selfish and so class-conscious, or a proletariat so fawning, so lacking in all solidarity and sense of corporate honor. But perhaps one hardly needs to cite experience for a truth so obvious a priori. As Aristotle remarked, men do not become dictators in order to keep warm. If a ruling class has some other source of strength, why need it bother about money? Most of what it wants will be pressed upon it by emulous flatterers; the rest can be taken by force.

There were two blessings at Wyvern that wore no disguise; one of them was my form master, Smewgy as we called him. I spell the name so as to insure the right pronunciation — the first syllable should rhyme exactly with *Fugue* — though the Wyvern spelling was "Smugy."

Except at Oldie's I had been fortunate in my teachers ever since I was born; but Smewgy was "beyond expectation, beyond hope." He was a gray-head with large spectacles and a wide mouth which combined to give him a froglike expression, but nothing could be less froglike than his voice. He was honey-tongued. Every verse he read turned into music on his lips: something midway between speech and song. It is not the only good way of reading verse, but it is the way to enchant boys; more dramatic and less rhythmical ways can be learned later. He first taught me the right sensuality of poetry, how it should be savored and mouthed in solitude. Of Milton's "Thrones, Dominations, Princedoms, Virtues, Powers" he said, "That line made me happy for a week." It was not the sort of thing I had heard anyone say before. Nor had I ever met before perfect courtesy in a teacher. It had nothing to do with softness; Smewgy could be very severe, but it was the severity of a judge, weighty and measured, without taunting —

> *He never yet no vileinye ne sayde*
> *In all his lyf unto no maner wight.*

He had a difficult team to drive, for our form consisted partly of youngsters, New Bugs with scholarships, starting there like myself, and partly of veterans who had arrived there at the end of their slow journey up the school. He made us a unity by his good manners. He always addressed us as "gentlemen" and the possibility of behaving otherwise seemed thus to be ruled out from the beginning; and in that room at least the distinction between fags and Bloods never raised its head. On a hot day, when he had given us permission to remove our coats, he asked our permission before removing his gown. Once for bad work I was sent by him to the Headmaster to be threatened and rated. The Headmaster misunderstood Smewgy's report and thought there had been some complaint about my manners. Afterward Smewgy got wind of the Head's actual words and at once corrected the mistake, drawing me aside and saying, "There has been some curious misunderstanding. I said nothing of the sort about you. You will have to be whipped if you don't do better at your Greek Grammar next week, but naturally that has nothing to do with your manners or mine." The idea that the tone of conversation between one gentleman and another should be altered by a flogging (any more than by a duel) was ridiculous. His manner was perfect: no familiarity, no hostility, no threadbare humor; mutual respect; decorum. "Never let us live with *amousia,*" was one of his favorite maxims: *amousia,* the absence of the Muses. And he knew, as Spenser knew, that courtesy was of the Muses.

Thus, even had he taught us nothing else, to be in Smewgy's form was to be in a measure ennobled. Amidst all the banal ambition and flashy splendors of school life he stood as a permanent reminder of things more gracious, more humane, larger and cooler. But his teaching, in the narrower sense, was equally good. He could enchant but he could also analyze. An idiom or a textual crux, once expounded by Smewgy, became clear as day. He made us feel that the scholar's demand for accuracy was not merely pedantic, still less an arbitrary moral discipline, but rather a niceness, a delicacy, to lack which argued "a gross and swainish disposition." I began to see that the reader who misses syntactical points in a poem is missing aesthetic points as well.

In those days a boy on the classical side officially did almost nothing but classics. I think this was wise; the greatest service we can do to education today is to teach fewer subjects. No one has time to do more than a very few things well before he is twenty, and when we force a boy to be a mediocrity in a dozen subjects we destroy his standards, perhaps for life. Smewgy taught us Latin and Greek, but everything else came in incidentally. The books I liked best under his teaching were Horace's Odes, Aeneid IV, and Euripides' *Bacchae.* I had always in one sense "liked" my classical work, but hitherto this had only been the pleasure that everyone feels in mastering a craft. Now I tasted the classics as poetry. Euripides' picture of Dionysus was closely linked in my mind with the whole mood of Mr. Stephens' *Crock of Gold,* which I had lately read for the first time with great excitement. Here was something very different from the Northernness. Pan and Dionysus lacked the cold, piercing appeal of Odin and Frey. A new quality entered my imagination: something Mediterranean and volcanic, the orgiastic drum beat. Orgiastic, but not, or not strongly, erotic. It was perhaps unconsciously connected with my growing hatred of the public school orthodoxies and conventions, my desire to break and tear it all.

The other undisguised blessing of the Coll was "the Gurney," the school library; not only because it was a library, but because it was sanctuary. As the Negro used to become free on touching English soil, so the meanest boy was "unfaggable" once he was inside the Gurney. It was not, of course, easy to get there. In the winter terms if you were not on the list for "Clubs" you had to go out for a run. In summer you could reach sanctuary of an afternoon only under favorable conditions. You might be put down for Clubs, and that excluded you. Or there might be either a House match or a Coll match which you were compelled to watch. Thirdly, and most probably, on your way to the Gurney you might be caught and fagged for the whole afternoon. But sometimes one succeeded in running the gauntlet of all these dangers; and then – the books, silence, leisure, the distant sound of bat and ball ("Oh the brave music of a *distant* drum"), bees buzzing at the open windows, and freedom. In the Gurney I found *Corpus Poeticum Boreale* and tried, vainly but happily, to hammer out the originals from the translation at the bottom of the page. There too I found Milton, and Yeats, and a book on Celtic mythology, which soon became, if not a rival, yet a humble companion, to Norse. That did me good; to enjoy two mythologies (or three, now that I had begun to love the Greek), fully aware of their differing flavors, is a balancing thing, and makes for catholicity. I felt keenly the difference between the stony and fiery sublimity of Asgard, the green, leafy, amorous, and elusive world of Cruachan and the Red Branch and Tir-nan-Og, the harder, more defiant, sun-bright beauty of Olympus. I began (presumably in the holidays) an epic on Cuchulain and another on Finn, in English hexameters and in fourteeners respectively. Luckily they were abandoned before these easy and vulgar metres had time to spoil my ear.

But the Northernness still came first and the only work I completed at this time was a tragedy, Norse in subject and Greek in form. It was called *Loki Bound* and was as classical as any Humanist could have desired, with Prologos, Parodos, Epeisodia, Stasima, Exodos, Stichomythia, and (of course) one passage in trochaic *septenarii* — with rhyme. I never enjoyed anything more. The content is significant. My Loki was not merely malicious. He was against Odin because Odin had created a world though Loki had clearly warned him that this was a wanton cruelty. Why should creatures have the burden of existence forced on them without their consent? The main contrast in my play was between the sad wisdom of Loki and the brutal orthodoxy of Thor. Odin was partly sympathetic; he could at least see what Loki meant and there had been old friendship between those two before cosmic politics forced them apart. Thor was the real villain, Thor with his hammer and his threats, who was always egging Odin on against Loki and always complaining that Loki did not sufficiently respect the major gods; to which Loki replied

I pay respect to wisdom not to strength.

Thor was, in fact, the symbol of the Bloods; though I see that more clearly now than I did at the time. Loki was a projection of myself; he voiced that sense of priggish superiority whereby I was, unfortunately, beginning to compensate myself for my unhappiness.

The other feature in *Loki Bound* which may be worth commenting on is the pessimism. I was at this time living, like so many Atheists or Antitheists, in a whirl of contradictions. I maintained that God did not exist. I was also very angry with God for not existing. I was equally angry with Him for creating a world.

How far was this pessimism, this desire not to have been, sincere? Well, I must confess that this desire quite slipped out of my mind during the seconds when I was covered by the wild Earl's revolver. By the Chestertonian test, then, the test of *Manalive,* it was not sincere at all. But I am still not convinced by Chesterton's argument. It is true that when a pessimist's life is threatened he behaves like other men; his impulse to preserve life is stronger than his judgment that life is not worth preserving. But how does this prove that the judgment was insincere or even erroneous? A man's judgment that whisky is bad for him is not invalidated by the fact that when the bottle is at hand he find desire stronger than reason and succumbs. Having once tasted life, we are subjected to the impulse of self-preservation. Life, in other words, is as habit-forming as cocaine. What then? If I still held creation to be "a great injustice" I should hold that this impulse to retain life aggravates the injustice. If it is bad to be forced to drink the potion, how does it mend matters that the potion turns out to be an addiction drug? Pessimism cannot be answered so. Thinking as I then thought about the universe, I was reasonable in condemning it. At the same time I now see that my view was closely connected with a certain lopsidedness of temperament. I had always been more violent in my negative than in my positive demands. Thus, in personal relations, I could forgive much neglect more easily than the least degree of what I regarded as interference. At table I could forgive much insipidity in my food more easily than the lease suspicion of what seemed to me excessive or inappropriate seasoning. In the course of life I could put up with any amount of monotony far more patiently than even the smallest disturbance, bother, bustle, or what the Scotch call *kurfuffle*. Never at any age did I clamor to be amused; always and at all ages (where I dared) I hotly demanded not to be interrupted. The pessimism, or cowardice, which would prefer non-existence itself to even the mildest unhappiness was thus merely the generalization of all these pusillanimous preferences. And it remains true that I have, almost all my life, been quite unable to feel that horror of nonentity, of annihilation, which, say, Dr. Johnson felt so strongly. I felt it for the first time only in 1947. But that was after I had long been re-converted and thus begun to know what life really is and what would have been lost by missing it.

VIII

RELEASE

As Fortune is wont, at her chosen hour,
Whether she sends us solace or sore,
The wight to whom she shows her power
Will find that he gets still more and more.

PEARL

A few chapters ago I warned the reader that the return of Joy had introduced into my life a duality which makes it difficult to narrate. Reading through what I have just written about Wyvern, I find myself exclaiming, "Lies, lies! This was really a period of ecstasy. It consisted chiefly of moments when you were too happy to speak, when the gods and heroes rioted through your head, when satyrs danced and Maenads roared on the mountains, when Brynhild and Sieglinde, Deirdre, Maeve and Helen were all about you, till sometimes you felt that it might break you with mere richness." And all that is true. There were more Leprechauns than fags in that House. I have seen the victories of Cuchulain more often than those of the first eleven. Was Borage the Head of the Coll? or was it Conachar MacNessa? And the world itself — can I have been unhappy, living in Paradise? What keen, tingling sunlight there was! The mere smells were enough to make a man tipsy — cut grass, dew-dabbled mosses, sweet pea, autumn woods, wood burning, peat, salt water. The sense ached. I was sick with desire; that sickness better than health. All this is true, but it does not make the other version a lie. I am telling a story of two lives. They have nothing to do with each other: oil and vinegar, a river running beside a canal, Jekyll and Hyde. Fix your eye on either and it claims to be the sole truth. When I remember my outer life I see clearly that the other is but momentary flashes, seconds of gold scattered in months of dross, each instantly swallowed up in the old, familiar, sordid, hopeless weariness. When I remember my inner life I see that everything mentioned in the last two chapters was merely a coarse curtain which at any moment might be drawn aside to reveal all the heavens I then knew. The same duality perplexes the story of my home life, to which I must now turn.

Once my brother had left Wyvern and I had gone to it, the classic period of our boyhood was at an end. Something not so good succeeded it, but this had long been prepared by slow development within the classic age itself. All began, as I have said, with the fact that our father was out of the house from nine in the morning till six at night. From the very first we built up for ourselves a life that excluded him. He on his part demanded a confidence even more boundless, perhaps, than a father usually, or wisely, demands. One instance of this, early in my life, had far-reaching effects. Once when I was at Oldie's and had just begun to try to live as a Christian I wrote out a set of rules for myself and put them in my pocket. On the first day of the holidays, noticing that my pockets bulged with all sorts of papers and that my coat was being pulled out of all shape, he plucked out the whole pile of rubbish and began to go through it. Boylike, I would have died rather than let him see my list of good resolutions. I managed to keep them out of his reach and get them into the fire. I do not see that either of us was to blame; but never from that moment until the hour of his death did I enter his house without first going through my own pockets and removing anything that I wished to keep private.

A habit of concealment was thus bred before I had anything guilty to conceal. By now I had plenty. And even what I had no wish to hide I could not tell. To have told him what Wyvern or even Chartres was really like would have been risky (he might write to Headmaster) and intolerably embarrassing. It would also have been impossible; and here I must touch on one of his strangest characteristics.

My father — but these words, at the head of a paragraph, will carry the reader's mind inevitably to *Tristram Shandy*. On second thoughts I am content that they should. It is only in a Shandean spirit that my matter can be approached. I have to describe something as odd and whimsical as ever entered the brain of Sterne; and if I could, I would gladly lead you to the same affection for my father as you have for Tristram's. And now for the thing itself. You will have grasped that my father was no fool. He had even a streak of genius in him. At the same time he had — when seated in his own armchair after a heavy midday dinner on an August afternoon with all the windows shut — more power of confusing an issue or taking up a fact wrongly than any man I have ever known. As a result it was impossible to drive into his head any of the realities of our school life, after which (nevertheless) he repeatedly enquired. The first and simplest barrier to communication was that, having earnestly asked, he did not "stay for an answer" or forgot it the moment it was uttered. Some facts must have been asked for and told him, on a moderate computation, once a week, and were received by him each time as perfect novelties. But this was the simplest barrier. Far more often he retained something, but something very unlike what you had said. His mind so bubbled over with humor, sentiment, and indignation that, long before he had understood or even listened to your words, some accidental hint had set his imagination to work, he had produced his own version of the facts, and believed that he was getting it from you. As he invariably got proper names wrong (no name seemed to him less probable than another) his *textus receptus* was often almost unrecognizable. Tell him that a boy called Churchwood had caught a field mouse and kept it as a pet, and a year, or ten years later, he would ask you, "Did you ever hear what became of poor Chickweed who was so afraid of the rats?" For his own version, once adopted, was indelible, and attempts to correct it only produced an incredulous "Hm! Well, that's not the story you *used* to tell." Sometimes, indeed, he took in the facts you had stated; but truth fared none the better for that. What are facts without interpretation? It was axiomatic to my father (in theory) that nothing was said or done from an obvious motive. Hence he who in his real life was the most honorable and impulsive of men, and the easiest victim that any knave or imposter could hope to meet, became a positive Machiavel when he knitted his brows and applied to the behavior of people he had never seen the spectral and labyrinthine operation which he called "reading between the lines." Once embarked upon that, he might make his landfall anywhere in the wide world: and always with unshakable conviction. "I see it all" – "I understand it perfectly" – "It's as plain as a pikestaff," he would say; and then, as we soon learned, he would believe till his dying day in some deadly quarrel, some slight, some secret sorrow or some immensely complex machination, which was not only improbable but impossible. Dissent on our part was attributed, with kindly laughter, to our innocence, gullibility, and general ignorance of life. And besides all these confusions, there were the sheer *non sequiturs* when the ground seemed to open at one's feet. "Did Shakespeare spell his name with an e at the end?" asked my brother. "I believe," said I – but my father interrupted: "I very much doubt if he used the Italian calligraphy *at all*." A certain church in Belfast has both a Greek inscription over the door and a curious tower. "That church is a great landmark," said I, "I can pick it out from all sorts of places – even from the top of Cave Hill." "Such nonsense," said my father, "how could you make out Greek letters three or four miles away?"

One conversation, held several years later, may be recorded as a specimen of these continual cross-purposes. My brother had been speaking of a reunion dinner for the officers of the Nth Division which he had lately attended. "I suppose your friend Collins was there," said my father.

B. Collins? Oh no. He wasn't in the Nth, you know.
F. (After a pause.) Did these fellows not like Collins then?
B. I don't quite understand. What fellows?
F. The Johnnies that got up the dinner.
B. Oh no, not at all. It was nothing to do with liking or not liking. You see, it was a purely Divisional affair. There'd be no question of asking anyone who hadn't been in the Nth.
F. (After a long pause.) Hm! Well, I'm sure poor Collins was very much hurt.

There are situations in which the very genius of Filial Piety would find it difficult not to let some sign of impatience escape him.

I would not commit the sin of Ham. Nor would I, as historian, reduce a complex character to a false simplicity. The man who, in his armchair, sometimes appeared not so much incapable of understanding anything as determined to misunderstand everything, was formidable in the police court and, I presume, efficient in his office. He was a humorist, even on occasion, a wit. When he was dying, the pretty nurse, rallying him, said, "What an old pessimist you are! You're just like my father." "I suppose," replied her patient, "he has *several* daughters."

The hours my father spent at home were thus hours of perplexity for us boys. After an evening of the sort of conversation I have been describing one felt as if one's head were spinning like a top. His presence put an end to all our innocent as well as to all our forbidden occupations. It is a hard thing – nay, a wicked thing – when a man is felt to be an intruder in his own house. And yet, as Johnson said, "Sensation is sensation." I am sure it was not his fault, I believe much of it was ours; what is certain is that I increasingly found it oppressive to be with him. One of his most amiable qualities helped to make it so. I have said before that he "conned no state"; except during his Philippics he treated us as equals. The theory was that we lived together more like three brothers than like a father and two sons. That, I say, was the theory. But of course it was not and could not be so; indeed ought not to have been so. That relation cannot really exist between schoolboys and a middle-aged man of overwhelming personality and of habits utterly unlike theirs. And the pretense that it does ends by putting a curious strain on the juniors. Chesterton has laid his finger on the weak point of all such factitious equality: "If a boy's aunts are his pals, will it not soon follow that a boy needs no pals but his aunts?" That was not, of course, the question for us; we wanted no pals. But we did want liberty, if only liberty to walk about the house. And my father's theory that we were three boys together actually meant that while he was at home we were as closely bound to his presence as if the three of us had been chained together; and all our habits were frustrated. Thus if my father came home unexpectedly at midday, having allowed himself an extra half-holiday, he might, if it were summer, find us with chairs and books in the garden. An austere parent, of the formal school, would have gone in to his own adult occupations. Not so my father. Sitting in the garden? An excellent idea. But would not all three of us be better on the summer seat? Thither, after he had assumed one of his "light spring overcoats," we would go. (I do not know how many overcoats he had; I am still wearing two of them.) After sitting for a few minutes, thus clad, on a shadeless seat where the noonday sun was blistering the paint, he not unnaturally began to perspire. "I don't know what you two think," he would say, "but I'm finding this almost *too* hot. What about moving indoors?" That meant an adjournment to the study, where even the smallest chink of open window was rather grudgingly allowed. I say "allowed," but there was no question of authority. In theory, everything was decided by the general Will. "Liberty Hall, boys, Liberty Hall," as he delighted to quote. "What time would you like lunch?" But we knew only too well that the meal which would otherwise have been at one had already been shifted, in obedience to his lifelong preference, to two or even two-thirty; and that the cold meats which we liked had already been withdrawn in favor of the only food our father ever voluntarily ate – hot butcher's meat, boiled, stewed or roast... and this to be eaten in mid-afternoon in a dining room that faced south. For the whole of the rest of the day, whether sitting or walking, we were inseparable; and the speech (you see that it could hardly be called conversation), the speech with its cross-purposes, with its tone (inevitably) always set by him, continued intermittently till bedtime. I should be worse than a dog if I blamed my lonely father for thus desiring the friendship of his sons; or even if the miserable return I made him did not to this day lie heavy on my conscience. But "sensation is sensation." It was extraordinarily tiring. And in my own contributions to these endless talks — which were indeed too adult for me, too anecdotal, too prevailingly jocular — I was increasingly aware of an artificiality. The anecdotes were, indeed, admirable in their kind: business stories, Mahaffy stories (many of which I found attached to Jowett at Oxford) stories of ingenious swindles, social blunders, police-court "drunks." But I was acting when I responded to them. Drollery, whimsicality, the kind of humor that borders on the fantastic, was my line. I had to act. My father's geniality and my own furtive disobediences both helped to drive me into hypocrisy. I could not "be myself" while he was at home. God forgive me, I thought Monday morning, when he went back to his work, the brightest jewel in the week.

Such was the situation which developed during the classic period. Now, when I had gone to Wyvern and my brother to a tutor to prepare for Sandhurst, there came a change. My brother had liked Wyvern as much as I loathed it. There were many reasons for this: his more adaptable temper, his face which bore no such smack-inviting signature as mine, but most of all the fact that he had gone there straight from Oldie's and I from preparatory school where I had been happy. No school in England but would have appeared a heaven on earth after Oldie's. Thus in one of his first letters from Wyvern my brother communicated the startling fact that you could really eat as much (or as little) as you wanted at table. To a boy fresh from the school at Belsen, this alone would have outweighed almost everything else. But by the time I went to Wyvern I had learned to take decent feeding for granted. And now a terrible thing happened. My reaction to Wyvern was perhaps the first great disappointment my brother had ever experienced. Loving the place as he did, he had looked forward to the days when this too could be shared between us — an *idem sentire* about Wyvern succeeding an *idem sentire* about Boxen. Instead he heard, from me, blasphemies against all his gods; from Wyvern, that his young brother looked like becoming a Coll Punt. The immemorial league between us was strained, all but broken.

All this was cruelly complicated by the fact that relations between my father and my brother were never before or since so bad as at this time; and Wyvern was behind that too. My brother's reports had grown worse and worse; and the tutor to whom he had now been sent confirmed them to the extent of saying that he seemed to have learned almost nothing at school. Nor was that all. Sentences savagely underlined in my father's copy of *The Lancaster Tradition* reveal his thoughts. They are passages about a certain glazed insolence, an elaborate, heartless flippancy, which the reforming Headmaster in that story encountered in the Bloods of the school he wished to reform. That was how my father envisaged my brother at this period: flippant, languid, emptied of the intellectual interests which had appeared in his earlier boyhood, immovable, indifferent to all real values, and urgent in his demand for a motor bicycle.

It was, of course, to turn us into public-school boys that my father had originally sent us to Wyvern; the finished product appalled him. It is a familiar tragicomedy and you can study it in Lockhart; Scott labored hard to make his son a hussar, but when the actual hussar was presented to him, Scott sometimes forgot the illusion of being an aristocrat and became once more a respectable Edinburgh lawyer with strong views about Puppyism. So in our family. Mispronunciation was one of my father's favorite rhetorical weapons. He now always sounded the first syllable of Wyvern wrongly. I can still hear him growl, "Wyvernian affectation." In proportion as my brother's tone became languid and urbanely weary, so my father's voice became more richly and energetically Irish, and all manner of strange music from his boyhood in Cork and Dublin forced its way up through the more recent Belfastian crust.

During these miserable debates I occupied a most unfortunate position. To have been on my father's side and against my brother I should have had to unmake myself; it was a state of parties outside my whole philosophy of domestic politics. It was all very disagreeable.

Yet out of this "unpleasantness" (a favorite word of my father's) there sprang what I still reckon, by merely natural standards, the most fortunate thing that ever happened to me. The tutor (in Surrey) to whom my brother had been sent was one of my father's oldest friends. He had been headmaster of Lurgan when my father was a boy there. In a surprisingly short time he so rebuilt and extended the ruins of my brother's education that he not only passed into Sandhurst but was placed among those very few candidates at the top of the list who received prize cadetships. I do not think my father ever did justice to my brother's achievement; it came at a time when the gulf between them was too wide, and when they were friends again it had become ancient history. But he saw very clearly what it proved about the exceptional powers of his teacher. At the same time, he was almost as sick as I of the very name of Wyvern. And I never ceased, by letter and by word of mouth, to beg that I might be taken away. All these factors urged him to the decision which he now made. Might it not after all be best to give me my desire? to have done with school for good and send me also to Surrey to read for the University with Mr. Kirkpatrick? He did not form this plan without much doubt and hesitation. He did his best to put all the risks before me: the dangers of solitude, the sudden change from the life and bustle of a great school (which change I might not like so much as I anticipated), the possibly deadening effect of living with only an old man and his old wife for company. Should I really be happy with no companions of my own age? I tried to look very grave at these questions. But it was all imposture. My heart laughed. Happy without other boys? Happy without toothache, without chilblains, happy without pebbles in my shoes? And so the arrangement was made. If it had had nothing else to recommend it, the mere thought, "Never, never,

never, shall I have to play games again," was enough to transport me. If you want to know how I felt, imagine your own feelings on waking one morning to find that income tax or unrequited love had somehow vanished from the world.

I should be sorry if I were understood to think, or if I encouraged any reader in thinking, that this invincible dislike of doing things with a bat or a ball were other than a misfortune. Not, indeed, that I allow to games any of the moral and almost mystical virtues which schoolmasters claim for them; they seem to me to lead to ambition, jealousy, and embittered partisan feeling, quite as often as to anything else. Yet not to like them is a misfortune, because it cuts you off from companionship with many excellent people who can be approached in no other way. A misfortune, not a vice; for it is involuntary. I had tried to like games and failed. That impulse had been left out of my make-up; I was to games as the proverb has it, like an ass to the harp.

It is a curious truth, noticed by many writers, that good fortune is nearly always followed by more good fortune, and bad, by more bad. About the same time that my father decided to send me to Mr. Kirkpatrick, another great good came to me. Many chapters ago I mentioned a boy who lived near us and who had tried, quite unsuccessfully, to make friends with my brother and myself. His name was Arthur and he was my brother's exact contemporary; he and I had been at Campbell together though we never met. I think it was shortly before the beginning of my last term at Wyvern that I received a message saying that Arthur was in bed, convalescent, and would welcome a visit. I can't remember what led me to accept this invitation, but for some reason I did.

I found Arthur sitting up in bed. On the table beside him lay a copy of *Myths of the Norsemen.*

"Do *you* like that?" said I.

"Do *you* like that? said he.

Next moment the book was in our hands, our heads were bent close together, we were pointing, quoting, talking — soon almost shouting — discovering in a torrent of questions that we liked not only the same thing, but the same parts of it and in the same way; that both knew the stab of Joy and that, for both, the arrow was shot from the North. Many thousands of people have had the experience of finding the first friend, and it is none the less a wonder; as great a wonder (*pace* the novelists) as first love, or even a greater. I had been so far from thinking such a friend possible that I had never even longed for one; no more than I longed to be King of England. If I had found that Arthur had independently built up an exact replica of the Boxonian world I should not really have been much more surprised. Nothing, I suspect, is more astonishing in any man's life than the discovery that there do exist people very, very like himself.

During my last few weeks at Wyvern strange stories began to appear in the papers, for this was the summer of 1914. I remember how a friend and I puzzled over a column that bore the headline "Can England keep out of it?" "Keep out of it?" said he, "I don't see how she can get into it." Memory paints the last hours of that term in slightly apocalyptic colors, and perhaps memory lies. Or perhaps for me it was apocalyptic enough to know that I was leaving, to see all those hated things for the last time; yet not simply (at that moment) to hate them. There is a "rumness," a ghostliness, about even a Windsor chair when it says, "You will not see me again." Early in the holidays we declared war. My brother, then on leave from Sandhurst, was recalled. Some weeks later I went to Mr. Kirkpatrick at Great Bookham in Surrey.

IX

THE GREAT KNOCK

You will often meet with characters in nature so extrava-
gant that a discreet poet would not venture to set them upon
the stage.

LORD CHESTERFIELD

On a September day, having crossed to Liverpool and reached London, I made my
way to Waterloo and ran down to Great Bookham. I had been told that Surrey was
"suburban," and the landscape that actually flitted past the windows astonished me. I
saw steep little hills, watered valleys, and wooded commons which ranked by my
Wyvernian and Irish standards as forest; bracken everywhere; a world of red and rus-
set and yellowish greens. Even the sprinkling of suburban villas (much rarer then
than now) delighted me. These timbered and red-tiled houses, embosomed in trees,
were wholly unlike the stuccoed monstrosities which formed the suburbs of Belfast.
Where I had expected gravel drives and iron gates and interminable laurels and monkey puzzlers, I saw crooked paths running up or down hill from wicket gates, between fruit trees and birches. By a severer taste than mine these houses would all be
mocked perhaps; yet I cannot help thinking that those who designed them and their
gardens achieved their object, which was to suggest Happiness. They filled me with a
desire for that domesticity which, in its full development, I had never known; they set
one thinking of tea trays.

At Bookham I was met by my new teacher — "Kirk" or "Knock" or the Great
Knock as my father, my brother, and I all called him. We had heard about him all our
lives and I therefore had a very clear impression of what I was in for. I came prepared
to endure a perpetual lukewarm shower bath of sentimentality. That was the price I
was ready to pay for the infinite blessedness of escaping school; but a heavy price.
One story of my father's, in particular, gave me the most embarrassing forebodings.
He had loved to tell how once at Lurgan, when he was in some kind of trouble or
difficulty, the Old Knock, or the dear Old Knock, had drawn him aside and there

74

"quietly and naturally" slid his arm round him and rubbed his dear old whiskers against my father's youthful cheek and whispered a few words of comfort.... And here was Bookham at last, and there was the arch-sentimentalist himself waiting to meet me.

He was over six feet tall, very shabbily dressed (like a gardener, I thought), lean as a rake, and immensely muscular. His wrinkled face seemed to consist entirely of muscles, so far as it was visible; for he wore mustache and side whiskers with a clean-shaven chin like the Emperor Franz Joseph. The whiskers, you will understand, concerned me very much at that moment. My cheek already tingled in anticipation. Would be begin at once? There would be tears for certain; perhaps worse things. It is one of my lifelong weaknesses that I never could endure the embrace or kiss of my own sex. (An unmanly weakness, by the way; Aeneas, Beowulf, Roland, Launcelot, Johnson, and Nelson knew nothing of it.)

Apparently, however, the old man was holding his fire. We shook hands, and though his grip was like iron pincers it was not lingering. A few minutes later we were walking away from the station.

"You are now," said Kirk, "proceeding along the principal artery between Great and Little Bookham."

I stole a glance at him. Was this geographical exordium a heavy joke? Or was he trying to conceal his emotions? His face, however, showed only an inflexible gravity. I began to "make conversation" in the deplorable manner which I had acquired at those evening parties and indeed found increasingly necessary to use with my father. I said I was surprised at the "scenery" of Surrey; it was much "wilder" than I had expected.

"Stop!" shouted Kirk with a suddenness that made me jump. "What do you mean by wildness and what grounds had you for not expecting it?"

I replied I don't know what, still "making conversation." As answer after answer was torn to shreds it at last dawned upon me that he really wanted to know. He was not making conversation, nor joking, nor snubbing me; he wanted to know. I was stung into attempting a real answer. A few passes sufficed to show that I had no clear and distinct idea corresponding to the word "wildness," and that, in so far as I had any idea at all, "wildness" was a singularly inept word. "Do you not see, then," concluded the Great Knock, "that your remark was meaningless?" I prepared to sulk a little, assuming that the subject would now be dropped. Never was I more mistaken in my life. Having analyzed my terms, Kirk was proceeding to deal with my proposition as a whole. On what had I based (but he pronounced it *baized*) my expectations about the Flora and Geology of Surrey? Was it maps, or photographs, or books? I could produce none. It had, heaven help me, never occurred to me that what I called my thoughts needed to be "baized" on anything. Kirk once more drew a con-clusion — without the slightest sign of emotion, but equally without the slightest con-cession to what I thought good manners: "Do you now see, then, that you had no right to have any opinion whatever on the subject?"

By this time our acquaintance had lasted about three and a half minutes; but the tone set by this first conversation was preserved without a single break during all the years I spent at Bookham. Anything more grotesquely unlike the "dear Old Knock" of my father's reminiscences could not be conceived. Knowing my father's invariable intention of veracity and also knowing what strange transformations every truth underwent when once it entered his mind, I am sure he did not mean to deceive us. But if Kirk at any time of his life took a boy aside and there "quietly and naturally" rubbed the boy's face with his whiskers, I shall as easily believe that he sometimes varied the treatment by quietly and naturally standing on his venerable and egg-bald head.

If ever a man came near to being a purely logical entity, that man was Kirk. Born a little later, he would have been a Logical Positivist. The idea that human beings should exercise their vocal organs for any purpose except that of communicating or discovering truth was to him preposterous. The most casual remark was taken as a summons to disputation. I soon came to know the differing values of his three openings. The loud cry of "Stop!" was flung in to arrest a torrent of verbiage which could not be endured a moment longer; not because it fretted his patience (he never thought of that) but because it was wasting time, darkening counsel. The hastier and quieter "Excuse!" (*i.e.*, "Excuse me") ushered in a correction or distinction merely parenthetical and betokened that, thus set right, your remark might still, without absurdity, be allowed to reach completion. The most encouraging of all was, "I hear you." This meant that your remark was significant and only required refutation; it had risen to the dignity of error. Refutation (when we got so far) always followed the same lines. Had I read this? Had I studied that? Had I any statistical evidence? Had I any evidence in my own experience? And so to the almost inevitable conclusion, "Do you not see then that you had no right, etc."

Some boys would not have liked it; to me it was red beef and strong beer. I had taken it for granted that my leisure hours at Bookham would be passed in "grown-up conversation." And that, as you know already, I had no taste for. In my experience it meant conversation about politics, money, deaths, and digestion. I assumed that a taste for it, as for eating mustard or reading newspapers, would develop in me when I grew older (so far, all three expectations have been disappointed). The only two kinds of talk I wanted were the almost purely imaginative and the almost purely rational; such talk as I had about Boxen with my brother or about Valhalla with Arthur, on the one hand, or such talk as I had had with my uncle Gussie about astronomy on the other. I could never have gone far in any science because on the path of every science the lion Mathematics lies in wait for you. Even in Mathematics, whatever could be done by mere reasoning (as in simple geometry) I did with delight; but the moment calculation came in I was helpless. I grasped the principles but my answers were always wrong. Yet though I could never have been a scientist, I had scientific as well as imaginative impulses, and I loved ratiocination. Kirk excited and satisfied one side of me. Here was talk that was really about something. Here was a man who thought not about you but about what you said. No doubt I snorted and bridled a little at some of my tossings; but, taking it all in all, I loved the treatment. After being knocked down sufficiently often I began to know a few guards and blows, and to put on intellectual muscle. In the end, unless I flatter myself, I became a not contemptible sparring partner. It was a great day when the man who had so long been engaged in exposing my vagueness at last cautioned me against the dangers of excessive subtlety.

If Kirk's ruthless dialectic had been merely a pedagogic instrument I might have resented it. But he knew no other way of talking. No age or sex was spared the elenchus. It was continuous astonishment to him that anyone should not desire to be clarified or corrected. When a very dignified neighbor, in the course of a Sunday call, observed with an air of finality, "Well, well, Mr. Kirkpatrick, it takes all sorts to make a world. You are a Liberal and I am a Conservative; we naturally look at the facts from different angles," Kirk replied, "What do you mean? Are you asking me to picture Liberals and Conservatives playing peep-bo at a rectangular Fact from opposite sides of a table?" If an unwary visitor, hoping to waive a subject, observed, "Of course, I know opinions differ — " Kirk would raise both his hands and exclaim, "Good heavens! I have no *opinions* on any subject whatsoever." A favorite maxim was, "You can have enlightenment for ninepence but you prefer ignorance." The commonest metaphors would be questioned till some bitter truth had been forced from its hiding place. "These fiendish German atrocities — " "But are not fiends a figment of the imagination?" — "Very well, then; these brutal atrocities — " "But none of the brutes does anything of the kind!" — "Well, what am I to call them?" "Is it not plain that we must call them simply *Human?*" What excited his supreme contempt was the conversation of other Headmasters, which he had sometimes had to endure at conferences when he himself was Head of Lurgan. "They would come and ask me, 'What attitude do you adopt to a boy who does so-and-so?' Good Heavens! As if I ever adopted an attitude to anybody or anything!" Sometimes, but rarely, he was driven to irony. On such occasions his voice became even weightier than usual and only the distention of his nostrils betrayed the secret to those who knew him. It was in such fashion that he produced his *dictum,* "The Master of Balliol is one of the most important beings in the universe."

It will be imagined that Mrs. Kirkpatrick led a somewhat uneasy life: witness the occasion on which her husband by some strange error found himself in the drawing room at the beginning of what his lady had intended to be a bridge party. About half an hour later she was observed to leave the room with a remarkable expression on her face; and many hours later still the Great Knock was discovered sitting on a stool in the midst of seven elderly ladies ("ful drery was hire chere") begging them to clarify their terms.

I have said that he was almost wholly logical; but not quite. He had been a Presbyterian and was now an Atheist. He spent Sunday, as he spent most of his time on weekdays, working in his garden. But one curious trait from his Presbyterian youth survived. He always, on Sundays, gardened in a different, and slightly more respectable, suit. An Ulster Scot may come to disbelieve in God, but not to wear his weekday clothes on the Sabbath.

Having said that he was an Atheist, I hasten to add that he was a "Rationalist" of the old, high and dry nineteenth-century type. For Atheism has come down in the world since those days, and mixed itself with politics and learned to dabble in dirt. The anonymous donor who now sends me anti-God magazines hopes, no doubt, to hurt the Christian in me; he really hurts the ex-Atheist. I am ashamed that my old mates and (which matters much more) Kirk's old mates should have sunk to what they are now. It was different then; even McCabe wrote like a man. At the time when I knew him, the fuel of Kirk's Atheism was chiefly of the anthropological and pessi-mistic kind. He was great on *The Golden Bough* and Schopenhauer.

The reader will remember that my own Atheism and Pessimism were fully formed before I went to Bookham. What I got there was merely fresh ammunition for the defense of a position already chosen. Even this I got indirectly from the tone of his mind or independently from reading his books. He never attacked religion in my presence. It is the sort of fact that no one would infer from an outside knowledge of my life, but it is a fact.

I arrived at Gastons (so the Knock's house was called) on a Saturday, and he an-nounced that we would begin Homer on Monday. I explained that I had never read a word in any dialect but the Attic, assuming that when he knew this he would approach Homer through some preliminary lessons on the Epic language. He replied merely with a sound very frequent in his conversation which I can only spell "Huh." I found this rather disquieting; and I woke on Monday saying to myself, "Now for Homer. Golly!" The name struck awe into my soul. At nine o'clock we sat down to work in the little upstairs study which soon became so familiar to me. It contained a sofa (on which we sat side by side when he was working with me), a table and chair (which I used when I was alone), a bookcase, a gas stove, and a framed photograph of Mr. Gladstone. We opened our books at *Iliad,* Book I. Without a word of introduction Knock read aloud the first twenty lines or so in the "new" pronunciation, which I had never heard before. Like Smewgy, he was a chanter; less mellow in voice, yet full gutturals and rolling r's and more varied vowels seemed to suit the Bronze Age epic as well as Smewgy's honey tongue had suited Horace. For Kirk, even after years of residence in England, spokes the purest Ulster. He then translated, with a few, a very few explanations, about a hundred lines. I had never seen a classical author taken in such large gulps before. When he had finished he handed me over Crusius' *Lexicon* and, having told me to go through again as much as I could of what he had done, left the room. It seems an odd method of teaching, but it worked. At first I could travel only a very short way along the trail he had blazed, but every day I could travel further. Presently I could travel the whole way. Then I could go a line or two beyond his furthest North. Then it became a kind of game to see how far beyond. He appeared at this stage to value speed more than absolute accuracy. The great gain was that I very soon became able to understand a great deal without (even mentally) translating it; I was beginning to think in Greek. That is the great Rubicon to cross in learning any language. Those in whom the Greek word lives only while they are hunting for it in the lexicon, and who then substitute the English word for it, are not reading the Greek at all; they are only solving a puzzle. The very formula, *"Naus* means a ship," is wrong. *Naus* and *ship* both mean a thing, they do not mean one another. Behind *Naus,* as behind *navis* or *naca,* we want to have a picture of a dark, slender mass with sail or oars, climbing the ridges, with no officious English word intruding.

We now settled into a routine which has ever since served in my mind as an archetype, so that what I still mean when I speak of a "normal" day (and lament that normal days are so rare) is a day of the Bookham pattern. For if I could please myself I would always live as I lived there. I would choose always to breakfast at exactly eight and to be at my desk by nine, there to read or write till one. If a cup of good tea or coffee could be brought me about eleven, so much the better. A step or so out of doors for a pint of beer would not do quite so well; for a man does not want to drink alone and if you meet a friend in the taproom the break is likely to be extended beyond its ten minutes. At one precisely lunch should be on the table; and by two at the latest I would be on the road. Not, except at rare intervals, with a friend. Walking and talking are two very great pleasures, but it is a mistake to combine them. Our own noise blots out the sounds and silences of the outdoor world; and talking leads almost inevitably to smoking, and then farewell to nature as far as one of our senses is concerned. The only friend to walk with is one (such as I found, during the holidays, in Arthur) who so exactly shares your taste for each mood of the countryside that a glance, a halt, or at most a nudge, is enough to assure us that the pleasure is shared. The return from the walk, and the arrival of tea, should be exactly coincident, and not later than a quarter past four. Tea should be taken in solitude, as I took it at Bookham on those (happily numerous) occasions when Mrs. Kirkpatrick was out; the Knock himself disdained this meal. For eating and reading are two pleasures that combine admirably. Of course not all books are suitable for mealtime reading. It would be a kind of blasphemy to read poetry at table. What one wants is a gossipy, formless book which can be opened anywhere. The ones I learned so to use at Bookham were Boswell, and a translation of Herodotus, and Lang's *History of English Literature.* *Tristram Shandy, Elia* and the *Anatomy of Melancholy* are all good for the same purpose. At five a man should be at work again, and at it till seven. Then, at the evening meal and after, comes the time for talk, or, failing that, for lighter reading; and unless you are making a night of it with your cronies (and at Bookham I had none) there is no reason why you should ever be in bed later than eleven. But when is a man to write his letters? You forget that I am describing the happy life I led with Kirk or the ideal life I would live now if I could. And it is an essential of the happy life that a man would have almost no mail and never dread the postman's knock. In those blessed days I received, and answered, only two letters a week; one from my father, which was a matter of duty, and one from Arthur which was the highlight of the week, for we poured out to each other on paper all the delight that was intoxicating us both. Letters from my brother, now on active service, were longer and rarer, and so were my replies.

Such is my ideal, and such then (almost) was the reality of "settled, calm, Epicurean life." It is no doubt for my own good that I have been so generally prevented from leading it, for it is a life almost entirely selfish. Selfish, not self-centered: for in such a life my mind would be directed toward a thousand things, not one of which is myself. The distinction is not unimportant. One of the happiest men and the most pleasing companions I have known was intensely selfish. On the other hand I have known people capable of real sacrifice whose lives were nevertheless a misery to themselves and to others, because self-concern and self-pity filled all their thoughts. Either condition will destroy the soul in the end. But till the end, give me the man who takes the best of everything (even at my expense) and then talks of other things, rather than the man who serves me and talks of himself, and whose very kindnesses are a continual reproach, a continual demand for pity, gratitude, and admiration.

Kirk did not, of course, make me read nothing but Homer. The Two Great Bores (Demosthenes and Cicero) could not be avoided. There were (oh glory!) Lucretius, Catullus, Tacitus, Herodotus. There was Virgil, for whom I still had no true taste. There were Greek and Latin compositions. (It is a strange thing that I have contrived to reach my late fifties without ever reading one word of Caesar.) There were Euripides, Sophocles, Aeschylus. In the evenings there was French with Mrs. Kirkpatrick, treated much as her husband treated Homer. We got through a great many good novels in this way and I was soon buying French books on my own. I had hoped there would be English essays, but whether because he felt he could not endure mine or because he soon guessed that I was already only too proficient in that art (which he almost certainly despised) Kirk never set me one. For the first week or so he gave me directions about my English reading, but when he discovered that, left to myself, I was not likely to waste my time, he gave me absolute freedom. Later in my career we branched out into German and Italian. Here his methods were the same. After the very briefest contact with Grammars and Exercises I was plunged into *Faust* and the *Inferno.* In Italian we succeeded. In German I have little doubt that we should equally have succeeded if I had stayed with him a little longer. But I left too soon and my German has remained all my life that of a schoolboy. Whenever I have set about rectifying this, some other and more urgent task has always interrupted me.

But Homer came first. Day after day and month after month we drove gloriously onward, tearing the whole *Achilleid* out of the *Illiad* and tossing the rest on one side, and then reading the *Odyssey* entire, till the music of the thing and the clear, bitter brightness that lives in almost every formula had become part of me. Of course my appreciation was very romanticized – the appreciation of a boy soaked in William Morris. But this slight error saved me from that far deeper error of "classicism" with which the Humanists have hoodwinked half the world. I cannot therefore deeply regret the days when I called Circe a "wise-wife" and every marriage a "high-tide." That has all burned itself out and left no snuff, and I can now enjoy the *Odyssey* in a maturer way. The wanderings mean as much as ever they did; the great moment of "eucatastrophe" (as Professor Tolkien would call it) when Odysseus strips off his rags and bends the bow, means more; and perhaps what now pleases me best of all is those exquisite, Charlotte M. Yonge families at Pylos and elsewhere. How rightly Sir Maurice Powicke says, "There have been civilised people in all ages." And let us add, "In all ages they have been surrounded by barbarism."

Meanwhile, on afternoons and on Sundays, Surrey lay open to me. County Down in the holidays and Surrey in the term — it was an excellent contrast. Perhaps, since their beauties were such that even a fool could not force them into competition, this cured me once and for all of the pernicious tendency to compare and to prefer — an operation that does little good even when we are dealing with works of art and endless harm when we are dealing with nature. Total surrender is the first step toward the fruition of either. Shut your mouth; open your eyes and ears. Take in what is there and give no thought to what might have been there or what is somewhere else. That can come later, if it must come at all. (And notice here how the true training for anything whatever that is good always prefigures and, if submitted to, will always help us in the true training for the Christian life. That is a school where they can always use your previous work whatever subject it was on.) What delighted me in Surrey was its intricacy. My Irish walks commanded large horizons and the general lie of land and sea could be taken in at a glance; I will try to speak of them later. But in Surrey the contours were so tortuous, the little valleys so narrow, there was so much timber, so many villages concealed in woods or hollows, so many field paths, sunk lanes, dingles, copses, such an unpredictable variety of cottage, farmhouse, villa, and country seat, that the whole thing could never lie clearly in my mind, and to walk in it daily gave one the same sort of pleasure that there is in the labyrinthine complexity of Malory or the *Faerie Queene*. Even where the prospect was tolerably open, as when I sat looking down on the Leatherhead and Dorking valley from Polesdan Lacey, it always lacked the classic comprehensibility of the Wyvern landscape. The valley twisted away southward into another valley, a train thudded past invisible in a wooded cutting, the opposite ridge concealed its bays and promontories. This, even on a summer morning. But I remember more dearly autumn afternoons in bottoms that lay intensely silent under old and great trees, and especially the moment, near Friday Street, when our party (that time I was not alone) suddenly discovered, from recognizing a curiously shaped stump, that we had traveled round in a circle for the last half-hour; or one frosty sunset over the Hog's Back at Guildford. On a Saturday afternoon in winter, when nose and fingers might be pinched enough to give an added relish to the anticipation of tea and fireside, and the whole weekend's reading lay ahead, I suppose I reached as much happiness as is ever to be reached on earth. And especially if there were some new, long-coveted book awaiting me.

For I had forgotten. When I spoke of the post I forgot to tell you that it brought parcels as well as letters. Every man of my age has had in his youth one blessing for which our juniors may well envy him: we grew up in a world of cheap and abundant books. Your *Everyman* was then a bare shilling, and what is more always in stock; your *World's Classic, Muses' Library, Home University Library, Temple Classic,* Nelson's French series, Bohn, and Longman's Pocket Library, at proportionate prices. All the money I could spare went in postal orders to Messrs. Denny of the Strand. No days, even at Bookham, were happier than those on which the afternoon post brought me a neat little parcel in dark gray paper. Milton, Spenser, Malory, *The High History of the Holy Grail,* the *Laxdale Saga,* Ronsard, Chénier, Voltaire, *Beowulf* and *Gawain and the Green Knight* (both in translations), Apuleius, the *Kalevala,* Herrick, Walton, Sir John Mandeville, Sidney's *Arcadia,* and nearly all of Morris, came volume by volume into my hands. Some of my purchases proved disappointments and some went beyond my hopes, but the undoing of the parcel always remained a delicious moment. On my rare visits to London I looked at Messrs. Denny in the Strand with a kind of awe; so much pleasure had come from it.

Smewgy and Kirk were my two greatest teachers. Roughly, one might say (in medieval language) that Smewgy taught me Grammar and Rhetoric and Kirk taught me Dialectic. Each had, and gave me, what the other lacked. Kirk had none of Smewgy's graciousness or delicacy, and Smewgy had less humor than Kirk. It was a saturnine humor. Indeed he was very like Saturn — not the dispossessed King of Italian legend, but grim old Cronos, Father Time himself with scythe and hourglass. The bitterest, and also funniest, things came out when he had risen abruptly from table (always before the rest of us) and stood ferreting in a villainous old tobacco jar on the mantelpiece for the dottles of former pipes which it was his frugal habit to use again. My debt to him is very great, my reverence to this day undiminished.

X

FORTUNE'S SMILE

The fields, the floods, the heavens, with one consent
Did seeme to laugh on me, and favour mine intent.

SPENSER

At the same time that I exchanged Wyvern for Bookham I also exchanged my brother for Arthur as my chief companion. My brother, as you know, was serving in France. From 1914 to 1916, which is the Bookham period, he becomes a figure that at rare intervals appears unpredicted on leave, in all the glory of a young officer, with what then seemed unlimited wealth at his command, and whisks me off to Ireland. Luxuries hitherto unknown to me, such as first-class railway carriages and sleeping cars, glorify these journeys. You will understand that I had been crossing the Irish sea six times a year since I was nine. My brother's leaves now often added journeys extraordinary. That is why my memory is stored with ship's-side images to a degree unusual for such an untraveled man. I have only to close my eyes to see if I choose, and sometimes whether I choose or no, the phosphorescence of a ship's wash, the mast unmoving against the stars though the water is rushing past us, the long salmon-colored rifts of dawn or sunset on the horizon of cold gray-green water, or the astonishing behavior of land as you approach it, the promontories that walk out to meet you, the complex movements and final disappearance of the mountains further inland.

These leaves were of course a great delight. The strains that had been developing (thanks to Wyvern) before my brother went to France were forgotten. There was a tacit determination on both sides to revive, for the short time allowed us, the classic period of our boyhood. As my brother was in the R.A.S.C., which in those days was reckoned a safe place to be, we did not feel that degree of anxiety about him which most families were suffering at this time. There may have been more anxiety in the unconscious than came out in fully waking thought. That, at least, would explain an experience I had, certainly once, and perhaps more often; not a belief, nor quite a dream, but an impression, a mental image, a haunting, which on a bitter winter night at Bookham represented my brother hanging about the garden and calling — or rather trying to call, but as in Virgil's Hell *inceptus clamor frustratur hiantem,* a bat's cry is all that comes. There hung over this image an atmosphere which I dislike as much as any I ever breathed, a blend of the macabre and the weakly, wretchedly, hopelessly pathetic — the dreary miasma of the Pagan Hades.

Though my friendship with Arthur began from an identity of taste on a particular point, we were sufficiently different to help one another. His home life was almost the opposite of mine. His parents were members of the Plymouth Brothers, and he was the youngest of a large family; his home, nevertheless, was almost as silent as ours was noisy. He was at this time working in the business of one of his brothers, but his health was delicate and after an illness or two he was withdrawn from it. He was a man of more than one talent: a pianist and, in hope, a composer, and also a painter. One of our earliest schemes was that he should make an operatic score for *Loki Bound* — a project which, of course, after an extremely short and happy life, died a painless death. In literature he influenced me more, or more permanently, than I did him. His great defect was that he cared very little for verse. Something I did to mend this, but less than I wished. He, on the other hand, side by side with his love for myth and marvel, which I fully shared, had another taste which I lacked till I met him and with which, to my great good, he infected me for life. This was the taste for what he called "the good, solid, old books," the classic English novelists. It is astonishing how I had avoided them before I met Arthur. I had been persuaded by my father to read *The Newcomes* when I was rather too young for it and never tried Thackeray again till I was at Oxford. He is still antipathetic to me, not because he preaches but because he preaches badly. Dickens I looked upon with a feeling of horror, engendered by long poring over the illustrations before I had learned to read. I still think them depraved. Here, as in Walt Disney, it is not the ugliness of the ugly figures but the simpering dolls intended for our sympathy which really betray the secret (not that Walt Disney is not far superior to the illustrators of Dickens). Of Scott I knew only a few of the medieval, that is, the weakest, novels. Under Arthur's influence I read at this time all the best Waverleys, all the Brontës, and all the Jane Austens. They provided an admirable complement to my more fantastic reading, and each was the more enjoyed for its contrast to the other. The very qualities which had previously deterred me from such books Arthur taught me to see as their charm. What I would have called their "stodginess" or "ordinariness" he called "Homeliness" — a key word in his imagination. He did not mean merely Domesticity, though that came into it. He meant the rooted quality which attaches them to all our simple experiences, to weather, food, the family, the neighborhood. He could get endless enjoyment out of the opening sentence of *Jane Eyre*, or that other opening sentence in one of Hans Andersen's stories, "How it did rain, to be sure." The mere word "beck" in the Brontës was a feast to him; and so were the schoolroom and kitchen scenes. This love of the "Homely" was not confined to literature; he looked for it in out-of-door scenes as well and taught me to do the same.

Hitherto my feelings for nature had been too narrowly romantic. I attended almost entirely to what I thought awe-inspiring, or wild, or eerie, and above all to distance. Hence mountains and clouds were my especial delight; the sky was, and still is, to me one of the principal elements in any landscape, and long before I had seen them all named and sorted out in *Modern Painters* I was very attentive to the different qualities, and different heights, of the cirrus, the cumulus, and the raincloud. As for the Earth, the country I grew up in had everything to encourage a romantic bent, had indeed done so ever since I first looked at the unattainable Green Hills through the nursery window. For the reader who knows those parts it will be enough to say that my main haunt was the Holywood Hills – the irregular polygon you would have described if you drew a line from Stormont to Comber, from Comber to Newtownards, from Newtownards to Scrabo, from Scrabo to Craigantlet, from Craigantlet to Holywood, and thence through Knocknagonney back to Stormont. How to suggest it all to a foreigner I hardly know.

First of all, it is by Southern English standards bleak. The woods, for we have a few, are of small trees, rowan and birch and small fir. The fields are small, divided by ditches with ragged sea-nipped hedges on top of them. There is a good deal of gorse and many outcroppings of rock. Small abandoned quarries, filled with cold-looking water, are surprisingly numerous. There is nearly always a wind whistling through the grass. Where you see a man plowing there will be gulls following him and pecking at the furrow. There are no field paths or rights of way, but that does not matter for everyone knows you – or if they do not know you, they know your kind and understand that you will shut gates and not walk over crops. Mushrooms are still felt to be common property, like the air. The soil has none of the rich chocolate or ocher you find in parts of England: it is pale – what Dyson calls "the ancient, bitter earth." But the grass is soft, rich, and sweet, and the cottages, always whitewashed and single storied and roofed with blue slate, light up the whole landscape.

Although these hills are not very high, the expanse seen from them is huge and various. Stand at the northeastern extremity where the slopes go steeply down to Holywood. Beneath you is the whole expanse of the Lough. The Antrim coast twists sharply to the north and out of sight; green, and humble in comparison, Down curves away southward. Between the two the Lough merges into the sea, and if you look carefully on a good day you can even see Scotland, phantom-like on the horizon. Now come further to the south and west. Take your stand at the isolated cottage which is visible from my father's house and overlooks our whole suburb, and which everyone calls the Shepherd's Hut, though we are not really a shepherd country. You are still looking down on the Lough, but its mouth and the sea are now hidden by the shoulder you have just come from, and it might (for all you see) be a land-locked lake. And here we come to one of those great contrasts which have bitten deeply into my mind – Niflheim and Asgard, Britain and Logres, Handramit and Harandra, air and ether, the low world and the high. Your horizon from here is the Antrim Mountains, probably a uniform mass of grayish blue, though if it is a sunny day you may just trace on the Cave Hill the distinction between the green slopes that climb two-thirds of the way to the summit and the cliff wall that perpendicularly accomplishes the rest. That is one beauty; and here where you stand is another, quite different and even more dearly loved — sunlight and grass and dew, crowing cocks and gaggling ducks. In between them, on the flat floor of the Valley at your feet, a forest of factory chimneys, gantries, and giant cranes rising out of a welter of mist, lies Belfast. Noises come up from it continually, whining and screeching of trams, clatter of horse traffic on uneven sets, and, dominating all else, the continual throb and stammer of the great shipyards. And because we have heard this all our lives it does not, for us, violate the peace of the hilltop; rather, it emphasizes it, enriches the contrast, sharpens the dualism. Down in that "smoke and stir" is the hated office to which Arthur, less fortunate than I, must return tomorrow: for it is only one of his rare holidays that allows us to stand here together on a weekday morning. And down there too are the barefoot old women, the drunken men stumbling in and out of the "spirit grocers" (Ireland's horrible substitute for the kindly English "pub"), the straining, overdriven horses, the hard-faced rich women — all the world which Alberich created when he cursed love and twisted the gold into a ring.

Now step a little way — only two fields and across a lane and up to the top of the bank on the far side — and you will see, looking south with a little east in it, a different world. And having seen it, blame me if you can for being a romantic. For here is the thing itself, utterly irresistible, the way to the world's end, the land of longing, the breaking and blessing of hearts. You are looking across what may be called, in a certain sense, the plain of Down, and seeing beyond it the Mourne Mountains.

It was K. — that is, Cousin Quartus' second daughter, the Valkyrie — who first expounded to me what this plain of Down is really like. Here is the recipe for imagining it. Take a number of medium-sized potatoes and lay them down (one layer of them only) in a flat-bottomed tin basin. Now shake loose earth over them till the potatoes themselves, but not the shape of them, is hidden; and of course the crevices between them will now be depressions of earth. Now magnify the whole thing till those crevices are large enough to conceal each its stream and its huddle of trees. And then, for coloring, change your brown earth into the checkered pattern of fields, always small fields (a couple of acres each), with all their normal variety of crop, grass, and plow. You have now got a picture of the "plain" of Down, which is a plain only in the sense that if you were a very large giant you would regard it as level but very ill to walk on — like cobbles. And now remember that every cottage is white. The whole expanse laughs with these little white dots; it is like nothing so much as the assembly of white foam caps when a fresh breeze is on a summer sea. And the roads are white too; there is no tarmac yet. And because the whole country is a turbulent democracy of little hills, these roads shoot in every direction, disappearing and reappearing. But you must not spread over this landscape your hard English sunlight; make it paler, make it softer, blur the edges of the white cumuli, cover it with watery gleams, deepening it, making all unsubstantial. And beyond all this, so remote that they seem fantastically abrupt, at the very limit of your vision, imagine the mountains. They are no stragglers. They are steep and compact and pointed and toothed and jagged. They seem to have nothing to do with the little hills and cottages that divide you from them. And sometimes they are blue, sometimes violet; but quite often they look transparent — as if huge sheets of gauze had been cut out into mountainous shapes and hung up there, so that you could see through them the light of the invisible sea at their backs.

I number it among my blessings that my father had no car, while yet most of my friends had, and sometimes took me for a drive. This meant that all these distant objects could be visited just enough to clothe them with memories and not impossible desires, while yet they remained ordinarily as inaccessible as the Moon. The deadly power of rushing about wherever I pleased had not been given me. I measured distances by the standard of man, man walking on his two feet, not by the standard of the internal combustion engine. I had not been allowed to deflower the very idea of distance; in return I possessed "infinite riches" in what would have been to motorists "a little room." The truest and most horrible claim made for modern transport is that it "annihilates space." It does. It annihilates one of the most glorious gifts we have been given. It is a vile inflation which lowers the value of distance, so that a modern boy travels a hundred miles with less sense of liberation and pilgrimage and adventure than his grandfather got from traveling ten. Of course if a man hates space and wants it to be annihilated, that is another matter. Why not creep into his coffin at once? There is little enough space there.

Such were my outdoor delights before I met Arthur, and all these he shared and confirmed. And in his search for the Homely he taught me to see other things as well. But for him I should never have known the beauty of the ordinary vegetables that we destine to the pot. "Drills," he used to say. "Just ordinary drills of cabbages — what can be better?" And he was right. Often he recalled my eyes from the horizon just to look through a hole in a hedge, to see nothing more than a farmyard in its mid-morning solitude, and perhaps a gray cat squeezing its way under a barn door, or a bent old woman with a wrinkled, motherly face coming back with an empty bucket from the pigsty. But best of all we liked it when the Homely and the unhomely met in sharp juxtaposition; if a little kitchen garden ran steeply up a narrowing enclave of fertile ground surrounded by outcroppings and furze, or some shivering quarry pool under a moonrise could be seen on our left, and on our right the smoking chimney and lamp-lit window of a cottage that was just settling down for the night.

Meanwhile, on the Continent, the unskilled butchery of the first German War went on. As it did so and as I began to foresee that it would probably last till I reached military age, I was compelled to make a decision which the law had taken out of the hands of English boys of my own age; for in Ireland we had no conscription. I did not much plume myself even then for deciding to serve, but I did feel that the decision absolved me from taking any further notice of the war. For Arthur, whose heart hopelessly disqualified him, there was no such question. Accordingly I put the war on one side to the degree which some people will think shameful and some incredible. Others will call it a flight from reality. I maintain that it was rather a treaty with reality, the fixing of a frontier. I said to my country, in effect, "You shall have me on a certain date, not before. I will die in your wars if need be, but till then I shall live my own life. You may have my body, but not my mind. I will take part in battles but not read about them." If this attitude needs excusing I must say that a boy who is unhappy at school inevitably learns the habit of keeping the future in its place; if once he began to allow infiltrations from the coming term into the present holidays he would despair. Also, the Hamilton in me was always on guard against the Lewis; I had seen enough of the self-torturing temperament.

No doubt, even if the attitude was right, the quality in me which made it so easy to adopt is somewhat repellent. Yet, even so, I can hardly regret having escaped the appalling waste of time and spirit which would have been involved in reading the war news or taking more than an artificial and formal part in conversations about the war. To read without military knowledge or good maps accounts of fighting which were distorted before they reached the Divisional general and further distorted before they left him and then "written up" out of all recognition by journalists, to strive to master what will be contradicted the next day, to fear and hope intensely on shaky evidence, is surely an ill use of the mind. Even in peacetime I think those are very wrong who say that schoolboys should be encouraged to read the newspapers. Nearly all that a boy reads there in his teens will be known before he is twenty to have been false in emphasis and interpretation, if not in fact as well, and most of it will have lost all importance. Most of what he remembers he will therefore have to unlearn; and he will probably have acquired an incurable taste for vulgarity and sensationalism and the fatal habit of fluttering from paragraph to paragraph to learn how an actress has been divorced in California, a train derailed in France, and quadruplets born in New Zealand.

I was now happier than I had ever been. All the sting had been drawn from the beginning of term. Yet the homecoming at its end remained almost as joyful as before. The holidays grew better and better. Our grown-up friends, and especially my cousins at Mountbracken, now seemed less grown up — for one's immediate elders grow downward or backward to meet one at that age. There were many merry meetings, much good talk. I discovered that other people besides Arthur loved books that I loved. The horrible old "social functions," the dances, were at an end, for my father now allowed me to refuse the invitations. All my engagements were now pleasant ones, within a small circle of people who were all intermarried, or very old neighbors, or (the women anyway) old school fellows. I am shy of mentioning them. Of Mountbracken I have had to speak because the story of my life could not be told without it; beyond that I hesitate to go. Praise of one's friends is near impertinence. I cannot tell you here of Janie M. nor of her mother, nor of Bill and Mrs. Bill. In novels, provincial-suburban society is usually painted gray to black. I have not found it so. I think we Strandtown and Belmont people had among us as much kindness, wit, beauty, and taste as any circle of the same size that I have ever known.

At home the real separation and apparent cordiality between my father and myself continued. Every holiday I came back from Kirk with my thoughts and my speech a little clearer, and this made it progressively less possible to have any real conversation with my father. I was far too young and raw to appreciate the other side of the account, to weigh the rich (if vague) fertility, the generosity and humor of my father's mind against the dryness, the rather deathlike lucidity, of Kirk's. With the cruelty of youth I allowed myself to be irritated by traits in my father which, in other elderly men, I have since regarded as lovable foibles. There were so many unbridgeable mis-understandings. Once I received a letter from my brother in my father's presence which he immediately demanded to see. He objected to some expressions in it about a third person. In defense of them I pleaded that they had not been addressed to him. "What nonsense!" answered my father. "He knew you would show me the letter, and intended you to show me the letter." In reality, as I well knew, my brother had foolishly gambled on the chance that it would arrive when my father was out. But this my father could not conceive. He was not overriding by authority a claim to privacy which he disallowed; he could not imagine anyone making such a claim.

My relations to my father help to explain (I am not suggesting that they excuse) one of the worst acts of my life. I allowed myself to be prepared for confirmation, and confirmed, and to make my first Communion, in total disbelief, acting a part, eating and drinking my own condemnation. As Johnson points out, where courage is not, no other virtue can survive except by accident. Cowardice drove me into hypocrisy and hypocrisy into blasphemy. It is true that I did not and could not then know the real na-ture of the thing I was doing: but I knew very well that I was acting a lie with the greatest possible solemnity. It seemed to me impossible to tell my father my real views. Not that he would have stormed and thundered like the traditional orthodox parent. On the contrary, he would (at first) have responded with the greatest kindness. "Let's talk the whole thing over," he would have said. But it would have been quite impossible to drive into his head my real position. The thread would have been lost almost at once, and the answer implicit in all the quotations, anecdotes, and rem-iniscences which would have poured over me would have been one I then valued not a straw – the beauty of the Authorized Version, the beauty of the Christian tradition and sentiment and character. And later, when this failed, when I still tried to make my exact points clear, there would have been anger between us, thunder from him and a thin, peevish rattle from me. Nor could the subject, once raised, ever have been dropped again. All this, of course, ought to have been dared rather than the thing I did. But at the time it seemed to me impossible. The Syrian captain was forgiven for bowing in the house of Rimmon. I am one of many who have bowed in the house of the real God when I believed Him to be no more than Rimmon.

During the weekends and evenings I was closely tethered to my father and felt this something of a hardship, since these were the times when Arthur was most often ac-cessible. My weekdays continued to supply me with a full ration of solitude. I had, to be sure, the society of Tim, who ought to have been mentioned far sooner. Tim was our dog. He may hold a record for longevity among Irish terriers since he was already with us when I was at Oldie's and did not die till 1922. But Tim's society did not amount to much. It had long since been agreed between him and me that he should not be expected to accompany me on walks. I went a good deal further than he liked, for his shape was already that of a bolster, or even a barrel, on four legs. Also, I went to places where other dogs might be met; and though Tim was no coward (I have seen him fight like a demon on his home ground) he hated dogs. In his walking days he had been known, on seeing a dog far ahead, to disappear behind the hedge and re-emerge a hundred yards later. His mind had been formed during our schooldays and he had perhaps learned his attitude to other dogs from our attitude to other boys. By now he and I were less like master and dog than like two friendly visitors in the same hotel. We met constantly, passed the time of day, and parted with much esteem to follow our own paths. I think he had one friend of his own species, a neighboring red setter; a very respectable, middle-aged dog. Perhaps a good influence; for poor Tim, though I loved him, was the most undisciplined, unaccomplished, and dissipated-looking creature that ever went on four legs. He never exactly obeyed you; he sometimes agreed with you.

The long hours in the empty house passed delightfully in reading and writing. I was in the midst of the Romantics now. There was a humility in me (as a reader) at that time which I shall never recapture. Some poems I could not enjoy as well as others. It never occurred to me that these might be the inferior ones; I merely thought that I was getting tired of my author or was not in the right mood. The *longueurs* of Endymion I attributed wholly to myself. The "swoony" element in Keats' sensuality (as when Porphyro grows "faint") I tried hard to like, and failed. I thought—though I have forgotten why—that Shelley must be better than Keats and was sorry I liked him less. But my great author at this period was William Morris. I had met him first in quotation in books on Norse Mythology; that led me to *Sigurd the Volsung*. I did not really like this as much as I tried to, and I think I now know why: the metre does not satisfy my ear. But then, in Arthur's bookcase, I found *The Well at the World's End*. I looked—I read chapter headings—I dipped—and next day I was off into town to buy a copy of my own. Like so many new steps it appeared to be partly a revival—"Knights in Armor" returning from a very early period of my childhood. After that I read all the Morris I could get, *Jason, The Earthly Paradise,* the prose romances. The growth of the new delight is marked by my sudden realization, almost with a sense of disloyalty, that the letters WILLIAM MORRIS were coming to have at least as potent a magic in them as WAGNER.

One other thing that Arthur taught me was to love the bodies of books. I had always respected them. My brother and I might cut up stepladders without scruple; to have thumb-marked or dog's-eared a book would have filled us with shame. But Arthur did not merely respect, he was enamored; and soon, I too. The set up of the page, the feel and smell of the paper, the differing sounds that different papers make as you turn the leaves, became sensuous delights. This revealed to me a flaw in Kirk. How often have I shuddered when he took a new classical text of mine in his gardener's hands, bent back the boards till they creaked, and left his sign on every page.

"Yes, I remember," said my father. "That was old Knock's one fault."

"A bad one," said I.

"An all but unforgivable one," said my father.

XI

CHECK

When bale is at highest, boote is at next.
SIR ALDINGAR

The History of Joy, since it came riding back to me on huge waves of Wagnerian music and Norse and Celtic mythology several chapters ago, must now be brought up to date.

I have already hinted how my first delight in Valhalla and Valkyries began to turn itself imperceptibly into a scholar's interest in them. I got about as far as a boy who knew no old Germanic language could get. I could have faced a pretty stiff examination in my subject. I would have laughed at popular bunglers who confused the late mythological Sagas with the classic Sagas, or the Prose with the Verse Edda, or even, more scandalously, Edda with Saga. I knew my way about the Eddaic cosmos, could locate each of the roots of the Ash and knew who ran up and down it. And only very gradually did I realize that all this was something quite different from the original Joy. And I went on adding detail to detail, progressing toward the moment when "I should know most and should least enjoy." Finally I woke from building the temple to find that the God had flown. Of course I did not put it that way. I would have said simply that I didn't get the old thrill. I was in the Wordsworthian predicament, lamenting that "a glory" had passed away.

Thence arose the fatal determination to recover the old thrill, and at last the moment when I was compelled to realize that all such efforts were failures. I had no lure to which the bird would come. And now, notice my blindness. At that very moment there arose the memory of a place and time at which I had tasted the lost Joy with unusual fullness. It had been a particular hill walk on a morning of white mist. The other volumes of the *Ring* (*The Rheingold* and *The Valkyrie*) had just arrived as a Christmas present from my father, and the thought of all the reading before me, mixed with the coldness and loneliness of the hillside, the drops of moisture on every

92

branch, and the distant murmur of the concealed town, had produced a longing (yet it was also fruition) which had flowed over from the mind and seemed to involve the whole body. That walk I now remembered. It seemed to me that I had tasted heaven then. If only such a moment could return! But what I never realized was that it had returned — that the remembering of that walk was itself a new experience of just the same kind. True, it was desire, not possession. But then what I had felt on the walk had also been desire, and only possession in so far as that kind of desire is itself desirable, is the fullest possession we can know on earth; or rather, because the very nature of Joy makes nonsense of our common distinction between having and wanting. There, to have is to want and to want is to have. Thus, the very moment when I longed to be so stabbed again, was itself again such a stabbing. The Desirable which had once alighted on Valhalla was now alighting on a particular moment of my own past; and I would not recognize him there because, being an idolater and a formalist, I insisted that he ought to appear in the temple I had built him; not knowing that he cares only for temples building and not at all for temples built. Wordsworth, I believe, made this mistake all his life. I am sure that all that sense of the loss of vanished vision which fills *The Prelude* was itself vision of the same kind, if only he could have believed it.

In my scheme of thought it is not blasphemous to compare the error which I was making with that error which the angel at the Sepulchre rebuked when he said to the women, "Why seek ye the living among the dead? He is not here, He is risen." The comparison is of course between something of infinite moment and something very small; like comparison between the Sun and the Sun's reflection in a dewdrop. Indeed, in my view, very like it, for I do not think the resemblance between the Christian and the merely imaginative experience is accidental. I think that all things, in their way, reflect heavenly truth, the imagination not least. "Reflect" is the important word. This lower life of the imagination is not[1] a beginning of, nor a step toward, the higher life of the spirit, merely an image. In me, at any rate, it contained no element either of belief or of ethics; however far pursued, it would never have made me either wiser or better. But it still had, at however many removes, the shape of the reality it reflected.

If nothing else suggests this resemblance it is at least suggested by the fact that we can make exactly the same mistakes on both levels. You will remember how, as a schoolboy, I had destroyed my religious life by a vicious subjectivism which made "realizations" the aim of prayer; turning away from God to seek states of mind, and trying to produce those states of mind by "maistry." With unbelievable folly I now proceeded to make exactly the same blunder in my imaginative life; or rather the same pair of blunders. The first was made at the very moment when I formulated the complaint that the "old thrill" was becoming rarer and rarer. For by that complaint I smuggled in the assumption that what I wanted was a "thrill," a state of my own mind. And there lies the deadly error. Only when your whole attention and desire are fixed

[1]*I.e.,* not necessarily and by its own nature. God can cause it to be such a beginning.

on something else — whether a distant mountain, or the past, or the gods of Asgard — does the "thrill" arise. It is a by-product. Its very existence presupposes that you desire not it but something other and outer. If by any perverse askesis or the use of any drug it could be produced from within, it would at once be seen to be of no value. For take away the object, and what, after all, would be left? — a whirl of images, a fluttering sensation in the diaphragm, a momentary abstraction. And who could want that? This, I say, is the first and deadly error, which appears on every level of life and is equally deadly on all, turning religion into a self-caressing luxury and love into auto-eroticism. And the second error is, having thus falsely made a state of mind your aim, to attempt to produce it. From the fading of the Northernness I ought to have drawn the conclusion that the Object, the Desirable, was further away, more external, less subjective, than even such a comparatively public and external thing as a system of mythology — had, in fact, only shone through that system. Instead, I concluded that it was a mood or state within myself which might turn up in any context. To "get it again" became my constant endeavor; while reading every poem, hearing every piece of music, going for every walk, I stood anxious sentinel at my own mind to watch whether the blessed moment was beginning and to endeavor to retain it if it did. Because I was still young and the whole world of beauty was opening before me, my own officious obstructions were often swept aside and, startled into self-forgetfulness, I again tasted Joy. But far more often I frightened it away by my greedy impatience to snare it, and, even when it came, instantly destroyed it by introspection, and at all times vulgarized it by my false assumption about its nature.

One thing, however, I learned, which has since saved me from many popular confusions of mind. I came to know by experience that it is not a disguise of sexual desire. Those who think that if adolescents were all provided with suitable mistresses we should soon hear no more of "immortal longings" are certainly wrong. I learned this mistake to be a mistake by the simple, if discreditable, process of repeatedly making it. From the Northernness one could not easily have slid into erotic fantasies without noticing the difference; but when the world of Morris became the frequent medium of Joy, this transition became possible. It was quite easy to think that one desired those forests for the sake of their female inhabitants, the garden of Hesperus for the sake of his daughters, Hylas' river for the river nymphs. I repeatedly followed that path — to the end. And at the end one found pleasure; which immediately resulted in the discovery that pleasure (whether that pleasure or any other) was not what you had been looking for. No moral question was involved; I was at this time as nearly non-moral on that subject as a human creature can be. The frustration did not consist in finding a "lower" pleasure instead of a "higher." It was the irrelevance of the conclusion that marred it. The hounds had changed scent. One had caught the wrong quarry. You might as well offer a mutton chop to a man who is dying of thirst as offer sexual pleasure to the desire I am speaking of. I did not recoil from the erotic conclusion with chaste horror, exclaiming, "Not that!" My feelings could rather have been expressed in the words, "Quite. I see. But haven't we wandered from the real point?"

Joy is not a substitute for sex; sex is very often a substitute for Joy. I sometimes wonder whether all pleasures are not substitutes for Joy.

Such, then, was the state of my imaginative life; over against it stood the life of my intellect. The two hemispheres of my mind were in the sharpest contrast. On the one side a many-islanded sea of poetry and myth; on the other a glib and shallow "rationalism." Nearly all that I loved I believed to be imaginary; nearly all that I believe to be real I thought grim and meaningless. The exceptions were certain people (whom I loved and believed to be real) and nature herself. That is, nature as she appeared to the senses. I chewed endlessly on the problem: "How can it be so beautiful and also so cruel, wasteful and futile?" Hence at this time I could almost have said with Santayana, "All that is good is imaginary; all that is real is evil." In one sense nothing less like a "flight from reality" could be conceived. I was so far from wishful thinking that I hardly thought anything true unless it contradicted my wishes.

Hardly, but not quite. For there was one way in which the world, as Kirk's rationalism taught me to see it, gratified my wishes. It might be grim and deadly but at least it was free from the Christian God. Some people (not all) will find it hard to understand why this seemed to me such an overwhelming advantage. But you must take into account both my history and my temperament. The period of faith which I had lived through at Oldie's had contained a good deal of fear. And by now, looking back on that fear, and egged on by Shaw and Voltaire and Lucretius with his *Tantum religio,* I greatly exaggerated that element in my memory and forgot the many other elements which had been combined with it. At all costs I was anxious that those full-moonlit nights in the dormitory should never come again. I was also, as you may remember, one whose negative demands were more violent that his positive, far more eager to escape pain than to achieve happiness, and feeling it something of an outrage that I had been created without my own permission. To such a craven the materialist's universe had the enormous attraction that it offered you limited liabilities. No strictly infinite disaster could overtake you in it. Death ended all. And if ever finite disasters proved greater than one wished to bear, suicide would always be possible. The horror of the Christian universe was that it had no door marked *Exit*. It was also perhaps not unimportant that the externals of Christianity made no appeal to my sense of beauty. Oriental imagery and style largely repelled me; and for the rest, Christianity was mainly associated for me with ugly architecture, ugly music, and bad poetry. Wyvern Priory and Milton's verse were almost the only points at which Christianity and beauty had overlapped in my experience. But, of course, what mattered most of all was my deep-seated hatred of authority, my monstrous individualism, my lawlessness. No word in my vocabulary expressed deeper hatred than the word *Interference*. But Christianity placed at the center what then seemed to me a transcendental Interferer. If its picture were true then no sort of "treaty with reality" could ever be possible. There was no region even in the innermost depth of one's soul (nay, there least of all) which one could surround with a barbed wire fence and guard with a notice No Admittance. And that was what I wanted; some area, however small, of which I could say to all other beings, "This is my business and mine only."

In this respect, and this only at first, I may have been guilty of wishful thinking. Almost certainly I was. The materialist conception would not have seemed so immensely probable to me if it had not favored at least one of my wishes. But the difficulty of explaining even a boy's thought entirely in terms of his wishes is that on such large questions as these he always has wishes on both sides. Any conception of reality which a sane mind can admit must favor some of its wishes and frustrate others. The materialistic universe had one great, negative attraction to offer me. It had no other. And this had to be accepted; one had to look out on a meaningless dance of atoms (remember, I was reading Lucretius), to realize that all the apparent beauty was a subjective phosphorescence, and to relegate everything one valued to the world of mirage. That price I tried loyally to pay. For I had learned something from Kirk about the honor of the intellect and the shame of voluntary inconsistency. And, of course, I exulted with youthful and vulgar pride in what I thought my enlightenment. In argument with Arthur I was a very swashbuckler. Most of it, as I now see, was incredibly crude and silly. I was in that state of mind in which a boy thinks it extremely telling to call God *Jahveh* and Jesus *Yeshua*.

Looking back on my life now, I am astonished that I did not progress into the opposite orthodoxy – did not become a Leftist, Atheist, satiric Intellectual of the type we all know so well. All the conditions seem to be present. I had hated my public school. I hated whatever I knew or imagined of the British Empire. And though I took very little notice of Morris's socialism (there were too many things in him that interested me far more), continual reading of Shaw had brought it about that such embryonic political opinions as I had were vaguely socialistic. Ruskin had helped me in the same direction. My lifelong fear of sentimentalism ought to have qualified me to become a vigorous "debunker." It is true that I hated the Collective as much as any man can hate anything; but I certainly did not then realize its relations to socialism. I suppose that my Romanticism was destined to divide me from the orthodox Intellectuals as soon as I met them; and also that a mind so little sanguine as mine about the future and about common action could only with great difficulty be made revolutionary.

Such, then, was my position: to care for almost nothing but the gods and heroes, the garden of the Hesperides, Launcelot and the Grail, and to believe in nothing but atoms and evolution and military service. At times the strain was severe, but I think this was a wholesome severity. Nor do I believe that the intermittent wavering in my materialistic "faith" (so to call it) which set in toward the end of the Bookham period would ever have arisen simply from my wishes. It came from another source.

Among all the poets whom I was reading at this time (I read *The Faerie Queene* and *The Earthly Paradise* entire) there was one who stood apart from the rest. Yeats was this poet. I had been reading him for a long time before I discovered the difference, and perhaps I should never have discovered it if I had not read his prose as well:

things like *Rosa Alchemica* and *Per Amica Silentia Lunae*. The difference was that Yeats believed. His "ever living ones" were not merely feigned or merely desired. He really thought that there was a world of being more or less like them, and that contact between that world and ours was possible. To put it quite plainly, he believed seriously in Magic. His later career as a poet has somewhat obscured that phase in popular estimates of him, but there is no doubt about the fact – as I learned when I met him some years later. Here was a pretty kettle of fish. You will understand that my rationalism was inevitably based on what I believed to be the findings of the sciences, and those findings, not being a scientist, I had to take on trust – in fact, on authority. Well, here was an opposite authority. If he had been a Christian I should have discounted his testimony, for I thought I had the Christians "placed" and disposed of forever. But I now learned that there were people, not traditionally orthodox, who nevertheless rejected the whole Materialist philosophy out of hand. And I was still very ingenuous. I had no conception of the amount of nonsense written and printed in the world. I regarded Yeats as a learned, responsible writer: what he said must be worthy of consideration. And after Yeats I plunged into Maeterlinck; quite innocently and naturally since everyone was reading him at that time and since I made a point of including a fair amount of French in my diet. In Maeterlinck I came up against Spiritualism, Theosophy, and Pantheism. Here once more was a responsible adult (and not a Christian) who believed in a world behind, or around, the material world. I must do myself the justice of saying that I did not give my assent categorically. But a drop of disturbing doubt fell into my Materialism. It was merely a "Perhaps." Perhaps (oh joy!) there was, after all, "something else"; and (oh reassurance!) perhaps it had nothing to do with Christian Theology. And as soon as I paused on that "Perhaps," inevitably all the old Occultist lore, and all the old excitement which the Matron of Chartres had innocently aroused in me, rose out of the past.

Now the fat was in the fire with a vengeance. Two things hitherto widely separated in my mind rushed together: the imaginative longing for Joy, or rather the longing which *was* Joy, and the ravenous, quasi-prurient desire for the Occult, the Preternatural as such. And with these there came (less welcome) some stirring of unease, some of the immemorial fear we have all known in the nursery, and (if we are honest) long after the nursery age. There is a kind of gravitation in the mind whereby good rushes to good and evil to evil. This mingled repulsion and desire drew toward them everything else in me that was bad. The idea that if there were Occult knowledge it was known to very few and scorned by the many became an added attraction: "We few," you will remember, was an evocative expression for me. That the means should be Magic – the most exquisitely unorthodox thing in the world, unorthodox both by Christian and by Rationalist standards – of course appealed to the rebel in me. I was already acquainted with the more depraved side of Romanticism; had read *Anactoria*, and Wilde, and pored upon Beardsley, not hitherto attracted, but making no moral judgment. Now I thought I began to see the point of it. In a word, you have already had in this story the World and the Flesh; now came the Devil. If there had been in the neighborhood some elder person who dabbled in dirt of the Magical kind (such have a good nose for potential disciples) I might now be a Satanist or a maniac.

In actual fact I was wonderfully protected, and this spiritual debauch had in the end one rather good result. I was protected, first, by ignorance and incapacity. Whether Magic were possible or not, I at any rate had no teacher to start me on the path. I was protected also by cowardice; the reawakened terrors of childhood might add a spice to my greed and curiosity as long as it was daylight. Alone, and in darkness, I used my best endeavors to become a strict Materalist again; not always with success. A "Perhaps" is quite enough for the nerves to work upon. But my best protection was the known nature of Joy. This ravenous desire to break the bounds, to tear the curtain, to be in the secret, revealed itself, more and more clearly the longer I indulged it, to be quite different from the longing that is Joy. Its coarse strength betrayed it. Slowly, and with many relapses, I came to see that the magical conclusion was just as irrelevant to Joy as the erotic conclusion has been. Once again one had changed scents. If circles and pentangles and the Tetragrammaton had been tried and had in fact raised, or seemed to raise, a spirit, that might have been – if a man's nerves could stand it – extremely interesting; but the real Desirable would have evaded one, the real Desire would have been left saying, "What is this to me?"

What I like about experience is that it is such an honest thing. You may take any number of wrong turnings; but keep your eyes open and you will not be allowed to go very far before the warning signs appear. You may have deceived yourself, but experience is not trying to deceive you. The universe rings true wherever you fairly test it.

The other results of my glance into the dark room were as follows. First, I now had both a fresh motive for wishing Materialism to be true and a decreased confidence that it was. The fresh motive came as you have divined, from those fears which I had so wantonly stirred up from their sleeping place in the memories of childhood; behaving like a true Lewis who will not leave well alone. Every man who is afraid of spooks will have a reason for wishing to be a Materialist; that creed promises to exclude the bogies. As for my shaken confidence, it remained in the form of a "Perhaps," stripped of its directly and grossly magical "affect" – a pleasing possibility that the Universe might combine the snugness of Materialism here and now with . . . well, with I didn't know what; somewhere or something beyond, "the unimaginable lodge for solitary thinkings." This was very bad. I was beginning to try to have it both ways: to get the comforts both of a materialist and of a spiritual philosophy without the rigors of either. But the second result was better. I had learned a wholesome antipathy to everything occult and magical which was to stand me in good stead when, at Oxford, I came to meet Magicians, Spiritualists, and the like, Not that the ravenous lust was never to tempt me again but that I now knew it for a temptation. And above all, I now knew that Joy did not point in that direction.

You might sum up the gains of this whole period by saying that henceforward the Flesh and the Devil, though they could still tempt, could no longer offer me the su-

preme bribe. I had learned that it was not in their gift. And the World had never even
pretended to have it.

And then, on top of this, in superabundance of mercy, came that event which I
have already more than once attempted to describe in other books. I was in the habit of
walking over to Leatherhead about once a week and sometimes taking the train back.
In summer I did so chiefly because Leatherhead boasted a tiny swimming bath; better
than nothing to me who had learned to swim almost before I can remember and who,
till middle age and rheumatism crept upon me, was passionately fond of being in
water. But I went in winter, too, to look for books and to get my hair cut. The evening
that I now speak of was in October. I and one porter had the long, timbered platform
of Leatherhead station to ourselves. It was getting just dark enough for the smoke of
an engine to glow red on the underside with the reflection of the furnace. The hills
beyond the Dorking Valley were of a blue so intense as to be nearly violet and the sky
was green with frost. My ears tingled with the cold. The glorious weekend of reading
was before me. Turning to the bookstall, I picked out an Everyman in a dirty jacket,
Phantastes, a Faerie Romance, George MacDonald. Then the train came in. I can
still remember the voice of the porter calling out the village names, Saxon and sweet
as a nut— "Bookham, Effingham, Horsley train." That evening I began to read my
new book.

The woodland journeyings in that story, the ghostly enemies, the ladies both
good and evil, were close enough to my habitual imagery to lure me on without the
perception of a change. It is as if I were carried sleeping across the frontier, or as if I
had died in the old country and could never remember how I came alive in the new.
For in one sense the new country was exactly like the old. I met there all that had already charmed me in Malory, Spenser, Morris, and Yeats. But in another sense all
was changed. I did not yet know (and I was long in learning) the name of the new
quality, the bright shadow, that rested on the travels of Andodos. I do now. It was
Holiness. For the first time the song of the sirens sounded like the voice of my mother
or my nurse. Here were old wives' tales; there was nothing to be proud of in enjoying
them. It was as though the voice which had called to me from the world's end were
now speaking at my side. It was with me in the room, or in my own body, or behind
me. If it had once eluded me by its distance, it now eluded me by proximity – something too near to see, too plain to be understood, on this side of knowledge. It seemed
to have been always with me; if I could ever have turned my head quick enough I
should have seized it. Now for the first time I felt that it was out of reach not because
of something I could not do but because of something I could not stop doing. If I
could only leave off, let go, unmake myself, it would be there. Meanwhile, in this
new region all the confusions that had hitherto perplexed my search for Joy were disarmed. There was no temptation to confuse the scenes of the tale with light that
rested upon them, or to suppose that they were put forward as realities, or even to
dream that if they had been realities and I could reach the woods where Anodos jour-

neyed I should thereby come a step nearer to my desire. Yet, at the same time, never had the wind of Joy blowing through any story been less separable from the story itself. Where the god and the *idolon* were most nearly one there was least danger of confounding them. Thus, when the great moments came I did not break away from the woods and cottages that I read of to seek some bodiless light shining beyond them, but gradually, with a swelling continuity (like the sun at mid-morning burning through a fog) I found the light shining on those woods and cottages, and then on my own past life, and on the quiet room where I sat and on my old teacher where he nodded above his little *Tacitus*. For I now perceived that while the air of the new region made all my erotic and magical perversions of Joy look like sordid trumpery, it had no such disenchanting power over the bread upon the table or the coals in the grate. That was the marvel. Up till now each visitation of Joy had left the common world momentarily a desert— "The first touch of the earth went nigh to kill." Even when real clouds or trees had been the material of the vision, they had been so only by reminding me of another world; and I did not like the return to ours. But now I saw the bright shadow coming out of the book into the real world and resting there, transforming all common things and yet itself unchanged. Or, more accurately, I saw the common things drawn into the bright shadow. *Unde hoc mihi?* In the depth of my disgraces, in the then invincible ignorance of my intellect, all this was given me without asking, even without consent. That night my imagination was, in a certain sense, baptized; the rest of me. not unnaturally, took longer. I had not the faintest notion what I had let myself in for by buying *Phantastes*.

XII

GUNS AND GOOD COMPANY

*La compagnie, de tant d'hommes vous plaist, nobles, jeunes,
actifs; la liberté de cette conversation sans art, et une façon
de vie masle et sans cérémonie.*

MONTAIGNE

The old pattern began to repeat itself. The Bookham days, like a longer and more glorious holiday, drew to their end; a scholarship examination and, after that, the army, loomed behind them like a grimmer term. The good time had never been better than in its last months. I remember, in particular, glorious hours of bathing in Donegal. It was surf bathing: not the formal affair with boards that you have now, but mere rough and tumble, in which the waves, the monstrous, emerald, deafening waves, are always the winner, and it is at once a joke, a terror, and a joy to look over your shoulder and see (too late) one breaker of such sublime proportions that you would have avoided him had you known he was coming. But they gather themselves up, pre-eminent above their fellows, as suddenly and unpredictably as a revolution.

It was late in the winter term of 1916 that I went to Oxford to sit for my scholarship examination. Boys who have faced this ordeal in peacetime will not easily imagine the indifference with which I went. This does not mean that I underestimated the importance (in one sense) of succeeding. I knew very well by now that there was hardly any position in the world save that of a don in which I was fitted to earn a living, and that I was staking everything on a game in which few won and hundreds lost. As Kirk had said of me in a letter to my father (I did not, of course, see it till many years later), "You may make a writer or a scholar of him, but you'll not make anything else. You may make up your mind to *that*." And I knew this myself; sometimes it terrified me. What blunted the edge of it now was that whether I won a scholarship or no I should next year go into the army; and even a temper more sanguine than mine could feel in 1916 that an infantry subaltern would be insane to waste anxiety on anything so hypothetical as his postwar life. I once tried to explain this to my father;

it was one of the attempts I often made (though doubtless less often than I ought) to break through the artificiality of our intercourse and admit him to my real life. It was a total failure. He replied at once with fatherly counsels about the necessity of hard work and concentration, the amount that he had already spent in educating me, the very moderate, nay negligible, assistance he would be able to give me in later life. Poor man! He misjudged me sadly if he thought that idleness at my book was among my many vices. And how, I asked myself, could he expect the winning or losing of a scholarship to lose none of its importance when life and death were the real issues? The truth is, I think, that while death (mine, his, everyone's) was often vividly present to him as a subject of anxiety and other emotions, it had no place in his mind as a sober, matter-of-fact contingency from which consequences could be drawn. At any rate the conversation was a failure. It shipwrecked on the old rock. His intense desire for my total confidence co-existed with an inability to listen (in any strict sense) to what I said. He could never empty, or silence, his own mind to make room for an alien thought.

My first taste of Oxford was comical enough. I had made no arrangements about quarters and, having no more luggage than I could carry in my hand, I sallied out of the railway station on foot to find either a lodging house or a cheap hotel; all agog for "dreaming spires" and "last enchantments." My first disappointment at what I saw could be dealt with. Towns always show their worst face to the railway. But as I walked on and on I became more bewildered. Could this succession of mean shops really be Oxford? But I still went on, always expecting the next turn to reveal the beauties, and reflecting that it was a much larger town than I had been led to suppose. Only when it became obvious that there was very little town left ahead of me, that I was, in fact, getting to open country, did I turn round and look. There, behind me, far away, never more beautiful since, was the fabled cluster of spires and towers. I had come out of the station on the wrong side and been all this time walking into what was even then the mean and sprawling suburb of Botley. I did not see to what extent this little adventure was an allegory of my whole life. I merely walked back to the station, somewhat footsore, took a hansom, and asked to be driven to "some place where I can get rooms for a week, please." The method, which I should now think hazardous, was a complete success, and I was soon at tea in comfortable lodgings. The house is still there, the first on the right as you turn into Mansfield Road out of Holywell. I shared the sitting room with another candidate, a man from Cardiff College, which he pronounced to be architecturally superior to anything in Oxford. His learning terrified me, but he was an agreeable man. I have never seen him since.

It was very cold and the next day snow began to fall, turning pinnacles into wedding-cake decorations. The examination was held in the Hall of Oriel, and we all wrote in greatcoats and mufflers and wearing at least our left-hand gloves. The Provost, old Phelps, gave out the papers. I remember very little about them, but I suppose I was outshone in pure classics by many of my rivals and succeeded on my general knowledge and dialectics. I had the impression that I was doing badly. Long years (or years that seemed long) with the Knock had cured me of my defensive Wyvernian priggery, and I no longer supposed other boys to be ignorant of what I knew. Thus the essay was on a quotation from Johnson. I had read several times the Boswellian conversation in which it occurred and was able to replace the whole question in that context; but I never thought that this (any more than a fairish knowledge of Schopenhauer) would gain me any particular credit. It was a blessed state to be in, but for the moment depressing. As I left the Hall after that essay I heard one candidate say to his friend, "I worked in all my stuff about Rousseau and the Social Contract." That struck dismay into my soul, for though I had dabbled (not to my good) in the *Confessions* I knew nothing of the *Contrat Social.* At the beginning of the morning a nice Harrovian had whispered to me, "I don't even know if it's Sam or Ben." In my innocence I explained to him that it was Sam and could not be Ben because Ben was spelled without an h. I did not think there could be any harm in giving away such information.

When I arrived home I told my father that I had almost certainly failed. It was an admission calculated to bring out all his tenderness and chivalry. The man who could not understand a boy's taking his own possible, or probable, death into account could very well understand a child's disappointment. Not a word was now heard of expenses and difficulties; nothing but consolation, reassurance and affection. Then, almost on Christmas Eve, we heard that "Univ" (University College) had elected me.

Though I was now a scholar of my College I still had to pass "Responsions," which involved elementary mathematics. To prepare for this I returned after Christmas for one last term with Kirk—a golden term, poignantly happy under the approaching shadow. At Easter I was handsomely plowed in Responsions, having been unable as usual to get my sums right. "Be more careful," was the advice that everyone gave me, but I found it useless. The more care I took the more mistakes I made; just as, to this day, the more anxiously I fair copy a piece of writing the more certain I am to make a ghastly clerical error in the very first line.

In spite of this I came into residence in the summer (Trinity) term of 1917; for the real object now was simply to enter the University Officers' Training Corps as my most promising route into the army. My first studies at Oxford, nevertheless, still had Responsions in view. I read algebra (devil take it!) with old Mr. Campbell of Hertford who turned out to be a friend of our dear friend Janie M. That I never passed Responsions is certain, but I cannot remember whether I again sat for it and was again plowed. The question became unimportant after the war, for a benevolent decree exempted ex-servicemen from taking it. Otherwise, no doubt, I should have had to abandon the idea of going to Oxford.

I was less than a term at Univ when my papers came through and I enlisted; and the conditions made it a most abnormal term. Half the College had been converted into a hospital and was in the hands of the R.A.M.C. In the remaining portion lived a tiny community of undergraduates—two of us not yet of military age, two unfit, one a Sinn-Feiner who would not fight for England, and a few other oddments which I never quite placed. We dined in the little lecture room which is now a passage between Common Room and Hall. Small though our numbers were (about eight) we were rather distinguished, for we included E.V. Gordon, afterward Professor of English at Manchester, and A.C. Ewing, the Cambridge philosopher; also that witty and kindly man, Theobald Butler, skilled in turning the most lurid limericks into Greek verse. I enjoyed myself greatly; but it bore little resemblance to normal undergraduate life and was for me an unsettled, excited, and generally useless period. Then came the army. By a remarkable turn of fate this did not mean removal from Oxford. I was drafted into a Cadet Battalion whose billet was Keble.

I passed through the ordinary course of training (a mild affair in those days compared with that of the recent war) and was commissioned as a Second Lieutenant in the Somerset Light Infantry, the old XIIIth Foot. I arrived in the front line trenches on my nineteenth birthday (November 1917), saw most of my service in the villages before Arras — Fampoux and Monchy — and was wounded at Mt. Bernenchon, near Lillers, in April, 1918.

I am surprised that I did not dislike the army more. It was, of course, detestable. But the words "of course" drew the sting. That is where it differed from Wyvern. One did not expect to like it. Nobody said you ought to like it. Nobody pretended to like it. Everyone you met took it for granted that the whole thing was an odious necessity, a ghastly interruption of rational life. And that made all the difference. Straight tribulation is easier to bear than tribulation which advertises itself as pleasure. The one breeds camaraderie and even (when intense) a kind of love between the fellow sufferers; the other, mutual distrust, cynicism, concealed and fretting resentment. And secondly, I found my military elders and betters incomparably nicer than the Wyvern Bloods. This is no doubt because Thirty is naturally kinder to Nineteen than Nineteen is to Thirteen: it is really grown up and does not need to reassure itself. But I am inclined to think that my face had altered. That "look" which I had so often been told to "take off it" had apparently taken itself off — perhaps when I read *Phantastes*. There is even some evidence that it had been succeeded by a look which excited either pity or kindly amusement. Thus, on my very first night in France, in a vast marquee or drill hall where about a hundred officers were to sleep on plank beds, two middle-aged Canadians at once took charge of me and treated me, not like a son (that might have given offence) but like a long-lost friend. Blessings upon them! Once, too, in the Officers' Club at Arras where I was dining alone, and quite happy with my book and my wine (a bottle of Heidsieck then cost 8 francs, and a bottle of Perrier Jouet, 12) two immensely senior officers, all covered with ribbons and red tabs, came over to my table toward the end of the meal, and hailing me as "Sunny Jim" carried me off to their own for brandy and cigars. They weren't drunk either; nor did they make me drunk. It was pure good will. And though exceptional, this was not so very exceptional. There were nasty people in the army; but memory fills those months with pleasant, transitory contacts. Every few days one seemed to meet a scholar, an original, a poet, a cheery buffoon, a raconteur, or at the least a man of good will.

Some time in the middle of that winter I had the good luck to fall sick with what the troops called "trench fever" and the doctors P.U.O. (Pyrexia, unknown origin) and was sent for a wholly delightful three weeks to hospital at Le Tréport. Perhaps I ought to have mentioned before that I had had a weak chest ever since childhood and had very early learned to make a minor illness one of the pleasures of life, even in peace-time. Now, as an alternative to the trenches, a bed and a book were "very heaven." The hospital was a converted hotel and we were two in a room. My first week was marred by the fact that one of the night nurses was conducting a furious love affair with my rooommate. I had too high a temperature to be embarrassed, but the human whisper is a very tedious and unmusical noise; especially at night. After that my fortune mended. The amorous man was sent elsewhere and replaced by a musical misogynist from Yorkshire, who on our second morning together said to me, "Eh lad, if we make beds ourselves dom b— —s won't stay in room so long" (or words to that effect). Accordingly, we made our own beds every day, and every day when the two V.A.D.'s looked in they said, "Oh, they've made their beds! Aren't these two good?" and rewarded us with their brightest smiles. I think they attributed our action to gallantry.

It was here that I first read a volume of Chesterton's essays. I had never heard of him and had no ida of what he stood for; nor can I quite understand why he made such an immediate conquest of me. It might have been expected that my pessimism, my atheism, and my hatred of sentiment would have made him to me the least congenial of all authors. It would almost seem that Providence, or some "second cause" of a very obscure kind, quite overrules our previous tastes when it decides to bring two minds together. Liking an author may be as involuntary and improbable as falling in love. I was by now a sufficiently experienced reader to distinguish liking from agreement. I did not need to accept what Chesterton said in order to enjoy it. His humor was of the kind which I like best — not "jokes" imbedded in the page like currants in a cake, still less (what I cannot endure), a general tone of flippancy and jocularity, but the humor which is not in any way separable from the argument but is rather (as Aristotle would say) the "bloom" on dialectic itself. The sword glitters not because the swordsman set out to make it glitter but because he is fighting for his life and therefore moving it very quickly. For the critics who think Chesterton frivolous or "paradoxical" I have to work hard to feel even pity; sympathy is out of the question. Moreover, strange as it may seem, I liked him for his goodness. I can attribute this taste to myself freely (even at that age) because it was a liking for goodness which had nothing to do with any attempt to be good myself. I have never felt the dislike of goodness which seems to be quite common in better men than me. "Smug" and "smugness" were terms of disapprobation which had never had a place in my critical vocabulary. I lacked the cynic's nose, the *odora canum vis* or bloodhound sensitivity for hypocrisy or Pharisaism. It was a matter of taste: I felt the "charm" of goodness as a man feels the charm of a woman he has no intention of marrying. It is, indeed, at that distance that its "charm" is most apparent.

In reading Chesterton, as in reading MacDonald, I did not know what I was

letting myself in for. A young man who wishes to remain a sound Atheist cannot be
too careful of his reading. There are traps everywhere – "Bibles laid open, millions of
surprises," as Herbert says, "fine nets and stratagems." God is, if I may say it, very
unscrupulous.

In my own battalion also I was assailed. Here I met one Johnson (on whom be
peace) who would have been a lifelong friend if he had not been killed. He was, like
me, already a scholar of an Oxford college (Queen's) who hopd to take up his
scholarship after the war, but a few years my senior and at that time in command of a
company. In him I found dialectical sharpness such as I had hitherto known only in
Kirk, but coupled with youth and whim and poetry. He was moving toward Theism
and we had endless arguments on that and every other topic whenever we were out of
the line. But it was not this that mattered. The important thing was that he was a man
of conscience. I had hardly till now encountered principles in anyone so nearly of my
own age and my own sort. The alarming thing was that he took them for granted. It
crossed my mind for the first time since my apostasy that the severer virtues might
have some relevance to one's own life. I say "the severer virtues" because I already had
some notion of kindness and faithfulness to friends and generosity about money
– as who has not till he meets the temptation which gives all their opposite vices new
and more civil names? But it had not seriously occurred to me that people like ourselves, people like Johnson and me who wanted to know whether beauty was objective or how Aeschylus handled the reconcilation of Zeus and Prometheus, should be
attempting strict veracity, chastity, or devotion to duty. I had taken it that they were
not our subjects. There was not discussion between us on the point and I do not think
he ever suspected the truth about me. I was at no pains to display it. If this is hypocrisy, then I must conclude that hypocrisy can do a man good. To be ashamed of what
you were about to say, to pretend that something which you had meant seriously was
only a joke – this is an ignoble part. But it is better than not to be ashamed at all. And
the distinction between pretending you are better than you are and beginning to be
better in reality is finer than moral sleuthhounds conceive. I was, in intention, con-
cealing only a part: I accepted his principles at once, made no attempt internally to
defend my own "unexamined life." When a boor first enters the society of courteous
people what can he do, for a while, except imitate the motions? How can he learn except by imitation?

You will have divined that ours was a very nice battalion; a minority of good regulars ruling a pleasantly mixed population of promoted rankers (west country farmers, these), barristers, and university men. You could get as good talk there as anywhere. Perhaps the best of us all was our butt, Wallie. Wallie was a farmer, a Roman
Catholic, a passionate soldier (the only man I met who really longed for fighting) and
gullible to any degree by the rawest subaltern. The technique was to criticize the Yeomanry. Poor Wallie knew that it was the bravest, the most efficient, the hardest and
cleanest corps that ever sat on horses. He knew all that inside, having learned it from
an uncle in Yeomanry when he was a child. But he could not get it out. He stammered

and contradicted himself and always came at last to his trump card: "I wish my Uncle Ben was here to talk to you. Uncle Ben'd talk to you. He'd tell you." Mortals must not judge; but I doubt whether any man fought in France who was more likely to go straight to Heaven if he were killed. I would have been better employed cleaning his boots than laughing at him. I may add that I did not enjoy the short time I spent in the company he commanded. Wallie had a genuine passion for killing Germans and a complete disregard of his own or anyone else's safety. He was always striking out bright ideas at which the hair of us subalterns stood on end. Luckily he could be very easily dissuaded by any plausible argument that occurred to us. Such was his valor and innocence that he never for a moment suspected us of any but a military motive. He could never grasp the neighborly principles which, by the tacit agreement of the troops, were held to govern trench warfare, and to which I was introduced at once by my sergeant. I had suggested "pooping" a rifle grenade into a German post where we had seen heads moving. "Just as 'ee like, zir," said the sergeant, scratching his head, "but once 'ee start doing that kind of thing, 'ee'll get zummit back, zee?"

I must not paint the wartime army all gold. I met there both the World and the great goddess Nonsense. The world presented itself in a very ridiculous form on that night (my nineteenth birthday) when I first arrived "up the line." As I emerged from the shaft into the dugout and blinked in the candlelight I noticed that the Captain to whom I was reporting was a master whom I had liked more than I had respected at one of my schools. I ventured to claim acquaintance. He admitted in a low, hurried voice that he had once been a schoolmaster, and the topic was never raised between us again. The impact of the Great Goddess was even funnier, and I met it long before I had reached my own battalion. The troop train from Rouen — that interminable, twelve-mile-an-hour train, in which no two coaches were alike — left at about ten in the evening. Three other officers and I were allotted a compartment. There was no heating; for light we brought our own candles; for sanitation there were the windows. The journey would last about fifteen hours. It was freezing hard. In the tunnel just outside Rouen (all my generation remember it) there was a sudden wrenching and grating noise and one of our doors dropped off bodily into the dark. We sat with chattering teeth till the next stop, where the officer commanding the train came bustling up and demanded what we had done with our door. "It came off, sir," said we. "Don't talk nonsense," said he, "it wouldn't have come off if there hadn't been some horseplay!" — as if nothing were more natural than that four officers (being, of course, provided with screwdrivers) should begin a night journey in mid-winter by removing the door of their carriage.

The war itself has been so often described by those who saw more of it than I that I shall here say little about it. Until the great German attack came in the Spring we had a pretty quiet time. Even then they attacked not us but the Canadians on our right, merely "keeping us quiet" by pouring shells into our line about three a minute all day. I think it was that day I noticed how a greater terror overcomes a less: a mouse that I met (and a poor shivering mouse it was, as I was a poor shivering man) made no

attempt to run from me. Through the winter, weariness and water were our chief enemies. I have gone to sleep marching and woken again and found myself marching
still. One walked in the trenches in thigh gum boots with water above the knee; one
remembers the icy stream welling up inside the boot when you punctured it on concealed barbed wire. Familiarity both with the very old and the very recent dead confirmed that view of corpses which had been formed the moment I saw my dead
mother. I came to know and pity and reverence the ordinary man: particularly dear
Sergeant Ayres, who was (I suppose) killed by the same shell that wounded me. I was
a futile officer (they gave commissions too easily then), a puppet moved about by
him, and he turned this ridiculous and painful relation into something beautiful,
became to me almost like a father. But for the rest, the war — the frights, the cold, the
smell of H.E., the horribly smashed men still moving like half-crushed beetles, the
sitting or standing corpses, the landscape of sheer earth without a blade of grass, the
boots worn day and night till they semed to grow to your feet — all this shows rarely
and faintly in memory. It is too cut off from the rest of my experience and often seems
to have happened to someone else. It is even in a way unimportant. One imaginative
moment seems now to matter more than the realities that followed. It was the first
bullet I heard — so far from me that it "whined" like a journalist's or a peacetime poet's
bullet. At that moment there was something not exactly like fear, much less like
indifference: a little quavering signal that said, "This is War. This is what Homer
wrote about."

XIII

THE NEW LOOK

This wall I was many a weary month in finishing, and yet never thought myself safe till it was done.
DEFOE, *Robinson Crusoe*

The rest of my war experiences have little to do with this story. How I "took" about sixty prisoners — that is, discovered to my great relief that the crowd of field-gray figures who suddenly appeared from nowhere, all had their hands up — is not worth telling, save as a joke. Did not Falstaff "take" Sir Colville of the Dale? Nor does it concern the reader to know how I got a sound "Blighty" from an English shell, or how the exquisite Sister N. in the C.C.S. has ever since embodied my idea of Artemis. Two things stand out. One is the moment, just after I had been hit, when I found (or thought I found) that I was not breathing and concluded that this was death. I felt no fear and certainly no courage. It did not seem to be an occasion for either. The proposition "Here is a man dying" stood before my mind as dry, as factual, as unemotional as something in a textbook. It was not even interesting. The fruit of this experience was that when, some years later, I met Kant's distinction between the Noumenal and the Phenomenal self, it was more to me than an abstraction. I had tasted it; I had proved that here was a fully conscious "I" whose connections with the "me" of introspection were loose and transitory. The other momentous experience was that of reading Bergson in a Convalescent Camp on Salisbury Plain. Intellectually this taught me to avoid the snares that lurk about the word *Nothing*. But it also had a revolutionary effect on my emotional outlook. Hitherto my whole bent had been toward things pale, remote, and evanescent; the water-color world of Morris, the leafy recesses of Malory,[1] the twilight of Yeats. The word "life" had for me pretty much the same associations it had for Shelley in *The Triumph of Life*. I would not have understood what Goethe meant by *des Lebens goldnes Baum*. Bergson showed me. He did not abolish my old loves, but he gave me a new one. From him I first

---

[1] The irony in Malory, the tragedy of contrition, I did not yet at all perceive.

learned to relish energy, fertility, and urgency; the resource, the triumphs, and even the insolence, of things that grow. I became capable of appreciating artists who would, I believe, have meant nothing to me before; all the resonant, dogmatic, flaming, unanswerable people like Beethoven, Titian (in his mythological pictures), Goethe, Dunbar, Pindar, Christopher Wren, and the more exultant Psalms.

I returned to Oxford — "demobbed" — in January 1919. But before I say anything of my life there I must warn the reader that one huge and complex episode will be omitted. I have no choice about this reticence. All I can or need say is that my earlier hostility to the emotions was very fully and variously avenged. But even were I free to tell the story, I doubt if it has much to do with the subject of the book.

The first lifelong friend I made at Oxford was A. K. Hamilton Jenkin, since known for his books on Cornwall. He continued (what Arthur had begun) my education as a seeing, listening, smelling, receptive creature. Arthur had had his preference for the Homely. But Jenkin seemed to be able to enjoy everything; even ugliness. I learned from him that we should attempt a total surrender to whatever atmosphere was offering itself at the moment; in a squalid town to seek out those very places where its squalor rose to grimness and almost grandeur, on a dismal day to find the most dismal and dripping wood, on a windy day to seek the windiest ridge. There was no Betjemannic irony about it; only a serious, yet gleeful, determination to rub one's nose in the very quiddity of each thing, to rejoice in its being (so magnificently) what it was.

My next was Owen Barfield. There is a sense in which Arthur and Barfield are the types of every man's First Friend and Second Friend. The First is the *alter ego*, the man who first reveals to you that you are not alone in the world by turning out (beyond hope) to share all your most secret delights. There is nothing to be overcome in making him your friend; he and you join like raindrops on a window. But the Second Friend is the man who disagrees with you about everything. He is not so much the *alter ego* as the antiself. Of course he shares your interests; otherwise he would not become your friend at all. But he has approached them all at a different angle. He has read all the right books but has got the wrong thing out of every one. It is as if he spoke your language but mispronounced it. How can he be so nearly right and yet, invariably, just not right? He is as fascinating (and infuriating) as a woman. When you set out to correct his heresies, you find that he forsooth has decided to correct yours! And then you go at it, hammer and tongs, far into the night, night after night, or walking through fine country that neither gives a glance to, each learning the weight of the other's punches, and often more like mutually respectful enemies than friends. Actually (though it never seems so at the time) you modify one another's thought; out of this perpetual dogfight a community of mind and a deep affection emerge. But I think he changed me a good deal more than I him. Much of the thought which he afterward put into *Poetic Diction* had already become mine before that important little book appeared. It would be strange if it had not. He was of course not so learned then as he has since become; but the genius was already there.

Closely linked with Barfield of Wadham was his friend (and soon mine), A. C. Harwood of The House, later a pillar of Michael Hall, the Steinerite school at Kidbrooke. He was different from either of us; a wholly imperturbable man. Though poor (like most of us) and wholly without "prospects," he wore the expression of a nineteenth-century gentleman with something in the Funds. On a walking tour when the last light of a wet evening had just revealed some ghastly error in map-reading (probably his own) and the best hope was "Five miles to Mudham (if we could find it) and we *might* get beds there," he still wore that expression. In the heat of argument he wore it still. You would think that he, if anyone, would have been told to "take that look off his face." But I don't believe he ever was. It was no mask and came from no stupidity. He has been tried since by all the usual sorrows and anxieties. He is the sole Horatio known to me in this age of Hamlets; no "stop for Fortune's finger."

There is one thing to be said about these and other friends whom I made at Oxford. They were all, by decent Pagan standards (much more, by so low a standard as mine), "good." That is, they all, like my friend Johnson, believed, and acted on the belief, that veracity, public spirit, chastity, and sobriety were obligatory – "to be attempted," as the examiners say, "by all candidates." Johnson had prepared me to be influenced by them. I accepted their standards in principle and perhaps (this part I do not very well remember) tried to act accordingly.

During my first two years at Oxford I was busily engaged (apart from "doing Mods" and "beginning Greats") in assuming what we may call an intellectual "New Look." There was to be no more pessimism, no more self-pity, no flirtations with any idea of the supernatural, no romantic delusions. In a word, like the heroine of *Northanger Abbey,* I formed the resolution "of always judging and acting in future with the greatest good sense." And good sense meant, for me at that moment, a retreat, almost a panic-stricken flight, from all that sort of romanticism which had hitherto been the chief concern of my life. Several causes operated together.

For one thing, I had recently come to know an old, dirty, gabbling, tragic, Irish parson who had long since lost his faith but retained his living. By the time I met him his only interest was the search for evidence of "human survival." On this he read and talked incessantly, and, having a highly critical mind, could never satisfy himself. What was especially shocking was that the ravenous desire for personal immortality co-existed in him with (apparently) a total indifference to all that could, on a sane view, make immortality desirable. He was not seeking the Beatific Vision and did not even believe in God. He was not hoping for more time in which to purge and improve his own personality. He was not dreaming of reunion with dead friends or lovers; I never heard him speak with affection of anybody. All he wanted was the assurance that something he could call "himself" would, on almost any terms, last longer than his bodily life. So, at least, I thought. I was too young and hard to suspect that what secretly moved him was a thirst for the happiness which had been wholly denied him on earth. And his state of mind appeared to me the most contemptible I had ever encountered. Any thoughts or dreams which might lead one into that fierce monomania were, I decided, to be utterly shunned. The whole question of immortality became rather disgusting to me. I shut it out. All one's thought must be confined to

> *the very world, which is the world*
> *Of all of us — the place where, in the end,*
> *We find our happiness, or not at all.*

Secondly, it had been my chance to spend fourteen days, and most of the fourteen nights as well, in close contact with a man who was going mad. He was a man whom I had dearly loved, and well he deserved love. And now I helped to hold him while he kicked and wallowed on the floor, screaming out that devils were tearing him and that he was that moment falling down into Hell. And this man, as I well knew, had not kept the beaten track. He had flirted with Theosophy, Yoga, Spiritualism, Psychoanalysis, what not? Probably these things had in fact no connection with his insanity, for which (I believe) there were physical causes. But it did not seem so to me at the time. I thought I had seen a warning; it was to this, this raving on the floor, that all romantic longings and unearthly speculations led a man in the end—

> *Be not too wildly amorous of the far*
> *Nor lure thy fantasy to its utmost scope.*

Safety first, thought I: the beaten track, the approved road, the center of the road, the lights on. For some months after that nightmare fortnight, the words "ordinary" and "humdrum" summed up everything that appeared to me most desirable.

Thirdly, the new Psychology was at that time sweeping through us all. We did not swallow it whole (few people then did) but we were all influenced. What we were most concerned about was "Fantasy" or "wishful thinking." For (of course) we were all poets and critics and set a very great value on "Imagination" in some high Coleridgean sense, so that it became important to distinguish Imagination, not only (as Coleridge did) from Fancy, but also from Fantasy as the psychologists understand that term. Now what, I asked myself, were all my delectable mountains and western gardens but sheer Fantasies? Had they not revealed their true nature by luring me, time and again, into undisguisedly erotic reverie or the squalid nightmare of Magic? In reality, of course, as previous chapters have told, my own experience had repeatedly shown that these romantic images had never been more than a sort of flash, or even slag, thrown off by the occurrence of Joy, that those mountains and gardens had never been what I wanted but only symbols which professed themselves to be no more, and that every effort to treat them as the real Desirable soon honestly proved itself to be a failure. But now, busy with my New Look, I managed to forget this. Instead of repenting my idolatry I vilified the unoffending images on which I had lavished it. With the confidence of a boy I decided I had done with all that. No more Avalon, no more Hesperides. I had (this was very precisely the opposite of the truth) "seen through" them. And I was never going to be taken in again.

Finally, there was of course Bergson. Somehow or other (for it does not seem very clear when I reopen his books today) I found in him a refutation of the old haunting idea, Schopenhauer's idea, that the universe "might not have existed." In other words one Divine attribute, that of necessary existence, rose above my horizon. It was still, and long after, attached to the wrong subject; to the universe, not to God. But the mere attribute was itself of immense potency. When once one has dropped the absurd notion that reality is an arbitrary alternative to "nothing," one gives up being a pessimist (or even an optimist). There is no sense in blaming or praising the Whole, nor, indeed, in saying anything about it. Even if you persist in hurling Promethean or Hardyesque defiances at it, then, since you are part of it, it is only that same Whole which through you "quietly declaims the cursings of itself" — a futility which seems to me to vitiate Lord Russell's stirring essay on "The Worship of a Free Man." Cursings were as futile, and as immature, as dreams about the western garden. One must (like Carlyle's lady) "accept" the universe; totally, with no reservations, loyally. This sort of Stoical Monism was the philosophy of my New Look. And it gave me a great sense of peace. It was perhaps the nearest thing to a religious experience which I had had since my prep-school days. It ended (I hope forever) any idea of a treaty or compromise with reality. So much the perception of even one Divine attribute can do.

As for Joy, I labeled it "aesthetic experience" and talked much about it under that name and said it was very "valuable." But it came very seldom and when it came it didn't amount to much.

Those early days of the New Look were on the whole happy ones. Very gradually the sky changed. There came to be more unhappiness and anxiety in my own life; and Barfield was living through

> *that whole year of youth*
> *When life ached like an aching tooth.*

Our generation, the generation of the returned soldiers, began to pass. Oxford was full of new faces. Freshmen began to make historical allowances for our warped point of view. The problem of one's career loomed larger and grimmer.

It was then that a really dreadful thing (dreadful to me) happened. First Harwood (still without changing his expression), and then Barfield, embraced the doctrines of Steiner and became Anthroposophists. I was hideously shocked. Everything that I had labored so hard to expel from my own life seemed to have flared up and met me in my best friends. Not only my best friends but those whom I would have thought safest; the one so immovable, the other brought up in a free-thinking family and so immune from all "superstition" that he had hardly heard of Christianity itself until he went to school. (The gospel first broke on Barfeld in the form of a dictated list of Parables Peculiar to St. Matthew.) Not only in my seeming-safest friends but at a moment when we all had most need to stand together. And as I came to learn (so far as I ever have learned) what Steiner thought, my horror turned into disgust and resentment. For here, apparently, were all the abominations; none more abominable than those which had once attracted me. Here were gods, spirits, after-life and pre-existence, initiates, occult knowledge, meditation. "Why — damn it — it's *medieval*," I exclaimed; for I still had all the chronological snobbery of my period and used the names of earlier periods as terms of abuse. Here was everything which the New Look had been designed to exclude; everything that might lead one off the main road into those dark places where men wallow on the floor and scream that they are being dragged down into Hell. Of course it was all arrant nonsense. There was no danger of *my* being taken in. But then, the loneliness, the sense of being deserted.

Naturally, I attributed to my friends the same desires which, had I become an Anthroposophist, would have been operative in me. I thought they were falling under that ravenous, salt lust for the occult. I now see that, from the very first, all the evidence was against this. They were not that sort. Nor does Anthroposophy, so far as I can see, cater for that sort. There is a difficulty and (to me) a reassuring Germanic dullness about it which would soon deter those who were looking for thrills. Nor have I ever seen that it had a deleterious effect on the character of those who embraced it; I have once known it to have a very good one.

I say this, not because I ever came within a hundred miles of accepting the thing myself, but in common fairness, and also as a tardy amends for the many hard, unjust and bitter things I once said about it to my friends. For Barfield's conversion to Anthroposophy marked the beginning of what I can only describe as the Great War between him and me. It was never, thank God, a quarrel, though it could have become one in a moment if he had used to me anything like the violence I allowed myself to him. But it was an almost incessant disputation, sometimes by letter and sometimes face to face, which lasted for years. And this Great War was one of the turning points of my life.

Barfield never made me an Anthroposophist, but his counterattacks destroyed forever two elements in my own thought. In the first place he made short work of what I have called my "chronological snobbery," the uncritical acceptance of the intellectual climate common to our own age and the assumption that whatever has gone out of date is on that account discredited. You must find why it went out of date. Was it ever refuted (and if so by whom, where, and how conclusively) or did it merely die away as fashions do? If the latter, this tells us nothing about its truth or falsehood. From seeing this, one passes to the realization that our own age is also "a period," and certainly has, like all periods, its own characteristic ilusions. They are likeliest to lurk in those widespread assumptions which are so ingrained in the age that no one dares to attack or feels it necessary to defend them. In the second place he convinced me that the positions we had hitherto held left no room for any satisfactory theory of knowledge. We had been, in the technical sense of the term, "realists"; that is, we accepted as rock-bottom reality the universe revealed by the senses. But at the same time we continued to make for certain phenomena of consciousness all the claims that really went with a theistic or idealistic view. We maintained that abstract thought (if obedient to logical rules) gave indisputable truth, that our moral judgment was "valid," and our aesthetic experience not merely pleasing but "valuable." The view was, I think, common at the time; it runs through Bridges' *Testament of Beauty*, the work of Gilbert Murray, and Lord Russell's "Worship of a Free Man." Barfield convinced me that it was inconsistent. If thought were a purely subjective event, these claims for it would have to be abandoned. If one kept (as rock-bottom reality) the universe of the senses, aided by instruments and co-ordinated so as to form "science," then one would have to go much further – as many have since gone – and adopt a Behavioristic theory of logic, ethics, and aesthetics. But such a theory was, and is, unbelievable to me. I am using the word "unbelievable," which many use to mean "improbable" or even "undesirable," in a quite literal sense. I mean that the act of believing what the behaviorist believes is one that my mind simply will not perform. I cannot force my thought into that shape any more than I can scratch my ear with my big toe or pour wine out of a bottle into the cavity at the base of that same bottle. It is as final as a physical impossibility. I was therefore compelled to give up realism. I had been trying to defend it ever since I began reading philosophy. Partly, no doubt, this was mere "cussedness." Idealism was then the dominant philosophy at Oxford and I was by nature "against Government." But partly, too, realism satisfied an emotional need. I wanted Nature to be quite independent of our observation; something other, indifferent, self-existing. (This went with the Jenkinian zest for rubbing one's nose in the mere quiddity.) But now, it seemed to me, I had to give that up. Unless I were to accept an unbelievable alternative, I must admit that mind was no late-come epiphenomenon; that the whole universe was, in the last resort, mental; that our logic was participation in a cosmic *Logos*.

It is astonishing (at this time of day) that I could regard this position as something quite distinct from Theism. I suspect there was some willful blindness. But there were in those days all sorts of blankets, insulators, and insurances which enabled one to get all the conveniences of Theism, without believing in God. The English Hegelians, writers like T. H. Green, Bradley, and Bosanquet (then mighty names), dealt in precisely such wares. The Absolute Mind – better still, the Absolute – was impersonal, or it knew itself (but not us?) only in us, and it was so absolute that it wasn't really much more like a mind than anything else. And anyway, the more muddled one got about it and the more contradictions one committed, the more this proved that our discursive thought moved only on the level of "Appearance," and "Reality" must be somewhere else. And where else but, of course, in the Absolute? There, not here, was "the fuller splendor" behind the "sensuous curtain." The emotion that went with all this was certainly religious. But this was a religion that cost nothing. We could talk religiously about the Absolute: but there was no danger of Its doing anything about us. It was "there"; safely and immovably "there." It would never come "here," never (to be blunt) made a nuisance of Itself. This quasi-religion was all a one-way street; all *eros* (as Dr. Nygren would say) steaming up, but no *agape* darting down. There was nothing to fear; better still, nothing to obey.

Yet there was one really wholesome element in it. The Absolute was "there," and that "there" contained the reconciliation of all contraries, the transcendence of all finitude, the hidden glory which was the only perfectly real thing there is. In fact, it had much of the quality of Heaven. But it was a Heaven none of us could ever get to.

For we are appearances. To be "there" is, by definition, not to be we. All who embrace such a philosophy live, like Dante's virtuous Pagans, "in desire without hope." Or like Spinoza they so love their God as to be unable even to wish that He should love them in return. I should be very sorry not to have passed through that experience. I think it is more religious than many experiences that have been called Christian. What I learned from the Idealists (and still most strongly hold) is this maxim: It is more important that Heaven should exist than that any of us should reach it.

And so the great Angler played His fish and I never dreamed that the hook was in my tongue. But two great advances had been made. Bergson had showed me necessary existence; and from Idealism I had come one step nearer to understanding the words, "We give thanks to thee for thy great glory." The Norse gods had given me the first hint of it; but then I didn't believe in them, and I did believe (so far as one can believe an *Unding*) in the Absolute.

XIV

CHECKMATE

The one principle of hell is — "I am my own."
GEORGE MACDONALD

In the summer of 1922 I finished Greats. As there were no philosophical posts going, or none that I could get, my long-suffering father offered me a fourth year at Oxford during which I read English so as to get a second string to my bow. The Great War with Barfield had, I think, begun at this time.

No sooner had I entered the English School than I went to George Gordon's discussion class. And there I made a new friend. The very first words he spoke marked him out from the ten or twelve others who were present; a man after my own heart, and that too at an age when the instantaneous friendships of earlier youth were becoming rather rare events. His name was Nevill Coghill. I soon had the shock of discovering that he — clearly the most intelligent and best informed man in that class — was a Christian and a thorough-going supernaturalist. There were other traits that I liked but found (for I was still very much a modern) oddly archaic; chivalry, honor, courtesy, "freedom," and "gentillesse." One could imagine him fighting a duel. He spoke much "ribaldry" but never "villeinye." Barfield was beginning to overthrow my chronological snobbery; Coghill gave it another blow. Had something really dropped out of our lives? Was the archaic simply the civilized, and the modern simply the barbaric? It will seem strange to many of my critics who regard me as a typical *laudator temporis acti* that this question should have arisen so comparatively late in my life. But then the key to my books is Donne's maxim, "The heresies that men leave are hated most." The things I assert most vigorously are those that I resisted long and accepted late.

These disturbing factors in Coghill ranged themselves with a wider disturbance which was now threatening my whole earlier outlook. All the books were beginning to turn against me. Indeed, I must have been as blind as a bat not to have seen, long before, the ludicrous contradiction between my theory of life and my actual experi-

117

ences as a reader. George MacDonald had done more to me than any other writer; of course it was a pity he had that bee in his bonnet about Christianity. He was good *in spite of it.* Chesterton had more sense than all the other moderns put together; bating, of course, his Christianity. Johnson was one of the few authors whom I felt I could trust utterly; curiously enough, he had the same kink. Spenser and Milton by a strange coincidence had it too. Even among ancient authors the same paradox was to be found. The most religious (Plato, Aeschylus, Virgil) were clearly those on whom I could really feed. On the other hand, those writers who did not suffer from religion and with whom in theory my sympathy ought to have been complete — Shaw and Wells and Mill and Gibbon and Voltaire — all seemed a little thin; what as boys we called "tinny." It wasn't that I didn't like them. They were all (especially Gibbon) entertaining; but hardly more. There seemed to be no depth in them. They were too simple. The roughness and density of life did not appear in their books.

Now that I was reading more English, the paradox began to be aggravated. I was deeply moved by the *Dream of the Road;* more deeply still by Langland: intoxicated (for a time by Donne; deeply and lastingly satisfied by Thomas Browne. But the most alarming of all was George Herbert. Here was a man who seemed to me to excel all the authors I had ever read in conveying the very quality of life as we actually live it from moment to moment, but the wretched fellow, instead of doing it all directly, insisted on mediating it through what I would still have called "the Christian mythology." On the other hand most of the authors who might be claimed as precursors of modern enlightenment seemed to me very small beer and bored me cruelly. I thought Bacon (to speak frankly) a solemn, pretentious ass, yawned my way through Restoration Comedy, and, having manfully struggled on to the last line of *Don Juan,* wrote on the end leaf "Never again." The only non-Christians who seemed to me really to know anything were the Romantics; and a good many of them were dangerously tinged with something like religion, even at times with Christianity. The upshot of it all could nearly be expressed in a perversion of Roland's great line in the *Chanson* —

> *Christians are wrong, but all the rest are bores.*

The natural step would have been to inquire a little more closely whether the Christians were, after all, wrong. But I did not take it. I thought I could explain their superiority without that hypothesis. Absurdly (yet many Absolute Idealists have shared this absurdity) I thought that "the Christian myth" conveyed to unphilosophic minds as much of the truth, that is of Absolute Idealism, as they were capable of grasping, and that even that much put them above the irreligious. Those who could not rise to the notion of the Absolute would come nearer to the truth by belief in "a God" than by disbelief. Those who could not understand how, as Reasoners, we participated in a timeless and therefore deathless world, would get a symbolic shadow of the truth by believing in a life after death. The implication — that something which I and most other undergraduates could master without extrordinary pains would have been too hard for Plato, Dante, Hooker, and Pascal — did not yet strike me as absurd. I hope this is because I never looked it squarely in the face.

As the plot quickens and thickens toward its end, I leave out more and more of such matters as would go into a full autobiography. My father's death, with all the fortitude (even playfulness) which he displayed in his last illness, does not really come into the story I am telling. My brother was at that time in Shanghai. Nor would it be relevant to tell in detail how I became a temporary lecturer at Univ for a year and was elected a fellow of Magdalen in 1925. The worst is that I must leave undescribed many men whom I love and to whom I am deeply in debt; G. H. Stevenson and E. F. Carritt, my tutors, the Fark (but who could paint him anyway?), and five great Magdalen men who enlarged my very idea of what a learned life should be – P. V. M. Benecke, C. C. J. Webb, J. A. Smith, F. E. Brightman, and C. T. Onions. Except for Oldie, I have always been blessed both in my official and my unofficial teachers. In my earlier years at Magdalen I inhabited a world where hardly anything I wanted to know needed to be found out by my own unaided efforts. One or other of these could always give you a clue. ("You'll find something about it in Alanus. . . . " – "Macrobius would be the man to try. . . . " – "Doesn't Comparetti mention it?" . . . "Have you looked for it in Du Cange?") I found, as always, that the ripest are kindest to the raw and the most studious have most time to spare. When I began teaching for the English Faculty, I made two other friends, both Christians (these queer people seemed now to pop up on every side) who were later to give me much help in getting over the last stile. They were H. V. V. Dyson (then of Reading) and J. R. R. Tolkien. Friendship with the latter marked the breakdown of two old prejudices. At my first coming into the world I had been (implicitly) warned never to trust a Papist, and at my first coming into the English Faculty (explicitly) never to trust a philologist. Tolkien was both.

Realism had been abandoned; the New Look was somewhat damaged; and chronological snobbery was seriously shaken. All over the board my pieces were in the most disadvantageous positions. Soon I could no longer cherish even the illusion that the initiative lay with me. My Adversary began to make His final moves.

The first Move annihilated the last remains of the New Look. I was suddenly impelled to reread (which was certainly no business of mine at the moment) the *Hippolytus* of Euripides. In one chorus all that world's end imagery which I had rejected when I assumed my New Look rose before me. I liked, but did not yield; I tried to patronize it. But next day I was overwhelmed. There was a transitional moment of delicious uneasiness, and then – instantaneously – the long inhibition was over, the dry desert lay behind. I was off once more into the land of longing, my heart at once broken and exalted as it had never been since the old days at Bookham. There was nothing whatever to do about it; no question of returning to the desert. I had simply been ordered – or, rather, compelled – to "take that look off my face." And never to resume it either.

The next Move was intellectual, and consolidated the first Move. I read in Alexander's *Space Time and Deity* his theory of "Enjoyment" and "Contemplation." These are technical terms in Alexander's philosophy; "Enjoyment" has nothing to do with pleasure, nor "contemplation" with the contemplative life. When you see a table you "enjoy" the act of seeing and "contemplate" the table. Later, if you took up Optics and thought about Seeing itself, you would be contemplating and seeing and enjoying the thought. In bereavement you contemplate the beloved and the beloved's death and, in Alexander's sense, "enjoy" the loneliness and grief but a psychologist, if he were considering you as a case of melancholia, would be contemplating your grief and enjoying psychology. We do not "think a thought" in the same sense in which we "think that Herodotus is unreliable." When we think a thought, "thought" is a cognate accusative (like "blow" in "strike a blow"). We enjoy the thought (that Herodotus is unreliable) and, in so doing, contemplate the unreliability of Herodotus.

I accepted this distinction at once and have ever since regarded it as an indispensable tool of thought. A moment later its consequences – for me quite catastrophic – began to appear. It seemed to me self-evident that one essential property of love, hate, fear, hope, or desire was attention to their object. To cease thinking about or attending to the woman is, so far, to cease loving; to cease thinking about or attending to the dreaded thing is, so far, to cease being afraid. But to attend to your own love or fear is to cease attending to the loved or dreaded object. In other words the enjoyment and the contemplation of our inner activities are incompatible. You cannot hope and also think about hoping at the same moment; for in hope we look to hope's object and we interrupt this by (so to speak) turning round to look at the hope itself. Of course the two activities can and do alternate with great rapidity; but they are distinct and incompatible. This was not merely a logical result of Alexander's analysis, but could be verified in daily and hourly experience. The surest means of disarming an anger or a lust was to turn your attention from the girl or the insult and start examining the passion itself. The surest way of spoiling a pleasure was to start examing your satisfaction. But if so, it followed that all introspection is in one respect misleading. In introspection we try to look "inside ouselves" and see what is going on. But nearly everything that was going on a moment before is stopped by the very act of our turning to look at it. Unfortunately this does not mean that introspection finds nothing. On the contrary, it finds precisely what is left behind by the suspension of all our normal activities; and what is left behind is mainly mental images and physical sensations. The great error is to mistake this mere sediment or track or by-product for the activities themselves. That is how men may come to believe that thought is only unspoken words, or the appreciation of poetry only a collection of mental pictures, when these in reality are what the thought or the appreciation, when interrupted, leave behind – like the swell at sea, working after the wind has dropped. Not, of course, that these activities, before we stopped them by introspection, were unconscious. We do not love, fear, or think without knowing it. Instead of the twofold division into Conscious and Unconscious, we need a threefold division: the Unconscious, the Enjoyed, and the Contemplated.

This discovery flashed a new light back on my whole life. I saw that all my waitings and watchings for Joy, all my vain hopes to find some mental content on which I could, so to speak, lay my finger and say, "This is it," had been a futile attempt to contemplate the enjoyed. All that such watching and waiting ever *could* find would be either an image (Asgard, the Western Garden, or what not) or a quiver in the diaphragm. I should never have to bother again about these images or sensations. I knew now that they were merely the mental track left by the passage of Joy – not the wave but the wave's imprint on the sand. The inherent dialectic of desire itself had in a way already shown me this; for all images and sensations, if idolatrously mistaken for Joy itself, soon honestly confessed themselves inadequate. All said, in the last resort, "It is not I. I am only a reminder. Look! Look! What do I remind you of?"

So far, so good. But it is at the next step that awe overtakes me. There was no doubt that Joy was a desire (and, in so far as it was also simultaneously a good, it was also a kind of love). But a desire is turned not to itself but to its object. Not only that, but it owes all its character to its object. Erotic love is not like desire for food, nay, a love for one woman differs from a love for another woman in the very same way and the very same degree as the two women differ from one another. Even our desire for one wine differs in tone from our desire for another. Our intellectual desire (curiosity) to know the true answer to a question is quite different from our desire to find that one answer, rather than another, is true. The form of the desired is in the desire. It is the object which makes the desire harsh or sweet, coarse or choice, "high" or "low." It is the object that makes the desire itself desirable or hateful. I perceived (and this was a wonder of wonders) that just as I had been wrong in supposing that I really desired the Garden of the Hesperides, so also I had been equally wrong in supposing that I desired Joy itself, considered simply as an event in my own mind, turned out to be of no value at all. All the value lay in that of which Joy was the desiring. And that object, quite clearly, was no state of my own mind or body at all. In a way, I had proved this by elimination. I had tried everything in my own mind and body; as it were, asking myself, "Is it this you want? Is it this?" Last of all I had asked if Joy itself was what I wanted; and labelling it "aesthetic experience," had pretended I could answer Yes. But that answer too had broken down. Inexorably Joy proclaimed, "You want – I myself am your want of – something other, outside, not you nor any state of you." I did not yet ask, Who is the desired? only What is it? But this brought me already into the region of awe, for I thus understood that in deepest solitude there is a road right out of the self, a commerce with something which, by refusing to identify itself with any object of the senses, or anything whereof we have biological or social need, or anything imagined, or any state of our own minds, proclaims itself sheerly objective. Far more objective than bodies, for it is not, like them, clothed in our senses; the naked Other, imageless (though our imagination salutes it with a hundred images), unknown, undefined, desired.

That was the second Move; equivalent, perhaps, to the loss of one's last remaining bishop. The third Move did not seem to me dangerous at the time. It consisted merely in linking up this new *éclaircissement* about Joy with my idealistic philosophy. I saw that Joy, as I now understood it, would fit in. We mortals, seen as the sciences see us and as we commonly see one another, are mere "appearances." But appearances of the Absolute. In so far as we really are at all (which isn't saying much) we have, so to speak, a root in the Absolute, which is the utter reality. And that is why we experience Joy: we yearn, rightly, for that unity which we can never reach except by ceasing to be the separate phenomenal beings called "we." Joy was not a deception. Its visitations were rather the moments of clearest consciousness we had, when we became aware of our fragmentary and phantasmal nature and ached for that impossible reunion which would annihilate us or that self-contradictory waking which would reveal, not that we had had, but that we *were,* a dream. This seemed quite satisfactory intellectually. Even emotionally too; for it matters more that Heaven should exist than that we should ever get there. What I did not notice was that I had passed an important milestone. Up till now my thoughts had been centrifugal; now the centripetal movement had begun. Considerations arising from quite different parts of my experience were beginning to come together with a click. This new dovetailing of my desire-life with my philosophy foreshadowed the day, now fast approaching, when I should be forced to take my "philosophy" more seriously than I ever intended. I did not foresee this. I was like a man who has lost "merely a pawn" and never dreams that this (in that state of the game) means mate in a few moves.

The fourth Move was more alarming. I was now teaching philosophy (I suspect very badly) as well as English. And my watered Hegelianism wouldn't serve for tutorial purposes.[1] A tutor must make things clear. Now the Absolute cannot be made clear. Do you mean Nobody-knows-what, or do you mean a superhuman mind and therefore (we may as well admit) a Person? After all, did Hegel and Bradley and all the rest of them ever do more than add mystifications to the simple, workable, theistic idealism of Berkeley? I thought not. And didn't Berkeley's "God" do all the same work as the Absolute, with the added advantage that we had at least some notion of what we meant by Him? I thought He did. So I was driven back into something like Berkeleyanism; but Berkeleyanism with a few top dressings of my own. I distinguished this philosophical "God" very sharply (or so I said) from "the God of popular religion." There was, I explained, no possibility of being in a personal relation with Him. For I thought He projected us as a dramatist projects his characters, and I could no more "meet" Him, than Hamlet could meet Shakespeare. I didn't call Him "God" either; I called Him "Spirit." One fights for one's remaining comforts.

Then I read Chesterton's *Everlasting Man* and for the first time saw the whole Christian outline of history set out in a form that seemed to me to make sense. Somehow I contrived not to be too badly shaken. You will remember that I already thought Chesterton the most sensible man alive "apart from his Christianity." Now, I veritably believe, I thought — I didn't of course *say;* words would have revealed the nonsense — that Christianity itself was very sensible "apart from its Christianity." But I hardly remember, for I had not long finished *The Everlasting Man* when something far more alarming happened to me. Early in 1926 the hardest boiled of all the atheists I ever knew sat in my room on the other side of the fire and remarked that the evidence for

---

[1]Not, of course, that I thought it a tutor's business to make converts to his own philosophy. But I found I needed a position of my own as a basis from which to criticize my pupils' essays.

the historicity of the Gospels was really surprisingly good. "Rum thing," he went on. "All that stuff of Frazer's about the Dying God. Rum thing. It almost looks as if it had really happened once." To understand the shattering impact of it, you would need to know the man (who has certainly never since shown any interest in Christianity). If he, the cynic of cynics, the toughest of the toughs, were not — as I would still have put it — "safe," where could I turn? Was there then no escape?

The odd thing was that before God closed in on me, I was in fact offered what now appears a moment of wholly free choice. In a sense. I was going up Headington Hill on the top of a bus. Without words and (I think) almost without images, a fact about myself was somehow presented to me. I became aware that I was holding something at bay, or shutting something out. Or, if you like, that I was wearing some stiff clothing, like corsets, or even a suit of armor, as if I were a lobster. I felt myself being, there and then, given a free choice. I could open the door or keep it shut; I could unbuckle the armor or keep it on. Neither choice was presented as a duty; no threat or promise was attached to either, though I knew that to open the door or to take off the corslet meant the incalculable. The choice appeared to be momentous but it was also strangely unemotional. I was moved by no desires or fears. In a sense I was not moved by anything. I chose to open, to unbuckle, to loosen the rein. I say, "I chose," yet it did not really seem possible to do the opposite. On the other hand, I was aware of no motives. You could argue that I was not a free agent, but I am more inclined to think that this came nearer to being a perfectly free act than most that I have ever done. Necessity may not be the opposite of freedom, and perhaps a man is most free when, instead of producing motives, he could only say, "I am what I do." Then came the repercussion on the imaginative level. I felt as if I were a man of snow at long last beginning to melt. The melting was starting in my back — drip-drip and presently trickle-trickle. I rather disliked the feeling.

The fox had been dislodged from Hegelian Wood and was now running in the open, "with all the woe in the world," bedraggled and weary, hounds barely a field behind. And nearly everyone was now (one way or another) in the pack; Plato, Dante, MacDonald, Herbert, Barfield, Tolkien, Dyson, Joy itself. Everyone and everything had joined the other side. Even my own pupil Griffiths — now Dom Bede Griffiths — though not yet himself a believer, did his share. Once, when he and Barfield were lunching in my room, I happened to refer to philosophy as "a subject." "It wasn't a *subject* to Plato," said Barfield, "it was a way." The quiet but fervent agreement of Griffiths, and the quick glance of understanding between these two, revealed to me my own frivolity. Enough had been thought, and said, and felt, and imagined. It was about time that something should be done.

For of course there had long been an ethic (theoretically) attached to my Idealism. I thought the business of us finite and half-unreal souls was to multiply the consciousness of Spirit by seeing the world from different positions while yet remaining qualitatively the same as Spirit; to be tied to a particular time and place and set of circumstances, yet there to will and think as Spirit itself does. This was hard; for the very act whereby Spirit projected souls and a world gave those souls different and competitive interests, so that there was a temptation to selfishness. But I thought each of us had it in his power to discount the emotional perspective produced by his own particular selfhood, just as we discount the optical perspective produced by our position in space. To prefer my own happiness to my neighbor's was like thinking that the nearest telegraph post was really the largest. The way to recover, and act upon, this universal and objective vision was daily and hourly to remember our true nature, to reascend or return into that Spirit which, in so far as we really were at all, we still were. Yes; but I now felt I had better try to do it. I faced at last (in MacDonald's words) "some thing to be neither more nor less nor other than *done."* An attempt at complete virtue must be made.

Really, a young Atheist cannot guard his faith too carefully. Dangers lie in wait for him on every side. You must not do, you must not even try to do, the will of the Father unless you are prepared to "know of the doctrine." All my acts, desires, and thoughts were to be brought into harmony with universal Spirit. For the first time I examined myself with a seriously practical purpose. And there I found what appalled me; a zoo of lusts, a bedlam of ambitions, a nursery of fears, a harem of fondled hatreds. My name was legion.

Of course I could do nothing – I could not last out one hour – without continual conscious recourse to what I called Spirit. But the fine, philosophical distinction between this and what ordinary people call "prayer to God" breaks down as soon as you start doing it in earnest. Idealism can be talked, and even felt; it cannot be lived. It became patently absurd to go on thinking of "Spirit" as either ignorant of, or passive to, my approaches. Even if my own philosophy were true, how could the initiative lie on my side? My own analogy, as I now first perceived, suggested the opposite: if Shakespeare and Hamlet could ever meet, it must be Shakespeare's doing.[1] Hamlet could initiate nothing. Perhaps, even now, my Absolute Spirit still differed in some way from the God of religion. The real issue was not, or not yet, there. The real terror was that if you seriously believed in even such a "God" or 'Spirit' as I admitted, a wholly new situation developed. As the dry bones shook and came together in that dreadful valley of Ezekiel's, so now a philosophical theorem, cerebrally entertained, began to stir and heave and throw off its grave-clothes, and stood upright and became a living presence. I was to be allowed to play at philosophy no longer. It might, as I say, still be true that my "Spirit" differed in some way from "the God of popular religion." My Adversary waived the point. It sank into utter unimportance. He would not argue about it. He only said, "I am the Lord"; "I am that I am"; "I am."

People who are naturally religious find difficulty in understanding the horror of such a revelation. Amiable agnostics will talk cheerfully about "man's search for God." To me, as I then was, they might as well have talked about the mouse's search

---

[1] *I.e.,* Shakespeare could, in principle, make himself appear as Author within the play, and write a dialogue between Hamlet and himself. The "Shakespeare" within the play would of course be at once Shakespeare and one of Shakespeare's creatures. It would bear some analogy to Incarnation.

for the cat. The best image of my predicament is the meeting of Mime and Wotan in the first act of *Siegfried; hier brauch' ich nicht Spärer, noch Späher, Einsam will ich. . . .* (I've no use for spies and snoopers. I would be private. . . .)

Remember, I had always wanted, above all things, not to be "interfered with." I had wanted (mad wish) "to call my soul my own." I had been far more anxious to avoid suffering than to achieve delight. I had always aimed at limited liabilities. The supernatural itself had been to me, first, an illicit dram, and then, as by a drunkard's reaction, nauseous. Even my recent attempt to live my philosophy had secretly (I now knew) been hedged round by all sorts of reservations. I had pretty well known that my ideal of virtue would never be allowed to lead me into anything intolerably painful; I would be "reasonable." But now what had been an ideal became a command; and what might not be expected of one? Doubtless, by definition, God was Reason itself. But would He also be "reasonable" in that other, more comfortable, sense? Not the slightest assurance on that score was offered me. Total surrender, the absolute leap in the dark, were demanded. The reality with which no treaty can be made was upon me. The demand was not even "All or nothing." I think that stage had been passed, on the bus top when I unbuckled my armor and the snowman started to melt. Now, the demand was simply "All."

You must picture me alone in that room in Magdalen, night after night, feeling, whenever my mind lifted even for a second from my work, the steady, unrelenting approach of Him whom I so earnestly desired not to meet. That which I greatly feared had at last come upon me. In the Trinity Term of 1929 I gave in, and admitted that God was God, and knelt and prayed: perhaps, that night, the most dejected and reluctant convert in all England. I did not then see what is now the most shining and obvious thing; the Divine humility which will accept a convert even on such terms. The Prodigal Son at least walked home on his own feet. But who can duly adore that Love which will open the high gates to a prodigal who is brought in kicking, struggling, resentful, and darting his eyes in every direction for a chance of escape? The words *compelle intrare,* compel them to come in, have been so abused by wicked men that we shudder at them; but, properly understood, they plumb the depth of the Divine mercy. The hardness of God is kinder than the softness of men, and His compulsion is our liberation.

XV

THE BEGINNING

Aliud est de silvestri cacumine videre patriam pacis...et aliud tenere viam illuc ducentem.

ST. AUGUSTINE, *Confessions*, VII, xxi

For it is one thing to see the land of peace from a wooded ridge...and another to tread the road that leads to it.

It must be understood that the conversion recorded in the last chapter was only to Theism, pure and simple, not to Christianity. I knew nothing yet about the Incarnation. The God to whom I surrendered was sheerly nonhuman.

It may be asked whether my terror was at all relieved by the thought that I was now approaching the source from which those arrows of Joy had been shot at me ever since childhood. Not in the least. No slightest hint was vouchsafed me that there ever had been or ever would be any connection between God and Joy. If anything, it was the reverse. I had hoped that the heart of reality might be of such a kind that we can best symbolize it as a place; instead, I found it to be a Person. For all I knew, the total rejection of what I called Joy might be one of the demands, might be the very first demand, He would make upon me. There was no strain of music from within, no smell of eternal orchards at the threshold, when I was dragged through the doorway. No kind of desire was present at all.

My conversion involved as yet no belief in a future life. I now number it among my greatest mercies that I was permitted for several months, perhaps for a year, to know God and to attempt obedience without even raising that question. My training was like that of the Jews, to whom He revealed Himself centuries before there was a whisper of anything better (or worse) beyond the grave than shadowy and featureless *Sheol*. And I did not dream even of that. There are men, far better men than I, who have made immortality almost the central doctrine of their religion; but for my own part I have never seen how a preoccupation with that subject at the outset could fail to

126

corrupt the whole thing. I had been brought up to believe that goodness was goodness only if it were disinterested, and that any hope of reward or fear of punishment contaminated the will. If I was wrong in this (the question is really much more complicated than I then perceived) my error was most tenderly allowed for. I was afraid that threats or promises would demoralize me; no threats or promises were made. The commands were inexorable, but they were backed by no "sanctions." God was to be obeyed simply because he was God. Long since, through the gods of Asgard, and later through the notion of the Absolute, He had taught me how a thing can be revered not for what it can do to us but for what it is in itself. That is why, though it was a terror, it was no surprise to learn that God is to be obeyed because of what He is in Himself. If you ask why we should obey God, in the last resort the answer is, "I am." To know that our obedience is due to Him. In His nature His sovereignty *de jure* is revealed.

Of course, as I have said, the matter is more complicated than that. The primal and necessary Being, the Creator, has sovereignty *de facto* as well as *de jure*. He has the power as well as the kingdom and the glory. But the *de jure* sovereignty was made known to me before the power, the right before the might. And for this I am thankful. I think it is well, even now, sometimes to say to ourselves, "God is such that if (*per impossibile*) his power could vanish and His other attributes remain, so that the supreme right were forever robbed of the supreme might, we should still owe Him precisely the same kind and degree of allegiance as we now do." On the other hand, while it is true to say that God's own nature is the real sanction of His commands, yet to understand this must, in the end, lead us to the conclusion that union with that Nature is bliss and separation from it horror. Thus Heaven and Hell come in. But it may well be that to think much of either except in this context of thought, to hypostatize them as if they had a substantial meaning apart from the presence or absence of God, corrupts the doctrine of both and corrupts us while we so think of them.

The last stage in my story, the transition from mere Theism to Christianity, is the one on which I am now least informed. Since it is also the most recent, this ignorance may seem strange. I think there are two reasons. One is that as we grow older we remember the more distant past better than what is nearer. But the other is, I believe, that one of the first results of my Theistic conversion was a marked decrease (and high time, as all readers of this book will agree) in the fussy attentiveness which I had so long paid to the progress of my own opinions and the states of my own mind. For many healthy extroverts self-examination first begins with conversion. For me it was almost the other way round. Self-examination did of course continue. But it was (I suppose, for I cannot quite remember) at stated intervals, and for a practical purpose; a duty, a discipline, an uncomfortable thing, no longer a hobby or a habit. To believe and to pray were the beginning of extroversion. I had been, as they say, "taken out of myself." If Theism had done nothing else for me, I should still be thankful that it cured me of the time-wasting and foolish practice of keeping a diary. (Even for autobiographical purposes a diary is nothing like so useful as I had hoped. You put down each day what you think important; but of course you cannot each day see what will prove to have been important in the long run.[1])

As soon as I became a Theist I started attending my parish church on Sundays and my college chapel on weekdays; not because I believed in Christianity, nor because I thought the difference between it and simple Theism a small one, but because I thought one ought to "fly one's flag" by some unmistakable overt sign. I was acting in obedience to a (perhaps mistaken) sense of honor. The idea of churchmanship was to me wholly unattractive. I was not in the least anticlerical, but I was deeply antiecclesiastical. That curates and archdeacons and churchwardens should exist was admirable. They gratified my Jenkinian love of everything which has its own strong flavor. And (apart from Oldie) I had been fortunate in my clerical acquaintances; especially in Adam Fox, the Dean of Divinity at Magdalen, and in Arthur Barton (later Archbishop of Dublin) who had been our Rector at home in Ireland. (He, by the by, had once suffered under Oldie at Belsen. Speaking of Oldie's death, I had said to him, "Well, we shan't see *him* again." "You mean," he answered with a grim smile, "we *hope* we shan't.") But though I liked clergymen as I liked bears, I had as little wish to be in the Church as in the zoo. It was, to begin with, a kind of collective; a wearisome "get-together" affair. I couldn't yet see how a concern of that sort should have anything to do with one's spiritual life. To me, religion ought to have been a matter of good men praying alone and meeting by twos and threes to talk of spiritual matters. And then the fussy, time-wasting botheration of it all! the bells, the crowds, the umbrellas, the notices, the bustle, the perpetual arranging and organizing. Hymns were (and are) extremely disagreeable to me. Of all musical instruments I liked (and like) the organ least. I have, too, a sort of spiritual *gaucherie* which makes me unapt to participate in any rite.

Thus my churchgoing was a merely symbolical and provisional practice. If it in fact helped to move me in the Christian direction, I was and am unaware of this. My chief companion on this stage of the road was Griffiths, with whom I kept up a copious correspondence. Both now believed in God, and were ready to hear more of Him from any source, Pagan or Christian. In my mind (I cannot now answer for his, and he has told his own story admirably in *The Golden String*) the perplexing multiplicity of "religions" began to sort itself out. The real clue had been put into my hand by that hard-boiled Atheist when he said, "Rum thing, all that about the Dying God. Seems to have really happened once"; by him and by Barfield's encouragement of a more respectful, if not more delighted, attitude to Pagan myth. The question was no longer to find the one simply true religion among a thousand religions simply false. It was rather, "Where has religion reached its true maturity? Where, if

[1]The only real good I got from keeping a diary was that it taught me a just appreciation of Boswell's amazing genius. I tried very hard to reproduce conversations, in some of which very amusing and striking people had taken part. But none of these people came to life in the diary at all. Obviously something quite different from mere accurate reporting went to the presentation of Boswell's Langton, Beauclerk, Wilkes, and the rest.

anywhere, have the hints of all Paganism been fulfilled?" With the irreligious I was no longer concerned; their view of life was henceforth out of court. As against them, the whole mass of those who had worshiped — all who had danced and sung and sacrificed and trembled and adored — were clearly right. But the intellect and the conscience, as well as the orgy and the ritual, must be our guide. There could be no question of going back to primitive, untheologized and unmoralized, Paganism. The God whom I had at last acknowledged was one, and was righteous. Paganism had been only the childhood of religion, or only a prophetic dream. Where was the thing full grown? or where was the awakening? (*The Everlasting Man* was helping me here.) There were really only two answers possible: either in Hinduism or in Christianity. Everything else was either a preparation for, or else (in the French sense) a *vulgarization* of, these. Whatever you could find elsewhere you could find better in one of these. But Hinduism seemed to have two disqualifications. For one thing, it appeared to be not so much a moralized and philosophical maturity of Paganism as a mere oil-and-water coexistence of philosophy side by side with Paganism unpurged; the Brahmin meditating in the forest, and, in the village a few miles away, temple prostitution, *sati,* cruelty, monstrosity. And secondly, there was no such historical claim as in Christianity. I was by now too experienced in literary criticism to regard the Gospels as myths. They had not the mythical taste. And yet the very matter which they set down in their artless, historical fashion — those narrow, unattractive Jews, too blind to the mythical wealth of the Pagan world around them — was precisely the matter of the great myths. If ever a myth had become fact, had been incarnated, it would be just like this. And nothing else in all literature was just like this. Myths were like it in one way. Histories were like it in another. But nothing was simply like it. And no person was like the Person it depicted; as real, as recognizable, through all that depth of time, as Plato's Socrates or Boswell's Johnson (ten times more so than Eckermann's Goethe or Lockhart's Scott), yet also numinous, lit by a light from beyond the world, a god. But if a god — we are no longer polytheists — then not a god, but God. Here and here only in all time the myth must have become fact; the Word, flesh; God, Man. This is not "a religion," nor "a philosophy." It is the summing up and actuality of them all.

As I have said, I speak of this last transition less certainly than of any which went before it, and it may be that in the preceding paragraph I have mixed thoughts that came later. But I can hardly be wrong about the main lines. Of one thing I am sure. As I drew near the conclusion, I felt a resistance almost as strong as my previous resistance to Theism. As strong, but shorter-lived, for I understood it better. Every step I had taken, from the Absolute to "Spirit" and from "Spirit" to "God," had been a step toward the more concrete, the more imminent, the more compulsive. At each step one had less chance "to call one's soul one's own." To accept the Incarnation was a further step in the same direction. It brings God nearer, or near in a new way. And this, I found, was something I had not wanted. But to recognize the ground for my evasion was of course to recognize both its shame and its futility. I know very well when, but hardly how, the final step was taken. I was driven to Whipsnade one sunny morning. When we set out I did not believe that Jesus Christ is the Son of God, and when we reached the zoo I did. Yet I had not exactly spent the journey in thought. Nor in great emotion. "Emotional" is perhaps the last word we can apply to some of the most important events. It was more like when a man, after long sleep, still lying motionless in bed, becomes aware that he is now awake. And it was, like that moment on top of the bus, ambiguous. Freedom, or necessity? Or do they differ at their maximum? At that maximum a man is what he does; there is nothing of him left over or outside the act. As for what we commonly call Will, and what we commonly call Emotion, I fancy these usually talk too loud, protest too much, to be quite believed, and we have a secret suspicion that the great passion or the iron resolution is partly a put-up job.

They have spoiled Whipsnade since then. Wallaby Wood, with the birds singing overhead and the bluebells underfoot and the Wallabies hopping all round one, was almost Eden come again.

But what, in conclusion, of Joy? for that, after all, is what the story has mainly been about. To tell you the truth, the subject has lost nearly all interest for me since I became a Christian. I cannot, indeed, complain, like Wordsworth, that the visionary gleam has passed away. I believe (if the thing were at all worth recording) that the old stab, the old bittersweet, has come to me as often and as sharply since my conversion as at any time of my life whatever. But I now know that the experience, considered as a state of my own mind, had never had the kind of importance I once gave it. It was valuable only as a pointer to something other and outer. While that other was in doubt, the pointer naturally loomed large in my thoughts. When we are lost in the woods the sight of a signpost is a great matter. He who first sees it cries, "Look!" The whole party gathers round and stares. But when we have found the road and are passing signposts every few miles, we shall not stop and stare. They will encourage us and we shall be grateful to the authority that set them up. But we shall not stop and stare, or not much; not on this road, though their pillars are of silver and their lettering of gold. "We would be at Jerusalem."

Not, of course, that I don't often catch myself stopping to stare at roadside objects of even less importance.

Reflections
on the Psalms

I

INTRODUCTORY

This is not a work of scholarship. I am no Hebraist, no higher critic, no ancient historian, no archaeologist. I write for the unlearned about things in which I am unlearned myself. If an excuse is needed (and perhaps it is) for writing such a book, my excuse would be something like this. It often happens that two schoolboys can solve difficulties in their work for one another better than the master can. When you took the problem to a master, as we all remember, he was very likely to explain what you understood already, to add a great deal of information which you didn't want, and say nothing at all about the thing that was puzzling you. I have watched this from both sides of the net; for when, as a teacher myself, I have tried to answer questions brought me by pupils, I have sometimes, after a minute, seen that expression settle down on their faces which assured me that they were suffering exactly the same frustration which I had suffered from my own teachers. The fellow-pupil can help more than the master because he knows less. The difficulty we want him to explain is one he has recently met. The expert met it so long ago that he has forgotten. He sees the whole subject, by now, in such a different light that he cannot conceive what is really troubling the pupil; he sees a dozen other difficulties which ought to be troubling him but aren't.

In this book, then, I write as one amateur to another, talking about difficulties I have met, or lights I have gained, when reading the Psalms, with the hope that this might at any rate interest, and sometimes even help, other inexpert readers. I am "comparing notes", not presuming to instruct. It may appear to some that I have used the Psalms merely as pegs on which to hang a series of miscellaneous essays. I do not know that it would have done any harm if I had written the book that way, and I shall have no grievance against anyone who reads it that way. But that is not how it was in fact written. The thoughts it contains are those to which I found myself driven in reading the Psalms; sometimes by my enjoyment of them, sometimes by meeting with what at first I could not enjoy.

The Psalms were written by many poets and at many different dates. Some, I believe, are allowed to go back to the reign of David; I think certain scholars allow that Psalm 18 (of which a slightly different version occurs in I *Samuel* 22) might be by

133

David himself. But many are later than the "captivity", which we should call the deportation to Babylon. In a scholarly work, chronology would be the first thing to settle: In a book of this sort nothing more need, or can, be said about it.

What must be said, however, is that the Psalms are poems, and poems intended to be sung: not doctrinal treatises, nor even sermons. Those who talk of reading the Bible "as literature" sometimes mean, I think, reading it without attending to the main thing it is about; like reading Burke with no interest in politics, or reading the *Aeneid* with no interest in Rome. That seems to me to be nonsense. But there is a saner sense in which the Bible, since it is after all literature, cannot properly be read except as literature; and the different parts of it as the different sorts of literature they are. Most emphatically the Psalms must be read as poems; as lyrics, with all the licences and all the formalities, the hyperboles, the emotional rather than logical connections, which are proper to lyric poetry. They must be read as poems if they are to be understood; no less than French must be read as French or English as English. Otherwise we shall miss what is in them and think we see what is not.

Their chief formal characteristic, the most obvious element of pattern, is fortunately one that survives in translation. Most readers will know that I mean what the scholars call "parallelism"; that is, the practice of saying the same thing twice in different words. A perfect example is "He that dwelleth in heaven shall laugh them to scorn: the Lord shall have them in derision" (2, *4*), or again, "He shall make thy righteousness as clear as the light; and thy just dealing as the noon-day" (37, *6*). If this is not recognised as pattern, the reader will either find mares' nests (as some of the older preachers did) in his effort to get a different meaning out of each half of the verse or else feel that it is rather silly.

In reality it is a very pure example of what all pattern, and therefore all art, involves. The principle of art has been defined by someone as "the same in the other". Thus in a country dance you take three steps and then three steps again. That is the same. But the first three are to the right and the second three to the left. That is the other. In a building there may be a wing on one side and a wing on the other, but both of the same shape. In music the composer may say ABC, and then abc, and then $\alpha\beta\gamma$. Rhyme consists in putting together two syllables that have the same sound except for their initial consonants, which are other. "Parallelism" is the characteristically Hebrew form of the same in the other, but it occurs in many English poets too: for example, in Marlowe's

> *Cut is the branch that might have grown full straight*
> *And burned is Apollo's laurel bough,*

or in the childishly simple form used by the *Cherry Tree Carol*,

> *Joseph was an old man and an old man was he.*

Of course the Parallelism is often partially concealed on purpose (as the balances between masses in a picture may be something far subtler than complete symmetry).

And of course other and more complex patterns may be worked in across it, as in Psalm 119, or in 107 with its refrain. I mention only what is most obvious, the Parallelism itself. It is (according to one's point of view) either a wonderful piece of luck or a wise provision of God's that poetry which was to be turned into all languages should have as its chief formal characteristic one that does not disappear (as mere metre does) in translation.

If we have any taste for poetry we shall enjoy this feature of the Psalms. Even those Christians who cannot enjoy it will respect it; for Our Lord, soaked in the poetic tradition of His country, delighted to use it. "For with what judgement ye judge, ye shall be judged; and with what measure ye mete, it shall be measured to you again" (*Matthew* 7, 2). The second half of the verse makes no logical addition; it echoes, with variation, the first, "Ask, and it shall be given you; seek, and ye shall find; knock and it shall be opened unto you" (7, 7). The advice is given in the first phrase, then twice repeated with different images. We may, if we like, see in this an exclusively practical and didactic purpose; by giving to truths which are infinitely worth remembering this rhythmic and incantatory expression, He made them almost impossible to forget. I like to suspect more. It seems to me appropriate, almost inevitable, that when that great Imagination which in the beginning, for Its own delight and for the delight of men and angels and (in their proper mode) of beasts, had invented and formed the whole world of Nature, submitted to express Itself in human speech, that speech should sometimes be poetry. For poetry too is a little incarnation, giving body to what had been before invisible and inaudible.

I think, too, it will do us no harm to remember that, in becoming Man, He bowed His neck beneath the sweet yoke of a heredity and early environment. Humanly speaking, He would have learned his style, if from no one else (but it was all about Him) from His Mother. "That we should be saved from our enemies and from the hands of all that hate us; to perform the mercy promised to our fathers, and to remember his holy covenant." Here is the same parallelism. (And incidentally, is this the only aspect in which we can say of His human nature "He was His Mother's own son"? There is a fierceness, even a touch of Deborah, mixed with the sweetness in the *Magnificat* to which most painted Madonnas do little justice; matching the frequent severity of His own sayings. I am sure the private life of the holy family was, in many senses, "mild" and "gentle", but perhaps hardly in the way some hymn writers have in mind. One may suspect, on proper occasions, a certain astringency; and all in what people at Jerusalem regarded as a rough north-country dialect.)

I have not attempted of course to "cover the subject" even on my own amateurish level. I have stressed, and omitted, as my own interests led me. I say nothing about the long historical Psalms, partly because they have meant less to me, and partly because they seem to call for little comment. I say the least I can about the history of the Psalms as parts of various "services"; a wide subject, and not for me. And I begin with those characteristics of the Psalter which are at first most repellent. Other men of my age will know why. Our generation was brought up to eat everything on the plate; and it was the sound principle of nursery gastronomy to polish off the nasty things first and leave the titbits to the end.

I have worked in the main from the translation which Anglicans find in their Prayer Book; that of Coverdale. Even of the old translators he is by no means the most accurate; and of course a sound modern scholar has more Hebrew in his little finger than poor Coverdale had in his whole body. But in beauty, in poetry, he, and St. Jerome, the great Latin translator, are beyond all whom I know. I have usually checked, and sometimes corrected, his version from that of Dr. Moffatt.

Finally, as will soon be apparent to any reader, this is not what is called an "apologetic" work. I am nowhere trying to convince unbelievers that Christianity is true. I address those who already believe it, or those who are ready, while reading, to "suspend their disbelief". A man can't be always defending the truth; there must be a time to feed on it.

I have written, too, as a member of the Church of England, but I have avoided controversial questions as much as possible. At one point I had to explain how I differed on a certain matter both from Roman Catholics and from Fundamentalists: I hope I shall not for this forfeit the goodwill or the prayers of either. Nor do I much fear it. In my experience the bitterest opposition comes neither from them nor from any other thoroughgoing believers, and not often from atheists, but from semi-believers of all complexions. There are some enlightened and progressive old gentlemen of this sort whom no courtesy can propitiate and no modesty disarm. But then I dare say I am a much more annoying person than I know. (Shall we, perhaps, in Purgatory, see our own faces and hear our own voices as they really were?)

II

"JUDGEMENT"
IN THE PSALMS

If there is any thought at which a Christian trembles it is the thought of God's "judgement". The "Day" of Judgement is "that day of wrath, that dreadful day". We pray for God to deliver us "in the hour of death and at the day of judgement". Christian art and literature for centuries have depicted its terrors. This note in Christianity certainly goes back to the teaching of Our Lord Himself; especially to the terrible parable of the Sheep and the Goats. This can leave no conscience untouched, for in it the "Goats" are condemned entirely for their sins of omission; as if to make us fairly sure that the heaviest charge against each of us turns not upon the things he has done but on those he never did—perhaps never dreamed of doing.

It was therefore with great surprise that I first noticed how the Psalmists talk about the judgements of God. They talk like this; "O let the nations rejoice and be glad, for thou shalt judge the folk righteously (67, *4*), "Let the field be joyful... all the trees of the wood shall rejoice before the Lord, for he cometh, for he cometh to judge the earth" (96, *12, 13*). Judgement is apparently an occasion of universal rejoicing. People ask for it: "Judge me, O Lord my God, according to thy righteousness" (35, *24*).

The reason for this soon becomes very plain. The ancient Jews, like ourselves, think of God's judgement in terms of an earthly court of justice. The difference is that the Christian pictures the case to be tried as a criminal case with himself in the dock; the Jew pictures it as a civil case with himself as the plaintiff. The one hopes for acquittal, or rather for pardon; the other hopes for a resounding triumph with heavy damages. Hence he prays "judge my quarrel", or "avenge my cause" (35, *23*). And though, as I said a minute ago, Our Lord in the parable of the Sheep and the Goats painted the characteristically Christian picture, in another place He is very characteristically Jewish. Notice what He means by "an unjust judge". By those words most of us would mean someone like Judge Jeffreys or the creatures who sat on the benches of German tribunals during the Nazi *régime*: someone who bullies witnesses and jurymen in order to convict, and then savagely to punish, innocent men. Once again, we are thinking of a criminal trial. We hope we shall never appear in the dock before such a judge. But the Unjust Judge in the parable is quite a different character. There is no danger of appearing in his court against your will: the difficulty is the opposite – to get into it. It is clearly a civil action. The poor woman (*Luke* 18, *1–5*) has had her little strip of land – room for a pigsty or a hen-run – taken away from her by a richer and more powerful neighbour (nowadays it would be Town-Planners or some other "Body"). And she knows she has a perfectly watertight case. If once she could get it into court and have it tried by the laws of the land, she would be bound to get that strip back. But no one will listen to her, she can't get it tried. No wonder she is anxious for "judgement".

Behind this lies an age-old and almost world-wide experience which we have been spared. In most places and times it has been very difficult for the "small man" to get his case heard. The judge (and, doubtless, one or two of his underlings) has to be bribed. If you can't afford to "oil his palm" your case will never reach court. Our judges do not receive bribes. (We probably take this blessing too much for granted; it will not remain with us automatically). We need not therefore be surprised if the Psalms, and the Prophets, are full of the longing for judgement, and regard the announcement that "judgement" is coming as good news. Hundreds and thousands of people who have the right entirely on their side will at least be heard. Of course they are not afraid of judgement. They know their case is unanswerable – if only it could be heard. When God comes to judge, at last it will.

Dozens of passages make the point clear. In Psalm 9 we are told that God will "minister true judgement" *(8)*, and that is because He "forgetteth not the complaint of the poor" *(12)*. He "defendeth the cause" (that is, the "case") "of the widows" (68, 5). The good king in Psalm 72, 2, will "judge" the people rightly; that is, he will "defend the poor". When God "arises to judgement" he will "help all the meek upon earth" (76, 9), all the timid, helpless people whose wrongs have never been righted yet. When God accuses earthly judges of "wrong judgement", He follows it up by telling them to see that the poor "have right" (82, 2, 3).

The "just" judge, then, is primarily he who rights a wrong in a civil case. He would, no doubt, also try a criminal case justly, but that is hardly ever what the Psalmists are thinking of. Christians cry to God for mercy instead of justice; *they* cried to God for justice instead of injustice. The Divine Judge is the defender, the rescuer. Scholars tell me that in the *Book of Judges* the word we so translate might almost be rendered "champions"; for though these "judges" do sometimes perform what we should call judicial functions many of them are much more concerned with rescuing the oppressed Israelites from Philistines and others by force of arms. They are more like Jack the Giant Killer than like a modern judge in a wig. The knights in romances of chivalry who go about rescuing distressed damsels and widows from giants and other tyrants are acting almost as "judges" in the old Hebrew sense: so is the modern solicitor (and I have known such) who does unpaid work for poor clients to save them from wrong.

I think there are very good reasons for regarding the Christian picture of God's judgement as far more profound and far safer for souls than the Jewish. But this does not mean that the Jewish conception must simply be thrown away. I, at least, believe I can still get a good deal of nourishment out of it.

It supplements the Christian picture in one important way. For what alarms us in the Christian picture is the infinite purity of the standard against which our actions will be judged. But then we know that none of us will ever come up to that standard. We are all in the same boat. We must all pin our hopes on the mercy of God and the work of Christ, not on our own goodness. Now the Jewish picture of a civil action sharply reminds us that perhaps we are faulty not only by the Divine standard (that is a matter of course) but also by a very human standard which all reasonable people admit and which we ourselves usually wish to enforce upon others. Almost certainly there are unsatisfied claims, human claims, against each one of us. For who can really believe that in all his dealings with employers and employees, with husband or wife, with parents and children, in quarrels and in collaborations, he has always attained (let alone charity or generosity) mere honesty and fairness? Of course we forget most of the injuries we have done. But the injured parties do not forget even if they forgive. And God does not forget. And even what we can remember is formidable enough. Few of us have always, in full measure, given our pupils or patients or clients (or whatever our particular "consumers" may be called) what we were being paid for. We have not always done quite our fair share of some tiresome work if we found a colleague or partner who could be beguiled into carrying the heavy end.

Our quarrels provide a very good example of the way in which the Christian and Jewish conceptions differ, while yet both should be kept in mind. As Christians we must of course repent of all the anger, malice, and self-will which allowed the discussion to become, on our side, a quarrel at all. But there is also the question on a far lower level: "granted the quarrel (we'll go into that later) did you fight fair?" Or did we not quite unknowingly falsify the whole issue? Did we pretend to be angry about one thing when we knew, or could have known, that our anger had a different and much less presentable cause? Did we pretend to be "hurt" in our sensitive and tender feelings (fine natures like ours are so vulnerable) when envy, ungratified vanity, or thwarted self-will was our real trouble? Such tactics often succeed. The other parties give in. They give in not because they don't know what is really wrong with us but because they have long known it only too well, and that sleeping dog can be roused, that skeleton brought out of its cupboard, only at the cost of imperilling their whole relationship with us. It needs surgery which they know we will never face. And so we win; by cheating. But the unfairness is very deeply felt. Indeed what is commonly called "sensitiveness" is the most powerful engine of domestic tyranny, sometimes a lifelong tyranny. How we should deal with it in others I am not sure; but we should be merciless to its first appearances in ourselves.

The constant protests in the Psalms against those who oppress "the poor" might seem at first to have less application to our own society than to most. But perhaps this is superficial; perhaps what changes is not the oppression but only the identity of "the poor". It often happens that someone in my acquaintance gets a demand from the Income Tax people which he queries. As a result it sometimes comes back to him reduced by anything up to fifty per cent. One man whom I knew, a solicitor, went round to the office and asked what they had meant by the original demand. The creature behind the counter tittered and said, "Well there's never any harm trying it on." Now when the cheat is thus attempted against men of the world who know how to look after themselves, no great harm is done. Some time has been wasted, and we all in some measure share the disgrace of belonging to a community where such practices are tolerated, but that is all. When, however, that kind of publican sends a similarly dishonest demand to a poor widow, already half starving on a highly taxable "unearned" income (actually earned by years of self-denial on her husband's part) which inflation has reduced to almost nothing, a very different result probably follows. She cannot afford legal help; she understands nothing; she is terrified, and pays – cutting down on the meals and the fuel which were already wholly insufficient. The publican who has successfully "tried it on" with her is precisely "the ungodly" who "for his own lust doth persecute the poor" (10, 2). To be sure, he does this, not like the ancient publican, for his own immediate rakeoff; only to advance himself in the service or to please his masters. This makes a difference. How important that difference is in the eyes of Him who avenges the fatherless and the widow I do not know. The publican may consider the question in the hour of death and will learn the answer at the day of "judgement". (But – who knows? – I may be doing the publicans an injustice. Perhaps they regard their work as a sport and observe game laws; and as other sportsmen will not shoot a sitting bird, so they may reserve their illegal demands for those who can defend themselves and hit back, and would never dream of "trying it on" with the helpless. If so, I can only apologise for my error. If what I have said is unjustifed as a rebuke of what they are, it may still be useful as a warning of what they may yet become. Falsehood is habit-forming.)

It will be noticed, however, that I make the Jewish conception of a civil judgement available for my Christian profit by picturing myself as the defendant, not the plaintiff. The writers of the Psalms do not do this. They look forward to "judgement" because they think they have been wronged and hope to see their wrongs righted. There are, indeed, some passages in which the Psalmists approach to Christian humility and wisely lose their self-confidence. Thus in Psalm 50 (one of the finest) God is the accuser (6 – 21); and in 143,2, we have the words which most Christians often repeat – "Enter not into judgement with Thy servant, for in Thy sight shall no man living be justified." But these are exceptional. Nearly always the Psalmist is the indignant plaintiff.

He is quite sure, apparently, that his own hands are clean. He never did to others the horrid things that others are doing to him. "If I have done any such thing" – if I ever behaved like so-and-so, then let so-and-so "tread my life down upon the earth" (7, 3 – 5). But of course I haven't. It is not as if my enemies are paying me out for any ill turn I ever did them. On the contrary, they have "rewarded me evil for good". Even after that, I went on exercising the utmost charity towards them. When they were ill I prayed and fasted on their behalf (35, *12 – 14*).

All this of course has its spiritual danger. It leads into that typically Jewish prison of self-righteousness which Our Lord so often terribly rebuked. We shall have to consider that presently. For the moment, however, I think it is important to make a distinction: between the conviction that one is in the right and the conviction that one is "righteous" is a good man. Since none of us is righteous, the second conviction is always a delusion. But any of us may be, probably all of us at one time or another are, in the right about some particular issue. What is more, the worse man may be in the right against the better man. Their general characters have nothing to do with it. The question whether the disputed pencil belongs to Tommy or Charles is quite distinct from the question which is the nicer little boy, and the parents who allowed the one to influence their decision about the other would be very unfair. (It would be still worse if they said Tommy ought to let Charles have the pencil whether it belonged to him or not, because this would show he had a nice disposition. That may be true, but it is an untimely truth. An exhortation to charity should not come as rider to a refusal of justice. It is likely to give Tommy a lifelong conviction that charity is a sanctimonious dodge for condoning theft and whitewashing favouritism.) We need therefore by no means assume that the Psalmists are deceived or lying when they assert that, as against their particular enemies at some particular moment, they are completely in the right. Their voices while they say so may grate harshly on our ear and suggest to us that they are unamiable people. But that is another matter. And to be wronged does not commonly make people amiable.

But of course the fatal confusion between being in the right and being righteous soon falls upon them. In 7, from which I have already quoted, we see the transition. In verses *3* to *5* the poet is merely in the right; by verse *8* he is saying "give sentence with me, O Lord, according to my righteousness and according to the innocency that is in me." There is also in many of the Psalms a still more fatal confusion – that between the desire for justice and the desire for revenge. These important topics will have to be treated separately. The self-righteous Psalms can be dealt with only at a much later stage; the vindictive Psalms, the cursings, we may turn to at once. It is these that have made the Psalter largely a closed book to many modern church-goers. Vicars, not unnaturally, are afraid to set before their congregations poems so full of that passion to which Our Lord's teaching allows no quarter. Yet there must be some Christian use to be made of them; if, at least, we still believe (as I do) that all Holy Scripture is in some sense – though not all parts of it in the same sense – the word of God. (The sense in which I understand this will be explained later.)

III

THE CURSINGS

In some of the Psalms the spirit of hatred which strikes us in the face is like the heat from a furnace mouth. In others the same spirit ceases to be frightful only by becoming (to a modern mind) almost comic in its naîveté.

Examples of the first can be found all over the Psalter, but perhaps the worst is in 109. The poet prays that an ungodly man may rule over his enemy and that "Satan" may stand at his right hand (5). This probably does not mean what a Christian reader naturally supposes. The "Satan" is an accuser, perhaps an informer. When the enemy is tried, let him be convicted and sentenced, "and let his prayer be turned into sin" (6). This again means, I think, not his prayers to God, but his supplications to a human judge, which are to make things all the hotter for him (double the sentence because he begged for it to be halved). May his days be few, may his job be given to someone else (7). When he is dead may his orphans be beggars (9). May he look in vain for anyone in the world to pity him (11). Let God always remember against him the sins of his parents (13). Even more devilish in one verse is the, otherwise beautiful, 137 where a blessing is pronounced on anyone who will snatch up a Babylonian baby and beat its brains out against the pavement (9). And we get the refinement of malice in 69, 23, "Let their table be made a snare to take themselves withal; and let the things that should have been for their wealth be unto them an occasion of falling."

The examples which (in me at any rate) can hardly fail to produce a smile may occur most disquietingly in Psalms we love; 143, after proceeding for eleven verses in a strain that brings tears to the eyes, adds in the twelfth, almost like an afterthought "and of thy goodness slay mine enemies." Even more naîvely, almost childishly, 139, in the middle of its hymn of praise throws in (19) "Wilt thou not slay the wicked, O God?" —as if it were surprising that such a simple remedy for human ills had not occurred to the Almighty. Worst of all in "The Lord is my shepherd" (23), after the green pasture, the waters of comfort, the sure confidence in the valley of the shadow, we suddenly run across (5) "Thou shalt prepare a table for me *against them that trouble me*" —or, as Dr. Moffatt translates it, "Thou art my host, spreading a feast for me *while my enemies have to look on.*" The poet's enjoyment of his present prosperity would not be complete unless those horrid Joneses (who used to look down their noses at him) were watching it all and hating it. This may not be so diabolical as the passages I have quoted above; but the pettiness and vulgarity of it, especially in such surroundings, are hard to endure.

One way of dealing with these terrible or (dare we say?) contemptible Psalms is simply to leave them alone. But unfortunately the bad parts will not "come away clean"; they may, as we have noticed, be intertwined with the most exquisite things. And if we still believe that all Holy Scripture is "written for our learning" or that the age-old use of the Psalms in Christian worship was not entirely contrary to the will of God, and if we remember that Our Lord's mind and language were clearly steeped in the Psalter, we shall prefer, if possible, to make some use of them. What use can be made?

Part of the answer to this question cannot be given until we come to consider the subject of allegory. For the moment I can only describe, on the chance that it may help others, the use which I have, undesignedly and gradually, come to make of them myself.

At the outset I felt sure, and I feel sure still, that we must not either try to explain them away or to yield for one moment to the idea that, because it comes in the Bible, all this vindictive hatred must somehow be good and pious. We must face both facts squarely. The hatred is there — festering, gloating, undisguised — and also we should be wicked if we in any way condoned or approved it, or (worse still) used it to justify similar passions in ourselves. Only after these two admissions have been made can we safely proceed.

The first thing that helped me — this is a common experience — came from an angle that did not seem to be religious at all. I found that these maledictions were in one way extremely interesting. For here one saw a feeling we all know only too well, Resentment, expressing itself with perfect freedom, without disguise, without self-consciousness, without shame — as few but children would express it today. I did not of course think that this was because the ancient Hebrews had no conventions or restraints. Ancient and oriental cultures are in many ways more conventional, more ceremonious, and more courteous than our own. But their restraints came in different places. Hatred did not need to be disguised for the sake of social decorum or for fear anyone would accuse you of a neurosis. We therefore see it in its "wild" or natural condition.

One might have expected that this would immediately, and usefully, have turned my attention to the same thing in my own heart. And that, of course, is one very good use we can make of the maledictory Psalms. To be sure, the hates which we fight against in ourselves do not dream of quite such appalling revenges. We live — at least, in some countries we still live — in a milder age. These poets lived in a world of savage punishments, of massacre and violence, of blood sacrifice in all countries and human sacrifice in many. And of course, too, we are far more subtle than they in disguising our ill will from others and from ourselves. "Well," we say, "he'll live to be sorry for it," as if we were merely, even regretfully, predicting; not noticing, certainly not admitting, that what we predict gives us a certain satisfaction. Still more in the Psalmists' tendency to chew over and over the cud of some injury, to dwell in a kind of self-torture on every circumstance that aggravates it, most of us can recognise something we have met in ourselves. We are, after all, blood-brothers to these ferocious, self-pitying, barbaric men.

That, as I say, is a good use to make of the cursings. In fact, however, something else occurred to me first. It seemed to me that, seeing in them hatred undisguised, I saw also the natural result of injuring a human being. The word *natural* is here important. This result can be obliterated by grace, suppressed by prudence or social convention, and (which is dangerous) wholly disguised by self-deception. But just as the natural result of throwing a lighted match into a pile of shavings is to produce a fire—though damp or the intervention of some more sensible person may prevent it—so the natural result of cheating a man, or "keeping him down" or neglecting him, is to arouse resentment; that is, to impose upon him the temptation of becoming what the Psalmists were when they wrote the vindictive passages. He may succeed in resisting the temptation; or he may not. If he fails, if he dies spiritually because of his hatred for me, how do I, who provoked that hatred, stand? For in addition to the original injury I have done him a far worse one. I have introduced into his inner life, at best a new temptation, at worst a new besetting sin. If that sin utterly corrupts him, I have in a sense debauched or seduced him. I was the tempter.

There is no use in talking as if forgiveness were easy. We all know the old joke, "You've given up smoking once; I've given it up a dozen times." In the same way I could say of a certain man, "Have I forgiven him for what he did that day? I've forgiven him more times than I can count." For we find that the work of forgiveness has to be done over and over again. We forgive, we mortify our resentment; a week later some chain of thought carries us back to the original offence and we discover the old resentment blazing away as if nothing had been done about it at all. We need to forgive our brother seventy times seven not only for 490 offences but for one offence. Thus the man I am thinking of has introduced a new and difficult temptation into a soul which had the devil's plenty of them already. And what he has done to me, doubtless I have done to others; I, who am exceptionally blessed in having been allowed a way of life in which, having little power, I have had little opportunity of oppressing and embittering others. Let all of us who have never been school prefects, N.C.O.s, schoolmasters, matrons of hospitals, prison warders, or even magistrates, give hearty thanks for it.

It is monstrously simple-minded to read the cursings in the Psalms with no feeling except one of horror at the uncharity of the poets. They are indeed devilish. But we must also think of those who made them so. Their hatreds are the reaction to something. Such hatreds are the kind of thing that cruelty and injustice, by a sort of natural law, produce. This, among other things, is what wrong doing means. Take from a man his freedom or his goods and you may have taken his innocence, almost his humanity, as well. Not all the victims go and hang themselves like Mr. Pilgrim; they may live and hate.

Then another thought occurred which led me in an unexpected, and at first unwelcome, direction. The reaction of the Psalmists to injury, though profoundly natural, is profoundly wrong. One may try to excuse it on the ground that they were not Christians and knew no better. But there are two reasons why this defence, though it will go some way, will not go very far.

The first is that within Judaism itself the corrective to this natural reaction already existed. "Thou shalt not avenge or bear any grudge against the children of thy people, but thou shalt love thy neighbour as thyself," says *Leviticus* (19, *17, 18*). In *Exodus* we read, "If thou seest the ass of him that hateth thee lying under his burden . . . thou shalt surely help with him," and "if thou meet thine enemy's ox or his ass going astray, thou shalt surely bring it back to him" (*23,* 4,5). "Rejoice not when thine enemy falleth, and let not thy heart be glad when he stumbleth" (*Proverbs* 24, *17*). And I shall never forget my surprise when I first discovered that St. Paul's "If thine enemy hunger, give him bread", etc., is a direct quotation from the same book (*Proverbs* 25, *21*). But this is one of the rewards of reading the Old Testament regularly. You keep on discovering more and more what a tissue of quotations from it the New Testament is; how constantly Our Lord repeated, reinforced, continued, refined, and sublimated, the Judaic ethics, how very seldom He introduced a novelty. This of course was perfectly well-known — was indeed axiomatic — to millions of unlearned Christians as long as Bible reading was habitual. Nowadays it seems to be so forgotten that people think they have somehow discredited Our Lord if they can show that some pre-Christian document (or what they take to be pre-Christian) such as the Dead Sea Scrolls has "anticipated" Him. As if we supposed Him to be a cheapjack like Nietzsche inventing a new ethics! Every good teacher, within Judaism as without, has anticipated Him. The whole religious history of the pre-Christian world, on its better side, anticipates Him. It could not be otherwise. The Light which has lightened every man from the beginning may shine more clearly but cannot change. The Origin cannot suddenly start being, in the popular sense of the word, "original".

The second reason is more disquieting. If we are to excuse the poets of the Psalms on the ground that they were not Christians, we ought to be able to point to the same sort of thing, and worse, in Pagan authors. Perhaps if I knew more Pagan literature I should be able to do this. But in what I do know (a little Greek, a little Latin, and of Old Norse very little indeed) I am not at all sure that I can. I can find in them lasciviousness, much brutal insensibility, cold cruelties taken for granted, but not this fury or luxury of hatred. I mean, of course, where writers are speaking in their own person; speeches put into the mouths of angry characters in a play are a different matter. One's first impression is that the Jews were much more vindictive and vitriolic than the Pagans.

If we are not Christians we shall dismiss this with the old gibe "How odd of God to choose the Jews". That is impossible for us who believe that God chose that race for the vehicle of His own Incarnation, and who are indebted to Israel beyond all possible repayment.

Where we find a difficulty we may always expect that a discovery awaits us.

Where there is cover we hope for game. This particular difficulty is well worth exploring.

It seems that there is a general rule in the moral universe which may be formulated "The higher, the more in danger". The "average sensual man" who is sometimes unfaithful to his wife, sometimes tipsy, always a little selfish, now and then (within the law) a trifle sharp in his deals, is certainly, by ordinary standards, a "lower" type than the man whose soul is filled with some great Cause, to which he will subordinate his appetites, his fortune, and even his safety. But it is out of the second man that something really fiendish can be made; an Inquisitor, a Member of the Committee of Public Safety. It is great men, potential saints, not little men, who become merciless fanatics. Those who are readiest to die for a cause may easily become those who are readiest to kill for it. One sees the same principle at work in a field (comparatively) so unimportant as literary criticism; the most brutal work, the most rankling hatred of all other critics and of nearly all authors, may come from the most honest and disinterested critic, the man who cares most passionately and selflessly about literature. The higher the stakes, the greater the temptation to lose your temper over the game. We must not over-value the relative harmlessness of the little, sensual, frivolous people. They are not above, but below, some temptations.

If I am never tempted, and cannot even imagine myself being tempted, to gamble, this does not mean that I am better than those who are. The timidity and pessimism which exempt me from that temptation themselves tempt me to draw back from those risks and adventures which every man ought to take. In the same way we cannot be certain that the comparative absence of vindictiveness in the Pagans, though certainly a good thing in itself, is a good symptom. This was borne in upon me during night journey taken early in the Second War in a compartment full of young soldiers. Their conversation made it clear that they totally disbelieved all that they had read in the papers about the wholesale cruelties of the Nazi régime. They took it for granted, without argument, that this was all lies, all propaganda put out by our own government to "pep up" our troops. And the shattering thing was, that, believing this, they expressed not the slightest anger. That our rulers should falsely attribute the worst of crimes to some of their fellow-men in order to induce others of their fellow-men to shed their blood seemed to them a matter of course. They weren't even particularly interested. They saw nothing wrong in it. Now it seemed to me that the most violent of the Psalmists — or, for that matter any child wailing out "But it's not fair" — was in a more hopeful condition than these young men. If they had perceived, and felt as a man should feel, the diabolical wickedness which they believed our rulers to be committing, and then forgiven them, they would have been saints. But not to perceive it at all — not even to be tempted to resentment — to accept it as the most ordinary thing in the world — argues a terrifying insensibility. Clearly these young men had (on that subject anyway) no conception of good and evil whatsoever.

Thus the absence of anger, especially that sort of anger which we call *indignation*, can, in my opinion, be a most alarming symptom. And the presence of indignation may be a good one. Even when that indignation passes into bitter personal vindictiveness, it may still be a good symptom, though bad in itself. It is a sin; but it at least shows that those who commit it have not sunk below the level at which the temptation to that sin exists — just as the sins (often quite appalling) of the great patriot or great reformer point to something in him above mere self. If the Jews cursed more bitterly than the Pagans this was, I think, at least in part because they took right and wrong more seriously. For if we look at their railings we find they are usually angry not simply because these things have been done to them but because these things are manifestly wrong, are hateful to God as well as to the victim. The thought of the "righteous Lord" — who surely must hate such doings as much as they do, who surely therefore must (but how terribly He delays!) "judge" or avenge, is always there, if only in the background. Sometimes it comes into the foreground; as in 58, *9, 10,* "The righteous shall rejoice when he seeth the vengeance . . . so that a man shall say . . . Doubtless there is a God that judgeth the earth." This is something different from mere anger without indignation — the almost animal rage at finding that a man's enemy has done to him exactly what he would have done to his enemy if he had been strong enough or quick enough.

Different, certainly higher, a better symptom; yet also leading to a more terrible sin. For it encourages a man to think that his own worst passions are holy. It encourages him to add, explicitly or implicitly, "Thus saith the Lord" to the expression of his own emotion or even his own opinions; as Carlyle and Kipling and some politicans, and even in their own way, some modern critics, so horribly do. (It is this, by the way, rather than mere idle "profane swearing" that we ought to mean by "taking God's name in vain". The man who says "Damn that chair!" does not really wish that it should first be endowed with an immortal soul and then sent to eternal perdition.) For here also it is true "the higher, the more in danger". The Jews sinned in this matter worse than the Pagans not because they were further from God but because they were nearer to Him. For the Supernatural, entering a human soul, opens to it new possibilities both of good and evil. From that point the road branches: one way to sanctity, love, humility, the other to spiritual pride, self-righteousness, persecuting zeal. And no way back to the mere humdrum virtues and vices of the unawakened soul. If the Divine call does not make us better, it will make us very much worse. Of all bad men religious bad men are the worst. Of all created beings the wickedest is one who originally stood in the immediate presence of God. There seems no way out of this. It gives a new application to Our Lord's words about "counting the cost."

For we can still see, in the worst of their maledictions, how these old poets were, in a sense, near to God. Though hideously distorted by the human instrument, something of the Divine voice can be heard in these passages. Not, of course, that God looks upon their enemies as they do: He "desireth not the death of a sinner". But doubtless He has for the sin of those enemies just the implacable hostility which the poets express. Implacable? Yes, not to the sinner but to the sin. It will not be tolerated nor condoned, no treaty will be made with it. That tooth must come out, that right hand must be amputated, if the man is to be saved. In that way the relentlessness of the Psalmists is far nearer to one side of the truth than many modern attitudes which can be mistaken, by those who hold them, for Christian charity. It is, for example, obviously nearer than the total moral indifference of the young soldiers. It is nearer than the pseudo-scientific tolerance which reduces all wickedness to neurosis (though of course some apparent wickedness is). It even contains a streak of sanity absent from the old woman presiding at a juvenile court who — I heard it myself — told some young hooligans, convicted of a well-planned robbery for gain (they had already sold the swag and some had previous convictions against them) that they must, they really must, give up such "stupid pranks". Against all this the ferocious parts of the Psalms serve as a reminder that there is in the world such a thing as wickedness and that it (if not its perpetrators) is hateful to God. In that way, however dangerous the human distortion may be, His word sounds through these passages too.

But can we, besides learning from these terrible Psalms also use them in our devotional life? I believe we can; but that topic must be reserved for a later chapter.

IV

DEATH IN THE PSALMS

According to my policy of taking first what is most unattractive, I should now proceed to the self-righteousness in many of the Psalms. But we cannot deal with that properly until some other matters have been noticed. I turn first to a very different subject.

Our ancestors seem to have read the Psalms and the rest of the Old Testament under the impression that the author wrote with a pretty full understanding of Christian Theology; the main difference being that the Incarnation, which for us is something recorded, was for them something predicted. In particular, they seldom doubted that the old authors were, like ourselves, concerned with a life beyond death, that they feared damnation and hoped for eternal joy.

In our own Prayer Book version, and probably in many others, some passages make this impression almost irresistibly. Thus in 17, *14*, we read of wicked men "which have their portion in this life." The Christian reader inevitably reads into this (and Coverdale, the translator, obviously did so too) Our Lord's contrast between the Rich Man who had his good things here and Lazarus who had them hereafter; the same contrast which is implied in Luke 6, *24* – "Woe unto you that are rich, for ye have received your consolation." But modern translators can find nothing like this in the actual Hebrew. In reality this passage is merely one of the cursings we were considering in the previous chapter. In 17, *13* the poet prays God to "cast down" (in Dr. Moffatt, "crush") the ungodly; in verse *14*, a refinement occurs to him. Yes, crush them, but first let them "have their portion in this life". Kill them, but first give them a bad time while alive.

Again, in 49, we have "No man may deliver his brother...for it cost more to redeem their souls; so that he must let that alone forever" *(7, 8)*. Who would not think that this referred to the redeeming work of Christ? No man can "save" the soul of another. The price of salvation is one that only the Son of God could pay; as the hymn says, there was no other "good enough to pay the price". The very phrasing of our version strengthens the effect – the verb "redeem" which (outside the pawnbroking business) is now used only in a theological sense, and the past tense of "cost". Not it

149

"costs," but it did cost, more, once and for all on Calvary. But apparently the Hebrew poet meant something quite different and much more ordinary. He means merely that death is inevitable. As Dr. Moffatt translates: "None can buy himself off. Not one can purchase for a price from God (soul's ransom is too dear) life that shall never end."

At this point I can imagine a lifelong lover of the Psalms exclaiming: "Oh bother the great scholars and modern translators! I'm not going to let them spoil the whole Bible for me. At least let me ask two questions. (i) Is it not stretching the arm of coincidence rather far to ask me to believe that, not once but twice, in the same book, mere accident (wrong translations, bad manuscripts, or what not) should have so successfully imitated the language of Christianity? (ii) Do you mean that the old meanings which we have always attached to these verses simply have to be scrapped?" Both questions will come up for consideration in a later chapter. For the moment I will only say that, to the second, my personal answer is a confident No. I return to what I believe to be the fact.

It seems quite clear that in most parts of the Old Testament there is little or no belief in a future life; certainly no belief that is of any religious importance. The word translated "soul" in our version of the Psalms means simply "life"; the word translated "hell" means simply "the land of the dead", the state of all the dead, good and bad alike, *Sheol*.

It is difficult to know how an ancient Jew thought of *Sheol*. He did not like thinking about it. His religion did not encourage him to think about it. No good could come of thinking about it. Evil might. It was a condition from which very wicked people like the Witch of Endor were believed to be able to conjure up a ghost. But the ghost told you nothing about Sheol; it was called up solely to tell you things about our own world. Or again, if you allowed yourself an unhealthly interest in Sheol you might be lured into one of the neighbouring forms of Paganism and "eat the offerings of the dead" (106, *28*).

Behind all this one can discern a conception not specifically Jewish but common to many ancient religions. The Greek Hades is the most familiar example to modern people. Hades is neither Heaven or Hell; it is almost nothing. I am speaking of the popular beliefs; of course philosophers like Plato have a vivid and positive doctrine of immortality. And of course poets may write fantasies about the world of the dead. These have often no more to do with the real Pagan religion than the fantasies we may write about other planets have to do with real astronomy. In real Pagan belief, Hades was hardly worth talking about; a world of shadows, of decay. Homer (probably far closer to actual beliefs than the later and more sophisticated poets) represents the ghosts as witless. They gibber meaninglessly until some living man gives them sacrificial blood to drink. How the Greeks felt about it in his time is startlingly shown at the beginning of the *Iliad* where he says of men killed in battle that "their souls" went to Hades but "the men themselves" were devoured by dogs and carrion birds. It is the body, even the dead body which is the man himself; the ghost is only a sort of reflection or echo. (The grim impulse sometimes has crossed my mind to wonder whether all this was, is, in fact true; that the merely natural fate of humanity, the fate of unredeemed humanity, is just this — to disintegrate in soul as in body, to be a witless psychic sediment. If so, Homer's idea that only a drink of sacrificial blood can restore a ghost to rationality would be one of the most striking among many Pagan anticipations of the truth.)

Such a conception, vague and marginal even in Paganism, becomes more so in Judaism. Sheol is even dimmer, further in the background, than Hades. It is a thousand miles away from the centre of Jewish religion; especially in the Psalms. They speak of Sheol (or "hell" or "the pit") very much as a man speaks of "death" or "the grave" who has no belief in any sort of future state whatever — a man to whom the dead are simply dead, nothing, and there's no more to be said.

In many passages this is quite clear, even in our translation, to every attentive reader. The clearest of all is the cry in 89, *46*: "O remember how short my time is: why has thou made all men for nought?" We all come to nothing in the end. Therefore "every man living is altogether vanity" (39, *6*). Wise and foolish have the same fate (49, *10*). Once dead, a man worships God no more; "Shall the dust give thanks unto thee?" (30, *10*); "for in death no man remembereth thee" (6, *5*). Death is "the land" where, not only worldly things, but all things, "are forgotten" (88, *19*). When a man dies "all his thoughts perish" (146, *3*). Every man will "follow the generation of his fathers, and shall never see light" (49, *19*): he goes into a darkness which will never end.

Elsewhere of course it sounds as if the poet were praying for the "salvation of his soul" in the Christian sense. Almost certainly he is not. In 30, *3*, "Thou hast brought my soul out of hell" means "you have saved me from death". The snares of death compassed me round about, the pains of hell gat hold upon me" (116, *3*) means "Death was setting snares for me, I felt the anguish of a dying man" — as we should say, "I was at death's door."

As we all know from our New Testaments Judaism had greatly changed in this respect by Our Lord's time. The Sadducees held to the old view. The Pharisees, and apparently many more, believed in the life of the world to come. When, and by what stages, and (under God) from what sources, this new belief crept in, is not part of our present subject. I am more concerned to try to understand the absence of such a belief, in the midst of intense religious feeling, over the earlier period. To some it may seem astonishing that God, having revealed so much of Himself to that people, should not have taught them this.

It does not now astonish me. For one thing there were nations close to the Jews whose religion was overwhelmingly concerned with the afterlife. In reading about ancient Egypt one gets the impression of a culture in which the main business of life was the attempt to secure the well-being of the dead. It looks as if God did not want the chosen people to follow that example. We may ask why. Is it possible for men to be too much concerned with their eternal destiny? In one sense, paradoxical though it sounds, I should reply, Yes.

For the truth seems to me to be that happiness or misery beyond death, simply in themselves, are not even religious subjects at all. A man who believes in them will of course be prudent to seek the one and avoid the other. But that seems to have no more to do with religion than looking after one's health or saving money for one's old age. The only difference here is that the stakes are so very much higher. And this means that, granted a real and steady conviction, the hopes and anxieties aroused are overwhelming. But they are not on that account the more religious. They are hopes for oneself, anxieties for oneself. God is not in the centre. He is still important only for the sake of something else. Indeed such a belief can exist without a belief in God at all. Buddhists are much concerned with what will happen to them after death, but are not, in any true sense, Theists.

It is surely, therefore, very possible that when God began to reveal Himself to men, to show them that He and nothing else is their true goal and the satisfaction of their needs, and that He has a claim upon them simply by being what He is, quite apart from anything He can bestow or deny, it may have been absolutely necessary that this revelation should not begin with any hint of future Beatitude or Perdition. These are not the right point to begin at. An effective belief in them, coming too soon, may even render almost impossible the development of (so to call it) the appetite for God; personal hopes and fears, too obviously exciting, have got in first. Later, when, after centuries of spiritual training, men have learned to desire and adore God, to pant after Him "as pants the hart", it is another matter. For then those who love God will desire not only to enjoy Him but "to enjoy Him forever", and will fear to lose Him. And it is by that door that a truly religious hope of Heaven and fear of Hell can enter; as corollaries to a faith already centred upon God, not as things of any independent or intrinsic weight. It is even arguable that the moment "Heaven" ceases to mean union with God and "Hell" to mean separation from Him, the belief in either is a mischievous superstition; for then we have, on the one hand, a merely "compensatory" belief (a "sequel" to life's sad story, in which everything will "come all right") and, on the other, a nightmare which drives men into asylums or makes them persecutors.

Fortunately, by God's good providence, a strong and steady belief of that self-seeking and subreligious kind is extremely difficult to maintain, and is perhaps possible only to those who are slightly neurotic. Most of us find that our belief in the future life is strong only when God is in the center of our thoughts; that if we try to use the hope of "Heaven" as a compensation (even for the most innocent and natural misery, that of bereavement) it crumbles away. It can, on those terms, be maintained only by arduous efforts of controlled imagination; and we know in our hearts that the imagination is our own. As for Hell, I have often been struck, in reading the "hell-fire sermons" of our older divines, at the desperate efforts they make to render these horrors vivid to their hearers, at their astonishment that men, with such horrors hanging over them, can live as carelessly as they do. But perhaps it is not really astonishing. Perhaps the divines are appealing, on the level of self-centred prudence and self-centered terror, to a belief which, on that level, cannot really exist as a permanent influence on conduct – though of course it may be worked up for a few excited minutes or even hours.

All this is only one man's opinion. And it may be unduly influenced by my own experience. For I (I have said it in another book, but the repetition is unavoidable) was allowed for a whole year to believe in God and try – in some stumbling fashion – to obey Him before any belief in the future life was given me. And that year always seems to me to have been of very great value. It is therefore perhaps natural that I should suspect a similar value in the centuries during which the Jews were in the same position. Other views no doubt can be taken.

Of course among ancient Jews, as among us, there were many levels. They were not all of them, not perhaps any of them at all times, disinterested, any more than we. What then filled the place which was later taken by the hope of Heaven (too often, I am afraid, desired chiefly as an escape from Hell) was of course the hope of peace and plenty on earth. This was in itself no less (but really no more) sub-religious than prudential cares about the next world. It was not quite so personal and self-centred as our own wishes for earthly prosperity. The individual, as such, seems to have been less aware of himself, much less separated from others, in those ancient times. He did not so sharply distingush his own prosperity from that of the nation and especially of his own descendants. Blessings on one's remote posterity were blessings on oneself. Indeed it is not always easy to know whether the speaker in a Psalm is the individual poet or Israel itself. I suspect that sometimes the poet had never raised the question.

But we should be quite mistaken if we supposed that these worldly hopes were the only thing in Judaism. They are not the characteristic thing about it, the thing that sets it apart from ancient religion in general. And notice here the strange roads by which God leads His people. Century after century, by blows which seem to us merciless, by defeat, deportation, and massacre, it was hammered into the Jews that earthly prosperity is not in fact the certain, or even the probable, reward of seeing God. Every hope was disappointed. The lesson taught in the *Book of Job* was grimly illustrated in practice. Such experience would surely have destroyed a religion which had no other centre than the hope of peace and plenty with "every man under his own vine and his own fig tree". And of course many did "fall off". But the astonishing thing is that the religion is not destroyed. In its best representatives it grows purer, stronger, and more profound. It is being, by this terrible discipline, directed more and more to its real centre. That will be the subject of the next chapter.

V

"THE FAIR BEAUTY
OF THE LORD"

"Now let us stint all this and speak of mirth." So far — I couldn't help it — this book has been what the old woman in Scott described as "a cauld clatter o' morality". At last we can turn to better things. If we think "mirth" an unsuitable word for them, that may show how badly we need something which the Psalms can give us perhaps better than any other book in the world.

David, we know, danced before the Ark. He danced with such abandon that one of his wives (presumably a more modern, though not a better, type than he) thought he was making a fool of himself. David didn't care whether he was making a fool of himself or not. He was rejoicing in the Lord. This helps to remind us at the outset that Judaism, though it is the worship of the one true and eternal God, is an ancient religion. That means that its externals, and many of its attitudes, were much more like those of Paganism that they were like all that stuffiness — all that regimen of tiptoe tread and lowered voice — which the word "religion" suggests to so many people now. In one way, of course, this puts a barrier between it and us. We should not have enjoyed the ancient rituals. Every temple in the world, the elegant Parthenon at Athens and the holy Temple at Jerusalem, was a sacred slaughterhouse. (Even the Jews seem to shrink from a return to this. They have not rebuilt the Temple nor revived the sacrifices.) But even that has two sides. If temples smelled of blood, they also smelled of roast meat; they struck a festive and homely note, as well as a sacred.

When I read the Bible as a boy I got the idea that the Temple of Jerusalem was related to the local synagogues very much as a great cathedral is related to the parish churches in a Christian country. In reality there is no such parallel. What happened in the synagogues was quite unlike what happened in the Temple. The synagogues were meeting-houses where the Law was read and where an address might be given — often by some distinguished visitor (as in *Luke* 4, *20* or *Acts* 13, *15*). The Temple was the place of sacrifice, the place where the essential worship of Jahweh was enacted. Every parish church is the descendant of both. By its sermons and lessons it shows its ancestry in the synagogue. But because the Eucharist is

154

celebrated and all other sacraments administered in it, it is like the Temple; it is a place where the adoration of the Deity can be fully enacted. Judaism without the Temple was mutilated, deprived of its central operation; any church, barn, sick-room, or field, can be the Christian's temple.

The most valuable thing the Psalms do for me is to express that same delight in God which made David dance. I am not saying that this is so pure or so profound a thing as the love of God reached by the greatest Christian saints and mystics. But I am not comparing it with that, I am comparing it with the merely dutiful "church-going" and laborious "saying our prayers" to which most of us are, thank God not always, but often, reduced. Against that it stands out as something astonishingly robust, virile, and spontaneous; something we may regard with an innocent envy and may hope to be infected by as we read.

For the reason I have given this delight is very much centered on the Temple. The simpler poets do not in fact distinguish between the love of God in what we might (rather dangerously) call "a spiritual sense" and their enjoyment of the festivals in the Temple. We must not misunderstand this. The Jews were not, like the Greeks, an analytical and logical people; indeed, except the Greeks, no ancient people were. The sort of distinction which we can easily make between those who are really worshipping God in church and those who enjoy "a beautiful service" for musical, antiquarian, or merely sentimental reasons, would have been impossible to them. We get nearest to their state of mind if we think of a pious modern farm-labourer at church on Christmas Day or at the harvest thanksgiving. I mean, of course, one who really believes, who is a regular communicant; not one who goes only on these occasions and is thus (not in the worst but in the best sense of that word) a Pagan, practising Pagan piety, making his bow to the Unknown — and at other times Forgotten — on the great annual festivals. The man I picture is a real Christian. But you would do him wrong by asking him to separate out, at such moments, some exclusively religious element in his mind from all the rest — from his hearty social pleasure in a corporate act, his enjoyment of the hymns (and the crowd), his memoryof other such services since childhood, his well-earned anticipation of rest after harvest or Christmas dinner after church. They are all one in his mind. This would have been even truer of any ancient man, and especially of an ancient Jew. He was a peasant, very close to the soil. He had never heard of music, or festivity, or agriculture as things separate from religion, nor of religion as something separate from them. Life was one. This of course laid him open to spiritual dangers which more sophisticated people can avoid; it also gave him privileges which they lack.

Thus when the Psalmists speak of "seeing" the Lord, or long to "see" Him, most of them mean something that happened to them in the Temple. The fatal way of putting this would be to say "they only mean they have seen the festival". It would be better to say "If we had been there we should have seen only the festival". Thus in 68 "It is well seen, O God, how thou goest[1]...in the sanctuary...the singers go before, the

[1]This was sung while the Ark itself was carried round.

minstrels follow after; in the midst are the damsels playing with the timbrels" (*24, 25*), it is almost as if the poet said "Look, here He comes". If I had been there I should have seen the musicians and the girls with the tambourines; in addition, as another thing, I might or might not have (as we say) "felt" the presence of God. The ancient worshipper would have been aware of no such dualism. Similarly, if a modern man wished to "dwell in the house of the Lord all the days of his life, to behold the fair beauty of the Lord" (*27, 4*) he would mean, I suppose, that he hoped to receive, not of course without the mediation of the sacraments and the help of other "services", but as something distinguishable from them and not to be presumed upon as their inevitable result, frequent moments of spiritual vision and the "sensible" love of God. But I suspect that the poet of that Psalm drew no distinction between "beholding the fair beauty of the Lord" and the acts of worship themselves.

When the mind becomes more capable of abstraction and analysis this old unity breaks up. And no sooner is it possible to distinguish the rite from the vision of God than there is a danger of the rite becoming a substitute for, and a rival to, God Himself. Once it can be thought of separately, it will; and it may then take on a rebellious, cancerous life of its own. There is a stage in a child's life at which it cannot separate the religious from the merely festal character of Chrismas or Easter. I have been told of a very small and very devout boy who was heard murmuring to himself on Easter morning a poem of his own composition which began "Chocolate eggs and Jesus risen". This seems to me, for his age, both admirable poetry and admirable piety. But of course the time will soon come when such a child can no longer effortlessly and spontaneously enjoy that unity. He wll become able to distinguish the spiritual from the ritual and festal aspect of Easter; chocolate eggs will no longer be sacramental. And once he has distinguished he must put one or the other first. If he puts the spiritual first he can still taste something of Easter in the chocolate eggs; if he puts the eggs first they will soon be no more than any other sweetmeat. They have taken on an independent, and therefore a soon withering, life. Either at some period in Judaism, or else in the experience of some Jews, a roughly parallel situation occurred. The unity falls apart; the sacrificial rites become distinguishable from the meeting with God. This does not unfortunately mean that they will cease or become less important. They may, in various evil modes, become even more important than before. They may be valued as a sort of commercial transaction with a greedy God who somehow really wants or needs large quantities of carcasses and whose favours cannot be secured on any other terms. Worse still, they may be regarded as the only thing He wants, so that their punctual performance will satisfy Him without obedience to His demands for mercy, "judgement", and truth. To the priests themselves the whole system will seem important simply because it is both their art and their livelihood; all their pedantry, all their pride, all their economic position, is bound up with it. They will elaborate their art more and more. And of course the corrective to these views of sacrifice can be found within Judaism itself. The prophets continually fulminate against it. Even the Psalter, though largely a Temple collection, can do so; as in Psalm 50 where God tells His people that all this Temple worship, considered in itself, is not the real point at all, and particularly ridicules the genuinely Pagan notion that He really needs to be fed with roast meat. "If I were hungry, do you think I would apply to *you?*" (*12*). I have sometimes fancied He might similarly ask a certain type of modern clergyman, "If I wanted music – if I were conducting research into the more recondite details of the history of the Western Rite – do you really think *you* are the source I would rely on?"

This possible degradation of sacrifice and the rebukes of it are, however, so well known that there is no need to stress them here. I want to stress what I think that we (or at least I) need more; the joy and delight in God which meet us in the Psalms, however loosely or closely, in this or that instance, they may be connected with the Temple. This is the living centre of Judaism. These poets knew far less reason than we for loving God. They did not know that He offered them eternal joy; still less that He would die to win it for them. Yet they express a longing for Him, for His mere presence, which comes only to the best Christians or to Christians in their best moments. They long to live all their days in the Temple so that they may constantly see "the fair beauty of the Lord" (*27, 4*). Their longing to go up to Jerusalem and "appear before the presence of God" is like a physical thirst (*42*). From Jerusalem His presence flashes out "in perfect beauty" (*50, 2*). Lacking that encounter with Him, their souls are parched like a waterless countryside (*63, 2*). They crave to be "satisfied with the pleasures" of His house (*65, 4*). Only there can they be at ease, like a bird in the nest (*84, 3*). One day of those "pleasures" is better than a lifetime spent elsewhere (*10*).

I have rather – though the expression may seem harsh to some – called this the "appetite for God" than "the love of God". The "Love of God" too easily suggests the word "spiritual" in all those negative or restrictive senses which it has unhappily acquired. These old poets do not seem to think that they are meritorious or pious for having such feelings; nor, on the other hand, that they are privileged in being given the grace to have them. They are at once less priggish about it than the worst of us and less humble – one might almost say, less surprised – than the best of us. It has all the cheerful spontaneity of a natural, even a physical, desire. It is gay and jocund. They are glad and rejoice (*9, 2*). Their fingers itch for the harp (*43, 4*), for the lute and the harp – wake up, lute and harp! – (*57, 9*); let's have a song, bring the tambourine, bring the "merry harp with the lute", we're going to sing merrily and make a cheerful noise (*81, 1, 2*). Noise, you may well say. Mere music is not enough. Let everyone, even the benighted gentiles,[1] clap their hands (*47, 1*). Let us have clashing cymbals, not only well tuned, but *loud*, and dances too (*150, 5*). Let even the remote islands (all islands were remote, for the Jews were no sailors) share the exultation (*97, 1*).

I am not saying that this gusto – if you like, this rowdiness – can or should be revived. Some of it cannot be revived because it is not dead but with us still. It would be idle to pretend that we Anglicans are a striking example. The Romans, the

[1] Not "all ye people" as in our version, but "all ye nations" (Goyim).

Orthodox, and the Salvation Army all, I think, have retained more of it than we. We have a terrible concern about good taste. Yet even we can still exult. The second reason goes far deeper. All Christians know something the Jews did not know about what it "cost to redeem their souls". Our life as Christians begins by being baptised into a death; our most joyous festivals begin with, and centre upon, the broken body and the shed blood. There is thus a tragic depth in our worship which Judaism lacked. Our joy has to be the sort of joy which can coexist with that; there is for us a spiritual conterpoint where they had simple melody. But this does not in the least cancel the delighted debt which I, for one, feel that I owe to the most jocund Psalms. There, despite the presence of elements we should now find it hard to regard as religious at all, and the absence of elements which some might think essential to religion, I find an experience fully God-centred, asking of God no gift more urgently than His presence, the gift of Himself, joyous to the highest degree, and unmistakably real. What I see (so to speak) in the faces of these old poets tells me more about the God whom they and we adore.

But this characteristically Hebraic delight or gusto finds also another channel. We must follow it in the next chapter.

VI

"SWEETER THAN HONEY"

In Racine's tragedy of *Athalie* the chorus of Jewish girls sing an ode about the original giving of the Law on Mount Sinai, which has the remarkable refrain *ô charmante loi* (Act I, scene iv). Of course it will not do—it will border on the comic—to translate this "oh charming Law". *Charming* in English has come to be a tepid and even patronising word; we use it of a pretty cottage, of a book that is something less than great or a woman who is something less than beautiful. How we should translate *chamante* I don't know; "enchanting?"—"delightful?"—"beautiful?" None of them quite fits. What is, however, certain is that Racine (a mighty poet and steeped in the Bible) is here coming nearer than any modern writer I know to a feeling very characteristic of certain Psalms. And it is a feeling which I at first found utterly bewildering.

"More to be desired are they than gold, yea than much fine gold: sweeter also than honey and the honeycomb" (19, *10*). One can well understand this being said of God's mercies, God's visitations, His attributes. But what the poet is actually talking about is God's law, His commands; His "ruling" as Dr. Moffatt well translates in verse *9* (for "judgements" here plainly means decisions about conduct). What is being compared to gold and honey is those "statutes" (in the Latin version "decrees") which, we are told, "rejoice the heart" (*8*). For the whole poem is about the Law, not about "Judgement" in the sense to which Chapter I was devoted.

This was to me at first very mysterious. "Thou shalt not steal, thou shalt not commit adultery"—I can understand that a man can, and must, respect these "statutes", and try to obey them, and assent to them in his heart. But it is very hard to find how they could be, so to speak, delicious, how they exhilarate. If this is difficult at any time, it is doubly so when obedience to either is opposed to some strong, and perhaps *in itself* innocent, desire. A man held back by his unfortunate previous marriage to some lunatic or criminal who never dies from some woman whom he faithfully loves, or a hungry man left alone, without money, in a shop filled with the smell and sight of new bread, roasting coffee, or fresh strawberries—can these find the prohibition of adultery or of theft at all like honey? They may obey, they may still respect the "statute". But surely it could be more aptly compared to the dentist's forceps or the front line than to anything enjoyable and sweet.

A fine Christian and a great scholar to whom I once put this question said he thought that the poets were referring to the satisfaction men felt in knowing they had obeyed the Law; in other words, to the "pleasures of a good conscience". They would, on his view, be meaning something very like what Wordsworth meant when he said we know nothing more beautiful than the "smile" on Duty's face — her smile when her orders have been carried out. It is rash for me to differ from such a man, and his view certainly makes excellent sense. The difficulty is that the Psalmists never seem to me to say anything very like this.

In 1, 2 we are told that the good man's "delight is in the law of the Lord, and in his law will he exercise himself day and night". To "exercise himself" in it apparently does not mean to obey it (though of course the good man will do that too) but to study it, as Dr. Moffatt says to "pore over it". Of course "the Law" does not here mean simply the ten commandments, it means the whole complex legislation (religious, moral, civil, criminal and even constitutional) contained in *Leviticus*, *Numbers* and *Deuteronomy*. The man who "pores upon it" is obeying Joshua's command (*Joshua 1, 8*), "the book of the Law shall not depart out of thy mouth; but thou shalt meditate therein day and night." This means, among other things, that the Law was a study or, as we should say, a "subject"; a thing on which there would be commentaries, lectures, and examinations. There were. Thus part (religiously, the least important part) of what an ancient Jew meant when he said "delighted in the Law" was very like what one of us would mean if he said that somebody "loved" history, or physics, or archaeology. This might imply a wholly innocent — though, of course, merely natural — delight in one's favourite subject; or, on the other hand, the pleasures of conceit, pride in one's own learning and consequent contempt for the outsiders who don't share it, or even a venal admiration for the studies which secure one's own stipend and social position.

The danger of this second development is of course increased tenfold when the study in question is from the outset stamped as sacred. For then the danger of spiritual pride is added to that of mere ordinary pedantry and conceit. One is sometimes (not often) glad not to be a great theologian; one might so easily mistake it for being a good Christian. The temptations to which a great philologist or a great chemist is exposed are trivial in comparison. When the subject is sacred, proud and clever men may come to think that the outsiders who don't know it are not merely inferior to them in skill but lower in God's eyes; as the priests said (*John 7, 49*), "All that rabble who are not experts in the Torah are accursed." And as this pride increases, the "subject" or study which confers such privilege will grow more and more complicated, the list of things forbidden will increase, till to get through a single day without supposed sin becomes like an elaborate step-dance, and this horrible network breeds self-righteousness in some and haunting anxiety in others. Meanwhile the "weightier matters of the Law", righteousness itself, shrinks into insignificance under this vast overgrowth, so that the legalists strain at a gnat and swallow a camel.

Thus the Law, like the sacrifice, can take on a cancerous life of its own and work against the thing for whose sake it existed. As Charles Williams wrote, "When the means are autonomous they are deadly." This morbid condition of the Law contributed to—I do not suggest it is the sole or main cause of—St. Paul's joyous sense of Christ as the Deliverer from Law. It is against this same morbid condition that Our Lord uttered some of His sternest words; it is the sin, and simultaneously the punishment, of the Scribes and Pharisees. But that is not the side of the matter I want to stress here, nor does it by this time need stressing. I would rather let the Psalms show me again the good thing of which this bad thing is the corruption.

As everyone knows, the Psalm specially devoted to the Law is 119, the longest in the whole collection. And everyone has probably noticed that from the literary or technical point of view, it is the most formal and elaborate of them all. The technique consists in taking a series of words which are all, for purposes of this poem, more or less synonyms (*word, statutes, commandments, testimonies,* etc.), and ringing the changes on them through each of its eight-verse sections—which themselves correspond to the letters of the alphabet. (This may have given an ancient ear something of the same sort of pleasure we get from the Italian metre called the *Sestina*, where instead of rhymes we have the same end words repeated in varying orders in each stanza.) In other words, this poem is not, and does not pretend to be, a sudden outpouring of the heart like, say, Psalm 18. It is a pattern, a thing done like embroidery, stitch by stitch, through long, quiet hours, for love of the subject and for the delight in leisurely, disciplined craftsmanship.

Now this, in itself, seems to me very important because it lets us into the mind and mood of the poet. We can guess at once that he felt abut the Law somewhat as he felt about his poetry; both involved exact and loving conformity to an intricate pattern. This at once suggests an attitude from which the Pharisaic conception could later grow but which in itself, though not nessarily religious, is quite innocent. It will look like priggery or pedantry (or else like a neurotic fussiness) to those who cannot sympathise with it, but it need not be any of these things. It may be the delight in Order, the pleasure in getting a thing "just so"—as in dancing a minuet. Of course the poet is well aware that something incomparably more serious than a minuet is here in question. He is also aware that he is very unlikely, himself, to achieve this perfection of discipline: "O that my ways *were* made so straight that I *might* keep thy statutes!" (*5*). At present they aren't and he can't. But his effort to do so does not spring from servile fear. The Order of the Divine mind, embodied in the Divine Law, is beautiful. What should a man do but try to reproduce it, so far as possible, in his daily life? His "delight" is in those statutes (*16*); to study them is like finding treasure (*14*); they affect him like music, are his "songs" (*54*); they taste like honey (*103*); they are better than silver and gold (*72*). As one's eyes are more and more opened, one sees more and more in them, and it excites wonder (*18*). This is not priggery nor even scrupulosity; it is the language of a man ravished by a moral beauty. If we cannot at all share his experience, we shall be the losers. Yet I cannot help fancying that a Chinese Christian — one whose own traditional culture had been the "schoolmaster to bring him to Christ" — would appreciate this Psalm more than most of us; for it is an old idea in that culture that life should above all things be ordered and that its order should reproduce a Divine order.

But there is something else to our purpose in this grave poem. On three occasions the poet asserts that the Law is "true" or "the truth" (*86, 138, 142*). We find the same in III,7, "all his commandments are true". (The word, I understand, could also be translated "faithful", or "sound"; what is, in the Hebrew sense, "true" is what "holds water", what doesn't "give way" or collapse.) A modern logician would say that the Law is a command and that to call a command "true" makes no sense; "The door is shut" may be true or false but "Shut the door" can't. But I think we all see pretty well what the Psalmists mean. They mean that in the Law you find the "real" or "correct" or stable, well-grounded, directions for living. The law answers the question "Wherewithal shall a young man cleanse his way?" (119, *9*). It is like a lamp, a guide (*105*). There are many rival directions for living, as the Pagan cultures all round us show. When the poets call the directions or "rulings" of Jahweh "true" they are expressing the assurance that these, and not those others, are the "real" or "valid" or unassailable ones; that they are based on the very nature of things and the very nature of God.

By this assurance they put themselves, implicitly, on the right side of a controversy which arose far later among Christians. There were in the eighteenth century terrible theologians who held that "God did not command certain things because they are right, but certain things are right because God commanded them". To make the position perfectly clear, one of them even said that though God has, as it happens, commanded us to love Him and one another, He might equally well have commanded us to hate Him and one another, and hatred would then have been right. It was apparently a mere toss-up which He decided on. Such a view of course makes God a mere arbitrary tyrant. It would be better and less irreligious to believe in no God and to have ethics than to have such an ethics and such a theology as this. The Jews of course never discuss this in abstract and philosophical terms. But at once, and completely, they assume the right view, knowing better than they know. They know that the Lord (not merely obedience to the Lord) is "righteous" and commands "righteousness" because He loves it (II, *8*). He enjoins what is good because it is good, because He is good. Hence His laws have *emeth* "truth," intrinsic validity, rock-bottom reality, being rooted in His own nature, and are therefore as solid as that Nature which He has created. But the Psalmists themselves can say it best; "thy righteousness standeth like the strong mountains, thy judgements are like the great deep" (36, *6*).[1] Their delight in the Law is a delight in having touched firmness; like

[1]See Appendix I, page 203.

the pedestrian's delight in feeling the hard road beneath his feet after a false short cut has long entangled him in muddy fields.

For there were other roads, which lacked "truth". The Jews had as their immediate neighbours, close to them in race as well as in position, Pagans of the worst kind, Pagans whose religion was marked by none of that beauty or (sometimes) wisdom which we can find among the Greeks. That background made the "beauty" or "sweetness" of the Law more visible; not least because these neighbouring Paganisms were a constant temptation to the Jew and may in some of their externals have been not unlike his own religion. The temptation was to turn to those terrible rites in times of terror – when, for example, the Assyrians were pressing on. We who not so long ago waited daily for invasion by enemies, like the Assyrians, skilled and constant in systematic cruelty, know how they may have felt. They were tempted, since the Lord seemed deaf, to try those appalling deities who demanded so much more and might therefore perhaps give more in return. But when a Jew in some happier hour, or a better Jew even in that hour, looked at those worships – when he thought of sacred prostitution, sacred sodomy, and the babies thrown into the fire for Moloch – his own "Law" as he turned back to it must have shone with an extraordinary radiance. Sweeter than honey; or if that metaphor does not suit us who have not such a sweet tooth as all ancient peoples (partly because we have plenty of sugar), let us say like mountain water, like fresh air after a dungeon, like sanity after a nightmare. But once again, the best image is in a Psalm, the 19th.[1]

I take this to be the greatest poem in the Psalter and one of the greatest lyrics in the world. Most readers will remember its structure; six verses about Nature, five about the Law, and four of personal prayer. The actual words supply no logical connection between the first and second movements. In this way its technique resembles that of the most modern poetry. A modern poet would pass with similar abruptness from one theme to another and leave you to find out the connecting link for yourself. But then he would possibly be doing this quite deliberately; he might have, though he chose to conceal, a perfectly clear and conscious link in his own mind which he could express to you in logical prose if he wanted to. I doubt if the ancient poet was like that. I think he felt, effortlessly and without reflecting on it, so close a connection, indeed (for his imagination) such an identity, between his first theme and his second that he passed from the one to the other without realising that he had made any transititon. First he thinks of the sky; how, day after day, the pageantry we see there shows us the splendour of its Creator. Then he thinks of the sun, the bridal joyousness of its rising, the unimaginable speed of its daily voyage from east to west. Finally, of its heat; not of course the mild heats of our climate but the cloudless, blinding, tyrannous rays hammering the hills, searching every cranny. The key phrase on which the whole poem depends is "there is nothing hid from the heat thereof". It pierces everwhere with its strong, clean ardour. Then at once, in verse 7 he is talking of something else, which hardly seems to him something else because it is so like the all-piercing, all-

[1] See Appendix I, page 202.

detecting sunshine. The Law is "undefiled", the Law gives light, it is clean and everlasting, it is "sweet". No one can improve on this and nothing can more fully admit us to the old Jewish feeling about the Law; luminous, severe, disinfectant, exultant. One hardly needs to add that this poet is wholly free from self-righteousness and the last section is concerned with his "secret faults." As he has felt the sun, perhaps in the desert, searching him out in every nook of shade where he attempted to hide from it, so he feels the Law searching out all the hiding-places of his soul.

In so far as this idea of the Law's beauty, sweetness, or preciousness, arose from the contrast of the surrounding Paganisms, we may soon find occasion to recover it. Christians increasingly live on a spiritual island; new and rival ways of life surround it in all directions and their tides come further up the beach every time. None of these new ways is yet so filthy or cruel as some Semitic Paganism. But many of them ignore all individual rights and are already cruel enough. Some give morality a wholly new meaning which we cannot accept, some deny its possibility. Perhaps we shall all learn, sharply enough, to value the clean air and "sweet reasonableness" of the Christian ethics which in a more Christian age we might have taken for granted. But of course, if we do, we shall then be exposed to the danger of priggery. We might come to "thank God that we are not as other men". This introduces the greatest difficulty which the Psalms have raised in my mind.

VII

CONNIVANCE

Every attentive reader of the Psalms will have noticed that they speak to us severely not merely about doing evil ourselves but about something else. In 26, *4,* the good man is not only free from "vanity" (falsehood) but has not even "dwelled with", been on intimate terms with, those who are "vain". He has " hated" them *(5).* So in 31, *7,* he has "hated" idolaters. In 50, *18,* God blames a man not for being a thief but for "consenting to" (in Dr. Moffatt, "you are a friend to any thief you see"). In 141, *4 – 6,* where our translation appears to be rather wrong, the general sense nevertheless comes through and expresses the same attitude. Almost comically the Psalmist of 139 asks "Don't I hate those who hate thee, Lord?. . . . Why, I hate them as if they were *my* enemies!" *(21, 22).*

Now obviously all this – taking upon oneself to hate those whom one thinks God's enemies, avoiding the society of those one thinks wicked, judging our neighbours, thinking oneself "too good" for some of them (not in the snobbish way, which is a trivial sin in comparison, but in the deepest meaning of the words "too good") – is an extremely dangerous, almost a fatal, game. It leads straight to "Pharisaism" in the sense which Our Lord's own teaching has given to that word. It leads not only to the wickedness but to the absurdity of those who in later times came to be called the "unco guid". This I assume from the outset, and I think that even in the Psalms this evil is already at work. But we must not be Pharisaical even to the Pharisees. It is foolish to read such passages without realising that a quite genuine problem is involved. And I am not at all confident about the solution.

We hear it said again and again that the editor of some newspaper is a rascal, that some politician is a liar, that some official person is a tyrannical Jack-in-office and even dishonest, that someone has treated his wife abominably, that some celebrity (film-star, author, or what not) leads a most vile and mischievous life. And the general rule in modern society is that no one refuses to meet any of these people and to behave towards them in the friendliest and most cordial manner. People will even go out of their way to meet them. They will not even stop buying the rascally newspaper, thus paying the owner for the lies, the detestable intrusions upon private

165

life and private tragedy, the blasphemies and the pornography, which they profess to condemn.

I have said there is a problem here, but there are really two. One is social and almost political. It may be asked whether that state of society in which rascality undergoes no social penalty is a healthy one; whether we should not be a happier country if certain important people were pariahs as the hangman once was — blackballed at every club, dropped by every acquaintance, and liable to the print of riding-crop or fingers across the face if they were ever bold enough to speak to a respectable woman. It leads into the larger question whether the great evil of our civil life is not the fact that there seems now no medium between hopeless submission and full-dress revolution. Rioting has died out, moderate rioting. It can be argued that if the windows of various ministries and newspapers were more often broken, if certain people were more often put under pumps and (mildly — mud, not stones) pelted in the streets, we should get on a great deal better. It is not wholly desirable that any man should be allowed at once the pleasures of a tyrant or a wolf's- head and also those of an honest freeman among his equals. To this question I do not know the answer. The dangers of a change in the direction I have outlined are very great; so are the evils of our present tameness.

I am concerned here only with the problem that appears in our individual and private lives. How ought we to behave in the presence of very bad people? I will limit this by changing "very bad people" to "very bad people who are powerful, prosperous and impenitent." If they are outcasts, poor and miserable, whose wickedness obviously has not "paid", then every Christian knows the answer. Christ speaking to the Samaritan woman at the well, Christ with the woman taken in adultery, Christ dining with publicans, is our example. I mean, of course, that His humility, His love. His total indifference to the social discredit and misrepresentation He might incur are examples for us; not, Heaven knows, that any of us who was not specially qualified to do so by priesthood, age, old acquaintance, or the earnest request of the sinners themselves, could without insolence and presumption assume the least trace of His authority to rebuke and pardon. (One has to be very careful lest the desire to patronise and the itch to be a busybody should disguise itself as a vocation to help the "fallen", or tend to obscure our knowledge that we are fallen — perhaps in God's eyes far more so — ourselves.) But of course there were probably others who equally consorted with "publicans and sinners" and whose motives were very unlike those of our Lord.

The publicans were the lowest members of what may be called the Vichy or Collaborationist movement in Palestine; men who fleeced their fellow countrymen to get money for the occupying power in return for a fat percentage of the swag. As such they were like the hangman, outside all decent social intercourse. But some of them did pretty well financially, and no doubt most of them enjoyed, up to a point, the protection and contemptuous favors of the Roman government. One may guess that some consorted with them for very bad reasons — to get "pickings", to be on good terms with such dangerous neighbours. Besides Our Lord there would have been among their guests toadies and those who wanted to be "on the band-wagon"; people in fact like a young man I once knew.

He had been a strict socialist at Oxford. Everything ought to be run by the State; private enterprise and independent professions were for him the great evil. He then went away and became a schoolmaster. After about ten years of that he came to see me. He said his political views had been wholly reversed. You never heard a fuller recantation. He now saw that State interference was fatal. What had converted him was his experience as a schoolmaster of the Ministry of Education – a set of ignorant meddlers armed with insufferable powers to pester, hamper and interrupt the work of real, practical teachers who knew the subjects they taught, who knew boys, parents, and all the real conditions of their work. It makes no difference to the point of the story whether you agree with his view of the Ministry; the important thing is that he held that view. For the real point of the story, and of his visit, when it came, nearly took my breath away. Thinking thus, he had come to see whether I had any influence which might help him to get a job in the Ministry of Education.

Here is the perfect band-wagoner. Immediately on the decision "This is a revolting tyranny," follows the question "How can I as quickly as possible cease to be one of the victims and become one of the tyrants?" If I had been able to introduce the young man to someone in the Ministry, I think we may be sure that his manners to that hated "meddler" would have been genial and friendly in the extreme. Thus someone who had heard his previous invective against the meddling and then witnessed his actual behavior to the meddler, might possibly (for clarity "believeth all things") have concluded that this young man was full of the purest Christianity and loved one he thought a sinner while hating what he thought his sin.

Of course this is an instance of band-wagoning so crude and unabashed as to be farcical. Not many of us perhaps commit the like. But there are subtler, more social or intellectual forms of band-wagoning which might deceive us. Many people have a very strong desire to meet celebrated or "important" people, including those of whom they disapprove, from curiosity or vanity. It gives them something to talk or even (anyone may produce a book of reminiscences) to write about. It is felt to confer distinction if the great, though odious, man recognises you in the street. And where such motives are in play it is better still to know him quite well, to be intimate with him. It would be delightful if he shouted out "Hello Bill" while you were walking down the Strand with an impressionable country cousin. I don't know that the desire is itself a very serious defect. But I am incllined to think a Christian would be wise to avoid, where he decently can, any meeting with people who are bullies, lascivious, cruel, dishonest, spiteful and so forth.

Not because we are "too good" for them. In a sense because we are not good enough. We are not good enough to cope with all the temptations, nor clever enough to cope with all the problems, which an evening spent in such society produces. The temptation is to condone, to connive at; by our words, looks and laughter, to "consent". The temptation was never greater than now when we are all (and very rightly) so afraid of priggery or "smugness." And of course, even if we do not seek them out, we shall constantly be in such company whether we wish it or not. This is the real and unavoidable difficulty.

We shall hear vile stories told as funny; not merely licentious stories but (to me far more serious and less noticed) stories which the teller could not be telling unless he was betraying someone's confidence. We shall hear infamous detraction of the absent, often disguised as pity or humour. Things we hold sacred will be mocked. Cruelty will be slyly advocated by the assumption that its only opposite is "sentimentality". The very presuppositions of any possible good life—all disinterested motives, all heroism, all genuine forgiveness—will be, not explicitly denied (for then the matter could be discussed), but assumed to be phantasmal, idiotic, believed in only by children.

What is one to do? For on the one hand, quite certainly, there is a degree of unprotesting participation in such talk which is very bad. We are strengthening the hands of the enemy. We are encouraging him to believe that "those Christians", once you get them off their guard and round a dinner table, really think and feel exactly as he does. By implication we are denying our Master; behaving as if we "knew not the Man". On the other hand is one to show that, like Queen Victoria, one is "not amused"? Is one to be contentious, interrupting the flow of conversation at every moment with "I don't agree, I don't agree"? Or rise and go away? But by these courses we may also confirm some of their worst suspicions of "those Christians". We are just the sort of ill-mannered prigs they always said.

Silence is a good refuge. People will not notice it nearly so easily as we tend to suppose. And (better still) few of us enjoy it as we might be in danger of enjoying more forcible methods. Disagreement can, I think, sometimes be expressed without the appearance of priggery, if it is done argumentatively, not dictatorially; support will often come from some most unlikely member of the party, or from more than one, till we discover that those who were silently dissentient were actually a majority. A discussion of real interest may follow. Of course the right side may be defeated in it. That matters very much less than I used to think. The very man who has argued you down will sometimes be found, years later, to have been influenced by what you said.

There comes of course a degree of evil against which a protest will have to be made, however little chance it has of success. There are cheery agreements in cynicism or brutality which one must contract out of unambiguously. If it can't be done without seeming priggish, then priggish we must seem.

For what really matters is not seeming but being a prig. If we sufficiently dislike making the protest, if we are strongly tempted not to, we are unlikely to be priggish in reality. Those who positively enjoy, as they call it, "testifying" are in a different and more dangerous position. As for the mere seeming—well, though it is very bad to be a prig, there are social atmospheres so foul that in them it is almost an alarming symptom if a man has never been called one. Just in the same way, though pedantry is a folly and snobbery a vice, yet there are circles in which only a man indifferent to all accuracy will escape being called a pedant, and others where manners are so coarse, flashy and shameless that a man (whatever his social position) of any natural good taste will be called a snob.

What makes this contact with wicked people so difficult is that to handle the situation successfully requires not merely good intentions, even with humility and courage thrown in; it may call for social and even intellectual talents which God has not given us. It is therefore not self-righteousness but mere prudence to avoid it when we can. The Psalmists were not quite wrong when they described the good man as avoiding "the seat of the scornful" and fearing to consort with the ungodly lest he should "eat of" (shall we say, laugh at, admire, approve, justify?) "such things as please them". As usual in their attitude, with all its dangers, there is a core of very good sense. "Lead us not into temptation" often means, among other things "Deny me those gratifying invitations, those highly interesting contacts, that participation in the brilliant movements of our age, which I so often, at such risk, desire."

Closely connected with these warnings against what I have called "connivance" are the protests of the Psalter[1] against other sins of the tongue. I think that when I began to read it these surprised me a little; I had half expected that in a simpler and more violent age when more evil was done with the knife, the big stick, and the firebrand, less would be done by talk. But in reality the Psalmists mention hardly any kind of evil more often than this one, which the most civilised societies share. "Their throat is an open sepulchre, they flatter" (5, *10*), "under his tongue is ungodliness and vanity", or "perjury" as Dr. Moffatt translates it (10, *7*), "deceitful lips" (12, *3*), "lying lips" (31, *20*). "words full of deceit" (36, *3*) the "whispering" of evil men (41, *7*), cruel lies that "cut like a razor" (52, *3*), talk that sounds "smooth as oil" and will wound like a sword (55, *22*), pitiless jeering (102, *8*). It is all over the Psalter. One almost hears the incessant whispering, tattling, lying, scolding, flattery, and circulation of rumours. No historical readjustments are here required, we are in the world we know. We even detect in that muttering and wheedling chorus voices which are familiar. One of them may be too familiar for recognition.

[1]Some of these probably involve archaic, and even magical, ideas of a power intrinsic in words themselves, so that all blessings and cursings would be efficacious.

VIII

NATURE

Two factors determine the Psalmists' approach to Nature. The first they share with the vast majority of ancient writers; the second was in their time, if not absolutely unique, extremely rare.

i. They belong to a nation chiefly of peasants. For us the very name Jew is associated with finance, shopkeeping, money-lending and the like. This however, dates from the Middle Ages when the Jews were not allowed to own land and were driven into occupations remote from the soil. Whatever characteristics the modern Jew has acquired from millennia of such occupations, they cannot have been those of his ancient ancestors. Those were peasants or farmers. When even a king covets a piece of his neighbour's property, the piece is a vineyard; he is more like a wicked squire than a wicked king. Everyone was close to the land; everyone vividly aware of our dependence on soils and weather. So, till a late age, was every Greek and Roman. Thus part of what we should now, perhaps, call "appreciation of Nature" could not then exist – all that part which is really delight in "the country" as a contrast to the town. Where towns are few and very small and where nearly everyone is on the land, one is not aware of any special thing called "the country". Hence a certain sort of "nature poetry" never existed in the ancient world till really vast cities like Alexandria arose; and, after the fall of ancient civilisation, it never existed again until the eighteenth century. At other periods what we call "the country" is simply the world, what water is to a fish. Nevertheless appreciation of Nature can exist; a delight which is both utilitarian and poetic. Homer can enjoy a landscape, but what he means by a beautiful landscape is one that is useful – good deep soil, plenty of fresh water, pasture that will make the cows really fat, and some nice timber. Being one of a seafaring race he adds, as a Jew would not, a good harbour. The Psalmists, who are writing lyrics not romances, naturally give us little landscape. What they do give us, far more sensuously and delightedly than anything I have seen in Greek, is the very feel of weather – weather seen with a real countryman's eyes, enjoyed almost as a

170

vegetable might be supposed to enjoy it. "Thou art good to the earth . . . thou waterest her furrows . . . thou makest it soft with the drops of rain . . . the little hills shall rejoice on every side . . . the valleys shall stand so thick with corn that they shall laugh and sing" (65, *9-14*). In 104, *16* (better in Dr. Moffatt than in the Prayer Book), "the great trees drink their fill".

ii. The Jews, as we all know, believed in one God, maker of heaven and earth. Nature and God were distinct; the One had made the other; the One ruled and the other obeyed. This, I say, we all know. But for various reasons its real significance can easily escape a modern reader if his studies happen not to have led him in certain directions.

In the first place it is for us a platitude. We take it for granted. Indeed I suspect that many people assume that some clear doctrine of creation underlies all religions: that in Paganism the gods, or one of the gods, usually created the world; even that religions normally begin by answering the question, "Who made the world?" In reality, creation, in any unambiguous sense, seems to be a surprisingly rare doctrine; and when stories about it occur in Paganism they are often religiously unimportant, not in the least central to the religions in which we find them. They are on the fringe where religion tails off into what was perhaps felt, even at the time, to be more like fairy-tale. In one Egyptian story a god called Atum came up out of the water and, being apparently a hermaphrodite, begot and bore the two next gods; after that, things could get on. In another, the whole senate of the gods came up out of Nun, the Deep. According to a Babylonian myth, before heaven and earth were made a being called Aspu begot, and a being called Tiamat bore, Lahmu and Lahamu, who in their turn produced Anshar and Kishar. We are expressly told that this pair were greater than their parents, so that it is more like a myth of evolution than of creation. In the Norse myth we begin with ice and fire, and indeed with a north and south, amidst all of which, somehow, a giant comes to life, who bears (from his arm-pit) a son and daughter. Greek mythology starts with heaven and earth already in existence.

I do not mention these myths to indulge in a cheap laugh at their crudity. All our language about such things, that of the theologian as well as that of the child, is crude. The real point is that the myths, even in their own terms, do not reach the idea of Creation in our sense at all. Things "come up out of" something or "are formed in" something. If the stories could, for the moment, be supposed true, they would still be stories about very early events in a process of development, a world-history, which was already going on. When the curtain rises in these myths there are always some "properties" already on the stage and some sort of drama is proceeding. You may say they answer the question "How did the play begin?" But that is an ambiguous question. Asked by the man who arrived ten minutes late it would be properly answered, say, with the words, "Oh, first three witches came in, and then there was a scene between an old king and a wounded soldier." That is the sort of question the myths are in fact answering. But the very different question: "How does a play originate? Does it write itself? Do the actors make it up as they go along? Or is there someone — not on the stage, not like the people on the stage — someone we don't see — who invented it all and caused it to be?" — this is rarely asked or answered.

We do of course find in Plato a clear Theology of Creation in the Judaic and Christian sense; the whole universe — the very conditions of time and space under which it exists — are produced by the will of a perfect, timeless, unconditioned God who is above and outside all that He makes. But this is an amazing leap (though not made without the help of Him who is the Father of lights) by an overwhelming theological genius; it is not ordinary Pagan religion.

Now we all understand of course the importance of this peculiarity in Judaic thought from a strictly and obviously religious point of view. But its total consequences, the ways in which it changes a man's whole mind and imagination, might escape us.

To say that God created Nature, while it brings God and Nature into relation, also separates them. What makes and what is made must be two, not one. Thus the doctrine of Creation in one sense empties Nature of divinity. How very hard this was to do and, still more, to keep on doing, we do not now easily realise. A passage from *Job* (not without its own wild poetry in it) may help us: if I beheld the sun when it shined, or the moon walking in brightness: and my heart hath been secretly enticed, or my mouth kissed my hand; this also would be an iniquity" (31, *26 – 28*). There is here no question of turning, in a time of desperate need, to devilish gods. The speaker is obviously referring to an utterly spontaneous impulse, a thing you might find yourself acting upon almost unawares. To pay some reverence to the sun or moon is apparently so natural; so apparently innocent. Perhaps in certain times and places it was really innocent. I would gladly believe that the gesture of homage offered to the moon was sometimes accepted by her Maker; in those times of ignorance which God "winked at" (*Acts* 17, *30*). The author of Job, however, was not in that ignorance. If he had kissed his hand to the Moon it would have been iniquity. The impulse was a temptation; one which no European has felt for the last thousand years.

But in another sense the same doctrine which empties Nature of her divinity also makes her an index, a symbol, a manifestation, of the Divine. I must recall two passages quoted in an earlier chapter. One is that from Psalm 19 where the searching and cleansing sun becomes an image of the searching and cleansing Law. The other is from 36: "Thy mercy, O Lord, reacheth unto the heavens, and thy faithfulness unto the clouds. Thy righteousness standeth like the strong mountains, thy judgements are like the great deep" (5, *6*). It is surely just because the natural objects are no longer taken to be themselves Divine that they can now be magnificent symbols of Divinity. There is little point in comparing a Sun-god with the Sun or Neptune with the great deep; there is much in comparing the Law with the Sun or saying that God's judgements are an abyss and a mystery like the sea.

But of course the doctrine of Creation leaves Nature full of manifestations which show the presence of God, and created energies which serve Him. The light is His garment, the thing we partially see Him through (104, 2), the thunder can be His voice (29, 3−5). He dwells in the dark thundercloud (18, *11*), the eruption of a volcano comes in answer to His touch (104, 32). The world is full of his emissaries and executors. He makes winds His messengers and flames His servants (104, 4), rides upon cherubim (18, *10*), commands the army of angels.

All this is of course in one way very close to Paganism. Thor and Zeus also spoke in the thunder; Hermes or Iris was the messenger of the gods. But the difference, though subtle, is momentous, between hearing in the thunder the voice of God or the voice of a god. As we have seen, even in the creation-myths, gods have beginnings. Most of them have fathers and mothers; often we know their birth-places. There is no question of self-existence or the timeless. Being is imposed upon them, as upon us, by preceding causes. They are, like us, creatures or products; though they are luckier than we in being stronger, more beautiful, and exempt from death. They are, like us, actors in the cosmic drama, not its authors. Plato fully understood this. His God creates the gods and preserves them from death by His own power; they have no inherent immortality. In other words, the difference between believing in God and in many gods is not one of arithmetic. As someone has said "gods" is not really the plural of God; God has no plural. Thus, when you hear in the thunder the voice of a god, you are stopping short, for the voice of a god is not really a voice from beyond the world, from the uncreated. By taking the god's voice away — or envisaging the god as an angel, a servant of that Other — you go further. The thunder becomes not less divine but more. By emptying Nature of divinity — or, let us say, of divinities — you may fill her with Deity, for she is now the bearer of messages. There is a sense in which Nature-worship silences her — as if a child or a savage were so impressed with the postman's uniform that he omitted to take in the letters.

Another result of believing in Creation is to see Nature not as a mere datum but as an achievement. Some of the Psalmists are delighted with its mere solidity and permanence. God has given to His works His own character of *emeth*; they are watertight, faithful, reliable, not at all vague or phantasmal. "All His works are *faithful* — He spake and it was done, He commanded and it stood fast" (33, 4, 9). By His might (Dr. Moffatt's version) "the mountains are made firm and strongly fixed" (65, 6). God has laid the foundations of the earth with perfect thoroughness (104, 5). He has made everything firm and permanent and imposed boundaries which limit each thing's operation (148, 6). Notice how in Psalm 136 the poet passes from God's creation of Nature to the delivering of Israel out of Egypt: both are equally great deeds, great victories.

But the most surprising result of all is still to be mentioned. I said that the Jews, like nearly all the ancients, were agricultural and approached Nature with a gardener's and a farmer's interest, concerned with rain, with grass "for the service of man," wine to cheer man up and olive-oil to make his face shine — to make it look, as Homer says somewhere, like a peeled onion (104, *14, 15*). But we find them led on beyond this. Their gusto, or even gratitude, embraces things that are no use to man. In the great Psalm especially devoted to Nature, from which I have just quoted (104),[1] we have not only the useful cattle, the cheering vine, and the nourishing corn. We have springs where the wild asses quench their thirst (*11*), fir trees for the storks (*17*), hill country for the wild goats and "conies" (perhaps marmots, *18*), finally even the lions (*21*); and even with a glance far out to sea, where no Jew willingly went, the great whales playing, enjoying themselves (*26*).

Of course this appreciation of, almost this sympathy with, creatures useless or hurtful or wholly irrelevant to man, is not our modern "kindness to animals". That is a virtue most easily practised by those who have never, tired and hungry, had to work with animals for a bare living, and who inhabit a country where all dangerous wild beasts have been exterminated.[2] The Jewish feeling, however, is vivid, fresh, and impartial. In Norse stories a pestilent creature such as a dragon tends to be conceived as the enemy not only of men but of gods. In classical stories, more disquietingly, it tends to be sent by a god for the destruction of men whom he has a grudge against. The Psalmist's clear objective view — noting the lions and whales side by side with men and men's cattle — is unusual. And I think it is certainly reached through the idea of God as Creator and sustainer of all. In 104, *21*, the point about the lions is that they, like us, "do seek their meat from God". All these creatures, like us, "wait upon" God at feeding-time (*27*). It is the same in 147, *9*; though the raven was an unclean bird to Jews, God "feedeth the young ravens that call upon him". The thought which gives these creatures a place in the Psalmist's gusto for Nature is surely obvious. They are our fellow-dependents; we all, lions, storks, ravens, whales — live, as our fathers said, "as God's charges," and the mention of all equally redounds to His praise.

One curious bit of evidence strengthens my belief that there is such a connection between this sort of nature poetry and the doctrine of creation; and it is also so interesting in itself that I think it worth a digression. I have said that Paganism in general fails to get out of nature something that the Jews got. There is one apparent instance to the contrary; one ancient Gentile poem which provides a fairly close parallel to Psalm 104. But then, when we come to examine it, we find that this poem is not Pagan in the sense of Polytheistic at all. It is addressed to a Monotheistic God and salutes Him as the Creator of the whole earth. It is therefore no exception to my generalisation. Where ancient Gentile literature (in some measure) anticipates the nature poetry of the Jews, it has also (in some measure) anticipated their theology. And that, in my view, is what we might have expected.

The poem in question is an Egyptian *Hymn to the Sun* dating from the fourteenth

[1] See Appendix I, page 000.

[2] Heaven forbid, however, that I should be thought to slight it. I only mean that for those of us who meet beasts solely as pets it is not a costly virtue. We may properly be kicked if we lack it, but must not pat ourselves on the back for having it. When a hardworked shepherd or carter remains kind to animals his back may well be patted; not ours.

century B.C. Its author is that Pharaoh whose real name was Amenhetep IV, but who called himself Akhenaten. Many of my readers will know his story already. He was a spiritual revolutionary. He broke away from the Polytheism of his fathers and nearly tore Egypt into shreds in his efforts to establish by force the worship of a single God. In the eyes of the established priesthood, whose property he transferred to the service of this new religion, he must have seemed a monster; a sort of Henry VIII plundering the abbeys. His Monotheism appears to have been of an extremely pure and conceptual kind. He did not, as a man of that age might have been expected to do, even identify God with the Sun. The visible disc was only His manifestation. It is an astonishing leap, more astonishing in some ways than Plato's, and, like Plato's, in sharp contrast to ordinary Paganism. And as far as we can see, it was a total failure. Akhenaten's religion died with him. Nothing, apparently, came of it.

Unless of course, as is just possible, Judaism itself partly came of it. It is conceivable that ideas derived from Akhenaten's system formed part of that Egyptian "Wisdom" in which Moses was bred. There is nothing to disquiet us in such a possibility. Whatever was true in Akhenaten's creed came to him, in some mode or other, as all truth comes to all men, from God. There is no reason why traditions descending from Akhenaten should not have been among the instruments which God used in making Himself known to Moses. But we have no evidence that this is what actually happened. Nor do we know how fit Akhenatenism would really have been to serve as an instrument for this purpose. Its inside, its spirituality, the quality of life from which it sprang and which it encouraged, escape us. The man himself still has the power, after thirty-four centuries, to evoke the most violent, and contradictory, reactions. To one modern scholar he is the "first individual" whom history records; to another, he is a crank, a faddist, half insane, possibly cretinous. We may well hope that he was accepted and blessed by God; but that his religion, at any rate on the historical level, was not so blessed and so accepted, is pretty clear. Perhaps the seed was good seed but fell on stony ground. Or perhaps it was not after all exactly the right sort of seed. To us moderns, no doubt, such a simple, enlightened, reasonable Monotheism looks very much more like the good seed than those earliest documents of Judaism in which Jahveh seems little more than a tribal deity. We might be wrong. Perhaps if Man is finally to know the bodiless, timeless, transcendent Ground of the whole universe not as a mere philosophical abstraction but as the Lord who, despite this transcendence, is "not far from any one of us", as an utterly concrete Being (far more concrete than we) whom Man can fear, love, address, and "taste", he must begin far more humbly and far nearer home, with the local altar, the traditional feast, and the treasured memories of God's judgements, promises, and mercies. It is possible that a certain sort of enlightenment can come too soon and too easily. At that early stage it may not be fruitful to typify God by anything so remote, so neutral, so international and (as it were) interdenominational, so featureless, as the solar disc. Since in the end we are to come to baptism and the Eucharist, to the stable at Bethlehem, the hill of Calvary, and the emptied rock-tomb, perhaps it is better to begin with circumcision, the Passover, the Ark, and the Temple. For "the highest does not stand without the lowest." Does not stand, does not stay; rises, rather, and expands, and finally loses itself in endless space. For the entrance is low: we must stoop till we are no taller than children in order to get in.

It would therefore be rash to assume that Akhenaten's Monotheism was, in those ways which are religiously most important, an exact anticipation of the Judaic; so that if only the priests and people of Egypt had accepted it, God could have dispensed with Israel altogether and revealed Himself to us henceforward through a long line of Egyptian prophets. What concerns us at the moment, however, is simply to note that Akhenaten's religion, being certainly in some respects like that of the Jews, sets him free to write nature-poetry in some degree like theirs. The degree could be exaggerated. The *Hymn to the Sun* remains different from the Psalms. It is magnificently like Psalm 139 (*13 – 16*) when it praises God for making the embryo grow in the mother's body, so that He is "our nurse even in the womb": or for teaching the chick to break the eggshell and come forth "chirping as loud as he can". In the verse "Thous didst create the earth, according to thy desire" Akhenaten even anticipates the New Testament — "thou hast created all things, and for thy pleasure they are, and were created" (*Revelation* 4, *11*). But he does not quite see the lions as our fellow-pensioners. He brings them in, to be sure, but notice how: "when thou settest, the world is in darkness like the dead. Out come the lions: all serpents sting." Thus coupled with death and poisonous snakes, they are clearly envisaged in their capacity of enemies. It almost sounds as if the night itself were an enemy, out of God's reach. There is just a trace of dualism. But if there is difference, the likeness also is real. And it is the likeness which is relevant to the theme of this chapter. In Akhenaten as in the Psalms, a certain kind of poetry seems to go with a certain kind of theology. But the full and abiding development of both is Jewish.

(Meanwhile, what gentle heart can leave the topic without a prayer that this lonely ancient king, crank and doctrinaire though perhaps he was, has long seen and now enjoys the truth which so far transcends his own glimpse of it?)

IX

A WORD ABOUT PRAISING

It is possible (and it is to be hoped) that this chapter will be unnecessary for most people. Those who were never thick-headed enough to get into the difficulty it deals with may even find it funny. I have not the least objection to their laughing; a little comic relief in a discussion does no harm, however serious the topic may be. (In my own experience the funniest things have occurred in the gravest and most sincere conversations.)

When I first began to draw near to belief in God and even for some time after it had been given to me, I found a stumbling block in the demand so clamorously made by all religious people that we should "praise" God; still more in the suggestion that God Himself demanded it. We all despise the man who demands continued assurance of his own virtue, intelligence or delightfulness; we despise still more the crowd of people round every dictator, every millionaire, every celebrity, who gratify that demand. Thus a picture, at once ludicrous and horrible, both of God and of His worshippers, threatened to appear in my mind. The Psalms were especially troublesome in this way — "Praise the Lord," "O praise the Lord with me," "Praise Him." (And why, incidentally, did praising God so often consist in telling other people to praise Him? Even in telling whales, snowstorms, etc., to go on doing what they would certainly do whether we told them or not?) Worse still was the statement put into God's own mouth, "whoso offereth me thanks and praise, he honoureth me" (50, 23). It was hideously like saying, "What I most want is to be told that I am good and great." Worst of all was the suggestion of the very silliest Pagan bargaining, that of the savage who makes offerings to his idol when the fishing is good and beats it when he has caught nothing. More than once the Psalmists seemed to be saying, "You like praise. Do this for me, and you shall have some." Thus in 54 the poet begins "save me" (*1*), and in verse *6* adds an inducement, "An offering of a free heart will I give thee, and praise thy Name." Again and again the speaker asks to be saved from death on the ground that if God lets His suppliants die He will get no more praise from them, for the ghosts in Sheol cannot praise (30,*10;* 88, *10;* 119, *175*). And mere quantity of praise seemed to count; "seven times a day do I praise thee" (119, *164*). It was extremely distressing. It made one think what one least wanted to think. Gratitude to God, reverence to Him, obedience to Him, I thought I could understand; not this perpetual eulogy. Nor were matters mended by a modern author who talked of God's "right" to be praised.

I still think "right" is a bad way of expressing it, but I believe I now see what that author meant. It is perhaps easiest to begin with inanimate objects which can have no rights. What do we mean when we say that a picture is "admirable"? We certainly don't mean that it is admired (that's as may be) for bad work is admired by thousands and good work may be ignored. Nor that it "deserves" admiration in the sense in which a candidate "deserves" a high mark from the examiners—i.e. that a human being will have suffered injustice if it is not awarded. The sense in which the picture "deserves" or "demands" admiration is rather this; that admiration is the correct, adequate or appropriate, response to it, that if paid, admiration will not be "thrown away", and that if we do not admire we shall be stupid, insensible, and great losers, we shall have missed something. In that way many objects both in Nature and in Art may be said to deserve, or merit, or demand, admiration. It was from this end, which will seem to some irreverent, that I found it best to approach the idea that God "demands" praise. He is that Object to admire which (or, if you like, to appreciate which) is simply to be awake, to have entered the real world; not to appreciate which is to have lost the greatest experience, and in the end to have lost all. The incomplete and crippled lives of those who are tone deaf, have never been in love, never known true friendship, never cared for a good book, never enjoyed the feel of the morning air on their cheeks, never (I am one of these) enjoyed football, are faint images of it.

But of course this is not all. God does not only "demand" praise as the supremely beautiful and all-satisfying Object. He does apparently command it as lawgiver. The Jews were told to sacrifice. We are under an obligation to go to church. But this was a difficulty only because I did not then understand any of what I have tried to say above in Chapter V. I did not see that it is in the process of being worshipped that God communicates His presence to men. It is not of course the only way. But for many people at many times the "fair beauty of the Lord" is revealed chiefly or only while they worship Him together. Even in Judaism the essence of the sacrifice was not really that men gave bulls and goats to God, but that by their so doing God gave Himself to men; in the central act of our own worship of course this is far clearer— there it is manifestly, even physically, God who gives and we who receive. The miserable idea that God should in any sense need, or crave for, our worship like a vain woman wanting compliments, or a vain author presenting his new books to people who never met or heard of him, is implicitly answered by the words "If I be hungry I will not tell *thee*" (50, *12*). Even if such an absurd Deity could be conceived, He would hardly come to *us*, the lowest of rational creatures, to gratify His appetite. I don't want my dog to bark approval of my books. Now that I come to think of it, there are some humans whose enthusiastically favourable criticism would not much gratify me.

But the most obvious fact about praise – whether of God or anything – strangely escaped me. I thought of it in terms of compliment, approval, or the giving of honour. I have never noticed that all enjoyment spontaneously overflows into praise unless (sometimes even if) shyness or the fear of boring others is deliberately brought in to check it. The world rings with praise – lovers praising their mistresses, readers their favorite poet, walkers praising the countryside, players praising their favourite game – praise of weather, wines, dishes, actors, motors, horses, colleges, countries, historical personages, children, flowers, mountains, rare stamps, rare beetles, even sometimes politicians or scholars. I had not noticed how the humblest, and at the same time most balanced and capacious, praised most, while the cranks, misfits and malcontents praised least. The good critics found something to praise in many imperfect works; the bad ones continually narrowed the list of books we might be allowed to read. The healthy and unaffected man, even if luxuriously brought up and widely experienced in good cookery, could praise a very modest meal: the dyspeptic and the snob found fault with all. Except where intolerably adverse circumstances interfere, praise almost seems to be inner health made audible. Nor does it cease to be so when, through lack of skill, the forms of its expression are very uncouth or even ridiculous. Heaven knows, many poems of praise addressed to an earthly beloved are as bad as our bad hymns, and an anthology of love poems for public and perpetual use would probably be as sore a trial to literary taste as *Hymns Ancient and Modern*. I had not noticed either that just as men spontaneously praise whatever they value, so they spontaneously urge us to join them in praising it: "Isn't she lovely? Wasn't it glorious? Don't you think that magnificent?" The Psalmists in telling everyone to praise God are doing what all men do when they speak of what they care about. My whole, more general, difficulty about the praise of God depended on my absurdly denying to us, as regards the supremely Valuable, what we delight to do, what indeed we can't help doing, about everything else we value.

I think we delight to praise what we enjoy because the praise not merely expresses but completes the enjoyment; it is its appointed consummation. It is not out of compliment that lovers keep on telling one another how beautiful they are; the delight is incomplete till it is expressed. It is frustrating to have discovered a new author and not to be able to tell anyone how good he is; to come suddenly, at the turn of the road, upon some mountain valley of unexpected grandeur and then to have to keep silent because the people with you care for it no more than for a tin can in the ditch; to hear a good joke and find no one to share it with (the perfect hearer died a year ago). This is so even when our expressions are inadequate, as of course they usually are. But how if one could really and fully praise even such things to perfection – utterly "get out" in poetry or music or paint the upsurge of appreciation which almost bursts you? Then indeed the object would be fully appreciated and our delight would have attained perfect development. The worthier the object, the more intense this delight would be. If it were possible for a created soul fully (I mean, up to the full measure conceivable in a finite being) to "appreciate", that is to love and delight in, the worthiest object of all, and simultaneously at every moment to give this delight perfect expression, then that soul would be in supreme beatitude. It is along these lines that I find it easiest to understand the Christian doctrine that "Heaven" is a state in which angels now, and men hereafter, are perpetually employed in praising God. This does not mean, as it can so dismally suggest, that it is like "being in Church". For our "services" both in their conduct and in our power to participate, are merely attempts at worship; never fully successful, often 99.9 per cent failures, sometimes total failures. We are not riders but pupils in the riding school; for most of us the falls and bruises, the aching muscles and the severity of the exercise, far outweigh those few moments in which we were, to our own astonishment, actually galloping without terror and without disaster. To see what the doctrine really means, we must suppose ourselves to be in perfect love with God—drunk with, drowned in, dissolved by, that delight which, far from remaining pent up within ourselves as incommunicable, hence hardly tolerable, bliss, flows out from us incessantly again in effortless and perfect expression, our joy no more separable from the praise in which it liberates and utters itself than the brightness a mirror receives is separable from the brightness it sheds. The Scotch catechism says that man's chief end is "to glorify God and enjoy Him forever". But we shall then know that these are the same thing. Fully to enjoy is to glorify. In commanding us to glorify Him, God is inviting us to enjoy Him.

Meanwhile of course we are merely, as Donne says, tuning our instruments. The tuning up of the orchestra can be itself delightful, but only to those who can in some measure, however little, anticipate the symphony. The Jewish sacrifices, and even our own most sacred rites, as they actually occur in human experience, are, like the tuning, promise, not performance. Hence, like the tuning, they may have in them much duty and little delight; or none. But the duty exists for the delight. When we carry out our "religious duties" we are like people digging channels in a waterless land, in order that when at last the water comes, it may find them ready. I mean, for the most part. There are happy moments, even now, when a trickle creeps along the dry beds; and happy souls to whom this happens often.

As for the element of bargaining in the Psalms (Do this and I will praise you), that silly dash of Paganism certainly existed. The flame does not ascend pure from the altar. But the impurities are not its essence. And we are not all in a position to despise even the crudest Psalmist on this score. Of course we would not blunder in our words like them. But there is, for ill as well as for good, a wordless prayer. I have often, on my knees, been shocked to find what sort of thoughts I have, for a moment, been addressing to God; what infantile placations I was really offering, what claims I have really made, even what absurd adjustments or compromises I was, half-consciously, proposing. There is a Pagan, savage heart in me somewhere. For unfortunately the folly and idiot-cunning of Paganism seem to have far more power of surviving than its innocent or even beautiful elements. It is easy, once you have power, to silence the pipes, still the dances, disfigure the statues, and forget the stories; but not easy to kill the savage, the greedy, frightened creature now cringing, now blustering, in one's soul – the creature to whom God may well say, "thou thoughtest I am even such a one as thyself" (50, *21*).

But all this, as I have said, will be illuminating to only a few of my readers. To the others, such a comedy of errors, so circuitous a journey to reach the obvious, will furnish occasion for charitable laughter.

X

SECOND MEANINGS

I must now turn to something far more difficult. Hitherto we have been trying to read the Psalms as we suppose – or I suppose – their poets meant them to be read. But this of course is not the way in which they have chiefly been used by Christians. They have been believed to contain a second or hidden meaning, an "allegorical" sense, concerned with the central truths of Christianity, with the Incarnation, the Passion, the Resurrection, the Ascension, and with the Redemption of man. All the Old Testament has been treated in the same way. The full significance of what the writers are saying is, on this view, apparent only in the light of events which happened after they were dead.

Such a doctrine, not without reason, arouses deep distrust in a modern mind. Because, as we know, almost anything can be read into any book if you are determined enough. This will be especially impressed on anyone who has written fantastic fiction. He will find reviewers, both favourable and hostile, reading into his stories all manner of allegorical meanings which he never intended. (Some of the allegories thus imposed on my own books have been so ingenious and interesting that I often wish I had thought of them myself.) Apparently it is impossible for the wit of man to devise a narrative in which the wit of some other man cannot, and with some plausibility, find a hidden sense.

The field for self-deception, once we accept such methods of interpretation, is therefore obviously very wide. Yet in spite of this I think it impossible – for a reason I will give later – to abandon the method wholly when we are dealing, as Christians, with the Bible. We have, therefore, a steep hill before us. I will not attempt the cliffs. I must take a roundabout route which we will look at first as if it could never lead us to the top at all.

I begin far away from Scripture and even from Christianity, with instances of something said or written which takes on a new significance in the light of later events.

One of the Roman historians tells us about a fire in a provincial town which was thought to have originated in the public baths. What gave some colour to the suspicion of deliberate incendiarism was the fact that, earlier that day, a gentleman had complained that the water in the hot bath was only lukewarm and had received from an attendant the reply, *it will soon be hot enough*. Now of course if there really had been a plot, and the slave was in it, and fool enough to risk discovery by this veiled threat, then the story would not concern us. But let us suppose the fire was an accident (i.e. was intended by nobody). In that case the slave would have said something truer, or more importantly true, than he himself supposed. Clearly, there need be nothing here but chance coincidence. The slave's reply is fully explained by the customer's complaint; it is just what any bath attendant would say. The deeper significance which his words turned out to have during the next few hours was, as we should say, accidental.

Now let us take a somewhat tougher instance. (The non-classical reader needs to know that to a Roman the "age" or "reign" of Saturn meant the lost age of innocence and peace. That is, it roughly corresponded to the Garden of Eden before the Fall; though it was never, except among the Stoics, of anything like comparable importance.) Virgil, writing not very long before the birth of Christ, begins a poem thus: "The great procession of the ages begins anew. Now the Virgin returns, the reign of Saturn returns, and the new child is sent down from high heaven." It goes on to describe the paradisal age which this nativity will usher in. And of course throughout the Middle Ages it was taken that some dim prophetic knowledge of the birth of Christ had reached Virgil, probably through the Sibylline Books. He ranked as a pagan prophet. Modern scholars would, I suppose, laugh at the idea. They might differ as to what noble or imperial couple were being thus extravagantly complimented by a court poet on the birth of a son; but the resemblances to the birth of Christ would be regarded, once more, as an accident. To say the least of it, however, this is a much more striking accident that the slave's words to the man in the baths. If this is luck, it is extraordinary luck. If one were a fanatical opponent of Christianity one would be tempted to say, in an unguarded moment, that it was diabolically lucky.

I now turn to two examples which I think to be on a different level. In them, as in those we have been considering, someone says what is truer and more important than he knows; but it does not seem to me that he could have done so by chance. I hasten to add that the alternative to chance which I have in mind is not "prophecy" in the sense of clear prevision, miraculously bestowed. Nor of course have I the slightest intention of using the examples I shall cite as evidences for the truth of Christianity. Evidences are not here our subject. We are merely considering how we should regard those second meanings which things said or written sometimes take on in the light of fuller knowledge than their author possessed. And I am suggesting that different instances demand that we should regard them in different ways. Sometimes we may regard this overtone as the result of simple coincidence, however striking. But there are other cases in which the later truth (which the speaker did not know) is intimately related to the truth he did know; so that, in hitting out something like it, he was in touch with that very same reality in which the fuller truth is rooted. Reading his words in the light of that fuller truth and hearing it in them as an overtone or second meaning, we are not foisting on them something alien to his mind, an arbitrary addition. We are prolonging his meaning in a direction congenial to it. The basic reality behind his words and behind the full truth is one and the same.

The status I claim for such things, then, is neither that of coincidence on the one hand nor that of supernatural prevision on the other. I will try to illustrate it by three imaginable cases. i. A holy person, explicitly claiming to prophesy by the Spirit, tells us that there is in the universe such and such a creature. Later we learn (which God forbid) to travel in space and distribute upon new worlds the vomit of our own corruption; and, sure enough, on the remote planet of some remote star, we find that very creature. This would be prophecy in the strictest sense. This would be evidence for the prophet's miraculous gift and strong presumptive evidence for the truth of anything else he had said. ii. A wholly unscientific writer of fantasies invents a creature for purely artistic reasons. Later on, we find a creature recognisably like it. This would be just the writer's luck. A man who knows nothing about racing may once in his life back a winner. iii. A great biologist, illustrating the relation between animal organisms and their environment, invents for this purpose a hypothetical animal adapted to a hypothetical environment. Later, we find a creature very like (of course in an environment very like the one he had supposed). This resemblance is not in the least accidental. Insight and knowledge, not luck, led to his invention. The real nature of life explains both why there is such a creature in the universe and also why there was such a creature in his lectures. If, while we re-read the lectures, we think of the reality, we are not bringing arbitrary fancies of our own to bear on the text. This second meaning is congenial to it. The examples I have in mind correspond to this third case; except of course that something more sensitive and personal than scientific knowledge is involved – what the writer or speaker was, not only what he knew.

Plato in his *Republic* is arguing that righteousness is often praised for the rewards it brings – honour, popularity, and the like – but that to see it in its true nature we must separate it from all these, strip it naked. He asks us therefore to imagine a perfectly righteous man treated by all around him as a monster of wickedness. We must picture him still perfect, while he is bound, scourged, and finally impaled (the Persian equivalent of crucifixion). At this passage a Christian reader starts and rubs his eyes. What is happening? Yet another of these lucky coincidences? But presently he sees that there is something here which cannot be called luck at all.

Virgil, in the poem I have quoted, may have been, and the slave in the baths almost certainly was, "talking about something else", some matter other than that of which their words were most importantly true. Plato is talking, and knows he is talking, about the fate of goodness in a wicked and misunderstanding world. But that is not something simply other than the Passion of Christ. It is the very same thing of which that Passion is the supreme illustration. If Plato was in some measure moved to write of it by the recent death – we may almost say the martyrdom – of his master Socrates then that again is not something simply other than the Passion of Christ.

The imperfect, yet very venerable, goodness of Socrates led to the easy death of the hemlock, and the perfect goodness of Christ led to the death of the cross, not by chance but for the same reason; because goodness is what it is, and because the fallen world is what it is. If Plato, starting from one example and from his insight into the nature of goodness and the nature of the world, was led on to see the possibility of a perfect example, and thus to depict something extremely like the Passion of Christ, this happened not because he was lucky but because he was wise. If a man who knew only England and had observed that, the higher a mountain was, the longer it retained the snow in early spring, were led on to suppose a mountain so high that it retained the snow all the year round, the similarity between his imagined mountain and the real Alps would not be merely a lucky accident. He might not know that there were any such mountains in reality; just as Plato probably did not know that the ideally perfect instance of crucified goodness which he had depicted would ever become actual and historical. But if that man ever saw the Alps he would not say "What a curious coincidence". He would be more likely to say "There! What did I tell you?"

And what are we to say of those gods in various Pagan mythologies who are killed and rise again and who thereby renew or transform the life of their worshippers or of nature? The odd thing is that here those anthropologists who are most hostile to our faith would agree with many Christians in saying "The resemblance is not accidental". Of course the two parties would say this for different reasons. The anthropologists would mean: "All these superstitions have a common source in the mind and experience, especially the agricultural experience, of early man. Your myth of Christ is like the myth of Balder because it has the same origin. The likeness is a family likeness." The Christians would fall into two schools of thought. The early Fathers (or some of them), who believed that Paganism was nothing but the direct work of the Devil, would say: "The Devil has from the beginning tried to mislead humanity with lies. As all accomplished liars do, he makes his lies as like the truth as he can; provided they lead man astray on the main issue, the more closely they imitate truth the more effective they will be. That is why we call him God's Ape; he is always imitating God. The resemblance of Adonis to Christ is therefore not at all accidental, it is the resemblance we expect to find between a counterfeit and the real thing, between a parody and the original, between imitation pearls and pearls." Other Christians who think, as I do, that in mythology divine and diabolical and human elements (the desire for a good story), all play a part, would say: "It is not accidental. In the sequence of night and day, in the annual death and rebirth of the crops, in the myths which these processes gave rise to, in the strong, if half-articulate, feeling (embodied in many Pagan 'Mysteries') that man himself must undergo some sort of death if he would truly live, there is already a likeness permitted by God to that truth on which all depends. The resemblance between these myths and the Christian truth is no more accidental than the resemblance between the sun and the sun's reflection in a pond, or that between a historical fact and the somewhat garbled version of it which lives in popular report, or between the trees and hills of the real world and the trees and hills in our dreams." Thus all three views alike would regard the "Pagan Christ" and the true Christ as things really related and would find the resemblance significant.

In other words, when we examine things said which take on, in the light of later knowledge, a meaning they could not have had for those who said them, they turn out to be of different sorts. To be sure, of whatever sort they may be, we can often profitably read them with that second meaning in mind. If I think (as I cannot help thinking) about the birth of Christ while I read that poem of Virgil's, or even if I make it a regular part of my Christmas reading, this may be quite a sensible and edifying thing to do. But the resemblance which makes such a reading possible may after all be a mere coincidence (though I am not sure that it is). I may be reading into Virgil what is wholly irrelevant to all he was, and did, and intended; irrelevant as the sinister meaning which the bathman's word in the Roman story acquired from later events may have been to anything that slave was or meant. But when I meditate on the Passion while reading Plato's picture of the Righteous One, or on the Resurrection while reading about Adonis or Balder, the case is altered. There is a real connection between what Plato and the myth-makers most deeply were and meant and what I believe to be the truth. I know that connection and they do not. But it is really there. It is not an arbitrary fancy of my own thrust upon the old words. One can, without any absurdity, imagine Plato or the myth-makers if they learned the truth, saying, "I see . . . so that was what I was really talking about. Of course. That is what my words really meant, and I never knew it." The bath attendant if innocent, on hearing the second meaning given to his words, would no doubt have said, "So help me, I never meant no such thing. Never come into my head. I hadn't a clue." What Virgil would have said, if he had learned the truth, I have no idea. (Or may we more charitably speak, not of what Plato and Virgil and the myth-makers "would have said" but of what they said? For we can pray with good hope that they now know and have long since welcomed the truth; "many shall come from the east and the west and sit down in the kingdom.")

Thus, long before we come to the Psalms or the Bible, there are good reasons for not throwing away all second meanings as rubbish. Keble said of the Pagan poets, "Thoughts beyond their thoughts to those high bards were given." But let us now turn to Scripture itself.

XI

SCRIPTURE

If even pagan utterances can carry a second meaning, not quite accidentally but because, in the sense I have suggested, they have a sort of right to it, we shall expect the Scriptures to do this more momentously and more often. We have two grounds for doing so if we are Christians.

i. For us these writings are "holy", or "inspired", or, as St. Paul says, "the Oracles of God". But this has been understood in more than one way, and I must try to explain how I understand it, at least so far as the Old Testament is concerned. I have been suspected of being what is called a Fundamentalist. That is because I never regard any narrative as unhistorical simply on the ground that it includes the miraculous. Some people find the miraculous so hard to believe that they cannot imagine any reason for my acceptance of it other than a prior belief that every sentence of the Old Testament has historical or scientific truth. But this I do not hold, any more than St. Jerome did when he said that Moses described Creation "after the manner of a popular poet" (as we should say, mythically) or than Calvin did when he doubted whether the story of Job were history or fiction. The real reason why I can accept as historical a story in which a miracle occurs is that I have never found any philosophical grounds for the universal negative proposition that miracles do not happen. I have to decide on quite other grounds (if I decide at all) whether a given narrative is historical or not. The *Book of Job* appears to me unhistorical because it begins about a man quite unconnected with all history or even legend, with no genealogy, living in a country of which the Bible elsewhere has hardly anything to say; because, in fact, the author quite obviously writes as a story-teller, not as a chronicler.

I have therefore no difficulty in accepting, say, the view of those scholars who tell us that the account of Creation in *Genesis* is derived from earlier Semitic stories which were Pagan and mythical. We must of course be quite clear what "derived from" means. Stories do not reproduce their species like mice. They are told by men. Each re-teller either repeats exactly what his predecessor had told him or else changes it. He may change it unknowingly or deliberately. If he changes it deliberately, his invention, his sense of form, his ethics, his ideas of what is fit, or edifying, or merely interesting, all come in. If unknowingly, then his unconscious (which is so largely responsible for our forgettings) has been at work. Thus at every step in what is called — a little misleadingly — the "evolution" of a story, a man, all he is and all his attitudes, are involved. And no good work is done anywhere without aid from the Father of Lights. When a series of such re-tellings turns a creation story which at first had almost no religious or metaphysical significance into a story which achieves the idea of true Creation and of a transcendent Creator (as *Genesis* does), then nothing will make me believe that some of the re-tellers, or some one of them, has not been guided by God.

Thus something originally merely natural — the kind of myth that is found among most nations — will have been raised by God above itself, qualified by Him and compelled by Him to serve purposes which of itself would not have served. Generalising this, I take it that the whole Old Testament consists of the same sort of material as any other literature — chronicle (some of it obviously pretty accurate), poems, moral and political diatribes, romances, and what not; but all taken into the service of God's word. Not all, I suppose, in the same way. There are prophets who write with the clearest awareness that Divine compulsion is upon them. There are chroniclers whose intention may have been merely to record. There are poets like those in the *Song of Songs* who probably never dreamed of any but a secular and natural purpose in what they composed. There is (and it is no less important) the work first of the Jewish and then of the Christian Church in preserving and canonising just these books. There is the work of redactors and editors in modifying them. On all of these I suppose a Divine pressure; of which not by any means all need have been conscious.

The human qualities of the raw materials show through. Naïveté, error, contradiction, even (as in the cursing Psalms) wickedness are not removed. The total result is not "the Word of God" in the sense that every passage, in itself, gives impeccable science or history. It carries the Word of God; and we (under grace, with attention to tradition and to interpreters wiser than ourselves, and with the use of such intelligence and learning as we may have) receive that word from it not by using it as an encyclopedia or an encyclical but by steeping ourselves in its tone or temper and so learning its overall message.

To a human mind this working-up (in a sense imperfectly), this sublimation (incomplete) of human material, seems, no doubt, an untidy and leaky vehicle. We might have expected, we may think we should have preferred, an unrefracted light giving us ultimate truth in systematic form — something we could have tabulated and memorised and relied on like the multiplication table. One can respect, and at moments envy, both the Fundamentalist's view of the Bible and the Roman Catholic's view of the Church. But there is one argument which we should beware of using for either position: God must have done what is best, this is best, therefore God has done this. For we are mortals and do not know what is best fo us, and it is dangerous to prescribe what God must have done — especially when we cannot, for the life of us, see that He has after all done it.

We may observe that the teaching of Our Lord Himself, in which there is no imperfection, is not given us in that cut-and-dried, fool-proof, systematic fashion we might have expected or desired. He wrote no book. We have only reported sayings, most of them uttered in answer to questions, shaped in some degree by their context. And when we have collected them all we cannot reduce them to a system. He preaches but He does not lecture. He uses paradox, proverb, exaggeration, parable, irony; even (I mean no irreverence) the "wisecrack". He utters maxims which, like popular proverbs, if rigorously taken, may seem to contradict one another. His teaching therefore cannot be grasped by the intellect alone, cannot be "got up" as if it were a "subject". If we try to do that with it, we shall find Him the most elusive of teachers. He hardly ever gave a straight answer to a straight question. He will not be, in the way we want, "pinned down". The attempt is (again, I mean no irreverence) like trying to bottle a sunbeam.

Descending lower, we find a somewhat similar difficulty with St. Paul. I cannot be the only reader who has wondered why God, having given him so many gifts, withheld from him (what would to us seem so necessary for the first Christian theologian) that of lucidity and orderly exposition.

Thus on three levels, in appropriate degrees, we meet the same refusal of what we might have thought best for us — in the Word Himself, in the Apostle of the Gentiles, in Scripture as a whole. Since this is what God has done, this, we must conclude, was best. It may be that what we should have liked would have been fatal to us if granted. It may be indispensable that Our Lord's teaching, by that elusiveness (to our systematising intellect), should demand a response from the whole man, should make it so clear that there is no question of learning a subject but of steeping ourselves in a Personality, acquiring a new outlook and temper, breathing a new atmosphere, suffering Him, in His own way, to rebuild in us the defaced image of Himself. So in St. Paul. Perhaps the sort of works I should wish him to have written would have been useless. The crabbedness, the appearance of inconsequence and even of sophistry, the turbulent mixture of petty detail, personal complaint, practical advice, and lyrical rapture, finally let through what matters more than ideas — a whole Christian life in operation — better say, Christ Himself operating in a man's life. And in the same way, the value of the Old Testament may be dependent on what seems its imperfection. It may repel one use in order that we may be forced to use it in another way — to find the Word in it, not without repeated and leisurely reading nor without discriminations made by our conscience and our critical faculties, to re-live, while we read, the whole Jewish experience of God's gradual and graded self-revelation, to feel the very contentions between the Word and the human material through which it works. For here again, it is our total response that has to be elicited.

Certainly it seems to me that from having had to reach what is really the Voice of God in the cursing Psalms through all the horrible distortions of the human medium,

I have gained something I might not have gained from a flawless, ethical exposition. The shadows have indicated (at least to my heart) something more about the light. Nor would I (now) willingly spare from my Bible something in itself so anti-religious as the nihilism of *Ecclesiastes*. We get there a clear, cold picture of man's life without God. That statement is itself part of God's word. We need to have heard it. Even to have assimilated *Ecclesiastes* and no other book in the Bible would be to have advanced further towards truth than some men do.

But of course these conjectures as to why God does what He does are probably of no more value than my dog's ideas of what I am up to when I sit and read. But though we can only guess the reasons, we can at least observe the consistency, of His ways. We read in *Genesis* (2, 7) that God formed man of the dust and breathed life into him. For all the first writer knew of it, this passage might merely illustrate the survival, even in a truly creational story, of the Pagan inability to conceive true Creation, the savage, pictorial tendency to imagine God making things "out of" something as the potter or the carpenter does. Nevertheless, whether by lucky accident or (as I think) by God's guidance, it embodies a profound principle. For on any view man is in one sense clearly made "out of" something else. He is an animal; but an animal called to be, or raised to be, or (if you like) doomed to be, something more than an animal. On the ordinary biological view (what difficulties I have about evolution are not religious) one of the primates is changed so that he becomes man; but he remains still a primate and an animal. He is taken up into a new life without relinquishing the old. In the same way, all organic life takes up and uses processes merely chemical. But we can trace the principle higher as well as lower. For we are taught that the Incarnation itself proceeded "not by the conversion of the god-head into flesh, but by taking of (the) manhood into God"; in it human life becomes the vehicle of Divine life. If the Scriptures proceed not by conversion of God's word into a literature but by taking up of a literature to be the vehicle of God's word, this is not anomalous.

Of course, on almost all levels, that method seems to us precarious or, as I have said, leaky. None of these up-gradings is, as we should have wished, self-evident. Because the lower nature, in being taken up and loaded with a new burden and advanced to a new privilege, remains, and is not annihilated, it will always be possible to ignore the up-grading and see nothing but the lower. Thus men can read the life of Our Lord (because it is a human life) as nothing but a human life. Many, perhaps most, modern philosophies read human life merely as an animal life of unusual complexity. The Cartesians read animal life as mechanism. Just in the same way Scripture can be read as merely human literature. No new discovery, no new method, will ever give a final victory to either interpretation. For what is required, on all these levels alike, is not merely knowledge but a certain insight; getting the focus right. Those who can see in each of these instances only the lower will always be plausible. One who contended that a poem was nothing but black marks on white paper would be unanswerable if he addressed an audience who couldn't read. Look at it through microscopes, analyse the printer's ink and the paper, study it (in that way) as long as you like; you will never find something over and above all the products of analysis whereof you can say "This is the poem". Those who can read, however, will continue to say the poem exists.

If the Old Testament is a literature thus "taken up", made the vehicle of what is more than human, we can of course set no limit to the weight or multiplicity of meanings which may have been laid upon it. If any writer may say more than he knows and mean more than he meant, then these writers will be especially likely to do so. And not by accident.

ii. The second reason for accepting the Old Testament in this way can be put more simply and is of course far more compulsive. We are committed to it in principle by Our Lord Himself. On that famous journey to Emmaus He found fault with the two disciples for not believing what the prophets had said. They ought to have known from their Bibles that the Anointed One, when He came, would enter his glory through suffering. He then explained, from "Moses" (i.e. the Pentateuch) down, all the places in the Old Testament "concerning Himself" (*Luke* 24, *25–27*). He clearly identified Himself with a figure often mentioned in the Scriptures; appropriated to Himself many passages where a modern scholar might see no such reference. In the predictions of His Own Passion which He had previously made to the disciples. He was obviously doing the same thing. He accepted – indeed He claimed to be – the second meaning of Scripture.

We do not know – or anyway I do not know – what all these passages were. We can be pretty sure about one of them. The Ethiopian eunuch who met Philip (*Acts* 8, *27–38*) was reading *Isaiah* 53. He did not know whether in that passage the prophet was talking about himself or about someone else. Philip, in answering his question, "preached unto him Jesus". The answer, in fact, was "Isaiah is speaking of Jesus". We need have no doubt that Philip's authority for this interpretation was Our Lord. (Our ancestors would have thought that Isaiah consciously foresaw the sufferings of Christ as people see the future in the sort of dreams recorded by Mr. Dunne. Modern scholars would say, that on the conscious level, he was referring to Israel itself, the whole nation personified. I do not see that it matters which view we take.) We can, again, be pretty sure, from the words on the cross (*Mark* 15, *34*), that Our Lord identified Himself with the sufferer in Psalm 22. Or when He asked (*Mark* 12, *35, 36*) how Christ could be both David's son and David's lord, He clearly identified Christ, and therefore Himself, with the "my Lord" of Psalm 110 – was in fact hinting at the mystery of the Incarnation by pointing out a difficulty which only it could solve. In *Matthew* 4, *6* the words of Psalm 91 *11, 12*, "He shall give his angels charge over thee . . . that thou hurt not thy foot against a stone," are applied to Him, and we may be sure the application was His own since only He could be the source of the temptation-story. In *Mark* 12, *10* He implicitly appropriates to Himself the words of Psalm 118 *22* about the stone which the builders rejected. "Thou shalt not leave my soul in hell, neither shalt thou suffer thy Holy One to see corruption" (16, *11*) is treated as a prophecy of His Resurrection in *Acts* 2, *27,* and was doubtless so taken by Himself, since we find it so taken in the earliest Christian tradition — that is, by people likely to be closer both to the spirit and to the letter of His words than any scholarship (I do not say, "any sanctity") will bring a modern. Yet it is, perhaps, idle to speak here of spirit and letter. There is almost no "letter" in the words of Jesus. Taken by a literalist, He will always prove the most elusive of teachers. Systems cannot keep up with that darting illumination. No net less wide than a man's whole heart, nor less fine of mesh than love, will hold the sacred Fish.

"Selfish, not self-centered .... The
distinction is not unimportant. One
of the happiest men + most pleasant
companions I have ever known was
intensely selfish. On the other hand, I
have known people capable of real
sacrifice whose lives were nevertheless
a misery to themselves + to others, bec.
self-concern + self-pity filled all their
thoughts. Either condition will destroy
the soul in the end. But till the end,
give me the man who takes the
best of everything (even at my expense)
+ then talks of other things, rather than
the man who serves me + talks of
himself, + whose very kindnesses are
a continual reproach, a continual demand for pity, gratitude, + admiration. "

157 - Moderns annihilation of space
via the car ....

start p. 165 - chap. XI 'Check'

XII

SECOND MEANINGS
IN THE PSALMS

In a certain sense Our Lord's interpretation of the Psalms was common ground between Himself and His opponents. The question we mentioned a moment ago, how David can call Christ "my Lord" (*Mark* 12, 35–37), would lose its point unless it were addressed to those who took it for granted that the "my Lord" referred to in Psalm 110 was the Messiah, the regal and anointed deliverer who would subject the world to Israel. This method was accepted by all. The "scriptures" all had a "spiritual" or second sense. Even a gentile "God-fearer"[1] like the Ethiopian eunuch (*Acts* 8, 27–38) knew that the sacred books of Israel could not be understood without a guide, trained in the Judaic tradition, who could open the hidden meanings. Probably all instructed Jews in the first century saw references to the Messiah in most of those passages where our Lord saw them; what was controversial was His identification of the Messianic King with another Old Testament figure and of both with Himself.

Two figures meet us in the Psalms, that of the sufferer and that of the conquering and liberating king. In 13, 28, 55 or 102, we have the Sufferer; in 2 or 72, the King. The Sufferer was, I think, by this time generally identified with (and may sometimes have originally been intended as) the whole nation, Israel itself—they would have said "himself". The King was the successor of David, the coming Messiah. Our Lord identified Himself with both these characters.

In principle, then, the allegorical way of reading the Psalms can claim the highest possible authority. But of course this does not mean that all the countless applications of it are fruitful, legitimate, or even rational. What we see when we think we are looking into the depths of Scripture may sometimes be only the reflection of our own silly faces. Many allegorical interpretations which were once popular seem to me, as perhaps to most moderns, to be strained, arbitrary and ridiculous. I think we may be sure that some of them really are; we ought to be much less sure that we know which.

---

[1]The "god-fearers" (*sebomenoi* or *metuentes*) were a recognised class of Gentiles who worshipped Jahveh without submitting to circumcision and the other ceremonial obligations of the Law. Cf. Psalm 118 (*2*, Jewish laity; *3* Jewish priests; *4* God-fearers) and Acts 10, 2.

What seems strained — a mere triumph of perverse ingenuity — to one age, seems plain and obvious to another, so that our ancestors would often wonder how we could possibly miss what we wonder how they could have been silly-clever enough to find. And between different ages there is no impartial judge on earth, for no one stands outside the historical process; and of course no one is so completely enslaved to it as those who take our own age to be, not one more period, but a final and permanent platform from which we can see all other ages objectively.

Interpretations which were already established in the New Testament of course have a special claim on our attention. We find in our Prayer Books that Psalm 110[1] is one of those appointed for Christmas Day. We may at first be surprised by this. There is nothing in it about peace and good-will, nothing remotely suggestive of the stable at Bethlehem. It seems to have been originally either a coronation ode for a new king, promising conquest and empire, or a poem addressed to some king on the eve of a war, promising victory. It is full of threats. The "rod" of the king's power is to go forth from Jerusalem, foreign kings are to be wounded, battle fields to be covered with carnage, skulls cracked. The note is not "Peace and good-will" but "Beware. He's coming". Two things attach it to Christ with an authority far beyond that of the Prayer Book. The first of course (already mentioned) is that He Himself did so; He is the "lord" whom "David" calls "my Lord". The second is the reference to Melchizedek (*4*). The identification of this very mysterious person as a symbol or prophecy of Christ is made in *Hebrews* 7. The exact form of the comment there made on *Genesis* 14 is of course alien to our minds, but I think the essentials can all be retained in our own idiom. We should certainly not argue from the failure of *Genesis* to give Melchizedek any genealogy or even parents that he has neither beginning nor end (if it comes to that, Job has no genealogy either); but we should be vividly aware that his unrelated, unaccounted for, appearance sets him strangely apart from the texture of the surrounding narrative. He comes from nowhere, blesses in the name of the "most high God, possessor of heaven and earth", and utterly disappears. This gives him the effect of belonging, if not to *the* Other World, at any rate to *another* world; other than the story of Abraham in general. He assumes without question, as the writer of *Hebrews* saw, a superiority over Abraham which Abraham accepts. He is an august, a "numinous" figure. What the teller, or last re-teller, of *Genesis* would have said if we asked him why he brought this episode in or where he had got it from, I do not know. I think, as I have explained, that a pressure from God lay upon these tellings and re-tellings. And one effect which the episode of Melchizedek was to have is quite clear. It puts in, with unforgettable impressiveness, the idea of a priesthood, not Pagan but a priesthood to the one God, far earlier than the Jewish priesthood which descends from Aaron, independent of the call to Abraham, somehow superior to Abraham's vocation. And this older, pre-Judaic, priesthood is united with royalty; Melchizedek is a priest-king. In some communities priest-kings were normal, but not in Israel. It is thus simply a fact that Melchizedek resembles (in his peculiar way

[1]See Appendix I, page 207.

he is the only Old Testament character who resembles) Christ Himself. For He, like Melchizedek claims to be Priest, though not of the priestly tribe, and also King. Melchizedek really does point to Him; and so of course does the hero of Psalm 110 who is a king but also has the same sort of priesthood.

For a Jewish convert to Christianity this was extremely important and removed a difficulty. He might be brought to see how Christ was the successor of David; it would be impossible to say that He was, in a similar sense, the successor of Aaron. The idea of His priesthood therefore involved the recognition of a priesthood independent of and superior to Aaron's. Melchizedek was there to give this conception the sanction of the Scriptures. For us gentile Christians it is rather the other way round. We are more likely to start from the priestly, sacrificial, and intercessory character of Christ and under-stress that of king and conqueror. Psalm 110, with three other Christmas Psalms, corrects this. In 45, we have again the almost threatening tone: "Gird thee with thy sword upon thy thigh, O thou most mighty . . . thy right hand shall teach thee terrible things . . . thy arrows are very sharp"(*4 – 6*). In 89 we have the promises to David (who would certainly mean all, or any, of David's successors, just as "Jacob" can mean all his descendants). Foes are to fall before him (*24*). "David will call God "Father", and God says "I will make him my firstborn" (*27, 28*), that is "I will make him an eldest son", make him my heir, give him the whole world. In 132 we have "David" again; "As for his enemies, I shall clothe them with shame, but upon himself shall his crown flourish" (*19*). All this emphasises an aspect of the Nativity to which our later sentiment about Christmas (excellent in itself) does less than justice. For those who first read these Psalms as poems about the birth of Christ, that birth primarily meant something very militant; the hero, the "judge" or champion or giant-killer, who was to fight and beat death, hell and the devils, had at last arrived, and the evidence suggests that Our Lord also thought of Himself in those terms. (Milton's poem on the *Nativity* well recaptures this side of Christmas.)

The assignment of Psalm 68[1] to Whitsunday has some obvious reasons, even at a first reading. Verse *8*, "The earth shook and the heavens dropped at the presence of God, even as Sinai also was moved," was, no doubt, for the original writer a reference to the miracles mentioned in *Exodus,* and this foreshadows that very different descent of God which came with the tongues of fire. Verse *11* is a beautiful instance of the way in which the old texts almost inevitably charge themselves with the new weight of meaning. The Prayer Book version gives it as "The Lord gave the word, great was the company of the preachers". The "word" would be the order for battle and its "preachers" (in rather a grim sense) the triumphant Jewish warriors. But that translation appears to be wrong. The verse really means that there were many to spread "word" (i.e. the news) of the victory. This will suit Pentecost quite as well. But I think the real New Testament authority for assigning this Psalm to Whitsunday appears in verse *18* (in the Prayer Book, "Thou art gone up on high, thou hast led captivity captive, and received gifts for men"). According to the scholars the Hebrew

[1]See Appendix I, page 204.

text here means that God, with the armies of Israel as his agents, had taken huge masses of prisoners and received "gifts" (booty or tribute) *from* men. St. Paul, however (*Ephesians* 4, *8*) quotes a different reading: "When He ascended up on high He led captivity captive and *gave* gifts *to* men." This must be the passage which first associated the Psalm with the coming of the Holy Ghost, for St. Paul is there speaking of the gifts of the Spirit *(4 — 7)* and stressing the fact that they come after the Ascension. After ascending, as a result of ascending, Christ gives these gifts to men, or receives these gifts (notice how the Prayer Book version will now do well enough) from His Father "for men", for the use of men, in order to transmit them to men. And this relation between the Ascension and the coming of the Spirit is of course in full accordance with Our Lord's own words, "It is expedient for you that I go away, for if I go not away the Comforter will not come unto you" (*John* 16, *7*); as if the one were somehow impossible without the other, as if the Ascension, the withdrawal from the space-time in which our present senses operate, of the incarnate God, were the necessary condition of God's presence in another mode. There is a mystery here that I will not even attempt to sound.

That Psalm has led us through some complications; those in which Christ appears as the sufferer are very much easier. And it is here too that the second meaning is most inevitable. If Christ "tasted death for all men", became the archetypal sufferer, then the expressions of all who ever suffered in the world are, from the very nature of things, related to His. Here (to speak in ludicrously human terms) we feel that it needed no Divine guidance to give the old texts their second meaning but would rather have needed a special miracle to keep it out. In Psalm 22, the terrible poem which Christ quoted in His final torture, it is not "they pierced my hands and my feet" *(17)*, striking though this anticipation must always be, that really matters most. It is the union of total privation with total adherence to God, to a God who makes no response, simply because of what God is: "and thou continuest holy" (*3*). All the sufferings of the righteous speak here; but in 40, *15,* all the sufferings of the guilty too — "my sins have taken such hold upon me that I am not able to look up." But this too is for us the voice of Christ, for we have been taught that He who was without sin became sin for our sakes, plumbed the depth of that worst suffering which comes to evil men who at last know their own evil. Notice how this, in the original or literal sense, is hardly consistent with verses *8, 9,* and what counterpoint of truth this apparent contradiction takes on once the speaker is understood to be Christ.

But to say more of these suffering Psalms would be to labour the obvious. What I, at any rate, took longer to see was the full richness of that Christmas Psalm we have already mentioned, Psalm 45,[1] which shows us so many aspects of the Nativity we could never get from the carols or even (easily) from the gospels. This in its original intention was obviously a laureate ode on a royal wedding. (We are nowadays surprised to find that such an official bit of work, made "to order" by a court poet for a special occasion, should be good poetry. But in ages when the arts had their full

[1]See Appendix I, page 203.

health no one would have understood our surprise. All the great poets, painters, and musicians of old could produce great work "to order". One who could not would have seemed as great a humbug as a captain who could navigate or a farmer who could farm only when the fit took him.) And simply as a marriage ode — what the Greeks call an *Epithalamium* — it is magnificent. But it is far more valuable for the light it throws on the Incarnation.

Few things once seemed to me more frigid and far-fetched than those interpretations, whether of this Psalm or of the *Song of Songs*, which identify the Bridegroom with Christ and the bride with the Church. Indeed, as we read the frank erotic poetry of the latter and contrast it with the edifying headlines in our Bibles, it is easy to be moved to a smile, even a cynically knowing smile, as if the pious interpreters were feigning an absurd innocence. I should still find it very hard to believe that anything like the "spiritual" sense was remotely intended by the original writers. But no one now (I fancy) who accepts that spiritual or second sense is denying, or saying anything against, the very plain sense which the writers did intend. The Psalm remains a rich, festive Epithalamium, the *Song* remains fine, sometimes exquisite, love poetry, and this is not in the least obliterated by the burden of the new meanings. (Man is still one of the primates; a poem is still black marks on white paper.) And later I began to see that the new meaning is not arbitrary and springs from depths I had not suspected. First, the language of nearly all great mystics, not even in a common tradition, some of them Pagan, some Islamic, most Christian, confronts us with evidence that the image of marriage, of sexual union, is not only profoundly natural but almost inevitable as a means of expressing the desired union between God and man. The very word "union" has already entailed some such idea. Secondly, the god as bridegroom, his "holy marriage" with the goddess, is a recurrent theme and a recurrent ritual in many forms of Paganism — Paganism not at what we should call its purest or most enlightened, but perhaps at its most religious, at its most serious and convinced. And if, as I believe, Christ, in transcending and thus abrogating, also fulfils, both Paganism and Judaism, then we may expect that He fulfils this side of it too. This, as well as all else, is to be "summed up" in Him. Thirdly, the idea appears, in a slightly different form, within Judaism. For the mystics God is the Bridegroom of the individual soul. For the Pagans, the god is the bridegroom of the mother-goddess, the earth, but his union with her also makes fertile the whole tribe and its livestock, so that in a sense he is their bridegroom too. The Judaic conception is in some ways closer to the Pagan than to that of the mystics, for in it the Bride of God is the whole nation, Israel. This is worked out in one of the most moving and graphic chapters of the whole Old Testament (*Ezekiel* 16). Finally, this is transferred in the Apocalypse from the old Israel to the new, and the Bride becomes the Church, "the whole blessed company of faithful people". It is this which has, like the unworthy bride in Ezekiel, been rescued, washed, clothed, and married by God — a marriage like King Cophetua's. Thus the allegory which at first seemed so arbitrary — the ingenuity of some prudish commentator who was determined to force flat edifications upon the most unpromising texts — turned out, when you seriously tugged at it, to have roots in the whole history of religion, to be loaded with poetry, to yield insights. To reject it because it does not immediately appeal to our own age is to be provincial, to have the self-complacent blindness of the stay-at-home.

Read in this sense, the Psalm restores Christmas to its proper complexity. The birth of Christ is the arrival of the great warrior and the great king. Also of the Lover, the Bridegroom, whose beauty surpasses that of man. But not only the bridegroom as the lover, the desired; the Bridegroom also as he who makes fruitful, the father of children still to be begotten and born. (Certainly the image of a Child in a manger by no mean suggests to us a king, giant-killer, bridegroom, and father. But it would not suggest the eternal Word either — if we didn't know. All alike are aspects of the same central paradox.) Then the poet turns to the Bride, with the exhortation, "forget also thine own people and thy father's house" (*II*). This of course has a plain, and to us painful, sense while we read the Psalm as the poet probably intended it. One thinks of home-sickness, of a girl (probably a mere child) secretly crying in a strange *hareem*, of all the miseries which may underlie any dynastic marriage, especially an Oriental one. The poet (who of course knew all about this — he probably had a daughter of his own) consoles her: "Never mind, you have lost your parents but you will presently have children instead, and children who will be great men." But all this has also its poignant relevance when the Bride is the Church. A vocation is a terrible thing. To be called out of nature into the supernatural life is at first (or perhaps not quite at first — the wrench of the parting may be felt later) a costly honour. Even to be called from one natural level to another is loss as well as gain. Man has difficulties and sorrows which the other primates escape. But to be called up higher still costs still more." Get thee out of thy country, and from thy kindred, and from thy father's house", said God to Abraham (*Genesis* 12, *I*). It is a terrible command; turn your back on all you know. The consolation (if it will at that moment console) is very like that which the Psalmist offers to the bride: "I will make of thee a great nation." This "turn you back" is of course terribly repeated, one may say aggravated, by Our Lord — "he that hateth not father and mother and his own life." He speaks, as so often in the proverbial, paradoxical manner; hatred (in cold prose) is not enjoined; only the resolute, the apparently ruthless, rejection of natural claims when, and if, the terrible choice comes to that point. (Even so, this text is, I take it, profitable only to those who read it with horror. The man who finds it easy enough to hate his father, the woman whose life is a long struggle not to hate her mother, had probably best keep clear of it.) The consolation of the Bride, in this allegory, consists, not (where the mystics would put it) in the embraces of the Spouse, but in her fruitfulness. If she does not bear fruit, is not the mother of saints and sanctity, it may be supposed that the marriage was an illusion — for "a god's embraces never are in vain".

The choice of Psalm 8[1] for Ascension Day again depends on an interpretation

[1]See Appendix I, page 202.

found in the New Testament. In its literal sense this short, exquisite lyric is simplicity itself – an expression of wonder at man and man's place in Nature (there is a chorus in Sophocles not unlike it) and therefore at God who appointed it. God is wonderful both as champion or "judge" and as Creator. When one looks up at the sky, and all the stars which are His work, it seems strange that He should be concerned at all with such things as man. Yet in fact, though He has made us inferior to the celestial beings, He has, down here on earth, given us extraordinary honour – made us lords of all the other creatures. But to the writer of *Hebrews* (2, 6 – 9) this suggested something which we, of ourselves, would never have thought of. The Psalmist said "Thou has put all things in subjection under his (man's) feet" (6). The Christian writer observes that, in the actual state of the universe, this is not strictly true. Man is often killed, and still more often defeated, by beasts, poisonous vegetables, weather, earthquakes, etc. It would seem to us merely perverse and captious thus to take a poetic expression as if it were intended for a scientific universal. We can get nearest to the point of view if we imagine the commentator arguing nòt (as I think he actually does) "Since this is not true of the present, and since all the scriptures must be true, the statement must really refer to the future", but rather, "This is of course true in the poetic – and therefore, to a logician, the loose – sense which the poet intended; but how if it were far truer than he knew?" This will lead us, by a route that is easier for our habits of mind, to what he thinks the real meaning – or I should say the "over-meaning", the new weight laid upon the poet's words. Christ has ascended into Heaven. And in due time all things, quite strictly all, will be subjected to Him. It is He who having been made (for a while) "lower than the angels", will become the conqueror and ruler of all things, including death and (death's patron) the devil.

To most of us this will seem a wire-drawn allegory. But it is the very same which St. Paul obviously has in mind in I *Corinthians* 15, 20 – 28. This, with the passage in *Hebrews*, makes it pretty certain that the interpretation was established in the earliest Christian tradition. It may even descend from Our Lord. There was, after all, no description of Himself which He delighted in more than the "Son of Man," and of course, just as "daughter of Babylon" means Babylon, so "Son of Man" means Man, the Man, the archetypal Man, in whose suffering, resurrection, and victories all men (unless they refuse) can share.

And it is this, I believe, that most modern Christians need to be reminded of. It seems to me that I seldom meet any strong or exultant sense of the continued, never-to-be-abandoned, Humanity of Christ in glory, in eternity. We stress the Humanity too exclusively at Christmas, and the Deity too exclusively after the Resurrection; almost as if Christ once became a man and then presently reverted to being simply God. We think of the Resurrection and Ascension (rightly) as great acts of God; less often as the triumph of Man. The ancient interpretation of Psalm 8, however arrived at, is a cheering corrective. Nor, on further consideration, is the analogy of humanity's place in the universe (its greatness and littleness, its humble origins and – even on the natural level – amazing destiny) to the humiliation and victories of

Christ, really strained and far-fetched. At least it does not seem so to me. As I have already indicated, there seems to me to be something more than analogy between the taking up of animality into man and the taking up of man into God.

But I walk in wonders beyond myself. It is time to conclude with a brief notice of some simpler things.

One is the apparent (and often no doubt real) self-righteousness of the Psalms: "Thou shalt find no wickedness in me" (17, *3*), "I have walked innocently" (26, *1*), "Preserve thou my soul, for I am holy" (86, *2*). For many people it will not much mend matters if we say, as we probably can with truth, that sometimes the speaker was from the first intended to be Israel, not the individual; and even, within Israel, the faithful remnant. Yet it makes some difference; up to a certain point that remnant was holy and innocent compared with some of the surrounding Pagan cultures. It was often an "innocent sufferer" in the sense that it had not deserved what was inflicted on it, nor deserved it at the hands of those who inflicted it. But of course there was to come a Sufferer who was in fact holy and innocent. Plato's imaginary case was to become actual. All these assertions were to become true in His mouth. And if true, it was necessary they should be made. The lesson that perfect, unretaliating, forgiving innocence can lead as the world is, not to love but to the screaming curses of the mob and to death, is essential. Our Lord therefore becomes the speaker in these passages when a Christian reads them; by right — it would be an obscuring of the real issue if He did not. For He denied all sin of Himself. (That, indeed, is no small argument of His Deity. For He has not often made even on the enemies of Christianity the impression of arrogance; many of them do not seem as shocked as we should expect at His claim to be "meek and lowly of heart". Yet He said such things as, on any hypothesis but one, would be the arrogance of a paranoiac. It is as if, even where the hypothesis is rejected, some of the reality which implies its truth "got across").

Of the cursing Psalms I suppose most of us make our own moral allegories — well aware that these are personal and on a quite different level from the high matters I have been trying to handle. We know the proper object of utter hostility — wickedness, especially our own. Thus in 36, "My heart showeth me the wickedness of the ungodly," each can reflect that his own heart is the specimen of that wickedness best known to him. After that, the upward plunge at verse *5* into the mercy high as heaven and the righteousness solid as the mountains takes on even more force and beauty. From this point of view I can use even the horrible passage in 137 about dashing the Babylonian babies against the stones. I know things in the inner world which are like babies; the infantile beginning of small indulgences, small resentments, which may one day become dipsomania or settled hatred, but which woo us and wheedle us with special pleadings and seem so tiny, so helpless that in resisting them we feel we are being cruel to animals. They begin whimpering to us "I don't ask much, but", or "I had at least hoped", or "you owe yourself *some* consideration". Against all such pretty infants (the dears have such winning ways) the advice of the Psalm is the best. Knock the little bastards' brains out. And "blessed" he who can, for it's easier said than done.

Sometimes with no prompting from tradition a second meaning will impose itself upon a reader irresistibly. When the poet of Psalm 84 said (*10*) "For one day in thy courts is better than a thousand", he doubtless meant that one day there was better than a thousand elsewhere. I find it impossible to exclude while I read this thought which, so far as I know, the Old Testament never quite reaches. It is there in the New, beautifully introduced not by laying a new weight on old words but more simply by adding to them. In Psalm 90 (*4*) it had been said that a thousand years were to God like a single yesterday; in 2 *Peter* 3, *8* — not the first place in the world where one would have looked for so metaphysical a theology — we read not only that a thousand years are as one day but also that "one day is as a thousand years". The Psalmist only meant, I think, that God was everlasting, that His life was infinite in time. But the epistle takes us out of the time-series altogether. As nothing outlasts God, so nothing slips away from Him into a past. The later conception (later in Christian thought — Plato had reached it) of the timeless as an eternal present has been achieved. Ever afterwards, for some of us, the "one day" in God's court which is better than a thousand, must carry a double meaning. The Eternal may meet us in what is, by our present measurements, a day, or (more likely) a minute or a second; but we have touched what is not in any way commensurable with lengths of time, whether long or short. Hence our hope finally to emerge, if not altogether from time (that might not suit our humanity) at any rate from the tyranny, the unilinear poverty, of time, to ride it not to be ridden by it, and so to cure that always aching wound ("the wound man was born for") which mere succession and mutability inflict on us, almost equally when we are happy and when we are unhappy. For we are so little reconciled to time that we are even astonished at it. "How he's grown!" we exclaim, "How time flies!" as though the universal form of our experience were again and again a novelty. It is as strange as if a fish were repeatedly surprised at the wetness of water. And that would be strange indeed; unless of course the fish were destined to become, one day, a land animal.

APPENDIX I:
SELECTED PSALMS

PSALM

8 *Domine, Dominus noster*

O Lord our Governor, how excellent is thy Name in all the world: thou that hast set thy glory above the heavens!

2. Out of the mouth of very babes and sucklings hast thou ordained strength, because of thine enemies: that thou mightest still the enemy and the avenger.

3. For I will consider thy heavens, even the works of thy fingers: the moon and the stars, which thou hast ordained.

4. What is man, that thou art mindful of him: and the son of man, that thou visitest him?

5. Thou madest him lower than the angels: to crown him with glory and worship.

6. Thou makest him to have dominion of the works of thy hands: and thou has put all things in subjection under his feet;

7. All sheep and oxen: yea, and the beasts of the field.

8. The fowls of the air, and the fishes of the sea: and whatsoever walketh through the paths of the seas.

9. O Lord our Governor: how excellent is thy Name in all the world!

19 *Coeli enarrant*

The heavens declare the glory of God: and the firmament showeth his handywork

2. One day telleth another: and one night certifieth another.

3. There is neither speech nor language: but their voices are heard among them.

4. Their sound is gone out into all lands: and their words into the ends of the world.

5. In them hath he set a tabernacle for the sun: which cometh forth as a bridegroom out of his chamber, and rejoiceth as a giant to run his course.

6. It goeth forth from the uttermost part of the heaven, and runneth about unto the end of it again: and there is nothing hid from the heat thereof.

7. The law of the Lord is an undefiled law, converting the soul: the testimony of the Lord is sure, and giveth wisdom unto the simple.

8. The statutes of the Lord are right, and rejoice the heart: the commandment of the Lord is pure, and giveth light unto the eyes.

9. The fear of the Lord is clean, and endureth for ever: the judgements of the Lord are true, and righteous altogether.

10. More to be desired are they than gold, yea, than much fine gold: sweeter also than honey, and the honeycomb.

PSALM

11. Moreover, by them is thy servant taught: and in keeping of them there is great reward.

12. Who can tell how oft he offendeth: O clense thou me from my secret faults.

13. Keep thy servant also from presumptuous sins, lest they get the dominion over me: so shall I be undefiled, and innocent from the great offence.

14. Let the words of my mouth, and the meditation of my heart: be always acceptable in thy sight.

15. O Lord: my strength, and my redeemer.

36 *Dixit injustus*

My heart sheweth me the wickedness of the ungodly: that there is no fear of God before his eyes.

2. For he flattereth himself in his own sight: until his abominable sin be found out.

3. The words of his mouth are unrighteous, and full of deceit: he hath left off to behave himself wisely, and to do good.

4. He imagineth mischief upon his bed, and hath set himself in no good way: neither doth he abhor any thing that is evil.

5. Thy mercy, O Lord, reacheth unto the heavens: and thy faithfulness unto the clouds.

6. Thy righteousness standeth like the strong mountains: thy judgements are like the great deep.

7. Thou, Lord, shalt save both man and beast; How excellent is thy mercy, O God: and the children of men shall put their trust under ths shadow of thy wings.

8. They shall be satisfied with the plenteousness of thy house: and thou shalt give them drink of thy pleasures, as out of the river.

9. For with thee is the well of life: and in thy light shall we see light.

10. O continue forth thy loving-kindness unto them that know thee: and thy righteousness unto them that are true of heart.

11. O let not the foot of pride come against me: and let not the hand of the ungodly cast me down.

12. There are they fallen, all that work wickedness: they are cast down, and shall not be able to stand.

45 *Eructavit cor meum*

My heart is inditing of a good matter: I speak of the things which I have made unto the King.

2. My tongue is the pen: of a ready writer.

3. Thou art fairer than the children of men: full of grace are thy lips, because God hath blessed thee for ever,

4. Gird thee with thy sword upon thy thigh, O thou most Mighty: according to thy worship and renown.

5. Good luck have thou with thine honour: ride on, because of the word of truth, of meekness, and righteousness; and thy right hand shall teach thee terrible things.

6. The arrows are very sharp, and the people shall be subdued unto thee: even in the midst among the King's enemies.

7. Thy seat, O God, endureth for ever: the sceptre of thy kingdom is a right sceptre.

8. Thou has loved righteousness, and hated iniquity: wherefore God , even thy God, hath anointed thee with the oil of gladness above thy fellows.

9. All the garments smell of myrrh, aloes, and cassia: out of the ivory palaces, whereby they have made thee glad.

10. Kings' daughters were among thy honourable women: upon thy right hand did stand the queen in a vesture of gold, wrought about with divers colours.

11. Hearken, O daughter, and consider, incline thine ear: forget also thine own people, and thy father's house.

12. So shall the King have pleasure in thy beauty: for he is thy Lord God, and worship thou him.

13. And the daughter of Tyre shall be there with a gift: like as the rich also among the people shall make their supplication before thee.

14. The King's daughter is all glorious within: her clothing is of wrought gold.

15. She shall be brought unto the King in raiment of needlework: the virgins that be her fellows shall bear her company, and shall be brought unto thee.

16. With joy and gladness shall they be brought: and shall enter into the King's palace.

17. Instead of thy fathers thou shalt have children: whom thou mayest make princes in all lands.

18. I will remember thy Name from one generation to another: therefore shall the people give thanks unto thee, world without end.

68 *Exurgat Deus*

Let God arise, and let his enemies be scattered: let them also that hate him flee before him.

2. Like as the smoke vanisheth, so shalt thou drive them away: and like as wax melteth at the fire, so let the ungodly perish at the presence of God.

3. But let the righteous be glad and rejoice before God: let them also be merry and joyful.

4. O sing unto God, and sing praises unto his Name: magnify him that rideth upon the heavens, as it were upon an horse; praise him in his Name JAH, and rejoice before him.

5. He is a Father of the fatherless, and defendeth the cause of the widows: even God in his Holy habitation.

6. He is the God that maketh men to be of one mind in an house, and bringeth the prisoners out of captivity: but letteth the runagates continue in scarceness.

7. O God, when thou wentest forth before the people: when thou wentest through the wilderness,

8. The earth shook, and the heavens dropped at the presence of God: even as Sinai also was moved at the presence of God, who is the God of Israel.

9. Thou, O God, sentest a gracious rain upon thine inheritance: and refreshedst it when it was weary.

10. Thy congregation shall dwell therein: for thou, O God, hast of thy goodness prepared for the poor.

11. The Lord gave the word: great was the company of the preachers.

12. Kings with their armies did flee, and were discomfited: and they of the household divided the spoil.

13. Though ye have lien among the pots, yet shall ye be as the wings of a dove: that is covered with silver wings, and her feathers like gold.

14. When the Almighty scattered kings for their sake: then were they as white as snow in Salmon.

15. As the hill of Basan, so is God's hill: even an high hill, as the hill of Basan.

16. Why hop ye so, ye high hills? this is God's hill, in the which it pleaseth him to dwell: yea, the Lord will abide in it for ever.

17. The chariots of God are twenty thousand, even thousands of angels: and the Lord is among them, as in the holy place of Sinai.

18. Thou art gone up on high, thou has led captivity captive, and received gifts for men: yea, even for thine enemies, that the Lord God might dwell among them.

19. Praised be the Lord daily: even the God who helpeth us, and poureth his benefits upon us.

20. He is our God, even the God of whom cometh salvation: God is the Lord, by whom we escape death.

21. God shall wound the head of his enemies: and the hairy scalp of such a one as goeth on still in wickedness.

22. The Lord hath said, I will bring my people again, as I did from Basan: mine own will I bring again, as I did sometime from the deep of the sea.

23. That thy foot may be dipped in the blood of thine enemies: and that the tongue of thy dogs may be red through the same.

24. It is well seen, O God, how thou goest: how thou, my God and King, goest in the sanctuary.

25. The singers go before, the minstrels follow after: in the midst are the damsels playing with the timbrels.

26. Give thanks, O Israel, unto God the Lord in the congregations: from the ground of the heart.

27. There is little Benjamin, their ruler, and the princes of Judah their counsel: the princes of Zabulon, and the princes of Nephthali.

28. Thy God hath sent forth strength for thee: establish the thing, O God, that thou hast wrought in us.

29. For thy temple's sake at Jerusalem: so shall kings bring presents unto thee.

30. When the company of the spear-men, and multitude of the mighty are scattered abroad among the beasts of the people, so that they humbly bring pieces of silver: and when he hath scattered the people that delight in war;

31. Then shall the princes come out of Egypt: the Morians' land shall soon stretch out her hands unto God.

32. Sing unto God, O ye kingdoms of the earth: O sing praises unto the Lord.

33. Who sitteth in the heavens over all from the beginning: lo, he doth send out his voice, yea, and that a mighty voice.

34. Ascribe ye the power to God over Israel: his worship and strength is in the clouds.

35. O God, wonderful art thou in thy holy places: even the God of Israel; he will give strength and power unto his people: blessed be God.

104 *Benedic, anima mea*

Praise the Lord, O my soul: O Lord my God, thou art become exceeding glorious; thou art clothed with majesty and honour.

2. Thou deckest thyself with light as it were with a garment: the spreadest out the heavens like a curtain.

3. Who layeth the beams of his chambers in the waters: and maketh the clouds his chariot, and walketh upon the wings of the wind.

4. He maketh his angels spirits: and his ministers a flaming fire.

5. He laid the foundations of the earth: that it never should move at any time.

6. Thou coveredst it with the deep like as with a garment: the waters stand in the hills.

7. At thy rebuke they flee: at the voice of thy thunder they are afraid.

8. They go up as high as the hills, and down to the valleys beneath: even unto the place which thou hast appointed for them.

9. Thou hast set them their bounds which they shall not pass: neither turn again to cover the earth.

10. He sendeth the springs into the rivers: which run among the hills.

11. All beasts of the field drink thereof: and the wild asses quench their thirst.

12. Beside them shall the fowls of the air have their habitation: and sing among the branches.

13. He watereth the hills from above: the earth is filled with the fruit of thy works.

14. He bringeth forth grass for the cattle: and green herb for the service of men.

15. That he may bring food out of the earth, and wine that maketh glad the heart of man: and oil to make him a cheerful countenance, and bread to strengthen man's heart.

16. The trees of the Lord also are full of sap: even the cedars of Libanus which he hath planted.

17. Wherein the birds make their nests: and the fir-trees are a dwelling for the stork.

18. The high hills are a refuge for the wild goats: and so are the stony rocks for the conies.

19. He appointed the mood for certain seasons: and the sun knoweth his going down.

20. Thou makest darkness that it may be night: wherein all the beasts of the forest do move.

21. The lions roaring after their prey: do seek their meat from God.

22. The sun ariseth, and they get them away together: and lay them down in their dens.

23. Man goeth forth to his work, and to his labour; until the evening.

24. O Lord, how manifold are thy works: in wisdom hast thou made them all; the earth is full of thy riches.

25. So is the great and wide sea also: wherein are things creeping innumerable, both small and great beasts.

26. There go the ships, and there is that Leviathan: whom thou hast made to take his pastime therein.

27. These wait all upon thee: that thou mayest give them their meat in due season.

28. When thou givest it them they gather it: and when thou openest thy hand they are filled with good.

29. When thou hidest thy face they are troubled: when thou takest away their breath they die, and are turned again to their dust.

30. When thou lettest thy breath go forth they shall be made: and thou shalt renew the face of the earth,

31. The glorious majesty of the Lord shall endure for ever: the Lord shall rejoice in his works.

32. The earth shall tremble at the look of him: if he do but touch the hills, they shall smoke.

33. I will sing unto the Lord as long as I live: I will praise my God while I have my being.

34. And so shall my words please him: my joy shall be in the Lord.

35. As for sinners, they shall be consumed out of the earth, and the ungodly shall come to an end: praise thou the Lord, O my soul, praise the Lord.

PSALM

110 *Dixit Dominus*

The Lord said unto my Lord: Sit thou on my right hand, until I make thine enemies thy footstool.

2. The Lord shall send the rod of thy power out of Sion: be thou ruler, even in the midst among thine enemies.

3. In the day of thy power shall the people offer thee free-will offerings with an holy worship: the dew of thy birth is of the womb of the morning.

4. The Lord sware, and will not repent: Thou art a Priest for ever after the order of Melchisedech.

5. The Lord upon thy right hand: shall wound even kings in the day of his wrath.

6. He shall judge among the heathen; he shall fill the places with the dead bodies: and smite in sunder the heads over divers countries.

7. He shall drink of the brook in the way: therefore shall he lift up his head.

APPENDIX II: PSALMS
DISCUSSED OR MENTIONED

The Four Loves

That our affections kill us not, nor dye.
— DONNE

I

INTRODUCTION

"God is love," says St. John. When I first tried to write this book I thought that his maxim would provide me with a very plain highroad through the whole subject. I thought I should be able to say that human loves deserved to be called loves at all just in so far as they resembled that Love which is God. The first distinction I made was therefore between what I called Gift-love and Need-love. The typical example of Gift-love would be that love which moves a man to work and plan and save for the future well-being of his family which he will die without sharing or seeing; of the second, that which sends a lonely or frightened child to its mother's arms.

There was no doubt which was more like Love Himself. Divine Love is Gift-love. The Father gives all He is and has to the Son. The Son gives Himself back to the Father, and gives Himself to the world, and for the world to the Father, and thus gives the world (in Himself) back to the Father too.

And what, on the other hand, can be less like anything we believe of God's life than Need-love? He lacks nothing, but our Need-love, as Plato saw, is "the son of Poverty." It is the accurate reflection in consciousness of our actual nature. We are born helpless. As soon as we are fully conscious we discover loneliness. We need others physically, emotionally, intellectually; we need them if we are to know anything, even ourselves.

I was looking forward to writing some fairly easy panegyrics on the first sort of love and disparagements of the second. And much of what I was going to say still seems to me to be true. I still think that if all we mean by our love is a craving to be loved, we are in a very deplorable state. But I would not now say (with my master, MacDonald) that if we mean only this craving we are mistaking for love something that is not love at all. I cannot now deny the name *love* to Need-love. Every time I have tried to think the thing out along those lines I have ended in puzzles and contradictions. The reality is more complicated than I supposed.

First of all, we do violence to most languages, including our own, if we do not call Need-love "love." Of course language is not an infallible guide, but it contains, with all its defects, a good deal of stored insight and experience. If you begin by flouting it, it has a way of avenging itself later on. We had better not follow Humpty Dumpty in making words mean whatever we please.

Secondly, we must be cautious about calling Need-love "mere selfishness." *Mere* is always a dangerous word. No doubt Need-love, like all our impulses, can be selfishly indulged. A tyrannous and gluttonous demand for affection can be a horrible thing. But in ordinary life no one calls a child selfish because it turns for comfort to its mother; nor an adult who turns to his fellow "for company." Those, whether children or adults, who do so least are not usually the most selfless. Where Need-love is felt there may be reasons for denying or totally mortifying it; but not to feel it is in general the mark of the cold egoist. Since we do in reality need one another ("it is not good for man to be alone"), then the failure of this need to appear as Need-love in consciousness — in other words, the illusory feeling that it *is* good for us to be alone — is a bad spiritual symptom; just as lack of appetite is a bad medical symptom because men do really need food.

But thirdly, we come to something far more important. Every Christian would agree that a man's spiritual health is exactly proportional to his love for God. But man's love for God, from the very nature of the case, must always be very largely, and must often be entirely, a Need-love. This is obvious when we implore forgiveness for our sins or support in our tribulations. But in the long run it is perhaps even more apparent in our growing — for it ought to be growing — awareness that our whole being by its very nature is one vast need; incomplete, preparatory, empty yet cluttered, crying out for Him who can untie things that are now knotted together and tie up things that are still dangling loose. I do not say that man can never bring to God anything at all but sheer Need-love. Exalted souls may tell us of a reach beyond that. But they would also, I think, be the first to tell us that those heights would cease to be true Graces, would become Neo-Platonic or finally diabolical illusions, the moment a man dared to think that he could live on them and henceforth drop out the element of need. "The highest," says the *Imitation*, "does not stand without the lowest." It would be a bold and silly creature that came before its Creator with the boast "I'm no beggar. I love you disinterestedly." Those who come nearest to a Gift-love for God will next moment, even at the very same moment, be beating their breasts with the publican and laying their indigence before the only real Giver. And God will have it so. He addresses our Need-love: "Come unto me all ye that travail and are heavy-laden," or, in the Old Testament, "Open your mouth wide and I will fill it."

Thus one Need-love, the greatest of all, either coincides with or at least makes a main ingredient in man's highest, healthiest, and most realistic spiritual condition. A very strange corollary follows. Man approaches God most nearly when he is in one sense least like God. For what can be more unlike than fullness and need, sovereignty and humility, righteousness and penitence, limitless power and a cry for help? This paradox staggered me when I first ran into it; it also wrecked all my previous attempts to write about love. When we face it, something like this seems to result.

We must distinguish two things which might both possibly be called "nearness to God." One is likeness to God. God has impressed some sort of likeness to Himself, I suppose, in all that He has made. Space and time, in their own fashion, mirror His greatness; all life, His fecundity; animal life, His activity. Man has a more important likeness than these by being rational. Angels, we believe, have likenesses which Man lacks: immortality and intuitive knowledge. In that way all men, whether good or bad, all angels including those that fell, are more like God than the animals are. Their natures are in this sense "nearer" to the Divine Nature. But, secondly, there is what we may call nearness of approach. If this is what we mean, the states in which a man is "nearest" to God are those in which he is most surely and swiftly approaching his final union with God, vision of God and enjoyment of God. And as soon as we distinguish nearness-by-likeness and nearness-of -approach, we see that they do not necessarily coincide. They may or may not.

Perhaps an analogy may help. Let us suppose that we are doing a mountain walk to the village which is our home. At mid-day we come to the top of a cliff where we are, in space, very near it because it is just below us. We could drop a stone into it. But as we are no cragsmen we can't get down. We must go a long way round; five miles, maybe. At many points during that *détour* we shall, statically, be farther from the village than we were when we sat above the cliff. But only statically. In terms of progress we shall be far "nearer" our baths and teas.

Since God is blessed, omnipotent, sovereign and creative, there is obviously a sense in which happiness, strength, freedom and fertility (whether of mind or body), wherever they appear in human life, constitute likenesses, and in that way proximities, to God. But no one supposes that the possession of these gifts has any necessary connection with our sanctification. No kind of riches is a passport to the Kingdom of Heaven.

At the cliff's top we are near the village, but however long we sit there we shall never be any nearer to our bath and our tea. So here; the likeness, and in that sense nearness, to Himself which God has conferred upon certain creatures and certain states of those creatures is something finished, built in. What is near Him by likeness is never, by that fact alone, going to be any nearer. But nearness of approach is, by definition, increasing nearness. And whereas the likeness is given to us – and can be received with or without thanks, can be used or abused – the approach, however initiated and supported by Grace, is something we must do. Creatures are made in their varying ways images of God without their own collaboration or even consent. It is not so that they become sons of God. And the likeness they receive by sonship is not that of images or portraits. It is in one way more than likeness, for it is union or unity with God in will; but this is consistent with all the differences we have been considering. Hence, as a better writer has said, our imitation of God in this life – that is, our willed imitation as distinct from any of the likenesses which He has impressed upon our natures or states – must be an imitation of God incarnate: our model is the Jesus, not only of Calvary, but of the workshop, the roads, the crowds, the clamorous demands and surly oppositions, the lack of all peace and privacy, the interruptions. For this, so strangely unlike anything we can attribute to the Divine life in itself, is apparently not only like, but is, the Divine life operating under human conditions.

I must now explain why I have found this distinction necessary to any treatment of our loves. St. John's saying that God is love has long been balanced in my mind against the remark of a modern author (M. Denis de Rougemont) that "love ceases to be a demon only when he ceases to be a god"; which of course can be re-stated in the form "begins to be a demon the moment he begins to be a god." This balance seems to me an indispensable safeguard. If we ignore it the truth that God is love may slyly come to mean for us the converse, that love is God.

I suppose that everyone who has thought about the matter will see what M. de Rougemont meant. Every human love, at its height, has a tendency to claim for itself a divine authority. Its voice tends to sound as if it were the will of God Himself. It tells us not to count the cost, it demands of us a total commitment, it attempts to over-ride all other claims and insinuates that any action which is sincerely done "for love's sake" is thereby lawful and even meritorious. That erotic love and love of one's country may thus attempt to "become gods" is generally recognized. But family affection may do the same. So, in a different way, may friendship. I shall not here elaborate the point, for it will meet us again and again in later chapters.

Now it must be noticed that the natural loves make this blasphemous claim not when they are in their worst, but when they are in their best, natural condition; when they are what our grandfathers called "pure" or "noble." This is especially obvious in the erotic sphere. A faithful and genuinely self-sacrificing passion will speak to us with what seems the voice of God. Merely animal or frivolous lust will not. It will corrupt its addict in a dozen ways, but not in that way; a man may act upon such feelings but he cannot revere them any more than a man who scratches reveres the itch. A silly woman's temporary indulgence, which is really self-indulgence, to a spoiled child – her living doll while the fit lasts – is much less likely to "become a god" than the deep, narrow devotion of a woman who (quite really) "lives for her son." And I am inclined to think that the sort of love for a man's country which is worked up by beer and brass bands will not lead him to do much harm (or much good) for her sake. It will probably be fully discharged by ordering another drink and joining in the chorus.

And this of course is what we ought to expect. Our loves do not make their claim to divinity until the claim becomes plausible. It does not become plausible until there is in them a real resemblance to God, to Love Himself. Let us here make no mistake. Our Gift-loves are really God-like; and among our Gift-loves those are most God-like which are most boundless and unwearied in giving. All the things the poets say about them are true. Their joy, their energy, their patience, their readiness to forgive, their desire for the good of the beloved – all this is a real and all but adorable image of the Divine life. In its presence we are right to thank God "who has given such power to men." We may say, quite truly and in an intelligible sense, that those who love greatly are "near" to God. But of course it is "nearness by likeness." It will not of itself produce "nearness of approach." The likeness has been given us. It has no necessary connection with that slow and painful approach which must be our own (though by no means our unaided) task. Meanwhile, however, the likeness is a splendour. That is why we may mistake Like for Same. We may give our human loves the unconditional allegiance which we owe only to God. Then they become gods: then they become demons. Then they will destroy us, and also destroy themselves. For natural loves that are allowed to become gods do not remain loves. They are still called so, but can become in fact complicated forms of hatred.

Our Need-loves may be greedy and exacting but they do not set up to be gods. They are not near enough (by likeness) to God to attempt that.

It follows from what has been said that we must join neither the idolaters nor the "debunkers" of human love. Idolatry both of erotic love and of "the domestic affections" was the great error of nineteenth-century literature. Browning, Kingsley, and Patmore sometimes talk as if they thought that falling in love was the same thing as sanctification; the novelists habitually oppose to "the World" not the Kingdom of Heaven but the home. We live in the reaction against this. The debunkers stigmatise as slush and sentimentality a very great deal of what their fathers said in praise of love. They are always pulling up and exposing the grubby roots of our natural loves. But I take it we must listen neither "to the over-wise nor to the over-foolish giant." The highest does not stand without the lowest. A plant must have roots below as well as sunlight above and roots must be grubby. Much of the grubbiness is clean dirt if only you will leave it in the garden and not keep on sprinkling it over the library table. The human loves can be glorious images of Divine love. No less than that: but also no more — proximities of likeness which in one instance may help, and in another may hinder, proximity of approach. Sometimes perhaps they have not very much to do with it either way.

II

LIKINGS AND LOVES
FOR THE SUB-HUMAN

Most of my generation were reproved as children for saying that we "loved" straw-berries, and some people take a pride in the fact that English has the two verbs *love* and *like* while French has to get on with *aimer* for both. But French has a good many other languages on its side. Indeed it very often has actual English usage on its side too. Nearly all speakers, however pedantic or however pious, talk every day about "loving" a food, a game, or a pursuit. And in fact there is a continuity between our elementary likings for things and our loves for people. Since "the highest does not stand without the lowest" we had better begin at the bottom, with mere likings; and since to "like" anything means to take some sort of pleasure in it, we must begin with pleasure.

Now it is a very old discovery that pleasures can be divided into two classes; those which would not be pleasures at all unless they were preceded by desire, and those which are pleasures in their own right and need no such preparation. An ex-ample of the first would be a drink of water. This is a pleasure if you are thirsty and a great one if you are very thirsty. But probably no one in the world, except in obedi-ence to thirst or to a doctor's orders, ever poured himself out a glass of water and drank it just for the fun of the thing. An example of the other class would be the un-sought and unexpected pleasures of smell — the breath from a bean-field or a row of sweet-peas meeting you on your morning walk. You were in want of nothing, com-pletely contented, before it; the pleasure, which may be very great, is an unsolicited, super-added gift. I am taking very simple instances for clarity's sake, and of course there are many complications. If you are given coffee or beer where you expected (and would have been satisfied with) water, then of course you get a pleasure of the first kind (allaying of thirst) and one of the second (a nice taste) at the same time. Again, an addiction may turn what was once a pleasure of the second kind into one of the first. For the temperate man an occasional glass of wine is a treat — like the smell of the bean-field. But to the alcoholic, whose palate and digestion have long since

218

been destroyed, no liquor gives any pleasure except that of relief from an unbearable craving. So far as he can still discern tastes at all, he rather dislikes it; but it is better than the misery of remaining sober. Yet through all their permutations and combinations the distinction between the two glasses remains tolerably clear. We may call them Need-pleasures and Pleasures of Appreciation.

The resemblance between these Need-pleasures and the "Need-loves" in my first chapter will occur to everyone. But there, you remember, I confessed that I had had to resist a tendency to disparage the Need-loves or even to say they were not loves at all. Here, for most people, there may be an opposite inclination. It would be very easy to spread ourselves in laudation of the Need-pleasures and to frown upon those that are Appreciative: the one so natural (a word to conjure with), so necessary, so shielded from excess by their very naturalness, the other unnecessary and opening the door to every kind of luxury and vice. If we were short of matter on this theme we could turn on the tap by opening the works of the Stoics and it would run till we had a bathful. But throughout this inquiry we must be careful never to adopt prematurely a moral or evaluating attitude. The human mind is generally far more eager to praise and dispraise than to describe and define. It wants to make every distinction a distinction of value; hence those fatal critics who can never point out the differing quality of two poets without putting them in an order of preference as if they were candidates for a prize. We must do nothing of the sort about the pleasures. The reality is too complicated. We are already warned of this by the fact that Need-pleasure is the state in which Appreciative pleasures end up when they go bad (by addiction).

For us at any rate the importance of the two sorts of pleasure lies in the extent to which they foreshadow characteristics in our "loves" (properly so called).

The thirsty man who has just drunk off a tumbler of water may say, "By Jove, I *wanted* that." So may the alcoholic who has just had his "nip." The man who passes the sweet-peas in his morning walk is more likely to say, "How lovely the smell *is*." The connoisseur after his first sip of the famous claret, may similarly say, "This *is* a great wine." When Need-pleasures are in question we tend to make statements about ourselves in the past tense; when Appreciative pleasures are in question we tend to make statements about the object in the present tense. It is easy to see why.

Shakespeare has described the satisfaction of a tyrannous lust as something

> *Past reason hunted and, no sooner had,*
> *Past reason hated.*

But the most innocent and necessary of Need-pleasures have about them something of the same character — only something, of course. They are not hated once we have had them, but they certainly "die on us" with extraordinary abruptness, and completely. The scullery tap and the tumbler are very attractive indeed when we come in parched from mowing the grass; six seconds later they are emptied of all interest. The smell of frying food is very different before and after breakfast. And, if you will forgive me for citing the most extreme instance of all, have there not for most of us been moments (in a strange town) when the sight of the word GENTLEMEN over a door has roused a joy almost worthy of celebration in verse?

Pleasures of Appreciation are very different. They make us feel that something has not merely gratified our senses in fact but claimed our appreciation by right. The connoisseur does not merely enjoy his claret as he might enjoy warming his feet when they were cold. He feels that here is a wine that deserves his full attention; that justifies all the tradition and skill that have gone to its making and all the years of training that have made his own palate fit to judge it. There is even a glimmering of unselfishness in his attitude. He wants the wine to be preserved and kept in good condition, not entirely for his own sake. Even if he were on his death-bed and was never going to drink wine again, he would be horrified at the thought of this vintage being spilled or spoiled or even drunk by clods (like myself) who can't tell a good claret from a bad. And so with the man who passes the sweet-peas. He does not simply enjoy, he feels that this fragrance somehow deserves to be enjoyed. He would blame himself if he went past inattentive and undelighted. It would be blockish, insensitive. It would be a shame that so fine a thing should have been wasted on him. He will remember the delicious moment years hence. He will be sorry when he hears that the garden past which his walk led him that day has now been swallowed up by cinemas, garages, and the new by-pass.

Scientifically both sorts of pleasure are, no doubt, relative to our organisms. But the Need-pleasures loudly proclaim their relativity not only to the human frame but to its momentary condition, and outside that relation have no meaning or interest for us at all. The objects which afford pleasures of appreciation give us the feeling — whether irrational or not — that we somehow owe it to them to savour, to attend to and praise it. "It would be a sin to set a wine like that before Lewis," says the expert in claret. "How can you walk past this garden taking no notice of the smell?" we ask. But we should never feel this about a Need-pleasure: never blame ourselves or others for not having been thirsty and therefore walking past a well without taking a drink of water.

How the Need-pleasures foreshadow our Need-loves is obvious enough. In the latter the beloved is seen in relation to our own needs, just as the scullery tap is seen by the thirsty man or the glass of gin by the alcoholic. And the Need-love, like the Need-pleasure, will not last longer than the need. This does not, fortunately, mean that all affections which begin in Need-love are transitory. The need itself may be permanent or recurrent. Another kind of love may be grafted on the Need-love. Moral principles (conjugal fidelity, filial piety, gratitude, and the like) may preserve the relationship for a lifetime. But where Need-love is left unaided we can hardly expect it not to "die on us" once the need is no more. That is why the world rings with the complaints of mothers whose grown-up children neglect them and of forsaken mistresses whose lovers' love was pure need — which they have satisfied. Our Need-love for God is in a different position because our need of Him can never end either in this world or in any other. But our awareness of it can, and then the Need-love dies too. "The Devil was sick, the Devil a monk would be." There seems no reason for describing as hypocritical the short-lived piety of those whose religion fades away once they have emerged from "danger, necessity, or tribulation." Why should they not have been sincere?. They were desperate and they howled for help. Who wouldn't?

What Appreciative pleasure foreshadows is not so quickly described.

First of all, it is the starting point for our whole experience of beauty. It is impossible to draw a line below which such pleasures are "sensual" and above which they are "aesthetic." The experiences of the expert in claret already contain elements of concentration, judgement, and disciplined perceptiveness, which are not sensual; those of the musician still contain elements which are. There is no frontier – there is seamless continuity – between the sensuous pleasure of garden smells and an enjoyment of the countryside (or "beauty") as a whole, or even our enjoyment of the painters and poets who treat it.

And, as we have seen, there is in these pleasures from the very beginning a shadow or dawn of, or an invitation to, disinterestedness. Of course in one way we can be disinterested or unselfish, and far more heroically so, about the Need-pleasures: it is a cup of water that the wounded Sidney sacrifices to the dying soldier. But that is not the sort of disinterestedness I now mean. Sidney loves his neighbour. But in the Appreciative pleasures, even at their lowest, and more and more as they grow up into the full appreciation of all beauty, we get something that we can hardly help calling *love* and hardly help calling *disinterested,* towards the object itself. It is the feeling which would make a man unwilling to deface a great picture even if he were the last man left alive and himself about to die; which makes us glad of unspoiled forests that we shall never see; which makes us anxious that the garden or bean-field should continue to exist. We do not merely like the things; we pronounce them, in a momentarily God-like sense, "very good."

And now our principle of starting at the lowest – without which "the highest does not stand" – begins to pay a dividend. It has revealed to me a deficiency in our previous classification of the loves into those of Need and those of Gift. There is a third element in love, no less important than these, which is foreshadowed by our Appreciative pleasures. This judgment that the object is very good, this attention (almost homage) offered to it as a kind of debt, this wish that it should be and should continue being what it is even if we were never to enjoy it, can go out not only to things but to persons. When it is offered to a woman we call it admiration; when to a man, hero-worship; when to God, worship simply.

Need-love cries to God from our poverty; Gift-love longs to serve, or even to suffer for, God; Appreciative love says: "We give thanks to thee for thy great glory." Need-love says of a woman "I cannot live without her"; Gift-love longs to give her happiness, comfort, protection – if possible, wealth; Appreciative love gazes and holds its breath and is silent, rejoices that such a wonder should exist even if not for him, will not be wholly dejected by losing her, would rather have it so than never to have seen her at all.

We murder to dissect. In actual life, thank God, the three elements of love mix and succeed one another, moment by moment. Perhaps none of them except Need-love ever exists alone, in "chemical" purity, for more than a few seconds. And perhaps that is because nothing about us except our neediness is, in this life, permanent.

Two forms of love for what is not personal demand special treatment.

For some people, perhaps especially for Englishmen and Russians, what we call "the love of nature" is a permanent and serious sentiment. I mean here that love of nature which cannot be adequately classified simply as an instance of our love for beauty. Of course many natural objects — trees, flowers and animals — are beautiful. But the nature-lovers whom I have in mind are not very much concerned with individual beautiful objects of that sort. The man who is distracts them. An enthusiastic botanist is for them a dreadful companion on a ramble. He is always stopping to draw their attention to particulars. Nor are they looking for "views" or landscapes. Wordsworth, their spokesman, strongly deprecates this. It leads to "a comparison of scene with scene," makes you "pamper" yourself with "meagre novelties of colour and proportion." While you are busying yourself with this critical and discriminating activity you lose what really matters — the "moods of time and season," the "spirit" of the place. And of course Wordsworth is right. That is why, if you love nature in his fashion, a landscape painter is (out of doors) an even worse companion than a botanist.

It is the "moods" or the "spirit" that matter. Nature-lovers want to receive as fully as possible whatever nature, at each particular time and place, is, so to speak, saying. The obvious richness, grace, and harmony of some scenes are no more precious to them than the grimness, bleakness, terror, monotony, or "visionary dreariness" of others. The featureless itself gets from them a willing response. It is one more word uttered by nature. They lay themselves bare to the sheer quality of every countryside, every hour of the day. They want to absorb it into themselves, to be coloured through and through by it.

This experience, like so many others, after being lauded to the skies in the nineteenth century, has been debunked by the moderns. And one must certainly concede to the debunkers that Wordsworth, not when he was communicating it as a poet, but when he was merely talking about it as a philosopher (or philosophaster), said some very silly things. It is silly, unless you have found any evidence, to believe that flowers enjoy the air they breathe, and sillier not to add that, if this were true, flowers would undoubtedly have pains as well as pleasures. Nor have many people been taught moral philosophy by an "impulse from a vernal wood."

If they were, it would not necessarily be the sort of moral philosophy Wordsworth would have approved. It might be that of ruthless competition. For some moderns I think it is. They love nature in so far as, for them, she calls to "the dark gods in the blood"; not although, but because, sex and hunger and sheer power there operate without pity or shame.

If you take nature as a teacher she will teach you exactly the lessons you had already decided to learn; this is only another way of saying that nature does not teach. The tendency to take her as a teacher is obviously very easily grafted on to the experience we call "love of nature." But it is only a graft. While we are actually subjected to them, the "moods" and "spirits" of nature point no morals. Overwhelming gaiety, insupportable grandeur, sombre desolation are flung at you. Make what you can of them, if you must make at all. The only imperative that nature utters is, "Look. Listen. Attend."

The fact that this imperative is so often misinterpreted and sets people making theologies and pantheologies and antitheologies — all of which can be debunked — does not really touch the central experience itself. What nature-lovers — whether they are Wordsworthians or people with "dark gods in their blood" — get from nature is an iconography, a language of images. I do not mean simply visual images; it is the "moods" or "spirits" themselves — the powerful expositions of terror, gloom, jocundity, cruelty, lust, innocence, purity — that are the images. In them each man can clothe his own belief. We must learn our theology or philosophy elsewhere (not surprisingly, we often learn them from theologians and philosophers).

But when I speak of "clothing" our belief in such images I do not mean anything like using nature for similes or metaphors in the manner of the poets. Indeed I might have said "filling" or "incarnating" rather than clothing. Many people — I am one myself — would never, but for what nature does to us, have had any content to put into the words we must use in confessing our faith. Nature never taught me that there exists a God of glory and of infinite majesty. I had to learn that in other ways. But nature gave the word "glory" a meaning for me. I still do not know where else I could have found one. I do not see how the "fear" of God could have ever meant to me anything but the lowest prudential efforts to be safe, if I had never seen certain ominous ravines and unapproachable crags. And if nature had never awakened certain longings in me, huge areas of what I can now mean by the "love" of God would never, so far as I can see, have existed.

Of course the fact that a Christian can so use nature is not even the beginning of a proof that Christianity is true. Those suffering from Dark Gods can equally use her (I suppose) for their creed. That is precisely the point. Nature does not teach. A true philosophy may sometimes validate an experience of nature; an experience of nature cannot validate a philosophy. Nature will not verify any theological or metaphysical proposition (or not in the manner we are now considering); she will help to show what it means.

And not, on the Christian premises, by accident. The created glory may be expected to give us hints of the uncreated; for the one is derived from the other and in some fashion reflects it.

In some fashion. But not perhaps in so direct and simple a fashion as we at first might suppose. For of course all the facts stressed by nature-lovers of the other school are facts too; there are worms in the belly as well as primroses in the wood. Try to reconcile them, or to show that they don't really need reconciliation, and you are turning from direct experience of nature—our present subject—to metaphysics or theodicy or something of that sort. That may be a sensible thing to do; but I think it should be kept distinct from the love of nature. While we are on that level, while we are still claiming to speak of what nature has directly "said" to us, we must stick to it. We have seen an image of glory. We must not try to find a direct path through it and beyond it to an increasing knowledge of God. The path peters out almost at once. Terrors and mysteries, the whole depth of God's counsels and the whole tangle of the history of the universe, choke it. We can't get through; not that way. We must make a *détour*—leave the hills and woods and go back to our studies, to church, to our Bibles, to our knees. Otherwise the love of nature is beginning to turn into a nature religion. And then, even if it does not lead us to the Dark Gods, it will lead us to a great deal of nonsense.

But we need not surrender the love of nature—chastened and limited as I have suggested—to the debunkers. Nature cannot satisfy the desires she arouses nor answer theological questions nor sanctify us. Our real journey to God involves constantly turning our backs on her; passing from the dawn-lit fields into some poky little church, or (it might be) going to work in an East End parish. But the love of her has been a valuable and, for some people, an indispensable initiation.

I need not say "has been." For in fact those who allow no more than this love of nature seem to be those who retain it. This is what one should expect. This love, when it sets up as a religion, is beginning to be a god—therefore to be a demon. And demons never keep their promises. Nature "dies" on those who try to live for a love of nature. Coleridge ended by being insensible to her; Wordsworth, by lamenting that the glory had passed away. Say your prayers in a garden early, ignoring steadfastly the dew, the birds and the flowers, and you will come away overwhelmed by its freshness and joy; go there in order to be overwhelmed and, after a certain age, nine times out of ten nothing will happen to you.

I turn now to the love of one's country. Here there is no need to labour M. de Rougemont's maxim; we all know now that this love becomes a demon when it becomes a god. Some begin to suspect that it is never anything but a demon. But then they have to reject half the high poetry and half the heroic action our race has achieved. We cannot keep even Christ's lament over Jerusalem. He too exhibits love for His country.

Let us limit our field. There is no need here for an essay on international ethics. When this love becomes demoniac it will of course produce wicked acts. But others, more skilled, may say what acts between nations are wicked. We are only considering the sentiment itself in the hope of being able to distinguish its innocent from its demoniac condition. Neither of these is the efficient cause of national behavior. For strictly speaking it is rulers, not nations, who behave internationally. Demoniac patriotism in their subjects—I write only for subjects—will make it easier for them to act wickedly; healthy patriotism may make it harder: when they are wicked they may by propaganda encourage a demoniac condition of our sentiments in order to secure our acquiescence in their wickedness. If they are good, they could do the opposite. That is one reason why we private persons should keep a wary eye on the health or disease of our own love for our country. And that is what I am writing about.

How ambivalent patriotism is may be gauged by the fact that no two writers have expressed it more vigorously than Kipling and Chesterton. If it were one element two such men could not both have praised it. In reality it contains many ingredients, of which many different blends are possible.

First, there is love of home, of the place we grew up in or the places, perhaps many, which have been our homes; and of all places fairly near these and fairly like them; love of old acquaintances, of familiar sights, sounds and smells. Note that at its largest this is, for us, a love of England, Wales, Scotland, or Ulster. Only foreigners and politicians talk about "Britain." Kipling's "I do not love my empire's foes" strikes a ludicrously false note. *My* empire! With this love for the place there goes a love for the way of life; for beer and tea and open fires, trains with compartments in them and an unarmed police force and all the rest of it; for the local dialect and (a shade less) for our native language. As Chesterton says, a man's reasons for not wanting his country to be ruled by foreigners are very like his reasons for not wanting his house to be burned down; because he "could not even begin" to enumerate all the things he would miss.

It would be hard to find any legitimate point of view from which this feeling could be condemned. As the family offers us the first step beyond self-love, so this offers us the first step beyond family selfishness. Of course it is not pure charity; it involves love of our neighbours in the local, not of our Neighbour, in the Dominical, sense. But those who do not love the fellow-villagers or fellow-townsmen whom they *have* seen are not likely to have got very far towards loving "Man" whom they have not. All natural affections, including this, can become rivals to spiritual love: but they can also be preparatory imitations of it, training (so to speak) of the spiritual muscles which Grace may later put to a higher service; as women nurse dolls in childhood and later nurse children. There may come an occasion for renouncing this love; pluck out your right eye. But you need to have an eye first: a creature which had none — which had only got so far as a "photo-sensitive" spot — would be very ill employed in meditation on that severe text.

Of course patriotism of this kind is not in the least aggressive. It asks only to be let alone. It becomes militant only to protect what it loves. In any mind which has a pennyworth of imagination it produces a good attitude towards foreigners. How can I love my home without coming to realise that other men, no less rightly, love theirs? Once you have realised that the Frenchmen like *café complet* just as we like bacon and eggs — why, good luck to them and let them have it. The last thing we want is to make everywhere else just like our own home. It would not be home unless it were different.

The second ingredient is a particular attitude to our country's past. I mean to that past as it lives in popular imagination; the great deeds of our ancestors. Remember Marathon. Remember Waterloo. "We must be free or die who speak the tongue that Shakespeare spoke." This past is felt both to impose an obligation and to hold out an assurance; we must not fall below the standard our fathers set us, and because we are their sons there is good hope we shall not.

This feeling has not quite such good credentials as the sheer love of home. The actual history of every country is full of shabby and even shameful doings. The heroic stories, if taken to be typical, give a false impression of it and are often themselves open to serious historical criticism. Hence a patriotism based on our glorious past is fair game for the debunker. As knowledge increases it may snap and be converted into disillusioned cynicism, or may be maintained by a voluntary shutting of the eyes. But who can condemn what clearly makes many people, at many important moments, behave so much better than they could have done without its help?

I think it is possible to be strengthened by the image of the past without being either deceived or puffed up. The image becomes dangerous in the precise degree to which it is mistaken, or substituted, for serious and systematic historical study. The stories are best when they are handed on and accepted as stories. I do not mean by this that they should be handed on as mere fictions (some of them are after all true). But the emphasis should be on the tale as such, on the picture which fires the imagination, the example that strengthens the will. The schoolboy who hears them should dimly feel – though of course he cannot put it into words – that he is hearing *saga*. Let him be thrilled – preferably "out of school" – by the "Deeds that won the Empire"; but the less we mix this up with his "history lessons" or mistake it for a serious analysis – worse still, a justification – of imperial policy, the better. When I was a child I had a book full of coloured pictures called *Our Island Story*. That title has always seemed to me to strike exactly the right note. The book did not look at all like a text-book either. What does seem to me poisonous, what breeds a type of patriotism that is pernicious if it lasts but not likely to last long in an educated adult, is the perfectly serious indoctrination of the young in knowably false or biased history – the heroic legend drably disguised as text-book fact. With this creeps in the tacit assumption that other nations have not equally their heroes; perhaps even the belief – surely it is very bad biology – that we can literally "inherit" a tradition. And these almost inevitably lead on to a third thing that is sometimes called patriotism.

This third thing is not a sentiment but a belief: a firm, even prosaic belief that our own nation, in sober fact, has long been, and still is markedly superior to all others. I once ventured to say to an old clergyman who was voicing this sort of patriotism, "But, sir, aren't we told that *every* people thinks its own men the bravest and its own women the fairest in the world?" He replied with total gravity – he could not have been graver if he had been saying the Creed at the altar – "Yes, but in England it's true." To be sure, this conviction had not made my friend (God rest his soul) a villain; only an extremely lovable old ass. It can however produce asses that kick and bite. On the lunatic fringe it may shade off into that popular Racialism which Christianity and science equally forbid.

This brings us to the fourth ingredient. If our nation is really so much better than others it may be held to have either the duties or the rights of a superior being towards them. In the nineteenth century the English became very conscious of such duties: the "white man's burden." What we called *natives* were our wards and we their self-appointed guardians. This was not all hypocrisy. We did do them some good. But our habit of talking as if England's motives for acquiring an empire (or any youngster's motives for seeking a job in the Indian Civil Service) had been mainly altruistic nauseated the world. And yet this showed the sense of superiority working at its best. Some nations who have also felt it have stressed the rights not the duties. To them, some foreigners were so bad that one had the right to exterminate them. Others, fitted only to be hewers of wood and drawers of water to the chosen people, had better be made to get on with their hewing and drawing. Dogs, know your betters! I am far from suggesting that the two attitudes are on the same level. But both are fatal. Both demand that the area in which they operate should grow "wider still and wider." And both have about them this sure mark of evil: only by being terrible do they avoid being comic. If there were no broken treaties with Redskins, no extermination of the Tasmanians, no gas-chambers and no Belsen, no Amritsar, Black and Tans or Apartheid, the pomposity of both would be roaring farce.

Finally we reach the stage where patriotism in its demoniac form unconsciously denies itself. Chesterton picked on two lines from Kipling as the perfect example. It was unfair to Kipling, who knew — wonderfully, for so homeless a man — what the love of home can mean. But the lines, in isolation, can be taken to sum up the thing. They run:

> *If England was what England seems*
> *'Ow quick we'd drop 'er. But she ain't!*

Love never spoke that way. It is like loving your children only "if they're good," your wife only while she keeps her looks, your husband only so long as he is famous and successful. "No man," said one of the Greeks, "loves his city because it is great, but because it is his." A man who really loves his country will love her in her ruin and degeneration — "England, with all thy faults, I love thee still." She will be to him "a poor thing but mine own." He may think her good and great, when she is not, because he loves her; the delusion is up to a point pardonable. But Kipling's soldier reverses it; he loves her because he thinks her good and great — loves her on her merits. She is a fine going concern and it gratifies his pride to be in it. How if she ceased to be such? The answer is plainly given: "'Ow quick we'd drop 'er." When the ship begins to sink he will leave her. Thus that kind of patriotism which sets off with the greatest swagger of drums and banners actually sets off on the road that can lead to Vichy. And this is a phenomenon which will meet us again. When the natural loves become lawless they do not merely do harm to other loves; they themselves cease to be the loves they were – to be loves at all.

Patriotism has, then, many faces. Those who would reject it entirely do not seem to have considered what will certainly step – has already begun to step – into its place. For a long time yet, or perhaps forever, nations will live in danger. Rulers must somehow nerve their subjects to defend them or at least to prepare for their defence. Where the sentiment of patriotism has been destroyed this can be done only by presenting every international conflict in a purely ethical light. If people will spend neither sweat nor blood for "their country" they must be made to feel that they are spending them for justice, or civilisation, or humanity. This is a step down, not up. Patriotic sentiment did not of course need to disregard ethics. Good men needed to be convinced that their country's cause was just; but it was still their country's cause, not the cause of justice as such. The difference seems to me important. I may without self-righteousness or hypocrisy think it just to defend my house by force against a burglar; but if I start pretending that I blacked his eye purely on moral grounds – wholly indifferent to the fact that the house in question was mine – I become insufferable. The pretence that when England's cause is just we are on England's side – as some neutral Don Quixote might be – for that reason alone, is equally spurious. And nonsense draws evil after it. If our country's cause is the cause of God, wars must be wars of annihilation. A false transcendence is given to things which are very much of this world.

The glory of the old sentiment was that while it could steel men to the utmost endeavour, it still knew itself to be a sentiment. Wars could be heroic without pretending to be Holy Wars. The hero's death was not confused with the martyr's. And (delightfully) the same sentiment which could be so serious in a rearguard action could also in peacetime take itself as lightly as all happy loves often do. It could laugh at itself. Our older patriotic songs cannot be sung without a twinkle in the eye; later ones sound more like hymns. Give me "The British Grenadiers" (*with a tow-row-row-row*) any day rather than "Land of Hope and Glory."

It will be noticed that the sort of love I have been describing, and all its ingredients, can be for something other than a country: for a school, a regiment, a great family, or a class. All the same criticisms will still apply. It can also be felt for bodies that claim more than a natural affection: for a Church or (alas) a party in a Church, or for a religious order. This terrible subject would require a book to itself. Here it will be enough to say that the Heavenly Society is also an earthly society. Our (merely natural) patriotism towards the latter can very easily borrow the transcendent claims of the former and use them to justify the most abominable actions. If ever the book which I am not going to write is written it must be the full confession by Christendom of Christendom's specific contribution to the sum of human cruelty and treachery. Large areas of "the World" will not hear us till we have publicly disowned much of our past. Why should they? We have shouted the name of Christ and enacted the service of Moloch.

It may be thought that I should not end this chapter without a word about our love for animals. But that will fit in better in the next. Whether animals are in fact sub-personal or not, they are never loved as if they were. The fact or the illusion of personality is always present, so that love for them is really an instance of that Affection which is the subject of the following chapter.

III

AFFECTION

I begin with the humblest and most widely diffused of loves, the love in which our experience seems to differ least from that of the animals. Let me add at once that I do not on that account give it a lower value. Nothing in Man is either worse or better for being shared with the beasts. When we blame a man for being "a mere animal," we mean not that he displays animal characteristics (we all do) but that he displays these, and only these, on occasions where the specifically human was demanded. (When we call him "brutal" we usually mean that he commits cruelties impossible to most real brutes; they're not clever enough.)

The Greeks called this love *storge* (two syllables and the g is "hard"). I shall here call it simply Affection. My Greek Lexicon defines *storge* as "affection, especially of parents to offspring"; but also of offspring to parents. And that, I have no doubt, is the original form of the thing as well as the central meaning of the word. The image we must start with is that of a mother nursing a baby, a bitch or a cat with a basketful of puppies or kittens; all in a squeaking, nuzzling heap together; purrings, lickings, baby-talk, milk, warmth, the smell of young life.

The importance of this image is that it presents us at the very outset with a certain paradox. The Need and Need-love of the young is obvious; so is the Gift-love of the mother. She gives birth, gives suck, gives protection. On the other hand, she must give birth or die. She must give suck or suffer. That way, her Affection too is a Need-love. There is the paradox. It is a Need-love but what it needs is to give. It is a Gift-love but it needs to be needed. We shall have to return to this point.

But even in animal life, and still more in our own, Affection extends far beyond the relation of mother and young. This warm comfortableness, this satisfaction in being together, takes in all sorts of objects. It is indeed the least discriminating of loves. There are women for whom we can predict few wooers and men who are likely to have few friends. They have nothing to offer. But almost anyone can become an object of Affection; the ugly, the stupid, even the exasperating. There need be no apparent fitness between those whom it unites. I have seen it felt for an imbecile not only by his parents but by his brothers. It ignores the barriers of age, sex, class and educa-

230

tion. It can exist between a clever young man from the university and an old nurse, though their minds inhabit different worlds. It ignores even the barriers of species. We see it not only between dog and man but, more surprisingly, between dog and cat. Gilbert White claims to have discovered it between a horse and a hen.

Some of the novelists have seized this well. In *Tristram Shandy* "my father" and Uncle Toby are so far from being united by any community of interests or ideas that they cannot converse for ten minutes without cross-purposes; but we are made to feel their deep mutual affection. So with Don Quixote and Sancho Panza, Pickwick and Sam Weller, Dick Swiveller and the Marchioness. So too, though probably without the author's conscious intention, in *The Wind in the Willows*; the quaternion of Mole, Rat, Badger, and Toad suggests the amazing heterogeneity possible between those who are bound by Affection.

But Affection has its own criteria. Its objects have to be familiar. We can sometimes point to the very day and hour when we fell in love or began a new friendship. I doubt if we ever catch Affection beginning. To become aware of it is to become aware that it has already been going on for some time. The use of "old" or *vieux* as a term of Affection is significant. The dog barks at strangers who have never done it any harm and wags its tail for old acquaintances even if they never did it a good turn. The child will love a crusty old gardener who has hardly ever taken any notice of it and shrink from the visitor who is making every attempt to win its regard. But it must be an *old* gardener, one who has "always" been there – the short but seemingly immemorial "always" of childhood.

Affection, as I have said, is the humblest love. It gives itself no airs. People can be proud of being "in love," or of friendship. Affection is modest – even furtive and shame-faced. Once when I had remarked on the affection quite often found between cat and dog, my friend replied, "Yes. But I bet no dog would ever confess it to the other dogs." That is at least a good caricature of much human Affection. "Let homely faces stay at home," says Comus. Now Affection has a very homely face. So have many of those for whom we feel it. It is no proof of our refinement or perceptiveness that we love them; nor that they love us. What I have called Appreciative love is no basic element in Affection. It usually needs absence or bereavement to set us praising those to whom only Affection binds us. We take them for granted: and this taking for granted, which is an outrage in erotic love, is here right and proper up to a point. It fits the comfortable, quiet nature of the feeling. Affection would not be affection if it was loudly and frequently expressed; to produce it in public is like getting your household furniture out for a move. It did very well in its place, but it looks shabby or tawdry or grotesque in the sunshine. Affection almost slinks or seeps through our lives. It lives with humble, un-dress, private things; soft slippers, old clothes, old jokes, the thump of a sleepy dog's tail on the kitchen floor, the sound of a sewing-machine, a gollywog left on the lawn.

But I must at once correct myself. I am talking of Affection as it is when it exists apart from the other loves. It often does so exist; often not. As gin is not only a drink in itself but also a base for many mixed drinks, so Affection, besides being a love it-self, can enter into the other loves and colour them all through and become the very medium in which from day to day they operate. They would not perhaps wear very well without it. To make a friend is not the same as to become affectionate. But when your friend has become an old friend, all those things about him which had originally nothing to do with the friendship become familiar and dear with familiarity. As for erotic love, I can imagine nothing more disagreeable than to experience it for more than a very short time without this homespun clothing of affection. That would be a most uneasy condition, either too angelic or too animal or each by turn; never quite great enough or little enough for man. There is indeed a peculiar charm, both in friendship and in Eros, about those moments when Appreciative love lies, as it were, curled up asleep, and the mere ease and ordinariness of the relationship (free as soli-tude, yet neither is alone) wraps us round. No need to talk. No need to make love. No needs at all except perhaps to stir the fire.

This blending and overlapping of the loves is well kept before us by the fact that at most times and places all three of them had in common, as their expression, the kiss. In modern England friendship no longer uses it, but Affection and Eros do. It belongs so fully to both that we cannot now tell which borrowed it from the other or whether there were borrowing at all. To be sure, you may say that the kiss of Affection differs from the kiss of Eros. Yes; but not all kisses between lovers are lovers' kisses. Again, both these loves tend — and it embarrasses many moderns — to use a "little language" or "baby talk." And this is not peculiar to the human species. Professor Lorenz has told us that when jackdaws are amorous their calls "consist chiefly of infantile sounds reserved by adult jackdaws for these occasions" (*King Solomon's Ring,* p. 158). We and the birds have the same excuse. Different sorts of tenderness are both tenderness and the language of the earliest tenderness we have ever known is recalled to do duty for the new sort.

One of the most remarkable by-products of Affection has not yet been mentioned. I have said that is not primarily an Appreciative love. It is not discriminating. It can "rub along" with the most unpromising people. Yet oddly enough this very fact means that it can in the end make appreciations possible which, but for it, might never have existed. We may say, and not quite untruly, that we have chosen our friends and the woman we love for their various excellences — for beauty, frankness, goodness of heart, wit, intelligence, or what not. But it had to be the particular kind of wit, the particular kind of beauty, the particular kind of goodness that we like, and we have our personal tastes in these matters. That is why friends and lovers feel that they were "made for one another." The especial glory of Affection is that it can unite those who most emphatically, even comically, are not; people who, if they had not found themselves put down by fate in the same household or community, would have had nothing to do with each other. If Affection grows out of this — of course it often does not — their eyes begin to open. Growing fond of "old so-and-so," at first simply because he happens to be there, I presently begin to see that there is "something in him" after all. The moment when one first says, really meaning it, that though he is not "my sort of man" he is a very good man "in his own way" is one of liberation. It does not feel like that; we may feel only tolerant and indulgent. But really we have crossed a frontier. That "in his own way" means that we are getting beyond our own idiosyncrasies, that we are learning to appreciate goodness or intelligence in themselves, not merely goodness or intelligence flavoured and served to suit our own palate.

"Dogs and cats should always be brought up together," said someone, "it broadens their minds so." Affection broadens ours; of all natural loves it is the most catholic, the least finical, the broadest. The people with whom you are thrown together in the family, the college, the mess, the ship, the religious house, are from this point of view a wider circle than the friends, however numerous, whom you have made for yourself in the outer world. By having a great many friends I do not prove that I have a wide appreciation of human excellence. You might as well say I prove the width of my literary taste by being able to enjoy all the books in my own study. The answer is the same in both cases – "You chose those books. You chose those friends. Of course they suit you." The truly wide taste in reading is that which enables a man to find something for his needs on the sixpenny tray outside any secondhand bookshop. The truly wide taste in humanity will similarly find something to appreciate in the cross-section of humanity whom one has to meet every day. In my experience it is Affection that creates this taste, teaching us first to notice, then to endure, then to smile at, then to enjoy, and finally to appreciate, the people who "happen to be there." Made for us? Thank God, no. They are themselves, odder than you could have believed and worth far more than we guessed.

And now we are drawing nearer the point of danger. Affection, I have said, gives itself no airs; charity, said St. Paul, is not puffed up. Affection can love the unattractive: God and His saints love the unlovable. Affection "does not expect too much," turns a blind eye to faults, revives easily after quarrels; just so charity suffers long and is kind and forgives. Affection opens our eyes to goodness we could not have seen, or should not have appreciated without it. So does humble sanctity. If we dwelled exclusively on these resemblances we might be led on to believe that this Affection is not simply one of the natural loves but is Love Himself working in our human hearts and fulfilling the law. Were the Victorian novelists right after all? Is love (of this sort) really enough? Are the "domestic affections," when in their best and fullest development, the same thing as the Christian life? The answer to all these questions, I submit, is certainly No.

I do not mean simply that those novelists sometimes wrote as if they had never heard the text about "hating" wife and mother and one's own life also. That of course is true. The rivalry between all natural loves and the love of God is something a Christian dare not forget. God is the great Rival, the ultimate object of human jealousy; that beauty, terrible as the Gorgon's, which may at any moment steal from me – or it seems like stealing to me – my wife's or husband's or daughter's heart. The bitterness of some unbelief, though disguised even from those who feel it as anti-clericalism or hatred of superstition, is really due to this. But I am not at present thinking of that rivalry; we shall have to face it in a later chapter. For the moment our business is more down to earth.

How many of these "happy homes" really exist? Worse still; are all the unhappy ones unhappy because Affection is absent? I believe not. It can be present, causing the unhappiness. Nearly all the characteristics of this love are ambivalent. They may work for ill as well as for good. By itself, left simply to follow its own bent, it can darken and degrade human life. The debunkers and anti-sentimentalists have not said all the truth about it, but all they have said is true.

Symptomatic of this, perhaps, is the odiousness of nearly all those treacly tunes and saccharine poems in which popular art expresses Affection. They are odious because of their falsity. They represent as a ready-made recipe for bliss (and even for goodness) what is in fact only an opportunity. There is no hint that we shall have to do anything: only let Affection pour over us like a warm shower-bath and all, it is implied, will be well.

Affection, we have seen, includes both Need-love and Gift-love. I begin with the Need – our craving for the Affection of others.

Now there is a clear reason why this craving, of all love-cravings, easily becomes the most unreasonable. I have said that almost anyone may be the object of Affection. Yes; and almost everyone expects to be. The egregious Mr. Pontifex in *The Way of All Flesh* is outraged to discover that his son does not love him; it is "unnatural" for a boy not to love his own father. It never occurs to him to ask whether, since the first day the boy can remember, he has ever done or said anything that could excite love. Similarly, at the beginning of *King Lear* the hero is shown as a very unlovable old man devoured with a ravenous appetite for Affection. I am driven to literary examples because you, the reader, and I do not live in the same neighbourhood; if we did, there would unfortunately be no difficulty about replacing them with examples from real life. The thing happens every day. And we can see why. We all know that we must do something, if not to merit, at least to attract, erotic love or friendship. But Affection is often assumed to be provided, ready made, by nature; "built-in," "laid-on," "on the house." We have a right to expect it. If the others do not give it, they are "unnatural."

This assumption is no doubt the distortion of a truth. Much has been "built-in." Because we are a mammalian species, instinct will provide at least some degree, often a high one, of maternal love. Because we are a social species familiar association provides a *milieu* in which, if all goes well, Affection will arise and grow strong without demanding any very shining qualities in its objects. If it is given us it will not necessarily be given us on our merits; we may get it with very little trouble. From a dim perception of the truth (many are loved with Affection far beyond their deserts) Mr. Pontifex draws the ludicrous conclusion, "Therefore I, without desert, have a right to it." It is as if, on a far higher plane, we argued that because no man by merit has a right to the Grace of God, I, having no merit, am entitled to it. There is no question of rights in either case. What we have is not "a right to expect" but a "reasonable expectation" of being loved by our intimates if we, and they, are more or less ordinary people. But we may not be. We may be intolerable. If we are, "nature" will work against us. For the very same conditions of intimacy which make Affection possible also — and no less naturally — make possible a peculiarly incurable distaste; a hatred as immemorial, constant, unemphatic, almost at times unconscious, as the corresponding form of love. Siegfried, in the opera, could not remember a time before every shuffle, mutter, and fidget of his dwarfish foster-father had become odious. We never catch this kind of hatred, any more than Affection, at the moment of its beginning. It was always there before. Notice that *old* is a term of wearied loathing as well as of endearment: "at his old tricks," "in his old way," "the same old thing."

It would be absurd to say that Lear is lacking in Affection. In so far as Affection is Need-love he is half-crazy with it. Unless, in his own way, he loved his daughters he would not so desperately desire their love. The most unlovable parent (or child) may be full of such ravenous love. But it works to their own misery and everyone else's. The situation becomes suffocating. If people are already unlovable a continual demand on their part (as of right) to be loved — their manifest sense of injury, their reproaches, whether loud and clamorous or merely implicit in every look and gesture of resentful self-pity — produce in us a sense of guilt (they are intended to do so) for a fault we could not have avoided and cannot cease to commit. They seal up the very fountain for which they are thirsty. If ever, at some favoured moment, any germ of Affection for them stirs in us, their demand for more and still more petrifies us again. And of course such people always desire the same proof of our love; we are to join their side, to hear and share their grievance against someone else. If my boy really loved me he would see how selfish his father is . . . if my brother loved me he would make a party with me against my sister . . . if you loved me you wouldn't let me be treated like this . . .

And all the while they remain unaware of the real road. "If you would be loved, be lovable," said Ovid. That cheery old reprobate only meant, "If you want to attract the girls you must be attractive," but his maxim has a wider application. The amorist was wiser in his generation than Mr. Pontifex and King Lear.

The really surprising thing is not that these insatiable demands made by the unlovable are sometimes made in vain, but that they are so often met. Sometimes one sees a woman's girlhood, youth and long years of her maturity up to the verge of old age spent in tending, obeying, caressing, and perhaps supporting, a maternal vampire who can never be caressed and obeyed enough. The sacrifice — but there are two opinions about that — may be beautiful; the old woman who exacts it is not.

The "built-in" or unmerited character of Affection thus invites a hideous misinterpretation. So does its ease and informality.

We hear a great deal about the rudeness of the rising generation. I am an oldster myself and might be expected to take the oldsters' side, but in fact I have been far more impressed by the bad manners of parents to children than by those of children to parents. Who has not been the embarrassed guest at family meals where the father or mother treated their grown-up offspring with an incivility which, offered to any other young people, would simply have terminated the acquaintance? Dogmatic assertions on matters which the children understand and their elders don't, ruthless inter-ruptions, flat contradictions, ridicule of things the young take seriously — sometimes of their religion — insulting references to their friends, all provide an easy answer to the question "Why are they always out? Why do they like every house better than their home?" Who does not prefer civility to barbarism?

If you asked any of these insufferable people — they are not all parents of course — why they behaved that way at home, they would reply, "Oh, hang it all, one comes home to relax. A chap can't be always on his best behaviour. If a man can't be himself in his own house, where can he? Of course we don't want Company Manners at home. We're a happy family. We can say *anything* to one another here. No one minds. We all understand."

Once again it is so nearly true yet so fatally wrong. Affection is an affair of old clothes, and ease, of the unguarded moment, of liberties which would be ill-bred if we took them with strangers. But old clothes are one thing; to wear the same shirt till it stank would be another. There are proper clothes for a garden party; but the clothes for home must be proper too, in their own different way. Similarly there is a distinc-tion between public and domestic courtesy. The root principle of both is the same: "that no one give any kind of preference to himself." But the more public the occasion, the more our obedience to this principle has been "taped" or formalised. There are "rules" of good manners. The more intimate the occasion, the less the formalisation; but not therefore the less need for courtesy. On the contrary, Affection at its best practises a courtesy which is incomparably more subtle, sensitive, and deep than the public kind. In public a ritual would do. At home you must have the reality which that ritual represented, or else the deafening triumphs of the greatest egoist present. You must really give no kind of preference to yourself; at a party it is enough to conceal the preference. Hence the old proverb "come live with me and you'll know me." Hence a man's familiar manners first reveal the true value of his (significantly odious phrase!) "Company" or "Party" manners. Those who leave their manners behind them when they come home from the dance or the sherry party have no real courtesy even there. They were merely aping those who had.

"We can say *anything* to one another." The truth behind this is that Affection at its best can say whatever Affection at its best wishes to say, regardless of the rules that govern public courtesy; for Affection at its best wishes neither to wound nor to hu-miliate nor to domineer. You may address the wife of your bosom as "Pig!" when she has inadvertently drunk your cocktail as well as her own. You may roar down the story which your father is telling once too often. You may tease and hoax and banter. You can say "Shut up. I want to read." You can do anything in the right tone and at the right moment — the tone and moment which are not intended to, and will not, hurt. The better the Affection the more unerringly it knows which these are (every love has its *art of love*). But the domestic Rudesby means something quite different when he claims liberty to say "anything." Having a very imperfect sort of Affection himself, or perhaps at that moment none, he arrogates to himself the beautiful liberties which only the fullest affection has a right to or knows how to manage. He then uses them spitefully in obedience to his resentments; or ruthlessly in obedience to his egoism; or at best stupidly, lacking the art. And all the time he may have a clear conscience. He knows that Affection takes liberties. He is taking liberties. Therefore (he concludes) he is being affectionate. Resent anything and he will say that the defect of love is on your side. He is hurt. He has been misunderstood.

He then sometimes avenges himself by getting on his high horse and becoming elaborately "polite." The implication is of course, "Oh! So we are not to be intimate? We are to behave like mere acquaintances? I had hoped – but no matter. Have it your own way." This illustrates prettily the difference between intimate and formal courtesy. Precisely what suits the one may be a breach of the other. To be free and easy when you are presented to some eminent stranger is bad manners; to practice formal and ceremonial courtesies at home ("public faces in private places") is – and is always intended to be – bad manners. There is a delicious illustration of really good domestic manners in *Tristram Shandy*. At a singularly unsuitable moment Uncle Toby has been holding forth on his favourite theme of fortification. "My Father," driven for once beyond endurance, violently interrupts. Then he sees his brother's face; the utterly unretaliating face of Toby, deeply wounded, not by the slight to himself – he would never think of that – but by the slight to the noble art. My Father at once repents. There is an apology, a total reconciliation. Uncle Toby, to show how complete is his forgiveness, to show that he is not on his dignity, resumes the lecture on fortification.

But we have not yet touched on jealousy. I suppose no one now believes that jealousy is especially connected with erotic love. If anyone does, the behaviour of children, employees, and domestic animals ought soon to undeceive him. Every kind of love, almost every kind of association, is liable to it. The jealousy of affection is closely connected with its reliance on what is old and familiar. So also with the total, or relative, unimportance for Affection of what I call Appreciative love. We don't want the "old, familiar faces" to become brighter or more beautiful, the old ways to be changed even for the better, the old jokes and interests to be replaced by exciting novelties. Change is a threat to Affection.

A brother and sister, or two brothers – for sex here is not at work – grow to a certain age sharing everything. They have read the same comics, climbed the same trees, been pirates or spacemen together, taken up and abandoned stamp-collecting at the same moment. Then a dreadful thing happens. One of them flashes ahead – discovers poetry or science or serious music or perhaps undergoes a religious conversion. His life is flooded with the new interest. The other cannot share it; he is left behind. I doubt whether even the infidelity of a wife or husband raises a more miserable sense of desertion or a fiercer jealousy than this can sometimes do. It is not yet jealousy of the new friends whom the deserter will soon be making. That will come;

at first it is jealousy of the thing itself — of this science, this music, of God (always called "religion" or "all this religion" in such contexts). The jealousy will probably be expressed by ridicule. The new interest is "all silly nonsense," contemptibly childish (or contemptibly grown-up), or else the deserter is not really interested in it at all — he's showing off, swanking; it's all affectation. Presently the books will be hidden, the scientific specimens destroyed, the radio forcibly switched off the classical programmes. For Affection is the most instinctive, in that sense the most animal, of the loves; its jealousy is proportionately fierce. It snarls and bares its teeth like a dog whose food has been snatched away. And why would it not? Something or someone has snatched away from the child I am picturing his lifelong food, his second self. His world is in ruins.

But it is not only children who react thus. Few things in the ordinary peacetime life of a civilised country are more nearly fiendish than the rancour with which a whole unbelieving family will turn on the one member of it who has become a Christian, or a whole lowbrow family on the one who shows signs of becoming an intellectual. This is not, as I once thought, simply the innate and, as it were, disinterested hatred of darkness for light. A church-going family in which one has gone atheist will not always behave any better. It is the reaction to a desertion, even to robbery. Someone or something has stolen "our" boy (or girl). He who was one of Us has become one of Them. What right had anybody to do it? He is *ours*. But once change has thus begun, who knows where it will end? (And we all so happy and comfortable before and doing no harm to no one!)

Sometimes a curious double jealousy is felt, or rather two inconsistent jealousies which chase each other round in the sufferer's mind. On the one hand "This" is "All nonsense, all bloody high-brow nonsense, all canting humbug." But on the other, "Supposing — it can't be, it mustn't be, but just supposing — there were something in it?" Supposing there really were anything in literature, or in Christianity? How if the deserter has really entered a new world which the rest of us never suspected? But, if so, how unfair! Why him? Why was it never opened to us? "A chit of a girl — a whipper-snapper of a boy — being shown things that are hidden from their elders?" And since that is clearly incredible and unendurable, jealousy returns to the hypothesis "All nonsense."

Parents in this state are much more comfortably placed than brothers and sisters. Their past is unknown to their children. Whatever the deserter's new world is, they can always claim that they have been through it themselves and have come out the other end. "It's a phase," they say. "It'll blow over." Nothing could be more satisfactory. It cannot be there and then refuted, for it is a statement about the future. It stings, yet — so indulgently said — is hard to resent. Better still, the elders may really believe it. Best of all, it may finally turn out to have been true. It won't be their fault if it doesn't.

"Boy, boy, these wild courses of yours will break your mother's heart." That eminently Victorian appeal may often have been true. Affection was bitterly wounded when one member of the family fell from the homely *ethos* into something worse — gambling, drink, keeping an opera girl. Unfortunately it is almost equally possible to break your mother's heart by rising above the homely *ethos*. The conservative tenacity of Affection works both ways. It can be a domestic counterpart to that nationally suicidal type of education which keeps back the promising child because the idlers and dunces might be "hurt" if it were undemocratically moved into a higher class than themselves.

All these perversions of Affection are mainly connected with Affection as a Need-love. But Affection as a Gift-love has its perversions too.

I am thinking of Mrs. Fidget, who died a few months ago. It is really astonishing how her family have brightened up. The drawn look has gone from her husband's face; he begins to be able to laugh. The younger boy, whom I had always thought an embittered, peevish little creature, turns out to be quite human. The elder, who was hardly ever at home except when he was in bed, is nearly always there now and has begun to reorganise the garden. The girl, who was always supposed to be "delicate" (though I never found out what exactly the trouble was), now has the riding lessons which were once out of the question, dances all night, and plays any amount of tennis. Even the dog who was never allowed out except on a lead is now a well-known member of the Lamp-post Club in their road.

Mrs. Fidget very often said that she lived for her family. And it was not untrue. Everyone in the neighbourhood knew it. "She lives for her family," they said; "what a wife and mother!" She did all the washing; true, she did it badly, and they could have afforded to send it out to a laundry, and they frequently begged her not to do it. But she did. There was always a hot lunch for anyone who was at home and always a hot meal at night (even in midsummer). They implored her not to provide this. They protested almost with tears in their eyes (and with truth) that they liked cold meals. It made no difference. She was living for her family. She always sat up to "welcome" you home if you were out late at night; two or three in the morning, it made no odds; you would always find the frail, pale, weary face awaiting you, like a silent accusation. Which meant of course that you couldn't with any decency go out very often. She was always making things too; being in her own estimation (I'm no judge myself) an excellent amateur dressmaker and a great knitter. And of course, unless you were a heartless brute, you had to wear the things. (The Vicar tells me that, since her death, the contributions of that family alone to "sales of work" outweigh those of all his other parishioners put together.) And then her care for their health! She bore the whole burden of that daughter's "delicacy" alone. The Doctor — an old friend, and it was not being done on National Health — was never allowed to discuss matters with his patient. After the briefest examination of her, he was taken into another room by the mother. The girl was to have no worries, no responsibility for her own health. Only loving care; caresses, special foods, horrible tonic wines, and breakfast in bed. For Mrs. Fidget, as she so often said, would "work her fingers to the bone" for her family. They couldn't stop her. Nor could they — being decent people — quite sit still and watch her do it. They had to help. Indeed they were always having to help. That is, they did things for her to help her to do things for them which they didn't want done. As for the dear dog, it was to her, she said, "Just like one of the children." It was in fact, as like one of them as she could make it. But since it had no scruples it got on rather better than they, and though vetted, dieted and guarded within an inch of its life, contrived sometimes to reach the dustbin or the dog next door.

The Vicar says Mrs. Fidget is now at rest. Let us hope she is. What's quite certain is that her family are.

It is easy to see how liability to this state is, so to speak, congenital in the maternal instinct. This, as we saw, is a Gift-love, but one that needs to give; therefore needs to be needed. But the proper aim of giving is to put the recipient in a state where he no longer needs our gift. We feed children in order that they may soon be able to feed themselves; we teach them in order that they may soon not need our teaching. Thus a heavy task is laid upon this Gift-love. It must work towards its own abdication. We must aim at making ourselves superfluous. The hour when we can say "They need me no longer" should be our reward. But the instinct, simply in its own nature, has no power to fulfil this law. The instinct desires the good of its object, but not simply; only the good it can itself give. A much higher love — a love which desires the good of the object as such, from whatever source that good comes — must step in and help or tame the instinct before it can make the abdication. And of course it often does. But where it does not, the ravenous need to be needed will gratify itself either by keeping its objects needy or by inventing for them imaginary needs. It will do this all the more ruthlessly because it thinks (in one sense truly) that it is a Gift-love and therefore regards itself as "unselfish."

It is not only mothers who can do this. All those other Affections which, whether by derivation from parental instinct or by similarity of function, need to be needed may fall into the same pit. The Affection of patron for *protégé* is one. In Jane Austen's novel, Emma intends that Harriet Smith should have a happy life; but only the sort of happy life which Emma herself has planned for her. My own profession — that of a university teacher — is in this way dangerous. If we are any good we must always be working towards the moment at which our pupils are fit to become our critics and rivals. We should be delighted when it arrives, as the fencing master is delighted when his pupil can pink and disarm him. And many are.

But not all. I am old enough to remember the sad case of Dr. Quartz. No university boasted a more effective or devoted teacher. He spent the whole of himself on his pupils. He made an indelible impression on nearly all of them. He was the object of much well merited hero-worship. Naturally, and delightfully, they continued to visit him after the tutorial relation had ended — went round to his house of an evening and had famous discussions. But the curious thing is that this never lasted. Sooner or later — it might be within a few months or even a few weeks — came the fatal evening when they knocked on his door and were told that the Doctor was engaged. After that he would always be engaged. They were banished from him forever. This was because, at their last meeting, they had rebelled. They had asserted their independence — differed from the master and supported their own view, perhaps not without success. Faced with that very independence which he had laboured to produce and which it was his duty to produce if he could, Dr. Quartz could not bear it. Wotan had toiled to create the free Siegfried; presented with the free Siegfried, he was enraged. Dr. Quartz was an unhappy man.

This terrible need to be needed often finds its outlet in pampering an animal. To learn that someone is "fond of animals" tells us very little until we know in what way. For there are two ways. On the one hand the higher and domesticated animal is, so to speak, a "bridge" between us and the rest of nature. We all at times feel somewhat painfully our human isolation from the sub-human world — the atrophy of instinct which our intelligence entails, our excessive self-consciousness, the innumerable complexities of our situation, our inability to live in the present. If only we could shuffle it all off! We must not — and incidentally we can't — become beasts. But we can be *with* a beast. It is personal enough to give the word *with* a real meaning; yet it remains very largely an unconscious little bundle of biological impulses. It has three legs in nature's world and one in ours. It is a link, an ambassador. Who would not wish, as Bosanquet put it, "to have a representative at the court of Pan"? Man with dog closes a gap in the universe. But of course animals are often used in a worse fashion. If you need to be needed and if your family, very properly, decline to need you, a pet is the obvious substitute. You can keep it all its life in need of you. You can keep it permanently infantile, reduce it to permanent invalidism, cut it off from all genuine animal well-being, and compensate for this by creating needs for countless little indulgences which only you can grant. The unfortunate creature thus becomes very useful to the rest of the household; it acts as a sump or drain — you are too busy spoiling a dog's life to spoil theirs. Dogs are better for this purpose than cats: a monkey, I am told, is best of all. Also it is more like the real thing. To be sure, it's all very bad luck for the animal. But probably it cannot fully realise the wrong you have done it. Better still, you would never know if it did. The most down-trodden human, driven too far, may one day turn and blurt out a terrible truth. Animals can't speak.

Those who say "The more I see of men the better I like dogs" — those who find in animals a *relief* from the demands of human companionship — will be well advised to examine their real reasons.

I hope I am not being misunderstood. If this chapter leads anyone to doubt that the lack of "natural affection" is an extreme depravity I shall have failed. Nor do I question for a moment that Affection is responsible for nine-tenths of whatever solid and durable happiness there is in our natural lives. I shall therefore have some sympathy with those whose comment on the last few pages takes the form "Of course. Of course. These things do happen. Selfish or neurotic people can twist anything, even love, into some sort of misery or exploitation. But why stress these marginal cases? A little common sense, a little give and take, prevents their occurrence among decent people." But I think this comment itself needs a commentary.

Firstly, as to *neurotic.* I do not think we shall see things more clearly by classify-ing all these malefical states of Affection as pathological. No doubt there are really pathological conditions which make the temptation to these states abnormally hard or even impossible to resist for particular people. Send those people to the doctors by all means. But I believe that everyone who is honest with himself will admit that he has felt these temptations. Their occurrence is not a disease; or if it is, the name of that disease is Being a Fallen Man. In ordinary people the yielding to them – and who does not sometimes yield? – is not disease, but sin. Spiritual direction will here help us more than medical treatment. Medicine labours to restore "natural" structure or "normal" function. But greed, egoism, self-deception and self-pity are not unnatural or abnormal in the same sense as astigmatism or a floating kidney. For who, in Heaven's name, would describe as natural or normal the man from whom these failings were wholly absent? "Natural," if you like, in a quite different sense; archnatural, unfallen. We have seen only one such Man. And He was not at all like the psychologist's picture of the integrated, balanced, adjusted, happily married, em-ployed, popular citizen. You can't really be very well "adjusted" to your world if it says you "have a devil" and ends by nailing you up naked to a stake of wood.

But secondly, the comment in its own language admits the very thing I am trying to say. Affection produces happiness if – and only if – there is common sense and give and take and "decency." In other words, only if something more, and other, than Affection is added. The mere feeling is not enough. You need "common sense," that is, reason. You need "give and take"; that is, you need justice, continually stimulating mere Affection when it fades and restraining it when it forgets or would defy the *art* of love. You need "decency." There is no disguising the fact that this means goodness; patience, self-denial, humility, and the continual intervention of a far higher sort of love than Affection, in itself, can ever be. That is the whole point. If we try to live by Affection alone, Affection will "go bad on us."

How bad, I believe we seldom recognise. Can Mrs. Fidget really have been quite unaware of the countless frustrations and miseries she inflicted on her family? It passes belief. She knew – of course she knew – that it spoiled your whole evening to know that when you came home you would find her uselessly, accusingly, "sitting up for you." She continued all these practices because if she had dropped them she would have been faced with the fact she was determined not to see; would have known that she was not necessary. That is the first motive. Then too, the very laboriousness of her life silenced her secret doubts as to the quality of her love. The more her feet burned and her back ached, the better, for this pain whispered in her ear "How much I must love them if I do all this!" That is the second motive. But I think there is a lower depth. The unappreciativeness of the others, those terrible, wounding words – anything will "wound" a Mrs. Fidget – in which they begged her to send the washing out, enabled her to feel ill-used, therefore, to have a continual grievance, to enjoy the pleasures of resentment. If anyone says he does not know those pleasures he is a liar or a saint. It is true that they are pleasures only to those who hate. But then a love like Mrs. Fidget's contains a good deal of hatred. It was of erotic love that the Roman poet said, "I love and hate," but other kinds of love admit the same mixture. They carry in them the seeds of hatred. If Affection is made the absolute sovereign of a human life the seeds will germinate. Love, having become a god, becomes a demon.

IV

FRIENDSHIP

When either Affection or Eros is one's theme, one finds a prepared audience. The importance and beauty of both have been stressed and almost exaggerated again and again. Even those who would debunk them are in conscious reaction against this laudatory tradition and, to that extent, influenced by it. But very few modern people think Friendship a love of comparable value or even a love at all. I cannot remember that any poem since *In Memoriam,* or any novel, has celebrated it. Tristan and Isolde, Antony and Cleopatra, Romeo and Juliet, have innumerable counterparts in modern literature: David and Jonathan, Pylades and Orestes, Roland and Oliver, Amis and Amile, have not. To the Ancients, Friendship seemed the happiest and most fully human of all loves; the crown of life and the school of virtue. The modern world, in comparison, ignores it. We admit of course that besides a wife and family a man needs a few "friends." But the very tone of the admission, and the sort of acquaintanceships which those who make it would describe as "friendships," show clearly that what they are talking about has very little to do with that *Philia* which Aristotle classified among the virtues or that *Amicitia* on which Cicero wrote a book. It is something quite marginal; not a main course in life's banquet; a diversion; something that fills up the chinks of one's time. How has this come about?

The first and most obvious answer is that few value it because few experience it. And the possibility of going through life without the experience is rooted in the fact which separates Friendship so sharply from both the other loves. Friendship is – in a sense not at all derogatory to it – the least *natural* of loves; the least instinctive, organic, biological, gregarious and necessary. It has least commerce with our nerves; there is nothing throaty about it; nothing that quickens the pulse or turns you red and pale. It is essentially between individuals; the moment two men are friends they have in some degree drawn apart together from the herd. Without Eros none of us would have been begotten and without Affection none of us would have been reared; but we can live and breed without Friendship. The species, biologically considered, has no need of it. The pack or herd – the community – may even dislike and mistrust it. Its leaders very often do. Headmasters and Headmistresses and Heads of religious com-

244

munities, colonels and ships' captains, can feel uneasy when close and strong friendships arise between little knots of their subjects.

This (so to call it) "non-natural" quality in Friendship goes far to explain why it was exalted in ancient and medieval times and has come to be made light of in our own. The deepest and most permanent thought of those ages was ascetic and world-renouncing. Nature and emotion and the body were feared as dangers to our souls, or despised as degradations of our human status. Inevitably that sort of love was most prized which seemed most independent, or even defiant, of mere nature. Affection and Eros were too obviously connected with our nerves, too obviously shared with the brutes. You could feel these tugging at your guts and fluttering in your diaphragm. But in Friendship — in that luminous, tranquil, rational world of relationships freely chosen — you got away from all that. This alone, of all the loves, seemed to raise you to the level of gods or angels.

But then came Romanticism and "tearful comedy" and the "return to nature" and the exaltation of Sentiment; and in their train all that great wallow of emotion which, though often criticised, has lasted ever since. Finally, the exaltation of instinct, the dark gods in the blood; whose hierophants may be incapable of male friendship. Under this new dispensation all that had once commended this love now began to work against it. It had not tearful smiles and keepsakes and baby-talk enough to please the sentimentalists. There was not blood and guts enough about it to attract the primitivists. It looked thin and etiolated; a sort of vegetarian substitute for the more organic loves.

Other causes have contributed. To those — and they are now the majority — who see human life merely as a development and complication of animal life all forms of behaviour which cannot produce certificates of an animal origin and of survival value are suspect. Friendship's certificates are not very satisfactory. Again, that outlook which values the collective above the individual necessarily disparages Friendship; it is a relation between men at their highest level of individuailty. It withdraws men from collective "togetherness" as surely as solitude itself could do; and more dangerously, for it withdraws them by two's and three's. Some forms of democratic sentiment are naturally hostile to it because it is selective and an affair of the few. To say "These are my friends" implies "Those are not." For all these reasons if a man believes (as I do) that the old estimate of Friendship was the correct one, he can hardly write a chapter on it except as a rehabilitation.

This imposes on me at the outset a very tiresome bit of demolition. It has actually become necessary in our time to rebut the theory that every firm and serious friendship is really homosexual.

The dangerous word *really* is here important. To say that every Friendship is consciously and explicitly homosexual would be too obviously false; the wiseacres take refuge in the less palpable charge that it is *really* — unconsciously, cryptically, in some Pickwickian sense — homosexual. And this, though it cannot be proved, can never of course be refuted. The fact that no positive evidence of homosexuality can be discovered in the behaviour of two Friends does not disconcert the wiseacres at all: "That," they say gravely, "is just what we should expect." The very lack of evidence is thus treated as evidence; the absence of smoke proves that the fire is very carefully hidden. Yes — if it exists at all. But we must first prove its existence. Otherwise we are arguing like a man who should say "If there were an invisible cat in that chair, the chair would look empty; but the chair does look empty; therefore there is an invisible cat in it."

A belief in invisible cats cannot perhaps be logically disproved, but it tells us a good deal about those who hold it. Those who cannot conceive Friendship as a sub-stantive love but only as a disguise or elaboration of Eros betray the fact that they have never had a Friend. The rest of us know that though we can have erotic love and friendship for the same person yet in some ways nothing is less like a Friendship than a love-affair. Lovers are always talking to one another about their love; Friends hardly ever about their Friendship. Lovers are normally face to face, absorbed in each other; Friends, side by side, absorbed in some common interest. Above all, Eros (while it lasts) is necessarily between two only. But two, far from being the necessary number for Friendship, is not even the best. And the reason for this is important.

Lamb says somewhere that if, of three friends (A, B, and C), A should die, then B loses not only A but "A's part in C, while C loses not only A but A's part in B." In each of my friends there is something that only some other friend can fully bring out. By myself I am not large enough to call the whole man into activity; I want other lights than my own to show all his facets. Now that Charles is dead, I shall never again see Ronald's reaction to a specifically Caroline joke. Far from having more of Ronald, having him "to myself" now that Charles is away, I have less of Ronald. Hence true Friendship is the least jealous of loves. Two friends delight to be joined by a third, and three by a fourth, if only the newcomer is qualified to become a real friend. They can then say, as the blessed souls say in Dante, "Here comes one who will augment our loves." For in this love "to divide is not to take away." Of course the scarcity of kindred souls — not to mention practical considerations about the size of rooms and the audi-bility of voices — set limits to the enlargement of the circle; but within those limits we possess each friend not less but more as the number of those with whom we share him increases. In this, Friendship exhibits a glorious "nearness by resemblance" to Hea-ven itself where the very multitude of the blessed (which no man can number) in-creases the fruition which each has of God. For every soul, seeing Him in her own way, doubtless communicates that unique vision to all the rest. That, says an old author, is why the Seraphim in Isaiah's vision are crying "Holy, Holy, Holy" *to one another* (Isaiah VI, 3) The more we thus share the Heavenly Bread between us, the more we shall all have.

The homosexual theory therefore seems to me not even plausible. This is not to say that Friendship and abnormal Eros have never been combined. Certain cultures at certain periods seem to have tended to the contamination. In war-like societies it was, I think, especially likely to creep into the relation between the mature Brave and his young armour-bearer or squire. The absence of the women while you were on the war-path had no doubt something to do with it. In deciding, if we think we need or can decide, where it crept in and where it did not, we must surely be guided by the evidence (when there is any) and not by an *a priori* theory. Kisses, tears and embraces are not in themselves evidence of homosexuality. The implications would be, if nothing else, too comic. Hrothgar embracing Beowulf, Johnson embracing Boswell (a pretty flagrantly heterosexual couple) and all those hairy old toughs of centurions in Tacitus, clinging to one another and begging for last kisses when the legion was broken up...all pansies? If you can believe that you can believe anything. On a broad historical view it is, of course, not the demonstrative gestures of Friendship among our ancestors but the absence of such gestures in our own society that calls for some special explanation. We, not they, are out of step.

I have said that Friendship is the least biological of our loves. Both the individual and the community can survive without it. But there is something else, often confused with Friendship, which the community does need; something which, though not Friendship, is the matrix of Friendship.

In early communities the co-operation of the males as hunters or fighters was no less necessary than the begetting and rearing of children. A tribe where there was no taste for the one would die no less surely than a tribe where there was no taste for the other. Long before history began we men have got together apart from the women and done things. We had to. And to like doing what must be done is a characteristic that has survival value. We not only had to do the things, we had to talk about them. We had to plan the hunt and the battle. When they were over we had to hold a *post mortem* and draw conclusions for future use. We liked this even better. We ridiculed or punished the cowards and bunglers, we praised the star-performers. We revelled in technicalities. ("He might have known he'd never get near the brute, not with the wind that way"..."You see, I had a lighter arrowhead; that's what did it"..."What I always say is—"..."stuck him just like that, see? Just the way I'm holding this stick"...) In fact, we talked shop. We enjoyed one another's society greatly: we Braves, we hunters, all bound together by shared skill, shared dangers and hardships, esoteric jokes—away from the women and children. As some wag has said, palaeolithic man may or may not have had a club on his shoulder but he certainly had a club of the other sort. It was probably part of his religion; like that sacred smoking-club where the savages in Melville's *Typee* were "famously snug" every evening of their lives.

What were the women doing meanwhile? How should I know? I am a man and never spied on the mysteries of the Bona Dea. They certainly often had rituals from which men were excluded. When, as sometimes happened, agriculture was in their hands, they must, like the men, have had common skills, toils and triumphs. Yet perhaps their world was never as emphatically feminine as that of their menfolk was masculine. The children were with them; perhaps the old men were there too. But I am only guessing. I can trace the pre-history of Friendship only in the male line.

This pleasure in co-operation, in talking shop, in the mutual respect and understanding of men who daily see one another tested, is biologically valuable. You may, if you like, regard it as a product of the "gregarious instinct." To me that seems a round-about way of getting at something which we all understand far better already than anyone has ever understood the word *instinct* — something which is going on at this moment in dozens of ward-rooms, bar-rooms, common-rooms, messes and golf-clubs. I prefer to call it Companionship — or Clubbableness.

This Companionship is, however, only the matrix of Friendship. It is often called Friendship, and many people when they speak of their "friends" mean only their companions. But it is not Friendship in the sense I give to the word. By saying this I do not at all intend to disparage the merely Clubbable relation. We do not disparage silver by distinguishing it from gold.

Friendship arises out of mere Companionship when two or more of the companions discover that they have in common some insight or interest or even taste which the others do not share and which, till that moment, each believed to be his own unique treasure (or burden). The typical expression of opening Friendship would be something like, "What? You too? I thought I was the only one." We can imagine that among those early hunters and warriors single individuals — one in a century? one in a thousand years? — saw what others did not; saw that the deer was beautiful as well as edible, that hunting was fun as well as necessary, dreamed that his gods might be not only powerful but holy. But as long as each of these percipient persons dies without finding a kindred soul, nothing (I suspect) will come of it; art or sport or spiritual religion will not be born. It is when two such persons discover one another, when, whether with immense difficulties and semi-articulate fumblings or with what would seem to us amazing and elliptical speed, they share their vision — it is then that Friendship is born. And instantly they stand together in an immense solitude.

Lovers seek for privacy. Friends find this solitude about them, this barrier between them and the herd, whether they want it or not. They would be glad to reduce it. The first two would be glad to find a third.

In our own time Friendship arises in the same way. For us of course the shared activity and therefore the companionship on which Friendship supervenes will not often be a bodily one like hunting or fighting. It may be a common religion, common studies, a common profession, even a common recreation. All who share it will be our companions; but one or two or three who share something more will be our Friends. In this kind of love, as Emerson said, *Do you love me?* means *Do you see the same truth?* — Or at least, "Do you *care about* the same truth?" The man who agrees with us that some question, little regarded by others, is of great importance can be our Friend. He need not agree with us about the answer.

Notice that Friendship thus repeats on a more individual and less socially necessary level the character of the Companionship which was its matrix. The Companionship was between two people who were doing something together — hunting, studying, painting or what you will. The Friends will still be doing something together, but something more inward, less widely shared and less easily defined; still hunters, but of some immaterial quarry; still collaborating, but in some work the world does not, or not yet, take account of; still travelling companions, but on a different kind of journey. Hence we picture lovers face to face but Friends side by side; their eyes look ahead.

That is why those pathetic people who simply "want friends" can never make any. The very condition of having Friends is that we should want something else besides Friends. Where the truthful answer to the question *Do you see the same truth?* would be "I see nothing and I don't care about the truth; I only want a Friend," no Friendship can arise — though Affection of course may. There would be nothing for the Friendship to be *about*; and Friendship must be about something, even if it were only an enthusiasm for dominoes or white mice. Those who have nothing can share nothing; those who are going nowhere can have no fellow-travellers.

When the two people who thus discover that they are on the same secret road are of different sexes, the friendship which arises between them will very easily pass — may pass in the first half-hour — into erotic love. Indeed, unless they are physically repulsive to each other or unless one or both already loves elsewhere, it is almost certain to do so sooner or later. And conversely, erotic love may lead to Friendship between the lovers. But this, so far from obliterating the distinction between the two loves, puts it in a clearer light. If one who was first, in the deep and full sense, your Friend, is then gradually or suddenly revealed as also your lover you will certainly not want to share the Beloved's erotic love with any third. But you will have no jealousy at all about sharing the Friendship. Nothing so enriches an erotic love as the discovery that the Beloved can deeply, truly and spontaneously enter into Friendship with the Friends you already had: to feel that not only are we two united by erotic love but we three or four or five are all travellers on the same quest, have all a common vision.

The co-existence of Friendship and Eros may also help some moderns to realise that Friendship is in reality a love, and even as great a love as Eros. Suppose you are fortunate enough to have "fallen in love with" and married your Friend. And now suppose it possible that you were offered the choice of two futures: "*Either* you two will cease to be lovers but remain forever joint seekers of the same God, the same beauty, the same truth, *or else,* losing all that, you will retain as long as you live the raptures and ardours, all the wonder and the wild desire of Eros. Choose which you please." Which should we choose? Which choice should we not regret after we had made it?

I have stressed the "unnecessary" character of Friendship, and this of course requires more justification than I have yet given it.

It could be argued that Friendships are of practical value to the Community. Every civilised religion began in a small group of friends. Mathematics effectively began when a few Greek friends got together to talk about numbers and lines and angles. What is now the Royal Society was originally a few gentlemen meeting in their spare time to discuss things which they (and not many others) had a fancy for.

What we now call "the Romantic Movement" once *was* Mr. Wordsworth and Mr. Coleridge talking incessantly (at least Mr. Coleridge was) about a secret vision of their own. Communism, Tractarianism, Methodism, the movement against slavery, the Reformation, the Renaissance, might perhaps be said, without much exaggeration, to have begun in the same way.

There is something in this. But nearly every reader would probably think some of these movements good for society and some bad. The whole list, if accepted, would tend to show, at best, that Friendship is both a possible benefactor and a possible danger to the community. And even as a benefactor it would have, not so much survival value, as what we may call "civilisation-value"; would be something (in Aristotelian phrase) which helps the community not to live but to live well. Survival value and civilisation value coincide at some periods and in some circumstances, but not in all. What at any rate seems certain is that when Friendship bears fruit which the community can use it has to do so accidentally, as a by-product. Religions devised for a social purpose, like Roman emperor-worship or modern attempts to "sell" Christianity as a means of "saving civilisation," do not come to much. The little knots of Friends who turn their backs on the "World" are those who really transform it. Egyptian and Babylonian Mathematics were practical and social, pursued in the service of Agriculture and Magic. But the free Greek Mathematics, pursued by Friends as a leisure occupation, have mattered to us more.

Others again would say that Friendship is extremely useful, perhaps necessary for survival, to the individual. They could produce plenty of authority: "bare is back without brother behind it" and "there is a friend that sticketh closer than a brother." But when we speak thus we are using *friend* to mean "ally." In ordinary usage *friend* means, or should mean, more than that. A Friend will, to be sure, prove himself to be also an ally when alliance becomes necessary; will lend or give when we are in need, nurse us in sickness, stand up for us among our enemies, do what he can for our widows and orphans. But such good offices are not the stuff of Friendship. The occasions for them are almost interruptions. They are in one way relevant to it, in another not. Relevant, because you would be a false friend if you would not do them when the need arose; irrelevant, because the role of benefactor always remains accidental, even a little alien, to that of Friend. It is almost embarrassing. For Friendship is utterly free from Affection's need to be needed. We are sorry that any gift or loan or night-watching should have been necessary — and now, for heaven's sake, let us forget all about it and go back to the things we really want to do or talk of together. Even gratitude is no enrichment to this love. The stereotyped "Don't mention it" here expresses what we really feel. The mark of perfect Friendship is not that help will be given when the pinch comes (of course it will) but that, having been given, it makes no difference at all. It was a distraction, an anomaly. It was a horrible waste of the time, always too short, that we had together. Perhaps we had only a couple of hours in which to talk and, God bless us, twenty minutes of it has had to be devoted to *affairs!*

For of course we do not want to know our Friend's affairs at all. Friendship, unlike

Eros, is uninquisitive. You become a man's Friend without knowing or caring whether he is married or single or how he earns his living. What have all these "unconcerning things, matters of fact" to do with the real question, *Do you see the same truth?* In a circle of true Friends each man is simply what he is: stands for nothing but himself. No one cares twopence about any one else's family, profession, class, income, race, or previous history. Of course you will get to know about most of these in the end. But casually. They will come out bit by bit, to furnish an illustration or an analogy, to serve as pegs for an anecdote; never for their own sake. That is the kingliness of Friendship. We meet like sovereign princes of independent states, abroad, on neutral ground, freed from our contexts. This love (essentially) ignores not only our physical bodies but that whole embodiment which consists of our family, job, past and connections. At home, besides being Peter or Jane, we also bear a general character; husband or wife, brother or sister, chief, colleague, or subordinate. Not among our Friends. It is an affair of disentangled, or stripped, minds. Eros will have naked bodies; Friendship naked personalities.

Hence (if you will not misunderstand me) the exquisite arbitrariness and irresponsibility of this love. I have no duty to be anyone's Friend and no man in the world has a duty to be mine. No claims, no shadow of necessity. Friendship is unnecessary, like philosophy, like art, like the universe itself (for God did not need to create). It has no survival value; rather it is one of those things which give value to survival.

When I spoke of Friends as side by side or shoulder to shoulder I was pointing a necessary contrast between their posture and that of the lovers whom we picture face to face. Beyond that contrast I do not want the image pressed. The common quest or vision which unites Friends does not absorb them in such a way that they remain ignorant or oblivious of one another. On the contrary it is the very medium in which their mutual love and knowledge exist. One knows nobody so well as one's "fellow." Every step of the common journey tests his mettle; and the tests are tests we fully understand because we are undergoing them ourselves. Hence, as he rings true time after time, our reliance, our respect and our admiration blossom into an Appreciative love of a singularly robust and well-informed kind. If, at the outset, we had attended more to him and less to the thing our Friendship is "about," we should not have come to know or love him so well. You will not find the warrior, the poet, the philosopher or the Christian by staring in his eyes as if he were your mistress: better fight beside him, read with him, argue with him, pray with him.

In a perfect Friendship this Appreciative love is, I think, often so great and so firmly based that each member of the circle feels, in his secret heart, humbled before all the rest. Sometimes he wonders what he is doing there among his betters. He is lucky beyond desert to be in such company. Especially when the whole group is together, each bringing out all that is best, wisest, or funniest in all the others. Those are the golden sessions; when four or five of us after a hard day's walking have come to our inn; when our slippers are on, our feet spread out towards the blaze and our drinks at our elbows; when the whole world, and something beyond the world, opens itself to our minds as we talk; and no one has any claim on or any responsibility for another, but all are freemen and equals as if we had first met an hour ago, while at the same time an Affection mellowed by the years enfolds us. Life — natural life — has no better gift to give. Who could have deserved it?

From what has been said it will be clear that in most societies at most periods Friendships will be between men and men or between women and women. The sexes will have met one another in Affection and in Eros but not in this love. For they will seldom have had with each other the companionship in common activities which is the matrix of Friendship. Where men are educated and women not, where one sex works and the other is idle, or where they do totally different work, they will usually have nothing to be Friends about. But we can easily see that it is this lack, rather than anything in their natures, which excludes Friendship; for where they can be companions they can also become Friends. Hence in a profession (like my own) where men and women work side by side, or in the mission field, or among authors and artists, such Friendship is common. To be sure, what is offered as Friendship on one side may be mistaken for Eros on the other, with painful and embarrassing results. Or what begins as Friendship in both may become also Eros. But to say that something can be mistaken for, or turn into, something else is not to deny the difference between them. Rather it implies it; we should not otherwise speak of "turning into" or being "mistaken for."

In one respect our own society is unfortunate. A world where men and women never have common work or a common education can probably get along comfortably enough. In it men turn to each other, and only to each other, for Friendship, and they enjoy it very much. I hope the women enjoy their feminine Friends equally. Again, a world where all men and women had sufficient common ground for this relationship could also be comfortable. At present, however, we fall between two stools. The necessary common ground, the matrix, exists between the sexes in some groups but not in others. It is notably lacking in many residential suburbs. In a plutocratic neighbourhood where the men have spent their whole lives in acquiring money some at least of the women have used their leisure to develop an intellectual life — have become musical or literary. In such places the men appear among the women as barbarians among civilised people. In another neighbourhood you will find the situation reversed. Both sexes have, indeed, "been to school." But since then the men have had a much more serious education; they have become doctors, lawyers, clergymen, architects, engineers, or men of letters. The women are to them as children to adults. In neither neighbourhood is real Friendship between the sexes at all probable. But this, though an impoverishment, would be tolerable if it were admitted and accepted. The peculiar trouble of our own age is that men and women in this situation, haunted by rumours and glimpses of happier groups where no such chasm between the sexes exists, and bedevilled by the egalitarian idea that what is possible for some ought to be (and therefore is) possible to all, refuse to acquiesce in it. Hence, on the one hand, we get the wife as school-marm, the "cultivated" woman who is always trying to bring her husband "up to her level." She drags him to concerts and would like him to learn morris-dancing and invites "cultivated" people to the house. It often does surprisingly little harm. The middle-aged male has great powers of passive resistance and (if she but knew) of indulgence; "women will have their fads." Something much more painful happens when it is the men who are civilised and the women not, and when all the women, and many of the men too, simply refuse to recognise the fact.

When this happens we get a kind, polite, laborious and pitiful pretence. The women are "deemed" (as lawyers say) to be full members of the male circle. The fact — in itself not important — that they now smoke and drink like men seems to simple-minded people a proof that they really are. No stag-parties are allowed. Wherever the men meet, the women must come too. The men have learned to live among ideas. They know what discussion, proof and illustration mean. A woman who has had merely school lessons and has abandoned soon after her marriage whatever tinge of "culture" they gave her — whose reading is the Women's Magazines and whose general conversation is almost wholly narrative — cannot really enter such a circle. She can be locally and physically present with it in the same room. What of that? If the men are ruthless, she sits bored and silent through a conversation which means nothing to her. If they are better bred, of course, they try to bring her in. Things are explained to her: people try to sublimate her irrelevant and blundering observations into some kind of sense. But the efforts soon fail and, for manners' sake, what might have been a real discussion is deliberately diluted and peters out in gossip, anecdotes, and jokes. Her presence has thus destroyed the very thing she was brought to share. She can never really enter the circle because the circle ceases to be itself when she enters it — as the horizon ceases to be the horizon when you get there. By learning to drink and smoke and perhaps to tell *risqué* stories, she has not, for this purpose, drawn an inch nearer to the men than her grandmother. But her grandmother was far happier and more realistic. She was at home talking real women's talk to other women and perhaps doing so with great charm, sense and even wit. She herself might be able to do the same. She may be quite as clever as the men whose evening she has spoiled, or cleverer. But she is not really interested in the same things, nor mistress of the same methods. (We all appear as dunces when feigning an interest in things we care nothing about.)

The presence of such women, thousands strong, helps to account for the modern disparagement of Friendship. They are often completely victorious. They banish male companionship, and therefore male Friendship, from whole neighbourhoods. In the only world they know, an endless prattling "Jolly" replaces the intercourse of minds. All the men they meet talk like women while women are present.

This victory over Friendship is often unconscious. There is, however, a more militant type of woman who plans it. I have heard one say "Never let two men sit together or they'll get talking about some *subject* and then there'll be no fun." Her point could not have been more accurately made. Talk, by all means; the more the better; unceasing cascades of the human voice; but not, please, a subject. The talk must not be about anything.

This gay lady — this lively, accomplished, "charming," unendurable bore — was seeking only each evening's amusement, making the meeting "go." But the conscious war against Friendship may be fought on a deeper level. There are women who regard it with hatred, envy and fear as the enemy of Eros and, perhaps even more, of Affection. A woman of that sort has a hundred arts to break up her husband's Friendships. She will quarrel with his Friends herself or, better still, with their wives. She will sneer, obstruct and lie. She does not realise that the husband whom she succeeds in isolating from his own kind will not be very well worth having; she has emasculated him. She will grow to be ashamed of him herself. Nor does she remember how much of his life lies in places where she cannot watch him. New Friendships will break out, but by this time they will be secret. Lucky for her, and lucky beyond her deserts, if there are not soon other secrets as well.

All these, of course, are silly women. The sensible women who, if they wanted, would certainly be able to qualify themselves for the world of discussion and ideas, are precisely those who, if they are not qualified, never try to enter it or to destroy it. They have other fish to fry. At a mixed party they gravitate to one end of the room and talk women's talk to one another. They don't want us, for this sort of purpose, any more than we want them. It is only the riff-raff of each sex that wants to be incessantly hanging on the other. Live and let live. They laugh at us a good deal. That is just as it should be. Where the sexes, having no real shared activities, can meet only in Affection and Eros — cannot be Friends — it is healthy that each should have a lively sense of the other's absurdity. Indeed it is always healthy. No one ever really appreciated the other sex — just as no one really appreciates children or animals — without at times feeling them to be funny. For both sexes are. Humanity is tragi-comical; but the division into sexes enables each to see in the other the joke that often escapes it in itself — and the pathos too.

I gave warning that this chapter would be largely a rehabilitation. The preceding pages have, I hope, made clear why to me at least it seems no wonder if our ancestors regarded Friendship as something that raised us almost above humanity. This love, free from instinct, free from all duties but those which love has freely assumed, almost wholly free from jealousy, and free without qualification from the need to be needed, is eminently spiritual. It is the sort of love one can imagine between angels. Have we here found a natural love which is Love itself?

Before we rush to any such conclusion let us beware of the ambiguity in the word *spiritual*. There are many New Testament contexts in which it means "pertaining to the (Holy) Spirit," and in such contexts the spiritual is, by definition, good. But when *spiritual* is used simply as the opposite of corporeal, or instinctive, or animal, this is not so. There is spiritual evil as well as spiritual good. There are unholy, as well as holy, angels. The worst sins of men are spiritual. We must not think that in finding

Friendship to be *spiritual* we have found it to be in itself holy or inerrant. Three significant facts remain to be taken into account.

The first, already mentioned, is the distrust which Authorities tend to have of close Friendships among their subjects. It may be unjustified; or there may be some basis for it.

Secondly, there is the attitude of the majority towards all circles of close Friends. Every name they give such a circle is more or less derogatory. It is at best a "set"; lucky if not a *coterie,* a "gang," a "little senate," or a "mutal admiration society." Those who in their own lives know only Affection, Companionship and Eros, suspect Friends to be "stuck-up prigs who think themselves too good for us." Of course this is the voice of Envy. But Envy always brings the truest charge, or the charge nearest to the truth, that she can think up; it hurts more. This charge, therefore, will have to be considered.

Finally, we must notice that Friendship is very rarely the image under which Scripture represents the love between God and Man. It is not entirely neglected; but far more often, seeking a symbol for the highest love of all, Scripture ignores this seemingly almost angelic relation and plunges into the depth of what is most natural and instinctive. Affection is taken as the image when God is represented as our Father; Eros, when Christ is represented as the Bridgroom of the Church.

Let us begin with the suspicions of those in Authority. I think there is a ground for them and that a consideration of this ground brings something important to light. Friendship, I have said, is born at the moment when one man says to another "What! You too? I thought that no one but myself . . . " But the common taste or vision or point of view which is thus discovered need not always be a nice one. From such a moment art, or philosophy, or an advance in religion or morals might well take their rise; but why not also torture, cannibalism, or human sacrifice?. Surely most of us have experienced the ambivalent nature of such moments in our own youth? It was wonderful when we first met someone who cared for our favourite poet. What we had hardly understood before now took clear shape. What we had been half ashamed of we now freely acknowledged. But it was no less delightful when we first met someone who shared with us a secret evil. This too became far more palpable and explicit; of this too, we ceased to be ashamed. Even now, at whatever age, we all know the perilous charm of a shared hatred or grievance. (It is difficult not to hail as a Friend the only other man in College who really sees the faults of the Sub-Warden.)

Alone among unsympathetic companions, I hold certain views and standards timidly, half ashamed to avow them and half doubtful if they can after all be right. Put me back among my Friends and in half an hour — in ten minutes — these same views and standards become once more indisputable. The opinion of this little circle, while I am in it, outweighs that of a thousand outsiders: as Friendship strengthens, it will do this even when my Friends are far away. For we all wish to be judged by our peers, by the men "after our own heart." Only they really know our mind and only they judge it by standards we fully acknowledge. Theirs is the praise we really covet and the blame we really dread. The little pockets of early Christians survived because they cared exclusively for the love of "the brethren" and stopped their ears to the opinion of the Pagan society all round them. But a circle of criminals, cranks, or perverts survives in just the same way; by becoming deaf to the opinion of the outer world, by discounting it as the chatter of outsiders who "don't understand," of the "conventional," "the bourgeois," the "Establishment," of prigs, prudes and humbugs.

It is therefore easy to see why Authority frowns on Friendship. Every real Friendship is a sort of secession, even a rebellion. It may be a rebellion of serious thinkers against accepted clap-trap or of faddists against accepted good sense; of real artists against popular ugliness or of charlatans against civilised taste; of good men against the badness of society or of bad men against its goodness. Whichever it is, it will be unwelcome to Top People. In each knot of Friends there is a sectional "public opinion" which fortifies its members against the public opinion of the community in general. Each therefore is a pocket of potential resistance. Men who have real Friends are less easy to manage or "get at"; harder for good Authorities to correct or for bad Authorities to corrupt. Hence if our masters, by force or by propaganda about "Togetherness" or by unobtrusively making privacy and unplanned leisure impossible, ever succeed in producing a world where all are Companions and none are Friends, they will have removed certain dangers, and will also have taken from us what is almost our strongest safeguard against complete servitude.

But the dangers are perfectly real. Friendship (as the ancients saw) can be a school of virtue; but also (as they did not see) a school of vice. It is ambivalent. It makes good men better and bad men worse. It would be a waste of time to elaborate the point. What concerns us is not to expatiate on the badness of bad Friendships but to become aware of the possible danger in good ones. This love, like the other natural loves, has its congenital liability to a particular disease.

It will be obvious that the element of secession, of indifference or deafness (at least on some matters) to the voices of the outer world, is common to all Friendships, whether good, bad, or merely innocuous. Even if the common ground of the Friendship is nothing more momentous than stamp-collecting, the circle rightly and inevitably ignores the views of the millions who think it a silly occupation and of the thousands who have merely dabbled in it. The founders of meteorology rightly and inevitably ignored the views of the millions who still attributed storms to witchcraft. There is no offence in this. As I know that I should be an Outsider to a circle of golfers, mathematicians, or motorists, so I claim the equal right of regarding them as Outsiders to mine. People who bore one another should meet seldom; people who interest one another, often.

The danger is that this partial indifference or deafness to outside opinion, justified and necessary though it is, may lead to a wholesale indifference or deafness. The most spectacular instances of this can be seen not in a circle of Friends but in a Theocratic or aristocratic class. We know what the Priests in Our Lord's time thought of the common people. The Knights in Froissart's chronicles had neither sympathy nor mercy for the "outsiders," the churls or peasantry. But this deplorable indifference was very closely intertwined with a good quality. They really had, among themselves, a very high standard of valour, generosity, courtesy and honour. This standard the cautious, close-fisted churl would have thought merely silly. The Knights, in maintaining it, were, and had to be, wholly indifferent to his views. They "didn't give a damn" what he thought. If they had, our own standard today would be the poorer and the coarser for it. But the habit of "not giving a damn" grows on a class. To discount the voice of the peasant where it really ought to be discounted makes it easier to discount his voice when he cries for justice or mercy. The partial deafness which is noble and necessary encourages the wholesale deafness which is arrogant and inhuman.

A circle of Friends cannot of course oppress the outer world as a powerful social class can. But it is subject, on its own scale, to the same danger. It can come to treat as "outsiders" in a general (and derogatory) sense those who were quite properly outsiders for a particular purpose. Thus, like an aristocracy, it can create around it a vacuum across which no voice will carry. The literary or artistic circle which began by discounting, perhaps rightly, the plain man's ideas about literature or art may come to discount equally his idea that they should pay their bills, cut their nails and behave civilly. Whatever faults the circle has — and no circle is without them — thus become incurable. But that is not all. The partial and defensible deafness was based on some kind of superiority — even if it were only a superior knowledge about stamps. The sense of superiority will then get itself attached to the total deafness. The group will disdain as well as ignore those outside it. It will, in effect, have turned itself into something very like a class. A *coterie* is a self-appointed aristocracy.

I said above that in a good Friendship each member often feels humility towards the rest. He sees that they are splendid and counts himself lucky to be among them. But unfortunately the *they* and *them* are also, from another point of view *we* and *us*. Thus the transition from individual humility to corporate pride is very easy.

I am not thinking of what we should call a social or snobbish pride: a delight in knowing, and being known to know, distinguished people. That is quite a different thing. The snob wishes to attach himself to some group because it is already regarded as an *élite*; friends are in danger of coming to regard themselves as an *élite* because they are already attached. We seek men after our own heart for their own sake and are then alarmingly or delightfully surprised by the feeling that we have become an aristocracy. Not that we'd call it that. Every reader who has known Friendship will probably feel inclined to deny with some heat that his own circle was ever guilty of such an absurdity. I feel the same. But in such matters it is best not to begin with ourselves. However it may be with us, I think we have all recognised some such tendency in those other circles to which we are the Outsiders.

I was once at some kind of conference where two clergymen, obviously close friends, began talking about "uncreated energies" other than God. I asked how there could be any uncreated things except God if the Creed was right in calling Him the

"maker of all things visible and invisible." Their reply was to glance at one another
and laugh. I had no objection to their laughter, but I wanted an answer in words as
well. It was not at all a sneering or unpleasant laugh. It expressed very much what
Americans would express by saying "Isn't he cute?" It was like the laughter of jolly
grown-ups when an *enfant terrible* asks the sort of question that is never asked. You
can hardly imagine how inoffensively it was done, nor how clearly it conveyed the
impression that they were fully aware of living habitually on a higher plane than the
rest of us, of coming among us as Knights among churls or as grown-ups among children. Very possibly they had an answer to my question and knew that I was too ignorant to follow it. If they had said in so many words "I'm afraid it would take too long to
explain," I would not be attributing to them the pride of Friendship. The glance and
the laugh are the real point – the audible and visible embodiment of a corporate superiority taken for granted and unconcealed. The almost complete inoffensiveness,
the absence of any apparent wish to wound or exult (they were very nice young men)
really underline the Olympian attitude. Here was a sense of superiority so secure that
it could afford to be tolerant, urbane, unemphatic.

This sense of corporate superiority is not always Olympian; that is, tranquil and
tolerant. It may be Titanic; restive, militant and embittered. Another time, when I had
been addressing an undergraduate society and some discussion (very properly)
followed my paper, a young man with an expression as tense as that of a rodent so
dealt with me that I had to say, "Look, sir. Twice in the last five minutes you have as
good as called me a liar. If you cannot discuss a question of criticism without that kind
of thing I must leave." I expected he would do one of two things; lose his temper and
redouble his insults, or else blush and apologise. The startling thing is that he did
neither. No new perturbation was added to the habitual *malaise* of his expression. He
did not repeat the Lie Direct; but apart from that he went on just as before. One had
come up against an iron curtain. He was forearmed against the risk of any strictly
personal relation, either friendly or hostile, with such as me. Behind this, almost certainly, there lies a circle of the Titanic sort – self-dubbed Knights Templars perpetually in arms to defend a critical Baphomet. We – who are *they* to them – do not exist
as persons at all. We are specimens; specimens of various Age Groups, Types, Cli-
mates of Opinion, or Interests, to be exterminated. Deprived of one weapon, they
coolly take up another. They are not, in the ordinary human sense, meeting us at all;
they are merely doing a job of work – spraying (I have heard one use that image)
insecticide.

My two nice young clergymen and my not so nice Rodent were on a high intellectual level. So were that famous set who in Edwardian times reached the sublime fatuity of calling themselves "the Souls." But the same feeling of corporate superiority
can possess a group of much more commonplace friends. It will then be flaunted in a
cruder way. We have all seen this done by the "old hands" at school talking in the
presence of a new boy, or two Regulars in the Army talking before a "Temporary";
sometimes by very loud and vulgar friends to impress mere strangers in a bar or a

railway carriage. Such people talk very intimately and esoterically in order to be overheard. Everyone who is not in the circle must be shown that he is not in it. Indeed the Friendship may be "about" almost nothing except the fact that it excludes. In speaking to an Outsider each member of it delights to mention the others by their Christian names or nicknames; not although, but because, the Outsider won't know who he means. A man I once knew was even subtler. He simply referred to his friends as if we all knew, certainly ought to know, who they were. "As Richard Button once said to me...," he would begin. We were all very young. We never dared to admit that we hadn't heard of Richard Button. It seemed so obvious that to everyone who was anyone he must be a household word; "not to know him argued ourselves unknown." Only much later did we come to realise that no one else had heard of him either. (Indeed I now have a suspicion that some of these Richard Buttons, Hezekiah Cromwells, and Eleanor Forsyths had no more existence than Mrs. Harris. But for a year or so we were completely overawed.)

We can thus detect the pride of Friendship — whether Olympian, Titanic, or merely vulgar — in many circles of Friends. It would be rash to assume that our own is safe from its danger; for of course it is in our own that we should be slowest to recognise it. The danger of such pride is indeed almost inseparable from Friendly love. Friendship must exclude. From the innocent and necessary act of excluding to the spirit of exclusiveness is an easy step; and thence to the degrading pleasure of exclusiveness. If that is once admitted the downward slope will grow rapidly steeper. We may never perhaps become Titans or plain cads; we might — which is in some ways worse — become "Souls." The common vision which first brought us together may fade quite away. We shall be a *coterie* that exists for the sake of being a *coterie*; a little self-elected (and therefore absurd) aristocracy, basking in the moonshine of our collective self-approval.

Sometimes a circle in this condition begins to dabble in the world of practice. Judiciously enlarging itself to admit recruits whose share in the original common interest is negligible but who are felt to be (in some undefined sense) "sound men," it becomes a power in the land. Membership of it comes to have a sort of political importance, though the politics involved may be only those of a regiment, a college, or a cathedral close. The manipulation of committees, the capture of jobs (for sound men) and the united front against the Have-nots now become its principal occupation, and those who once met to talk about God or poetry now meet to talk about lectureships or livings. Notice the justice of their doom. "Dust thou art and unto dust shalt thou return," said God to Adam. In a circle which has thus dwindled into a coven of wanglers Friendship has sunk back again into the mere practical Companionship which was its matrix. They are now the same sort of body as the primitive horde of hunters. Hunters, indeed, is precisely what they are; and not the kind of hunters I most respect.

The mass of the people, who are never quite right, are never quite wrong. They are hopelessly mistaken in their belief that every knot of friends came into existence for the sake of the pleasures of conceit and superiority. They are, I trust, mistaken in their belief that every Friendship actually indulges in these pleasures. But they would seem to be right in diagnosing pride as the danger to which Friendships are naturally liable. Just because this is the most spiritual of loves the danger which besets it is spiritual too. Friendship is even, if you like, angelic. But man needs to be triply protected by humility if he is to eat the bread of angels without risk.

Perhaps we may now hazard a guess why Scripture uses Friendship so rarely as an image of the highest love. It is already, in actual fact, too spiritual to be a good symbol of Spiritual things. The highest does not stand without the lowest. God can safely represent Himself to us as Father and Husband because only a lunatic would think that He is physically our sire or that His marriage with the Church is other than mystical. But if Friendship were used for this purpose we might mistake the symbol for the thing symbolized. The danger inherent in it would be aggravated. We might be further encouraged to mistake that nearness (by resemblance) to the heavenly life which Friendship certainly displays for a nearness of approach.

Friendship, then, like the other natural loves, is unable to save itself. In reality, because it is spiritual and therefore faces a subtler enemy, it must, even more wholeheartedly than they, invoke the divine protection if it hopes to remain sweet. For consider how narrow its true path is. It must not become what the people call a "mutual admiration society"; yet if it is not full of mutual admiration, of Appreciative love, it is not Friendship at all. For unless our lives are to be miserably impoverished it must be for us in our Friendships as it was for Christiana and her party in *The Pilgrim's Progress:*

> They seemed to be a terror one to the other, for that they could not see that glory each one on herself which they could see in each other. Now therefore they began to esteem each other better than themselves. For you are fairer than I am, said one; and you are more comely than I am, said another.

There is in the long run only one way in which we can taste this illustrious experience with safety. And Bunyan has indicated it in the same passage. It was in the House of the Interpreter, after they had been bathed, sealed and freshly clothed in "White Raiment" that the women saw one another in this light. If we remember the bathing, sealing and robing, we shall be safe. And the higher the common ground of the Friendship is, the more necessary the remembrance. In an explicitly religious Friendship, above all, to forget it would be fatal.

For then it will seem to us that we – we four or five – have chosen one another, the insight of each finding the intrinsic beauty of the rest, like to like, a voluntary nobility; that we have ascended above the rest of mankind by our native powers. The other loves do not invite the same illusion. Affection obviously requires kinships or at least proximities which never depended on our own choice. And as for Eros, half the love songs and half the love poems in the world will tell you that the Beloved is your fate or destiny, no more your choice than a thunderbolt, for "it is not in our power to love or hate." Cupid's archery, genes – anything but ourselves. But in

Friendship, being free of all that, we think we have chosen our peers. In reality, a few years' difference in the dates of our births, a few more miles between certain houses, the choice of one university instead of another, posting to different regiments, the accident of a topic being raised or not raised at a first meeting — any of these chances might have kept us apart. But, for a Christian, there are, strictly speaking, no chances. A secret Master of the Ceremonies has been at work. Christ, who said to the disciples "Ye have not chosen me, but I have chosen you," can truly say to every group of Christian friends "You have not chosen one another but I have chosen you for one another." The Friendship is not a reward for our discrimination and good taste in finding one another out. It is the instrument by which God reveals to each the beauties of all the others. They are no greater than the beauties of a thousand other men; by Friendship God opens our eyes to them. They are, like all beauties, derived from Him, and then, in a good Friendship, increased by Him through the Friendship itself, so that it is His instrument for creating as well as for revealing. At this feast it is He who has spread the board and it is He who has chosen the guests. It is He, we may dare to hope, who sometimes does, and always should, preside. Let us not reckon without our Host.

Not that we must always partake of it solemnly. "God who made good laughter" forbid. It is one of the difficult and delightful subtleties of life that we must deeply acknowledge certain things to be serious and yet retain the power and will to treat them often as lightly as a game. But there will be a time for saying more about this in the next chapter. For the moment I will only quote Dunbar's beautifully balanced advice:

> *Man, please thy Maker, and be merry,*
> *And give not for this world a cherry.*

V

EROS

By Eros I mean of course that state which we call "being in love"; or, if you prefer, that kind of love which lovers are "in." Some readers may have been surprised when, in an earlier chapter, I described Affection as the love in which our experience seems to come closest to that of the animals. Surely, it might be asked, our sexual functions bring us equally close? This is quite true as regards human sexuality in general. But I am not going to be concerned with human sexuality simply as such. Sexuality makes part of our subject only when it becomes an ingredient in the complex state of "being in love." That sexual experience can occur without Eros, without being "in love," and that Eros includes other things besides sexual activity, I take for granted. If you prefer to put it that way, I am inquiring not into the sexuality which is common to us and the beasts or even common to all men but into one uniquely human variation of it which develops within "love" — what I call Eros. The carnal or animally sexual element within Eros, I intend (following an old usage) to call Venus. And I mean by Venus what is sexual not in some cryptic or rarefied sense — such as a depth-psychologist might explore — but in a perfectly obvious sense; what is known to be sexual by those who experience it; what could be proved to be sexual by the simplest observations.

Sexuality may operate without Eros or as part of Eros. Let me hasten to add that I make the distinction simply in order to limit our inquiry and without any moral implications. I am not at all subscribing to the popular idea that it is the absence or presence of Eros which makes the sexual act "impure" or "pure," degraded or fine, unlawful or lawful. If all who lay together without being in the state of Eros were abominable, we all come of tainted stock. The times and places in which marriage depends on Eros are in a small minority. Most of our ancestors were married off in early youth to partners chosen by their parents on grounds that had nothing to do with Eros. They went to the act with no other "fuel," so to speak, than plain animal desire. And they did right; honest Christian husbands and wives, obeying their fathers and mothers, discharging to one another their "marriage debt," and bringing up families in the fear of the Lord. Conversely, this act, done under the influence of a soaring and iridescent Eros which reduces the role of the senses to a minor consideration, may yet be plain adultery, may involve breaking a wife's heart, deceiving a husband, betraying a friend, polluting hospitality and deserting your children. It has not pleased God that the distinction between a sin and a duty should turn on fine feelings. This act, like any other, is justified (or not) by far more prosaic and definable criteria; by the keeping or breaking of promises, by justice or injustice, by charity or selfishness, by obedience or disobedience. My treatment rules out mere sexuality — sexuality without Eros — on grounds that have nothing to do with morals; because it is irrelevant to our purpose.

To the evolutionist Eros (the human variation) will be something that grows out of Venus, a late complication and development of the immemorial biological impulse. We must not assume, however, that this is necessarily what happens within the consciousness of the individual. There may be those who have first felt mere sexual appetite for a woman and then gone on at a later stage to "fall in love with her." But I doubt if this is at all common. Very often what comes first is simply a delighted pre-occupation with the Beloved — a general, unspecified pre-occupation with her in her totality. A man in this state really hasn't leisure to think of sex. He is too busy thinking of a person. The fact that she is a woman is far less important than the fact that she is herself. He is full of desire, but the desire may not be sexually toned. If you asked him what he wanted, the true reply would often be, "To go on thinking of her." He is love's contemplative. And when at a later stage the explicitly sexual element awakes, he will not feel (unless scientific theories are influencing him) that this had all along been the root of the whole matter. He is more likely to feel that the incoming tide of Eros, having demolished many sand-castles and made islands of many rocks, has now at last with a triumphant seventh wave flooded this part of his nature also — the little pool of ordinary sexuality which was there on his beach before the tide came in. Eros enters him like an invader, taking over and reorganising, one by one, the institutions of a conquered country. It may have taken over many others before it reaches the sex in him; and it will reorganise that too.

No one has indicated the nature of that reorganisation more briefly and accurately than George Orwell, who disliked it and preferred sexuality in its native condition, uncontaminated by Eros. In *Nineteen Eighty-Four* his dreadful hero (how much less human than the four-footed heroes of his excellent *Animal Farm*!), before towsing the heroine, demands a reassurance, "You like doing this?" he asks, "I don't mean simply me; I mean the thing in itself." He is not satisfied till he gets the answer, "I adore it." This little dialogue defines the reorganisation. Sexual desire, without Eros, wants *it*, the *thing in itself*; Eros wants the Beloved.

The *thing* is a sensory pleasure; that is, an event occurring within one's own body. We use a most unfortunate idiom when we say, of a lustful man prowling the streets, that he "wants a woman." Strictly speaking, a woman is just what he does not want. He wants a pleasure for which a woman happens to be the necessary piece of apparatus. How much he cares about the woman as such may be gauged by his attitude to her five minutes after fruition (one does not keep the carton after one has smoked the cigarettes). Now Eros makes a man really want, not a woman, but one particular woman. In some mysterious but quite indisputable fashion the lover desires the Beloved herself, not the pleasure she can give. No lover in the world ever sought the embraces of the woman he loved as a result of a calculation, however unconscious, that they would be more pleasurable than those of any other woman. If he raised the question he would, no doubt, expect that this would be so. But to raise it would be to step outside the world of Eros altogether. The only man I know of who ever did raise it was Lucretius, and he was certainly not in love when he did. It is interesting to note his answer. That austere voluptuary gave it as his opinion that love actually impairs sexual pleasure. The emotion was a distraction. It spoiled the cool and critical receptivity of his palate. (A great poet; but "Lord, what beastly fellows these Romans were!")

The reader will notice that Eros thus wonderfully transforms what is *par excellence* a Need-pleasure into the most Appreciative of all pleasures. It is the nature of a Need-pleasure to show us the object solely in relation to our need, even our momentary need. But in Eros, a Need, at its most intense, sees the object most intensely as a thing admirable in herself, important far beyond her relation to the lover's need.

If we had not all experienced this, if we were mere logicians, we might boggle at the conception of desiring a human being, as distinct from desiring any pleasure, comfort, or service that human beings can give. And it is certainly hard to explain. Lovers themselves are trying to express part of it (not much) when they say they would like to "eat" one another. Milton has expressed more when he fancies angelic creatures with bodies made of light who can achieve total interpenetration instead of our mere embraces. Charles Williams has said something of it in the words, "Love you? I *am* you."

Without Eros sexual desire, like every other desire, is a fact about ourselves. Within Eros it is rather about the Beloved. It becomes almost a mode of perception, entirely a mode of expression. It feels objective; something outside us, in the real world. That is why Eros, though the king of pleasures, always (at his height) has the air of regarding pleasure as a by-product. To think about it would plunge us back in ourselves, in our own nervous system. It would kill Eros, as you can "kill" the finest mountain prospect by locating it all in your own retina and optic nerves. Anyway, whose pleasure? For one of the first things Eros does is to obliterate the distinction between giving and receiving.

Hitherto I have been trying merely to describe, not to evaluate. But certain moral questions now inevitably arise, and I must not conceal my own view of them. It is submitted rather than asserted, and of course open to correction by better men, better lovers and better Christians.

It has been widely held in the past, and is perhaps held by many unsophisticated people to-day, that the spiritual danger of Eros arises almost entirely from the carnal element within it; that Eros is "noblest" or "purest" when Venus is reduced to the minimum. The older moral theologians certainly seem to have thought that the danger we chiefly had to guard against in marriage was that of a soul-destroying surrender to the senses. It will be noticed, however, that this is not the Scriptural approach. St. Paul, dissuading his converts from marriage, says nothing about that side of the matter except to discourage prolonged abstinence from Venus (I *Cor.* VII, 5). What he fears is pre-occupation, the need of constantly "pleasing" – that is, considering – one's partner, the multiple distractions of domesticity. It is marriage itself, not the marriage bed, that will be likely to hinder us from waiting uninterruptedly on God. And surely St. Paul is right? If I may trust my own experience it is (within marriage as without) the practical and prudential cares of this world, and even the smallest and most prosaic of those cares, that are the great distraction. The gnat-like cloud of petty anxieties and decisions about the conduct of the next hour have interfered with my prayers more often than any passion or appetite whatever. The great, permanent temptation of marriage is not to sensuality but (quite bluntly) to avarice. With all proper respect to the medieval guides, I cannot help remembering that they were all celibates, and probably did not know what Eros does to our sexuality; how, far from aggravating, he reduces the nagging and addictive character of mere appetite. And that not simply by satisfying it. Eros, without diminishing desire, makes abstinence easier. He tends, no doubt, to a pre-occupation with the Beloved which can indeed be an obstacle to the spiritual life; but not chiefly a sensual pre-occupation.

The real spiritual danger in Eros as a whole lies, I believe, elsewhere. I will return to the point. For the moment, I want to speak of the danger which at present, in my opinion, especially haunts the act of love. This is a subject on which I disagree, not with the human race (far from it), but with many of its gravest spokesmen. I believe we are all being encouraged to take Venus too seriously; at any rate, with a wrong kind of seriousness. All my life a ludicrous and portentous solemnisation of sex has been going on.

One author tells us that Venus should recur through the married life in "a solemn, sacramental rhythm." A young man to whom I had described as "pornographic" a novel that he much admired, replied with genuine bewilderment, "Pornographic? But how can it be? It treats the whole thing so seriously" – as if a long face were a sort of moral disinfectant. Our friends who harbour Dark Gods, the "pillar of blood" school, attempt seriously to restore something like the Phallic religion. Our advertisements, at their sexiest, paint the whole business in terms of the rapt, the intense, the swoony-devout; seldom a hint of gaiety. And the psychologists have so bedevilled us with the infinite importance of complete sexual adjustment and the all but impossibility of achieving it, that I could believe some young couples now go to it with the complete works of Freud, Kraft-Ebbing, Havelock Ellis and Dr. Stopes spread out on bed-tables all round them. Cheery old Ovid, who never either ignored a mole-hill or made a mountain of it, would be more to the point. We have reached the stage at which nothing is more needed than a roar of old-fashioned laughter.

But, it will be replied, the thing *is* serious. Yes; quadruply so. First, theologically, because this is the body's share in marriage which, by God's choice, is the mystical image of the union between God and Man. Secondly, as what I will venture to call a sub-Christian, or Pagan or natural sacrament, our human participation in, and exposition of, the natural forces of life and fertility — the marriage of Sky-Father and Earth-Mother. Thirdly, on the moral level, in view of the obligations involved and the incalculable momentousness of being a parent and ancestor. Finally it has (sometimes, not always) a great emotional seriousness in the minds of the participants.

But eating is also serious; theologically, as the vehicle of the Blessed Sacrament; ethically in view of our duty to feed the hungry; socially, because the table is from time immemorial the place for talk; medically, as all dyspeptics know. Yet we do not bring bluebooks to dinner nor behave there as if we were in church. And it is *gourmets,* not saints, who come nearest to doing so. Animals are always serious about food.

We must not be totally serious about Venus. Indeed we can't be totally serious without doing violence to our humanity. It is not for nothing that every language and literature in the world is full of jokes about sex. Many of them may be dull or disgusting and nearly all of them are old. But we must insist that they embody an attitude to Venus which in the long run endangers the Christian life far less than a reverential gravity. We must not attempt to find an absolute in the flesh. Banish play and laughter from the bed of love and you may let in a false goddess. She will be even falser than the Aphrodite of the Greeks; for they, even while they worshipped her, knew that she was "laughter-loving." The mass of the people are perfectly right in their conviction that Venus is a partly comic spirit. We are under no obligation at all to sing all our love-duets in the throbbing, world-without-end, heart-breaking manner of Tristan and Isolde; let us often sing like Papageno and Papagena instead.

Venus herself will have a terrible revenge if we take her (occasional) seriousness at its face value. And that in two ways. One is most comically — though with no comic intention — illustrated by Sir Thomas Browne when he says that her service is "the foolishest act a wise man commits in all his life, nor is there anything that will more deject his cool'd imagination, when he shall consider what an odd and unworthy piece of folly he hath committed." But if he had gone about that act with less solemnity in the first place he would not have suffered this "dejection." If his imagination had not been misled, its cooling would have brought no such revulsion. But Venus has another and worse revenge.

She herself is a mocking, mischievous spirit, far more elf than deity, and makes game of us. When all external circumstances are fittest for her service she will leave one or both the lovers totally indisposed for it. When every overt act is impossible and even glances cannot be exchanged — in trains, in shops, and at interminable parties — she will assail them with all her force. An hour later, when time and place agree, she will have mysteriously withdrawn; perhaps from only one of them. What a pother this must raise — what resentments, self-pities, suspicions, wounded vanities and all the current chatter about "frustration" — in those who have deified her! But sensible lovers laugh. It is all part of the game; a game of catch-as-catch-can, and the escapes and tumbles and head-on collisions are to be treated as a romp.

For I can hardly help regarding it as one of God's jokes that a passion so soaring, so apparently transcendent, as Eros, should thus be linked in incongruous symbiosis with a bodily appetite which, like any other appetite, tactlessly reveals its connections with such mundane factors as weather, health, diet, circulation and digestion. In Eros at times we seem to be flying; Venus gives us the sudden twitch that reminds us we are really captive balloons. It is a continual demonstration of the truth that we are composite creatures, rational animals, akin on one side to the angels, on the other to tom-cats. It is a bad thing not to be able to take a joke. Worse, not to take a divine joke; made, I grant you, at our expense, but also (who doubts it?) for our endless benefit.

Man has held three views of his body. First there is that of those ascetic Pagans who called it the prison or the "tomb" of the soul, and of Christians like Fisher to whom it was a "sack of dung," food for worms, filthy, shameful, a source of nothing but temptation to bad men and humiliation to good ones. Then there are the Neo-Pagans (they seldom know Greek), the nudists and the sufferers from Dark Gods, to whom the body is glorious. But thirdly we have the view which St. Francis expressed by calling his body "Brother Ass." All three may be — I am not sure — defensible; but give me St. Francis for my money.

Ass is exquisitely right because no one in his senses can either revere or hate a donkey. It is a useful, sturdy, lazy, obstinate, patient, lovable and infuriating beast; deserving now the stick and now a carrot; both pathetically and absurdly beautiful. So the body. There's no living with it till we recognise that one of its functions in our lives is to play the part of buffoon. Until some theory has sophisticated them, every man, woman and child in the world knows this. The fact that we have bodies is the oldest joke there is. Eros (like death, figure-drawing, and the study of medicine) may at moments cause us to take it with total seriousness. The error consists in concluding that Eros should always do so and permanently abolish the joke. But this is not what happens. The very faces of all the happy lovers we know make it clear. Lovers, unless their love is very short-lived, again and again feel an element not only of comedy, not only of play, but even of buffoonery, in the body's expression of Eros. And the body would frustrate us if this were not so. It would be too clumsy an instrument to render love's music unless its very clumsiness could be felt as adding to the total experience its own grotesque charm — a sub-plot or antimasque miming with its own hearty rough-and-tumble what the soul enacts in statelier fashion. (Thus in old comedies the lyric loves of the hero and heroine are at once parodied and corroborated by some much more earthy affair between a Touchstone and an Audrey or a valet and a chambermaid.)The highest does not stand without the lowest. There is indeed at certain moments a high poetry in the flesh itself; but also, by your leave, an irreducible element of obstinate and ludicrous unpoetry. If it does not make itself felt on one occasion, it will on another. Far better plant it foursquare within the drama of Eros as comic relief than pretend you haven't noticed it.

For indeed we require this relief. The poetry is there as well as the un-poetry; the gravity of Venus as well as her levity, the *gravis ardor* or burning weight of desire.

Pleasure, pushed to its extreme, shatters us like pain. The longing for a union which only the flesh can mediate while the flesh, our mutually excluding bodies, renders it forever unattainable can have the grandeur of a metaphysical pursuit. Amorousness as well as grief can bring tears to the eyes. But Venus does not always come thus "entire, fastened to her prey," and the fact that she sometimes does so is the very reason for preserving always a hint of playfulness in our attitude to her. When natural things look most divine, the demoniac is just round the corner.

This refusal to be quite immersed — this recollection of the levity even when, for the moment, only the gravity is displayed — is especially relevant to a certain attitude which Venus, in her intensity, evokes from most (I believe, not all) pairs of lovers. This act can invite the man to an extreme, though short-lived, masterfulness, to the dominance of a conqueror or a captor, and the woman to a correspondingly extreme subjection and surrender. Hence the roughness, even fierceness, of some erotic play; the "lover's pinch which hurts and is desired." How should a sane couple think of this? or a Christian couple permit it?

I think it is harmless and wholesome on one condition. We must recognise that we have here to do with what I called "the Pagan sacrament" in sex. In Friendship, as we noticed, each participant stands for precisely himself — the contingent individual he is. But in the act of love we are not merely ourselves. We are also representatives. It is here no impoverishment but an enrichment to be aware that forces older and less personal than we work through us. In us all the masculinity and femininity of the world, all that is assailant and responsive, are momentarily focused. The man does play the Sky-Father and the woman the Earth-Mother; he does play Form, and she Matter. But we must give full value to the word *play*. Of course neither "plays a part" in the sense of being a hypocrite. But each plays a part or role in — well, in something which is comparable to a mystery-play or ritual (at one extreme) and to a masque or even a charade (at the other).

A woman who accepted as literally her own this extreme self-surrender would be an idolatress offering to a man what belongs only to God. And a man would have to be the coxcomb of all coxcombs, and indeed a blasphemer, if he arrogated to himself, as the mere person he is, the sort of sovereignty to which Venus for a moment exalts him. But what cannot lawfully be yielded or claimed can be lawfully enacted. Outside this ritual or drama he and she are two immortal souls, two free-born adults, two citizens. We should be much mistaken if we supposed that those marriages where this mastery is most asserted and acknowledged in the act of Venus were those where the husband is most likely to be dominant in the married life as a whole; the reverse is perhaps more probable. But within the rite or drama they become a god and goddess between whom there is no equality — whose relations are asymmetrical.

Some will think it strange I should find an element of ritual or masquerade in that action which is often regarded as the most real, the most unmasked and sheerly genuine, we ever do. Are we not our true selves when naked? In a sense, no. The word *naked* was originally a past participle; the naked man was the man who had under-gone a process of *naking*, that is, of stripping or peeling (you used the verb of nuts and fruit). Time out of mind the naked man has seemed to our ancestors not the natural but the abnormal man; not the man who has abstained from dressing but the man who has been for some reason undressed. And it is a simple fact — anyone can observe it at a men's bathing place — that nudity emphasises common humanity and soft-pedals what is individual. In that way we are "more ourselves" when clothed. By nudity the lovers cease to be solely John and Mary; the universal He and She are emphasised. You could almost say they *put* on nakedness as a ceremonial robe — or as the costume for a charade. For we must still beware — and never more than when we thus partake of the Pagan sacrament in our love-passages — of being serious in the wrong way. The Sky-Father himself is only a Pagan dream of One far greater than Zeus and far more masculine than the male. And a mortal man is not even the Sky-Father, and cannot really wear his crown. Only a copy of it, done in tinselled paper. I do not call it this in contempt. I like ritual; I like private theatricals; I even like charades. Paper crowns have their legitimate, and (in the proper context) their serious, uses. They are not in the last resort much flimsier ("if imagination mend them") than all earthly dignities.

But I dare not mention this Pagan sacrament without turning aside to guard against any danger of confusing it with an incomparably higher mystery. As nature crowns man in that brief action, so the Christian law has crowned him in the perma-nent relationship of marriage, bestowing — or should I say, inflicting? — a certain "headship" on him. This is a very different coronation. And as we could easily take the natural mystery too seriously, so we might take the Christian mystery not serious-ly enough. Christian writers (notably Milton) have sometimes spoken of the hus-band's headship with a complacency to make the blood run cold. We must go back to our Bibles. The husband is the head of the wife just in so far as he is to her what Christ is to the Church. He is to love her as Christ loved the Church — read on — *and give his life for her.* (*Eph.* V, 25). This headship, then, is most fully embodied not in the husband we should all wish to be but in him whose marriage is most like a cruci-fixion; whose wife receives most and gives least, is most unworthy of him, is — in her own mere nature — least lovable. For the Church has no beauty but what the Bride-groom gives her; he does not find, but makes her, lovely. The chrism of this terrible coronation is to be seen not in the joys of any man's marriage but in its sorrows, in the sickness and sufferings of a good wife or the faults of a bad one, in his unwearying (never paraded) care or his inexhaustible forgiveness: forgiveness, not acquiescence. As Christ sees in the flawed, proud, fanatical or lukewarm Church on earth that Bride who will one day be without spot or wrinkle, and labours to produce the latter, so the husband whose headship is Christ-like (and he is allowed no other sort) never despairs. He is a King Cophetua who after twenty years still hopes that the beggar-girl will one day learn to speak the truth and wash behind her ears.

To say this is not to say that there is any virtue or wisdom in making a marriage

that involves such misery. There is no wisdom or virtue in seeking unnecessary martyrdom or deliberately courting persecution; yet it is, none the less, the persecuted or
martyred Christian in whom the pattern of the Master is most unambiguously realised. So, in these terrible marriages, once they have come about, the "headship" of the
husband, if only he can sustain it, is most Christ-like.

The sternest feminist need not grudge my sex the crown offered to it either in the
Pagan or in the Christian mystery. For the one is of paper and the other of thorns. The
real danger is not that husbands may grasp the latter too eagerly; but that they will allow or compel their wives to usurp it.

From Venus, the carnal ingredient within Eros, I now turn to Eros as a whole.
Here we shall see the same pattern repeated. As Venus within Eros does not really
aim at pleasure, so Eros does not aim at happiness. We may think he does, but when
he is brought to the test it proves otherwise. Everyone knows that it is useless to try to
separate lovers by proving to them that their marriage will be an unhappy one. This is
not only because they will disbelieve you. They usually will, no doubt. But even if
they believed, they would not be dissuaded. For it is the very mark of Eros that when
he is in us we had rather share unhappiness with the Beloved than be happy on any
other terms. Even if the two lovers are mature and experienced people who know that
broken hearts heal in the end and can clearly foresee that, if they once steeled themselves to go through the present agony of parting, they would almost certainly be happier ten years hence than marriage is at all likely to make them—even then, they
would not part. To Eros all these calculations are irrelevant—just as the coolly brutal
judgment of Lucretius is irrelevant to Venus. Even when it becomes clear beyond all
evasion that marriage with the Beloved cannot possibly lead to happiness—when it
cannot even profess to offer any other life than that of tending an incurable invalid, of
hopeless poverty, of exile, or of disgrace—Eros never hesitates to say, "Better this
than parting. Better to be miserable with her than happy without her. Let our hearts
break provided they break together." If the voice within us does not say this, it is not
the voice of Eros.

This is the grandeur and terror of love. But notice, as before, side by side with this
grandeur, the playfulness. Eros, as well as Venus, is the subject of countless jokes.
And even when the circumstances of the two lovers are so tragic that no bystander
could keep back his tears, they themselves —in want, in hospital wards, on visitors'
days in jail—will sometimes be surprised by a merriment which strikes the onlooker
(but not them) as unbearably pathetic. Nothing is falser than the idea that mockery is
necessarily hostile. Until they have a baby to laugh at, lovers are always laughing at
each other.

It is in the grandeur of Eros that the seeds of danger are concealed. He has spoken
like a god. His total commitment, his reckless disregard of happiness, his transcendence of self-regard, sound like a message from the eternal world.

And yet it cannot, just as it stands, be the voice of God Himself. For Eros, speaking with that very grandeur and displaying that very transcendence of self, may urge to evil as well as to good. Nothing is shallower than the belief that a love which leads to sin is always qualitatively lower – more animal or more trivial – than one which leads to faithful, fruitful and Christian marriage. The love which leads to cruel and perjured unions, even to suicide-pacts and murder, is not likely to be wandering lust or idle sentiment. It may well be Eros in all his splendour; heartbreakingly sincere; ready for every sacrifice except renunciation.

There have been schools of thought which accepted the voice of Eros as something actually transcendent and tried to justify the absoluteness of his commands. Plato will have it that "falling in love" is the mutual recognition on earth of souls which have been singled out for one another in a previous and celestial existence. To meet the Beloved is to realise "We loved before we were born." As a myth to express what lovers feel this is admirable. But if one accepted it literally one would be faced by an embarrassing consequence. We should have to conclude that in that heavenly and forgotten life affairs were no better managed than here. For Eros may unite the most unsuitable yokefellows; many unhappy, and predictably unhappy, marriages were love-matches.

A theory more likely to be accepted in our own day is what we may call Shavian – Shaw himself might have said "metabiological" – Romanticism. According to Shavian Romanticism the voice of Eros is the voice of the *élan vital* or Life Force, the "evolutionary appetite." In overwhelming a particular couple it is seeking parents (or ancestors) for the superman. It is indifferent both to their personal happiness and to the rules of morality because it aims at something which Shaw thinks very much more important: the future perfection of our species. But if all this were true it hardly makes clear whether – and if so, why – we should obey it. All pictures yet offered us of the superman are so unattractive that one might well vow celibacy at once to avoid the risk of begetting him. And secondly, his theory surely leads to the conclusion that the Life Force does not very well understand its (or her? or his?) own business. So far as we can see the existence or intensity of Eros between two people is no warrant that their offspring will be especially satisfactory, or even that they will have offspring at all. Two good "strains" (in the stockbreeders' sense), not two good lovers, is the recipe for fine children. And what on earth was the Life Force doing through all those countless generations when the begetting of children depended very little on mutual Eros and very much on arranged marriages, slavery, and rape? Has it only just thought of this bright idea for improving the species?

Neither the Platonic nor the Shavian type of erotic transcendentalism can help a Christian. We are not worshippers of the Life Force and we know nothing of previous existences. We must not give unconditional obedience to the voice of Eros when he speaks most like a god. Neither must we ignore or attempt to deny the god-like quality. This love is really and truly like Love Himself. In it there is a real nearness to God (by Resemblance); but not, therefore and necessarily, a nearness of Approach. Eros, honoured so far as love of God and charity to our fellows will allow, may become for us a means of Approach. His total commitment is a paradigm or example, built into our natures, of the love we ought to exercise towards God and Man. As nature, for the nature-lover, gives a content to the word *glory,* so this gives a content to the word *Charity.* It is as if Christ said to us through Eros, "Thus — just like this — with this prodigality — not counting the cost — you are to love me and the least of my brethren." Our conditional honour to Eros will of course vary with our circumstances. Of some a total renunciation (but not a contempt) is required. Others, with Eros as their fuel and also as their model, can embark on the married life. Within which Eros, of himself, will never be enough — will indeed survive only in so far as he is continually chastened and corroborated by higher principles.

But Eros, honoured without reservation and obeyed unconditionally, becomes a demon. And this is just how he claims to be honoured and obeyed. Divinely indifferent to our selfishness, he is also demoniacally rebellious to every claim of God or Man that would oppose him. Hence as the poet says:

> *People in love cannot be moved by kindness,*
> *And opposition makes them feel like martyrs.*

Martyrs is exactly right. Years ago when I wrote about medieval love-poetry and described its strange, half make-believe, "religion of love," I was blind enough to treat this as an almost purely literary phenomenon. I know better now. Eros by his nature invites it. Of all loves he is, at his height, most god-like; therefore most prone to demand our worship. Of himself he always tends to turn "being in love" into a sort of religion.

Theologians have often feared, in this love, a danger of idolatry. I think they meant by this that the lovers might idolise one another. That does not seem to me to be the real danger; certainly not in marriage. The deliciously plain prose and businesslike intimacy of married life render it absurd. So does the Affection in which Eros is almost invariably clothed. Even in courtship I question whether anyone who has felt the thirst for the Uncreated, or even dreamed of feeling it, ever supposed that the Beloved could satisfy it. As a fellow-pilgrim pierced with the very same desire, that is, as a Friend, the Beloved may be gloriously and helpfully relevant; but as an object for it — well (I would not be rude), ridiculous. The real danger seems to me not that the lovers will idolise each other but that they will idolise Eros himself.

I do not of course mean that they will build altars or say prayers to him. The idolatry I speak of can be seen in the popular misinterpretation of Our Lord's words "Her sins, which are many, are forgiven her, for she loved much" (*Luke* VII, 47). From the context, and especially from the preceding parable of the debtors, it is clear that this must mean: "The greatness of her love for Me is evidence of the greatness of the sins I have forgiven her." (The *for* here is like the *for* in "He can't have gone out, *for* his hat is still hanging in the hall"; the presence of the hat is not the cause of his being in the house but a probable proof that he is.) But thousands of people take it quite differently. They first assume, with no evidence, that her sins were sins against chastity, though, for all we know, they may have been usury, dishonest shopkeeping, or cruelty to children. And they then take Our Lord to be saying, "I forgive her unchastity because she was so much in love." The implication is that a great Eros extenuates — almost sanctions — almost sanctifies — any actions it leads to.

When lovers say of some act that we might blame, "Love made us do it," notice the tone. A man saying, "I did it because I was frightened," or "I did it because I was angry," speaks quite differently. He is putting forward an excuse for what he feels to require excusing. But the lovers are seldom doing quite that. Notice how tremulously, almost how devoutly, they say the word *love,* not so much pleading an "extenuating circumstance" as appealing to an authority. The confession can be almost a boast. There can be a shade of defiance in it. They "feel like martyrs." In extreme cases what their words really express is a demure yet unshakable allegiance to the god of love.

"These reasons in love's law have passed for good," says Milton's Dalila. That is the point; *in love's law.* "In love," we have our own "law," a religion of our own, our own god. Where a true Eros is present resistance to his commands feels like apostasy, and what are really (by the Christian standard) temptations speak with the voice of duties — quasi-religious duties, acts of pious zeal to love. He builds his own religion round the lovers. Benjamin Constant has noticed how he creates for them, in a few weeks or months, a joint past which seems to them immemorial. They recur to it continually with wonder and reverence, as the Psalmists recur to the history of Israel. It is in fact the Old Testament of Love's religion; the record of love's judgments and mercies towards his chosen pair up to the moment when they first knew they were lovers. After that, its New Testament begins. They are now under a new law, under what corresponds (in this religion) to Grace. They are new creatures. The "spirit" of Eros supersedes all laws, and they must not "grieve" it.

It seems to sanction all sorts of actions they would not otherwise have dared. I do not mean solely, or chiefly, acts that violate chastity. They are just as likely to be acts of injustice or uncharity against the outer world. They will seem like proofs of piety and zeal towards Eros. The pair can say to one another in an almost sacrificial spirit, "It is for love's sake that I have neglected my parents — left my children — cheated my partner — failed my friend at his greatest need." These reasons in love's law have passed for good. The votaries may even come to feel a particular merit in such sacrifices; what costlier offering can be laid on love's altar than one's conscience?

And all the time the grim joke is that this Eros whose voice seems to speak from the eternal realm is not himself necessarily even permanent. He is notoriously the most mortal of our loves. The world rings with complaints of his fickleness. What is baffling is the combination of this fickleness with his protestations of permanency. To be in love is both to intend and to promise lifelong fidelity. Love makes vows unasked; can't be deterred from making them. "I will be ever true," are almost the first words he utters. Not hypocritically but sincerely. No experience will cure him of the delusion. We have all heard of people who are in love again every few years; each time sincerely convinced that "*this* time it's the real thing," that their wanderings are over, that they have found their true love and will themselves be true till death.

And yet Eros is in a sense right to make this promise. The event of falling in love is of such a nature that we are right to reject as intolerable the idea that it should be transitory. In one high bound it has overleaped the massive wall of our selfhood; it has made appetite itself altruistic, tossed personal happiness aside as a triviality and planted the interests of another in the centre of our being. Spontaneously and without effort we have fulfilled the law (towards one person) by loving our neighbour as ourselves. It is an image, a foretaste, of what we must become to all if Love Himself rules in us without a rival. It is even (well used) a preparation for that. Simply to relapse from it, merely to "fall out of" love again, is – if I may coin the ugly word – a sort of *disredemption.* Eros is driven to promise what Eros of himself cannot perform.

Can we be in this selfless liberation for a lifetime? Hardly for a week. Between the best possible lovers this high condition is intermittent. The old self soon turns out to be not so dead as he pretended – as after a religious conversion. In either he may be momentarily knocked flat; he will soon be up again; if not on his feet, at least on his elbow, if not roaring, at least back to his surly grumbling or his mendicant whine. And Venus will often slip back into mere sexuality.

But these lapses will not destroy a marriage between two "decent and sensible" people. The couple whose marriage will certainly be endangered by them, and possibly ruined, are those who have idolised Eros. They thought he had the power and truthfulness of a god. They expected that mere feeling would do for them, and permanently, all that was necessary. When this expectation is disappointed they throw the blame on Eros or, more usually, on their partners. In reality, however, Eros, having made his gigantic promise and shown you in glimpses what its performance would be like, has "done his stuff." He, like a godparent, makes the vows; it is we who must keep them. It is we who must labour to bring our daily life into even closer accordance with what the glimpses have revealed. We must do the works of Eros when Eros is not present. This all good lovers know, though those who are not reflective or articulate will be able to express it only in a few conventional phrases about "taking the rough along with the smooth," not "expecting too much," having "a little common sense," and the like. And all good Christian lovers know that this programme, modest as it sounds, will not be carried out except by humility, charity and divine grace; that it is indeed the whole Christian life seen from one particular angle.

Thus Eros, like the other loves, but more strikingly because of his strength, sweetness, terror and high port, reveals his true status. He cannot of himself be what, nevertheless, he must be if he is to remain Eros. He needs help; therefore needs to be ruled. The god dies or becomes a demon unless he obeys God. It would be well if, in such case, he always died. But he may live on, mercilessly chaining together two mutual tormentors, each raw all over with the poison of hate-in-love, each ravenous to receive and implacably refusing to give, jealous, suspicious, resentful, struggling for the upper hand, determined to be free and to allow no freedom, living on "scenes." Read *Anna Karenina,* and do not fancy that such things happen only in Russia. The lovers' old hyperbole of "eating" each other can come horribly near to the truth.

VI

CHARITY

William Morris wrote a poem called "Love Is Enough" and someone is said to have reviewed it briefly in the words "It isn't." Such has been the burden of this book. The natural loves are not self-sufficient. Something else, at first vaguely described as "decency and common sense," but later revealed as goodness, and finally as the whole Christian life in one particular relation, must come to the help of the mere feeling if the feeling is to be kept sweet.

To say this is not to belittle the natural loves but to indicate where their real glory lies. It is no disparagement to a garden to say that it will not fence and weed itself, nor prune its own fruit trees, nor roll and cut its own lawns. A garden is a good thing but that is not the sort of goodness it has. It will remain a garden, as distinct from a wilderness, only if someone does all these things to it. Its real glory is of quite a different kind. The very fact that it needs constant weeding and pruning bears witness to that glory. It teems with life. It glows with colour and smells like heaven and puts forward at every hour of a summer day beauties which man could never have created and could not even, on his own resources, have imagined. If you want to see the difference between its contribution and the gardener's, put the commonest weed it grows side by side with his hoes, rakes, shears, and packet of weed killer; you have put beauty, energy and fecundity beside dead, sterile things. Just so, our "decency and common sense" show grey and deathlike beside the geniality of love. And when the garden is in its full glory the gardener's contributions to that glory will still have been in a sense paltry compared with those of nature. Without life springing from the earth, without rain, light and heat descending from the sky, he could do nothing. When he has done all, he has merely encouraged here and discouraged there, powers and beauties that have a different source. But his share, though small, is indispensable and laborious. When God planted a garden He set a man over it and set the man under Himself. When He planted the garden of our nature and caused the flowering, fruiting loves to grow there, He set our will to "dress" them. Compared with them it is dry and cold. And unless His grace comes down, like the rain and the sunshine, we shall use this tool to little purpose. But its laborious — and largely negative — services

276

are indispensable. If they were needed when the garden was still Paradisal, how much more now when the soil has gone sour and the worst weeds seem to thrive on it best? But heaven forbid we should work in the spirit of prigs and Stoics. While we hack and prune we know very well that what we are hacking and pruning is big with a splendour and vitality which our rational will could never of itself have supplied. To liberate that splendour, to let it become fully what it is trying to be, to have tall trees instead of scrubby tangles, and sweet apples instead of crabs, is part of our purpose.

But only part. For now we must face a topic that I have long postponed. Hitherto hardly anything has been said in this book about our natural loves as rivals to the love of God. Now the question can no longer be avoided. There were two reasons for my delay.

One — already hinted — is that this question is not the place at which most of us need begin. It is seldom, at the outset, "addressed to our condition." For most of us the true rivalry lies between the self and the human Other, not yet between the human Other and God. It is dangerous to press upon a man the duty of getting beyond earthly love when his real difficulty lies in getting so far. And it is no doubt easy enough to love the fellow-creature less and to imagine that this is happening because we are learning to love God more, when the real reason may be quite different. We may be only "mistaking the decays of nature for the increase of Grace." Many people do not find it really difficult to hate their wives or mothers. M. Mauriac, in a fine scene, pictures the other disciples stunned and bewildered by this strange command, but not Judas. He laps it up easily.

But to have stressed the rivalry earlier in this book would have been premature in another way also. The claim to divinity which our loves so easily make can be refuted without going so far as that. The loves prove that they are unworthy to take the place of God by the fact that they cannot even remain themselves and do what they promise to do without God's help. Why prove that some petty princeling is not the lawful Emperor when without the Emperor's support he cannot even keep his subordinate throne and make peace in his little province for half a year? Even for their own sakes the loves must submit to be second things if they are to remain the things they want to be. In this yoke lies their true freedom; they "are taller when they bow." For when God rules in a human heart, though He may sometimes have to remove certain of its native authorities altogether, He often continues others in their offices and, by subjecting their authority to His, gives it for the first time a firm basis. Emerson has said, "When half-gods go, the gods arrive." That is a very doubtful maxim. Better say, "When God arrives (and only then) the half-gods can remain." Left to themselves they either vanish or become demons. Only in His name can they with beauty and security "wield their little tridents." The rebellious slogan "All for love" is really love's death warrant (date of execution, for the moment, left blank).

But the question of the rivalry, for these reasons long postponed, must now be treated. In any earlier period, except the nineteenth century, it would have loomed large throughout a book on this subject. If the Victorians needed the reminder that love is not enough, older theologians were always saying very loudly that (natural) love is likely to be a great deal too much. The danger of loving our fellow-creatures too little was less present to their minds than that of loving them idolatrously. In every wife, mother, child and friend they saw a possible rival to God. So of course does Our Lord (*Luke* XIV, 26).

There is one method of dissuading us from inordinate love of the fellow-creature which I find myself forced to reject at the very outset. I do so with trembling, for it met me in the pages of a great saint and a great thinker to whom my own glad debts are incalculable.

In words which can still bring tears to the eyes, St. Augustine describes the desolation in which the death of his friend Nebridius plunged him (*Confessions* IV, 10). Then he draws a moral. This is what comes, he says, of giving one's heart to anything but God. All human beings pass away. Do not let your happiness depend on something you may lose. If love is to be a blessing, not a misery, it must be for the only Beloved who will never pass away.

Of course this is excellent sense. Don't put your goods in a leaky vessel. Don't spend too much on a house you may be turned out of. And there is no man alive who responds more naturally than I do to such canny maxims. I am a safety-first creature. Of all arguments against love none makes so strong an appeal to my nature as "Careful! This might lead you to suffering."

To my nature, my temperament, yes. Not to my conscience. When I respond to that appeal I seem to myself to be a thousand miles away from Christ. If I am sure of anything I am sure that His teaching was never meant to confirm my congenital preference for safe investments and limited liabilities. I doubt whether there is anything in me that pleases Him less. And who could conceivably begin to love God on such a prudential ground — because the security (so to speak) is better? Who could even include it among the grounds for loving? Would you choose a wife or a Friend — if it comes to that, would you choose a dog — in this spirit? One must be outside the world of love, of all loves, before one thus calculates. Eros, lawless Eros, preferring the Beloved to happiness, is more like Love himself than this.

I think that this passage in the *Confessions* is less a part of St. Augustine's Christendom than a hangover from the high-minded Pagan philosophies in which he grew up. It is closer to Stoic "apathy" or neo-Platonic mysticism than to charity. We follow One who wept over Jerusalem and at the grave of Lazarus, and, loving all, yet had one disciple whom, in a special sense, he "loved." St. Paul has a higher authority with us than St. Augustine — St. Paul who shows no sign that he would not have suffered like a man, and no feeling that he ought not so to have suffered, if Epaphroditus had died (*Phil.* II, 27).

Even if it were granted that insurances against heartbreak were our highest wisdom, does God Himself offer them? Apparently not. Christ comes at last to say "Why hast thou forsaken me?"

There is no escape along the lines St. Augustine suggests. Nor along any other lines. There is no safe investment. To love at all is to be vulnerable. Love anything, and your heart will certainly be wrung and possibly be broken. If you want to make sure of keeping it intact, you must give your heart to no one, not even to an animal. Wrap it carefully round with hobbies and little luxuries; avoid all entanglements; lock it up safe in the casket or coffin of your selfishness. But in that casket – safe, dark, motionless, airless – it will change. It will not be broken; it will become unbreakable, impenetrable, irredeemable. The alternative to tragedy, or at least to the risk of tragedy, is damnation. The only place outside Heaven where you can be perfectly safe from all the dangers and perturbations of love is Hell.

I believe that the most lawless and inordinate loves are less contrary to God's will than a self-invited and self-protective lovelessness. It is like hiding the talent in a napkin and for much the same reason "I knew thee that thou wert a hard man." Christ did not teach and suffer that we might become, even in the natural loves, more careful of our own happiness. If a man is not uncalculating towards the earthly beloveds whom he has seen, he is none the more likely to be so towards God whom he has not. We shall draw nearer to God, not by trying to avoid the sufferings inherent in all loves, but by accepting them and offering them to Him; throwing away all defensive armour. If our hearts need to be broken, and if He chooses this as the way in which they should break, so be it.

It remains certainly true that all natural loves can be inordinate. *Inordinate* does not mean "insufficiently cautious." Nor does it mean "too big." It is not a quantitative term. It is probably impossible to love any human being simply "too much." We may love him too much *in proportion* to our love for God; but it is the smallness of our love for God, not the greatness of our love for the man, that constitutes the inordinacy. But even this must be refined upon. Otherwise we shall trouble some who are very much on the right road but alarmed because they cannot feel towards God so warm a sensible emotion as they feel for the earthly Beloved. It is much to be wished – at least I think so – that we all, at all times, could. We must pray that this gift should be given us. But the question whether we are loving God or the earthly Beloved "more" is not, so far as concerns our Christian duty, a question about the comparative intensity of two feelings. The real question is, which (when the alternative comes) do you serve, or choose, or put first? To which claim does your will, in the last resort, yield?

As so often, Our Lord's own words are both far fiercer and far more tolerable than those of the theologians. He says nothing about guarding against earthly loves for fear we might be hurt; He says something that cracks like a whip about trampling them all under foot the moment they hold us back from following Him. "If any man come to me and hate not his father and mother and wife . . . and his own life also, he cannot be my disciple" (*Luke* XIV, 26).

But how are we to understand the word *hate*? That Love Himself should be commanding what we ordinarily mean by hatred – commanding us to cherish resentment, to gloat over another's misery, to delight in injuring him – is almost a contradiction in terms. I think Our Lord, in the sense here intended, "hated" St. Peter when he said, "Get thee behind me." To hate is to reject, to set one's face against, to make no concession to, the Beloved when the Beloved utters, however sweetly and however pitiably, the suggestions of the Devil. A man, said Jesus, who tries to serve two masters, will "hate" the one and "love" the other. It is not, surely, mere feelings of aversion and liking that are here in question. He will adhere to, consent to, work for, the one and not for the other. Consider again, "I loved Jacob and I *hated* Esau" (*Malachi* I, 2-3). How is the thing called God's "hatred" of Esau displayed in the actual story? Not at all as we might expect. There is of course no ground for assuming that Esau made a bad end and was a lost soul; the Old Testament, here as elsewhere, has nothing to say about such matters. And, from all we are told, Esau's earthly life was, in every ordinary sense, a good deal more blessed than Jacob's. It is Jacob who has all the disappointments, humiliations, terrors, and bereavements. But he has something which Esau has not. He is a patriarch. He hands on the Hebraic tradition, transmits the vocation and the blessing, becomes an ancestor of Our Lord. The "loving" of Jacob seems to mean the acceptance of Jacob for a high (and painful) vocation; the "hating" of Esau, his rejection. He is "turned down," fails to "make the grade," is found useless for the purpose. So, in the last resort, we must turn down or disqualify our nearest and dearest when they come between us and our obedience to God. Heaven knows, it will seem to them sufficiently like hatred. We must not act on the pity we feel; we must be blind to tears and deaf to pleadings.

I will not say that this duty is hard; some find it too easy; some, hard almost beyond endurance. What is hard for all is to know when the occasion for such "hating" has arisen. Our temperaments deceive us. The meek and tender — uxorious husbands, submissive wives, doting parents, dutiful children — will not easily believe that it has ever arrived. Self-assertive people, with a dash of the bully in them, will believe it too soon. That is why it is of such extreme importance so to order our loves that it is unlikely to arrive at all.

How this could come about we may see on a far lower level when the Cavalier poet, going to the wars, says to his mistress:

> *I could not love thee, dear, so much*
> *Loved I not honour more.*

There are women to whom the plea would be meaningless. *Honour* would be just one of those silly things that Men talk about; a verbal excuse for, therefore an aggravation of, the offense against "love's law" which the poet is about to commit. Lovelace can use it with confidence because his lady is a Cavalier lady who already admits, as he does, the claims of Honour. He does not need to "hate" her, to set his face against her, for he and she acknowledge the same law. They have agreed and understood each other on this matter long before. The task of converting her to a belief in Honour is not now — now, when the decision is upon them — to be undertaken. It is this prior agreement which is so necessary when a far greater claim than that of Honour is at stake. It is too late, when the crisis comes, to begin telling a wife or husband or mother or friend, that your love all along had a secret reservation — "under God" or "so far as a higher Love permits." They ought to have been warned; not, to be sure, explicitly, but by the implication of a thousand talks, by the principle revealed in a hundred decisions upon small matters. Indeed, a real disagreement on this issue should make itself felt early enough to prevent a marriage or a Friendship from existing at all. The best love of either sort is not blind. Oliver Elton, speaking of Carlyle and Mill, said that they differed about justice, and that such a difference was naturally fatal "to any friendship worthy of the name." If "All" — quite seriously all — "for love" is implicit in the Beloved's attitude, his or her love is not worth having. It is not related in the right way to Love Himself.

And this brings me to the foot of the last steep ascent this book must try to make. We must try to relate the human activities called "loves" to that Love which is God a little more precisely than we have yet done. The precision can, of course, be only that of a model or a symbol, certain to fail us in the long run and, even while we use it, requiring correction from other models. The humblest of us, in a state of Grace, can have some "knowledge-by-acquaintance" (*connaître*), some "tasting," of Love Himself; but man even at his highest sanctity and intelligence has no direct "knowledge about" (*savoir*) the ultimate Being — only analogies. We cannot see light, though by light we can see things. Statements about God are extrapolations from the knowledge of other things which the divine illumination enables us to know. I labour these deprecations because, in what follows, my efforts to be clear (and not intolerably lengthy) may suggest a confidence which I by no means feel. I should be mad if I did. Take it as one man's reverie, almost one man's myth. If anything in it is useful to you, use it; if anything is not, never give it a second thought.

God is love. Again, "Herein is love, not that we loved God but that He loved us" (I *John* IV, 10). We must not begin with mysticism, with the creature's love for God, or with the wonderful foretastes of the fruition of God vouchsafed to some in their earthly life. We begin at the real beginning, with love as the Divine energy. This primal love is Gift-love. In God there is no hunger that needs to be filled, only plenteousness that desires to give. The doctrine that God was under no necessity to create is not a piece of dry scholastic speculation. It is essential. Without it we can hardly avoid the conception of what I can only call a "managerial" God; a Being whose function or nature is to "run" the universe, who stands to it as a head-master to a school or a hotelier to a hotel. But to be sovereign of the universe is no great matter to God. In Himself, at home in "the land of the Trinity," he is Sovereign of a far greater realm. We must keep always before our eyes that vision of Lady Julian's in which God carried in His hand a little object like a nut, and that nut was "all that is made." God, who needs nothing, loves into existence wholly superfluous creatures in order that He may love and perfect them. He creates the universe, already foreseeing — or should we say "seeing"? there are no tenses in God — the buzzing cloud of flies about the cross, the flayed back pressed against the uneven stake, the nails driven through the mesial nerves, the repeated incipient suffocation as the body droops, the repeated torture of back and arms as it is time after time, for breath's sake, hitched up. If I may dare the biological image, God is a "host" who deliberately creates His own parasites; causes us to be that we may exploit and "take advantage" of Him. Herein is love. This is the diagram of Love Himself, the inventor of all loves.

God, as Creator of nature, implants in us both Gift-loves and Need-loves. The Gift-loves are natural images of Himself; proximities to Him by resemblance which are not necessarily and in all men proximities of approach. A devoted mother, a beneficent ruler or teacher, may give and give, continually exhibiting the likeness, without making the approach. The Need-loves, so far as I have been able to see, have no resemblance to the Love which God is. They are rather correlatives, opposites; not as evil is the opposite of good, of course, but as the form of the blanc-mange is an opposite to the form of the mould.

But in addition to these natural loves God can bestow a far better gift; or rather, since our minds must divide and pigeon-hole, two gifts.

He communicates to men a share of His own Gift-love. This is different from the Gift-loves He has built into their nature. These never quite seek simply the good of the loved object for the object's own sake. They are biased in favour of those goods they can themselves bestow, or those which they would like best themselves, or those which fit in with a pre-conceived picture of the life they want the object to lead. But Divine Gift-love – Love Himself working in a man – is wholly disinterested and desires what is simply best for the beloved. Again, natural Gift-love is always directed to objects which the lover finds in some way intrinsically lovable – objects to which Affection or Eros or a shared point of view attracts him, or, failing that, to the grateful and the deserving, or perhaps to those whose helplessness is of a winning and appealing kind. But Divine Gift-love in the man enables him to love what is not naturally lovable; lepers, criminals, enemies, morons, the sulky, the superior and the sneering. Finally, by a high paradox, God enables men to have a Gift-love towards Himself. There is of course a sense in which no one can give to God anything which is not already His; and if it is already His what have you given? But since it is only too obvious that we can withhold ourselves, our wills and hearts, from God, we can, in that sense, also give them. What is His by right and would not exist for a moment if it ceased to be His (as the song is the singer's), He has nevertheless made ours in such a way that we can freely offer it back to Him. "Our wills are ours to make them Thine." And as all Christians know there is another way of giving to God; every stranger whom we feed or clothe is Christ. And this apparently is Gift-love to God whether we know it or not. Love Himself can work in those who know nothing of Him. The "sheep" in the parable has no idea either of the God hidden in the prisoner whom they visited or of the God hidden in themselves when they made the visit. (I take the whole parable to be about the judgment of the heathen. For it begins by saying, in the Greek, that the Lord will summon all "the nations" before Him – presumably, the Gentiles, the *Goyim.*)

That such a Gift-love comes by Grace and should be called Charity, everyone will agree. But I have to add something which will not perhaps be so easily admitted. God, as it seems to me, bestows two other gifts; a supernatural Need-love of Himself and a supernatural Need-love of one another. By the first I do not mean the Appreciative love of Himself, the gift of adoration. What little I have to say on that higher — that highest — subject will come later. I mean a love which does not dream of disinterestedness, a bottomless indigence. Like a river making its own channel, like a magic wine which in being poured out should simultaneously create the glass that was to hold it, God turns our need of Him into Need-love of Him. What is stranger still is that He creates in us a more than natural receptivity of Charity from our fellow-men. Need is so near greed and we are so greedy already that it seems a strange grace. But I cannot get it out of my head that this is what happens.

Let us consider first this supernatural Need-love of Himself, bestowed by Grace. Of course the Grace does not create the need. That is there already; "given" (as the mathematicians say) in the mere fact of our being creatures, and incalculably increased by our being fallen creatures. What the Grace gives is the full recognition, the sensible awareness, the complete acceptance — even, with certain reservations, the glad acceptance — of this Need. For, without Grace, our wishes and our necessities are in conflict.

All those expressions of unworthiness which Christian practice puts into the believer's mouth seem to the outer world like the degraded and insincere grovellings of a sycophant before a tyrant, or at best a *façon de parler* like the self-depreciation of a Chinese gentleman when he calls himself "this coarse and illiterate person." In reality, however, they express the continually renewed, because continually necessary, attempt to negate that misconception of ourselves and of our relation to God which nature, even while we pray, is always recommending to us. No sooner do we believe that God loves us than there is an impulse to believe that He does so, not because He is Love, but because we are intrinsically loveable. The Pagans obeyed this impulse unabashed; a good man was "dear to the gods" because he was good. We, being better taught, resort to subterfuge. Far be it from us to think that we have virtues for which God could love us. But then, how magnificently we have repented! As Bunyan says, describing his first and illusory conversion, "I thought there was no man in England that pleased God better than I." Beaten out of this, we next offer our own humility to God's admiration. Surely He'll like *that?* Or if not that, our clear-sighted and humble recognition that we still lack humility. Thus, depth beneath depth and subtlety within subtlety, there remains some lingering idea of our own, our very own, attractiveness. It is easy to acknowledge, but almost impossible to realise for long, that we are mirrors whose brightness, if we are bright, is wholly derived from the sun that shines upon us. Surely we must have a little — however little — native luminosity? Surely we can't be *quite* creatures?

For this tangled absurdity of a Need, even a Need-love, which never fully acknowledges its own neediness, Grace substitutes a full, childlike and delighted acceptance of our Need, a joy in total dependence. We become "jolly beggars." The good man is sorry for the sins which have increased his Need. He is not entirely sorry for the fresh Need they have produced. And he is not sorry at all for the innocent Need that is inherent in his creaturely condition. For all the time this illusion to which nature clings as her last treasure, this pretence that we have anything of our own or could for one hour retain by our own strength any goodness that God may pour into us, has kept us from being happy. We have been like bathers who want to keep their feet – or one foot – or one toe – on the bottom, when to lose that foothold would be to surrender themselves to a glorious tumble in the surf. The consequences of parting with our last claim to intrinsic freedom, power, or worth, are real freedom, power and worth, really ours just because God gives them and because we know them to be (in another sense) not "ours." Anodos has got rid of his shadow.

But God also transforms our Need-love for one another, and it requires equal transformation. In reality we all need at times, some of us at most times, that Charity from others which, being Love Himself in them, loves the unlovable. But this, though a sort of love we need, is not the sort we want. We want to be loved for our cleverness, beauty, generosity, fairness, usefulness. The first hint that anyone is offering us the highest love of all is a terrible shock. This is so well recognised that spiteful people will pretend to be loving us with Charity precisely because they know that it will wound us. To say to one who expects a renewal of Affection, Friendship, or Eros, "I forgive you as a Christian" is merely a way of continuing the quarrel. Those who say it are of course lying. But the thing would not be falsely said in order to wound unless, if it were true, it would be wounding.

How difficult it is to receive, and to go on receiving from others a love that does not depend on our own attraction can be seen from an extreme case. Suppose yourself a man struck down shortly after marriage by an incurable disease which may not kill you for many years; useless, impotent, hideous, disgusting; dependent on your wife's earnings; impoverishing where you hoped to enrich; impaired even in intellect and shaken by gusts of uncontrollable temper, full of unavoidable demands. And suppose your wife's care and pity to be inexhaustible. The man who can take this sweetly, who can receive all and give nothing without resentment, who can abstain even from those tiresome self-depreciations which are really only a demand for petting and reassurance, is doing something which Need-love in its merely natural condition could not attain. (No doubt such a wife will also be doing something beyond the reach of a natural Gift-love, but that is not the point at present.) In such a case to receive is harder and perhaps more blessed than to give. But what the extreme example illustrates is universal. We are all receiving Charity. There is something in each of us that cannot be naturally loved. It is no one's fault if they do not so love it. Only the lovable can be naturally loved. You might as well ask people to like the taste of rotten bread or the sound of a mechanical drill. We can be forgiven, and pitied, and loved in spite of it, with Charity; no other way. All who have good parents, wives, husbands, or children, may be sure that at some times – and perhaps at all times in respect of some one particular trait or habit – they are receiving Charity, are loved not because they are lovable but because Love Himself is in those who love them.

Thus God, admitted to the human heart, transforms not only Gift-love but Need-love; not only our Need-love of Him, but our Need-love of one another. This is of course not the only thing that can happen. He may come on what seems to us a more dreadful mission and demand that a natural love be totally renounced. A high and terrible vocation, like Abraham's, may constrain a man to turn his back on his own people and his father's house. Eros, directed to a forbidden object, may have to be sacrificed. In such instances, the process, though hard to endure, is easy to understand. What we are more likely to overlook is the necessity for a transformation even when the natural love is allowed to continue.

In such a case the Divine Love does not *substitute* itself for the natural — as if we had to throw away our silver to make room for the gold. The natural loves are summoned to become modes of Charity while also remaining the natural loves they were.

One sees here at once a sort of echo or rhyme or corollary to the Incarnation itself. And this need not surprise us, for the author of both is the same. As Christ is perfect God and perfect Man, the natural loves are called to become perfect Charity and also perfect natural loves. As God becomes Man "Not by conversion of the Godhead into flesh, but by taking of the Manhood into God," so here; Charity does not dwindle into merely natural love but natural love is taken up into, made the tuned and obedient instrument of, Love Himself.

How this can happen, most Christians know. All the activities (sins only excepted) of the natural loves can in a favoured hour become works of the glad and shameless and grateful Need-love or of the selfless, unofficious Gift-love, which are both Charity. Nothing is either too trivial or too animal to be thus transformed. A game, a joke, a drink together, idle chat, a walk, the act of Venus — all these can be modes in which we forgive or accept forgiveness, in which we console or are reconciled, in which we "seek not our own." Thus in our very instincts, appetites and recreations, Love has prepared for Himself "a body."

But I said "in a favoured hour." Hours soon pass. The total and secure transformation of a natural love into a mode of Charity is a work so difficult that perhaps no fallen man has ever come within sight of doing it perfectly. Yet the law that loves must be so transformed is, I suppose, inexorable.

One difficulty is that here, as usual, we can take a wrong turn. A Christian — a somewhat too vocally Christian — circle or family, having grasped this principle, can make a show, in their overt behaviour and especially in their words, of having achieved the thing itself — an elaborate, fussy, embarrassing and intolerable show. Such people make every trifle a matter of explicitly spiritual importance — out loud and to one another (to God, on their knees, behind a closed door, it would be another matter). They are always unnecessarily asking, or insufferably offering, forgiveness. Who would not rather live with those ordinary people who get over their tantrums (and ours) unempahtically, letting a meal, a night's sleep, or a joke mend all? The real work must be, of all our works, the most secret. Even as far as possible secret from ourselves. Our right hand must not know what our left is doing. We have not got far enough if we play a game of cards with the children "merely" to amuse them or to show that they are forgiven. If this is the best we can do we are right to do it. But it would be better if a deeper, less conscious, Charity threw us into a frame of mind in which a little fun with the children was the thing we should at that moment like best.

We are, however, much helped in this necessary work by that very feature of our experience at which we most repine. The invitation to turn our natural loves into Charity is never lacking. It is provided by those frictions and frustrations that meet us in all of them; unmistakable evidence that (natural) love is not going to be "enough" — unmistakable, unless we are blinded by egotism. When we are, we use them absurdly. "If only I had been more fortunate in my children (that boy gets more like his father every day) I could have loved them perfectly." But every child is sometimes infuriating; most children are not infrequently odious. "If only my husband were more considerate, less lazy, less extravagant"... "If only my wife had fewer moods and more sense, and were less extravagant"... "If my father wasn't so infernally prosy and close-fisted." But in everyone, and of course in ourselves, there is that which requires forbearance, tolerance, forgiveness. The necessity of practising these virtues first sets us, forces us, upon the attempt to turn—more strictly, to let God turn — our love into Charity. These frets and rubs are beneficial. It may even be that where there are fewest of them the conversion of natural love is most difficult. When they are plentiful the necessity of rising above it is obvious. To rise above it when it is as fully satisfied and as little impeded as earthly conditions allow — to see that we must rise when all seems so well already — this may require a subtler conversion and a more delicate insight. In this way also it may be hard for "the rich" to enter the Kingdom.

And yet, I believe, the necessity for the conversion is inexorable; at least, if our natural loves are to enter the heavenly life. That they can enter it most of us in fact believe. We may hope that the resurrection of the body means also the resurrection of what may be called our "greater body"; the general fabric of our earthly life with its affections and relationships. But only on a condition; not a condition arbitrarily laid down by God, but one necessarily inherent in the character of Heaven: nothing can enter there which cannot become heavenly. "Flesh and blood," mere nature, cannot inherit that Kingdom. Man can ascend to Heaven only because the Christ, who died and ascended to Heaven, is "formed in him." Must we not suppose that the same is true of a man's loves? Only those into which Love Himself has entered will ascend to Love Himself. And these can be raised with Him only if they have, in some degree and fashion, shared His death; if the natural element in them has submitted—year after year, or in some sudden agony—to transmutation. The fashion of this world passes away. The very name of nature implies the transitory. Natural loves can hope for eternity only in so far as they have allowed themselves to be taken into the eternity of Charity; have at least allowed the process to begin here on earth, before the night comes when no man can work. And the process will always involve a kind of death. There is no escape. In my love for wife or friend the only eternal element is the transforming presence of Love Himself. By that presence, if at all, the other elements may hope, as our physical bodies hope, to be raised from the dead. For this only is holy in them, this only is the Lord.

Theologians have sometimes asked whether we shall "know one another" in Heaven, and whether the particular love-relations worked out on earth would then continue to have any significance. It seems reasonable to reply: "It may depend what kind of love it had become, or was becoming, on earth." For, surely, to meet in the eternal world someone for whom your love in this, however strong, had been merely natural, would not be (on that ground) even interesting. Would it not be like meeting in adult life someone who had seemed to be a great friend at your preparatory school solely because of common interests and occupations? If there was nothing more, if he was not a kindred soul, he will now be a total stranger. Neither of you now plays conkers. You no longer want to swop your help with his French exercise for his help with your arithmetic. In Heaven I suspect, a love that had never embodied Love Himself would be equally irrelevant. For Nature has passed away. All that is not eternal is eternally out of date.

But I must not end on this note, I dare not — and all the less because longings and terrors of my own prompt me to do so — leave any bereaved and desolate reader confirmed in the widespread illusion that reunion with the loved dead is the goal of the Christian life. The denial of this may sound harsh and unreal in the ears of the broken hearted, but it must be denied.

"Thou hast made us for thyself," said St. Augustine, "and our heart has no rest till it comes to Thee." This, so easy to believe for a brief moment before the altar or, perhaps, half-praying, half-meditating in an April wood, sounds like mockery beside a deathbed. But we shall be far more truly mocked if, casting this way, we pin our comfort on the hope — perhaps even with the aid of *séance* and necromancy — of some day, this time forever, enjoying the earthly Beloved again, and no more. It is hard not to imagine that such an endless prolongation of earthly happiness would be completely satisfying.

But, if I may trust my own experience, we get at once a sharp warning that there is something wrong. The moment we attempt to use our faith in the other world for this purpose, that faith weakens. The moments in my life when it was really strong have all been moments when God Himself was central in my thoughts. Believing in Him, I could then believe in Heaven as a corollary. But the reverse process — believing first in reunion with the Beloved, and then, for the sake of that reunion, believing in Heaven, and finally, for the sake of Heaven, believing in God — this will not work. One can of course imagine things. But a self-critical person will soon be increasingly aware that the imagination at work is his own; he knows he is only weaving a fantasy. And simpler souls will find the phantoms they try to feed on void of all comfort and nourishment, only to be stimulated into some semblance of reality by pitiful efforts of self-hypnotism, and perhaps by the aid of ignoble pictures and hymns and (what is worse) witches.

We find thus by experience that there is no good applying to Heaven for earthly comfort. Heaven can give heavenly comfort; no other kind. And earth cannot give earthly comfort either. There is no earthly comfort in the long run.

For the dream of finding our end, the thing we were made for, in a Heaven of purely human love could not be true unless our whole Faith were wrong. We were made for God. Only by being in some respect like Him, only by being a manifestation of His beauty, lovingkindness, wisdom or goodness, has any earthly Beloved excited our love. It is not that we have loved them too much, but that we did not quite understand what we were loving. It is not that we shall be asked to turn from them, so dearly familiar, to a Stranger. When we see the face of God we shall know that we have always known it. He has been a party to, has made, sustained and moved moment by moment within, all our earthly experiences of innocent love. All that was true love in them was, even on earth, far more His than ours, and ours only because His. In Heaven there will be no anguish and no duty of turning away from our earthly Beloveds. First, because we shall have turned already; from the portraits to the Original, from the rivulets to the Fountain, from the creatures He made loveable to Love Himself. But secondly, because we shall find them all in Him. By loving Him more than them we shall love them more than we now do.

But all that is far away in "the land of the Trinity," not here in exile, in the weeping valley. Down here it is all loss and renunciation. The very purpose of the bereavement (so far as it affects ourselves) may have been to force this upon us. We are then compelled to try to believe, what we cannot yet feel, that God is our true Beloved. That is why bereavement is in some ways easier for the unbeliever than for us. He can storm and rage and shake his fist at the universe, and (if he is a genius) write poems like Houseman's or Hardy's. But we, at our lowest ebb, when the least effort seems too much for us, must begin to attempt what seem impossibilities.

"Is it easy to love God?" asks an old author. "It is easy," he replies, "to those who do it." I have included two Graces under the word Charity. But God can give a third. He can awake in man, towards Himself, a supernatural Appreciative love. This is of all gifts the most to be desired. Here, not in our natural loves, nor even in ethics, lies the true centre of all human and angelic life. With this all things are possible.

And with this, where a better book would begin, mine must end. I dare not proceed. God knows, not I, whether I have ever tasted this love. Perhaps I have only imagined the tasting. Those like myself whose imagination far exceeds their obedience are subject to a just penalty; we easily imagine conditions far higher than any we have really reached. If we describe what we have imagined we may make others, and make ourselves, believe that we have really been there. And if I have only imagined it, is it a further delusion that even the imagining has at some moments made all other objects of desire — yes, even peace, even to have no more fears — look like broken toys and faded flowers? Perhaps. Perhaps, for many of us, all experience merely defines, so to speak, the shape of that gap where our love of God ought to be. It is not enough. It is something. If we cannot "practice the presence of God," it is something to practice the absence of God, to become increasingly aware of our unawareness till we feel like men who should stand beside a great cataract and hear no noise, or like a man in a story who looks in a mirror and finds no face there, or a man in a dream who stretches out his hand to visible objects and gets no sensation of touch. To know that one is dreaming is to be no longer perfectly asleep. But for news of the fully waking world you must go to my betters.

The Business of Heaven

Daily Readings

PREFACE

'Humanity does not pass through phases as a train passes through stations: being alive, it has the privilege of always moving yet never leaving anything behind. Whatever we have been, in some sort we are still.' This comes from the opening paragraph of C.S. Lewis's *The Allegory of Love.* I had thought of this observation so often that, no sooner had I been asked to compile a day-to-day anthology of Lewis's theological writings than the two things were in my mind almost at the same moment. The idea of a train suggested a journey. A journey where? While thinking about this I remembered this passage from Lewis's *Reflections on the Psalms* – 'When we carry out our "religious duties" we are like people digging channels in a waterless land, in order that when at last the water comes, it may find them ready . . . There are happy moments, even now, when a trickle creeps along the dry beds; and happy souls to whom this happens often.'

The combination was irresistible and I began imagining what a pleasure it would be to pour the writings of C.S. Lewis into that 'channel' which is called the Christian Year. The Christian Year is like a train which *does* enjoy the 'privilege of always moving yet never leaving anything behind' because it is based on the two great events of history, the Birth and the Resurrection of Our Lord. Strictly speaking, the Christian Year begins with the first Sunday in Advent – which word means the 'coming' of Christ. The Christmas season reaches its culmination on January 6 in the Feast of the Epiphany which is the celebration of Christ's 'manifestation' to the Gentiles in the person of the Magi. The next and greatest Feast of the Church is that of Easter which lasts forty days and is followed by the feasts of the Ascension, Pentecost, and the Holy Trinity. It is customary to speak of the weeks between Pentecost and Advent as such and such a week 'after Pentecost' or 'after Trinity'. And so it goes on until we return to Advent and begin again. Those of us who take this annual circular journey of the Christian Year find it timeless and yet always refreshingly new.

There may be an odd individual here or there who will say 'New? What's so new about a train journey that returns to its original starting point?' But I doubt if such an objection will be raised by any one who has lived within the Christian fold. I realize that there are many Christians of churches less liturgical, but not less devout, to whom the ancient form of the Christian Year will seem a little confusing. But if they follow the order in which these readings are arranged I doubt that they will be confused for long. So far as I am able to judge, the Christian Year takes nothing away from what they already believe. More than that, I believe that they will find that what they hold best and dearest about the events in the earthly life of Our Lord will be strengthened. Surely it *does* strengthen both our belief and our appreciation of the Resurrection of Jesus to keep it in remembrance for forty days rather than to limit this great event to a single day.

I have never heard any Christian complain 'Christmas again! Easter again!' For most of us know that even the longest human life is not long enough for any attentive Christian to imagine that the Feast of the Resurrection is 'used up'. It was in his book *Letters to Malcolm* that C.S. Lewis said, 'It is well to have specifically holy places, and things and days, for, without these local points or reminders, the belief that all is holy and "big with God" will soon dwindle into a mere sentiment.' This he said in answer to Pantheism which is perhaps the most appealing heresy there is. At least Lewis found it so, as it delayed for some time his conversion to Christianity.

And Lewis, who drew so much nourishment from the Christian Year, praises it in the book where we are least likely to look for it – *The Screwtape Letters*. For those who may be meeting these letters for the first time in this anthology I should explain that Screwtape is a senior devil. His 'letters' are addressed to a young devil, Worm-wood, whose job it is to secure a young man's soul for Hell. You must remember that when Screwtape speaks of 'Our Father Below' he means Satan. When referring to 'He' or 'The Enemy' Screwtape means God. In the entry of this book for January 17 Screwtape is urging Wormwood to instil in us a horror of 'The Same Old Thing' along with an insatiable desire for Novelty. All this Screwtape admits would be easier if The Enemy had not balanced our 'love of change' by a 'love of permanence'. 'He gives them', complains Screwtape:

> the seasons, each season different yet every year the same, so that spring is always felt as a novelty yet always the recurrence of an immemorial theme. He gives them in His Church a spiritual year; they change from a fast to a feast, but it is the same feast as before.

It seemed, then, to me that the theme of the Christian Year would best serve those who like daily readings. And as I began selecting individual passages I came to believe that this theme could, if properly followed, make the most interesting and diversified use of C.S. Lewis's writings. I hoped, too, that it would go a long way towards defeating Screwtape's plans for destroying God's 'spiritual year' and inflaming our horror of 'The Same Old Thing'. 'The Enemy', Screwtape goes on to point out,

> loves platitudes. Of a proposed course of action He wants men, so far as I can see, to ask very simple questions; is it righteous? is it prudent? is it possible? Now if we can keep men asking 'Is it in accordance with the general movement of our time? Is it progressive or reactionary? Is this the way that History is going?' they will neglect the relevant questions. And the questions they *do* ask are, of course, unanswerable; for they do not know the future, and what the future will be depends very largely on just

those choices which they now invoke the future to help them make. As a result, while their minds are buzzing in this vacuum, we have the better chance to slip in and bend them to the action *we* have decided on.

A man would have to be very blind indeed not to see how many conquests Screwtape has made. I am thinking specially about the widespread apostasy among the clergy. I cannot forget my astonishment when I heard a bishop devote the whole of his Easter sermon to Psychical Research. He was delighted to report that some residue of what is now you and me might — just might — 'survive'. Lewis did not know this bishop, but there is a strikingly accurate portrait of him in the entries for May 22–25. You are fortunate if those entries are not a portrait of someone you know.

As it turned out, this 'Psychical Research Bishop' did me a favour. He made me remember something very important. If you know Church history you must know that whenever heresy has raised its head and pretended to be the way all sensible people think, it has resulted in a stimulation of orthodox Christian doctrine. Have you never noticed that such things as wars, diseases and famines usually have the effect of bringing out the best in many good people who do all they can to find solutions to these awful problems? Ever since the beginning of the Church, God has raised up great Christians to defeat heresy and strengthen the Faith once delivered. This is one of the reasons I have included entries for a number of those whom Lewis so frequently referred to as 'the great saints'.

I could not include entries for all the saints for the very pleasant reason that there are so many. And Lewis did not write about all of them. But there are two reasons why I've included those I have. First, they ought to be there as they stimulated or held fast to the Faith when the world (as now) seemed poised to lapse into Paganism. Second, they are a very necessary reminder that the Church did not begin with you or me, but is a great inheritance which might not be here today in the form Christ intended had it not been for these great ones. The names of the saints' days, and the Feasts and Fasts of the Church — what Lewis called 'holy days' — are printed in a different type to distinguish them from the titles I have given the other entries.

What are Fasts and Feasts? The different bodies of the Church are not agreed as to whether the two major Fasts of the Christian Year — Ash Wednesday, the first day of Lent, and Good Friday, the anniversary of the Crucifixion — should be marked by abstinence from all food or only from meat. Still, almost all believe that some acts of self-denial should be practised during the whole of Lent. When the Apostles witnessed Our Lord cast the evil spirit from the boy as recorded in St Mark 9:17–29 they asked why they could do nothing like this. 'This', replied Jesus, 'can come forth by nothing, but by prayer and fasting.' In the lives of the saints prayer and fasting nearly always go together. Fasting is a penitential practice designed to strengthen the spiritual life by weakening the attractions of sensual pleasures. The forty days of Lent commemorate Our Lord's forty days of temptation in the wilderness. For us the main purpose of Lent is to identify with Our Lord as He goes to the Cross.

Feasts are the anniversaries of the great events in the life of Our Lord and the occasions when we honour the saints. The Resurrection is the major Feast of the Christian Year. And here I suspect it would be a good idea to clear up a possible misunderstanding. When the New Testament writers referred to the Sabbath they meant both the day when God rested from His work of Creation as well as Israel's deliverance from Egypt. This is what the Jewish people still mean by the Sabbath. In New Testament times Sundays replaced Sabbaths. Even for the Apostles Sundays had come to mean a weekly commemoration of the Resurrection. This explains why fasting is never required on Sundays, not even during Lent, as every Sunday of the year is a commemoration of the Resurrection.

By now I expect you have spotted the one difficulty about arranging an anthology based on the Christian Year. It's plain sailing when one is dealing with what are called 'Immovable Feasts' – such as Christmas Day – because these days are fixed. However, because Easter Day is determined by the Paschal Full Moon it changes with the year, its extreme limits being March 21 and April 25. That causes it to be a 'Movable Feast'. There was no way I could give Easter Day and the fasts and feasts related to it a set place in this book. The solution was to put the readings for what I've called 'The Movable Fasts and Feasts' into a separate section at the end of the book. You should turn to that section for the appropriate readings from Lewis's writings for Ash Wednesday, Maundy Thursday, Good Friday, Holy Saturday, Easter Day, the Ascension, Pentecost, Holy Trinity, and The Body and Blood of Christ. I have provided a fifteen-year calendar in order to make it easy to know exactly when these special days occur.

There has been in recent years a movement to soft-pedal sin and to loud-pedal love, joy and peace. The result of this short cut has, so far as I can see, been disastrous. Those who are really guilty of something can't understand why it is, as they cannot be rid of the guilt which clings to them, that love, joy and peace never seem to amount to much. This effort to make us well without taking our medicine (repentance) seems to me like *looking* for happiness. As if happiness was something you could grasp if only you knew which bush it was hiding behind. You either get disillusioned, or you wake up to the fact that happiness has always been the *result* of something more important than itself.

I believe that those who follow these readings day by day as they were arranged to be read will discover what that 'something' beyond happiness is. You will find that I hammer away pretty hard with passages about morality. But you will find that I hammer away just as hard with passages which are meant to show us – as Lewis said – that 'Joy is the serious business of Heaven'. Lewis forces us to look at the whole of what we are. This is because he was one of the most realistic Christians we are ever likely to meet. He never makes a mountain of a mole hill. But he never pretends that a real mole hill isn't there. Not for a moment will he allow you to pretend that Christianity is less, or different, or other than what it is. Why should he? As he said, when writing of John Bunyan, 'To be born is to be exposed to delights and miseries greater than imagination could have anticipated; that the choice of ways at any cross-road may be more important than we think; and that short cuts may lead to very nasty places.'

But here's the surprise. As Lewis makes very clear in this book, morality — important though it is — was never intended as an end in itself. Morals are the 'ropes and axes' necessary for climbing those great heights from which a greater journey than even the Christian Year begins. That greater journey leads to the 'happy land of the Trinity'. It is there that joys, almost unimaginable in this world, begin. Begin — not *end* — for in that 'happy land' you won't need to have the 'serious business of Heaven' explained to you. You will have forgotten that there ever was anything else.

But C.S. Lewis's journey of the Christian Year comes first.

The Feast of St Mary Magdalen   WALTER HOOPER
1983, Oxford

READINGS FOR THE YEAR

Beginning the New Year JANUARY 1

I know all about the despair of overcoming chronic temptations. It is not serious, provided self-offended petulance, annoyance at breaking records, impatience etc. don't get the upper hand. *No amount* of falls will really undo us if we keep on picking ourselves up each time. We shall of course be very muddy and tattered children by the time we reach home. but the bathrooms are all ready, the towels put out, and the clean clothes in the airing cupboard. The only fatal thing is to lose one's temper and give it up. It is when we notice the dirt that God is most present in us: it is the very sign of His presence.

The First Job Each Morning JANUARY 2

The real problem of the Christian life comes where people do not usually look for it. It comes the very moment you wake up each morning. All your wishes and hopes for the day rush at you like wild animals. And the first job each morning consists simply in shoving them all back; in listening to that other voice, taking that other point of view, letting that other larger, stronger, quieter life come flowing in. And so on, all day. Standing back from all your natural fussings and frettings; coming in out of the wind.

   We can only do it for moments at first. But from those moments the new sort of life will be spreading through our system: because now we are letting Him work at the right part of us. It is the difference between paint, which is merely laid on the surface, and a dye or stain which soaks right through. He never talked vague, idealistic gas. When He said, 'Be perfect', he meant it. He meant that we must go in for the full treatment. It is hard; but the sort of compromise we are all hankering after is harder — in fact, it is impossible. It may be hard for an egg to turn into a bird: it would be a jolly sight harder for it to learn to fly while remaining an egg. We are like eggs at present. And you cannot go on indefinitely being just an ordinary, decent egg. We must be hatched or go bad.

Refreshments on the Journey

The settled happiness and security which we all desire, God withholds from us by the very nature of the world: but joy, pleasure, and merriment, He has scattered broadcast. We are never safe, but we have plenty of fun, and some ecstasy. It is not hard to see why. The security we crave would teach us to rest our hearts in this world and oppose an obstacle to our return to God: a few moments of happy love, a landscape, a symphony, a merry meeting with our friends, a bathe or a football match, have no such tendency. Our Father refreshes us on the journey with some pleasant inns, but will not encourage us to mistake them for home.

An Upside Down World

While we are in this 'valley of tears', cursed with labour, hemmed round with necessities, tripped up with frustrations, doomed to perpetual plannings, puzzlings, and anxieties, certain qualities that must belong to the celestial condition have no chance to get through, can project no image of themselves, except in activities which, for us here and now, are frivolous. For surely we must suppose the life of the blessed to be an end in itself, indeed The End: to be utterly spontaneous; to be the complete reconciliation of boundless freedom with order – with the most delicately adjusted, supple, intricate, and beautiful order? How can you find any image of this in the 'serious' activities either of our natural or of our (present) spiritual life? Either in our precarious and heartbroken affections or in the Way which is always, in some degree, a *via crucis*? No . . . . It is only in our 'hours-off', only in our moments of permitted festivity, that we find an analogy. Dance and game *are* frivolous, unimportant down here; for 'down here' is not their natural place. Here they are a moment's rest from the life we were placed here to live. But in this world everything is upside down. That which, if it could be prolonged here, would be a truancy, is likest that which in a better country is the End of ends. Joy is the serious business of Heaven.

The Road

When we are lost in the woods the sight of a signpost is a great matter. He who first sees it cries, 'Look!' The whole party gathers round and stares. But when we have found the road and are passing signposts every few miles, we shall not stop and stare.

They will encourage us and we shall be grateful to the authority that set them up. But we shall not stop and stare, or not much; not on this road, though their pillars are of silver and their lettering of gold. 'We would be at Jerusalem.'

The Epiphany of the Lord   JANUARY 6

We, with our modern democratic and arithmetical presuppositions would so have liked and expected all men to start equal in their search for God. One has the picture of great centripetal road coming from all directions, with well-disposed people, all meaning the same thing, and getting closer and closer together. How shockingly opposite to that is the Christian story! One people picked out of the whole earth; that people purged and proved again and again. Some are lost in the desert before they reach Palestine; some stay in Babylon; some becoming indifferent. The whole thing narrows and narrows, until at last it comes down to a little point, small as the point of a spear — a Jewish girl at her prayers. That is what the whole of human nature has narrowed down to before the Incarnation takes place. Very unlike what we expected, but, of course, not in the least unlike what seems, in general, as shown by Nature, to be God's way of working. . . . The people who are selected are, in a sense, unfairly selected for a supreme honour; but it is also a supreme burden. The People of Israel come to realize that it is their woes which are saving the world.

Waiting to be Called In   JANUARY 7

At present we are on the outside of the world, the wrong side of the door. We discern the freshness and purity of morning, but they do not make us fresh and pure. We cannot mingle with the splendours we see. But all the leaves of the New Testament are rustling with the rumour that it will not always be so. Some day, God willing, we shall get *in*. When human souls have become as perfect in voluntary obedience as the inanimate creation is in its lifeless obedience, then they will put on its glory, or rather that greater glory of which Nature is only the first sketch. For you must not think that I am putting forward any heathen fancy of being absorbed into Nature. Nature is mortal; we shall outlive her. When all the suns and nebulae have passed away, each one of you will still be alive. Nature is only the image, the symbol; but it is the symbol Scripture invites me to use. We are summoned to pass in through Nature, beyond her, into that splendour which she fitfully reflects.

Into the Presence of God

It is religion itself – prayer and sacrament and repentance and adoration – which is here, in the long run, our sole avenue to the real. Like mathematics, religion can grow from within, or decay. The Jew knows more than the Pagan, the Christian more than the Jew, the modern vaguely religious man less than any of the three. But, like mathematics, it remains simply itself, capable of being applied to any new theory of the material universe and outmoded by none.

When any man comes into the presence of God he will find, whether he wishes it or not, that all those things which seemed to make him so different from the men of other times, or even from his earlier self, have fallen off him. He is back where he always was, where every man always is.... No possible complexity which we can give to our picture of the universe can hide us from God: there is no copse, no forest, no jungle thick enough to provide cover.... In the twinkling of an eye, in a time too small to be measured, and in any place, all that seems to divide us from God can flee away, vanish, leaving us naked before Him, like the first man, like the only man, as if nothing but He and I existed. And since that contact cannot be avoided for long and since it means either bliss or horror, the business of life is to learn to like it. That is the first and great commandment.

Half-Hearted Creatures

If you asked twenty good men today what they thought the highest of the virtues, nineteen of them would reply, Unselfishness. But if you had asked almost any of the great Christians of old, he would have replied, Love. You see what has happened? A negative term has been substituted for a positive, and this is of more than philological importance. The negative idea of Unselfishness carries with it the suggestion not primarily of securing good things for others, but of going without them ourselves, as if our abstinence and not their happiness was the important point. I do not think this is the Christian virtue of Love. The New Testament has lots to say about self-denial, but not about self-denial as an end in itself. We are told to deny ourselves and to take up our crosses in order that we may follow Christ; and nearly every description of what we shall ultimately find if we do so contains an appeal to desire. If there lurks in most modern minds the notion that to desire our own good and earnestly to hope for the enjoyment of it is a bad thing, I submit that this notion has crept in from Kant and the Stoics and is no part of the Christian faith. Indeed, if we consider the unblushing promises of reward and the staggering nature of the rewards promised in the gospels, it would seem that Our Lord finds our desires, not too strong, but too weak. We are half-hearted creatures, fooling about with drink and sex and ambition when infinite joy is offered us, like an ignorant child who wants to go on making mud pies in a slum because he cannot imagine what is meant by the offer of a holiday at sea. We are far too easily pleased.

The Difference between Love and Kindness   JANUARY 10

By the goodness of God we mean nowadays almost exclusively His lovingness; and in this we may be right. And by Love, in this context, most of us mean kindness – the desire to see others than the self happy; not happy in this way or in that, but just happy. What would really satisfy us would be a God who said of anything we happened to like doing, 'What does it matter so long as they are contented?' We want, in fact, not so much a Father in Heaven as a grandfather in heaven – a senile benevolence who, as they say, 'liked to see young people enjoying themselves' and whose plan for the universe was simply that it might be truly said at the end of each day, 'a good time was had by all'. Not many people, I admit, would formulate a theology in precisely those terms: but a conception not very different lurks at the back of many minds. I do not claim to be an exception: I should very much like to love in a universe which was governed on such lines. But since it is abundantly clear that I don't, and since I have reason to believe, nevertheless, that God is Love, I conclude that my conception of love needs correction.

The Intolerable Compliment   JANUARY 11

There is kindness in Love: but Love and kindness are not coterminous, and when kindness . . . is separated from the other elements of Love, it involves a certain fundamental indifference to its object, and even something like contempt of it. Kindness consents very readily to the removal of its object – we have all met people whose kindness to animals is constantly leading them to kill animals lest they should suffer. Kindness, merely as such, cares not whether its object becomes good or bad, provided only that it escapes suffering. As Scripture points out, it is bastards who are spoiled: the legitimate sons, who are to carry on the family tradition, are punished. It is for people whom we care nothing about that we demand happiness on any terms: with our friends, our lovers, our children, we are exacting and would rather see them suffer much than be happy in contemptible and estranging modes. If God is Love, He is, by definition, something more than mere kindness. And it appears, from all the

records, that though He has often rebuked us and condemned us, He has never regarded us with contempt. He has paid us the intolerable compliment of loving us, in
the deepest, most tragic, most inexorable sense.

Objects of the Divine Love

When Christianity says that God loves man, it means that God *loves* man: not that He
has some 'disinterested', because really indifferent, concern for our welfare, but that,
in awful and surprising truth, we are the objects of His love. You asked for a loving
God: you have one. The great spirit you so lightly invoked, the 'lord of terrible aspect', is present: not a senile benevolence that drowsily wishes you to be happy in
your own way, not the cold philanthropy of a conscientious magistrate, nor the care of
a host who feels responsible for the comfort of his guests, but the consuming fire
Himself, the Love that made the worlds, persistent as the artist's love for his work and
despotic as a man's love for a dog, provident and venerable as a father's love for a
child, jealous, inexorable, exacting as love between the sexes. How this should be, I
do not know . . . . We were made not primarily that we may love God (though we were
made for that too) but that God may love us, that we may become objects in which the
Divine love may rest 'well pleased'. To ask that God's love should be content with us
as we are is to ask that God should cease to be God: because He is what He is, His
love must, in the nature of things, be impeded and repelled, by certain stains in our
present character, and because He already loves us He must labour to make us lovable. We cannot even wish, in our better moments, that He could reconcile Himself
to our present impurities.

The Visible Church

If He can be known it will be by self-revelation on His part, not by speculation on
ours. We, therefore, look for Him where it is claimed that He has revealed Himself by
miracle, by inspired teachers, by enjoined ritual. The traditions conflict, yet the
longer and more sympathetically we study them the more we become aware of a
common element in many of them: the theme of sacrifice, of mystical communion
through the shed blood, of death and rebirth, of redemption, is too clear to escape
notice. We are fully entitled to use moral and intellectual criticism. What we are not,
in my opinion, entitled to do is simply to abstract the ethical element and set that up
as a religion on its own. Rather in that tradition which is at once more completely

ethical and most transcends mere ethics . . . we may still most reasonably believe that we have the consummation of all religion, the fullest message from the wholly other, the living creator, who, if He is at all, must be the God not only of the philosophers, but of mystics and savages, not only of the head and heart, but also of the primitive emotions and the spiritual heights beyond all emotion. We may . . . attach ourselves to the Church, to the only concrete organization which has preserved down to this present time the core of all the messages, pagan and perhaps pre-pagan, that have ever come from beyond the world, and begin to practise the only religion which rests not upon some selection of certain supposedly 'higher' elements in our nature, but on the shattering and rebuilding, the death and rebirth, of that nature in every part: neither Greek nor Jew nor barbarian, but a new creation.

The Divisions of Christendom   JANUARY 14

If any man is tempted to think — as one might be tempted who read only contemporaries — that 'Christianity' is a word of so many meanings that it means nothing at all, he can learn beyond all doubt, by stepping out of his own century, that this is not so. Measured against the ages 'mere Christianity' turns out to be no insipid inter-denominational transparency, but something positive, self-consistent, and inexhaustible. I know it, indeed, to my cost. In the days when I still hated Christianity, I learned to recognize, like some all too familiar smell, that almost unvarying *something* which met me, now in Puritan Bunyan, now in Anglican Hooker, now in Thomist Dante . . . .

We are all rightly distressed, and ashamed also, at the divisions of Christendom. But those who have always lived within the Christian fold may be too easily dispirited by them. They are bad, but such people do not know what it looks like from without. Seen from there, what is left intact, despite all the divisions, still appears (as it truly is) an immensely formidable unity. I know, for I saw it; and well our enemies know it. That unity any of us can find by going out of his own age. It is not enough, but it is more than you had thought till then. Once you are well soaked in it, if you then venture to speak, you will have an amusing experience. You will be thought a Papist when you are actually reproducing Bunyan, a Pantheist when you are quoting Aquinas, and so forth. For you have now got on to the great level viaduct which crosses the ages and which looks so high from the valleys, so low from the mountains, so narrow compared with the swamps, and so broad compared with the sheeptracks.

The Reunion of Christ's Church JANUARY 15

It was never more needed. A united Christendom should be the answer to the new Paganism. But how reconciliation of the churches, as opposed to conversions of individuals from one church to another, is to come about, I confess I cannot see. I am inclined to think that the immediate task is vigorous co-operation on the basis of what even now is common — combined, of course, with full admission of the differences. An *experienced* unity on some things might then prove the prelude to a confessional unity on all things. Nothing would give such strong support to the Papal claims as the spectacle of a Pope actually functioning as head of Christendom.

Christianity v. Christianity-and-Water JANUARY 16

The time is always ripe for reunion. Divisions between Christians are a sin and a scandal, and Christians ought at all times to be making contributions towards reunion, if it is only by their prayers. I am only a layman and a recent Christian, and I do not know much about these things, but in all the things which I have written and thought I have always stuck to traditional dogmatic positions. The result is that letters of agreement reach me from what are ordinarily regarded as the most different kinds of Christians; for instance, I get letters from Jesuits, monks, nuns, and also from Quakers and Welsh Dissenters, and so on. So it seems to me that the 'extremist' elements in every church are nearest one another and the liberal and 'broad-minded' people in each Body could never be united at all. The world of 'broad-mindedness' and watered-down 'religion' is a world where a small number of people (all the same type) say totally different things and change their minds every few minutes. We shall never get reunion from them.

Screwtape on Hell's Plan for Christians JANUARY 17

My dear Wormwood,
    The real trouble about the set your patient is living in is that it is *merely* Christian. They all have individual interests, of course, but the bond remains mere Christianity. What we want, if men become Christians at all, is to keep them in the state of mind I call 'Christianity And'. You know — Christianity and the Crisis, Christianity and the New Psychology, Christianity and the New Order, Christianity and Faith

Healing, Christianity and Psychical Research, Christianity and Vegetarianism, Christianity and Spelling Reform. If they must be Christians let them at least be Christians with a difference. Substitute for the faith itself some Fashion with a Christian colouring. Work on their horror of the Same Old Thing.

The horror of the Same Old Thing is one of the most valuable passions we have produced in the human heart — an endless source of heresies in religion, folly in counsel, infidelity in marriage, and inconstancy in friendship. The humans live in time, and experience reality successively. To experience much of it, therefore, they must experience many different things; in other words, they must experience change. And since they need change, the Enemy (being a hedonist at heart) has made change pleasurable to them, just as He has made eating pleasurable. But since He does not wish them to make change, any more than eating, an end in itself, He has balanced the love of change in them by a love of permanence. He has contrived to gratify both tastes together in the very world He has made, by that union of change and permanence which we call Rhythm. He gives them the seasons, each season different yet every year the same, so that spring is always felt as a novelty yet always as the recurrence of an immemorial theme. He gives them in His Church a spiritual year; they change from a fast to a feast, but it is the same feast as before.... We pick out this natural pleasantness of change and twist it into a demand for absolute novelty.

The Theologian's Danger   JANUARY 18

There have been men...who got so interested in proving the existence of God that they came to care nothing for God Himself...as if the good Lord had nothing to do but *exist*! There have been some who were so occupied in spreading Christianity that they never gave a thought to Christ. Man! Ye see it in smaller matters. Did ye never know a lover of books that with all his first editions and signed copies had lost the power to read them? Or an organizer of charities that had lost all love for the poor? It is the subtlest of all snares.

Advice to the Clergy   JANUARY 19

There is a danger...of the clergy developing a special professional conscience which obscures the very plain moral issue. Men who have passed beyond these boundary lines...are apt to protest that they have come by their unorthodox opinions honestly. In defence of those opinions they are prepared to suffer obloquy and to forfeit professional advancement. They thus come to feel like martyrs. But this simply misses the point which so gravely scandalizes the layman. We never doubted that the unorthodox opinions were honestly held: what we complain of is your continuing your ministry after you have come to hold them. We always knew that a man who makes his living as a paid agent of the Conservative Party may honestly change his views and honestly become a Communist. What we deny is that he can honestly continue to be a Conservative agent and to receive money from one party while he supports the policy of another.

True – or False?   JANUARY 20

One of the great difficulties is to keep before the audience's mind the question of Truth. They always think you are recommending Christianity not because it is *true* but because it is *good*. And in the discussion they will at every moment try to escape from the issue 'True – or False' into stuff about the Spanish Inquisition, or France, or Poland – or anything whatever. You have to keep forcing them back, and again back, to the real point. Only thus will you be able to undermine . . . their belief that a certain amount of 'religion' is desirable but one mustn't carry it too far. One must keep on pointing out that Christianity is a statement which, if false, is of *no* importance, and, if true, of infinite importance. The one thing it cannot be is moderately important.

Defending the Faith   JANUARY 21

We are to defend Christianity itself – the faith preached by the Apostles, attested by the Martyrs, embodied in the Creeds, expounded by the Fathers. This must be clearly distinguished from the whole of what any one of us may think about God and Man. Each of us has his individual emphasis: each holds, in addition to the Faith, many opinions which seem to him to be consistent with it and true and important. And so perhaps they are. But as apologists it is not our business to defend *them*. We are defending Christianity; not 'my religion.' When we mention our personal opinions we must always make quite clear the difference between them and the Faith itself. . . .

    This distinction, which is demanded by honesty, also gives the apologist a great tactical advantage. The great difficulty is to get modern audiences to realize that you are preaching Christianity solely and simply because you happen to think it *true*; they always suppose you are preaching it because you like it or think it is good for society or something of that sort. . . . This immediately helps them to realize that what is being discussed is a question about objective fact — not gas about ideals and points of view. . . . Do not attempt to water Christianity down. There must be no pretence that you can have it with the Supernatural left out. So far as I can see Christianity is precisely the one religion from which the miraculous cannot be separated. You must frankly argue for supernaturalism from the very outset.

When the Temperature Drops   JANUARY 22

We who defend Christianity find ourselves constantly opposed not by the irreligion of our hearers but by their real religion. Speak about beauty, truth and goodness, or about a God who is simply the indwelling principle of these three, speak about a great spiritual force pervading all things, a common mind of which we are all parts, a pool of generalized spirituality to which we can all flow, and you will command friendly interest. But the temperature drops as soon as you mention a God who has purposes and performs particular actions, who does one thing and not another, a concrete, choosing, commanding, prohibiting God with a determinate character. People become embarrassed or angry. Such a conception seems to them primitive and crude and even irreverent. The popular 'religion' excludes miracles because it excludes the 'living God' of Christianity and believes instead in a kind of God who obviously would not do miracles, or indeed anything else.

Christian Education in Schools   JANUARY 23

If we had noticed that the young men of the present day found it harder and harder to get the right answers to sums, we should consider that this had been adequately explained the moment we discovered that schools had for some years ceased to teach arithmetic. After that discovery we should turn a deaf ear to people who offered explanations of a vaguer and larger kind — people who said that the influence of Einstein had sapped the ancestral belief in fixed numerical relations, or that gangster films had undermined the desire to get right answers, or that the evolution of consciousness was now entering on its post-arithmetical phase. Where a clear and simple explanation completely covers the facts no other explanation is in court. If the younger generation have never been told what the Christians say and never heard any arguments in defence of it, then their agnosticism or indifference is fully explained. There is no need to look any further: no need to talk about the general intellectual climate of the age, the influence of mechanistic civilization on the character of urban life. And having discovered that the cause of their ignorance is lack of instruction, we have also discovered the remedy. There is nothing in the nature of the younger generation which incapacitates them for receiving Christianity. If any one is prepared to tell them, they are apparently ready to hear.... The young people today are un-Christian because their teachers have been either unwilling or unable to transmit Christianity to them.... None can give to another what he does not possess himself.

St François de Sales

The crude picture of penitence as something like apology or even placation has, for me, the value of making penitence an act. The more high-minded views involve some danger of regarding it simply as a state of feeling.... The question is before my mind at present because I've been reading Alexander Whyte.... For him, one essential symptom of the regenerate life is a permanent, and permanently horrified, perception of one's natural and (it seems) unalterable corruption. The true Christian's nostril is to be continually attentive to the inner cesspool.... Another author, quoted in Haller's *Rise of Puritanism,* says that when he looked into his heart, it was 'as if I had in the heat of summer lookt down into the Filth of a Dungeon, where I discerned Millions of crawling living things in the midst of that Sink and liquid Corruption'.

I won't listen to those who describe that vision as merely pathological. I have seen the 'slimy things that crawled with legs' in my own dungeon. I thought the glimpse taught me sense. But Whyte seems to think it should not be a glimpse but a daily, lifelong scrutiny. Can he be right? It sounds so very unlike the New Testament fruits of the spirit — love, joy, peace. And very unlike the Pauline programme: 'forgetting those things which are behind and reaching forth unto those things that are before.' And very unlike St François de Sales' green, dewy chapter on *la douceur* towards one's self. Anyway, what's the use of laying down a programme of permanent emotions? They can be permanent only by being factitious.... I know that a spiritual emetic at the right moment may be needed. But not a regular diet of emetics! If one survived, one would develop a 'tolerance' of them. This poring over the 'sink' might breed its own perverse pride.

The Conversion of St Paul   JANUARY 25

In one sense the road back to God is a road of moral effort, of trying harder and harder. But in another sense it is not trying that is ever going to bring us home. All this
trying leads up to the vital moment at which you turn to God and say, 'You must do
this. I can't.' Do not, I implore you, start asking yourselves, 'Have I reached that
moment?' Do not sit down and start watching your own mind to see if it is coming
along. That puts a man quite on the wrong track. When the most important things in
our life happen we quite often do not know, at the moment, what is going on. A man
does not always say to himself, 'Hullo! I'm growing up.' It is often only when he looks
back that he realizes what has happened and recognizes it as what people call
'growing up'. You can see it even in simple matters. A man who starts anxiously
watching to see whether he is going to sleep is very likely to remain wide awake. As
well, the thing I am talking of now may not happen to every one in a sudden flash — as
it did to St Paul or Bunyan: It may be so gradual that no one could ever point to a particular hour or even a particular year. And what matters is the nature of the change in
itself, not how we feel while it is happening. It is the change from being confident
about our own efforts to the state in which we despair of doing anything for ourselves
and leave it to God.

St Timothy and St Titus   JANUARY 26

A most astonishing misconception has long dominated the modern mind on the subject of St Paul. It is to this effect: that Jesus preached a kindly and simple religion
(found in the Gospels) and that St Paul afterwards corrupted it into a cruel and complicated religion (found in the Epistles). This is really quite untenable. All the most
terrifying texts came from the mouth of Our Lord: all the texts on which we can base
such warrant as we have for hoping that all men will be saved come from St Paul. If it
could be proved that St Paul altered the teaching of his Master in any way, he altered it
in exactly the opposite way to that which is popularly supposed. But there is no real
evidence for a pre-Pauline doctrine different from St Paul's. The Epistles are, for the
most part, the earliest Christian documents we possess. The Gospels come later.
They are not 'the Gospel', the statement of the Christian belief. They were written for
those who had already been converted, who had already accepted 'the Gospel'. They
leave out many of the 'complications' (that is, the theology) because they are intended
for readers who have already been instructed in it. In that sense the Epistles are more
primitive and more central than the Gospels — though not, of course, than the great
events which the Gospels recount. God's act (the Incarnation, the Crucifixion, and

the Resurrection) comes first: the earliest theological analysis of it comes in the Epistles: then, when the generation who had known the Lord was dying out, the Gospels were composed to provide for believers a record of the great Act and of some of the Lord's sayings.

A Revolt Against Christ

In the earlier history of every rebellion there is a stage at which you do not yet attack the King in person. You say, 'The King is all right. It is his Ministers who are wrong. They misrepresent him and corrupt all his plans – which, I'm sure, are good plans if only the Ministers would let them take effect.' And the first victory consists in beheading a few Ministers: only at a later stage do you go on and behead the King himself. In the same way, the nineteenth-century attack on St Paul was really only a stage in the revolt against Christ. Men were not ready in large numbers to attack Christ Himself. They made the normal first move – that of attacking one of His principal ministers. Everything they disliked in Christianity was therefore attributed to St Paul. It was unfortunate that their case could not impress anyone who had really read the Gospels and the Epistles with attention: but apparently few people had, and so the first victory was won. St Paul was impeached and banished and the world went on to the next step – the attack on the King Himself.

St Thomas Aquinas

We may anticipate a revival of the allegorical sense in biblical criticism. But it will probably be dangerous, and in the Middle Ages I think it was dangerous, to appreciation of the Historical Books as plain heroic narrative.

St Thomas Aquinas throws a little more light on the . . . 'lowness' or 'simplicity' of the Bible. He explains why Scripture expresses divine truths not merely through corporeal images but even through images of vile bodies rather than noble. This is done, he says, to liberate the mind from error, to reduce the danger of any confusion between the symbol and the reality. It is an answer worthy of a profound theologian. At the same time, the passage in which it occurs reveals attitudes most hostile to aesthetic appreciation of the sacred text. It would seem, he says, that Scripture ought not to use metaphors. For what is proper to the lowest kind of learning (*infimae doctrinae*) does not seem suitable to the queen of the sciences. But metaphor is proper to poetry, and poetry is the lowest of all forms of learning. . . . The answer, so far as it concerns us here, is that poetry and Scripture use metaphor for quite different reasons; poetry for delight, and Scripture *propter necessitatem et utilitatem*. Where a nineteenth-century critic might have said that Scripture was itself the highest poetry, St Thomas says rather that the highest and the lowest *doctrinae* have, paradoxically, one point in common, but of course for different reasons.

Restoration of the Bible on its Own Terms   JANUARY 29

Unless the religious claims of the Bible are again acknowledged, its literary claims will, I think, be given only 'mouth honour' and that decreasingly. For it is, through and through, a sacred book. Most of its component parts were written, and all of them were brought together, for a purely religious purpose. It contains good litera-ture and bad literature. But even the good literature is so written that we can seldom disregard its sacred character. It is easy enough to read Homer while suspending our disbelief in the Greek pantheon; but then the *Iliad* was not composed chiefly, if at all, to enforce obedience to Zeus and Athene and Poseidon. The Greek tragedians are more religious than Homer, but even there we have only religious speculation or at least the poet's personal religious ideas; not dogma. That is why we can join in. Neither Aeschylus nor even Virgil tacitly prefaces his poetry with the formula 'Thus say the gods'. But in most parts of the Bible everything is implicitly or explicitly in-troduced with 'Thus saith the Lord'. It is, if you like to put it that way, not merely a sacred book but a book so remorselessly and continuously sacred that it does not in-vite, it excludes or repels, the merely aesthetic approach. You can read it as literature only by a *tour de force*. You are cutting the wood against the grain, using the tool for a purpose it was not intended to serve. It demands incessantly to be taken on its own terms: it will not continue to give literary delight very long except to those who go to it for something quite different. I predict that it will in the future be read as it always has been read, almost exclusively by Christians.

Other Religions   JANUARY 30

If you are a Christian you do not have to believe that all the other religions are simply wrong all through. If you are an atheist you do not have to believe that the main point in all the religions of the whole world is simply one huge mistake. If you are a Chris-tian, you are free to think that all these religions, even the queerest ones, contain at least some hint of the truth. When I was an atheist I had to try to persuade myself that most of the human race have always been wrong about the question that mattered to them most; when I became Christian I was able to take a more liberal view. But, of course, being a Christian does mean thinking that where Christianity differs from other religions, Christianity is right and they are wrong. As in arithmetic – there is only one right answer to a sum, and all other answers are wrong: but some of the wrong answers are much nearer being right that others.

No Half-Way House   JANUARY 31

There is no half-way house and there is no parallel in other religions. If you had gone to Buddha and asked him 'Are you the son of Bramah?' he would have said, 'My son, you are still in the vale of illusion.' If you had gone to Socrates and asked, 'Are you Zeus?' he would have laughed at you. If you had gone to Mohammed and asked, 'Are you Allah?' he would first have rent his clothes and then cut your head off. If you had asked Confucius, 'Are you Heaven?' I think he would have probably replied, 'Remarks which are not in accordance with nature are in bad taste.' The idea of a great moral teacher saying what Christ said is out of the question. In my opinion, the only person who can say that sort of thing is either God or a complete lunatic suffering from that form of delusion which undermines the whole mind of man. If you think you are a poached egg, when you are looking for a piece of toast to suit you, you may be sane, but if you think you are God, there is no chance for you. We may note in passing that He was never regarded as a mere moral teacher. He did not produce that effect on any of the people who actually met Him. He produced mainly three effects – Hatred – Terror – Adoration. There was no trace of people expressing mild approval.

What are We to Make of Christ?   FEBRUARY 1

'What are we to make of Christ?' There is no question of what we can make of Him, it is entirely a question of what He intends to make of us. You must accept or reject the story.

The things He says are very different from what any other teacher has said. Others say, 'This is the truth about the Universe. This is the way you ought to go', but He says, 'I am the Truth, and the Way, and the Life.' He says, 'No man can reach absolute reality, except through Me. Try to retain your own life and you will be inevitably ruined. Give yourself away and you will be saved.' He says, 'If you are ashamed of

Me, if, when you hear this call, you turn the other way, I also will look the other way when I come again as God without disguise. If anything whatever is keeping you from God and from Me, whatever it is, throw it away. If it is your eye, pull it out. If it is your hand, cut it off. If you put yourself first you will be last. Come to Me everyone who is carrying a heavy load, I will set that right. Your sins, all of them, are wiped out, I can do that. I am Re-birth, I am Life. Eat Me, drink Me, I am your Food. And finally, do not be afraid, I have overcome the whole Universe.' That is the issue.

The Presentation of the Lord   FEBRUARY 2

When we look into the Selectiveness which the Christians attribute to God we find in it none of that 'favouritism' which we were afraid of. The 'chosen' people are chosen not for their own sake (certainly not for their own honour or pleasure) but for the sake of the unchosen. Abraham is told that 'in his seed' (the chosen nation) 'all nations shall be blest'. That nation has been chosen to bear a heavy burden. Their sufferings are great: but, as Isaiah recognized, their sufferings heal others. On the finally selected Woman falls the utmost depth of maternal anguish. Her Son, the incarnate God, is a 'man of sorrows'; the one Man into whom Deity descended, the one Man who can be lawfully adored, is pre-eminent for suffering.

A Matter of Fairness   FEBRUARY 3

Is it not frightfully unfair that this new life should be confined to people who have heard of Christ and been able to believe in Him? But the truth is God has not told us what His arrangements about the other people are. We do know that no man can be saved except through Christ; we do not know that only those who know Him can be saved through Him. But in the meantime, if you are worried about the people outside, the most unreasonable thing you can do is to remain outside yourself. Christians are Christ's body, the organism through which He works. Every addition to that body enables Him to do more. If you want to help those outside you must add your own little cell to the body of Christ who alone can help them. Cutting off a man's fingers would be an odd way of getting him to do more work.

Dogma and the Universe   FEBRUARY 4

It is a common reproach against Christianity that its dogmas are unchanging, while human knowledge is in continual growth. Hence, to unbelievers, we seem to be always engaged in the hopeless task of trying to force the new knowledge into moulds which it has outgrown. I think this feeling alienates the outsider much more than any particular discrepancies between this or that doctrine and this or that scientific theory. We may, as we say, 'get over' dozens of isolated 'difficulties', but that does not alter his sense that the endeavour as a whole is doomed to failure and perverse: indeed, the more ingenious, the more perverse. For it seems to him clear that, if our ancestors had known what we know about the universe, Christianity would never have existed at all: and, however we patch and mend, no system of thought which claims to be immutable can, in the long run, adjust itself to our growing knowledge.

Science and the Dogma of Creation   FEBRUARY 5

In one respect, as many Christians have noticed, contemporary science has recently come into line with Christian doctrine, and parted company with the classical forms of materialism. If anything emerges clearly from modern physics, it is that nature is not everlasting. The universe had a beginning, and will have an end. But the great materialistic systems of the past all believed in the eternity, and thence in the self-existence of matter. As Professor Whittaker said in the Riddell Lectures of 1942, 'It was never possible to oppose seriously the dogma of the Creation except by maintaining that the world has existed from all eternity in more or less its present state.' This fundamental ground for materialism has now been withdrawn. We should not lean too heavily on this, for scientific theories change. But at the moment it appears that the burden of proof rests, not on us, but on those who deny that Nature has some cause beyond herself.

In popular thought, however, the origin of the universe has counted (I think) for less than its character — its immense size and its apparent indifference, if not hostility, to human life. And very often this impresses people all the more because it is supposed to be a modern discovery — an excellent example of those things which our ancestors did not know and which, if they had known them, would have prevented the very beginnings of Christianity. Here there is a simple historical falsehood. Ptolemy knew just as well as Eddington that the earth was infinitesimal in comparison with the whole content of space. There is no question here of knowledge having grown until the frame of archaic thought is no longer able to contain it. The real question is why the spatial insignificance of the earth, after being known for centuries, should suddenly in the last century have become an argument against Christianity.

The Argument about Space   FEBRUARY 6

When the doctor at a post-mortem diagnoses poison, pointing to the state of the dead man's organs, his argument is rational because he has a clear idea of that opposite state in which the organs would have been found if no poison were present. In the same way, if we use the vastness of space and the smallness of earth to disprove the existence of God, we ought to have a clear idea of the sort of universe we should expect if God did exist. But have we? Whatever space may be in itself — and, of course, some moderns think it finite — we certainly perceive it as three-dimensional, and to three-dimensional space we can conceive no boundaries. By the very forms of our perceptions, therefore, we must feel as if we lived somewhere in infinite space. If we discovered no objects in this infinite space except those which are of use to man (our own sun and moon), then this vast emptiness would certainly be used as a strong argument against the existence of God. If we discover other bodies, they must be habitable or uninhabitable: and the odd thing is that both these hypotheses are used as grounds for rejecting Christianity. If the universe is teeming with life, this, we are told, reduces to absurdity the Christian claim — or what is thought to be the Chrisian claim — that man is unique, and the Christian doctrine that to this one planet God came down and was incarnate for us men and our salvation. If, on the other hand, the earth is really unique, then that proves that life is only an accidental by-product in the universe, and so again disproves our religion. Really, we are hard to please. We treat God as the police treat a man when he is arrested; whatever he does will be used in evidence against Him. I do not think this is due to our wickedness. I suspect there is something in our very mode of thought which makes it inevitable that we should always be baffled by actual existence, *whatever* character actual existence may have.

Size and Value   FEBRUARY 7

The whole argument from size rests on the assumption that differences of size ought to coincide with differences of value: for unless they do, there is, of course, no reason why the minute earth and the yet smaller human creatures upon it should not be the most important thing in a universe that contains the spiral nebulae. Now, is this assumption rational or emotional? I feel, as well as anyone else, the absurdity of supposing that the galaxy could be of less moment in God's eyes than such an atom as a human being. But I notice that I feel no similar absurdity in supposing that a man of five feet high may be more important than another man who is five feet three and a half — nor that a man may matter more than a tree, or a brain more than a leg. In other words, the feeling of absurdity arises only if the differences of size are very great.

But where a relation is perceived by reason it holds good universally. If size and value had any real connection, small differences in size would accompany small differences in value as surely as large differences in size accompany large differences in value. But no sane man could suppose that this is so. I don't think the taller man *slightly* more valuable than the shorter one. I don't allow a slight superiority to trees over men, and then neglect it because it is too small to bother about. I perceive, as long as I am dealing with the small differences of size, that they have no connection with value whatsoever. I therefore conclude that the importance attached to the great differences of size is an affair, not of reason but of emotion — of that peculiar emotion which superiorities in size produce only after a certain point of absolute size has been reached.

We are Inveterate Poets FEBRUARY 8

When a quantity is very great, we cease to regard it as mere quantity. Our imaginations awake. Instead of mere quantity, we now have a quality — the sublime. Unless this were so, the merely arithmetical greatness of the galaxy would be no more impressive than the figures in a telephone directory. It is thus, in a sense, from ourselves that the material universe derives its power to overawe us. To a mind which did not share our emotions, and lacked our imaginative energies, the argument from size would be sheerly meaningless. Men look on the starry heavens with reverence: monkeys do not. The silence of the eternal spaces terrified Pascal, but it was the greatness of Pascal that enabled them to do so. When we are frightened by the greatness of the universe, we are (almost literally) frightened by our own shadows: for these light years and billions of centuries are mere arithmetic until the shadow of man, the poet, the maker of myth, falls upon them. I do not say we are wrong to tremble at his shadow; it is a shadow of an image of God. But if ever the vastness of matter threatens to overcross our spirits, one must remember that it is matter spiritualized which does so. To puny man, the great nebula in Andromeda owes in a sense its greatness.

What Sort of Universe Do We Demand? FEBRUARY 9

We are hard to please. If the world in which we found ourselves were not vast and strange enough to give us Pascal's terror, what poor creatures we should be! Being what we are, rational but also animate, amphibians who start from the world of sense and proceed through myth and metaphor to the world of spirit, I do not see how we could have come to know the greatness of God without that hint furnished by the greatness of the material universe. Once again, what sort of universe do we demand? If it were small enough to be cosy, it would not be big enough to be sublime. If it is large enough for us to stretch our spiritual limbs in, it must be large enough to baffle us. Cramped or terrified, we must, in any conceivable world, be one or the other. I prefer terror. I should be suffocated in a universe that I could see to the end of. Have you never, when walking in a wood, turned back deliberately for fear you should come out at the other side and thus make it ever after in your imagination a mere beggarly strip of trees?

Man is Not the Measure of All Things   FEBRUARY 10

I hope you do not think I am suggesting that God made the spiral nebulae solely or chiefly in order to give me the experience of awe and bewilderment. I have not the faintest idea why He made them; on the whole, I think it would be rather surprising if I had. As far as I understand the matter, Christianity is not wedded to an anthropocentric view of the universe as a whole. The first chapters of Genesis, no doubt, give the story of creation in the form of a folk-tale — a fact recognized as early as the time of St Jerome — and if you take them alone you might get that impression. But it is not confirmed by the Bible as a whole. There are few places in literature where we are more sternly warned against making man the measure of all things than in the Book of Job: 'Canst thou draw out leviathan with an hook? Will he make a covenant with thee? Wilt thou take him for a servant? Shall not one be cast down even at the sight of him?' In St Paul, the powers of the skies seem usually to be hostile to man. It is, of course, the essence of Christianity that God loves man and for his sake became man and died. But that does not prove that man is the sole end of nature. In the parable, it was the one lost sheep that the shepherd went in search of: it was not the only sheep in the flock, and we are not told that it was the most valuable — save in so far as the most desperately in need has, while the need lasts, a peculiar value in the eyes of Love.

God's Love Has no Limits   FEBRUARY 11

The doctrine of the Incarnation would conflict with what we know of this vast universe only if we knew also that there were other rational species in it who had, like us, fallen, and who needed redemption in the same mode, and that they had not been vouchsafed it. But we know none of these things. It may be full of life that needs no redemption. It may be full of life that has been redeemed. It may be full of things quite other than life which satisfy the Divine Wisdom in fashions one cannot conceive. We are in no position to draw up maps of God's psychology, and prescribe limits to His interests. We would not do so even for a man whom we knew to be greater than ourselves. The doctrines that God is Love and that He delights in men, are positive doctrines, not limiting doctrines. He is not less than this. What more He may be, we do not know; we know only that He must be more than we can conceive. It is to be expected that His creation should be, in the main, unintelligible to us.

Divine Revelation and Human Curiosity   FEBRUARY 12

Christians themselves have been much to blame for the misunderstanding on these matters. They have a bad habit of talking as if revelation existed to gratify curiosity by illuminating all creation so that it becomes self-explanatory and all questions are answered. But revelation appears to me to be purely practical, to be addressed to the particular animal, Fallen Man, for the relief of his urgent necessities — not to the spirit of inquiry in man for the gratification of his liberal curiosity. We know that God has visited and redeemed His people, and that tells us just as much about the general character of the creation as a dose given to one sick hen on a big farm tells us about the general character of farming in England. What we must do, which road we must take to the fountain of life, we know, and none who has seriously followed the directions complains that he has been deceived.But whether there are other creatures like ourselves, and how they are dealt with: whether inanimate matter exists only to serve living creatures or for some other reason: whether the immensity of space is a means to some end, or an illusion, or simply the natural mode in which infinite energy might be expected to create — on all these points I think we are left to our own speculations.

No. It is not Christianity which need fear the giant universe. It is those systems which place the whole meaning of existence in biological or social evolution on our own planet. It is the creative evolutionist, the Bergsonian or Shavian, or the Communist, who should tremble when he looks up at the night sky. For he really is committed to a sinking ship. He really is attempting to ignore the discovered nature of things, as though by concentrating on the possibly upward trend in a single planet he could make himself forget the inevitable downward trend in the universe as a whole, the trend to low temperatures and irrevocable disorganization.

Christianity and the Advance in Knowledge   FEBRUARY 13

How can an unchanging system survive the continual increase of knowledge? Now, in certain cases we know very well how it can. A mature scholar reading a great passage in Plato, and taking in at one glance the metaphysics, the literary beauty, and the place of both in the history of Europe, is in a very different position from a boy learning the Greek alphabet. Yet through that unchanging system of the alphabet all this vast mental and emotional activity is operating. It has not been broken by the new knowledge. It is not outworn. If it changed, all would be chaos. A great Christian statesman, considering the morality of a measure which will affect millions of lives, and which involves economic, geographical and political considerations of the utmost complexity, is in a different position from a boy first learning that one must not cheat or tell lies, or hurt innocent people. But only in so far as that first knowledge of the great moral platitudes survives unimpaired in the statesman will his deliberation be moral at all. If that goes, then there has been no progress, but ony mere change. For change is not progress unless the core remains unchanged. A small oak grows into a big oak: if it became a beech, that would not be growth, but mere change. And thirdly, there is a great difference between counting apples and arriving at the mathematical formulae of modern physics. But the multiplication table is used in both and does not grow out of date....

The very possibility of progress demands that there should be an unchanging element. New bottles for new wine, by all means: but not new palates, throats and stomachs, or it would not be, for us, 'wine' at all. I take it we should all agree to find this sort of unchanging element in the simple rules of mathematics. I would add to these the primary principles of morality. And I would also add the fundamental doctrines of Christianity. To put it in rather more technical language, I claim that the positive historical statements made by Christianity have the power, elsewhere found chiefly in formal principles, of receiving, without intrinsic change, the increasing complexity of meaning which increasing knowledge puts into them.

Is God in Outer Space?   FEBRUARY 14

The Russians, I am told, report that they have not found God in outer space. On the other hand, a good many people in many different times and countries claim to have found God, or been found by God, here on earth.

The conclusion some want us to draw from these data is that God does not exist. As a corollary, those who think they have met Him on earth were suffering from a delusion.

But other conclusions might be drawn:

1. We have not yet gone far enough in space. There had been ships on the Atlantic for a good time before America was discovered.

2. God does exist but is locally confined to this planet.

3. The Russians did find God in space without knowing it, because they lacked the requisite apparatus for detecting Him.

4. God does exist but is not an object either located in a particular part of space nor diffused, as we once thought 'ether' was, throughout space.

The first two conclusions do not interest me. The sort of religion for which they could be a defence would be a religion for savages: the belief in a local deity who can be contained in a particular temple, island or grove. That, in fact, seems to be the sort of religion about which the Russians – or some Russians, and a good many people in the West – are being irreligious. It is not in the least disquieting that no astronauts have discovered a god of that sort. The really disquieting thing would be if they had.

The Author of All Space and Time

Looking for God – or Heaven – by exploring space is like reading or seeing all Shakespeare's plays in the hope that you will find Shakespeare as one of the characters or Stratford as one of the places. Shakespeare is in one sense present at every moment in every play. But he is never present in the same way as Falstaff or Lady Macbeth. Nor is he diffused through the play like a gas. . . . My point is that, if God does exist, He is related to the universe more as an author is related to a play than as one object in the universe is related to another. If God created the universe, He created space-time, which is to the universe as the metre is to a poem or the key is to music. To look for Him as one item within the framework which He Himself invented is nonsensical. If God – such a God as any adult religion believes in – exists, mere movement in space will never bring you any nearer to Him or any farther from Him than you are at this very moment. You can neither reach Him nor avoid Him by travelling to Alpha Centauri or even to other galaxies. A fish is no more, and no less, in the sea after it has swum a thousand miles than it was when it set out. . . . Space-travel really has nothing to do with the matter. To some, God is discoverable everywhere; to others, nowhere. Those who do not find Him on earth are unlikely to find Him in space. (Hang it all, we're in space already; every year we go a huge circular tour in space.) But send a saint up in a spaceship and he'll find God in space as he found God on earth. Much depends on the seeing eye.

Life on Other Planets   FEBRUARY 16

If there are species, and rational species, other than man, are any or all of them, like us, fallen? This is the point non-Christians always seem to forget. They seem to think that the Incarnation implies some particular merit or excellence in humanity. But of course it implies just the reverse: a particular demerit and depravity. No creature that deserved Redemption would need to be redeemed. They that are whole need not the physician. Christ died for men precisely because men are *not* worth dying for; to make them worth it....

If we knew that Redemption by an Incarnation and Passion had been denied to creatures in need of it – is it certain that this is the only mode of Redemption that is possible? Here of course we ask for what is not merely unknown but, unless God should reveal it, wholly unknowable. It may be that the further we were permitted to see into His councils, the more clearly we should understand that thus and not other-wise – by the birth at Bethlehem, the cross on Calvary and the empty tomb – a fallen race could be rescued. There may be a necessity for this, insurmountable, rooted in the very nature of God and the very nature of sin. But we don't know. At any rate, I don't know. Spiritual as well as physical conditions might differ widely in different worlds. There might be different sorts and different degrees of fallenness. We must surely believe that the divine charity is as fertile in resource as it is measureless in condescension. To different diseases, or even to different patients sick with the same disease, the great Physician may have applied different remedies; remedies which we should probably not recognize as such even if we ever heard of them.

Missionaries in Outer Space   FEBRUARY 17

Can even missionaries be trusted? 'Gun and Gospel' have been horribly combined in the past. The missionary's holy desire to save souls has not always been kept quite distinct from the arrogant desire, the busybody's itch, to (as he calls it) 'civilize' the (as he calls them) 'natives'. Would all our missionaries recognize an unfallen race if they met it? Could they? Would they continue to press upon creatures that did not need to be saved that plan of Salvation which God has appointed to Man? Would they denounce as sins mere differences of behaviour which the spiritual and biological history of these strange creatures fully justified and which God Himself had blessed? Would they try to teach those from whom they had better learn? I do not know.

What I do know is that here and now, as our only possible practical preparation for such a meeting, you and I should resolve to stand firm against all exploitation and all theological imperialism. It will not be fun. We shall be called traitors to our own species. We shall be hated of almost all men; even of some religious men. And we must not give back one single inch. We shall probably fail, but let us go down fighting for the right side. Our loyalty is due not to our species but to God. Those who are, or can become, His sons, are our real brothers even if they have shells or tusks. It is spiritual, not biological, kinship that counts....

If I remember rightly, St Augustine raised a question about the theological position of satyrs, monopods, and other semi-human creatures. He decided it could wait till we knew there were any. So can this.

Chronological Snobbery   FEBRUARY 18

'Why — damn it — it's *medieval*,' I exclaimed; for I still had all the chronological snobbery of my period and used the names of earlier periods as terms of abuse... Barfield made short work of what I have called my 'chronological snobbery', the uncritical acceptance of the intellectual climate common to our own age and the assumption that whatever has gone out of date is on that account discredited. You must find why it went out of date. Was it refuted (and if so by whom, where, and how conclusively) or did it merely die away as fashions do? If the latter, this tells us nothing about its truth or falsehood. From seeing this, one passes to the realization that our own age is also 'a period', and certainly has, like all periods, its own characteristic illusions. They are likeliest to lurk in those widespread assumptions which are so ingrained in the age that no one dares to attack or feels it necessary to defend them... We had been, in the technical sense of the term, 'realists'; that is, we accepted as rock-bottom reality the universe revealed by the senses... We maintained that abstract thought (if obedient to logical rules) gave indisputable truth.

Approach of the Living God   FEBRUARY 19

Men are reluctant to pass over from the notion of an abstract and negative deity to the living God. I do not wonder.... The Pantheist's God does nothing, demands nothing. He is there if you wish for Him, like a book on a shelf. He will not pursue you. There is no danger that at any time heaven and earth should flee away at His glance. If He were the truth, then we could really say that all the Christian images of kingship were a historical accident of which our religion ought to be cleansed. It is with a shock that we discover them to be indispensable. You have had a shock like that before, in connection with smaller matters — when the line pulls at your hand, when something breathes beside you in the darkness. So here; the shock comes at the precise moment when the thrill of *life* is communicated to us along the clue we have been following. It is always shocking to meet life where we thought we were alone. 'Look out!' we cry, 'it's *alive*.' And therefore this is the very point at which so many draw back — I would have done so myself if I could — and proceed no further with Christianity. An 'impersonal God' — well and good. A subjective God of beauty, truth and goodness, inside our own heads — better still. A formless life-force surging through us, a vast power which we can tap — best of all. But God Himself, alive, pulling at the other end of the cord, perhaps approaching at an infinite speed, the hunter, king, husband — that is quite another matter. There comes a moment when the children who have been playing at burglars hush suddenly: was that a *real* footstep in the hall? There comes a moment when people who have been dabbling in religion ('Man's search for God'!) suddenly draw back. Supposing we really found Him? We never meant it to come to *that*! Worse still, supposing He had found us?

The Summons of Lent   FEBRUARY 20

It is a matter of common experience that, when one person has got himself into a hole, the trouble of getting him out usually falls on a kind friend. Now what was the sort of 'hole' man had got himself into? He had tried to set up on his own, to behave as if he belonged to himself. In other words, fallen man is not simply an imperfect creature who needs improvement: he is a rebel who must lay down his arms. Laying down your arms, surrendering, saying you are sorry, realizing that you have been on the wrong track and getting ready to start life over again from the ground floor — that is the only way out of a 'hole'. This process of surrender — this movement full speed astern — is what Christians call repentance. Now repentance is no fun at all. It is something much harder than merely eating humble pie. It means unlearning all the self-conceit and self-will that we have been training ourselves into for thousands of years. It means killing part of yourself, undergoing a kind of death. In fact, it needs a good man to repent. And here comes the catch. Only a bad person needs to repent: only a good person can repent perfectly. The worse you are the more you need it and the less you can do it. The only person who could do it perfectly would be a perfect person — and he would not need it.

Help from the Perfect Penitent

This repentance, this willing submission to humiliation and a kind of death, is not something God demands of you before He will take you back and which He could let you off if He chose: it is simply a description of what going back to Him is like. If you ask God to take you back without it, you are really asking Him to let you go back without going back. It cannot happen. Very well, then, we must go through with it. But the same badness which makes us need it, makes us unable to do it. Can we do it if God helps us? Yes, but what do we mean when we talk of God helping us? We mean God putting into us a bit of Himself, so to speak. He lends us a little of His reasoning powers and that is how we think: He puts a little of His love into us and that is how we love one another. When you teach a child writing, you hold its hand while it forms the letters: that is, it forms the letters because you are forming them. We love and reason because God loves and reasons and holds our hand while we do it.

A Complaint from the Ungracious

I have heard some people complain that if Jesus was God as well as man, then His suffering and death lose all value in their eyes, 'because it must have been so easy for him'. Others may (very rightly) rebuke the ingratitude and ungraciousness of this objection; what staggers me is the misunderstanding it betrays. In one sense, of course, those who make it are right. They have even understated their own case. The perfect submission, the perfect suffering, the perfect death were not only easier to Jesus because He was God, but were possible only because He was God. But surely that is a very odd reason for not accepting them? The teacher is able to form the letters for the child because the teacher is grown-up and knows how to write. That, of course, makes it easier for the teacher; and only because it is easier for him can he help the child. If it rejected him because 'it's easy for grown-ups' and waited to learn writing from another child who could not write itself (and so had no 'unfair' advantage), it would not get on very quickly. If I am drowning in a rapid river, a man who still has one foot on the bank may give me a hand which saves my life. Ought I to shout back (between my gasps) 'No, it's not fair! You have an advantage! You're keeping one foot on the bank'? That advantage – call it 'unfair' if you like – is the only reason why he can be of any use to me. To what will you look for help if you will not look to that which is stronger than yourself?

Contrition   FEBRUARY 23

The Lenten season is devoted especially to what theologians call contrition. . . . Contrite, as you know, is a word translated from the Latin, meaning crushed or pulverized. Now modern people complain that there is too much of that note in our Prayer Book. They do not wish their hearts to be pulverized, and they do not feel that they can sincerely say that they are 'miserable offenders'. I once knew a regular churchgoer who never repeated the words, 'the burden of them [i.e. his sins] is intolerable', because he did not feel that they were intolerable. But he was not understanding the words. I think the Prayer Book is very seldom talking primarily about our feelings; that is (I think) the first mistake we're apt to make about these words 'we are miserable offenders'. I do not think whether we are feeling miserable or not matters. I think it is using the word miserable in the old sense — meaning an object of pity. That a person can be a proper object of pity when he is not feeling miserable, you can easily understand if you imagine yourself looking down from a height on two crowded express trains that are travelling towards one another along the same line at sixty miles an hour. You can see that in forty seconds there will be a head-on collision. I think it would be very natural to say about the passengers of these trains, that they were objects of pity. This would not mean that they felt miserable themselves; but they would certainly be proper objects of pity.

Confession   FEBRUARY 24

It is not for me to decide whether you should confess your sins to a priest or not . . . but if you do not, you should at least make a list on a piece of paper, and make a serious act of penance about each one of them. There is something about the mere words, you know, provided you avoid two dangers, either of sensational exaggeration — trying to work things up and make melodramatic sins out of small matters — or the opposite danger of slurring things over. It is essential to use the plain, simple, old-fashioned words that you would use about anyone else. I mean words like theft, or fornication, or hatred, instead of 'I did not mean to be dishonest', or 'I was only a boy then', or 'I lost my temper'. I think that this steady facing of what one does know and bringing it before God, without excuses, and seriously asking for Forgiveness and Grace, and resolving as far as in one lies to do better, is the only way.

The Fatal Charm of National Repentance FEBRUARY 25

Men fail so often to repent their real sins that the occasional repentance of an imaginary sin might appear almost desirable. But what actually happens . . . to the youthful national penitent is a little more complicated than that. England is not a natural agent, but a civil society. When we speak of England's actions we mean the actions of the British Government. The young man who is called upon to repent of England's foreign policy is really being called upon to repent the acts of his neighbour; for a Foreign Secreaty or a Cabinet Minister is certainly a neighbour. And repentance presupposes condemnation. The first and fatal charm of national repentance is, therefore, the encouragement it gives us to turn from the bitter task of repenting our own sins to the congenial one of bewailing — but, first, of denouncing — the conduct of others. If it were clear to the young penitent that this is what he is doing, no doubt he would remember the law of charity. Unfortunately the very terms in which national repentance is recommended to him conceal its true nature. By a dangerous figure of speech, he calls the Government not 'they' but 'we'. And since, as penitents, we are not encouraged to be charitable to our own sins, nor to give ourselves the benefit of any doubt, a Government which is called 'we' is *ipso facto* placed beyond the sphere of charity or even of justice. You can say anything you please about it. You can indulge in the popular vice of detraction without restraint, and yet feel all the time that you are practising contrition.

The Forgiveness of Sins FEBRUARY 26

We say a great many things in church (and out of church too) without thinking of what we are saying. For instance, we say in the Creed 'I believe in the forgiveness of sins'. I had been saying it for several years before I asked myself why it was in the Creed. At first sight it seems hardly worth putting in. 'If one is a Christian,' I thought, 'of course one believes in the forgiveness of sins. It goes without saying.' But the people who compiled the Creed apparently thought that this was a part of our belief which we needed to be reminded of every time we went to church. And I have begun to see that, as far as I am concerned, they were right. To believe in the forgiveness of sins is not nearly so easy as I thought. Real belief in it is the sort of thing that very easily slips away if we don't keep on polishing it up.

We believe that God forgives us our sins; but also that He will not do so unless we forgive other people their sins against us. There is no doubt about the second part of this statement. It is in the Lord's Prayer: it was emphatically stated by Our Lord. If you don't forgive you will not be forgiven. No part of His teaching is clearer: and there are no exceptions to it. He doesn't say that we are to forgive other people's sins provided they are not too frightful, or provided there are extenuating circumstances, or anything of that sort. We are to forgive them all, however spiteful, however mean, however often they are repeated. If we don't, we shall be forgiven none of our own.

Forgiving and Excusing   FEBRUARY 27

Now it seems to me that we often make a mistake both about God's forgiveness of our sins and about the forgiveness we are told to offer to other people's sins. Take it first about God's forgiveness. I find that when I think I am asking God to forgive me I am often in reality (unless I watch myself very carefully) asking Him to do something quite different. I am asking Him not to forgive me but to excuse me. But there is all the difference in the world between forgiving and excusing. Forgiveness says 'Yes, you have done this thing, but I accept your apology, I will never hold it against you and everything between us two will be exactly as it was before.' But excusing says 'I see that you couldn't help it or didn't mean it, you weren't really to blame.' If one was not really to blame then there is nothing to forgive. In that sense forgiveness and excusing are almost opposites. Of course in dozens of cases, either between God and man, or between one man and another, there may be a mixture of the two. Part of what seemed at first to be the sins turns out to be really nobody's fault and is excused; the bit that is left over is forgiven. If you had a perfect excuse you would not need forgiveness: if the whole of your action needs forgiveness then there was no excuse for it. But the trouble is that what we call 'asking God's forgiveness' very often really consists in asking God to accept our excuses. What leads us into this mistake is the fact that there usually is some amount of excuse, some 'extenuating circumstances'. We are so very anxious to point these out to God (and to ourselves) that we are apt to forget the really important thing; that is, the bit left over, the bit which the excuses don't cover, the bit which is inexcusable but not, thank God, unforgivable. And if we forget this we shall go away imagining that we have repented and been forgiven when all that has really happened is that we have satisfied ourselves with our own excuses.

Our Mistakes and God's Remedy   FEBRUARY 28

There are two remedies for this danger. One is to remember that God knows all the real excuses very much better than we do. If there are real 'extenuating circumstances' there is no fear that He will overlook them. Often He must know many excuses that we have never thought of, and therefore humble souls will, after death, have the delightful surprise of discovering that on certain occasions they sinned much less than they had thought. All the real excusing He will do. What we have got to take to Him is the inexcusable bit, the sin. We are only wasting time by talking about all the parts which can (we think) be excused. When you go to a doctor you show him the bit of you that is wrong—say, a broken arm. It would be a mere waste of time to keep on explaining that your legs and eyes and throat are all right. You may be mistaken in thinking so; and anyway, if they are really all right, the doctor will know that.

The second remedy is really and truly to believe in the forgiveness of sins. A great deal of our anxiety to make excuses comes from not really believing in it: from thinking that God will not take us to Himself again unless He is satisfied that some sort of case can be made out in our favour. But that would not be forgiveness at all. Real forgiveness means looking steadily at the sin, the sin that is left over without any excuse, after all allowances have been made, and seeing it in all its horror, dirt, meanness and malice, and nevertheless being wholly reconciled to the man who has done it. That, and only that, is forgiveness; and that we can always have from God if we ask for it.

Charity and Fairness   MARCH 1

When it comes to a question of our forgiving other people, it is partly the same and partly different. It is the same because, here also, forgiving does not mean excusing. Many people seem to think it does. They think that if you ask them to forgive someone who has cheated or bullied them you are trying to make out that there was really no cheating or no bullying. But if that were so, there would be nothing to forgive. They keep on replying, 'But I tell you the man broke a most solemn promise.' Exactly: that is precisely what you have to forgive. (This doesn't mean you must necessarily believe his next promise. It does mean that you must make every effort to kill every trace of resentment in your own heart—every wish to humiliate or hurt him or to pay him out.) The difference between this situation and the one in which you are asking God's forgiveness is this. In our own case we accept excuses too easily, in other people's we do not accept them easily enough. As regards my own sins it is a safe bet (though not a certainty) that the excuses are not really so good as I think: as regards other men's sins against me it is a safe bet (though not a certainty) that the excuses are better than I think. One must therefore begin by attending carefully to everything which may show that the other man was not so much to blame as we thought. But even if he is absolutely fully to blame we still have to forgive him; and even if ninety-nine per cent of his apparent guilt can be explained away by really good excuses, the problem of forgiveness begins with the one per cent of guilt which is left over. To excuse what can really produce good excuses is not Christian charity; it is only fairness. To be a Christian means to forgive the inexcusable, because God has forgiven the inexcusable in you.

This is hard. It is perhaps not so hard to forgive a single great injury. But to forgive the incessant provocations of daily life — to keep on forgiving the bossy mother-in-law, the bullying husband, the nagging wife, the selfish daughter, the deceitful son — how can we do it? Only, I think, by remembering where we stand, by meaning our words when we say in our prayers each night 'Forgive us our trespasses as we forgive those that trespass against us.' We are offered forgiveness on no other terms. To refuse it is to refuse God's mercy for ourselves. There is no hint of exceptions and God means what He says.

The Three Parts of Morality   MARCH 2

There is a story about a schoolboy who was asked what he thought God was like. He replied that, as far as he could make out, God was 'The sort of person who is always snooping round to see if anyone is enjoying himself and then trying to stop it.' And I am afraid that is the sort of idea that the word Morality raises in a good many people's minds: something that interferes, something that stops you having a good time. In reality, moral rules are directions for running the human machine. Every moral rule is there to prevent a breakdown, or a strain, or a friction, in the running of that machine. That is why these rules at first seem to be constantly interfering with our natural inclinations. When you are being taught how to use any machine, the instructor keeps on saying, 'No, don't do it like that', because, of course, there are all sorts of things that look all right and seem to you the natural way of treating the machine, but do not really work....

There are two ways in which the human machine goes wrong. One is when human individuals drift apart from one another, or else collide with one another and do one another damage, by cheating or bullying. The other is when things go wrong inside the individual — when the different parts of him (his different faculties and desires and so on) either drift apart or interfere with one another.

Social Relations

When people say in the newspapers that we are striving for Christian moral standards, they usually mean that we are striving for kindness and fair play between nations, and classes, and individuals.... When a man says about something he wants to do, 'It can't be wrong because it doesn't do anyone else any harm', he is thinking... it does not matter what his ship is like inside provided that he does not run into the next ship. And it is quite natural, when we start thinking about morality, to begin with social relations. For one thing, the results of bad morality in that sphere are so obvious and press on us every day: war and poverty and graft and lies and shoddy work. ...Almost all people at all times have agreed (in theory) that human beings ought to be honest and kind and helpful to one another. But though it is natural to begin with all that, if our thinking about morality stops there, we might just as well not have thought at all. Unless we go on to the second thing – the tidying up inside each human being – we are only deceiving ourselves.

Immortality Makes a Great Difference

Religion involves a series of statements about facts, which must be either true or false. If they are true, one set of conclusions will follow about the right sailing of the human fleet: if they are false, quite a different set. For example, let us go back to the man who says that a thing cannot be wrong unless it hurts some other human being. He quite understands that he must not damage the other ships in the convoy, but he honestly thinks that what he does to his own ship is simply his own business. But does it not make a great difference whether his ship is his own property or not? Does it not make a great difference whether I am, so to speak, the landlord of my own mind and body, or only a tenant, responsible to the real landlord? If somebody else made me, for his own purposes, then I shall have a lot of duties which I should not have if I simply belonged to myself....

Christianity asserts that every individual human being is going to live for ever, and this must be either true or false. Now there are a good many things which would not be worth bothering about if I were going to live only seventy years, but which I had better bother about very seriously if I am going to live for ever. Perhaps my bad temper or my jealousy are gradually getting worse – so gradually that the increase in seventy years will not be very noticeable. But it might be absolute hell in a million years: in fact, if Christianity is true, Hell is the precisely correct technical term for what it would be.

Social Morality   MARCH 5

The first thing to get clear about Christian morality between man and man is that in
this department Christ did not come to preach any brand new morality. The Golden
Rule of the New Testament (Do as you would be done by) is a summing up of what
everyone, at bottom, had always known to be right. Really great moral teachers never
do introduce new moralities: it is quacks and cranks who do that. As Dr Johnson
said, 'People need to be reminded more often than they need to be instructed.' The
real job of every moral teacher is to keep on bringing us back, time after time, to the
old simple principles which we are all so anxious not to see; like bringing a horse
back and back to the fence it has refused to jump or bringing a child back and back to
the bit in its lesson that it wants to shirk.

The second thing to get clear is that Christianity has not, and does not profess to
have, a detailed political programme for applying 'Do as you would be done by' to a
particular society at a particular moment. It could not have. It is meant for all men at
all times and the particular programme which suited one place or time would not suit
another. And, anyhow, that is not how Christianity works. When it tells you to feed
the hungry it does not give you lessons in cookery. When it tells you to read the
Scriptures it does not give you lessons in Hebrew and Greek, or even in English
grammar. It was never intended to replace or supersede the ordinary human arts and
sciences: it is rather a director which will set them all to the right jobs, and a source
of energy which will give them all new life, if only they will put themselves at its
disposal.

The Duty of the Laymen   MARCH 6

People say, 'The Church ought to give us a lead.' That is true if they mean it in the
right way, but false if they mean it in the wrong way. By the Church they ought to
mean the whole body of practising Christians. And when they say that the Church
should give us a lead, they ought to mean that some Christians – those who happen to
have the right talents – should be economists and statesmen, and that all economists
and statesmen should be Christians, and that their whole efforts in politics and economics should be directed to putting 'Do as you would be done by' into action. If that
happened, and if we others were really ready to take it, then we should find the
Christian solution for our own social problems pretty quickly. But, of course, when
they ask for a lead from the Church most people mean they want the clergy to put out
a political programme. That is silly. The clergy are those particular people within the
whole Church who have been specially trained and set aside to look after what con-

cerns us as creatures who are going to live for ever: and we are asking them to do a quite different job for which they have not been trained. The job is really on us, on the laymen. The application of Christian principles, say, to trade unionism or education, must come from Christian trade unionists and Christian schoolmasters: just as Christian literature comes from Christian novelists and dramatists – not from the bench of bishops getting together and trying to write plays and novels in their spare time.

A Fully Christian Society MARCH 7

The New Testament, without going into details, gives us a pretty clear hint of what a fully Christian society would be like. Perhaps it gives us more than we can take. It tells us that there are to be no passengers or parasites: if a man does no work, he ought not to eat. Everyone is to work with his own hands, and what is more, everyone's work is to produce something good: there will be no manufacture of silly luxuries and then of sillier advertisements to persuade us to buy them. And there is to be no 'swank' or 'side', no putting on airs. To that extent a Christian society would be what we now call Leftist. On the other hand, it is always insisting on obedience – obedience (and outward marks of respect) from all of us to properly appointed magistrates, from children to parents, and (I am afraid this is going to be very unpopular) from wives to husbands. Thirdly, it is to be a cheerful society: full of singing and rejoicing, and regarding worry or anxiety as wrong. Courtesy is one of the Christian virtues; and the New Testament hates what it calls 'busybodies'.

If there were such a society in existence and you or I visited it, I think we should come away with a curious impression. We should feel that its economic life was very socialistic and, in that sense, 'advanced', but that its family life and its code of manners were rather old-fashioned – perhaps even ceremonious and aristocratic. Each of us would like some bits of it, but I am afraid very few of us would like the whole thing. That is just what one would expect if Christianity is the total plan for the human machine. We have all departed from that total plan in different ways, and each of us wants to make out that his own modification of the original plan is the plan itself. You will find this again and again about anything that is really Christian: everyone is attracted by bits of it and wants to pick out those bits and leave the rest. That is why we do not get much further: and that is why people who are fighting for quite opposite things can both say they are fighting for Christianity.

The Modern Economic System   MARCH 8

There is one bit of advice given to us by the ancient heathen Greeks, and by the Jews in the Old Testament, and by the great Christian teachers of the Middle Ages, which the modern economic system has completely disobeyed. All these people told us not to lend money at interest: and lending money at interest — what we call investment — is the basis of our whole system. Now it may not absolutely follow that we are wrong. Some people say that when Moses and Aristotle and the Christians agreed in forbidding interest (or 'usury' as they called it), they could not foresee the joint stock company, and were only thinking of the private moneylender, and that, therefore, we need not bother about what they said. That is a question I cannot decide on. I am not an economist and I simply do not know whether the investment system is responsible for the state we are in or not. That is where we want the Christian economist. But I should not have been honest if I had not told you that three great civilizations had agreed (or so it seems at first sight) in condemning the very thing on which we have based our whole life.

Giving to the Poor   MARCH 9

In the passage where the New Testament says that everyone must work, it gives as a reason 'in order that he may have something to give to those in need'. Charity — giving to the poor — is an essential part of Christian morality: in the frightening parable of the sheep and the goats it seems to be the point on which everything turns. Some people nowadays say that charity ought to be unnecessary and that instead of giving to the poor we ought to be producing a society in which there were no poor to give to. They may be quite right in saying that we ought to produce that kind of society. But if anyone thinks that, as a consequence, you can stop giving in the meantime, then he has parted company with all Christian morality. I do not believe one can settle how much we ought to give. I am afraid the only safe rule is to give more than we can spare. In other words, if our expenditure on comforts, luxuries, amusements, etc., is up to the standard common among those with the same income as our own, we are probably giving away too little. If our charities do not at all pinch or hamper us, I should say they are too small.

Morality and Psychoanalysis MARCH 10

You want to distinguish very clearly between two things: between the actual medical theories and technique of the psychoanalysts, and the general philosophical view of the world which Freud and some others have gone on to add to this. The second thing — the philosophy of Freud — is in direct contradiction to Christianity: and also in direct contradiction to the other great psychologist, Jung. And furthermore, when Freud is talking about how to cure neurotics he is speaking as a specialist on his own subject, but when he goes on to talk general philosophy he is speaking as an amateur. It is therefore quite sensible to attend to him with respect in the one case and not in the other — and that is what I do. I am all the readier to do it because I have found that when he is talking off his own subject and on a subject I do know something about (namely, languages) he is very ignorant. But psychoanalysis itself, apart from all the philosophical additions that Freud and others have made to it, is not in the least contradictory to Christianity. Its technique overlaps with Christian morality at some points and it would not be a bad thing if every parson knew something about it: but it does not run the same course all the way, for the two techniques are doing rather different things.

When a man makes a moral choice two things are involved. One is the act of choosing. The other is the various feelings, impulses and so on which his psychological outfit presents him with, and which are the raw material of his choice. Now this raw material may be of two kinds. Either it may be what we would call normal: it may consist of the sort of feelings that are common to all men. Or else it may consist of quite unnatural feelings due to things that have gone wrong in his subconscious.... Now what psychoanalysis undertakes to do is to remove the abnormal feelings, that is, to give the man better raw material for his acts of choice: morality is concerned with the acts of choice themselves.

Freedom of the Will MARCH 11

Imagine three men who go to war. One has the ordinary natural fear of danger that any man has and he subdues it by moral effort and becomes a brave man. Let us suppose that the other two have, as a result of things in their subconsciousness, exaggerated, irrational fears, which no amount of moral effort can do anything about. Now suppose that a psychoanalyst comes along and cures these two: that is, he puts them both back in the position of the first man. Well it is just then that the psychoanalytical problem is over and the moral problem begins. Because, now that they are cured, these two men might take quite different lines. The first might say, 'Thank goodness

I've got rid of all those doo-dahs. Now at last I can do what I always wanted to do —
my duty to the cause of freedom.' But the other might say, 'Well, I'm very glad that I
now feel moderately cool under fire, but, of course, that doesn't alter the fact that I'm
still jolly well determined to look after Number One and let the other chap do the
dangerous job whenever I can. Indeed one of the good things about feeling less
frightened is that I can now look after myself much more efficiently and can be much
cleverer at hiding the fact from the others.' Now this difference is a purely moral one
and psychoanalysis cannot do anything about it. However much you improve the
man's raw material, you have still got something else: the real, free choice of the man,
on the material presented to him, either to put his own advantage first or to put it last.
And this free choice is the only thing that morality is concerned with.

Screwtape on Will and Fantasy   MARCH 12

Do what you will, there is going to be some benevolence, as well as some malice, in
your patient's soul. The great thing is to direct the malice to his immediate neighbours whom he meets every day and to thrust his benevolence out to the remote cir-
cumference, to people he does not know. The malice thus becomes wholly real and
the benevolence largely imaginary. There is no good at all in inflaming his hatred of
Germans if, at the same time, a pernicious habit of charity is growing up between
him and his mother, his employer, and the man he meets in the train. Think of your
man as a series of concentric circles, his will being the innermost, his intellect coming next, and finally his fantasy. You can hardly hope, at once, to exclude from all the
circles everything that smells of the Enemy: but you must keep on shoving all the virtues outward till they are finally located in the circle of fantasy, and all the desirable
qualities inward into the will. It is only in so far as they reach the will and are there
embodied in habits that the virtues are really fatal to us.

Prudence   MARCH 13

Prudence means practical common sense, taking the trouble to think out what you
are doing and what is likely to come of it. Nowadays most people hardly think of Prudence as one of the 'virtues'. In fact, because Christ said we could only get into His
world by being like children, many Christians have the idea that, provided you are
'good', it does not matter being a fool. But that is a misunderstanding. In the first
place, most children show plenty of 'prudence' about doing the things they are really

interested in, and think them out quite sensibly. In the second place, as St Paul points out, Christ never meant that we were to remain children in *intelligence:* on the contrary, He told us to be not only 'as harmless as doves', but also 'as wise as serpents'. He wants a child's heart, but a grown-up's head. He wants us to be simple, single-minded, affectionate, and teachable, as good children are; but He also wants every bit of intelligence we have to be alert at its job, and in first-class fighting trim.

Temperance   MARCH 14

Temperance is, unfortunately, one of those words that has changed its meaning. It now usually means teetotalism. But in the days when the second Cardinal virtue was christened 'Temperance', it meant nothing of the sort. Temperance referred not specially to drink, but to all pleasures; and it meant not abstaining, but going the right length and no further. It is a mistake to think that Christians ought all to be teetotallers; Mohammedanism, not Christianity, is the teetotal religion. Of course it may be the duty of a particular Christian, or of any Christian, at a particular time, to abstain from strong drink, either because he is the sort of man who cannot drink at all without drinking too much, or because he wants to give the money to the poor, or because he is with people who are inclined to drunkenness and must not encourage them by drinking himself. But the whole point is that he is abstaining, for a good reason, from something which he does not condemn and which he likes to see other people enjoying. One of the marks of a certain type of bad man is that he cannot give up a thing himself without wanting everyone else to give it up. That is not the Christian way. An individual Christian may see fit to give up all sorts of things for special reasons — marriage, or meat, or beer, or the cinema; but the moment he starts saying the things are bad in themselves, or looking down his nose at other people who do use them, he has taken the wrong turning.

One great piece of mischief has been done by the modern restriction of the word Temperance to the question of drink. It helps people to forget that you can be just as intemperate about lots of other things. A man who makes his golf or his motor bicycle the centre of his life, or a woman who devotes all her thoughts to clothes or bridge or her dog, is being just as 'intemperate' as someone who gets drunk every evening. Of course, it does not show on the outside so easily: bridge-mania or golf-mania do not make you fall down in the middle of the road. But God is not deceived by externals.

Justice and Fortitude   MARCH 15

Justice means much more than the sort of thing that goes on in law courts. It is the old name for everything we should now call 'fairness'; it includes honesty, give and take, truthfulness, keeping promises, and all that side of life. And Fortitude includes both kinds of courage — the kind that faces danger as well as the kind that 'sticks it' under pain. 'Guts' is perhaps the nearest modern English. You will notice, of course, that you cannot practise any of the other virtues very long without bringing this one into play....

We might think that the 'virtues' were necessary only for this present life — that in the other world we could stop being just because there is nothing to quarrel about and stop being brave because there is no danger. Now it is quite true that there will probably be no occasion for just or courageous acts in the next world, but there will be every occasion for being the sort of people that we can become only as a result of doing such acts here. The point is not that God will refuse you admission to His eternal world if you have not got certain qualities of character: the point is that if people have not got at least the beginnings of those qualities inside them, then no possible external conditions could make a 'Heaven' for them — that is, could make them happy with the deep, strong, unshakable kind of happiness God intends for us.

Faith   MARCH 16

Faith seems to be used by Christians in two sense or on two levels.... In the first sense it means simply Belief — accepting or regarding as true the doctrines of Christianity. That is fairly simple. But what does puzzle people — at least it used to puzzle me — is the fact that Christians regard faith in this sense as a virtue. I used to ask how on earth it can be a virtue — what is there moral or immoral about believing or not believing a set of statements?... What I did not see then — and a good many people do not see still — was this. I was assuming that if the human mind once accepts a thing as true it will automatically go on regarding it as true, until some real reason for reconsidering it turns up. In fact, I was assuming that the human mind is completely ruled by reason. But that is not so. For example, my reason is perfectly convinced by good evidence that anaesthetics do not smother me and that properly trained surgeons do not start operating until I am unconscious. But that does not alter the fact that when they have me down on the table and clap their horrible mask over my face, a mere childish panic begins inside me. I start thinking I am going to choke, and I am afraid they will start cutting me up before I am properly under. In other words, I lose my faith in anaesthetics. It is not reason that is taking away my faith: on the contrary, my faith is based on reason. It is my imagination and emotions. The battle is between faith and reason on one side and emotion and imagination on the other.

Training the Habit of Faith MARCH 17

Faith, in the sense in which I am here using the word, is the art of holding on to things your reason has once accepted, in spite of your changing moods. For moods will change, whatever view your reason takes. I know that by experience. Now that I am a Christian I do have moods in which the whole thing looks very improbable: but when I was an atheist I had moods in which Christianity looked terribly probable. This re-bellion of your moods against your real self is going to come anyway. That is why Faith is such a necessary virtue: unless you teach your moods 'where they get off', you can never be either a sound Christian or even a sound atheist, but just a creature dithering to and fro, with its beliefs really dependent on the weather and the state of its digestion. Consequently one must train the habit of Faith.

The first step is to recognize the fact that your moods change. The next step is to make sure that, if you have once accepted Christianity, then some of its main doc-trines shall be deliberately held before your mind for some time every day. That is why daily prayers and religious readings and churchgoing are necessary parts of the Christian life. We have to be continually reminded of what we believe. Neither this belief nor any other will automatically remain alive in the mind. It must be fed. And as a matter of fact, if you examined a hundred people who had lost their faith in Christianity, I wonder how many of them would turn out to have been reasoned out of it by honest argument? Do not most people simply drift away?

Christ – the Only Complete Realist MARCH 18

No man knows how bad he is till he has tried very hard to be good. A silly idea is cur-rent that good people do not know what temptation means. This is an obvious lie. Only those who try to resist temptation know how strong it is. After all, you find out the strength of the German army by fighting it, not by giving in. You find out the strength of a wind by trying to walk against it, not by lying down. A man who gives in to temptation after five minutes simply does not know what it would have been like an hour later. That is why bad people, in one sense, know very little about badness.

They have lived a sheltered life by always giving in. We never find out the strength of the evil impulse inside us until we try to fight it: and Christ, because He was the only man who never yielded to temptation, is also the only man who knows to the full what temptation means – the only complete realist.

St Joseph, Husband of the Blessed Virgin Mary   MARCH 19

You will hear people say, 'The early Christians believed that Christ was the son of a virgin, but we know that this is a scientific impossibility.' Such people seem to have an idea that belief in miracles arose at a period when men were so ignorant of the course of nature that they did not perceive a miracle to be contrary to it. A moment's thought shows this to be nonsense: and the story of the Virgin Birth is a particularly striking example. When St Joseph discovered that his fiancée was going to have a baby, he not unnaturally decided to repudiate her. Why? Because he knew just as well as any modern gynaecologist that in the ordinary course of nature women do not have babies unless they have lain with men. No doubt the modern gynaecologist knows several things about birth and begetting which St Joseph did not know. But those things do not concern the main point – that a virgin birth is contrary to the course of nature. And St Joseph obviously knew *that*. In any sense in which it is true to say now, 'The thing is scientifically impossible', he would have said the same: the thing always was, and was always known to be, impossible *unless* the regular processes of nature were, in this particular case, being overruled or supplemented by something from beyond nature. When St Joseph finally accepted the view that his fiancée's pregnancy was due not to unchastity but to a miracle, he accepted the miracle as something contrary to the known order of nature. All records of miracles teach the same thing. . . . If they were not known to be contrary to the laws of nature how could they suggest the presence of the supernatural? How could they be surprising unless they were seen to be exceptions to the rule? . . . Nothing can seem extraordinary until you have discovered what is ordinary.

Hope   MARCH 20

We must not be troubled by unbelievers when they say that this promise of reward makes the Christian life a mercenary affair. There are different kinds of reward. There is the reward which has no natural connection with the things you do to earn it, and is quite foreign to the desires that ought to accompany those things. Money is not the natural reward of love; that is why we call a man mercenary if he marries a woman for the sake of her money. But marriage is the proper reward for a real lover, and he is not mercenary for desiring it. A general who fights well in order to get a peerage is mercenary; a general who fights for victory is not, victory being the proper reward of battle as marriage is the proper reward of love. The proper rewards are not simply tacked on to the activity for which they are given, but are the activity itself in consummation. There is also a third case, which is more complicated. An enjoyment of Greek poetry is certainly a proper, and not a mercenary, reward for learning Greek; but only those who have reached the stage of enjoying Greek poetry can tell from their own experience that this is so. The schoolboy beginning Greek grammar cannot look forward to his adult enjoyment of Sophocles as a lover looks forward to marriage or a general to victory . . . . But it is just in so far as he approaches the reward that he becomes able to desire it for its own sake; indeed, the power of so desiring it is itself a preliminary reward.

The Christian, in relation to Heaven, is in much the same position as this schoolboy. Those who have attained everlasting life in the vision of God doubtless know very well that it is no mere bribe, but the very consummation of their earthly discipleship; but we who have not yet attained it cannot know this in the same way, and cannot even begin to know it at all except by continuing to obey and finding the first reward of our obedience in our increasing power to desire the ultimate reward. Just in proportion as the desire grows, our fear lest it should be a mercenary desire will die away and finally be recognized as an absurdity. But probably this will not, for most of us, happen in a day; poetry replaces grammar, Gospel replaces Law, longing transforms obedience, as gradually as the tide lifts a grounded ship.

Loving and Liking   MARCH 21

Try to understand exactly what loving your neighbour as yourself means. I have to love him as I love myself. Well, how exactly do I love myself? Now that I come to think of it, I have not exactly got a feeling of fondness or affection for myself, and I do not even always enjoy my own society. So apparently 'Love your neighbour' does not mean 'feel fond of him' or 'find him attractive'. I ought to have seen that before, because, of course, you cannot feel fond of a person by trying. Do I think well of myself, think myself a nice chap? Well, I am afraid I sometimes do . . . but that is not why I love myself. So loving my enemies does not apparently mean thinking them nice either. That is an enormous relief. For a good many people imagine that forgiving your enemies means making out that they are really not such bad fellows after all, when it is quite plain that they are. Go a step further. In my most clearsighted moments not only do I not think myself a nice man, but I know that I am a very nasty one. I can look at some of the things I have done with horror and loathing. So apparently I am allowed to loathe and hate some of the things my enemies do. Now that I come to think of it, I remember Christian teachers telling me long ago that I must hate a bad man's actions, but not hate the bad man: or, as they would say, hate the sin but not the sinner.

Charity   MARCH 22

Though natural likings should normally be encouraged, it would be quite wrong to think that the way to become charitable is to sit trying to manufacture affectionate feelings. Some people are 'cold' by temperament; that may be a misfortune for them, but it is no more a sin than having a bad digestion is a sin; and it does not cut them out from the chance, or excuse them from the duty, of learning charity. The rule for all of us is perfectly simple. Do not waste time bothering whether you 'love' your neighbour; act as if you did. As soon as we do this we find one of the great secrets. When you are behaving as if you loved someone, you will presently come to love him. If you injure someone you dislike, you will find yourself disliking him more. If you do him a good turn, you will find yourself disliking him less. There is, indeed, one exception. If you do him a good turn, not to please God and obey the law of charity, but to show him what a fine forgiving chap you are, and to put him in your debt, and then sit down to wait for his 'gratitude', you will probably be disappointed. (People are not fools: they have a very quick eye for anything like showing off, or patronage.) But whenever we do good to another self, just because it is a self, made (like us) by God, and desiring its own happiness as we desire ours, we shall have learned to love it a little more or, at least, to dislike it less. . . .

Some writers use the word charity to describe not only Christian love between human beings, but also God's love for man and man's love for God. About the second of these two, people are often worried. They are told they ought to love God. They cannot find any such feeling in themselves. What are they to do? The answer is the same as before. Act as if you did. Do not sit trying to manufacture feelings. Ask yourself, 'If I were sure that I loved God, what would I do?' When you have found the answer, go and do it.

Faith or Good Works? MARCH 23

Christians have often disputed as to whether what leads the Christian home is good actions, or Faith in Christ. I have no right really to speak on such a difficult question, but it does seem to me like asking which blade in a pair of scissors is most necessary. A serious moral effort is the only thing that will bring you to the point where you throw up the sponge. Faith in Christ is the only thing to save you from despair at that point: and out of that Faith in Him good actions must inevitably come. There are two parodies of the truth which different sets of Christians have, in the past, been accused by other Christians of believing: perhaps they may make the truth clearer. One set were accused of saying, 'Good actions are all that matters. The best good action is charity. The best kind of charity is giving money. The best thing to give money to is the Church. So hand us over £10,000 and we will see you through.' The answer to that nonsense, of course, would be that good actions done for that motive, done with the idea that Heaven can be bought, would not be good actions at all, but only commercial speculations. The other set were accused of saying, 'Faith is all that matters. Consequently, if you have faith, it doesn't matter what you do. Sin away, my lad, and have a good time and Christ will see that it makes no difference in the end.' The answer to that nonsense is that, if what you call your 'faith' in Christ does not invoke taking the slightest notice of what He says, then it is not Faith at all – not faith or truth in Him, but only intellectual acceptance of some theory about Him.

Faith and Good Works are Inseparable MARCH 24

The Bible really seems to clinch the matter when it puts the two things together into one amazing sentence. The first half is, 'Work out your own salvation with fear and trembling' – which looks as if everything depended on us and our good actions: but the second half goes on, 'For it is God who worketh in you' – which looks as if God did everything and we did nothing. I am afraid that is the sort of thing we come up against in Christianity. I am puzzled, but I am not surprised. You see, we are now trying to understand, and to separate into watertight compartments, what exactly God does and what man does when God and man are working together. And, of course, we begin by thinking it is like two men working together, so that you could say, 'He did this bit and I did that.' But this way of thinking breaks down. God is not like that. He is inside you as well as outside: even if we could understand who did what, I do not think human language could properly express it. In the attempt to express it different churches say different things. But you will find that even those who insist most strongly on the importance of good actions tell you you need Faith; and even those who insist most strongly on Faith tell you to do good actions. At any rate that is as far as I go.

The Annunciation of the Lord   MARCH 25

The resemblance between the *Magnificat* and traditional Hebrew poetry . . . is not mere literary curiosity. There is, of course, a difference. There are no cursings here, no hatred, no self-righteousness. Instead, there is mere statement. He has scattered the proud, cast down the mighty, sent the rich empty away. I spoke . . . of the ironic contrast between the fierce psalmists and the choirboy's treble. The contrast is here brought up to a higher level. Once more we have the treble voice, a girl's voice, announcing without sin that the sinful prayers of her ancestors do not remain entirely unheard; and doing this, not indeed with fierce exultation, yet — who can mistake the tone? — in a calm and terrible gladness . . . .

Christians are unhappily divided about the kind of honour in which the Mother of the Lord should be held, but there is one truth about which no doubt seems admissible. If we believe in the Virgin Birth and if we believe in Our Lord's human nature, psychological as well as physical (for it is heretical to think Him a human body which had the Second Person of the Trinity *instead of* a human soul) we must also believe in a human heredity for that human nature. There is only one source for it (though in that source all the true Israel is summed up). If there is an iron element in Jesus may we not without irreverence guess whence, humanly speaking, it came? Did neighbours say, in His boyhood, 'He's His Mother's Son'? This might set in a new and less painful light the severity of some things He said to, or about His Mother. We may suppose that she understood them very well.

The Leap of Faith and Mother Kirk   MARCH 26

'I have come to give myself up', he said.

'It is well', said Mother Kirk. 'You have come a long way round to reach this place, whither I would have carried you in a few moments. But it is very well.'

'What must I do?' said John.

'You must take off your rags,' said she, 'as your friend has done already, and then you must dive into this water.'

'Alas,' said he, 'I have never learned to dive.'

'There is nothing to learn', said she. 'The art of diving is not to do anything new but simply to cease doing something. You have only to let yourself go.'

Chastity

Chastity is the most unpopular of the Christian virtues. There is no getting away from it: the old Christian rule is, 'Either marriage, with complete faithfulness to your partner, or else total abstinence.' Now this is so difficult and so contrary to our instincts, that obviously either Christianity is wrong or our sexual instinct, as it now is, has gone wrong. One or the other. Of course, being a Christian, I think it is the instinct which has gone wrong.

But I have other reasons for thinking so. The biological purpose of sex is children, just as the biological purpose of eating is to repair the body. Now if we eat whenever we feel inclined and just as much as we want, it is quite true that most of us will eat too much: but not terrifically too much. One man may eat enough for two, but he does not eat enough for ten. The appetite goes a little beyond its biological purpose, but not enormously. But if a healthy young man indulged his sexual appetite whenever he felt inclined, and if each act produced a baby, then in ten years he might easily populate a small village. This appetite is in ludicrous and preposterous excess of its function.

Or take it another way. You can get a large audience together for a striptease act – that is, to watch a girl undress on the stage. Now suppose you came to a country where you could fill a theatre by simply bringing a covered plate on to the stage and then slowly lifting the cover so as to let everyone see, just before the lights went out, that it contained a mutton chop or a bit of bacon, would you not think that in that country something had gone wrong with the appetite for food? And would not anyone who had grown up in a different world think there was something equally queer about the state of the sex instinct among us?

Sexual Morality

They tell you sex has become a mess because it was hushed up. But for the last twenty years it has not been hushed up. It has been chattered about all day long. Yet it is still in a mess. If hushing up had been the cause of the trouble, ventilation would have set it right. But it has not. I think it is the other way round. I think the human race orig-inally hushed it up because it had become such a mess. Modern people are always saying, 'Sex is nothing to be ashamed of.' They may mean two things. They may mean 'There is nothing to be ashamed of in the fact that the human race reproduces itself in a certain way, nor in the fact that it gives pleasure.' If they mean that, they are right. Christianity says the same. It is not the thing, nor the pleasure, that is the trouble. The old Christian teachers said that if man had never fallen, sexual pleasure, instead of being less than it is now, would actually have been greater. I know some muddle-headed Christians have talked as if Christianity thought that sex, or the body, or pleasure, were bad in themselves. But they were wrong. Christianity is almost the only one of the great religions which thoroughly approves of the body — which believes that matter is good, that God Himself once took on a human body, that some kind of body is going to be given to us even in Heaven and is going to be an essential part of our happiness, our beauty, and our energy. Christianity has glorified marriage more than any other religion: and nearly all the greatest love poetry in the world has been produced by Christians. If anyone says that sex, in itself, is bad, Christianity contradicts him at once. But, of course, when people say, 'Sex is nothing to be ashamed of', they may mean 'the state into which the sexual instinct has now got is nothing to be ashamed of'. . . .

I think it is everything to be ashamed of. There is nothing to be ashamed of in en-joying your food: there would be everything to be ashamed of if half the world made food the main interest of their lives. . . . There are people who want to keep our sex instinct inflamed in order to make money out of us. Because, of course, a man with an obsession is a man who has very little sales resistance.

Screwtape Explains Hell's View of Pleasures   MARCH 29

Never forget that when we are dealing with any pleasure in its healthy and normal and satisfying form, we are, in a sense, on the Enemy's ground. I know we have won many a soul through pleasure. All the same, it is His invention, not ours. He made the pleasures: all our research so far has not enabled us to produce one. All we can do is to encourage the humans to take the pleasures which our Enemy has produced, at times, or in ways, or in degrees, which He has forbidden. Hence we always try to work away from the natural condition of any pleasure to that in which it is least nat-ural, least redolent of its Maker, and least pleasurable. An ever-increasing craving for an ever-diminishing pleasure is the formula. It is more certain; and it's better *style*. To get the man's soul and give him *nothing* in return — that is what really glad-dens our Father's heart.

The Great Lie about Sex   MARCH 30

Our warped natures, the devils who tempt us, and all the contemporary propaganda
for lust, combine to make us feel that the desires we are resisting are so 'natural', so
'healthy', and so reasonable, that it is almost perverse and abnormal to resist them.
Poster after poster, film after film, novel after novel, associate the idea of sexual indulgence with the ideas of health, normality, youth, frankness, and good humour.
Now this association is a lie. Like all powerful lies, it is based on a truth – the truth
. . . that sex in itself (apart from the excesses and obsessions that have grown round it)
is 'normal' and 'healthy', and all the rest of it. The lie consists in the suggestion that
any sexual act to which you are tempted at the moment is also healthy and normal.
Now this, on any conceivable view, and quite apart from Christianity, must be nonsense. Surrender to all our desires obviously leads to impotence, disease, jealousies,
lies, concealment, and everything that is the reverse of health, good humour, and
frankness. For any happiness, even in this world, quite a lot of restraint is going to be
necessary; so the claim made by every desire, when it is strong, to be healthy and
reasonable, counts for nothing. Every sane and civilzed man must have some set of
principles by which he chooses to reject some of his desires and to permit others.
One man does this on Christian principles, another on hygienic principles, another
on sociological principles. The real conflict is not between Christianity and 'nature',
but between Christian principles and other principles in the control of 'nature'. For
'nature' (in the sense of natural desire) will have to be controlled anyway, unless you
are going to ruin your whole life.

The Animal Self and the Diabolical Self   MARCH 31

People often misunderstand what psychology teaches about 'repressions'. It teaches
us that 'repressed' sex is dangerous. But 'repressed' is here a technical term: it does
not mean 'suppressed' in the sense of 'denied' or 'resisted'. A repressed desire or
thought is one which has been thrust into the subconscious (usually at a very early
age) and can now come before the mind only in a disguised and unrecognizable form.
Repressed sexuality does not appear to the patient to be sexuality at all. When an
adolescent or an adult is engaged in resisting a conscious desire, he is not dealing
with a repression nor is he in the least danger of creating a repression. On the contrary, those who are seriously attempting chastity are more conscious, and soon
know a great deal more about their own sexuality than anyone else. They come to
know their desires as Wellington knew Napoleon, or as Sherlock Holmes knew Mor-
iarty; as a ratcatcher knows rats or a plumber knows about leaky pipes. Virtue – even
attempted virtue – brings light: indulgence brings fog.

Finally, though I have had to speak at some length about sex, I want to make it as clear as I possibly can that the centre of Christian morality is not here. If anyone thinks that Christians regard unchastity as the supreme vice, he is quite wrong. The sins of the flesh are bad, but they are the least bad of all sins. All the worst pleasures are purely spiritual: the pleasure of putting other people in the wrong, of bossing and patronizing and spoiling sport, and backbiting; the pleasures of power, of hatred. For there are two things inside me, competing with the human self which I must try to become. They are the Animal self, and the Diabolical self. The Diabolical self is the worse of the two. That is why a cold, self-righteous prig who goes regularly to church may be far nearer to hell than a prostitute. But, of course, it is better to be neither.

Pride   APRIL 1

According to Christian teachers, the essential vice, the utmost evil, is Pride. Unchastity, anger, greed, drunkenness, and all that, are mere fleabites in comparison: it was through Pride that the devil became the devil: Pride leads to every other vice: it is the complete anti-God state of mind....If you want to find out how proud you are the easiest way is to ask yourself, 'How much do I dislike it when other people snub me, or refuse to take any notice of me, or shove their oar in, or patronize me, or show off?' The point is that each person's pride is in competition with everyone else's pride. It is because I wanted to be the big noise at the party that I am so annoyed at someone else being the big noise. Two of a trade never agree. Now what you want to get clear is that Pride is *essentially* competitive – is competitive by its very nature – while the other vices are competitive only, so to speak, by accident. Pride gets no pleasure out of having something, only out of having more of it than the next man. We say that people are proud of being rich, or clever, or good-looking, but they are not. They are proud of being richer, or cleverer, or better-looking than others. If everyone else became equally rich, or clever, or good-looking there would be nothing to be proud about. It is the comparison that makes you proud: the pleasure of being above the rest. Once the element of competition has gone, pride has gone. That is why I say that Pride is essentially competitive in a way that the other vices are not.

The Chief Cause of Misery APRIL 2

It is Pride which has been the chief cause of misery in every nation and every family since the world began. Other vices may sometimes bring people together: you may find good fellowship and jokes and friendliness among drunken people or unchaste people. But Pride always means enmity – it *is* enmity. And not only enmity between man and man, but enmity to God.

In God you come up against something which is in every respect immeasurably superior to yourself. Unless you know God as that – and, therefore, know yourself as nothing in comparison – you do not know God. A proud man is always looking down on things and people: and, of course, as long as you are looking down, you cannot see something that is above you.

That raises a terrible question. How is it that people who are quite obviously eaten up with Pride can say they believe in God and appear to themselves very religious? I am afraid it means they are worshipping an imaginary God. They theoretically admit themselves to be nothing in the presence of this phantom God, but are really all the time imagining how He approves of them and thinks them far better than ordinary people: that is, they pay a pennyworth of imaginary humility to Him and get out of it a pound's worth of Pride towards their fellow men. I suppose it was of those people Christ was thinking when He said that some would preach about Him and cast out devils in His name, only to be told at the end of the world that He had never known them. And any of us may at any moment be in this deathtrap. Luckily, we have a test. Whenever we find that our religious life is making us feel that we are good – above all, that we are better than someone else – I think we may be sure that we are being acted on, not by God, but by the devil. The real test of being in the presence of God is that you either forget about yourself altogether or see yourself as a small, dirty object. It is better to forget about yourself altogether.

Direct from Hell APRIL 3

It is a terrible thing that the worst of all the vices can smuggle itself into the very centre of our religious life. But you can see why. The other, and less bad, vices come from the devil working on us through our animal nature. But this does not come through our animal nature at all. It comes direct from Hell. It is purely spiritual: consequently, it is far more subtle and deadly. For the same reason, Pride can often be used to beat down the simpler vices. Teachers, in fact, often appeal to a boy's Pride, or, as they call it, his self-respect, to make him behave decently: many a man has overcome cowardice, or lust, or ill-temper by learning to think that they are beneath his dignity — that is, by Pride. The devil laughs. He is perfectly content to see you become chaste and brave and self-controlled provided, all the time, he is setting up in you the Dictatorship of Pride — just as he would be quite content to see your chilblains cured if he was allowed, in return, to give you cancer. For Pride is spiritual cancer: it eats up the very possibility of love, or contentment, or even common sense.

The Difference between Pride and Vanity   APRIL 4

Pleasure in being praised is not Pride. The child who is patted on the back for doing a lesson well, the woman whose beauty is praised by her lover, the saved soul to whom Christ says 'Well done', are pleased and ought to be. For here the pleasure lies not in what you are but in the fact that you have pleased someone you wanted (and rightly wanted) to please. The trouble begins when you pass from thinking, 'I have pleased him; all is well', to thinking, 'What a fine person I must be to have done it.' The more you delight in yourself and the less you delight in the praise, the worse you are becoming. When you delight wholly in yourself and do not care about the praise at all, you have reached the bottom. That is why vanity, though it is the sort of Pride which shows most on the surface, is really the least bad and most pardonable sort. The vain person wants praise, applause, admiration, too much and is always angling for it. It is a fault, but a childlike and even (in an odd way) a humble fault. It shows that you are not yet completely contented with your own admiration. You value other people enough to want them to look at you. You are, in fact, still human. The real black, diabolical Pride comes when you look down on others so much that you do not care what they think of you.

Our Share in the Passion of Christ   APRIL 5

Some people feel guilty about their anxieties and regard them as a defect of faith. I don't agree at all. They are afflictions, not sins. Like all afflictions, they are, if we can so take them, our share in the Passion of Christ. For the beginning of the Passion — the first move, so to speak — is in Gethsemane. In Gethsemane a very strange and significant thing seems to have happened.

It is clear from many of His sayings that Our Lord had long foreseen His death. He knew what conduct such as His, in a world such as we have made of this, must inevitably lead to. But it is clear that this knowledge must somehow have been withdrawn from Him before he prayed in Gethsemane. He could not, with whatever reservation about the Father's will, have prayed that the cup might pass and simultaneously known that it would not. That is both a logical and a psychological impossibility. You see what this involves? Lest any trial incident to humanity should be lacking, the torments of hope — of suspense, anxiety — were at the last moment loosed upon Him — the supposed possibility that, after all, He might, He just conceivably might, be spared the supreme horror. There was precedent. Isaac had been spared: he too at the last moment, he also against all apparent probability. It was not quite impossible ...and doubtless He had seen other men crucified...a sight very unlike most of our religious pictures and images.

But for this last (and erroneous) hope against hope, and the consequent tumult of the soul, the sweat of blood, perhaps He would not have been very Man. To live in a fully predictable world is not to be a man.

At the end, I know, we are told that an angel appeared 'comforting' Him.... 'Strengthening' is more the word. May not the strengthening have consisted in the renewed certainty — cold comfort this — that the thing must be endured and therefore could be?

Christ Suffering for His World APRIL 6

Does not every movement in the Passion write large some common element in the sufferings of our race? First, the prayer of anguish; not granted. Then He turns to His friends. They are asleep — as ours, or we, are so often, or busy, or away, or preoccupied. Then He faces the Church; the very Church that He brought into existence. It condemns Him. This also is characteristic. In every Church, in every institution, there is something which sooner or later works against the very purpose for which it came into existence. But there seems to be another chance. There is the State; in this case, the Roman state. Its pretensions are far lower than those of the Jewish church, but for that very reason it may be free from local fanaticisms. It claims to be just on a rough, worldly level. Yes, but only so far as it is consistent with political expediency and *raison d'état*. One becomes a counter in a complicated game. But even now all is not lost. There is still an appeal to the People — the poor and simple whom He had blessed, whom He had healed and fed and taught, to whom He Himself belongs. But they have become overnight (it is nothing unusual) a murderous rabble shouting for His blood. There is, then, nothing left but God. And to God, God's last words are 'Why hast thou forsaken me?'

You see how characteristic, how representative, it all is. The human situation writ large. These are among the things it means to be a man. Every rope breaks when you seize it. Every door is slammed shut as you reach it. To be like the fox at the end of the run; the earths all staked.

The 'Hiddenness' of God   APRIL 7

As for the last dereliction of all, how can we either understand or endure it? Is it that God Himself cannot be Man unless God seems to vanish at His greatest need? And if so, why? I sometimes wonder if we have ever begun to understand what is involved in the very concept of creation. If God will create, He will make something to be, and yet to be not Himself. To be created is, in some sense, to be ejected or separated. Can it be that the more perfect the creature is, the further this separation must at some point be pushed? It is saints, not common people, who experience the 'dark night'. It is men and angels, not beasts, who rebel. Inanimate matter sleeps in the bosom of the Father. The 'hiddenness' of God perhaps presses most painfully on those who are in another way nearest to Him, and therefore God Himself, made man, will of all men be by God most forsaken? One of the seventeenth-century divines says, 'By pretending to be visible God could only deceive the world.' Perhaps He does pretend just a little to simple souls who need a full measure of 'sensible consolation'. Not deceiving them, but tempering the wind to the shorn lamb. Of course I'm not saying like Niebuhr that evil is inherent in finitude. That would identify the creation with the fall and make God the author of evil. But perhaps there is an anguish, an alienation, a crucifixion involved in the creative act. Yet He who alone can judge judges the far-off consummation to be worth it.

Miracles   APRIL 8

I have known only one person in my life who claimed to have seen a ghost. It was a woman; and the interesting thing is that she disbelieved in the immortality of the soul before seeing the ghost and still disbelieves after having seen it. She thinks it was a hallucination. In other words, seeing is not believing. This is the first thing to get clear in talking about miracles. Whatever experiences we may have, we shall not regard them as miraculous if we already hold a philosophy which excludes the supernatural. Any event which is claimed as a miracle is, in the last resort, an experience received from the senses; and the senses are not infallible. We can always say we have been the victims of an illusion; if we disbelieve in the supernatural this is what we always shall say. Hence, whether miracles have really ceased or not, they would certainly appear to cease in Western Europe as materialism became the popular creed. For let us make no mistake. If the end of the world appeared in all the literal trappings of the Apocalypse, if the modern materialist saw with his own eyes the heavens rolled up and the great white throne appearing, if he had the sensation of being himself hurled into the Lake of Fire, he would continue forever, in that lake itself, to regard his experience as an illusion and to find the explanation of it in psychoanalysis, or cerebral pathology. Experience by itself proves nothing. If a man doubts whether he is dreaming or waking, no experiment can solve his doubt, since every experiment may itself be part of the dream. Experience proves this, or that, or nothing, according to the preconceptions we bring to it.

The Snag about Materialism APRIL 9

If the solar system was brought about by an accidental collision, then the appearance of organic life on this planet was also an accident, and the whole evolution of Man was an accident too. If so, then all our present thoughts are mere accidents — the accidental by-product of the movement of atoms. And this holds for the thoughts of the materialists and astronomers as well as for anyone else's. But if *their* thoughts — i.e. of materialism and astronomy — are merely accidental by-products, why should we believe them to be true? I see no reason for believing that one accident should be able to give me a correct account of all the other accidents. It's like expecting that the accidental shape taken by the splash when you upset a milkjug should give you a correct account of how the jug was made and why it was upset.

The Natural and the Supernatural APRIL 10

The experience of a miracle in fact requires two conditions. First we must believe in a normal stability of Nature, which means we must recognize that the data offered by our senses recur in regular patterns. Secondly, we must believe in some reality beyond Nature. When both beliefs are held, and not till then, we can approach with an open mind the various reports which claim that this super- or extra-natural reality has sometimes invaded and disturbed the sensuous content of space and time which makes our 'natural' world. The belief in such a supernatural reality itself can neither be proved nor disproved by experience. The arguments for its existence are metaphysical, and to me conclusive. They turn on the fact that even to think and act in the natural world we have to assume something beyond it and even assume that we partly belong to that something. In order to think we must claim for our own reasoning a validity which is not credible if our own thought is merely a function of our brain, and our brains a by-product of irrational physical processes. In order to act, above the level of mere impulse, we must claim a similar validity for our judgements of good and evil. In both cases we get the same disquieting result. The concept of Nature itself is one we have reached only tacitly by claiming a sort of *super*-natural status for ourselves.

The Miracles of Our Lord   APRIL 11

This is what St Athanasius says in his little book *On the Incarnation:* 'Our Lord took a body like ours and lived as a man in order that those who had refused to recognize Him in His superintendence and captaincy of the whole universe might come to recognize from the works He did here below in the body that what dwelled in this body was the Word of God.' This accords exactly with Christ's account of His miracles: 'The Son can do nothing of Himself, but what He seeth the Father do.' The doctrine, as I understand it, is something like this:

There is an activity of God displayed throughout creation, a wholesale activity let us say which men refuse to recognize. The miracles done by God incarnate, living as a man in Palestine, perform the very same things as this wholesale activity, but at a different speed and on a smaller scale. One of their chief purposes is that men, having seen a thing done by personal power on the small scale, may recognize, when they see the same thing done on the larger scale, that the power behind it is also personal — is indeed the very same person who lived among us two thousand years ago. The miracles in fact are a retelling in small letters of the very same story which is written across the whole world in letters too large for some of us to see. Of that larger script part is already visible, part is still unsolved. In other words, some of the miracles do locally what God has already done universally: others do locally what He has not yet done, but will do. In that sense, and from our human point of view, some are reminders and others prophecies.

The Miracle at Cana   APRIL 12

Firstly to Miracles of *Fertility.* The earliest of these was the conversion of water into wine at the wedding feast in Cana. This miracle proclaims that the God of all wine is present. The vine is one of the blessings sent by Jahweh: He is the reality behind the false god Bacchus. Every year, as part of the Natural order, God makes wine. He does so by creating a vegetable organism that can turn water, soil, and sunlight into a juice which will, under proper conditions, become wine. Thus, in a certain sense, He constantly turns water into wine, for wine, like all drinks, is but water modified. Once, and in one year only, God, now incarnate, short-circuits the process: makes wine in a moment: uses earthenware jars instead of vegetable fibres to hold the water. But uses them to do what He is always doing. The Miracle consists in the short cut; but the event to which it leads is the usual one. If the thing happened, then we know that what has come into Nature is no anti-Natural spirit, no God who loves tragedy and tears and fasting *for their own sake* (however He may permit or demand them for special purposes) but the God of Israel who has through all these centuries given us wine to gladden the heart of man.

The Miraculous Feedings   APRIL 13

Other miracles that fall in this class are the two instances of miraculous feeding. They involve the multiplication of a little bread and a little fish into much bread and much fish. Once in the desert Satan had tempted Him to make bread of stones: He refused the suggestion. 'The Son does nothing except what He sees the Father do'; perhaps one may without boldness surmise that the direct change from stone to bread appeared to the Son to be not quite in the hereditary style. Little bread into much bread is quite a different matter. Every year God makes a little corn into much corn: the seed is sown and there is an increase. And men say, according to their several fashions, 'It is the laws of Nature', or 'It is Ceres, it as Adonis, it is the Corn-King.' But the laws of Nature are only a pattern: nothing will come of them unless they can, so to speak, take over the universe as a going concern. And as for Adonis, no man can tell us where he died or when he rose again. Here, at the feeding of the five thousand, is He whom we have ignorantly worshipped: the *real* Corn-King who will die once and rise once at Jerusalem during the term of office of Pontius Pilate.

That same day He also multiplied fish. Look down into every bay and almost every river. This swarming, undulating fecundity shows He is still at work 'thronging the seas with spawn innumerable'. The ancients had a god called Genius; the god of animal and human fertility, the patron of gynaecology, embryology, and the marriage bed – the 'genial' bed as they called it after its god Genius. But Genius is only another mask for the God of Israel, for it was He who at the beginning commanded all species 'to be fruitful and multiply and replenish the earth'. And now, that day, at the feeding of the thousands, incarnate God does the same: does close and small, under His human hands, a workman's hands, what He has always been doing in the seas, the lakes and the little brooks.

The Miracles of Healing   APRIL 14

Without deciding in detail which of the healings must (apart from acceptance of the Christian faith) be regarded as miraculous, we can however indicate the kind of miracle involved. Its character can easily be obscured by the somewhat magical view which many people still take of ordinary and medical healing. There is a sense in which no doctor ever heals. The doctors themselves would be the first to admit this. The magic is not in the medicine but in the patient's body — in the *vis medicatrix naturae,* the recuperative or self-corrective energy of Nature. What the treatment does is to stimulate Natural functions or to remove what hinders them. We speak for convenience of the doctor, or the dressing, healing a cut. But in another sense every cut heals itself: no cut can be healed in a corpse. The same mysterious force which we call gravitational when it steers the planets and biochemical when it heals a live body, is the efficient cause of all recoveries. And that energy proceeds from God in the first instance. All who are cured are cured by Him, not merely in the sense that His providence provides them with medical assistance and wholesome environments, but also in the sense that their very tissues are repaired by the far-descending energy which, flowing from Him, energizes the whole system of Nature. But once He did it visibly to the sick in Palestine, a Man meeting with men. What in its general operations we refer to laws of Nature or once referred to Apollo or Aesculapius thus reveals itself. The Power that always was behind all healings puts on a face and hands. Hence, of course, the apparent chanciness of the miracles. It is idle to complain that He heals those whom He happens to meet, not those whom He doesn't. To be a man means to be in one place and not in another. The world which would not know Him as present everywhere was saved by His becoming *local.*

The Miracle of Destruction   APRIL 15

Christ's single miracle of Destruction, the withering of the figtree, has proved troublesome to some people, but I think its significance is plain enough. The miracle is an acted parable, a symbol of God's sentence on all that is 'fruitless' and specially, no doubt, on the official Judaism of that age. That is its moral significance. As a miracle, it again does in focus, repeats small and close, what God does constantly and throughout Nature.... God, twisting Satan's weapon out of his hand, had become, since the Fall, the God even of human death. But much more, and perhaps ever since the creation, He has been the God of the death of organisms. In both cases, though in somewhat different ways, He is the God of death because He is the God of Life: the God of human death because through it increase of life now comes — the God of merely organic death because death is part of the very mode by which organic life spreads itself out in Time and yet remains new. A forest a thousand years deep is still collectively alive because some trees are dying and others are growing up. His human face, turned with negation in its eyes upon that one figtree, did once what His unincarnate action does to all trees. No tree died that year in Palestine, or any year anywhere, except because God did — or rather ceased to do — something to it.

What the Apostles Meant by the Resurrection

When modern writers talk of the Resurrection they usually mean one particular moment – the discovery of the Empty Tomb and the appearance of Jesus a few yards away from it. The story of that moment is what Christian apologists now chiefly try to support and sceptics chiefly try to impugn. But this almost exclusive concentration on the first five minutes or so of the Resurrection would have astonished the earliest Christian teachers. In claiming to have seen the Resurrection they were not necessarily claiming to have seen *that*. Some of them had, some of them had not. It had no more importance than any of the other appearances of the risen Jesus – apart from the poetic and dramatic importance which the beginnings of things must always have. What they were claiming was that they had all, at one time or another, met Jesus during the six or seven weeks that followed His death. Sometimes they seem to have been alone when they did so, but on one occasion twelve of them saw Him together, and on another occasion about five hundred of them. St Paul says that the majority of the five hundred were still alive when he wrote the *First Letter to the Corinthians,* i.e. in about A.D. 55.

The 'Resurrection' to which they bore witness was, in fact, not the action of rising from the dead but the state of having risen; a state, as they held, attested by intermittent meetings during a limited period.... This termination of the period is important, for, as we shall see, there is no possibility of isolating the doctrine of the Resurrection from that of the Ascension.

Christ's Triumph Over Death

The next point to notice is that the Resurrection was not regarded simply or chiefly as evidence for the immortality of the soul. It is, of course, often so regarded today: I have heard a man maintain that 'the importance of the Resurrection is that it proves *survival*. Such a view cannot at any point be reconciled with the language of the New Testament. On such a view Christ would simply have done what all men do when they die: the only novelty would have been that in His case we were allowed to see it happening. But there is not in Scripture the faintest suggestion that the Resurrection was new evidence for something that had *in fact* been always happening. The New Testament writers speak as if Christ's achievement in rising from the dead was the first event of its kind in the whole history of the universe. He is the 'first fruits', the 'pioneer of life'. He has forced open a door that has been locked since the death of the first man. He has met, fought, and beaten the King of Death. Everything is different because He has done so. This is the beginning of the New Creation: a new chapter in cosmic history has opened.

The Resurrection and 'Survival'   APRIL 18

I do not mean, of course, that the writers of the New Testament disbelieved in 'survival'. On the contrary they believed in it so readily that Jesus on more than one occasion had to assure them that He was not a ghost. From the earliest times the Jews, like many other nations, had believed that man possessed a 'soul' or *Nephesh* separable from the body, which went at death into the shadowy world called *Sheol*: a land of forgetfulness and imbecility where none called upon Jehovah any more, a land half unreal and melancholy like the Hades of the Greeks or the Niflheim of the Norsemen. From it shades could return and appear to the living, as Samuel's shade had done at the command of the Witch of Endor. In much more recent times there had arisen a more cheerful belief that the righteous passed at death to 'heaven'. Both doctrines are doctrines of 'the immortality of the soul' as a Greek or a modern Englishman understands it: and both are quite irrelevant to the story of the Resurrection. The writers look upon this event as an absolute novelty. Quite clearly they do not think they have been haunted by a ghost from Sheol, nor even that they have had a vision of a 'soul' in 'heaven'. It must be clearly understood that if the Psychical Researchers succeeded in proving 'survival' and showed that the Resurrection was an instance of it, they would not be supporting the Christian faith but refuting it. If that were all that had happened the original 'Gospel' would have been untrue.

Spiritualism and Psychical Research   APRIL 19

It seems to me that both beliefs, unless reinforced by something else, will be to modern man very shadowy and inoperative. If indeed we knew that God were righteous, that He had purposes for us, that He was the leader in a cosmic battle and that some real issue hung on our conduct in the field, then it would be something to the purpose. Or if, again, the utterances which purport to come from the other world ever had the accent which really *suggests* another world, ever spoke (as even the inferior actual religions do) with that voice before which our mortal nature trembles with awe or joy, then that also would be to the purpose. But the god of minimal Theism remains powerless to excite either fear or love . . . . As for the utterances of the mediums

...I do not wish to be offensive. But will even the most convinced spiritualist claim that one sentence from that source has ever taken its place among the golden sayings of mankind, has ever approached (much less equalled) in power to elevate, strengthen or correct even the second rank of such sayings? Will anyone deny that the vast majority of spirit messages sink pitiably below the best that has been thought and said even in this world?

The Appearances of the Risen Lord   APRIL 20

There are, I allow, certain respects in which the risen Christ resembles the 'ghost' of popular tradition. Like a ghost He 'appears' and 'disappears': locked doors are no obstacle to Him. On the other hand He Himself vigorously asserts that He is corporeal (Luke 24:39–40) and eats boiled fish. It is at this point that the modern reader becomes uncomfortable. He becomes more uncomfortable still at the words, 'Don't touch me; I have not yet gone up to the Father' (John 20:17). For voices and apparitions we are, in some measure, prepared. But what is this that must not be touched? What is all this about going 'up' to the Father? Is He not already 'with the Father' in the only sense that matters? What can 'going up' be except a metaphor for *that*? And if so, why has He 'not yet' gone? These discomforts arise because the story the apostles actually had to tell begins at this point to conflict with the story we expect and are determined beforehand to read into their narrative.

We expect them to tell of a risen life which is purely 'spiritual' in the negative sense of that word: that is, we use the word 'spiritual' to mean not what it is but what it is not. We mean a life without space, without history, without environment, with no sensuous elements in it. We also, in our heart of hearts, tend to slur over the risen *manhood* of Jesus, to conceive Him, after death, simply returning into Deity, so that the Resurrection would be no more than the reversal or undoing of the Incarnation. That being so, all references to the risen *body* make us uneasy: they raise awkward questions.

The Risen Christ — No Hallucination   APRIL 21

As long as we hold the negatively spiritual view, we have not really been believing in that body at all. We have thought (whether we acknowledged it or not) that the body was not objective: that it was an appearance sent by God to assure the disciples of truths otherwise incommunicable. But what truths? If the truth is that after death there comes a negatively spiritual life, an eternity of mystical experience, what more misleading way of communicating it could possibly be found than the appearance of a human form which eats boiled fish? Again, on such a view, the body would really be a hallucination. And any theory of hallucination breaks down on the fact (and if it is invention it is the oddest invention that ever entered the mind of man) that on three separate occasions this hallucination was not immediately recognized as Jesus (Luke 24:13–31; John 20:15, 21:4). Even granting that God sent a holy hallucination to teach truths already widely believed without it, and far more easily taught by other methods, and certain to be completely obscured by this, might we not at least hope that He would get the face of the hallucination *right*? Is He who made all faces such a bungler that He cannot even work up a recognizable likeness of the Man who was Himself?

The Imperishable Body of the Risen Lord   APRIL 22

The records represent Christ as passing after death (as no man had passed before) neither into a purely, that is, negatively, 'spiritual' mode of existence nor into a 'natural' life such as we know, but into a life which has its own, new Nature. It represents Him as withdrawing six weeks later, into some different mode of existence. It says — He says — that He goes 'to prepare a place for us'. This presumably means that He is about to create that whole new Nature which will provide the environment or conditions for His glorified humanity and, in Him, for ours. The picture is not what we expected — though whether it is less or more probable and philosophical on that account is another question. It is not the picture of an escape from any and every kind of Nature into some unconditioned and utterly transcendent life. It is the picture of a new human nature, and a new Nature in general, being brought into existence. We must, indeed, believe the risen body to be extremely different from the mortal body: but the existence, in that new state, of anything that could in any sense be described as 'body' at all, involves some sort of spatial relations and in the long run a whole new universe. That is the picture — not of unmaking but of remaking. The old field of space, time, matter, and the senses is to be weeded, dug, and sown for a new crop. We may be tired of that old field: God is not.

St George, Patron of England APRIL 23

A serious attack on the fairy tale as children's literature comes from those who do not wish children to be frightened.... Those who say that children must not be frightened may mean two things. They may mean (1) that we must not do anything likely to give the child those haunting, disabling, pathological fears against which ordinary courage is helpless: in fact, *phobias*.... Or they may mean (2) that we must try to keep out of his mind the knowledge that he is born into a world of death, violence, wounds, adventure, heroism and cowardice, good and evil. If they mean the first I agree with them: but not if they mean the second. The second would indeed be to give children a false impression and feed them on escapism in the bad sense. There is something ludicrous in the idea of so educating a generation which is born to the Ogpu and the atomic bomb. Since it is so likely that they will meet cruel enemies, let them at least have heard of brave knights and heroic courage.... By confining your child to blameless stories of child life in which nothing at all alarming ever happens, you would fail to banish the terrors, and would succeed in banishing all that can ennoble them or make them endurable. For in the fairy tales, side by side with the terrible figures, we find the immemorial comforters and protectors, the radiant ones; and the terrible figures are not merely terrible, but sublime. It would be nice if no little boy in bed, hearing, or thinking he hears, a sound, were ever at all frightened. But if he is going to be frightened, I think it better that he should think of giants and dragons than merely of burglars. And I think St George, or any bright champion in armour, is a better comfort than the idea of the police.

And So We Shall Rise APRIL 24

The miracles that have already happened are, of course, as Scripture so often says, the first fruits of that cosmic summer which is presently coming on. Christ has risen, and so we shall rise. St Peter for a few seconds walked on the water; and the day will come when there will be a remade universe, infinitely obedient to the will of glorified and obedient men, when we can do all things, when we shall be those gods that we are described as being in Scripture. To be sure, it feels wintry enough still: but often in the very early spring it feels like that. Two thousand years are only a day or two by this scale. A man really ought to say, 'The Resurrection happened two thousand years ago' in the same spirit in which he says, 'I saw a crocus yesterday.' Because we know what is coming behind the crocus. The spring comes slowly down this way; but the great thing is that the corner has been turned. There is, of course, this difference, that in the natural spring the crocus cannot choose whether it will respond or not. We can. We have the power either of withstanding the spring, and sinking back into the cosmic winter, or of going on into those 'high mid-summer pomps' in which our Leader, the Son of Man, already dwells, and to which He is calling us. It remains with us to follow or not, to die in this winter, or to go on into that spring and that summer.

St Mark, Evangelist   APRIL 25

'Say what you like,' we shall be told, 'the apocalyptic beliefs of the first Christians have been proved to be false. It is clear from the New Testament that they all expected the Second Coming in their own lifetime. And, worse still, they had a reason, and one you will find very embarrassing. Their Master had told them so. He shared, and indeed created, their delusion. He said in so many words, "This generation shall not pass till all these things be done." And He was wrong. He clearly knew no more about the end of the world than anyone else.'

It is certainly the most embarrassing verse in the Bible. Yet how teasing, also, that within fourteen words of it should come the statement 'But of that day and that hour knoweth no man, no, not the angels which are in heaven, neither the Son, but the Father.' The one exhibition of error and the one confession of ignorance grow side by side. That they stood thus in the mouth of Jesus Himself, and were not merely placed thus by the reporter, we surely need not doubt. Unless the reporter were perfectly honest he would never have recorded the confession of ignorance at all; he could have had no motive for doing so except a desire to tell the whole truth. And unless later copyists were equally honest they would never have preserved the (apparently) mistaken prediction about 'this generation' after the passage of time had shown the (apparent) mistake. This passage (Mark 13:30-32) and the cry 'Why hast thou forsaken me?' (Mark 15:34) together make up the strongest proof that the New Testament is historically reliable. The evangelists have the first great characteristic of honest witnesses: they mention facts which are, at first sight, damaging to their main contention.

The Full Healing of an Old Disease   APRIL 26

Let us confess that probably every Christian now alive finds a difficulty in reconciling the two things he has been told about 'heaven' – that it is, on the one hand, a life in Christ, a vision of God, a ceaseless adoration, and that it is, on the other hand, a bodily life. When we seem nearest to the vision of God in this life, the body seems al-most an irrelevance. And if we try to conceive our eternal life as one in a body (any kind of body) we tend to find that some vague dream of Platonic paradises and gardens of the Hesperides has substituted itself for that mystical approach which we feel (and I think rightly) to be more important. But if that discrepancy were final then it would follow — which is absurd — that God was originally mistaken when He introduced our spirits into the Natural order at all. We must conclude that the discrepancy itself is precisely one of the disorders which the New Creation comes to heal. The fact that the body, and locality and locomotion and time, now feel irrelevant to the highest reaches of the spiritual life is . . . a *symptom*. Spirit and Nature have quarrelled in us; that is our disease.

Heaven and Sexuality   APRIL 27

The letter and spirit of Scripture, and of all Christianity, forbid us to suppose that life in the New Creation will be a sexual life; and this reduces our imagination to the withering alternative either of bodies which are hardly recognizable as human bodies at all or else of a perpetual fast. As regards the fast, I think our present outlook might be like that of a small boy who, on being told that the sexual act was the highest bodily pleasure, should immediately ask whether you ate chocolates at the same time. On receiving the answer 'No', he might regard absence of chocolates as the chief characteristic of sexuality. In vain would you tell him that the reason why lovers in their carnal raptures don't bother about chocolates is that they have something better to think of. The boy knows chocolate: he does not know the positive thing that excludes it. We are in the same position. We know the sexual life; we do not know, except in glimpses, the other thing which, in Heaven, will leave no room for it. Hence where fulness awaits us we anticipate fasting. In denying that sexual life, as we now understand it, makes any part of the final beatitude, it is not of course necessary to suppose that the distinction of sexes will disappear. What is no longer needed for biological purposes may be expected to serve for splendour. Sexuality is the instrument both of virginity and of conjugal virtue; neither men nor women will be asked to throw away weapons they have used victoriously. It is the beaten and the fugitives who throw away their swords. The conquerors sheathe theirs and retain them. 'Transsexual' would be a better word than 'sexless' for the heavenly life.

Will We be Bored *by Heaven?*   APRIL 28

Our notion of Heaven involves perpetual negations: no food, no drink, no sex, no movement, no mirth, no events, no time, no art. Against all these, to be sure, we set one positive: the vision and enjoyment of God. And since this is an infinite good, we hold (rightly) that it outweighs them all. That is, the reality of the Beatific Vision would or will outweigh, would infinitely outweigh, the reality of the negations. But can our present notion of it outweigh our present notion of them? That is quite a different question. And for most of us at most times the answer is No. How it may be for great saints and mystics I cannot tell. But for others the conception of that Vision is a difficult, precarious, and fugitive extrapolation from a very few and ambiguous moments in our earthly experience, while our idea of the negated natural goods is vivid and persistent, loaded with the memories of a lifetime, built into our nerves and muscles and therefore into our imaginations.

Thus the negatives have, so to speak, an unfair advantage in every competition with the positive. What is worse, their presence — and most when we most resolutely try to suppress or ignore them — vitiates even such a faint and ghostlike notion of the positive as we might have had. The exclusion of the lower goods begins to seem the essential characteristic of the higher good. We feel, if we do not say, that the vision of God will come not to fulfil but to destroy our nature; this bleak fantasy often underlies our very use of such words as 'holy' or 'pure' or 'spiritual'.

We must not allow this to happen if we can possibly prevent it. We must believe — and therefore in some degree imagine — that every negation will be only the reverse side of a fulfilling. And we must mean by that the fulfilling, precisely, of our humanity; not our transformation into angels nor our absorption into Deity. For though we shall be 'as the angels' and made 'like unto' our Master, I think this means 'like with the likeness proper to men': as different instruments that play the same air but each in its own fashion. How far the life of the risen man will be sensory, we do not know. But I surmise that it will differ from the sensory life we know here, not as emptiness differs from water or water from wine but as a flower differs from a bulb or a cathedral from an architect's drawing.

A Fable about a Very Likely Misconception   APRIL 29

Let us picture a woman thrown into a dungeon. There she bears and rears a son. He grows up seeing nothing but the dungeon walls, the straw on the floor, and a little patch of the sky seen through the grating, which is too high up to show anything except sky. This unfortunate woman was an artist, and when they imprisoned her she managed to bring with her a drawing pad and a box of pencils. As she never loses the hope of deliverance she is constantly teaching her son about that outer world which he has never seen. She does it very largely by drawing him pictures. With her pencil she attempts to show him what fields, rivers, mountains, cities and waves on a beach are like. He is a dutiful boy and he does his best to believe her when she tells him that that outer world is far more interesting and glorious than anything in the dungeon. At times he succeeds. On the whole he gets on tolerably well until, one day, he says something that gives his mother pause. For a minute or two they are at cross-purposes. Finally it dawns on her that he has, all these years, lived under a misconception. 'But', she gasps, 'you didn't think that the real world was full of lines drawn in lead pencil?' 'What?' says the boy. 'No pencil marks there?' And instantly his whole notion of the outer world becomes a blank. For the lines, by which alone he was imagining it, have now been denied of it. He has no idea of that which will exclude and dispense with the lines, that of which the lines were merely a transposition — the waving treetops, the light dancing on the weir, the coloured three-dimensional realities which are not enclosed in lines but define their own shapes at every moment with a delicacy and multiplicity which no drawing could ever achieve. The child will get the idea that the real world is somehow less visible than his mother's pictures. In reality it lacks lines because it is incomparably more visible.

So with us. 'We know now what we shall be'; but we may be sure we shall be more, not less, than we were on earth. Our natural experiences (sensory, emotional, imaginative) are only like the drawing, like pencilled lines on flat paper. If they vanish in the risen life, they will vanish only as pencil lines vanish from the real landscape; not as a candle flame that is put out but as a candle flame which becomes invisible because someone has pulled up the blind, thrown open the shutters, and let in the blaze of the risen sun.

A Gallop with the King APRIL 30

The thought at the back of all this negative spirituality is really one forbidden to Christians. They, of all men, must not conceive spiritual joy and worth as things that need to be rescued or tenderly protected from time and place and matter and the senses. Their God is the God of corn and oil and wine. He is the glad Creator. He has become Himself incarnate. The Sacraments have been instituted. Certain spiritual gifts are offered us only on condition that we perform certain bodily acts. After that we cannot really be in doubt of His intention. To shrink back from all that can be called Nature into negative spirituality is as if we ran away from horses instead of learning to ride. There is in our present pilgrim condition plenty of room (more room than most of us like) for abstinence and renunciation and mortifying our natural desires. But behind all asceticism the thought should be, 'Who will trust us with the true wealth if we cannot be trusted even with the wealth that perishes?' Who will trust me with a spiritual body if I cannot control even an earthly body? These small and perishable bodies we now have were given to us as ponies are given to schoolboys. We must learn to manage: not that we may some day be free of horses altogether but that some day we may ride bareback, confident and rejoicing, those greater mounts, those winged, shining and world-shaking horses which perhaps even now expect us with impatience, pawing and snorting in the King's stables. Not that the gallop would be of any value unless it were a gallop with the King; but how else – since He has retained His own charger – should we accompany Him?

St Joseph the Worker   MAY 1

'Good Works' in the plural is an expression much more familiar to modern Christendom than 'good work'. Good works are chiefly alms-giving or 'helping' in the parish. They are quite separate from one's 'work'. And good works need not be good work, as anyone can see by inspecting some of the objects made to be sold at bazaars for charitable purposes. This is not according to our example. When Our Lord provided a poor wedding party with an extra glass of wine all round, He was doing good works. But also good work; it was a wine really worth drinking. Nor is the neglect of goodness in our 'work', our job, according to precept. The Apostle says every one must not only work but work to produce what is 'good'.

The idea of Good Work is not quite extinct among us, though it is not, I fear, especially characteristic of religious people. I have found it among cabinet-makers, cobblers, and sailors. It is no use at all trying to impress sailors with a new liner because she is the biggest or costliest ship afloat. They look for what they call her 'lines': they predict how she will behave in a heavy sea. Artists also talk of Good Work; but decreasingly. They begin to prefer words like 'significant', 'important', 'contemporary', or 'daring'. These are not, to my mind, good symptoms.

St Athanasius   MAY 2

His epitaph is *Athanasius contra mundum,* 'Athanasius against the world'. We are proud that our country has more than once stood against the world. Athanasius did the same. He stood for the Trinitarian doctrine, 'whole and undefiled', when it looked as if all the civilized world was slipping back from Christianity into the religion of

Arius — into one of those 'sensible' synthetic religions which are so strongly recommended today and which, then as now, included among their devotees many highly cultivated clergymen. It is his glory that he did not move with the times; it is his reward that he now remains when those times, as all times do, have moved away.

When I first opened *De Incarnatione* I soon discovered... that I was reading a masterpiece.... We cannot, I admit, appropriate all its confidence today. We cannot point to the high virtue of Christian living and the gay, almost mocking, courage of Christian martyrdom, as a proof of our doctrines with quite that assurance which Athanasius takes as a matter of course. But whoever may be to blame for that, it is not Athanasius.

St Philip and St James, Apostles MAY 3

We are taught that the Incarnation itself proceeded 'not by the conversion of the godhead into flesh, but by taking of [the] manhood into God'; in it human life becomes the vehicle of Divine life. If the Scriptures proceed not by conversion of God's word into a literature but by taking up of a literature to be the vehicle of God's word, this is not anomalous....

If the Old Testament is a literature thus 'taken up', made the vehicle of what is more than human, we can of course set no limit to the weight or multiplicity of meanings which may have been laid upon it .... We are committed to it in principle by Our Lord Himself. On that famous journey to Emmaus He found fault with two disciples for not believing what the prophets had said. They ought to have known from their Bibles that the Anointed One, when He came, would enter His glory through suffering. He then explained, from 'Moses' (i.e. the Pentateuch) down, all the places in the Old Testament 'concerning Himself'.... We do not know — or anyway I do not know — what all these passages were. We can be pretty sure about one of them. The Ethiopian eunuch who met Philip (Acts 8:27–38) was reading Isaiah 53. He did not know whether in that passage the prophet was talking about himself or about someone else. Philip, in answering his question, 'preached unto him Jesus'. The answer, in fact, was 'Isaiah is speaking of Jesus'. We need have no doubt that Philip's authority for this interpretation was Our Lord.

The Resurrection of Our Bodies   MAY 4

The raising of Lazarus differs from the Resurrection of Christ Himself because Lazarus, so far as we know, was not raised to a new and more glorious mode of existence but merely restored to the sort of life he had had before. The fitness of the miracle lies in the fact that He who will raise all men at the general resurrection here does it small and close, and in an inferior — a merely anticipatory — fashion. For the mere restoration of Lazarus is as inferior in splendour to the *glorious* resurrection of the New Humanity as stone jars are to the green and growing vine, or five little barley loaves to all the waving bronze and gold of a fat valley ripe for harvest. The resuscitation of Lazarus, so far as we can see, is simple reversal: a series of changes working in the direction opposite to that we have always experienced. At death, matter which has been organic begins to flow away into the inorganic, to be finally scattered and used (some of it) by other organisms. The resurrection of Lazarus involves the reverse process. The general resurrection involves the reverse process universalized — a rush of matter towards organization at the call of spirits which require it. It is presumably a foolish fancy (not justified by the words of Scripture) that each spirit should recover those particular units of matter which he ruled before. For one thing, they would not be enough to go round: we all live in secondhand suits and there are doubtless atoms in my chin which have served many another man, many a dog, many an eel, many a dinosaur. Nor does the unity of our bodies, even in this present life, consist in retaining the same particles. My form remains one, though the matter in it changes continually. I am, in that respect, like a curve in a waterfall.

The Resurrection of the Senses   MAY 5

The old picture of the soul re-assuming the corpse — perhaps blown to bits or long since usefully dissipated through Nature — is absurd. Nor is it what St Paul's words imply. And I admit that if you ask me what I substitute for this, I have only speculations to offer.

The principle behind these speculations is this. We are not, in this doctrine, concerned with matter as such at all; with waves and atoms and all that. What the soul cries out for is the resurrection of the senses. Even in this life matter would be nothing to us if it were not the source of sensations....

But don't run away with the idea that when I speak of the resurrection of the body I mean merely that the blessed dead will have excellent memories of their sensuous experience on earth. I mean it the other way round: that memory as we now know it is a dim foretaste, a mirage even, of a power which the soul, or rather Christ in the

soul (He went to 'prepare a place for us'), will exercise hereafter. It need no longer be intermittent. Above all, it need no longer be private to the soul in which it occurs....
At present we tend to think of the soul as somehow 'inside' the body. But the glorified body of the resurrection as I conceive it—the sensuous life raised from its death—will be inside the soul. As God is not in space but space is in God....

I don't say the resurrection of this body will happen at once. It may well be that this part of us sleeps in death, and the intellectual soul is sent to Lenten lands where she fasts in naked spirituality—a ghostlike and imperfectly human condition. I don't imply that an angel is a ghost. But naked spirituality is in accordance with his nature; not, I think, with ours. (A two-legged horse is maimed, but not a two-legged man.) Yet from that fact my hope is that we shall return and re-assume the wealth we have laid down.

Then the new earth and sky, the same yet not the same as these, will rise in us as we have risen in Christ. And once again, after who knows what aeons of the silence and the dark, the birds will sing and the waters flow, and lights and shadows move across the hills, and the faces of our friends laugh upon us with amazed recognition.

Guesses, of course, only guesses. If they are not true, something better will be. For 'we know that we shall be made like Him, for we shall see Him as He is'.

The Lenten Lands: Purgatory MAY 6

Our souls *demand* Purgatory, don't they? Would it not break the heart if God said to us, 'It is true, my son, that your breath smells and your rags drip with mud and slime, but we are charitable here and no one will upbraid you with these things, nor draw away from you. Enter into the joy'? Should we not reply, 'With submission, Sir, and if there is no objection, I'd *rather* be cleaned first.' 'It may hurt, you know.' — 'Even so, Sir.'

I assume that the process of purification will normally involve suffering. Partly from tradition; partly because most real good that has been done me in this life has involved it. But I don't think suffering is the purpose of the purgation. I can well believe that people neither much worse nor much better than I will suffer less than I or more. 'No nonsense about merit.' The treatment given will be the one required, whether it hurts little or much.

My favourite image on this matter comes from the dentist's chair. I hope that when the tooth of life is drawn and I am 'coming round' a voice will say, 'Rinse your mouth out with this.' *This* will be Purgatory.

The Second Coming   MAY 7

There are many reasons why the modern Christian and even the modern theologian may hesitate to give to the doctrine of Christ's Second Coming that emphasis which was usually laid on it by our ancestors. Yet it seems to me impossible to retain in any recognizable form our belief in the Divinity of Christ and the truth of the Christian revelation while abandoning, or even persistently neglecting, the promised, the threatened, Return. 'He shall come again to judge the quick and the dead', says the Apostles' Creed. 'This same Jesus', said the angels in Acts, 'shall so come in like manner as ye have seen Him go into heaven.' 'Hereafter', said Our Lord Himself (by those words inviting crucifixion), 'shall ye see the Son of Man...coming in the clouds of Heaven.' If this is not an integral part of the faith once given to the saints, I do not know what it is....

Many are shy of this doctrine because they are reacting against a school of thought which is associated with the great name of Dr Albert Schweitzer. According to that school, Christ's teaching about His own return and the end of the world — what theologians call His 'apocalyptic' — was the very essence of His message....Hence, from fear of that extreme, arises a tendency to soft-pedal what Schweitzer's school has over-emphasized.

For my own part I hate and distrust reactions not only in religion but in everything. Luther surely spoke very good sense when he compared humanity to a drunkard who, after falling off his horse on the right, falls off it next time on the left. I am convinced that those who find in Christ's apocalyptic the whole of His message are mistaken. But a thing does not vanish — it is not even discredited — because someone has spoken of it with exaggeration. It remains exactly where it was. The only difference is that if it has recently been exaggerated, we must now take special care not to overlook it; for that is the side on which the drunk man is now most likely to fall off.

The Modern Conception of Progress   MAY 8

No one looking at world history without some preconception in favour of progress could find in it a steady up gradient. There is often progress within a given field over a limited period. A school of pottery or painting, a moral effort in a particular direction, a practical art like sanitation or shipbuilding, may continuously improve over a number of years. If this process could spread to all departments of life and continue indefinitely, there would be 'Progress' of the sort our fathers believed in. But it never seems to do so. Either it is interrupted (by barbarian irruption or the even less resistible infiltration of modern industrialism) or else, more mysteriously, it decays. The idea which here shuts out the Second Coming from our minds, the idea of the world slowly ripening to perfection, is a myth, not a generalization from experience. And it is a myth which distracts us from our real duties and our real interest. It is our attempt to guess the plot of a drama in which we are the characters. But how can the characters in a play guess the plot? We are not the playwright, we are not the producer, we are not even the audience. We are on the stage. To play well the scenes in which we are 'on' concerns us much more than to guess about the scenes that follow it.

When the World Drama Ends MAY 9

In *King Lear* (III:vii) there is a man who is such a minor character that Shakespeare has not given him even a name: he is merely 'First Servant'. All the characters around him — Regan, Cornwall, and Edmund — have fine, longterm plans. They think they know how the story is going to end, and they are quite wrong. The servant has no such delusions. He has no notion how the play is going to go. But he understands the present scene. He sees an abomination (the blinding of old Gloucester) taking place. He will not stand it. His sword is out and pointed at his master's breast in a moment: then Regan stabs him dead from behind. That is his whole part: eight lines all told. But if it were real life and not a play, that is the part it would be best to have acted.

The doctrine of the Second Coming teaches us that we do not and cannot know when the world drama will end. The curtain may be rung down at any moment: say, before you have finished reading this paragraph. This seems to some people intolerably frustrating. So many things would be interrupted. Perhaps you were going to get married next month, perhaps you were going to get a rise next week: you may be on the verge of a great scientific discovery; you may be maturing great social and political reforms. Surely no good and wise God would be so very unreasonable as to cut all this short? Not *now*, of all moments!

The Play that God Wrote MAY 10

We think thus because we keep on assuming that we know the play. We do not know the play. We do not even know whether we are in Act I or Act V. We do not know who are the major and who the minor characters. The Author knows. The audience, if there is an audience (if angels and archangels and all the company of heaven fill the pit and the stalls), may have an inkling. But we, never seeing the play from outside, never meeting any characters except the tiny minority who are 'on' in the same scenes as ourselves, wholly ignorant of the future and very imperfectly informed about the past, cannot tell at what moment the end ought to come. That it will come when it ought, we may be sure; but we waste our time in guessing when that will be. That it has a meaning we may be sure, but we cannot see it. When it is over, we may be told. We are led to expect that the Author will have something to say to each of us on the part that each of us has played. The playing it well is what matters infinitely.

The doctrine of the Second Coming, then, is not to be rejected because it conflicts with our favourite modern mythology. It is, for that very reason, to be the more valued and made more frequently the subject of meditation. It is the medicine our condition especially needs.

Predictions of the Second Coming   MAY 11

Many people find it difficult to believe in this great event without trying to guess its date, or even without accepting as a certainty the date that any quack or hysteric offers them. To write a history of all these exploded predictions would need a book, and a sad, sordid, tragi-comical book it would be. One such prediction was circulating when St Paul wrote his second letter to the Thessalonians. Someone had told them that 'the Day' was 'at hand'. This was apparently having the result which such predictions usually have: people were idling and playing the busybody. One of the most famous predictions was that of poor William Miller in 1843. Miller (whom I take to have been an honest fanatic) dated the Second Coming to the year, the day, and the very minute. A timely comet fostered the delusion. Thousands waited for the Lord at midnight on March 21, and went home to a late breakfast on the 22nd followed by the jeers of a drunkard.

Clearly, no one wishes to say anything that will re-awaken such mass hysteria. We must never speak to simple, excitable people about 'the Day' without emphasizing again and again the utter impossibility of prediction. We must try to show them that that impossibility is an essential part of the doctrine. If you do not believe Our Lord's words, why do you believe in His return at all? And if you do believe them must you not put away from you, utterly and forever, any hope of dating that return? His teaching on the subject quite clearly consisted of three propositions: (1) That He will certainly return; (2) That we cannot possibly find out when; (3) And that therefore we must always be ready for Him.

We Must be Ready at All Times

Precisely because we cannot predict the moment, we must be ready at all moments. Our Lord repeated this practical conclusion again and again; as if the promise of the Return had been made for the sake of this conclusion alone. Watch, watch, is the burden of His advice. I shall come like a thief. You will not, I most solemnly assure you, you will not see me approaching. If the householder had known at which time the burglar would arrive, he would have been ready for him. If the servant had known when his absent employer would come home, he would not have been found drunk in the kitchen. But they didn't. Nor will you. Therefore you must be ready at all times. The point is surely simple enough. The schoolboy does not know which part of his Virgil lesson he will be made to translate: that is why he must be prepared to translate *any* passage. The sentry does not know at which time an enemy will attack, or an officer inspect, his post: that is why he must keep awake *all* the time. The Return is wholly unpredictable. There will be wars and rumours of wars and all kinds of catastrophes, as there always are. Things will be, in that sense, normal, the hour before the heavens roll up like a scroll. You cannot guess it. If you could, one chief purpose for which it was foretold would be frustrated. And God's purposes are not so easily frustrated as that. One's ears should be closed against any future William Miller in advance. The folly of listening to him at all is almost equal to the folly of believing him. He *couldn't* know what he pretends, or thinks, he knows.

Love and Fear

The doctrine of the Second Coming has failed, so far as we are concerned, if it does not make us realize that at every moment of every year in our lives Donne's question 'What if this present were the world's last night?' is equally relevant.

Sometimes this question has been pressed upon our minds with the purpose of exciting fear. I do not think that is its right use. I am, indeed, far from agreeing with those who think all religious fear barbarous and degrading, and demand that it should be banished from the spiritual life. Perfect love, we know, casteth out fear. But so do several other things — ignorance, alcohol, passion, presumption, and stupidity. It is very desirable that we should all advance to that perfection of love in which we shall fear no longer; but it is very undesirable, until we have reached that stage, that we should allow any inferior agent to cast out fear. The objection to any attempt at perpetual trepidation about the Second Coming is, in my view, quite a different one: namely, that it will certainly not succeed. Fear is an emotion: and it is quite impossible — even physically impossible — to maintain any emotion for very long. A perpetual excitement of hope about the Second Coming is impossible for the same reason. Crisis-feeling of any sort is essentially transitory. Feelings come and go, and when they come a good use can be made of them: they cannot be our regular spiritual diet.

St Matthias, Apostle   MAY 14

In the earliest days of Christianity an 'apostle' was first and foremost a man who claimed to be an eye-witness of the Resurrection. Only a few days after the Crucifixion when two candidates were nominated for the vacancy created by the treachery of Judas, their qualification was that they had known Jesus personally both before and after His death, and could offer first-hand evidence of the Resurrection in addressing the outer world (Acts 1:22). A few days later St Peter, preaching the first Christian sermon, makes the same claim – 'God raised Jesus, of which we all [we Christians] are witnesses' (Acts 2:32). In the first *Letter to the Corinthians* St Paul bases his claim to apostleship on the same ground – 'Am I not an apostle? Have I not seen the Lord Jesus?'

As this qualification suggests, to preach Christianity meant primarily to preach the Resurrection.... The Resurrection, and its consequences, were the 'Gospel' or good news which the Christians brought: what we call the 'gospels', the narratives of Our Lord's life and death, were composed later for the benefit of those who had already accepted the *Gospel.* They were in no sense the basis of Christianity: they were written for those already converted.... Nothing could be more unhistorical than to pick out selected sayings of Christ from the gospels and to regard those as the datum and the rest of the New Testament as a construction upon it. The first fact in the history of Christendom is a number of people who say they have seen the Resurrection. If they had died without making anyone else believe this 'Gospel' no gospels would ever have been written.

What if this Present were the World's Last Night?   MAY 15

What is important is not that we should always fear (or hope) about the End but that we should always remember, always take it into account. An analogy may help here. A man of seventy need not be always feeling (much less talking) about his approaching death: but a wise man of seventy should always take it into account. He would be foolish to embark on schemes which presuppose twenty more years of life: he would be criminally foolish not to make — indeed, not to have made long since — his will. Now, what death is to each man, the Second Coming is to the whole human race. We all believe, I suppose, that a man should 'sit loose' to his own individual life, should remember how short, precarious, temporary, and provisional a thing it is; should never give all his heart to anything which will end when his life ends. What modern Christians find it harder to remember is that the whole life of humanity in this world is also precarious, temporary, provisional.

The Death of Lazarus MAY 16

The world, knowing how all our real investments are beyond the grave, might expect us to be less concerned than other people who go in for what is called Higher Thought and tell us that 'death doesn't matter'; but we 'are not high-minded', and we follow One who stood and wept at the grave of Lazarus — not, surely, because He was grieved that Mary and Martha wept, and sorrowed for their lack of faith (though some thus interpret) but because death, the punishment of sin, is even more horrible in His eyes than in ours. The nature which He had created as God, the nature which He had assumed as Man, lay there before Him in its ignominy; a foul smell, food for worms. Though He was to revive it a moment later, He wept at the shame . . . . Of all men, we hope most of death; yet nothing will reconcile us to — well, its *unnaturalness*. We know that we were not made for it; we know how it crept into our destiny as an intruder; and we know Who has defeated it. Because Our Lord is risen we know that on one level it is an enemy already disarmed; but because we know that the natural level also is God's creation we cannot cease to fight against the death which mars it, as against all other blemishes upon it, against pain and poverty, barbarism and ignorance. Because we love something else more than this world we love even this world better than those who know no other.

Death MAY 17

As suicide is the typical expression of the stoic spirit, and battle of the warrior spirit, martyrdom always remains the supreme enacting and perfection of Christianity. This great action has been initiated for us, done on our behalf, exemplified for our imitation, and inconceivably communicated to all believers, by Christ on Calvary. There the degree of accepted Death reaches the utmost bounds of the imaginable and per-

haps goes beyond them; not only all natural supports, but the presence of the very
Father to whom the sacrifice is made deserts the victim, and surrender to God does
not falter though God 'forsakes' it....

Christianity teaches us that the terrible task has already in some sense been accomplished for us — that a master's hand is holding ours as we attempt to trace the
difficult letters and that our script need only be a 'copy', not an original. Again, where
other systems expose our total nature to death (as in Buddhist renunciation)
Christianity demands only that we set right a *misdirection* of our nature, and has no
quarrel, like Plato, with the body as such, nor with the psychical elements in our
make-up. And sacrifice in its supreme realization is not exacted of all. Confessors as
well as martyrs are saved, and some old people whose state of grace we can hardly
doubt seem to have got through their seventy years surprisingly easily. The sacrifice
of Christ is repeated, or re-echoed, among His followers in very varying degrees,
from the cruellest martyrdom down to a self-submission of intention whose outward
signs have nothing to distinguish them from the ordinary fruits of temperance and
'sweet reasonableness'. The causes of this distribution I do not know; but from our
present point of view it ought to be clear that the real problem is not why some
humble, pious, believing people suffer, but why some do *not*. Our Lord Himself, it
will be remembered, explained the salvation of those who are fortunate in this world
only by referring to the unsearchable omnipotence of God.

God's Verdict   MAY 18

Some moderns talk as though duties to posterity were the only duties we had. I can
imagine no man who will look with more horror on the End than a conscientious
revolutionary who has, in a sense sincerely, been justifying cruelties and injustices
inflicted on millions of his contemporaries by the benefits which he hopes to confer
on future generations: generations who, as one terrible moment now reveals to him,
were never going to exist. Then he will see the massacres, the faked trials, the depor-
tations, to be all ineffaceably real, an essential part, his part, in the drama that has
just ended: while the future Utopia had never been anything but a fantasy.

Frantic administration of panaceas to the world is certainly discouraged by the
reflection that 'this present' might be 'the world's last night'; sober work for the future, within the limits of ordinary morality and prudence, is not. For what comes is
Judgement: happy are those whom it finds labouring in their vocations, whether they
were merely going out to feed the pigs or laying good plans to deliver humanity a
hundred years hence from some great evil. The curtain has indeed now fallen. Those
pigs will never in fact be fed, the great campaign against White Slavery or Govern-

mental Tyranny will never in fact proceed to victory. No matter: you were at your post when the Inspection came.

Our ancestors had a habit of using the word 'Judgement' in this context as if it meant simply 'punishment': hence the popular expression, 'It's a judgement on him'. I believe we can sometimes render the thing more vivid to ourselves by taking a judgement in a stricter sense: not as the sentence or award, but as the Verdict. Some day (and 'What if this present were the world's last night?') an absolutely correct verdict – if you like, a perfect critique – will be passed on what each of us is.

The Final Judgement   MAY 19

It will be infallible judgement. If it is favourable we shall have no fear, if unfavourable, no hope, that it is wrong. We shall not only believe, we shall know, know beyond doubt in every fibre of our appalled or delighted being, that as the Judge has said, so we are: neither more nor less nor other. We shall perhaps even realize that in some dim fashion we could have known it all along. We shall know and all creation will know too: our ancestors, our parents, our wives or husbands, our children. The unanswerable and (by then) self-evident truth about each will be known to all.

I do not find that pictures of physical catastrophe – that sign in the clouds, those heavens rolled up like a scroll – help one so much as the naked idea of Judgement. We cannot always be excited. We can, perhaps, train ourselves to ask more and more often how the thing which we are saying or doing (or failing to do) at each moment will look when the irresistible light streams in upon it; that light which is so different from the light of this world – and yet, even now, we know just enough of it to take it into account. Women sometimes have the problem of trying to judge by artificial light how a dress will look by daylight. That is very like the problem of all of us: to dress our souls not for the electric lights of the present world but for the daylight of the next. The good dress is the one that will face that light. For that light will last longer.

The Divorce of Heaven and Hell   MAY 20

Blake wrote the Marriage of Heaven and Hell. If I have written of their Divorce, this is not because I think myself a fit antagonist for so great a genius, nor even because I feel at all sure that I know what he meant. But in some sense or other the attempt to make that marriage is perennial. The attempt is based on the belief that reality never presents us with an absolutely unavoidable 'either-or'; that, granted skill and patience and (above all) time enough, some way of embracing both alternatives can always be found; that mere development or adjustment or refinement will somehow turn evil into good without our being called on for a final and total rejection of anything we should like to retain. This belief I take to be a disastrous error. You cannot take all luggage with you on all journeys; on one journey even your right hand and your right eye may be among the things you have to leave behind. We are not living in a world where all roads are radii of a circle and where all, if followed long enough, will therefore draw gradually nearer and finally meet at the centre: rather in a world where every road, after a few miles, forks into two, and each of those two again, and at each fork you must make a decision. Even on the biological level life is not like a river but like a tree. It does not move towards unity but away from it and the creatures grow further apart as they increase in perfection. Good, as it ripens, becomes continually more different not only from evil but from other good.

Evil Cannot 'Develop' into Good   MAY 21

I do not think that all who choose wrong roads perish; but their rescue consists in being put back on the right road. A wrong sum can be put right: but only by going back till you find the error and working it afresh from that point, never by simply *going on*. Evil can be undone, but it cannot 'develop' into good. Time does not heal it. The spell must be unwound, bit by bit, 'with the backward mutters of dissevering power' – or else not. It is still 'either-or'. If we insist on keeping Hell (or even earth) we shall not see Heaven: if we accept Heaven we shall not be able to retain even the smallest and most intimate souvenirs of Hell. I believe, to be sure, that any man who reaches Heaven will find that what he abandoned (even in plucking out his right eye) has not been lost: that the kernel of what he was really seeking even in his most depraved wishes will be there, beyond expectation, waiting for him in 'the High Countries'. In that sense it will be true for those who have completed the journey (and for no others) to say that good is everything and Heaven everywhere. But we, at this end of the road, must not try to anticipate that retrospective vision. If we do, we are likely to embrace the false and disastrous converse and fancy that everything is good and everywhere is Heaven.

But what, you ask, of earth? Earth, I think, will not be found by anyone to be in the end a very distinct place. I think earth, if chosen instead of Heaven, will turn out to have been, all along, only a region in Hell: and earth, if put second to Heaven, to have been from the beginning a part of Heaven itself.

A Bishop from Hell Meets a Friend from Heaven   MAY 22

I saw another of the Bright People in conversation with a ghost. It was that fat ghost with the cultured voice . . . and it seemed to be wearing gaiters.

'My dear boy, I'm delighted to see you,' it was saying to the Spirit, who was naked and almost blindingly white. 'I was talking to your poor father the other day and wondering where you were.'

'You didn't bring him?' said the other.

'Well, no. He lives a long way from the bus, and, to be quite frank, he's been getting a little eccentric lately . . . . Ah, Dick, I shall never forget some of our talks. I expect you've changed your views a bit since then. You became rather narrow-minded towards the end of your life: but no doubt you've broadened out again.'

'How do you mean?'

'Well, it's obvious by now, isn't it, that you weren't quite right. Why, my dear boy, you were coming to believe in a literal Heaven and Hell!'

'But wasn't I right?'

'Oh, in a spiritual sense, to be sure. I still believe in them in that way. I am still, my dear boy, looking for the Kingdom. But nothing superstitious or mythological . . .'

'Excuse me. Where do you imagine you've been?'

'Ah, I see. You mean that the grey town with its continual hope of morning (we must all live by hope, must we not?), with its field for indefinite progress, is, in a sense, Heaven, if only we have eyes to see it? That is a beautiful idea.'

'I didn't mean that at all. Is it possible you don't know where you've been?'

'Now that you mention it, I don't think we ever do give it a name. What do you call it?'

'We call it Hell.'

'There is no need to be profane, my dear boy. I may not be very orthodox, in your sense of that word, but I do feel that these matters ought to be discussed simply, and seriously, and reverently.'

'Discuss Hell *reverently?* . . . . You have been in Hell: though if you don't go back you may call it Purgatory.'

The Bishop Questions His Friend   MAY 23

'Go on, my dear boy . . . . No doubt you'll tell me why I was sent there.'

'But don't you know? You went there because you are an apostate. . . .'

'Dick, this is unworthy of you. What are you suggesting?'

'Friend, I am not suggesting at all. You see, I *know* now. Let us be frank. Our opinions were not honestly come by. We simply found ourselves in contact with a certain current of ideas and plunged into it because it seemed modern and successful. ...When, in our whole lives, did we honestly face, in solitude, the one question on which all turned: whether after all the Supernatural might not in fact occur? When did we put up one moment's real resistance to the loss of our faith?'

'If this is meant to be a sketch of the genesis of liberal theology in general, I reply that it is a mere libel. Do you suggest that men like...'

'I have nothing to do with any generality. Nor with any man but you and me.... You know that you and I were playing with loaded dice. We didn't *want* the other to be true. We were afraid of crude salvationism, afraid of a breach with the spirit of the age, afraid of ridicule, afraid (above all) of real spiritual fears and hopes.'

'I'm far from denying that young men may make mistakes. They may well be influenced by current fashions of thought. But it's not a question of how the opinions are formed. The point is that they were my honest opinions, sincerely expressed.'

'Of course. Having allowed oneself to drift, unresisting, unpraying, accepting every half-conscious solicitation from our desires, we reached a point where we no longer believed the Faith. Just in the same way, a jealous man, drifting and unresisting, reaches a point at which he believes lies about his best friend: a drunkard reaches a point at which (for a moment) he actually believes that another glass will do him no harm. The beliefs are sincere in the sense that they do occur as psychological events in the man's mind. If that's what you mean by sincerity they are sincere, and so were ours. But errors which are sincere in that sense are not innocent.'

The Bishop is Urged to Come to Heaven   MAY 24

'Well, that is a plan. I am perfectly ready to consider it. Of course I should require some assurances....I should want a guarantee that you are taking me to a place where I shall find a wider sphere of usefulness—and scope for the talents that God has given me—and an atmosphere of free inquiry—in short, all that one means by civilization and—er—the spiritual life.'

'No', said the other. 'I can promise you none of these things. No sphere of usefulness: you are not needed there at all. No scope for your talents: only forgiveness for having perverted them. No atmosphere of inquiry, for I will bring you to the land not of questions but of answers, and you shall see the face of God.'

'Ah, but we must all interpret those beautiful words in our own way! For me there is no such thing as a final answer. The free wind of inquiry must *always* continue to blow through the mind, must it not? "Prove all things"...to travel hopefully is better than to arrive.'

'If that were true, and known to be true, how could anyone travel hopefully? There would be nothing to hope for'. . . .

'The suggestion that I should return at my age to the mere factual inquisitiveness of boyhood strikes me as preposterous. In any case, that question-and-answer conception of thought only applies to matters of fact. Religious and speculative questions are surely on a different level'. . . .

'Do you not even believe that He exists?'

'Exists? What does Existence mean? You *will* keep on implying some sort of static, ready-made reality which is, so to speak, "there", and to which our minds have simply to conform. These great mysteries cannot be approached in that way. If there were such a thing (there is no need to interrupt, my dear boy), quite frankly, I should not be interested in it. It would be of no *religious* significance. God, for me, is something purely spiritual. The spirit of sweetness and light and tolerance – and, er, Dick, service. We mustn't forget that, you know.'

The Bishop Makes up His Mind   MAY 25

'Happiness, my dear Dick,' said the Ghost placidly, 'happiness, as you will come to see when you are older, lies in the path of duty. Which reminds me. . . . Bless my soul, I'd nearly forgotten. Of course I can't come with you. I have to be back next Friday to read a paper. We have a little Theological Society down there. Oh, yes! there is plenty of intellectual life. Not of a very high quality, perhaps. One notices a certain lack of grip – a certain confusion of mind. That is where I can be of some use to them. There are even regrettable jealousies. . . . I don't know why, but tempers seem less controlled than they used to be. Still, one mustn't expect too much of human nature. I feel I can do a great work among them. But you've never asked me what my paper is about! I'm taking the text about growing up to the measure of the stature of Christ and working out an idea which I feel sure you'll be interested in. I'm going to point out how people always forget that Jesus [here the Ghost bowed] was a comparatively young man when he died. He would have outgrown some of his earlier views, you know, if he'd lived. As he might have done, with a little more tact and patience. I am going to ask my audience to consider what his mature views would have been. A profoundly interesting question. What a different Christianity we might have had if only the Founder had reached his full stature! I shall end up by pointing out how this deepens the significance of the Crucifixion. One feels for the first time what a disaster it was: what a tragic waste . . . so much promise cut short. Oh, must you be going? Well, so must I. Goodbye, my dear boy. It has been a great pleasure. Most stimulating and provocative. . . .'

The Ghost nodded its head and beamed on the Spirit with a bright clerical smile — or with the best approach to it which such unsubstantial lips could manage — and then turned away humming softly to itself 'City of God, how broad and far'.

Lewis's Guide on Good and Evil   MAY 26

'Son,' he said, 'ye cannot in your present state understand eternity. . . . But ye can get some likeness of it if ye say that both good and evil, when they are full grown, become retrospective. . . . That is what mortals misunderstand. They say of some temporal suffering, "No future bliss can make up for it", not knowing that Heaven, once attained, will work backwards and turn even that agony into a glory. And of some sinful pleasure they say, "Let me but have *this* and I'll take the consequences": little dreaming how damnation will spread back and back into their past and contaminate the pleasure of the sin. Both processes begin even before death. The good man's past begins to change so that his forgiven sins and remembered sorrows take on the quality of Heaven: the bad man's past already conforms to his badness and is filled only with dreariness. And that is why, at the end of all thing . . . the Blessed will say, "We have never lived anywhere except in Heaven", and the Lost, "We were always in Hell". And both will speak truly.'

Grumbling   MAY 27

'The whole difficulty of understanding Hell is that the thing to be understood is so nearly Nothing. But ye'll have had experiences. . . . It begins with a grumbling mood, and yourself still distinct from it: perhaps criticizing it. And yourself, in a dark hour, may will that mood, embrace it. Ye can repent and come out of it again. But there may come a day when you can do that no longer. Then there will be no *you* left to criticize the mood, nor even to enjoy it, but just the grumble itself going on forever like a machine.'

The Tyranny of 'Sensitivity' MAY 28

Did we pretend to be 'hurt' in our sensitive and tender feelings (fine natures like ours are so vulnerable) when envy, ungratified vanity, or thwarted self-will was our real problem? Such tactics often succeed. The other parties give in. They give in not because they don't know what is really wrong with us, but because they have long known it only too well, and that sleeping dog can be roused, that skeleton brought out of its cupboard, only at the cost of imperilling their whole relationship with us. It needs surgery which they know we will never face. And so we win; by cheating. But the unfairness is very deeply felt. Indeed what is commonly called 'sensitiveness' is the most powerful engine of domestic tyranny, sometimes a lifelong tyranny. How we should deal with it in others I am not sure; but we should be merciless to its first appearance in ourselves.

Can You be Happy when Some Reject God? MAY 29

'What some people say on earth is that the final loss of one soul gives the lie to all the joy of those who are saved.'

'Ye see it does not.'

'I feel in a way that it ought to.'

'That sounds very merciful: but see what lurks behind it.'

'What?'

'The demand of the loveless and the self-imprisoned that they should be allowed to blackmail the universe: that till they consent to be happy (on their own terms) no one else shall taste joy: that theirs should be the final power; that Hell should be able to *veto* Heaven.'

'I don't know what I want, Sir.'

'Son, son, it must be one way or the other. Either the day must come when joy prevails and all the makers of misery are no longer able to infect it: or else for ever and ever the makers of misery can destroy in others the happiness they reject for themselves. I know it has a grand sound to say ye'll accept no salvation which leaves even one creature in the dark outside. But watch that sophistry or ye'll make a Dog in a Manger the tyrant of the universe.'

Pity   MAY 30

'But dare one say — it is horrible to say — that Pity must ever die?'

'Ye must distinguish. The action of Pity will live for ever: but the passion of Pity will not. The passion of pity, the pity we merely suffer, the ache that draws men to concede what should not be conceded and to flatter when they should speak truth, the pity that has cheated many a woman out of her virginity and many a statesman out of his honesty — that will die. It was used as a weapon by bad men against good ones: their weapon will be broken.'

'And what is the other kind — the action?'

'It's a weapon on the other side. It leaps quicker than light from the highest place to the lowest to bring healing and joy, whatever the cost to itself. It changes darkness into light and evil into good. But it will not, at the cunning tears of Hell, impose on good the tyranny of evil. Every disease that submits to a cure shall be cured: but we will not call blue yellow to please those who insist on still having jaundice, nor make a midden out of the world's garden for the sake of some who cannot abide the smell of roses.'

Two Kinds of People in the End   MAY 31

There are only two kinds of people in the end: those who say to God, 'Thy will be done', and those to whom God says, in the end, '*Thy* will be done.' All that are in Hell, choose it. Without that self-choice there could be no Hell. No soul that seriously and constantly desires joy will ever miss it. Those who seek find. To those who knock it is opened.

The Choice   JUNE 1

As he lay there, still unable and perhaps unwilling to rise, it came into his mind that in certain old philosophers and poets he had read that the mere sight of the devils was one of the greatest among the torments of Hell. It had seemed to him till now merely a quaint fancy. And yet (as he now saw) even the children know better: no child would have any difficulty in understanding that there might be a face the mere beholding of which was final calamity. The children, the poets, and the philosophers were right. As there is one Face above all worlds merely to see which is irrevocable joy, so at the bottom of all worlds that face is waiting whose sight alone is the misery from which none who beholds it can recover. And though there seemed to be, and indeed were, a thousand roads by which a man could walk through the world, there was not a single one which did not lead sooner or later either to the Beatific or the Miserific Vision.

The Weight of Gold JUNE 2

In the end that Face which is the delight or the terror of the universe must be turned upon each of us either with one expression or with the other, either conferring glory inexpressible or inflicting shame that can never be cured or disguised. I read in a periodical the other day that the fundamental thing is how we think of God. By God Himself, it is not! How God thinks of us is not only more important, but infinitely more important. Indeed, how we think of Him is of no importance except in so far as it is related to how He thinks of us. It is written that we shall 'stand before' Him, shall appear, shall be inspected. The promise of glory is the promise, almost incredible and only possible by the work of Christ, that some of us, that any of us who really chooses, shall actually survive that examination, shall find approval, shall please God. To please God...to be a real ingredient in the divine happiness...to be loved by God, not merely pitied, but delighted in as an artist delights in his work or a father in a son—it seems impossible, a weight or burden of glory which our thoughts can hardly sustain. But so it is.

Heaven JUNE 3

We were made for God. Only by being in some respect like Him, only by being a manifestation of His beauty, lovingkindness, wisdom or goodness, has any earthly Beloved excited our love. It is not that we have loved them too much, but that we did not quite understand what we were loving. It is not that we shall be asked to turn from them, so dearly familiar, to a Stranger. When we see the face of God we shall know that we have always known it. He has been a party to, has made, sustained and moved moment by moment within, all our earthly experiences of innocent love. All that was true love in them was, even on earth, far more His than ours, and ours only because His. In Heaven there will be no anguish and no duty of turning away from our earthly Beloveds. First, because we shall have turned already; from the portraits to the Original, from the rivulets to the Fountain, from the creatures he made lovable to Love Himself. But secondly, because we shall find them all in Him. By loving Him more than them we shall love them more than we now do.

The Doctrine of Hell   JUNE 4

There is no doctrine which I would more willingly remove from Christianity than this, if it lay in my power. But it has the full support of Scripture and, specially, of Our Lord's own words; it has always been held by Christendom; and it has the support of reason. If a game is played, it must be possible to lose it. If the happiness of a creature lies in self-surrender, no one can make that surrender but himself (though many can help him to make it) and he may refuse. I would pay any price to be able to say truthfully 'All will be saved'. But my reason retorts, 'Without their will, or with it?' If I say 'Without their will', I at once perceive a contradiction; how can the supreme voluntary act of self-surrender be involuntary? If I say 'With their will', my reason replies 'How if they *will not* give in?'

The Dominical utterances about Hell, like all Dominical sayings, are addressed to the conscience and the will, not to our intellectual curiosity. When they have roused us into action by convincing us of a terrible possibility, they have done, probably, all they were intended to do; and if all the world were convinced Christians it would be unnecessary to say a word more on the subject. As things are, however, this doctrine is one of the chief grounds on which Christianity is attacked as barbarous, and the goodness of God impugned. We are told that it is a detestable doctrine – and indeed, I too detest it from the bottom of my heart – and are reminded of the tragedies in human life which have come from believing it. Of the other tragedies which come from not believing it we are told less.

We Cannot be More Merciful than God   JUNE 5

Let us try to be honest with ourselves. Picture to yourself a man who has risen to wealth or power by a continued course of treachery and cruelty, by exploiting for purely selfish ends the noble motions of his victims, laughing the while at their simplicity; who, having thus attained success, uses it for the gratification of lust and hatred and finally parts with the last rag of honour among thieves by betraying his own accomplices and jeering at their last moments of bewildered disillusionment. Suppose, further, that he does all this, not (as we like to imagine) tormented by remorse or even misgiving, but eating like a schoolboy and sleeping like a healthy infant – a jolly, ruddy-cheeked man, without a care in the world, unshakably confident to the very end that he alone has found the answer to the riddle of life, that God and man are fools whom he has got the better of, that his way of life is utterly successful, satisfactory, unassailable. We must be careful at this point. The least indulgence of the passion for revenge is very deadly sin. Christian charity counsels us to make every effort for the conversion of such a man: to prefer his conversion, at the peril of our own lives, perhaps of our own souls, to his punishment; to prefer it infinitely. But that is not the question. Supposing he *will* not be converted, what destiny in the eternal world can you regard as proper for him? Can you really desire that such a man, *remaining what he is* (and he must be able to do that if he has free will), should be confirmed forever in his present happiness — should continue, for all eternity, to be perfectly convinced that the laugh is on his side?

Hell   JUNE 6

The demand that God should forgive such a man while he remains what he is, is based on a confusion between condoning and forgiving. To condone an evil is simply to ignore it, to treat it as if it were good. But forgiveness needs to be accepted as well as offered if it is to be complete: and a man who admits no guilt can accept no forgiveness. . . .

I willingly believe that the damned are, in one sense, successful, rebels to the end; that the doors of Hell are locked on the *inside.* I do not mean that the ghosts may not *wish* to come out of Hell, in the vague fashion wherein an envious man 'wishes' to be happy: but they certainly do not will even the first preliminary stages of that self-abandonment through which alone the soul can reach any good. They enjoy forever the horrible freedom they have demanded, and are therefore self-enslaved: just as the blessed, forever submitting to obedience, become through all eternity more and more free.

In the long run the answer to all those who object to the doctrine of Hell, is itself a question: 'What are you asking God to do?' To wipe out their past sins and, at all costs, to give them a fresh start, smoothing every difficulty and offering every miraculous help? But He has done so, on Calvary. To forgive them? They will not be forgiven. To leave them alone? Alas, I am afraid that is what He does.

There are no Ordinary *People*   JUNE 7

It is a serious thing to live in a society of possible gods and goddesses, to remember that the dullest and most uninteresting person you can talk to may one day be a creature which, if you saw it now, you would be strongly tempted to worship, or else a horror and a corruption such as you now meet, if at all, only in a nightmare. All day long we are, in some degree, helping each other to one or other of these destinations.

It is in the light of these overwhelming possibilities, it is with the awe and the circum-spection proper to them, that we should conduct all our dealings with one another, all friendships, all loves, all play, all politics. There are no *ordinary* people. You have never talked to a mere mortal. Nations, cultures, arts, civilizations – these are mortal, and their life is to ours as the life of a gnat. But it is immortals whom we joke with, work with, marry, snub, and exploit – immortal horrors or everlasting splendours. This does not mean that we are to be perpetually solemn. We must play. But our merriment must be of that kind (and it is, in fact, the merriest kind) which exists between people who have, from the outset, taken each other seriously – no flippancy, no superiority, no presumption. And our charity must be a real and costly love, with deep feeling for the sins in spite of which we love the sinner – no mere tolerance, or indulgence which parodies love as flippancy parodies merriment. Next to the Blessed Sacrament itself, your neighbour is the holiest object presented to your senses. If he is your Christian neighbour, he is holy in almost the same way, for in him also Christ *vere latitat* – the glorifier and the glorified, Glory Himself – is truly hidden.

Gift-Love and Need-Love

'God is love', says St John. When I first tried to write this book [*The Four Loves*] I thought that his maxim would provide me with a very plain highroad through the whole subject. I thought I should be able to say that human loves deserved to be called loves at all just in so far as they resembled that Love which is God. The first distinction I made was therefore between what I called Gift-love and Need-love. The typical example of Gift-love would be that love which moves a man to work and plan and save for the future well-being of his family which he will die without sharing or seeing; of the second, that which sends a lonely or frightened child to its mother's arms.

There was no doubt which was more like Love Himself. Divine Love is Gift-love. The Father gives all He is and has to the Son. The Son gives Himself back to the Father, and gives Himself to the world, and for the world to the Father, and thus gives the world (in Himself) back to the Father too.

And what, on the other hand, can be less like anything we believe of God's life than Need-love? He lacks nothing, but our Need-love, as Plato saw, is 'the son of Poverty'. It is the accurate reflection in consciousness of our actual nature. We are born helpless. As soon as we are fully conscious we discover loneliness. We need others physically, emotionally, intellectually; we need them if we are to know any-thing, even ourselves.

God — the Only Real Giver

Every Christian would agree that a man's spiritual health is exactly proportional to his love for God. But man's love for God, from the very nature of the case, must always be very largely, and must often be entirely, a Need-love. This is obvious when we implore forgiveness for our sins or support in our tribulations. But in the long run it is perhaps even more apparent in our growing — for it ought to be growing — awareness that our whole being by its very nature is one vast need; incomplete, preparatory, empty yet cluttered, crying out for Him who can untie things that are now knotted together and tie up things that are still dangling loose. I do not say that man can never bring to God anything at all but sheer Need-love. Exalted souls may tell us of a reach beyond that. But they would also, I think, be the first to tell us that those heights would cease to be true Graces, would become Neo-Platonic or finally diabolical illusions, the moment a man dared to think that he could live on them and henceforth drop out the element of need. 'The highest', says the *Imitation,* 'does not stand without the lowest.' It would be a bold and silly creature that came before its Creator with the boast 'I'm no beggar. I love you disinterestedly.' Those who come nearest to a Gift-love for God will next moment, even at the very same moment, be beating their breasts with the publican and laying their indigence before the only real Giver. And God will have it so. He addresses our Need-love: 'Come unto me all ye that travail and are heavy-laden', or, in the Old Testament, 'Open your mouth wide and I will fill it.'

Nearness to God

We must distinguish two things which might both possibly be called 'nearness to God'. One is likeness to God. God has impressed some sort of likeness to Himself, I suppose, in all that He has made. Space and time, in their own fashion, mirror His greatness; all life, His fecundity; animal life, His activity. Man has a more important likeness than these by being rational. Angels, we believe, have likenesses which Man lacks: immortality and intuitive knowledge. In that way all men, whether good or bad, all angels including those that fell, are more like God than the animals are. Their natures are in this sense 'nearer' to the Divine Nature. But, secondly, there is what we may call nearness of approach. If this is what we mean, the states in which a man is 'nearest' to God are those in which he is most surely and swiftly approaching his final union with God, vision of God and enjoyment of God. And as soon as we distinguish nearness-by-likeness and nearness-of-approach, we see that they do not necessarily coincide. They may or may not.

Perhaps an analogy may help. Let us suppose that we are doing a mountain walk to the village which is our home. At midday we come to the top of a cliff where we are, in space, very near it because it is just below us. We could drop a stone into it. But as we are no cragsmen we can't get down. We must go a long way round; five miles, maybe. At many points during that detour we shall, statically, be farther from the village than we were when we sat above the cliff. But only statically. In terms of progress we shall be far 'nearer' our baths and teas.

St Barnabas, Apostle   JUNE 11

Why do we men need so much alteration? The Christian answer — that we have used our free will to become very bad — is so well known that it hardly needs to be stated. But to bring this doctrine into real life in the minds of modern men, and even of modern Christians, is very hard. When the Apostles preached, they could assume even in their Pagan hearers a real consciousness of deserving the Divine anger. The Pagan mysteries existed to allay this consciousness, and the Epicurean philosophy claimed to deliver men from the fear of eternal punishment. It was against this background that the Gospel appeared as good news. It brought news of possible healing to men who knew that they were mortally ill. But all this has changed. Christianity now has to preach the diagnosis — in itself very bad news — before it can win a hearing for the cure.

Affection   JUNE 12

I begin with the humblest and most widely diffused of loves, the love in which our experience seems to differ least from that of the animals. Let me add at once that I do not on that account give it a lower value. Nothing in Man is either worse or better for being shared with the beasts. When we blame a man for being 'a mere animal', we mean not that he displays animal characteristics (we all do) but that he displays these, and only these, on occasions where the specifically human was demanded. (When we call him 'brutal' we usually mean that he commits cruelties impossible to most real brutes; they're not clever enough.)

The Greeks called this love *storge* (two syllables and the g is 'hard'). I shall here call it simply Affection. My Greek Lexicon defines *storge* as 'affection, especially of parents to offspring'; but also of offspring to parents. And that, I have no doubt, is the original form of the thing as well as the central meaning of the word. The image we must start with is that of a mother nursing a baby, a bitch or a cat with a basketful of puppies or kittens; all in a squeaking, nuzzling heap together; purrings, lickings, baby-talk, milk, warmth, the smell of young life.

The importance of this image is that it presents us at the very outset with a certain paradox. The Need and Need-love of the young is obvious; so is the Gift-love of the mother. She gives birth, gives suck, gives protection. On the other hand, she must give birth or die. She must give suck or suffer. That way, her Affection too is a Need-love. There is the paradox. It is a Need-love but what it needs is to give. It is a Gift-love but it needs to be needed.

The Humblest Love   JUNE 13

Affection . . . is the humblest love. It gives itself no airs. People can be proud of being 'in love', or of friendship. Affection is modest — even furtive and shame-faced. Once when I had remarked on the affection quite often found between cat and dog, my friend replied, 'Yes. But I bet no dog would ever confess it to the other dogs.' That is at least a good caricature of much human Affection. 'Let homely faces stay at home', says Comus. Now Affection has a very homely face. So have many of those for whom we feel it. It is no proof of our refinement or perceptiveness that we love them; nor that they love us. What I have called Appreciative love is no basic element in Affection. It usually needs absence or bereavement to set us praising those to whom only Affection binds us. We take them for granted: and this taking for granted, which is an outrage in erotic love, is here right and proper up to a point. It fits the comfortable, quiet nature of the feeling. Affection would not be affection if it was loudly and frequently expressed; to produce it in public is like getting your household furniture out for a move. It did very well in its place, but it looks shabby or tawdry or grotesque in the sunshine. Affection almost slinks or seeps through our lives. It lives with humble, un-dress, private things; soft slippers, old clothes, old jokes, the thump of a sleepy dog's tail on the kitchen floor, the sound of a sewing-machine, a gollywog left on the lawn.

Affection with the Other Loves   JUNE 14

I am talking of Affection as it is when it exists apart from the other loves. It often does so exist; often not. As gin is not only a drink in itself but also a base for many mixed drinks, so Affection, besides being a love itself, can enter into the other loves and colour them all through and become the very medium in which from day to day they operate. They would not perhaps wear very well without it. To make a friend is not the same as to become affectionate. But when your friend has become an old friend, all those things about him which had originally nothing to do with the friendship become familiar and dear with familiarity. As for erotic love, I can imagine nothing more disagreeable than to experience it for more than a very short time without this homespun clothing of affection. That would be a most uneasy condition, either too angelic or too animal or each by turn; never quite great enough or little enough for man. There is indeed a peculiar charm, both in friendship and in Eros, about those moments when Appreciative love lies, as it were, curled up asleep, and the mere ease and ordinariness of the relationship (free as solitude, yet neither is alone) wraps us round. No need to talk. No need to make love. No needs at all except perhaps to stir the fire.

The Especial Glory of Affection   JUNE 15

Affection...can 'rub along' with the most unpromising people. Yet oddly enough this very fact means that it can in the end make appreciations possible which, but for it, might never have existed. We may say, and not quite untruly, that we have chosen our friends and the women we love for their various excellences – for beauty, frankness, goodness of heart, wit, intelligence, or what not. But it had to be the particular kind of wit, the particular kind of beauty, the particular kind of goodness that we like, and we have our personal tastes in these matters. That is why friends and lovers feel that they were 'made for one another'. The especial glory of Affection is that it can unite those who most emphatically, even comically, are not; people who, if they had not found themselves put down by fate in the same household or community, would have had nothing to do with each other. If Affection grows out of this – of course it often does not – their eyes begin to open. Growing fond of 'old so-and-so', at first simply because he happens to be there, I presently begin to see that there is 'something in him' after all. The moment when one first says, really meaning it, that though he is not 'my sort of man' he is a very good man 'in his own way' is one of liberation. It does not feel like that; we may feel only tolerant and indulgent. But really we have crossed a frontier. That 'in his own way' means that we are getting beyond our own idiosyncrasies, that we are learning to appreciate goodness or intelligence in themselves, not merely goodness or intelligence flavoured and served to suit our own palate.

'Dogs and cats should always be brought up together,' said someone, 'it broadens their minds so'. . . .It is Affection that creates this taste, teaching us first to notice, then to endure, then to smile at, then to enjoy, and finally to appreciate, the people who 'happen to be there'. Made for us? Thank God, no. They are themselves, odder than you could have believed and worth far more than we guessed.

Friendship

When either Affection or Eros is one's theme, one finds a prepared audience. The importance and beauty of both have been stressed and almost exaggerated again and again. Even those who would debunk them are in conscious reaction against this laudatory tradition and, to that extent, influenced by it. But very few modern people think Friendship a love of comparable value or even a love at all. I cannot remember that any poem since *In Memoriam,* or any novel, has celebrated it. Tristan and Isolde, Antony and Cleopatra, Romeo and Juliet, have innumerable counterparts in modern literature: David and Jonathan, Pylades and Orestes, Roland and Oliver, Amis and Amile, have not. To the Ancients, Friendship seemed the happiest and most fully human of all loves; the crown of life and the school of virtue. The modern world, in comparison, ignores it. We admit of course that besides a wife and family a man needs a few 'friends'. But the very tone of the admission, and the sort of acquaintanceships which those who make it would describe as 'friendships', show clearly that what they are talking about has very little to do with that *Philia* which Aristotle classified among the virtues or that *Amicitia* on which Cicero wrote a book. It is something quite marginal; not a main course in life's banquet; a diversion; something that fills up the chinks of one's time.

Friendship: the Love Valued by So Few

How has this come about? The first and most obvious answer is that few value it because few experience it. And the possibility of going through life without the experience is rooted in that fact which separates Friendship so sharply from both the other loves. Friendship is – in a sense not at all derogatory to it – the least *natural* of loves; the least instinctive, organic, biological, gregarious and necessary. It has least commerce with our nerves; there is nothing throaty about it; nothing that quickens the pulse or turns you red and pale. It is essentially between individuals; the moment two men are friends they have in some degree drawn apart together from the herd. Without Eros none of us would have been begotten and without Affection none of us would have been reared; but we can live and breed without Friendship...

This (so to call it) 'non-natural' quality in Friendship goes far to explain why it was exalted in ancient and medieval times and has come to be made light of in our own. The deepest and most permanent thought of those ages was ascetic and world-renouncing. Nature and emotion and the body were feared as dangers to our souls, or despised as degradations of our human status. Inevitably that sort of love was most prized which seemed most independent, or even defiant, of mere Nature. Affection and Eros were too obviously connected with our nerves, too obviously shared with the brutes. You could feel these tugging at your guts and fluttering in your diaphragm. But in Friendship—in that luminous, tranquil, rational world of relationships freely chosen—you got away from all that. This alone, of all the loves, seemed to raise you to the level of gods or angels.

The Exaltation of Instinct   JUNE 18

But then came Romanticism and 'tearful comedy' and the 'return to Nature' and the exaltation of Sentiment; and in their train all that great wallow of emotion which, though often criticized, has lasted ever since. Finally, the exaltation of instinct, the dark gods in the blood; whose hierophants may be incapable of male friendships. Under this new dispensation all that had once commended this love now began to work against it. It had not tearful smiles and keepsakes and baby-talk enough to please the sentimentalists. There was no blood and guts enough about it to attract the primitivists. It looked thin and etiolated; a sort of vegetarian substitute for the more organic loves.

Other causes have contributed. To those—and they are now the majority—who see human life merely as a development and complication of animal life all forms of behaviour which cannot produce certificates of an animal origin and of survival value are suspect. Friendship's certificates are not very satisfactory. Again, that outlook which values the collective above the individual necessarily disparages Friendship; it is a relation between men at their highest level of individuality. It withdraws men from collective 'togetherness' as surely as solitude itself could do; and more danger-ously, for it withdraws them by twos and threes. Some forms of democratic sentiment are naturally hostile to it because it is selective and an affair of the few. To say 'These are my friends' implies 'Those are not'. For all these reasons if a man believes (as I do) that the old estimate of Friendship was the correct one, he can hardly write... on it except as a rehabilitation.

Invisible Cats   JUNE 19

It has actually become necessary in our time to rebut the theory that every firm and serious friendship is really homosexual.

The dangerous word *really* is here important. To say that every Friendship is consciously and explicitly homosexual would be too obviously false; the wiseacres take refuge in the less palpable charge that it is *really* — unconsciously, cryptically, in some Pickwickian sense — homosexual. And this, though it cannot be proved, can never of course be refuted. The fact that no positive evidence of homosexuality can be discovered in the behaviour of two Friends does not disconcert the wiseacres at all: 'That', they say gravely, 'is just what we should expect.' The very lack of evidence is thus treated as evidence; the absence of smoke proves that the fire is very carefully hidden. Yes — if it exists at all. But we must first prove its existence. Otherwise we are arguing like a man who should say 'If there were an invisible cat in that chair, the chair would look empty; but the chair does look empty; therefore there is an invisible cat in it.'

A belief in invisible cats cannot perhaps be logically disproved, but it tells us a good deal about those who hold it. Those who cannot conceive Friendship as a sub-stantive love but only as a disguise or elaboration of Eros betray the fact that they have never had a Friend. The rest of us know that though we can have erotic love and friendship for the same person yet in some ways nothing is less like a Friendship than a love affair. Lovers are always talking to one another about their love; Friends hardly ever about their Friendship. Lovers are normally face to face, absorbed in each other; Friends, side by side, absorbed in some common interest.

The Least Jealous of Loves   JUNE 20

Lamb says somewhere that if, of three friends (A, B and C), A should die, then B loses not only A but 'A's part in C', while C loses not only A but 'A's part in B'. In each of my friends there is something that only some other friend can fully bring out. By myself I am not large enough to call the whole man into activity; I want other lights than my own to show all his facets. Now that Charles is dead, I shall never again see Ronald's reaction to a specifically Caroline joke. Far from having more of Ronald, having him 'to myself' now that Charles is away, I have less of Ronald. Hence true Friendship is the least jealous of loves. Two friends delight to be joined by a third, and three by a fourth, if only the newcomer is qualified to become a real friend. They can then say, as the blessed souls say in Dante, 'Here comes one who will augment our loves.' For in this love 'to divide is not to take away'. Of course the scarcity of kin-dred souls — not to mention practical considerations about the size of rooms and the audibility of voices — sets limits to the enlargement of the circle; but within those limits we possess each friend not less but more as the number of those with whom we share him increases. In this, Friendship exhibits a glorious 'nearness by resemblance' to Heaven itself where the very multitude of the blessed (which no man can number) increases the fruition which each has of God. For every soul, seeing Him in her own way, doubtless communicates that unique vision to all the rest. That, says an old author, is why the Seraphim in Isaiah's vision are crying 'Holy, Holy, Holy' to *one another* (Isaiah 6:3). The more we thus share the Heavenly Bread between us, the more we shall all have.

The Birth of a Friendship   JUNE 21

Friendship arises out of mere Companionship when two or more of the companions discover that they have in common some insight or interest or even taste which the others do not share and which, till that moment, each believed to be his own unique treasure (or burden). The typical expression of opening Friendship would be something like, 'What? You too? I thought I was the only one.' We can imagine that among those early hunters and warriors single individuals — one in a century? one in a thousand years? — saw what others did not; saw that the deer was beautiful as well as edible, that hunting was fun as well as necessary, dreamed that his gods might be not only powerful but holy. But as long as each of these percipient persons dies without finding a kindred soul, nothing (I suspect) will come of it; art or sport or spiritual religion will not be born. It is when two such persons discover one another, when, whether with immense difficulties and semi-articulate fumblings or with what would seem to us amazing and elliptical speed, they share their vision — it is then that Friendship is born. And instantly they stand together in an immense solitude....

In our own time Friendship arises in the same way. For us of course the shared activity and therefore the companionship on which Friendship supervenes will not often be a bodily one like hunting or fighting. It may be a common religion, common studies, a common profession, even a common recreation. All who share it will be our companions: but one or two or three who share something more will be our Friends. In this kind of love, as Emerson said, *Do you love me?* means *Do you see the same truth?* — Or at least, 'Do you *care about* the same truth?' The man who agrees with us that some question, little regarded by others, is of great importance can be our Friend. He need not agree with us about the answer.

Naked Personalities   JUNE 22

This love (essentially) ignores not only our physical bodies but that whole embodiment which consists of our family, job, past and connections. At home, besides being Peter or Jane, we also bear a general character; husband or wife, brother or sister, chief, colleague or subordinate. Not among our Friends. It is an affair of disentangled, or stripped, minds. Eros will have naked bodies; Friendship naked personalities.

Hence (if you will not misunderstand me) the exquisite arbitrariness and irresponsibility of this love. I have no duty to be anyone's Friend and no man in the world has a duty to be mine. No claims, no shadow of necessity. Friendship is unnecessary, like philosphy, like art, like the universe itself (for God did not need to create). It has no survival value; rather it is one of those things which give value to survival. . . .

In a perfect Friendship this Appreciative love is, I think, often so great and so firmly based that each member of the circle feels, in his secret heart, humbled before all the rest. Sometimes he wonders what he is doing there among his betters. He is lucky beyond desert to be in such company. Especially when the whole group is together, each bringing out all that is best, wisest, or funniest in all the others. Those are the golden sessions; when four or five of us after a hard day's walking have come to our inn; when our slippers are on, our feet spread out towards the blaze and our drinks at our elbows; when the whole world, and something beyond the world, opens itself to our minds as we talk; and no one has any claim on or any responsibility for another, but all are freemen and equals as if we had first met an hour ago, while at the same time an Affection mellowed by the years enfolds us. Life – natural life – has no better gift to give. Who could have deserved it?

Friendship Needs Divine Protection JUNE 23

Friendship, like the other natural loves, is unable to save itself. In reality, because it is spiritual and therefore faces a subtler enemy, it must, even more wholeheartedly than they, invoke the divine protection if it hopes to remain sweet. For consider how narrow its true path is. It must not become what the people call a 'mutual admiration society'; yet if it is not full of mutual admiration, of Appreciative love, it is not Friendship at all. . . .

For a Christian, there are, strictly speaking, no chances. A secret Master of the Ceremonies had been at work. Christ, who said to the disciples, 'Ye have not chosen me, but I have chosen you', can truly say to every group of Christian friends, 'You have not chosen one another but I have chosen you for one another.' The Friendship is not a reward for our discrimination and good taste in finding one another out. It is the instrument by which God reveals to each the beauties of all the others. They are no greater than the beauties of a thousand other men; by Friendship God opens our eyes to them. They are, like all beauties, derived from Him, and then, in a good Friendship, increased by Him through the Friendship itself, so that it is His instrument for creating as well as for revealing. At this feast it is He who has spread the board and it is He who has chosen the guests. It is He, we may dare to hope, who sometimes does, and always should, preside. Let us not reckon without our Host.

Eros   JUNE 24

By Eros I mean of course that state we call 'being in love'; or, if you prefer, that kind of love which lovers are 'in'. Some readers may have been surprised when...I described Affection as the love in which our experience seems to come closest to that of the animals. Surely, it might be asked, our sexual functions bring us equally close? That is quite true as regards human sexuality in general. But I am not going to be concerned with human sexuality simply as such. Sexuality makes part of our subject only when it becomes an ingredient in the complex state of 'being in love'. That sexual experience can occur without Eros, without being in 'love', and that Eros can include other things besides sexual activity,I take for granted. If you prefer to put it that way, I am inquiring not into the sexuality which is common to us and the beasts or even common to all men, but into one uniquely human variation of it which develops within 'love' – what I call Eros. The carnal or animally sexual element within Eros, I intend (following an old usage) to call Venus. And I mean by Venus what is sexual not in some cryptic or rarefied sense – such as a depth-psychologist might explore – but in a perfectly obvious sense; what is known to be sexual by those who experience it; what could be proved to be sexual by the simplest observations.

Eros and Obedience or Disobedience to God   JUNE 25

Sexuality may operate without Eros or as part of Eros. Let me hasten to add that I make the distinction simply in order to limit our inquiry and without any moral implications. I am not at all subscribing to the popular idea that it is the absence or presence of Eros which makes the sexual act 'impure' or 'pure', degraded or fine, unlawful or lawful. If all who lay together without being in the state of Eros were abominable, we all come of tainted stock. The times and places in which marriage depends on Eros are in a small minority. Most of our ancestors were married off in early youth to partners chosen by their parents on grounds that had nothing to do with Eros. They went to the act with no other 'fuel', so to speak, than plain animal desire. And they did right; honest Christian husbands and wives, obeying their fathers and mothers, discharging to one another their 'marriage debt', and bringing up families in the fear of the Lord. Conversely, this act, done under the influence of a soaring and iridescent Eros which reduces the role of the senses to a minor consideration, may yet be plain adultery, may involve breaking a wife's heart, deceiving a husband, betraying a friend, polluting hospitality and deserting your children. It has not pleased God that the distinction between a sin and a duty should turn on fine feelings. This act, like any other, is justified (or not) by far more prosaic and definable criteria; by the keeping or breaking of promises, by justice or injustice, by charity or selfishness, by obedience or disobedience.

Eros Admires the Beloved JUNE 26

To the evolutionist Eros (the human variation) will be something that grows out of Venus, a late complication and development of the immemorial biological impulse. We must not assume, however, that this is necessarily what happens within the consciousness of the individual. There may be those who have first felt mere sexual appetite for a woman and then gone on at a later stage to 'fall in love with her'. But I doubt if this is at all common. Very often what comes first is simply a delighted preoccupation with the Beloved – a general, unspecified preoccupation with her in her totality. A man in this state really hasn't leisure to think of sex. He is too busy thinking of a person. The fact that she is a woman is far less important than the fact that she is herself. He is full of desire, but the desire may not be sexually toned. If you asked him what he wanted, the true reply would often be, 'To go on thinking of her'. He is love's contemplative. And when at a later stage the explicitly sexual element awakes, he will not feel (unless scientific theories are influencing him) that this had all along been the root of the whole matter. He is more likely to feel that the incoming tide of Eros, having demolished many sandcastles and made islands of many rocks, has now at last with a triumphant seventh wave flooded this part of his nature also – the little pool of ordinary sexuality which was there on his beach before the tide came in. Eros enters him like an invader, taking over and reorganizing, one by one, the institutions of a conquered country.

Venus Wants 'It' JUNE 27

George Orwell…preferred sexuality in its native condition, uncontaminated by Eros. In *1984* his dreadful hero, before towsing the heroine, demands a reassurance: 'You like doing this?' he asks. 'I don't mean simply me; I mean the thing in itself.' He

is not satisfied till he gets the answer, 'I adore it.' This little dialogue defines the reor-
ganization. Sexual desire, without Eros, wants *it,* the *thing in itself,* Eros wants the
Beloved.

The *thing* is a sensory pleasure; that is, an event occurring within one's own body.
We use a most unfortunate idiom when we say, of a lustful man prowling the streets,
that he 'wants a woman'. Strictly speaking, a woman is just what he does not want. He
wants a pleasure for which a woman happens to be the necessary piece of apparatus.
How much he cares about the woman as such may be gauged by his attitude to her five
minutes after fruition (one does not keep the carton after one has smoked the
cigarettes). Now Eros makes a man really want, not a woman, but one particular
woman. In some mysterious but quite indisputable fashion the lover desires the
Beloved herself, not the pleasure she can give. No lover in the world ever sought the
embraces of the woman he loved as the result of a calculation, however unconscious,
that they would be more pleasurable than those of any other woman. If he raised the
question he would, no doubt, expect that this would be so. But to raise it would be to
step outside the world of Eros altogether.

One Spiritual Danger in Eros   JUNE 28

It has been widely held in the past, and is perhaps held by many unsophisticated
people today, that the spiritual danger of Eros arises almost entirely from the carnal
element within it; that Eros is 'noblest' or 'purest' when Venus is reduced to the minimum. The older moral theologians certainly seem to have thought that the danger
we chiefly had to guard against in marriage was that of a soul-destroying surrender to
the senses. It will be noticed, however, that this is not the Scriptural approach. St
Paul, dissuading his converts from marriage, says nothing about that side of the matter except to discourage prolonged abstinence from Venus (1 Corinthians 7:5). What
he fears is preoccupation, the need of constantly 'pleasing' — that is, considering —
one's partner, the multiple distractions of domesticity. It is marriage itself, not the
marriage bed, that will be likely to hinder us from waiting uninterruptedly on God.
And surely St Paul is right? If I may trust my own experience, it is (within marriage
as without) the practical and prudential cares of this world, and even the smallest and
most prosaic of those cares, that are the great distraction. The gnat-like cloud of petty anxieties and decisions about the conduct of the next hour have interfered with my
prayers more often than any passion or appetite whatever. The great, permanent
temptation of marriage is not to sensuality but (quite bluntly) to avarice.

St Peter and St Paul, Apostles JUNE 29

Peter has confessed Jesus to be the Anointed One. That flash of glory is hardly over before the dark prophecy begins – that the Son of Man must suffer and die. Then this contrast is repeated. Peter, raised for a moment by his confession, makes his false step; the crushing rebuff 'Get thee behind me' follows. Then, across that momentary ruin which Peter (as so often) becomes, the voice of the Master, turning to the crowd, generalizes the moral. All His followers must take up the cross. This avoidance of suffering, this self-preservation, is not what life is really about. Then, more definitely still, the summons to martyrdom. You must stand to your tackling. If you disown Christ here and now, He will disown you later.

I think the 'low' church milieu that I grew up in did tend to be too cosily at ease in Sion. My grandfather, I'm told, used to say that he 'looked forward to having some very interesting conversations with St Paul when he got to heaven'. Two clerical gentlemen talking at ease in a club! It never seemed to cross his mind that an encounter with St Paul might be rather an overwhelming experience even for an Evangelical clergyman of good family. But when Dante saw the great apostles in heaven they affected him like *mountains*. There's lots to be said against devotions to saints; but at least they keep on reminding us that we are very small people compared with them. How much smaller before their Master?

Angels, Tom-Cats, and the Marriage-Bed JUNE 30

We must not be totally serious about Venus. Indeed we can't be totally serious without doing violence to our humanity. It is not for nothing that every language and literature in the world is full of jokes about sex. Many of them may be dull or disgusting and nearly all of them are old. But we must insist that they embody an attitude to Venus which in the long run endangers the Christian life far less than a reverential gravity. . . .

She herself is a mocking, mischievous spirit, far more elf than deity, and make game of us. When all external circumstances are fittest for her service she will leave one or both the lovers totally indisposed for it. When every overt act is impossible and even glances cannot be exchanged – in trains, in shops and at interminable parties – she will assail them with all her force. An hour later, when time and place agree, she will have mysteriously withdrawn; perhaps from only one of them. What a pother this must raise – what resentments, self-pities, suspicions, wounded vanities and all the current chatter about 'frustration' – in those who have deified her! But sensible lovers laugh. . . .

I can hardly help regarding it as one of God's jokes that a passion so soaring, so apparently transcendent, as Eros, should thus be linked in incongruous symbiosis with a bodily appetite which, like any other appetite, tactlessly reveals its connections with such mundane factors as weather, health, diet, circulation, and digestion. In Eros at times we seem to be flying; Venus gives us the sudden twitch that reminds us we are really captive balloons. It is a continual demonstration of the truth that we are composite creatures, rational animals, akin on one side to the angels, on the other to tom-cats. It is a bad thing not to be able to take a joke. Worse, not to take a divine joke; made, I grant you, at our expense, but also (who doubts it?) for our endless benefit.

The 'Headship' of the Christian Husband   JULY 1

Christian law has crowned him in the permanent relationship of marriage, bestowing — or should I say, inflicting? — a certain 'headship' on him. . . . As we could easily take the natural mystery too seriously, so we might take the Christian mystery not seriously enough. Christian writers (notably Milton) have sometimes spoken of the husband's headship with a complacency to make the blood run cold. We must go back to our Bibles. The husband is the head of the wife just in so far as he is to her what Christ is to the Church. He is to love her as Christ loved the Church — read on — *and gave his life for her* (Ephesians 5:25). This headship, then, is most fully embodied not in the husband we should all wish to be but in him whose marriage is most like a crucifixion; whose wife receives most and gives least, is most unworthy of him, is — in her own mere nature — least lovable. For the Church has no beauty but what the Bridegroom gives her; he does not find, but makes her, lovely. The chrism of this terrible coronation is to be seen not in the joys of any man's marriage but in its sorrows, in the sickness and sufferings of a good wife or the faults of a bad one, in his unwearying (never paraded) care or his inexhaustible forgiveness: forgiveness, not acquiescence. As Christ sees in the flawed, proud, fanatical or lukewarm Church on earth that Bride who will one day be without spot or wrinkle, and labours to produce the latter, so the husband whose headship is Christ-like (and he is allowed no other sort) never despairs. . . .

To say this is not to say that there is any virtue or wisdom in making a marriage that involves such misery. There is no wisdom or virtue in seeking unnecessary martyrdom or deliberately courting persecution; yet it is, none the less, the persecuted or martyred Christian in whom the pattern of the Master is most unambiguously realized. So, in these terrible marriages, once they have come about, the 'headship' of the husband, if only he can sustain it, is most Christ-like.

The sternest feminist need not grudge my sex the crown offered to it either in the

Pagan or in the Christian mystery. For the one is of paper and the other of thorns. The real danger is not that husbands may grasp the latter too eagerly; but that they will allow or compel their wives to usurp it.

When Eros Speaks Like a God JULY 2

Eros, honoured without reservation and obeyed unconditionally, becomes a demon. And this is just how he claims to be honoured and obeyed. Divinely indifferent to our selfishness, he is also demoniacally rebellious to every claim of God or Man that would oppose him. . . . When lovers say of some act that we might blame, 'Love made us do it', notice the tone. A man saying, 'I did it because I was frightened', or 'I did it because I was angry', speaks quite differently. He is putting forward an excuse for what he feels to require excusing. But the lovers are seldom doing quite that. Notice how tremulously, almost how devoutly, they say the word *love,* not so much pleading an 'extenuating circumstance' as appealing to an authority. The confession can be almost a boast. There can be a shade of defiance in it. They 'feel like martyrs'. In extreme cases what their words really express is a demure yet unshakable allegiance to the god of love.

'These reasons in love's law have passed for good', says Milton's Dalila. That is the point; *in love's law.* . . . It seems to sanction all sorts of actions they would not otherwise have dared. I do not mean solely, or chiefly, acts that violate chastity. They are just as likely to be acts of injustice or uncharity against the outer world. They will seem like proofs of piety and zeal towards Eros. The pair can say to one another in an almost sacrificial spirit, 'It is for love's sake that I have neglected my parents – left my children – cheated my partner – failed my friend at his greatest need.' These reasons in love's law have passed for good. The votaries may even come to feel a particular merit in such sacrifices; what costlier offering can be laid on love's altar than one's conscience?

St Thomas, Apostle JULY 3

The saying 'Blessed are those that have not seen and have believed' has nothing to do with our original assent to the Christian propositions. It was not addressed to a philosopher inquiring whether God exists. It was addressed to a man who already believed that, who already had long acquaintance with a particular Person, and evidence that that Person could do very odd things, and who then refused to believe one odd thing more, often predicted by that Person and vouched for by all His closest friends. It is a rebuke not to scepticism in the philosophic sense but to the psychological quality of being 'suspicious'. It says in effect, 'You should have known me better.' There are cases between man and man where we should all, in our different ways, bless those who have not seen and have believed. Our relation to those who trusted us only after we were proved innocent in court cannot be the same as our relation to those who trusted us all through.

We Must Do What Eros Cannot Do   JULY 4

The couple whose marriage will certainly be endangered . . . and possibly ruined, are those who have idolized Eros. They thought he had the power and truthfulness of a god. They expected that mere feeling would do for them, and permanently, all that was necessary. When this expectation is disappointed they throw the blame on Eros or, more usually, on their partners. In reality, however, Eros, having made his gigantic promise and shown you in glimpses what its performance would be like, has 'done his stuff'. He, like a godparent, makes the vows; it is we who must keep them. It is we who must labour to bring our daily life into even closer accordance with what the glimpses have revealed. We must do the works of Eros when Eros is not present. This all good lovers know, though those who are not reflective or articulate must be able to express it only in a few conventional phrases about 'taking the rough along with the smooth', not 'expecting too much', having 'a little common sense', and the like. And all good Christian lovers know that this programme, modest as it sounds, will not be carried out except by humility, charity and divine grace; that it is indeed the whole Christian life seen from one particular angle.

Charity   JULY 5

William Morris wrote a poem called 'Love Is Enough' and someone is said to have reviewed it briefly in the words 'It isn't'. . . . The natural loves are not self-sufficient. Something else, at first vaguely described as 'decency and common sense', but later revealed as goodness, and finally as the whole Christian life in one particular relation, must come to the help of the mere feeling if the feeling is to be kept sweet.

To say this is not to belittle the natural loves but to indicate where their real glory lies. It is no disparagement to a garden to say that it will not fence and weed itself, nor prune its own fruit trees, nor roll and cut its own lawns. A garden is a good thing but that is not the sort of goodness it has. It will remain a garden, as distinct from a wilderness, only if someone does all these things to it. Its real glory is of quite a different kind. The very fact that it needs constant weeding and pruning bears witness to that glory. It teems with life. It glows with colour and smells like heaven and puts forward at every hour of a summer day beauties which man could never have created and could not even, on his own resources, have imagined. If you want to see the difference between its contribution and the gardener's, put the commonest weed it grows side by side with his hoes, rakes, shears, and packet of weed killer; you have put beauty, energy and fecundity beside dead, sterile things. Just so, our 'decency and common sense' show grey and deathlike beside the geniality of love.

Do Not Imagine You Have Come Further than You Have JULY 6

For most of us the true rivalry lies between the self and the human Other, not yet between the human Other and God. It is dangerous to press upon a man the duty of getting beyond earthly love when his real difficulty lies in getting so far. And it is no doubt easy enough to love the fellow creature less and to imagine that this is happening because we are learning to love God more, when the real reason may be quite different. We may be only 'mistaking the decays of nature for the increase of Grace'. Many people do not find it really difficult to hate their wives or mothers. Mr Mauriac, in a fine scene, pictures the other disciples stunned and bewildered by this strange command, but not Judas. He laps it up easily.

The Natural Loves' Claim to Divinity JULY 7

The loves prove that they are unworthy to take the place of God by the fact that they cannot even remain themselves and do what they promise to do without God's help. Why prove that some petty princeling is not the lawful Emperor when without the Emperor's support he cannot even keep his subordinate throne and make peace in his little province for half a year? Even for their own sakes the loves must submit to be second things if they are to remain the things they want to be. In this yoke lies their true freedom; they 'are taller when they bow'. For when God rules in a human heart, though He may sometimes have to remove certain of its native authorities altogether, He often continues others in their offices and, by subjecting their authority to His, gives it for the first time a firm basis. Emerson has said, 'When half-gods go, the gods arrive.' That is a very doubtful maxim. Better say, 'When God arrives (and only then) the half-gods can remain.' Left to themselves they either vanish or become demons. Only in His name can they with beauty and security 'wield their little tridents'. The rebellious slogan 'All for love' is really love's death warrant (date of execution, for the moment, left blank).

Safe Investments and Limited Liabilities   JULY 8

In words which can still bring tears to the eyes, St Augustine describes the desolation in which the death of his friend Nebridius plunged him *Confessions* IV, 10). Then he draws a moral. This is what comes, he says, of giving one's heart to anything but God. All human beings pass away. Do not let your happiness depend on something you may lose. If love is to be a blessing, not a misery, it must be for the only Beloved who will never pass away.

Of course this is excellent sense. Don't put your goods in a leaky vessel. Don't spend too much on a house you may be turned out of. And there is no man alive who responds more naturally than I do to such canny maxims. I am a safety-first creature. Of all arguments against love none makes so strong an appeal to my nature as 'Careful! This might lead you to suffering.'

To my nature, my temperament, yes. Not to my conscience. When I respond to that appeal I seem to myself to be a thousand miles away from Christ. If I am sure of anything I am sure that His teaching was never meant to confirm my congenital preference for safe investments and limited liabilities. I doubt whether there is anything in me that pleases Him less. And who could conceivably begin to love God on such a prudential ground – because the security (so to speak) is better? Who could even include it among the grounds for loving? Would you choose a wife or a Friend – if it comes to that, would you choose a dog – in this spirit? One must be outside the world of love, of all loves, before one thus calculates. Eros, lawless Eros, preferring the Beloved to happiness, is more like Love Himself than this.

No Insurances Against Heartbreak   JULY 9

Even if it were granted that insurances against heartbreak were our highest wisdom, does God Himself offer them? Apparently not. Christ comes at last to say 'Why hast thou forsaken me?' ...

To love at all is to be vulnerable. Love anything, and your heart will certainly be wrung and possibly be broken. If you want to make sure of keeping it intact, you must give your heart to no one, not even to an animal. Wrap it carefully round with hobbies and little luxuries; avoid all entanglements; lock it up safe in the casket or coffin of your selfishness. But in that casket – safe, dark, motionless, airless – it will change. It will not be broken; it will become unbreakable, impenetrable, irredeemable. The alternative to tragedy, or at least to the risk of tragedy, is damnation. The only place outside Heaven where you can be perfectly safe from all the dangers and perturbations of love is Hell.

I believe that the most lawless and inordinate loves are less contrary to God's will than a self-invited and self-protective lovelessness. It is like hiding the talent in a napkin and for much the same reason. 'I knew thee that thou wert a hard man.' Christ did not teach and suffer that we might become, even in the natural loves, more careful of our own happiness. If a man is not uncalculating towards the earthly beloveds whom he has seen, he is none the more likely to be so towards God whom he has not. We shall draw nearer to God, not by trying to avoid the sufferings inherent in all loves, but by accepting them and offering them to Him; throwing away all defensive armour. If our hearts need to be broken, and if He chooses this as the way in which they should break, so be it.

'Hating' the People We Love   JULY 10

As so often, Our Lord's own words are both far fiercer and far more tolerable than those of the theologians. He says nothing about guarding against earthly loves for fear we might be hurt; He says something that cracks like a whip about trampling them all under foot the moment they hold us back from following Him. 'If any man come to me and hate not his father and mother and wife... and his own life also, he cannot be my disciple' (Luke 14:26).

But how are we to understand the word *hate*? That Love Himself should be commanding what we ordinarily mean by hatred – commanding us to cherish resentment, to gloat over another's misery, to delight in injuring him – is almost a contradiction in terms. I think Our Lord, in the sense here intended, 'hated' St Peter when he said, 'Get thee behind me.' To hate is to reject, to set one's face against, to make no concession to, the Beloved when the Beloved utters, however sweetly and however pitiably, the suggestions of the Devil. A man, said Jesus, who tries to serve two masters, will 'hate' the one and 'love' the other. It is not, surely, mere feelings of aversion and liking that are here in question.... In the last resort, we must turn down or disqualify our nearest and dearest when they come between us and our obedience to God. Heaven knows, it will seem to them sufficiently like hatred. We must not act on the pity we feel; we must be blind to tears and deaf to pleadings.

I will not say that this duty is hard; some find it too easy; some, hard almost beyond endurance. What is hard for all is to know when the occasion for such 'hating' has arisen. Our temperaments deceive us. The meek and tender — uxorious husbands, submissive wives, doting parents, dutiful children — will not easily believe that it has ever arrived. Self-assertive people, with a dash of the bully in them, will believe it too soon. That is why it is of such extreme importance so to order our loves that it is unlikely to arrive at all.

The Raising of All Loves   JULY 11

We may hope that the resurrection of the body means also the resurrection of what may be called our 'greater body'; the general fabric of our earthly life with its affections and relationships. But only on a condition; not a condition arbitrarily laid down by God, but one necessarily inherent in the character of Heaven: nothing can enter there which cannot become heavenly. 'Flesh and blood', mere nature, cannot inherit that Kingdom. Man can ascend to Heaven only because the Christ, who died and ascended to Heaven, is 'formed in him'. Must we not suppose that the same is true of a man's loves? Only those into which Love Himself has entered will ascend to Love Himself. And these can be raised with Him only if they have, in some degree and fashion, shared His death; if the natural element in them has submitted — year after year, or in some sudden agony — to transmutation. The fashion of this world passes away. The very name of nature implies the transitory. Natural loves can hope for eternity only in so far as they have allowed themselves to be taken into the eternity of Charity; have at least allowed the process to begin here on earth, before the night comes when no man can work. And the process will always involve a kind of death. There is no escape. In my love for wife or friend the only eternal element is the transforming presence of Love Himself. By that presence, if at all, the other elements may hope, as our physical bodies hope, to be raised from the dead. For this only is holy in them, this only is the Lord.

Philautia: *Self-Love*   JULY 12

Self-renunciation is thought to be, and indeed is, very near the core of Christian ethics. When Aristotle writes in praise of a certain kind of self-love, we may feel, despite the careful distinctions which he draws between the legitimate and the illegitimate *Philautia*. that here we strike something essentially sub-Christian. It is more difficult, however, to decide what we think of St François de Sales's chapter *De la douceur envers nous-mesmes* ['Of meekness towards ourselves'], where we are forbidden to indulge resentment even against ourselves and advised to reprove even our own faults *avec des remonstrances douces et tranquilles* ['with mild and calm remonstrances'], feeling more compassion than passion. In the same spirit, Lady Julian of Norwich would have us 'loving and peaceable', not only to our 'even-Christians', but to 'ourself'. Even the New Testament bids me love my neighbour 'as myself', which would be a horrible command if the self were simply to be hated. Yet Our Lord also says that a true disciple must 'hate his own life'.

Two Kinds of Self-Hatred   JULY 13

We must not explain this apparent contradiction by saying that self-love is right up to a certain point and wrong beyond that point. The question is not one of degree. There are two kinds of self-hatred which look rather alike in their earlier stages, but of which one is wrong from the beginning and the other right to the end. When Shelley speaks of self-contempt as the source of cruelty, or when a later poet says that he has no stomach for the man 'who loathes his neighbour as himself', they are referring to a very real and very un-Christian hatred of the self which may make diabolical a man whom common selfishness would have left (at least, for a while) merely animal. The hardboiled economist or psychologist of our own day, recognizing the 'ideological taint' or Freudian motive in his own make-up, does not necessarily learn Christian humility. He may end in what is called a 'low view' of all souls, including his own, which expresses itself in cynicism or cruelty, or both. Even Christians, if they accept in certain forms the doctrine of total depravity, are not always free from the danger. The logical conclusion of the process is the worship of suffering — for others as well as for the self — which we see, if I read it aright, in Mr David Lindsay's *Voyage to Arcturus,* or that extraordinary vacancy which Shakespeare depicts at the end of *Richard III.* Richard in his agony tries to turn to self-love. But he has been 'seeing through' all emotions so long that he 'sees through' even this. It becomes a mere tautology: 'Richard loves Richard; that is, I am I.'

Two Ways with the Self   JULY 14

The self can be regarded in two ways. On the one hand, it is God's creature, an occasion of love and rejoicing; now, indeed, hateful in condition, but to be pitied and healed. On the other hand, it is that one self of all others which is called *I* and *me,* and which on that ground puts forward an irrational claim to preference. This claim is to be not only hated, but simply killed; 'never', as George MacDonald says, 'to be allowed a moment's respite from eternal death.' The Christian must wage endless war against the clamour of the *ego* as *ego*: but he loves and approves selves as such, though not their sins. The very self-love which he has to reject is to him a specimen of how he ought to feel to all selves; and he may hope that when he has truly learned (which will hardly be in this life) to love his neighbour as himself, he may then be able to love himself as his neighbour: that is, with charity instead of partiality. The other kind of self-hatred, on the contrary, hates selves as such. It begins by accepting the special value of the particular self called *me*; then, wounded in its pride to find that such a darling object should be so disappointing, it seeks revenge, first upon that self, then on all. Deeply egoistic, but now with an inverted egoism, it uses the reveal-ing argument, 'I don't spare myself' — with the implication 'then *a fortiori* I need not spare others' — and becomes like the centurion in Tacitus, *immitior quia toleraverat* ['more relentless because he had endured it himself'].

The wrong asceticism torments the self: the right kind kills the selfness. We must die daily: but it is better to love the self than to love nothing, and to pity the self than to pity no one.

Looking Beyond Ourselves   JULY 15

We should, I believe, distrust states of mind which turn our attention upon ourselves. Even at our sins we should look no longer than is necessary to know and to repent them; and our virtues or progress (if any) are certainly a dangerous object of contem-plation. When the sun is vertically above a man he casts no shadow: similarly when we have come to the Divine meridian our spiritual shadow (that is, our consciousness of self) will vanish. One will thus in a sense be almost nothing: a room to be filled by God and our blessed fellow creatures, who in their turn are rooms we help to fill.

A Dislocation of the Aesthetic Life   JULY 16

Until quite modern times — I think, until the time of the Romantics — nobody ever suggested that literature and the arts were an end in themselves. They 'belonged to the ornamental part of life', they provided 'innocent diversion'; or else they 'refined our manners' or 'incited us to virtue' or glorified the gods. The great music had been written for Masses, the great pictures painted to fill up a space on the wall of a noble patron's dining-room or to kindle devotion in a church; the great tragedies were pro-

duced either by religious poets in honour of Dionysius or by commercial poets to entertain Londoners on half-holidays.

It was only in the nineteenth century that we became aware of the full dignity of
art. We began to 'take it seriously'. . . . But the result seems to have been a dislocation
of the aesthetic life in which little is left for us but high-minded works which fewer
and fewer people want to read or hear or see, and 'popular' works of which both those
who make them and those who enjoy them are half ashamed. . . . By valuing too highly
a real, but subordinate good, we have come near to losing that good itself.

First and Second Things JULY 17

The longer I looked into it the more I came to suspect that I was perceiving a universal law. *On cause mieux quand on ne dit pas Causons* ['One converses better when
one does not say "Let us converse"]. The woman who makes a dog the centre of her
life loses, in the end, not only her human usefulness and dignity but even the proper
pleasure of dog-keeping. The man who makes alcohol his chief good loses not only
his job but his palate and all power of enjoying the earlier (and only pleasurable)
levels of intoxication. It is a glorious thing to feel for a moment or two that the whole
meaning of the universe is summed up in one woman — glorious so long as other
duties and pleasures keep tearing you away from her. But clear the decks and so ar-
range your life (it is sometimes feasible) that you will have nothing to do but contemplate her, and what happens? Of course this law has been discovered before, but it
will stand re-discovery. It may be stated as follows: every preference of a small good
to a great, or a partial good to a total good, involves the loss of the small or partial
good for which the sacrifice was made.

Apparently the world is made that way. If Esau really got the pottage in return for
his birthright, then Esau was a lucky exception. You can't get things only by putting
first things first. From which it would follow that the question, What things are first?
is of concern not only to philosophers but to everyone.

Is World Peace More Important than Salvation? JULY 18

It is impossible. . . not to inquire what our own civilization has been putting first for
the last thirty years. And the answer is plain. It has been putting itself first. To preserve civilization has been the great aim; the collapse of civilization, the great bugbear. Peace, a high standard of life, hygiene, transport, science and amusement — all

these, which are what we usually mean by civilization, have been our ends. It will be replied that our concern for civilization is very natural and very necessary at a time when civilization is so imperilled. But how if the shoe is on the other foot? – how if civilization has been imperilled precisely by the fact that we have all made civilization our *summum bonum?* Perhaps it can't be preserved in that way. Perhaps civilization will never be safe until we care for something else more than we care for it.

The hypothesis has certain facts to support it. As far as peace (which is one ingredient in our idea of civilization) is concerned, I think many would now agree that a foreign policy dominated by desire for peace is one of the many roads that lead to war. And was civilization ever seriously endangered until civilization became the exclusive aim of human activity? There is much rash idealization of past ages about, and I do not wish to encourage more of it. Our ancestors were cruel, lecherous, greedy and stupid, like ourselves. But while they cared for other things more than for civilization – and they cared at different times for all sorts of things, for the will of God, for glory, for personal honour, for doctrinal purity, for justice – was civilization often in serious danger of disappearing?

At least the suggestion is worth a thought. To be sure, if it were true that civilization will never be safe till it is put second, that immediately raises the question, second to what? What is the first thing? The only reply I can offer here is that if we do not know, then the first and only truly practical thing is to set about finding out.

The Bomb   JULY 19

Progress means movement in a desired direction, and we do not all desire the same things for our species. In 'Possible Worlds' Professor Haldane pictured a future in which Man, foreseeing that Earth would soon be uninhabitable, adapted himself for migration to Venus by drastically modifying his physiology and abandoning justice, pity and happiness. The desire here is for mere survival. Now I care far more how humanity lives than how long. Progress, for me, means increasing goodness and happiness of individual lives. For the species, as for each man, mere longevity seems to me a contemptible ideal.

I therefore go even further than C. P. Snow in removing the H-bomb from the centre of the picture. Like him, I am not certain whether if it killed one-third of us (the one-third I belong to), this would be a bad thing for the remainder; like him, I don't think it will kill us all. But suppose it did? As a Christian I take it for granted that human history will some day end; and I am offering Omniscience no advice as to the best date for that consummation. I am more concerned by what the Bomb is doing already.

One meets young people who make the threat of it a reason for poisoning every pleasure and evading every duty in the present. Don't they know that, Bomb or no Bomb, all men die (many in horrible ways)?

Equality JULY 20

It is idle to say that men are of equal value. If value is taken in a worldly sense — if we mean that all men are equally useful or beautiful or good or entertaining — then it is nonsense. If it means that all are of equal value as immortal souls then I think it conceals a dangerous error. The infinite value of each human soul is not a Christian doctrine. God did not die for man because of some value He perceived in him. The value of each human soul considered simply in itself, out of relation to God, is zero. As St Paul writes, to have died for valuable men would have been not divine but merely heroic; but God died for sinners. He loved us not because we were lovable, but because He is Love. It may be that He loves all equally — He certainly loved all to the death — and I am not certain what the expression means. If there is equality it is in His love, not in us.

Democracy JULY 21

I am a democrat because I believe in the Fall of Man. I think most people are democrats for the opposite reason. A great deal of democratic enthusiasm descends from the ideas of people like Rousseau, who believed in democracy because they thought mankind so wise and good that everyone deserved a share in the government. The danger of defending democracy on those grounds is that they are not true. And whenever their weakness is exposed, the people who prefer tyranny make capital out of the exposure. I find that they're not true without looking further than myself. I don't deserve a share in governing a henroost, much less a nation. Nor do most people — all the people who believe advertisements, and think in catchwords and spread rumours. The real reason for democracy is just the reverse. Mankind is so fallen that no man can be trusted with unchecked power over his fellows. . . .

This introduces a view of equality rather different from that in which we have been trained. I do not think that equality is one of those things (like wisdom or happiness) which are good simply in themselves and for their own sakes. I think it is in the same class as medicine, which is good because we are ill, or clothes, which are good because we are no longer innocent. . . . When equality is treated not as a medicine or a safety-gadget but as an ideal, we begin to breed that stunted and envious sort of mind which hates all superiority.

St Mary Magdalen   JULY 22

It is nice to be still under the care of St Mary Magdalen. . . . The allegorical sense of her great action dawned on me the other day. The precious alabaster box which one must *break* over the Holy Feet is one's *heart*. Easier said than done. And the contents become perfume only when it is broken. While they are safe inside they are more like sewage. All very alarming.

Monarchy: Our Taproot in Eden   JULY 23

We Britons should rejoice that we have contrived to reach much legal democracy (we still need more of the economic) without losing our ceremonial monarchy. For there, right in the midst of our lives, is that which satisfies the craving for inequality, and acts as a permanent reminder that medicine is not food. Hence a man's reaction to monarchy is a kind of test. Monarchy can easily be 'debunked'; but watch the faces, mark well the accents, of the debunkers. These are the men whose taproot in Eden has been cut: whom no rumour of the polyphony, the dance, can reach — men to whom pebbles laid in a row are more beautiful than an arch. Yet even if they desire mere equality they cannot reach it. Where men are forbidden to honour a king they honour millionaires, athletes or film stars instead: even famous prostitutes or gangsters. For spiritual nature, like bodily nature, will be served; deny it food and it will gobble poison.

Monarchy and Statecraft   JULY 24

Corineus compared modern Christianity with the modern English monarchy: the forms of kingship have been retained, but the reality has been abandoned. . . . 'Why not cut the cord?' asks Corineus. 'Everything would be much easier if you would free your thought from this vestigial mythology.' To be sure: far easier. Life would be far easier for the mother of an invalid child if she put it into an Institution and adopted someone else's healthy baby instead. Life would be far easier to many a man if he abandoned the woman he has actually fallen in love with and married someone else because she is more suitable. The only defect of the healthy baby and the suitable woman is that they leave out the patient's only reason for bothering about a child or wife at all. 'Would not conversation be much more rational than dancing?' said Jane Austen's Miss Bingley. 'Much more rational,' replied Mr Bingley, 'but much less like a ball.'

In the same way, it would be much more rational to abolish the English monarchy. But how if, by doing so, you leave out the one element in our State which matters most? How if the monarchy is the channel through which all the *vital* elements of citizenship – loyalty, the consecration of secular life, the hierarchical principle, splendour, ceremony, continuity – still trickle down to irrigate the dustbowl of modern economic Statecraft?

St James, Apostle   JULY 25

The New Testament contains embarrassing promises that what we pray for with faith we shall receive. Mark 11:24 is the most staggering. Whatever we ask for, believing that we'll get it, we'll get.... How is this astonishing promise to be reconciled (a) With the observed facts? and (b) with the prayer in Gethsemane, and (as a result of that prayer) the universally accepted view that we should ask everything with a reservation ('If it be Thy will')?

As regards (a), no evasion is possible. Every war, every famine or plague, almost every deathbed, is the monument to a petition that was not granted. At this very moment thousands of people in this one island are facing as a *fait accompli* the very thing against which they have prayed night and day....

But (b), though much less often mentioned, is surely an equal difficulty. How is it possible at one and the same moment to have a perfect faith – an untroubled or unhesitating faith as St James says (1:6) – that you will get what you ask for and yet also prepare yourself submissively in advance for a possible refusal? If you envisage a refusal as possible, how can you have simultaneously a perfect confidence that what you ask will not be refused? If you have that confidence, how can you take refusal into account at all?...

As regards the first difficulty, I'm not asking why our petitions are so often refused. Anyone can see in general that this must be so. In our ignorance we ask what is not good for us or for others, or not even intrinsically possible. Or again, to grant one man's prayer involves refusing another's. There is much here which it is hard for our will to accept but nothing that is hard for our intellect to understand. The real problem is different; not why refusal is so frequent, but why the opposite result is so lavishly promised.

Shall we...scrap the embarrassing promises as 'venerable archaisms' which have to be 'outgrown'? Surely, even if there were no other objection, that method is too easy. If we are free to delete all inconvenient data we shall certainly have no theological difficulties; but for the same reason no solutions and no progress. The very writers of the detective stories, not to mention the scientists, know better. The troublesome fact, the apparent absurdity which can't be fitted in to any synthesis we have yet made, is precisely the one we must not ignore. . . . There is always hope if we keep an unsolved problem fairly in view; there's none if we pretend it's not there.

Screwtape on Democracy JULY 26

Democracy is the word with which you must lead them by the nose. The good work which our philological experts have already done in the corruption of human language makes it unnecessary to warn you that they should never be allowed to give this word a clear and definable meaning. They won't. It will never occur to them that *democracy* is properly the name of a political system, even a system of voting, and that this has only the most remote and tenuous connection with what you are trying to sell them. Nor of course must they ever be allowed to raise Aristotle's question: whether 'democratic behaviour' means the behaviour that democracies like or the behaviour that will preserve a democracy. For if they did, it could hardly fail to occur to them that these need not be the same.

You are to use the word purely as an incantation; if you like, purely for its selling power. It is a name they venerate. And of course it is connected with the political ideal that men should be equally treated. You then make a stealthy transition in their minds from this political ideal to a factual belief that all men *are* equal. Especially the man you are working on. As a result you can use the word *democracy* to sanction in his thought the most degrading (and also the least enjoyable) of all human feelings. . . . The feeling I mean is of course that which prompts a man to say *I'm as good as you*. The first and most obvious advantage is that you thus induce him to enthrone at the centre of his life a good solid, resounding lie.

Screwtape's Encouragement of Envy JULY 27

Now, this useful phenomenon is in itself by no means new. Under the name of Envy it has been known to the humans for thousands of years. But hitherto they always regarded it as the most odious, and also the most comical, of vices. Those who were aware of feeling it felt it with shame; those who were not gave it no quarter in others. The delightful novelty of the present situation is that you can sanction it – make it respectable and even laudable – by the incantatory use of the word *democratic*.

Under the influence of this incantation those who are in any or every way inferior can labour more wholeheartedly and successfully than ever before to pull down everyone else to their own level. But that is not all. Under the same influence, those who come, or could come, nearer to a full humanity, actually draw back from it for fear of being undemocratic. I am credibly informed that young humans now sometimes suppress an incipient taste for classical music or good literature because it might prevent their Being Like Folks; that people who would really wish to be – and are offered the Grace which would enable them to be – honest, chaste, or temperate refuse it. To accept might make them Different, might offend against the Way of Life, take them out of Togetherness, impair their Integration with the Group. They might (horror of horrors!) become individuals.

Screwtape Explains the Disadvantages of War JULY 28

Of course a war is entertaining. . . . But, if we are not careful, we shall see thousands turning in this tribulation to the Enemy, while tens of thousands who do not go so far as that will nevertheless have their attention diverted from themselves to values and causes which they believe to be higher than the self. I know that the Enemy disapproves many of these causes. But that is where He is so unfair. He often makes prizes of humans who have given their lives for causes He thinks bad on the monstrously sophistical ground that the humans thought them good and were following the best they knew. Consider too what undesirable deaths occur in wartime. Men are killed in places where they knew they might be killed and to which they go, if they are at all of the Enemy's party, prepared. How much better for us if *all* humans died in costly nursing homes amid doctors who lie, nurses who lie, friends who lie, as we have trained them, promising life to the dying, encouraging the belief that sickness excuses every indulgence, and even, if our workers know their job, withholding all suggestion of a priest lest it should betray to the sick man his true condition! And how disastrous for us is the continual remembrance of death which war enforces. One of our best weapons, contented worldliness, is rendered useless. In wartime not even a human can believe that he is going to live forever.

St Martha   JULY 29

Human Death is the result of sin and the triumph of Satan. But it is also the means of redemption from sin, God's medicine for Man and His weapon against Satan. . . .

And one can see how it might have happened. The Enemy persuades Man to rebel against God: Man, by doing so, loses power to control that other rebellion which the Enemy now raises in Man's organism (both psychical and physical) against Man's spirit: just as that organism, in its turn, loses power to maintain itself against the rebellion of the inorganic. In that way, Satan produced human Death. But when God created Man he gave him such a constitution that, if the highest part of it rebelled against Himself, it would be bound to lose control over the lower parts: i.e. in the long run to suffer Death. This provision may be regarded equally as a punitive sentence ('In the day ye eat of that fruit ye shall die'), as a mercy, and as a safety-device. It is punishment because Death — that Death of which Martha says to Christ, 'But . . . Sir . . . it'll *smell'* — is horror and ignominy. . . . It is mercy because by willing and humble surrender to it Man undoes his act of rebellion and makes even this depraved and monstrous mode of Death an instance of that higher and mystical Death which is eternally good and a necessary ingredient in the highest life. . . . It is a safety-device because, once Man has fallen, natural immortality would be the one utterly hopeless destiny for him. Added to the surrender that he must make by no external necessity of Death, free (if you call it freedom) to rivet faster and faster about himself through unending centuries the chains of his own pride and lust and of the nightmare civilizations which these build up in ever-increasing power and complication, he would progress from being merely a fallen man to being a fiend, possibly beyond all modes of redemption.

Metaphors and Truth   JULY 30

An early peasant Christian might have thought that Christ's sitting at the right hand of the Father really implied two chairs of state, in a certain spatial relation, inside a sky palace. But if the same man afterwards received a philosophical education and discovered that God has no body, parts, or passions, and therefore neither a right hand nor a palace, he would not have felt that the essentials of his belief had been altered. What had mattered to him, even in the days of his simplicity, had not been supposed details about celestial furniture. It had been the assurance that the once crucified Master was now the supreme Agent of the unimaginable Power on whom the whole universe depends. And he would recognize that in this he had never been deceived.

The critic may still ask us why the imagery — which we admit to be untrue — should be used at all. But he has not noticed that any language we attempt to substitute for it would involve imagery that is open to all the same objections. To say that God 'enters' the natural order involves just as much spatial imagery as to say that He 'comes down'; one has simply substituted horizontal (or undefined) for vertical movement. To say that He is 're-absorbed' into the Noumenal is better than to say He 'ascended' into Heaven, only if the picture of something dissolving in warm fluid, or being sucked into a throat, is less misleading than the picture of a bird, or a balloon, going up. All language, except about objects of sense, is metaphorical through and through. To call God a 'Force' (that is, something like a wind or a dynamo) is as metaphorical as to call Him a Father or a King. On such matters we can make our language more polysyllabic and duller: we cannot make it more literal.

St. Ignatius Loyola   JULY 31

St Ignatius Loyola... advised his pupils to begin their meditations with what he called a *compositio loci*. The Nativity or the Marriage at Cana, or whatever the theme might be, was to be visualized in the fullest possible detail. One of his English followers would even have us look up 'what good Authors write of those places' so as to get the topography, 'the height of the hills and the situation of the townes', correct. Now for two different reasons this is not 'addressed to my condition'.

One is that I live in an archaeological age. We can no longer, as St Ignatius could, believingly introduce the clothes, furniture, and utensils of our own age into ancient Palestine. I'd know I wasn't getting them right. I'd know that the very sky and sunlight of those latitudes were different from any my northern imagination could supply. I could no doubt pretend to myself a naîveté I don't really possess; but that would cast an unreality over the whole exercise.

The second reason is more important. St Ignatius was a great master, and I am sure he knew what his pupils needed. I conclude that they were people whose visual imagination was weak and needed to be stimulated. But the trouble with people like ourselves is the exact reverse. We can say this to one another because, in our mouths, it is not a boast but a confession. We are agreed that the power — indeed, the compulsion — to visualize is not 'Imagination' in the higher sense, not the Imagination which makes a man either a great author or a sensitive reader. Ridden on a *very* tight rein, this visualizing power can sometimes serve true Imagination; very often it merely gets in the way.

If I started with a *compositio loci* I should never reach the meditation. The picture would go on elaborating itself indefinitely and becoming every moment of less spiritual relevance.

Looking 'Along' and Looking 'At'   AUGUST 1

I was standing today in the dark toolshed. The sun was shining outside and through the crack at the top of the door there came a sunbeam. From where I stood that beam of light, with the specks of dust floating in it, was the most striking thing in the place. Everything else was almost pitch black. I was seeing the beam, not seeing things by it.

Then I moved, so that the beam fell on my eyes. Instantly the whole previous picture vanished. I saw no toolshed, and (above all) no beam. Instead I saw, framed in the irregular cranny at the top of the door, green leaves moving on the branches of a tree outside and beyond that, ninety-odd million miles away, the sun. Looking along the beam, and looking at the beam are very different experiences.

But this is only a very simple example of the difference between looking at and looking along. A young man meets a girl. The whole world looks different when he sees her. Her voice reminds him of something he has been trying to remember all his life, and ten minutes' casual chat with her is more precious than all the favors that all other women in the world could grant. He is, as they say, 'in love'. Now comes a scientist and describes this young man's experience from the outside. For him it is all an affair of the young man's genes and a recognized biological stimulus. That is the difference between looking along the sexual impulse and looking *at* it.

Which Tells You Most about the Thing?   AUGUST 2

When you have got into the habit of making this distinction you will find examples of it all day long. The mathematician sits thinking, and to him it seems that he is contemplating timeless and spaceless truths about quantity. But the cerebral physiologist, if he could look inside the mathematician's head, would find nothing timeless and spaceless there—only tiny movements in the grey matter. The savage dances in ecstasy at midnight before Nyonga and feels with every muscle that his dance is helping to bring the new green crops and the spring rain and the babies. The anthropologist, observing that savage, records that he is performing a fertility ritual of the type so-and-so. The girl cries over her broken doll and feels that she has lost a real friend; the psychologist says that her nascent maternal instinct has been temporarily lavished on a bit of shaped and colored wax.

As soon as you have grasped this simple distinction, it raises a question. You get one experience of a thing when you look along it and another when you look at it. Which is the 'true' or 'valid' experience? Which tells you most about the thing? And you can hardly ask that question without noticing that for the last fifty years or so everyone has been taking the answer for granted. It has been assumed without discussion that if you want the true account of religion you must go, not to religious people, but to anthropologists; that if you want the true account of sexual love you must go, not to lovers, but to psychologists; that if you want to understand some 'ideology' (such as medieval chivalry or the nineteenth century idea of a 'gentleman'), you must listen not to those who lived inside it, but to sociologists.

The 'Modern' Type of Thought   AUGUST 3

The people who look *at* things have had it all their own way; the people who look *along* things have simply been browbeaten. It has even come to be taken for granted that the external account of a thing somehow refutes or 'debunks' the account given from inside. 'All these moral ideals which look so transcendental and beautiful from inside,' says the wiseacre, 'are really only a mass of biological instincts and inherited taboos.' And no one plays the game the other way round by replying, 'If you will only step inside, the things that look to you like instincts and taboos will suddenly reveal their real and transcendental nature.'

That, in fact, is the whole basis of the specifically 'modern' type of thought. And is it not, you will ask, a very sensible basis? For, after all, we are often deceived by things from the inside. For example, the girl who looks so wonderful while we're in love, may really be a very plain, stupid, and disagreeable person. The savage's dance to Nyonga does not really cause the crops to grow. Having been so often deceived by looking along, are we not well advised to trust only to looking at? – in fact to discount all these inside experiences ?

Well, no. There are two fatal objections to discounting them *all*. And the first is this. You discount them in order to think more accurately. But you can't think at all – and therefore, of course, can't think accurately – if you have nothing to think *about*. A physiologist, for example, can study pain and find out that it 'is' (whatever *is* means) such and such neural events. But the word *pain* would have no meaning for him unless he had 'been inside' by actually suffering. If he had never looked *along* pain he simply wouldn't know what he was looking *at*. The very subject for his inquiries from outside exists for him only because he has, at least once, been inside.

Thought Busily Working in a Vacuum   AUGUST 4

This case is not likely to occur, because every man has felt pain. But it is perfectly easy to go on all your life giving explanations of religion, love, morality, honour, and the like, without having been inside any of them. And if you do that, you are simply playing with counters. You go on explaining a thing without knowing what it is. That is why a great deal of contemporary thought is, strictly speaking, thought about nothing – all the apparatus of thought busily working in a vacuum.

The other objection is this: let us go back to the toolshed. I might have discounted what I saw when looking along the beam (i.e., the leaves moving and the sun) on the ground that it was 'really only a strip of dusty light in a dark shed'. That is, I might have set up as 'true' my 'side vision' of the beam. But then that side vision is itself an instance of the activity we call seeing. And this new instance could also be looked at from outside. I could allow a scientist to tell me that what seemed to be a beam of light in a shed was 'really only an agitation of my own optic nerves'. And that would be just as good (or as bad) a bit of debunking as the previous one. The picture of the beam in the toolshed would not have to be discounted, just as the previous picture of the trees and the sun had been discounted. And then, where are you?

In other words, you can step outside one experience only by stepping inside another. Therefore, if all inside experiences are misleading, we are always misled. The cerebral physiologist may say, if he chooses, that the mathematician's thought is 'only' tiny physical movements of the grey matter. But then what about the cerebral physiologist's own thought at that very moment? A second physiologist, looking at it, could pronounce it also to be only tiny physical movements in the first physiologist's skull. Where is the rot to end?

We Must Look Both 'Along' and 'At' Everything   AUGUST 5

The answer is that we must never allow the rot to begin. We must, on pain of idiocy, deny from the very outset the idea that looking *at* is, by its own nature 'intrinsically truer or better than looking *along*. One must look both *along* and *at* everything. In particular cases we shall find reason for regarding the one or the other vision as inferior. Thus the inside vision of rational thinking must be truer than the outside vision which sees only movements of the grey matter; for if the outside vision were the correct one all thought (including this thought itself) would be valueless, and this is self-contradictory. You cannot have a proof that no proofs matter. On the other hand, the inside vision of the savage's dance to Nyonga may be found deceptive because we find reason to believe that crops and babies are not really affected by it. In fact, we must take each case on its merits. But we must start with no prejudice for or against either kind of looking. We do not know in advance whether the lover or the psychologist is giving the more correct account of love, or whether both accounts are equally correct in different ways, or whether both are equally wrong. We just have to find out. But the period of browbeating has got to end.

The Transfiguration of the Lord AUGUST 6

The Transfiguration or 'Metamorphosis' of Jesus is...no doubt an anticipatory glimpse of something to come. He is seen conversing with two of the ancient dead. The change which His own human form had undergone is described as one to luminosity, to 'shining whiteness'. A similar whiteness characterizes His appearance at the beginning of the Book of Revelation. One rather curious detail is that this shining or whiteness affected His clothes as much as His body. St Mark indeed mentions the clothes more explicitly than the face, and adds, with his inimitable naïveté, that 'no laundry could do anything like it'. Taken by itself this episode bears all the marks of a 'vision': that is, of an experience which, though it may be divinely sent and may reveal great truth, yet is not, objectively speaking, the experience it seems to be. But if the theory of 'vision' (or holy hallucination) will not cover the Resurrection appearances, it would be only a multiplying of hypotheses to introduce it here. We do not know to what phase or feature of the New Creation this episode points. It may reveal some special glorifying of Christ's manhood at some phase of its history (since history it apparently has), or it may reveal the glory which that manhood always has in its New Creation: it may even reveal a glory which all risen men will inherit.

Using a Crucifix AUGUST 7

A particular toy or a particular ikon may be itself a work of art, but that is logically accidental; its artistic merits will not make it a better toy or a better ikon. They may make it a worse one. For its purpose is, not to fix attention upon itself, but to stimulate and liberate certain activities in the child or the worshiper. The teddy bear exists in order that the child may endow it with imaginary life and personality and enter into a quasi-social relationship with it. That is what 'playing with it' means. The better this activity succeeds the less the actual appearance of the object will matter. Too close or prolonged attention to its changeless and expressionless face impedes the play. A crucifix exists in order to direct the worshipper's thought and affections to the

Passion. It had better not have any excellences, subtleties, or originalities which will fix attention upon itself. Hence devout people may, for this purpose, prefer the crudest and emptiest ikon. The emptier, the more permeable; and they want, as it were, to pass through the material image and go beyond.

The Crucifixion as an Aid to Devotion   AUGUST 8

There is indeed one mental image which does not lure me away into trivial elaborations. I mean the Crucifixion itself; not seen in terms of all the pictures and crucifixes, but as we must suppose it to have been in its raw, historical reality. But even this is of less spiritual value than one might expect. Compunction, compassion, gratitude — all the fruitful emotions — are strangled. Sheer physical horror leaves no room for them. Nightmare. Even so, the image ought to be periodically faced. But no one could live with it. It did not become a frequent motive of Christian art until the generations which had seen real crucifixions were all dead. As for many hymns and sermons on the subject — endlessly harping on blood, as if that were all that mattered — they must be the work either of people so far above me that they can't reach me, or else of people with no imagination at all. (Some might be cut off from me by both these gulfs.)

Yet mental images play an important part in my prayers. I doubt if any act of will or thought or emotion occurs in me without them. But they seem to help me most when they are most fugitive and fragmentary — rising and bursting like bubbles in champagne or wheeling like rooks in a windy sky: contradicting one another (in logic) as the crowded metaphors of a swift poet may do. Fix on any one, and it goes dead. You must do as Blake would do with a joy; kiss it as it flies. And then, in their total effect, they do mediate to me something very important.

Our Holy Obligation   AUGUST 9

When I first became a Christian . . . I thought that I could do it on my own, by retiring to my rooms and reading theology, and I wouldn't go to the churches and gospel halls; and then later I found that it was the only way of flying your flag; and, of course, I found that this meant being a target. It is extraordinary how inconvenient to your family it becomes for you to get up early to go to church. It doesn't matter so much if you get up early for anything else, but if you get up early to go to church it's very selfish of you and you upset the house. If there is anything in the teaching of the New Testament which is in the nature of a command, it is that you are obliged to take the Sacrament, and you can't do it without going to church.

A Fixed Form of Service AUGUST 10

The advantage of a fixed form of service is that we know what is coming. *Ex tempore* public prayer has this difficulty: we don't know whether we can mentally join in it until we've heard it – it might be phoney or heretical. We are therefore called upon to carry on a critical and a *devotional* activity at the same moment: two things hardly compatible. In a fixed form we ought to have 'gone through the motions' before in our private prayers; the rigid form really sets our devotions *free*. I also find the more rigid it is, the easier it is to keep one's thoughts from straying. Also it prevents getting too completely eaten up by whatever happens to be the preoccupation of the moment (i.e. war, an election, or what not). The *permanent* shape of Christianity shows through.

The Proper Pleasure of Ritual AUGUST 11

This will be understood by any one who really understands the meaning of the Middle English word *solempne*. This means something different, but not quite different, from modern English *solemn*. Like *solemn* it implies the opposite of what is familiar, free and easy, or ordinary. But unlike *solemn* it does not suggest gloom, oppression, or austerity. The ball in the first act of *Romeo and Juliet* was a 'solemnity'. The feast at the beginning of *Gawain and the Green Knight* is very much of a solemnity. A great mass by Mozart or Beethoven is as much a solemnity in its hilarious *gloria* as in its poignant *crucifixus est*. Feasts are, in this sense, *more* solemn than fasts. Easter is *solempne,* Good Friday is not. The *solempne* is the festival which is also the stately and the ceremonial, the proper occasion for *pomp* – and the very fact that *pompous* is now used only in a bad sense measures the degree to which we have lost the old idea of 'solemnity'. To recover it you must think of a court ball, or a coronation, or a victory march, as these things appear to people who *enjoy* them; in an age when everyone puts on his oldest clothes to be happy in, you must re-awake the simpler state of mind in which people put on gold and scarlet to be happy in. Above all, you must be rid of the hideous idea, fruit of a widespread inferiority complex, that pomp, on the proper occasions, has any connection with vanity or self-conceit. A celebrant approaching the altar, a princess led out by a king to dance a minuet, a general officer on a ceremonial parade, a major domo preceding the boar's head at a Christmas feast —all these wear unusual clothes and move with calculated dignity. This does not mean that they are vain, but that they are obedient; they are obeying the *hoc age* which presides over every solemnity. The modern habit of doing ceremonial things unceremoniously is no proof of humility; rather it proves the offender's inability to forget himself in the rite, and his readiness to spoil for everyone else the proper pleasure of ritual.

Clerical One-Upmanship   AUGUST 12

I think our business as laymen is to take what we are given and make the best of it. And I think we should find this a great deal easier if what we were given was always and everywhere the same.

To judge from their practice, very few Anglican clergymen take this view. It looks as if they believed people can be lured to go to church by incessant brightenings, lightenings, lengthenings, abridgements, simplifications, and complications of the service. And it is probably true that a new, keen vicar will usually be able to form within his parish a minority who are in favour of his innovations. The majority, I believe, never are. Those who remain — many give up churchgoing altogether — merely endure.

Is this simply because the majority are hidebound? I think not. They have a good reason for their conservatism. Novelty, simply as such, can have only an entertainment value. And they don't go to church to be entertained. They go to *use* the service, or, if you prefer, to *enact* it. Every service is a structure of acts and words through which we receive a sacrament, or repent, or supplicate, or adore. And it enables us to do these things best — if you like, it 'works' best — when, through long familiarity, we don't have to think about it. As long as you notice, and have to count, the steps, you are not yet dancing but only learning to dance. A good shoe is a shoe you don't notice. Good reading becomes possible when you need not consciously think about eyes, or light, or print, or spelling. The perfect church service would be one we were almost unaware of; our attention would have been on God.

The Liturgical Fidget AUGUST 13

Novelty may fix our attention not even on the service but on the celebrant. You know what I mean. Try as one may to exclude it, the question 'What on earth is he up to now?' will intrude. It lays one's devotion waste. There is really some excuse for the man who said, 'I wish they'd remember that the charge to Peter was Feed my sheep; not Try experiments on my rats, or even, Teach my performing dogs new tricks.'

Thus my whole liturgiological position really boils down to an entreaty for permanence and uniformity. I can make do with almost any kind of service whatever, if only it will stay put. But if each form is snatched away just when I am beginning to feel at home in it, then I can never make any progress in the art of worship. You give me no chance to acquire the trained habit — *habito dell 'arte.*

It may well be that some variations which seem to me merely matters of taste really involve grave doctrinal differences. But surely not all? For if grave doctrinal differences are really as numerous as variations in practice, then we shall have to conclude that no such thing as the Church of England exists. And anyway, the Liturgical Fidget is not a purely Anglican phenomenon; I have heard Roman Catholics complain of it too.

Membership in the Body of Christ AUGUST 14

No Christian and, indeed, no historian could accept the epigram which defines religion as 'what a man does with his solitude'. It was one of the Wesleys, I think, who said that the New Testament knows nothing of solitary religion. We are forbidden to neglect the assembling of ourselves together. Christianity is already institutional in the earliest of its documents. The Church is the Bride of Christ. We are members of one another.

In our own age the idea that religion belongs to our private life — that it is, in fact, an occupation for the individual's hour of leisure — is at once paradoxical, dangerous, and natural. It is paradoxical because this exaltation of the individual in the religious field springs up in an age when collectivism is ruthlessly defeating the individual in every other field.... There is a crowd of busybodies, self-appointed masters of ceremonies, whose life is devoted to destroying solitude wherever solitude still exists. They call it 'taking the young people out of themselves', or 'waking them up', or 'overcoming their apathy'. If an Augustine, a Vaughan, a Traherne or a Wordsworth should be born in the modern world, the leaders of a Youth Organization would soon cure him. If a really good home, such as the home of Alcinous and Arete in the *Odys-*

sey or the Rostovs in *War and Peace* or any of Charlotte M. Yonge's families, existed today, it would be denounced as *bourgeois* and every engine of destruction would be levelled against it. And even where the planners fail and someone is left physically by himself, the wireless has seen to it that he will be — in a sense not intended by Scipio — never less alone than when alone. We live, in fact, in a world starved for solitude, silence, and privacy: and therefore starved for meditation and true friendship.

The Intrusion of Collectivism   AUGUST 15

That religion should be relegated to solitude in such an age is, then, paradoxical. But it is also dangerous for two reasons. In the first place, when the modern world says to us aloud, 'You may be religious when you are alone', it adds under its breath, 'and I will see to it that you never are alone.' To make Christianity a private affair while banishing all privacy is to relegate it to the rainbow's end or the Greek Calends. That is one of the enemy's stratagems. In the second place, there is the danger that real Christians who know that Christianity is not a solitary affair may react against that error by simply transporting into our spiritual life that same collectivism which has already conquered our secular life. That is the enemy's other stratagem. Like a good chess player he is always trying to manoeuvre you into a position where you can save your castle only by losing your bishop. In order to avoid the trap we must insist that though the private conception of Christianity is an error it is a profoundly natural one, and is clumsily attempting to guard a great truth. Behind it is the obvious feeling that our modern collectivism is an outrage upon human nature and that from this, as from all other evils, God will be our shield and buckler.

The Purpose of the Secular Community   AUGUST 16

As personal and private life is lower than participation in the Body of Christ, so the collective life is lower than the personal and private life and has no value save in its service. The secular community, since it exists for our natural good and not for our supernatural, has no higher end than to facilitate and safeguard the family, and friendship, and solitude. To be happy at home, said johnson, is the end of all human endeavour. As long as we are thinking only of natural values we must say that the sun looks down on nothing half so good as a household laughing together over a meal, or two friends talking over a pint of beer, or a man alone reading a book that interests him; and that all economics, politics, laws, armies, and institutions, save in so far as they prolong and multiply such scenes, are a mere ploughing the sand and sowing the ocean, a meaningless vanity and vexation of spirit. Collective activities are, of course, necessary; but this is the end to which they are necessary. Great sacrifices of this private happiness by those who have it may be necessary in order that it may be more widely distributed. All may have to be a little hungry in order that none may starve. But do not let us mistake necessary evils for good. The mistake is easily made. Fruit has to be tinned if it is to be transported, and has to lose thereby some of its good qualities. But one meets people who have learned actually to prefer the tinned fruit to the fresh. A sick society must think much about politics, as a sick man must think much about his digestion: to ignore the subject may be fatal cowardice for the one as for the other. But if either comes to regard it as the natural food of the mind — if either forgets that we think of such things only in order to be able to think of something else — then what was undertaken for the sake of health has become itself a new and deadly disease.

Our Only Safeguard Against Collectivism   AUGUST 17

There is, in fact, a fatal tendency in all human activities for the means to encroach upon the very ends which they were intended to serve. Thus money comes to hinder the exchange of commodities, and rules of art to hamper genius, and examinations to prevent young men from becoming learned. It does not, unfortunately, always follow that the encroaching means can be dispensed with. I think it probable that the collectivism of our life is necessary and will increase; and I think that our only safeguard against its deathly properties is in a Christian life; for we were promised that we could handle serpents and drink deadly things and yet live. That is the truth behind the erroneous definition of religion with which we started. Where it went wrong was in opposing to the collective mass mere solitude. The Christian is called, not to individualism but to membership in the mystical body. A consideration of the differences between the secular collective and the mystical body is therefore the first step to understanding how Christianity without being individualistic can yet counteract collectivism.

The Biblical Meaning of 'Members'   AUGUST 18

At the outset we are hampered by a difficulty of language. The very word *member-ship* is of Christian origin, but it has been taken over by the world and emptied of all meaning. In any book on logic you may see the expression 'members of a class'. It must be most emphatically stated that the items or particulars included in a homogeneous class are almost the reverse of what St Paul meant by *members*. By *members* ($\mu \epsilon \lambda \eta$) he meant what we should call *organs,* things essentially different from, and complementary to, one another: things differing not only in structure and function but also in dignity. Thus, in a club, the committee as a whole, and the servants as a whole, may both properly be regarded as 'members'; what we should call the members of the club are merely units. A row of identically dressed and identically trained soldiers set side by side, or a number of citizens listed as voters in a constituency, are not members of anything in the Pauline sense. I am afraid that when we describe a man as 'a member of the Church' we usually mean nothing Pauline: we mean only that he is a unit – that he is one more specimen of the same kind of thing as X and Y and Z. How true membership in a body differs from inclusion in a collective may be seen in the structure of a family. The grandfather, the parents, the grown-up son, the child, the dog, and the cat are true members (in the organic sense) precisely because they are not members or units of a homogeneous class. They are not interchangeable. Each person is almost a species in himself. The mother is not simply a different person from the daughter, she is a different kind of person. The grown-up brother is not simply one unit in the class children, he is a separate estate of the realm. The father and grandfather are almost as different as the cat and the dog. If you subtract any one member you have not simply reduced the family in number, you have inflicted an injury on its structure. Its unity is a unity of unlikes, almost of incommensurables.

Differences in Kind   AUGUST 19

A dim perception of the richness inherent in this kind of unity is one reason why we enjoy a book like *The Wind in* the *Willows*; a trio such as Rat, Mole, and Badger symbolizes the extreme differentiation of persons in harmonious union which we know intuitively to be our true refuge both from solitude and from the collective. The affection between such oddly matched couples as Dick Swiveller and the Marchioness, or Mr Pickwick and Sam Weller, pleases in the same way. That is why the modern notion that children should call their parents by their Christian names is so perverse. For this is an effort to ignore the difference in kind which makes for real organic unity. They are trying to inoculate the child with the preposterous view that one's mother is simply a fellow citizen like anyone else, to make it ignorant of what all men know and insensible to what all men feel. They are trying to drag the featureless repetitions of the collective into the fuller and more concrete world of the family.

A convict has a number instead of a name. That is the collective idea carried to its extreme.

Baptism: Our Entry into the Church   AUGUST 20

The society into which the Christian is called at baptism is not a collective but a Body. It is in fact that Body of which the family is an image on the natural level. If anyone came to it with the misconception that membership of the Church was membership in a debased modern sense – a massing together of persons as if they were pennies or counters – he would be corrected at the threshold by the discovery that the Head of this Body is so unlike the inferior members that they share no predicate with Him save by analogy. We are summoned from the outset to combine as creatures with our Creator, as mortals with immortal, as redeemed sinners with sinless Redeemer. His presence, the interaction between Him and us, must always be the overwhelmingly dominant factor in the life we are to lead within the Body; and any conception of Christian fellowship which does not mean primarily fellowship with Him is out of court. After that it seems almost trivial to trace further down the diversity of operations to the unity of the Spirit. But it is very plainly there. There are priests divided from the laity, catechumens divided from those who are in full fellowship. There is authority of husbands over wives and parents over children. There is, in forms too subtle for official embodiment, a continual interchange of complementary ministrations. We are all constantly teaching and learning, forgiving and being forgiven, representing Christ to man when we intercede, and man to Christ when others intercede for us. The sacrifice of selfish privacy which is daily demanded of us is daily repaid a hundredfold in the true growth of personality which the life of the Body encourages. Those who are members of one another become as diverse as the hand and the ear. That is why the worldlings are so monotonously alike compared with the almost fantastic variety of the saints. Obedience is the road to freedom, humility the road to pleasure, unity the road to personality.

Recovery of Our Real Inequalities   AUGUST 21

You have often heard that, though in the world we hold different stations, yet we are all equal in the sight of God. There are of course senses in which this is true. God is no accepter of persons: His love for us is not measured by our social rank or our intellectual talents. But I believe there is a sense in which this maxim is the reverse of the truth. I am going to venture to say that artificial equality is necessary in the life of the State, but that in the Church we strip off this disguise, we recover our real inequalities, and are thereby refreshed and quickened. . . .

I believe the authority of parent over child, husband over wife, learned over simple, to have been as much a part of the original plan as the authority of man over beast. I believe that if we had not fallen Filmer would be right, and patriarchal monarchy would be the sole lawful government. But since we have learned sin, we have found, as Lord Acton says, that 'all power corrupts, and absolute power corrupts absolutely'. The only remedy has been to take away the powers and substitute a legal fiction of equality. . . .

Equality is a quantitative term and therefore love often knows nothing of it. Authority exercised with humility, and obedience accepted with delight are the very lines along which our spirits live. Even in the life of the affections, much more in the Body of Christ, we step outside that world which says 'I am as good as you'. It is like turning from a march to a dance. It is like taking off our clothes. We become, as Chesterton said, taller when we bow; we become lowlier when we instruct. It delights me that there should be moments in the services of my own Church when the priest stands and I kneel. As democracy becomes more complete in the outer world and opportunities for reverence are successively removed, the refreshment, the cleansing, and invigorating returns to inequality, which the Church offers us, become more and more necessary.

Crucifixion of the Natural Self   AUGUST 22

A rejection, or in Scripture's strong language, a crucifixion of the natural self is the passport to everlasting life. Nothing that has not died will be resurrected. That is just how Christianity cuts across the antithesis between individualism and collectivism. There lies the maddening ambiguity of our faith as it must appear to outsiders. It sets its face relentlessly against our natural individualism; on the other hand, it gives back to those who abandon individualism an eternal possession of their own personal being, even of their bodies. As mere biological entities, each with its separate will to live and to expand, we are apparently of no account; we are cross-fodder. But as organs in the Body of Christ, as stones and pillars in the temple, we are assured of our eternal self-identity and shall live to remember the galaxies as an old tale.

This may be put in another way. Personality is eternal and inviolable. But then, personality is not a datum from which we start. The individualism in which we all begin is only a parody or shadow of it. True personality lies ahead – how far ahead, for most of us, I dare not say. And the key to it does not lie in ourselves. It will not be attained by development from within outwards. It will come to us when we occupy those places in the structure of the eternal cosmos for which we were designed or invented. As a colour first reveals its true quality when placed by an excellent artist in its pre-elected spot between certain others, as a spice reveals its true flavour when inserted just where and when a good cook wishes among the other ingredients, as the dog becomes really doggy only when he has taken his place in the household of man, so we shall then first be true persons when we have suffered ourselves to be fitted into our places.

Personality is the Gift of Christ

Starting with the doctrine that every individuality is 'of infinite value' we then picture God as a kind of employment committee whose business it is to find suitable careers for all souls, square holes for square pegs. In fact, however, the value of the individual does not lie in him. He is capable of receiving value. He receives it by union with Christ. There is no question of finding for him a place in the living temple which will do justice to his inherent value and give scope to his natural idiosyncrasy. The place was there first. The man was created for it. He will not be himself till he is there. We shall be true and everlasting and really divine persons only in Heaven. . . .

To say this is to repeat what everyone here admits already – that we are saved by grace, that in our flesh dwells no good thing, that we are, through and through, creatures not creators, derived beings, living not of ourselves but from Christ. If I seem to have complicated a simple matter, you will, I hope, forgive me. I have been anxious to bring out two points. I have wanted to try to expel that quite un-Christian worship of the human individual simply as such which is so rampant in modern thought side by side with our collectivism; for one error begets the opposite error and, far from neutralizing, they aggravate each other. I mean the pestilent notion (one sees it in literary criticism) that each of us starts with a treasure called 'Personality' locked up inside him, and that to expand and express this, to guard it from interference, to be 'original', is the main end of life. This is Pelagian, or worse, and it defeats even itself. No man who values originality will ever be original. But try to tell the truth as you see it, try to do any bit of work as well as it can be done for the work's sake, and what men call originality will come unsought. Even on that level, the submission of the individual to the function is already beginning to bring true Personality to birth. And secondly, I have wanted to show that Christianity is not, in the long run, concerned either with individuals or communities. Neither the individual nor the community as popular thought understands them can inherit eternal life: neither the natural self, nor the collective mass, but a new creature.

St Bartholomew, Apostle   AUGUST 24

Surely God saves different souls in different ways? To preach instantaneous conversion and eternal security as if they must be the experiences of all who are saved, seems to me very dangerous: the very way to drive some into presumption and others into despair. How very different were the callings of the disciples. I don't agree that if anyone were completely a new creature, you and I would necessarily recognize him as such. It takes holiness to detect holiness.

Modern Criticism   AUGUST 25

What are the key words of modern criticism? *Creative,* with its opposite *derivative*; *spontaneity,* with its opposite *convention*; *freedom,* contrasted with *rules.* Great authors are innovators, pioneers, explorers; bad authors bunch in schools and follow models. Or again, great authors are always 'breaking fetters' and 'bursting bonds'. They have personality, they 'are themselves'. I do not know whether we often think out the implication of such language into a consistent philosophy; but we certainly have a general picture of bad work flowing from conformity and discipleship, and of good work bursting out from certain centres of explosive force – apparently self-originating force – which we call men of genius.

Now the New Testament has nothing at all to tell us of literature. I know that there are some who like to think of Our Lord Himself as a poet and cite the parables to support their view. I admit freely that to believe in the Incarnation at all is to believe that every mode of human excellence is implicit in His historical human character: poethood, of course, included. But if all had been developed, the limitations of a single human life would have been transcended and He would not have been a man; therefore all excellences save the spiritual remained in varying degrees implicit.

Becoming Clean Mirrors AUGUST 26

In the New Testament the art of life itself is an art of imitation: can we, believing this, believe that literature, which must derive from real life, is to aim at being 'creative', 'original', and 'spontaneous'? 'Originality' in the New Testament is quite plainly the prerogative of God alone; even within the triune being of God it seems to be confined to the Father. The duty and happiness of every other being is placed in being derivative, in reflecting like a mirror. Nothing could be more foreign to the tone of Scripture than the language of those who describe a saint as a 'moral genius' or a 'spiritual genius' thus insinuating that his virtue or spirituality is 'creative' or 'original'. If I have read the New Testament aright, it leaves no room for 'creativeness' even in a modified or metaphorical sense. Our whole destiny seems to lie in the opposite direction, in being as little as possible ourselves, in acquiring a fragrance that is not our own but borrowed, in becoming clean mirrors filled with the image of a face that is not ours. I am not here supporting the doctrine of total depravity, and I do not say that the New Testament supports it; I am saying only that the highest good of a creature must be creaturely – that is, derivative or reflective – good. In other words, as St Augustine makes plain *(De Civ. Dei* xii, cap. I), pride does not only go before a fall but is a fall – a fall of the creature's attention from what is better, God, to what is worse, itself.

Two Attitudes Towards the Self AUGUST 27

The unbeliever may take his own temperament and experience, just as they happen to stand, and consider them worth communicating simply because they are facts or, worse still, because they are his. To the Christian his own temperament and experience, as mere fact, and as merely his, are of no value or importance whatsoever: he will deal with them, if at all, only because they are the medium through which, or the position from which, something universally profitable appeared to him. We can imagine two men seated in different parts of a church or theatre. Both, when they come out, may tell us their experiences, and both may use the first person. But the one is interested in his seat only because it was his – 'I was most uncomfortable', he will say. 'You would hardly believe what a draught comes in from the door in that corner. And the people! I had to speak pretty sharply to the woman in front of me.' The other will tell us what could be seen from his seat, choosing to describe this because this is what he knows, and because every seat must give the best view of something. 'Do you know,' he will begin, 'the moulding on those pillars goes on round at the back. It looks, too, as if the design on the back were the older of the two.' Here we have the expressionist and the Christian attitudes towards the self or temperament. Thus St Augustine and Rousseau both write *Confessions*; but to the one his own temperament is a kind of absolute (*au moins je suis autre*), to the other it is 'a narrow house too narrow for Thee to enter – oh make it wide. It is in ruins – oh rebuild it'. . . .

The Christian writer may be self-taught or original . . . but if his talents are such that he can produce good work by writing in an established form and dealing with experiences common to all his race, he will do so just as gladly. I even think he will do so more gladly. It is to him an argument not of strength but of weakness that he should respond fully to the vision only 'in his own way'. And always, of every idea and of every method he will ask not 'Is it mine?', but 'Is it good?'

St Augustine of Hippo   AUGUST 28

Everyone has noticed how hard it is to turn our thoughts to God when everything is going well with us. We 'have all we want' is a terrible saying when 'all' does not include God. We find God an interruption. As St Augustine says somewhere, 'God wants to give us something, but cannot, because our hands are full – there's nowhere for Him to put it.' Or as a friend of mine said, 'We regard God as an airman regards his parachute; it's there for emergencies but he hopes he'll never have to use it.' Now God, who has made us, knows what we are and that our happiness lies in Him. Yet we will not seek it in Him as long as He leaves us any other resort where it can even plausibly be looked for. While what we call 'our own life' remains agreeable we will not surrender it to Him. What then can God do in our interests but make 'our own life' less agreeable to us, and take away the plausible sources of false happiness? It is just here, where God's providence seems at first to be most cruel, that the Divine humility, the stooping down of the Highest, most deserves praise.

The Use of Our Talents   AUGUST 29

My own professional work, though conditioned by taste and talents, is immediately motivated by the need for earning my living. And on earning one's living I was relieved to note that Christianity, in spite of its revolutionary and apocalyptic elements, can be delightfully humdrum. The Baptist did not give the tax gatherers and soldiers lectures on the immediate necessity of turning the economic and military system of the ancient world upside down; he told them to obey the moral law – as they had presumably learned it from their mothers and nurses – and sent them back to their jobs.

St Paul advised the Thessalonians to stick to their work (I Thessalonians 4:11) and not to become busybodies (2 Thessalonians 3:11). The need for money is therefore *simpliciter* an innocent, though by no means a splendid, motive for any occupation. The Ephesians are warned to work professionally at something that is 'good' (Ephesians 4:28). I hoped that 'good' here did not mean much more than 'harmless,' and I was certain it did not imply anything very elevated. Provided, then, that there was a demand for culture, and that culture was not actually deleterious, I concluded I was justified in making my living by supplying that demand – and that all others in my position (dons, schoolmasters, professional authors, critics, reviewers) were similarly justified; especially if, like me, they had few or no talents for any other career – if their 'vocation' to a cultural profession consisted in the brute fact of not being fit for anything else.

The Lawful Use of Culture AUGUST 30

But is culture even harmless? It certainly can be harmful and often is. If a Christian found himself in the position of one inaugurating a new society *in vacuo* he might well decide not to introduce something whose abuse is so easy and whose use is, at any rate, not necessary. But that is not our position. The abuse of culture is already there, and will continue whether Christians cease to be cultured or not. It is therefore probably better that the ranks of the 'culture sellers' should include some Christians – as an antidote. It may even be the duty of some Christians to be culture sellers. Not that I have yet said anything to show that even the lawful use of culture stands very high. The lawful use might be no more than innocent pleasure; but if the abuse is common, the task of resisting that abuse might be not only lawful but obligatory....I must add that when I speak of 'resisting the abuse of culture' I do not mean that a Christian should take money for supplying one thing (culture) and use the opportunity thus gained to supply a quite different thing (homilectics and apologetics). That is stealing. The mere presence of Christians in the ranks of the culture sellers will inevitably provide an antidote....

When I ask what culture has done to me personally, the most obviously true answer is that it has given me quite an enormous amount of pleasure. I have no doubt at all that pleasure is in itself a good and pain in itself an evil; if not, then the whole Christian tradition about heaven and hell and the Passion of Our Lord seems to have no meaning. Pleasure, then, is good; a 'sinful' pleasure means a good offered, and accepted, under conditions which involve a breach of the moral law. The pleasures of culture are not intrinsically bound up with such conditions....Often, as Newman saw, they are an excellent diversion from guilty pleasures. We may, therefore, enjoy them ourselves, and lawfully, even charitably, teach others to enjoy them.

Some People's Road into Jerusalem   AUGUST 31

My general case may be stated...that culture is a storehouse of the best (sub-Christian) values. These values are in themselves of the soul, not the spirit. But God created the soul. Its values may be expected, therefore, to contain some reflection or antepast of the spiritual values. They will save no man. They resemble the regenerate life only as affection resembles charity, or honour resembles virtue, or the moon the sun. But though 'like is not the same', it is better than unlike. Imitation may pass into initiation. For some it is a good beginning. For others it is not; culture is not everyone's road into Jerusalem, and for some it is a road out.

There is another way in which it may predispose to conversion. The difficulty of converting an uneducated man nowadays lies in his complacency. Popularized science, the conventions or 'unconventions' of his immediate circle, party programmes, etc., enclose him in a tiny windowless universe which he mistakes for the only possible universe. There are no distant horizons, no mysteries. He thinks everything has been settled. A cultured person, on the other hand, is almost compelled to be aware that reality is very odd and that the ultimate truth, whatever it may be, *must* have the characteristics of strangeness — *must* be something that would seem remote and fantastic to the uncultured....On these grounds I conclude that culture has a distinct part to play in bringing certain souls to Christ. Not all souls — there is a shorter, and safer, way which has always been followed by thousands of simple affectional natures who begin, where we hope to end, with devotion to the person of Christ.

Sunlight at Second Hand   SEPTEMBER 1

Has it any part to play in the life of the converted? I think so, and in two ways. (a) If all the cultural values, on the way up to Christianity, were dim antepasts and ectypes of the truth, we can recognize them as such still. And since we must rest and play, where can we do so better than here — in the suburbs of Jerusalem? It is lawful to rest our eyes in moonlight — especially now that we know where it comes from, that it is only sunlight at second hand. (b) Whether the purely contemplative life is, or is not, desirable for any, it is certainly not the vocation of all. Most men must glorify God by doing to His glory something which is not *per se* an act of glorifying but which becomes so by being offered. If, as I now hope, cultural activities are innocent and even useful, then they also (like the sweeping of the room in Herbert's poem) can be done to the Lord. The work of a charwoman and the work of a poet become spiritual in the same way and on the same condition.

Two Kinds of Good and Bad   SEPTEMBER 2

Is there a kind of good which is not good? Is there any good that is not pleasing to God or any bad which is not hateful to Him? If you press me along these lines I end in doubts. But I will not get rid of those doubts by falsifying the little light I already have. That little light seems to compel me to say that there are two kinds of good and bad. The first, such as virtue and vice or love and hatred, besides being good or bad themselves make the possessor good or bad. The second do not. They include such things as physical beauty or ugliness, the possession or lack of a sense of humour, strength or weakness, pleasure or pain. But the two most relevant for us are . . . con- jugal *eros* (as distinct from *agape,* which, of course, is a good of the first class) and physical cleanliness. Surely we have all met people who said, indeed, that the latter was *next* to godliness, but whose unconscious attitude made it a *part* of godliness, and no small part? And surely we agree that any good of this second class, however good on its own level, becomes an enemy when it thus assumes demonic pretensions and erects itself into a quasi-spiritual value. As M. de Rougemount has recently told us, the conjugal *eros* 'ceases to be a devil only when it ceases to be a god'. My whole contention is that in literature, in addition to the spiritual good and evil which it car- ries, there is also a good and evil of this second class, a properly cultural or literary good and evil, which must not be allowed to masquerade as good and evil of the first class. . . . I enjoyed my breakfast this morning, and I think that was a good thing and do not think it was condemned by God. But I do not think myself a good man for en- joying it.

St Gregory The Great   SEPTEMBER 3

The glory of God, and, as our only means to glorifying Him, the salvation of human souls, is the real business of life. What, then, is the value of culture? It is, of course, no new question; but as a living question it was new to me. . . .

I found the famous saying, attributed to Gregory, that our use of secular culture was comparable to the action of the Israelites in going down to the Philistines to have their knives sharpened. This seems to me a most satisfactory argument as far as it goes, and very relevant to modern conditions. If we are to convert our heathen neigh- bours, we must understand their culture. We must 'beat them at their own game'. But of course, while this would justify Christian culture (at least for some Christians whose vocation lay in that direction) at the moment, it would come very far short of the claims made for culture in our modern tradition. On the Gregorian view culture is a weapon; and a weapon is essentially a thing we lay aside as soon as we safely can.

Do All to the Glory of God   SEPTEMBER 4

Religion cannot occupy the whole of life in the sense of excluding all our natural activities. For, of course, in some sense, it must occupy the whole of life. There is no
question of a compromise between the claims of God and the claims of culture, or
politics, or anything else. God's claim is infinite and inexorable. You can refuse it: or
you can begin to try to grant it. There is no middle way. Yet in spite of this it is clear
that Christianity does not exclude any of the ordinary human activities. St Paul tells
people to get on with their jobs. He even assumes that Christians may go to dinner
parties, and, what is more, dinner parties given by pagans. Our Lord attends a wedding and provides miraculous wine. Under the aegis of His Church, and in the most
Christian ages, learning and the arts flourish. The solution of this paradox is, of
course, well known to you. 'Whether ye eat or drink or whatsoever ye do, do all to the
glory of God.'

All our merely natural activities will be accepted, if they are offered to God, even
the humblest: and all of them, even the noblest, will be sinful if they are not. Christianity does not simply replace our natural life and substitute a new one: it is rather a
new organization which exploits, to its own supernatural ends, these natural
materials.

Our Need of Knowledge   SEPTEMBER 5

If all the world were Christian, it might not matter if all the world were uneducated.
But, as it is, a cultural life will exist outside the Church whether it exists inside or
not. To be ignorant and simple now – not to be able to meet the enemies on their own
ground – would be to throw down our weapons, and to betray our uneducated brethren who have, under God, no defense but us against the intellectual attacks of the
heathen. Good philosophy must exist, if for no other reason, because bad philosophy
needs to be answered. The cool intellect must work not only against cool intellect on
the other side, but against the muddy heathen mysticisms which deny intellect altogether. Most of all, perhaps, we need intimate knowledge of the past. Not that the
past has any magic about it, but because we cannot study the future, and yet need
something to set against the present, to remind us that the basic assumptions have
been quite different in different periods and that much which seems certain to the uneducated is merely temporary fashion. A man who has lived in many places is not
likely to be deceived by the local errors of his native village: the scholar has lived in
many times and is therefore in some degree immune from the great cataract of nonsense that pours from the press and the microphone of his own age.

Theology: the Science of God SEPTEMBER 6

In a way I quite understand why some people are put off by Theology. I remember once when I had been giving a talk to the R.A.F., an old, hardbitten officer got up and said, 'I've no use for all that stuff. But, mind you, I'm a religious man too. I *know* there's a God. I've *felt* Him: out alone in the desert at night: the tremendous mystery. And that's just why I don't believe all your neat little dogmas and formulas about Him. To anyone who's met the real thing they all seem so petty and pedantic and unreal!'

Now in a sense I quite agreed with that man. I think he had probably had a real experience of God in the desert. And when he turned from that experience to the Christian creeds, I think he really was turning from something real to something less real. In the same way, if a man has once looked at the Atlantic from the beach, and then goes and looks at a map of the Atlantic, he also will be turning from something real to something less real: turning from real waves to a bit of coloured paper. But here comes the point. The map is admittedly only coloured paper, but there are two things you have to remember about it. In the first place, it is based on what hundreds and thousands of people have found by sailing the real Atlantic. In that way it has behind it masses of experience just as real as the one you could have from the beach; only, while yours would be a single isolated glimpse, the map fits all those different experiences together. In the second place, if you want to go anywhere, the map is absolutely necessary. As long as you are content with walks on the beach, your own glimpses are far more fun than looking at a map. But the map is going to be more use than walks on the beach if you want to get to America.

Don't Go to Sea without a Map SEPTEMBER 7

Theology is like a map. Merely learning and thinking about the Christian doctrines, if you stop there, is less real and less exciting than the sort of thing my friend got in the desert. Doctrines are not God: they are only a kind of map. But that map is based on the experience of hundreds of people who really were in touch with God — experiences compared with which any thrills or pious feelings you and I are likely to get on our own are very elementary and very confused. And secondly, if you want to get any further, you must use the map. You see, what happened to that man in the desert may have been real, and was certainly exciting, but nothing comes of it. It leads nowhere. There is nothing to do about it. In fact, that is just why a vague religion — all about feeling God in nature, and so on — is so attractive. It is all thrills and no work; like watching the waves from the beach. But you will not get to Newfoundland by studying the Atlantic that way, and you will not get eternal life by simply feeling the presence of God in flowers or music. Neither will you get anywhere by looking at maps without going to sea. Nor will you be very safe If you go to sea without a map.

In other words, Theology is practical: especially now. In the old days, when there was less education and discussion, perhaps it was possible to get on with a very few simple ideas about God. But it is not so now. Everyone reads, everyone hears things discussed. Consequently, if you do not listen to Theology, that will not mean that you have no ideas about God. It will mean that you have a lot of wrong ones — bad, muddled, out-of-date ideas. For a great many of the ideas about God which are trotted out as novelties today are simply the ones which real Theologians tried centuries ago and rejected. To believe in the popular religion of modern England is retrogression — like believing the earth is flat.

The Creation   SEPTEMBER 8

I won't admit without a struggle that when I speak of God 'uttering' or 'inventing' the creatures I am 'watering down the concept of creation'. I am trying to give it, by remote analogies, some sort of content. I know that to create is defined as 'to make out of nothing', *ex nihilo*. But I take that to mean 'not out of any pre-existing material'. It can't mean that God makes what God has not thought of, or that He gives His creatures any powers or beauties which He Himself does not possess. Why, we think that even human work comes nearest to creation when the maker has 'got it all out of his own head'.

Nor am I suggesting a theory of 'emanations'. The differentia of an 'emanation' — literally an overflowing, a trickling out — would be that it suggests something involuntary. But my words — 'uttering' and 'inventing' — are meant to suggest an act.

This act, as it is for God, must always remain totally inconceivable to man. For we — even our poets and musicians and inventors — never, in the ultimate sense, *make*. We only build. We always have materials to build from. All we can know about the act of creation must be derived from what we can gather about the relation of the creatures to their Creator.

Divine Omnipotence

Omnipotence means 'power to do all, or everything'. And we are told in Scripture that 'with God all things are possible'. It is common enough, in argument with an un-believer, to be told that God, if He existed and were good, would do this or that; and then, if we point out that the proposed action is impossible, to be met with the retort, 'But I thought God was supposed to be able to do anything.' This raises the whole question of impossibility.

In ordinary usage the word *impossible* generally implies a suppressed clause be-ginning with the word *unless*. Thus it is impossible for me to see the street from where I sit writing at this moment; that is, it is impossible to see the street *unless* I go up to the top floor where I shall be high enough to overlook the intervening building. If I had broken my leg I should say 'But it is impossible to go up to the top floor' – meaning, however, that it is impossible *unless* some friends turn up who will carry me. Now let us advance to a different plane of impossibility, by saying, 'It is, at any rate, impossible to see the street *so long as* I remain where I am and the intervening building remains where it is.' Someone might add 'unless the nature of space, or of vision, were different from what it is'. I do not know what the best philosophers and scientists would say to this, but I should have to reply 'I don't know whether space and vision *could possibly* have been of such a nature as you suggest.' Now it is clear that the words could possibly here refer to some absolute kind of possibility or im-possibility which is different from the relative possibilities and impossibilities we have been considering. I cannot say whether seeing round corners is, in this new sense, possible or not, because I do not know whether it is self-contradictory or not. But I know very well that if it is self-contradictory it is absolutely impossible. The absolutely impossible may also be called the intrinsically impossible because it car-ries its impossibility within itself.

Omnipotence and Nonsense

Omnipotence means power to do all that is intrinsically possible, not to do the intrin-sically impossible. You may attribute miracles to Him, but not nonsense. This is no limit to His power. If you choose to say 'God can give a creature free will and at the same time withhold free will from it', you have not succeeded in saying *anything* about God: meaningless combinations of words do not suddenly acquire meaning simply because we prefix to them the two other words 'God can'. It remains true that all *things* are possible with God: the intrinsic impossibilities are not things but nonentities. It is no more possible for God than for the weakest of His creatures to carry out both of two mutually exclusive alternatives; not because His power meets an obstacle, but because nonsense remains nonsense even when we talk it about God.

The Context of Freedom SEPTEMBER 11

There is no reason to suppose that self-consciousness, the recognition of a creature by itself as a 'self', can exist except in contrast with an 'other', a something which is not the self. It is against an environment, and preferably a social environment, an environment of other selves, that the awareness of Myself stands out. This would raise a difficulty about the consciousness of God if we were mere theists: being Christians, we learn from the doctrine of the Blessed Trinity that something analogous to 'society' exists within the Divine being from all eternity – that God is Love, not merely in the sense of being the Platonic form of love, but because, within Him, the concrete reciprocities of love exist before all worlds and are thence derived to the creatures.

Again, the freedom of a creature must mean freedom to choose: and choice implies the existence of things to choose between. A creature with no environment would have no choices to make: so that freedom, like self-consciousness (if they are not, indeed, the same thing), again demands the presence to the self of something other than the self.

Competition or Courtesy SEPTEMBER 12

If the fixed nature of matter prevents it from being always, and in all its dispositions, equally agreeable even to a single soul, much less is it possible for the matter of the universe at any moment to be distributed so that it is equally convenient and pleasurable to each member of a society. If a man travelling in one direction is having a journey down hill, a man going in the opposite direction must be going up hill. If even a pebble lies where I want it to lie, it cannot, except by a coincidence, be where you want it to lie. And this is very far from being an evil: on the contrary, it furnishes occasion for all those acts of courtesy, respect, and unselfishness by which love and good humour and modesty express themselves. But it certainly leaves the way open to a great evil, that of competition and hostility. And if souls are free, they cannot be prevented from dealing with the problem by competition instead of by courtesy. And once they have advanced to actual hostility, they can then exploit the fixed nature of matter to hurt one another. The permanent nature of wood which enables us to use it as a beam also enables us to use it for hitting our neighbour on the head. The permanent nature of matter in general means that when human beings fight, the victory ordinarily goes to those who have superior weapons, skill, and number, even if their cause is unjust.

Fixed Laws and Man's Choice   SEPTEMBER 13

That God can and does, on occasions, modify the behaviour of matter and produce what we call miracles, is part of the Christian faith; but the very conception of a common, and therefore, stable, world, demands that these occasions should be extremely rare. In a game of chess you can make certain arbitrary concessions to your opponent, which stand to the ordinary rules of the game as miracles stand to the laws of nature. You can deprive yourself of a castle, or allow the other man sometimes to take back a move made inadvertently. But if you conceded everything that at any moment happened to suit him – if all his moves were revocable and if all your pieces disappeared whenever their position on the board was not to his liking – then you could not have a game at all. So it is with the life of souls in a world: fixed laws, consequences unfolding by causal necessity, the whole natural order, are at once the limits within which their common life is confined and also the sole condition under which any such life is possible. Try to exclude the possibility of suffering which the order of nature and the existence of free wills involve, and you find that you have excluded life itself.

Possible Worlds   SEPTEMBER 14

With every advance in our thought the unity of the creative act, and the impossibility of tinkering with the creation as though this or that element of it could have been removed, will become more apparent. Perhaps this is not the 'best of all possible' universes, but the only possible one. Possible worlds can mean only 'worlds that God could have made, but didn't'. The idea of that which God 'could have' done involves a too anthropomorphic conception of God's freedom. Whatever human freedom means, Divine freedom cannot mean indeterminacy between alternatives and choice of one of them. Perfect goodness can never debate about the end to be attained, and perfect wisdom cannot debate about the means most suited to achieve it. The freedom of God consists in the fact that no cause other than Himself produces His acts and no external obstacle impedes them—that His own goodness is the root from which they all grow and His own omnipotence the air in which they all flower. . . .

I shall not attempt to prove that to create was better than not to create: I am aware of no human scales in which such a portentous question can be weighed. Some comparison between one state of being and another can be made, but the attempt to compare being and not being ends in mere words. 'It would be better for me not to exist' — in what sense 'for me'? How should I, if I did not exist, profit by not existing?

God Intends to Give Us What We Need   SEPTEMBER 15

We are bidden to 'put on Christ', to become like God. That is, whether we like it or not, God intends to give us what we need, not what we now think we want. Once more, we are embarrassed by the intolerable compliment, by too much love, not too little.

Yet perhaps even this view falls short of the truth. It is not simply that God has arbitrarily made us such that He is our only good. Rather God is the only good of all creatures: and by necessity, each must find its good in that kind and degree of the fruition of God which is proper to its nature. The kind and degree may vary with the creature's nature: but that there ever could be any other good, is an atheistic dream. George MacDonald, in a passage I cannot now find, represents God as saying to men 'You must be strong with my strength and blessed with my blessedness, *for I have no other to give you.*' That is the conclusion of the whole matter. God gives what He has, not what He has not: He gives the happiness that there is, not the happiness that is not. To be God — to be like God and to share His goodness in creaturely response — to be miserable — these are the only three alternatives. If we will not learn to eat the only food that the universe grows — the only food that any possible universe ever can grow — then we must starve eternally.

Free Will   SEPTEMBER 16

Some people think they can imagine a creature which was free but had no possibility of going wrong; I cannot. If a thing is free to be good it is also free to be bad. And free will is what has made evil possible. Why, then, did God give them free will? Because free will, though it makes evil possible, is also the only thing that makes possible any love or goodness or joy worth having. A world of automata — of creatures that worked like machines — would hardly be worth creating. The happiness which God designs for His higher creatures is the happiness of being freely, voluntarily united to Him and to each other in an ecstasy of love and delight, compared with which the most rapturous love between a man and a woman on this earth is mere milk and water. And for that they must be free.

Satan   SEPTEMBER 17

How did the Dark Power go wrong? Here, no doubt, we ask a question to which human beings cannot give an answer with any certainty. A reasonable (and traditional) guess, based on our own experiences of going wrong, can, however, be offered. The moment you have a self at all, there is a possibility of putting yourself first — wanting to be the centre — wanting to be God, in fact. That was the sin of Satan: and that was the sin he taught the human race. Some people think the fall of man had something to do with sex, but that is a mistake. (The story in the Book of Genesis rather suggests that some corruption in our sexual nature followed the fall and was its result, not its cause.) What Satan put into the heads of our remote ancestors was the idea that they could 'be like gods' — could set up on their own as if they had created themselves — be their own masters — invent some sort of happiness for themselves outside God, apart from God. And out of that hopeless attempt has come nearly all that we call human history — money, poverty, ambition, war, prostitution, classes, empires, slavery — the long terrible story of man trying to find something other than God which will make him happy.

Satan and St Michael   SEPTEMBER 18

The commonest question is whether I really 'believe in the Devil'.

Now if by 'the Devil' you mean a power opposite to God and, like God, self-existent from all eternity, the answer is certainly 'No'. There is no uncreated being except God. God has no opposite. No being could attain a 'perfect badness' opposite to the perfect goodness of God; for when you have taken away every kind of good thing (intelligence, will, memory, energy, and existence itself) there would be none of him left.

The proper question is whether I believe in devils. I do. That is to say, I believe in angels and I believe that some of these, by the abuse of their free will, have become enemies to God and, as a corollary, to us. These we may call devils. They do not differ in nature from good angels, but their nature is depraved. *Devil* is the opposite of *angel* only as Bad Man is the opposite of Good Man. Satan, the leader or dictator of devils, is the opposite not of God but of Michael.

The Case Against Dualism   SEPTEMBER 19

If Dualism is true, then the bad Power must be a being who likes badness for its own sake. But in reality we have no experience of anyone liking badness just because it is bad. The nearest we can get to it is in cruelty. But in real life people are cruel for one of two reasons—either because they are sadists, that is, because they have a sensual perversion which makes cruelty a cause of sensual pleasure to them, or else for the sake of something they are going to get out of it—money, or power, or safety. But pleasure, money, power, and safety are all, as far as they go, good things. The badness consists in pursuing them by the wrong method, or in the wrong way, or too much. I do not mean, of course, that the people who do this are not desperately wicked. I do mean that wickedness, when you examine it, turns out to be the pursuit of some good in the wrong way. You can be good for the mere sake of goodness: you cannot be bad for the mere sake of badness. You can do a kind action when you are not feeling kind and when it gives you no pleasure, simply because kindness is right; but no one ever did a cruel action simply because cruelty is wrong—only because cruelty was pleasant or useful to him. In other words badness cannot succeed even in being bad in the same way in which goodness is good. Goodness is, so to speak, itself: badness is only spoiled goodness. And there must be something good first before it can be spoiled.

Satanic Blindness   SEPTEMBER 20

Satan is the best-drawn of Milton's characters. The reason is not hard to find. Of the major characters whom Milton attempted he is incomparably the easiest to draw. Set a hundred poets to tell the same story and in ninety of the resulting poems Satan will be the best character. In all but a few writers the 'good' characters are the least successful, and everyone who has ever tried to make even the humblest story ought to know why. To make a character worse than oneself it is only necessary to release imaginatively from control some of the bad passions which, in real life, are always straining at the leash; the Satan, the Iago, the Becky Sharp, within each of us, is always there and only too ready, the moment the leash is slipped, to come out and have in our books that holiday we try to deny them in our lives. But if you try to draw a character better than yourself, all you can do is to take the best moments you have had and to imagine them prolonged and more consistently embodied in action. But the real high virtues which we do not possess at all, we cannot depict except in a purely external fashion. We do not really know what it feels like to be a man much better than ourselves. His whole inner landscape is one we have never seen, and when we guess it we blunder. It is in their 'good' characters that novelists make, unawares, the most shocking self-revelations. Heaven understands Hell and Hell does not understand Heaven, and all of us, in our measure, share the Satanic, or at least the Napoleonic, blindness. To project ourselves into a wicked character, we have only to stop doing something, and something that we are already tired of doing: to project ourselves into a good one we have to do what we cannot and become what we are not. . . . The Satan in Milton enables him to draw the character well just as the Satan in us enables us to receive it.

Sin

SEPTEMBER 21

Is it still God speaking when a liar or a blasphemer speaks? In one sense, almost Yes. Apart from God he could not speak at all; there are no words not derived from the Word; no acts not derived from Him who is *Actus purus*. And indeed the only way in which I can make real to myself what theology teaches about the heinousness of sin is to remember that every sin is the distortion of an energy breathed into us — an energy which, if not thus distorted, would have blossomed into one of those holy acts whereof 'God did it' and 'I did it' are both true descriptions. We poison the wine as He decants it into us; murder a melody He would play with us as the instrument. We caricature the self-portrait He would paint. Hence all sin, whatever else it is, is sacrilege.

The Fall

SEPTEMBER 22

They wanted, as we say, to 'call their souls their own'. But that means to live a lie, for our souls are not, in fact, our own. They wanted some corner in the universe of which they could say to God, 'This is our business, not yours.' But there is no such corner. They wanted to be nouns, but they were, and eternally must be, mere adjectives. We have no idea in what particular act, or series of acts, the self-contradictory, impossible wish found expression. For all I can see, it might have concerned the literal eating of a fruit, but the question is of no consequence.

This act of self-will on the part of the creature, which constitutes an utter falseness to its true creaturely position, is the only sin that can be conceived as the Fall. For the difficulty about the first sin is that it must be very heinous, or its consequences would not be so terrible, and yet it must be something which a being free from the temptations of fallen man could conceivably have committed. The turning from God to self fulfills both conditions. It is a sin possible even to Paradisal man, because the mere existence of a self — the mere fact that we call it 'me' — includes, from the first, the danger of self-idolatry. Since I am I, I must make an act of self-surrender, however small or however easy, in living to God rather than to myself. This is, if you like, the 'weak spot' in the very nature of creation, the risk which God apparently thinks worth taking. But the sin was very heinous, because the self which Paradisal man had to surrender contained no natural recalcitrancy to being surrendered. His *data,* so to speak, were a psycho-physical organism wholly subject to the will and a will wholly disposed, though not compelled, to turn to God. The self-surrender which he practised before the Fall meant no struggle but only the delicious overcoming of an infinitesimal self-adherence which delighted to be overcome — of which we see a dim analogy in the rapturous mutual self-surrenders of lovers even now. He had, therefore, no *temptation* (in our sense) to choose the self — no passion or inclination obstinately inclining that way — nothing but the bare fact that the self was *him*self.

The Loss of Man's Original Nature   SEPTEMBER 23

Up to that moment the human spirit had been in full control of the human organism. It doubtless expected that it would retain this control when it had ceased to obey God. But its authority over the organism was a delegated authority which it lost when it ceased to be God's delegate. Having cut itself off, as far as it could, from the source of its being, it had cut itself off from the source of power. For when we say of created things that A rules B this must mean that God rules B through A. I doubt whether it would have been intrinsically possible for God to continue to rule the organism *through* the human spirit when the human spirit was in revolt against Him. At any rate He did not. He began to rule the organism in a more external way, not by the laws of spirit, but by those of nature. Thus the organs, no longer governed by man's will, fell under the control of ordinary biochemical laws and suffered whatever the inter-workings of those laws might bring about in the way of pain, senility and death. And desires began to come up into the mind of man, not as his reason chose, but just as the biochemical and environmental facts happened to cause them. And the mind itself fell under the psychological laws of association and the like which God had made to rule the psychology of the higher anthropoids. And the will, caught in the tidal wave of mere nature, had no resource but to force back some of the new thoughts and desires by main strength, and these uneasy rebels became the subconscious as we now know it. The process was not, I conceive, comparable to mere deterioration as it may now occur in a human individual; it was a loss of status as a *species*. What man lost by the Fall was his original specific nature. 'Dust thou art, and unto dust shalt thou return.'

Our Rebel Wills and Pain   SEPTEMBER 24

The proper good of a creature is to surrender itself to its Creator — to enact intellectually, volitionally, and emotionally, that relationship which is given in the mere fact of its being a creature. When it does so, it is good and happy. Lest we should think this a hardship, this kind of good begins on a level far above the creatures, for God Himself, as Son, from all eternity renders back to God as Father by filial obedience the being which the Father by paternal love eternally generates in the Son. This is the pattern which man was made to imitate — which Paradisal man did imitate — and wherever the will conferred by the Creator is thus perfectly offered back in delighted and delighting obedience by the creature, there, most undoubtedly, is Heaven, and there the Holy Ghost proceeds. In the world as we now know it, the problem is how to recover this self-surrender. We are not merely imperfect creatures who must be improved: we are, as Newman said, rebels who must lay down our arms. The first answer, then, to the question why our cure should be painful, is that to render back the will which we have so long claimed for our own, is in itself, wherever and however it is done, a grievous pain.

God's Megaphone   SEPTEMBER 25

The human spirit will not even begin to try to surrender self-will as long as all seems to be well with it. Now error and sin both have this property, that the deeper they are the less their victim suspects their existence; they are masked evil. Pain is unmasked, unmistakable evil; every man knows that something is wrong when he is being hurt. . . . And pain is not only immediately recognizable evil, but evil impossible to ignore.

We can rest contentedly in our sins and in our stupidities; and anyone who has watched gluttons shovelling down the most exquisite foods as if they did not know what they were eating, will admit that we can ignore even pleasure. But pain insists upon being attended to. God whispers to us in our pleasures, speaks in our conscience, but shouts in our pains: it is His megaphone to rouse a deaf world.

Pain as an Opportunity for Amendment   SEPTEMBER 26

When our ancestors referred to pains and sorrows as God's 'vengeance' upon sin they were not necessarily attributing evil passions to God; they may have been recognizing the good element in the idea of retribution. Until the evil man finds evil unmistakably present in his existence, in the form of pain, he is enclosed in illusion. Once pain has roused him, he knows that he is in some way or other 'up against' the real universe: he either rebels (with the possibility of a clearer issue and deeper repentance at some later stage) or else makes some attempt at an adjustment, which, if pursued, will lead him to religion. It is true that neither effect is so certain now as it was in ages when the existence of God (or even of the gods) was more widely known, but even in our own days we see it operating. Even atheists rebel and express, like Hardy and Housman, their rage against God although (or because) He does not, on their view, exist: and other atheists, like Mr Huxley, are driven by suffering to raise the whole problem of existence and to find some way of coming to terms with it which, if not Christian, is almost infinitely superior to fatuous contentment with a profane life. No doubt Pain as God's megaphone is a terrible instrument; it may lead to final and unrepented rebellion. But it gives the only opportunity the bad man can have for amendment. It removes the veil; it plants the flag of truth within the fortress of a rebel soul.

Divine Humility   SEPTEMBER 27

We are perplexed to see misfortune falling upon decent, inoffensive, worthy people — on capable, hardworking mothers of families or diligent, thrifty, little tradespeople, on those who have worked so hard, and so honestly, for their modest stock of happiness and now seem to be entering on the enjoyment of it with the fullest right. How can I say with sufficient tenderness what here needs to be said? It does not matter that I know I must become, in the eyes of every hostile reader, as it were personally responsible for all the sufferings I try to explain — just as, to this day, everyone talks as if St Augustine *wanted* unbaptized infants to go to Hell. But it matters enormously if I alienate anyone from the truth. Let me implore the reader to try to believe, if only for the moment, that God, who made these deserving people, may really be right when He thinks that their modest prosperity and the happiness of their children are not enough to make them blessed: that all this must fall from them in the end, and that if they have not learned to know Him they will be wretched. And therefore He troubles them, warning them in advance of an insufficiency that one day they will have to discover. The life to themselves and their families stands between them and the recognition of their need; He makes that life less sweet to them. I call this a Divine humility because it is a poor thing to strike our colours to God when the ship is going down under us; a poor thing to come to Him as a last resort, to offer up 'our own' when it is no longer worth keeping.

The Necessity of Tribulation　　　SEPTEMBER 28

I am progressing along the path of life in my ordinary contentedly fallen and godless condition, absorbed in a merry meeting with my friends for the morrow or a bit of work that tickles my vanity today, a holiday or a new book, when suddenly a stab of abdominal pain that threatens serious disease, or a headline in the newspapers that threatens us all with destruction, sends this whole pack of cards tumbling down. At first I am overwhelmed, and all my little happinesses look like broken toys. Then, slowly and reluctantly, bit by bit, I try to bring myself into the frame of mind that I should be in at all times. I remind myself that all these toys were never intended to possess my heart, that my true good is in another world and my only real treasure is Christ. And perhaps, by God's grace, I succeed, and for a day or two become a creature consciously dependent on God and drawing its strength from the right sources. But the moment the threat is withdrawn, my whole nature leaps back to the toys: I am even anxious, God forgive me, to banish from my mind the only thing that supported me under the threat because it is now associated with the misery of those few days. Thus the terrible necessity of tribulation is only too clear. God has had me for but forty-eight hours and then only by dint of taking everything else away from me. Let Him but sheathe that sword for a moment and I behave like a puppy when the hated bath is over — I shake myself as dry as I can and race off to reacquire my comfortable dirtiness, if not in the nearest manure heap, at least in the nearest flower bed. And that is why tribulations cannot cease until God either sees us remade or sees that our remaking is now hopeless.

St Michael and All Angels   SEPTEMBER 29

All angels, both the 'good' ones and the bad or 'fallen' ones which we call devils, are equally 'Supernatural' in relation to *this* spatio-temporal Nature: i.e. they are outside it and have powers and a mode of existence which it could not provide. But the good angels lead a life which is Supernatural in another sense as well. That is to say, they have, of their own free will, offered back to God in love the 'natures' He gave them at their creation. All creatures of course live from God in the sense that He made them and at every moment maintains them in existence. But there is a further and higher kind of 'life from God' which can be given only to a creature who voluntarily surrenders himself to it. This life the good angels have and the bad angels have not: and it is absolutely Supernatural because no creature in any world can have it by the mere fact of being the sort of creature it is.

St Jerome   SEPTEMBER 30

I do not maintain that God's creation of Nature can be proved as rigorously as God's existence, but it seems to me overwhelmingly probable, so probable that no one who approached the question with an open mind would very seriously entertain any other hypothesis. In fact one seldom meets people who have grasped the existence of a supernatural God and yet deny that He is the Creator. All the evidence we have points in that direction, and difficulties spring up on every side if we try to believe otherwise. No philosophical theory which I have yet come across is a radical improvement on the words of Genesis, that 'In the beginning God made Heaven and Earth'. I say 'radical' improvement, because the story in Genesis — as St Jerome said long ago — is told in the manner 'of a popular poet', or as we should say, in the form of folk tale. But if you compare it with the creation legends of other peoples — with all these delightful absurdities in which giants to be cut up and floods to be dried up are made to exist *before* creation — the depth and originality of this Hebrew folk tale will soon be apparent. The idea of *creation* in the rigorous sense of the word is there fully grasped.

The Law of Human Nature OCTOBER 1

Everyone has heard people quarrelling. Sometimes it sounds funny and sometimes it sounds merely unpleasant; but however it sounds, I believe we can learn something very important from listening to the kind of things they say. They say things like this: 'How'd you like it if anyone did the same to you?' — 'That's my seat, I was there first' — 'Leave him alone, he isn't doing you any harm' — 'Why should you shove in first?' — 'Give me a bit of your orange, I gave you a bit of mine' — 'Come on, you promised.' People say things like that every day, educated people as well as uneducated, and children as well as grown-ups.

Now what interests me about all these remarks is that the man who makes them is not merely saying that the other man's behaviour does not happen to please him. He is appealing to some kind of standard of behaviour which he expects the other man to know about. And the other man very seldom replies: 'To hell with your standard.' Nearly always he tries to make out that what he has been doing does not really go against the standard, or that if it does there is some special excuse....It looks, in fact, very much as if both parties had in mind some kind of Law or Rule of fair play or decent behaviour or morality or whatever you like to call it, about which they really agreed. And they have. If they had not, they might, of course, fight like animals, but they could not quarrel in the human sense of the word. Quarrelling means trying to show that the other man is in the wrong. And there would be no sense in trying to do that unless you and he had some sort of agreement as to what Right and Wrong are; just as there would be no sense in saying that a footballer had committed a foul unless there was some agreement about the rules of football.

Right and Wrong OCTOBER 2

The most remarkable thing is this. Whenever you find a man who says he does not believe in a real Right and Wrong, you will find the same man going back on this a moment later. He may break his promise to you, but if you try breaking one to him he will be complaining 'It's not fair' before you can say Jack Robinson. A nation may say treaties do not matter; but then, next minute, they spoil their case by saying that the particular treaty they want to break was an unfair one. But if treaties do not matter, and if there is no such thing as Right and Wrong — in other words, if there is no Law of Nature what is the difference between a fair treaty and an unfair one? Have they not let the cat out of the bag and shown that, whatever they say, they really know the Law of Nature just like anyone else?

It seems, then, we are forced to believe in a real Right and Wrong. People may be sometimes mistaken about them, just as people sometimes get their sums wrong; but they are not a matter of mere taste and opinion any more than the multiplication table.

The Moral Law and Instinct OCTOBER 3

Supposing you hear a cry for help from a man in danger. You will probably feel two desires – one a desire to give help (due to your herd instinct), the other a desire to keep out of danger (due to the instinct for self-preservation). But you will find inside you, in addition to these two impulses, a third thing which tells you that you ought to follow the impulse to help, and suppress the impulse to run away. Now this thing that judges between two instincts, that decides which should be encouraged, cannot itself be either of them. You might as well say that the sheet of music which tells you, at a given moment, to play one note on the piano and not another, is itself one of the notes on the keyboard. The Moral Law tells us the tune we have to play: our instincts are merely the keys.

Another way of seeing that the Moral Law is not simply one of our instincts is this. If two instincts are in conflict, and there is nothing in a creature's mind except those two instincts, obviously the stronger of the two must win. But at those moments when we are most conscious of the Moral Law, it usually seems to be telling us to side with the weaker of the two impulses. You probably *want* to be safe much more than you want to help the man who is drowning: but the Moral Law tells you to help him all the same. And surely it often tells us to try to make the right impulse stronger than it naturally is? I mean, we often feel it our duty to stimulate the herd instinct, by waking up our imaginations and arousing our pity and so on, so as to get up enough steam for doing the right thing. But clearly we are not acting *from* instinct when we set about making an instinct stronger than it is. The thing that says to you, 'Your herd instinct is asleep. Wake it up', cannot itself be the herd instinct. The thing that tells you which note on the piano needs to be played louder cannot itself be that note.

St Francis of Assisi OCTOBER 4

Man has held three views of his body. First there is that of those ascetic Pagans who called it the prison or the 'tomb' of the soul, and of Christians like Fisher to whom it was a 'sack of dung', food for worms, filthy, shameful, a source of nothing but temptation to bad men and humiliation to good ones. Then there are the Neo-Pagans (they seldom know Greek), the nudists and the sufferers from Dark Gods, to whom the body is glorious. But thirdly we have the view which St Francis expressed by calling his body 'Brother Ass'. All three may be — I am not sure — defensible; but give me St Francis for my money.

Ass is exquisitely right because no one in his senses can either revere or hate a donkey. It is a useful, sturdy, lazy, obstinate, patient, lovable and infuriating beast; deserving now the stick and now a carrot; both pathetically and absurdly beautiful. So the body.

The Moral Law is Universal OCTOBER 5

The Chinese . . . speak of a great thing (the greatest thing) called the *Tao*. It is the reality beyond all predicates, the abyss that was before the Creator Himself. It is Nature, it is the Way, the Road. It is the Way in which the universe goes on, the Way in which things everlastingly emerge, stilly and tranquilly, into space and time. It is also the Way which every man should tread in imitation of that cosmic and supercosmic progression, conforming all activities to that great exemplar. 'In ritual', say the Analects, 'it is harmony with Nature that is prized.' The ancient Jews likewise praise the Law as being 'true'.

This conception in all its forms, Platonic, Aristotelian, Stoic, Christian, and Oriental alike, I shall henceforth refer to for brevity simply as 'the *Tao*. . . . It is the doctrine of objective value, the belief that certain attitudes are really true, and others really false, to the kind of thing the universe is and the kind of things we are. Those who know the *Tao* can hold that to call children delightful or old men venerable is not simply to record a psychological fact about our own parental or filial emotions at the moment, but to recognize a quality which demands a certain response from us whether we make it or not. . . . And because our approvals and disapprovals are thus recognitions of objective value or responses to an objective order, therefore emotional states can be in harmony with reason (when we feel liking for what ought to be approved) or out of harmony with reason (when we perceive that liking is due but cannot feel it). No emotion is, in itself, a judgement: in that sense all emotions and sentiments are alogical. But they can be reasonable or unreasonable as they conform to Reason or fail to conform. The heart never takes the place of the head: but it can, and should, obey it.

The Sole Source of All Value Judgements   OCTOBER 6

This thing which I have called for convenience the *Tao,* and which others may call
Natural Law or Traditional Morality or the First Principles of Practical Reason or the
First Platitudes, is not one among a series of possible systems of value. It is the sole
source of all value judgements. If it is rejected, all value is rejected. If any value is retained, it is retained. The effort to refute it and raise a new system of value in its place
is self-contradictory. There never has been, and never will be, a radically new judgement of value in the history of the world. What purport to be new systems, or (as they
now call them) 'ideologies', all consist of fragments from the *Tao* itself, arbitrarily
wrenched from their context in the whole and then swollen to madness in their isolation, yet still owing to the *Tao* and to it alone such validity as they possess. If my duty
to my parents is a superstition, then so is my duty to my country or my race. If the
pursuit of scientific knowledge is a real value, then so is conjugal fidelity. The rebellion of new ideologies against the *Tao* is a rebellion of the branches against the tree: if
the rebels could succeed they would find that they had destroyed themselves. The
human mind has no more power of inventing a new value than of imagining a new primary colour, or, indeed, of creating a new sun and a new sky for it to move in.

Does the Moral Law Become Stagnant?   OCTOBER 7

The modern mind has two lines of defence. . . . The second claims that to tie ourselves
to an immutable moral code is to cut off all progress and acquiesce in 'stagnation'. . .

Let us strip it of the illegitimate emotional power it derives from the word 'stagnation' with its suggestion of puddles and mantled pools. If water stands too long it
stinks. To infer thence that whatever stands long must be unwholesome is to be the
victim of metaphor. Space does not stink because it has preserved its three dimensions from the beginning. The square on the hypotenuse has not gone mouldy by
continuing to equal the sum of the squares on the other two sides. Love is not dishon-
oured by constancy, and when we wash our hands we are seeking stagnation and
'putting the clock back', artificially restoring our hands to the *status quo* in which
they began the day and resisting the natural trend of events which would increase
their dirtiness steadily from our birth to our death. For the emotive term 'stagnant' let
us substitute the descriptive term 'permanent'. Does a permanent moral standard
preclude progress? On the contrary, except on the supposition of a changeless standard, progress is impossible. If good is a fixed point, it is at least possible that we
should get nearer and nearer to it; but if the terminus is as mobile as the train, how
can the train progress towards it? Our ideas of the good may change, but they cannot

change either for the better or the worse if there is no absolute and immutable good to which they can approximate or from which they can recede. We can go on getting a sum more and more nearly right only if the one perfectly right answer is 'stagnant'.

At the Back of the Moral Law — a Person   OCTOBER 8

Christianity tells people to repent and promises them forgiveness. It therefore has nothing (as far as I know) to say to people who do not know they have done anything to repent of and who do not feel that they need any forgiveness. It is after you have realized that there is a real Moral Law, and a Power behind the law, and that you have broken that law and put yourself wrong with that Power — it is after all this, and not a moment sooner, that Christianity begins to talk. When you know you are sick, you will listen to the doctor. When you have realized that our position is nearly desperate you will begin to understand what the Christians are talking about. They offer an explanation of how we got into our present state of both hating goodness and loving it. They offer an explanation of how God can be this impersonal mind at the back of the Moral Law and yet also a Person. They tell you how the demands of this law, which you and I cannot meet, have been met on our behalf, how God Himself becomes a man to save man from the disapproval of God. . . . I quite agree that the Christian religion is, in the long run, a thing of unspeakable comfort. But it does not begin in comfort; it begins in the dismay I have been describing, and it is no use at all trying to go on to that comfort without first going through that dismay. In religion, as in war and everything else, comfort is the one thing you cannot get by looking for it. If you look for truth, you may find comfort in the end: if you look for comfort you will not get either comfort or truth — only soft soap and wishful thinking to begin with and, in the end, despair.

Atheism   OCTOBER 9

My argument against God was that the universe seemed so cruel and unjust. But how had I got this idea of *just* and *unjust*? A man does not call a line crooked unless he has some idea of a straight line. What was I comparing this universe with when I called it unjust? If the whole show was bad and senseless from A to Z, so to speak, why did I, who was supposed to be part of the show, find myself in such violent reaction against it? A man feels wet when he falls into water, because man is not a water animal: a fish would not feel wet. Of course I could have given up my idea of justice by saying it was nothing but a private idea of my own. But if I did that, then my argument against God collapsed too – for the argument depended on saying that the world was really unjust, not simply that it did not happen to please my private fancies. Thus in the very act of trying to prove that God did not exist – in other words, that the whole of reality was senseless – I found I was forced to assume that one part of reality – namely my idea of justice – was full of sense. Consequently atheism turns out to be too simple. If the whole universe has no meaning, we should never have found out that it has no meaning: just as, if there were no light in the universe and therefore no creatures with eyes, we should never know it was dark. *Dark* would be without meaning.

Universal Evolutionism   OCTOBER 10

By universal evolutionism I mean the belief that the very formula of universal process is from imperfect to perfect, from small beginnings to great endings, from the rudimentary to the elaborate, the belief which makes people find it natural to think that morality springs from savage taboos, adult sentiment from infantile sexual maladjustments, thought from instinct, mind from matter, organic from inorganic, cosmos from chaos. This is perhaps the deepest habit of mind in the contemporary world. It seems to me immensely unplausible, because it makes the general course of nature so very unlike those parts of nature we can observe. You remember the old puzzle as to whether the owl came from the egg or the egg from the owl. The modern acquiescence in universal evolutionism is a kind of optical illusion, produced by attending exclusively to the owl's emergence from the egg. We are taught from childhood to notice how the perfect oak grows from the acorn and to forget that the acorn itself was dropped by a perfect oak. We are reminded constantly that the adult human being was an embryo, never that the life of the embryo came from two adult human beings. We love to notice that the express engine of today is the descendant of the 'Rocket'; we do not equally remember that the 'Rocket' springs not from some even more rudimentary engine, but from something much more perfect and complicated than itself – namely, a man of genius. The obviousness or naturalness which most people seem to find in the idea of emergent evolution thus seems to be a pure hallucination.

The Life Force

One reason why many people find Creative Evolution so attractive is that it gives one much of the emotional comfort of believing in God and none of the less pleasant consequences. When you are feeling fit and the sun is shining and you do not want to believe that the whole universe is a mere mechanical dance of atoms, it is nice to be able to think of this great mysterious Force rolling on through the centuries and carrying you on its crest. If, on the other hand, you want to do something rather shabby, the Life Force, being only a blind force, with no morals and no mind, will never interfere with you like that troublesome God we learned about when we were children. The Life Force is a sort of tame God. You can switch it on when you want, but it will not bother you. All the thrills of religion and none of the cost. Is the Life Force the greatest achievement of wishful thinking the world has yet seen?

Everythingism

You must really re-educate yourself: must work hard and consistently to eradicate from your mind the whole type of thought in which we have all been brought up. . . . It is technically called *Monism*; but perhaps the unlearned reader will understand me best if I call it *Everythingism*. I mean by this the belief that 'everything', or 'the whole show', must be self-existent, must be more important than every particular thing, and must contain all particular things in such a way that they cannot be really very different from one another — that they must be not merely 'at one', but one. Thus the Everythingist, if he starts from God, becomes a Pantheist; there must be nothing that is not God. If he starts from Nature he becomes a Naturalist; there must be nothing that is not Nature. He thinks that everything is in the long run 'merely' a precursor or a development or a relic or an instance or a disguise, of everything else. This philosophy I believe to be profoundly untrue. One of the moderns has said that reality is 'incorrigibly plural'. I think he is right. All things come from One. All things are related — related in different and complicated ways. But all things are not one. The word 'everything' should mean simply the total (a total to be reached, if we knew enough, by enumeration) of all the things that exist at a given moment. It must not be given a mental capital letter; must not (under the influence of picture thinking) be turned into a sort of pool in which particular things sink or even a cake in which they are the currants. Real things are sharp and knobbly and complicated and different. Everythingism is congenial to our minds because it is the natural philosophy of a totalitarian, mass-producing, conscripted age. That is why we must be perpetually on our guard against it.

Real Things are Not Simple OCTOBER 13

It is no good asking for a simple religion. After all, real things are not simple. They look simple, but they are not. The table I am sitting at looks simple: but ask a scientist to tell you what it is really made of—all about the atoms and how the light waves rebound from them and hit my eye and what they do to the optic nerve and what it does to my brain—and, of course, you find that what we call 'seeing a table' lands you in mysteries and complications which you can hardly get to the end of. A child saying a child's prayer looks simple. And if you are content to stop there, well and good. But if you are not — and the modern world usually is not — If you want to go on and ask what is really happening — then you must be prepared for something difficult. If we ask for something more than simplicity, it is silly then to complain that the something more is not simple.

Very often, however, this silly procedure is adopted by people who are not silly, but who, consciously or unconsciously, want to destroy Christianity. Such people put up a version of Christianity suitable for a child of six and make that the object of their attack. When you try to explain the Christian doctrine as it is really held by an instructed adult, they then complain that you are making their heads turn round and that it is all too complicated and that if there really were a God they are sure He would have made 'religion' simple, because simplicity is so beautiful, etc. You must be on your guard against these people for they will change their ground every minute and only waste your time. Notice, too, their idea of God 'making religion simple': as if 'religion' were something God invented, and not His statement to us of certain quite unalterable facts about His own nature.

The Unexpectedness about Reality OCTOBER 14

Besides being complicated, reality, in my experience, is usually odd. It is not neat, not obvious, not what you expect. For instance, when you have grasped that the earth and the other planets all go round the sun, you would naturally expect that all the planets were made to match — all at equal distances from each other, say, or distances that regularly increased, or all the same size, or else getting bigger or smaller as you go further from the sun. In fact, you find no rhyme or reason (that we can see) about either the sizes or the distances; and some of them have one moon, one has four, one has two, some have none, and one has a ring.

Reality, in fact, is usually something you could not have guessed. That is one of the reasons I believe Christianity. It is a religion you could not have guessed. If it offered us just the kind of universe we had always expected, I should feel we were making it up. But, in fact, it is not the sort of thing anyone would have made up. It has just that queer twist about it that real things have. So let us leave behind all these boys' philosophies – these over-simple answers. The problem is not simple and the answer is not going to be simple either.

Holy War OCTOBER 15

One of the things that surprised me when I first read the New Testament seriously was that it talked so much about a Dark Power in the universe – a mighty evil spirit who was held to be the Power behind death and disease, and sin. The difference is that Christianity thinks this Dark Power was created by God, and was good when he was created, and went wrong. Christianity agrees with Dualism that this universe is at war. But it does not think this is a war between independent powers. It thinks it is a civil war, a rebellion, and that we are living in a part of the universe occupied by the rebel.

Enemy-occupied territory – that is what this world is. Christianity is the story of how the rightful king has landed, you might say landed in disguise, and is calling us all to take part in a great campaign of sabotage. When you go to church you are really listening in to the secret wireless from our friends: that is why the enemy is so anxious to prevent us from going. He does it by playing on our conceit and laziness and intellectual snobbery. I know someone will ask me, 'Do you really mean, at this time of day, to re-introduce our old friend the devil – hoofs and horns and all?' Well, what the time of day has to do with it I do not know. And I am not particular about the hoofs and horns. But in other respects my answer is 'Yes, I do'. I do not claim to know anything about his personal appearance. If anybody really wants to know him better I would say to that person, 'Don't worry. If you really want to, you will. Whether you'll like it when you do is another question.'

Screwtape's Policy on Appearances OCTOBER 16

Our policy, for the moment, is to conceal ourselves. Of course this has not always been so. We are really faced with a cruel dilemma. When the humans disbelieve in our existence we lose all the pleasing results of direct terrorism and we make no magicians. On the other hand, when they believe in us, we cannot make them materialists and skeptics. At least, not yet. I have great hopes that we shall learn in due time how to emotionalize and mythologize their science to such an extent that what is, in effect, a belief in us (though not under that name), will creep in while the human mind remains closed to belief in the Enemy. The 'Life Force', the worship of sex, and some aspects of Psychoanalysis, may here prove useful. If once we can produce our perfect work — the Materialist Magician, the man, not using, but veritably worshipping, what he vaguely calls 'Forces' while denying the existence of 'spirits' — then the end of the war will be in sight. But in the meantime we must obey our orders. I do not think you will have much difficulty in keeping the patient in the dark. The fact that 'devils' are predominantly *comic* figures in the modern imagination will help you. If any faint suspicion of your existence begins to arise in his mind, suggest to him a picture of something in red tights, and persuade him that since he cannot believe in that (it is an old textbook method of confusing them) he therefore cannot believe in you.

The Price of Free Will   OCTOBER 17

Christians, then, believe that an evil power has made himself for the present the Prince of this World. And, of course, that raises problems. Is this state of affairs in accordance with God's will or not? If it is, He is a strange God, you will say: and if it is not, how can anything happen contrary to the will of a being with absolute power? God created things which had free will. That means creatures which can go either wrong or right. Some people think they can imagine a creature which was free but had no possibility of going wrong; I cannot. If a thing is free to be good it is also free to be bad. . . . Of course God knew what would happen if they used their freedom the wrong way: apparently He thought it worth the risk. Perhaps we feel inclined to disagree with Him. But there is a difficulty about disagreeing with God. He is the source from which all your reasoning power comes: you could not be right and He wrong any more than a stream can rise higher than its own source. When you are arguing against Him you are arguing against the very power that makes you able to argue at all: it is like cutting off the branch you are sitting on. If God thinks this state of war in the universe a price worth paying for free will — that is, for making a live world in which creatures can do real good or harm and something of real importance can happen, instead of a toy world which only moves when He pulls the strings — then we may take it it is worth paying.

St Luke, Evangelist OCTOBER 18

Surely there's no difficulty about the prayer in Gethsemane on the ground that if the disciples were asleep they couldn't have heard it and therefore couldn't have recorded it? The words they did record would hardly have taken three seconds to utter. He was only 'a stone's throw' away. The silence of night was around them. And we may be sure He prayed aloud. People did everything aloud in those days. . . .

There is a rather amusing instance of the same thing in Acts 24. The Jews had got down a professional orator called Tertullos to conduct the prosecution of St Paul. The speech as recorded by St Luke takes eighty-four words in the Greek, if I've counted correctly. Eighty-four words are impossibly short for a Greek advocate on a full-dress occasion. Presumably, then, they are a précis? But of those eighty-odd words forty are taken up with preliminary compliments to the bench — stuff which, in a précis on that tiny scale, ought not to have come in at all. It is easy to guess what has happened. St Luke, though an excellent narrator, was no good as a reporter. He starts off by trying to memorize, or to get down, the whole speech verbatim. And he succeeds in reproducing a certain amount of the exordium. (The style unmistakable. Only a practising *rhetor* ever talks that way.) But he is soon defeated. The whole of the rest of the speech has to be represented by a ludicrously inadequate abstract. But he doesn't tell us what has happened, and thus seems to attribute to Tertullos a performance which would have spelled professional ruin.

God's Answer to a Fallen World OCTOBER 19

What did God do? First of all He left us conscience, the sense of right and wrong: and all through history there have been people trying (some of them very hard) to obey it. None of them ever quite succeeded. Secondly, He sent the human race what I call good dreams: I mean those queer stories scattered all through the heathen religions about a god who dies and comes to life again and, by his death, has somehow given new life to men. Thirdly, He selected one particular people and spent several centuries hammering into their heads the sort of God He was — that there was only one of Him and that He cared about right conduct. Those people were the Jews, and the Old Testament gives an account of the hammering process.

Then comes the real shock. Among these Jews there suddenly turns up a man who goes about talking as if He was God. He claims to forgive sins. He says He has always existed. He says He is coming to judge the world at the end of time. Now let us get this clear. Among Pantheists, like the Indians, anyone might say that he was a part of God, or one with God: there would be nothing very odd about it. But this man, since He was a Jew, could not mean that kind of God. God, in their language, meant the Being outside the world Who had made it and was infinitely different from anything else. And when you have grasped that, you will see that what this man said was, quite simply, the most shocking thing that has ever been uttered by human lips.

An Extraordinary Claim   OCTOBER 20

One part of the claim tends to slip past us unnoticed because we have heard it so often that we no longer see what it amounts to. I mean the claim to forgive sins: any sins. Now unless the speaker is God, this is really so preposterous as to be comic. We can all understand how a man forgives offences against himself. You tread on my toe and I forgive you, you steal my money and I forgive you. But what should we make of a man, himself unrobbed and untrodden on, who announced that he forgave you for treading on other men's toes and stealing other men's money? Asinine fatuity is the kindest description we should give of his conduct. Yet this is what Jesus did. He told people that their sins were forgiven, and never waited to consult all the other people whom their sins had undoubtedly injured. He unhesitatingly behaved as if He was the party chiefly concerned, the person chiefly offended in all offences. This makes sense only if He really was the God whose laws are broken and whose love is wounded in every sin. In the mouth of any speaker who is not God, these words would imply what I can only regard as a silliness and conceit unrivaled by any other character in history.

The Shocking Alternative   OCTOBER 21

Christ says that He is 'humble and meek' and we believe Him; not noticing that, if He were merely a man, humility and meekness are the very last characteristics we could attribute to some of His sayings.

I am trying here to prevent anyone saying the really foolish thing that people often say about Him: 'I'm ready to accept Jesus as a great moral teacher, but I don't accept His claim to be God.' That is the one thing we must not say. A man who was merely a man and said the sort of things Jesus said would not be a great moral teacher. He would either be a lunatic — on a level with the man who says he is a poached egg — or else he would be the Devil of Hell. You must make your choice. Either this man was, and is, the Son of God: or else a madman or something worse. You can shut Him up for a fool, you can spit at Him and kill Him as a demon; or you can fall at His feet and call Him Lord and God. But let us not come with any patronizing nonsense about His being a great human teacher. He has not left that open to us. He did not intend to.

The Teaching of Our Lord OCTOBER 22

We might have expected, we may think we should have preferred, an unrefracted light giving us ultimate truth in systematic form — something we could have tabulated and memorized and relied on like the multiplication table. One can respect, and at moments envy, both the Fundamentalist's view of the Bible and the Roman Catholic's view of the Church. But there is one argument which we should beware of using for either position: God must have done what is best, this is best, therefore God has done this. For we are mortals and do not know what is best for us, and it is dangerous to prescribe what God must have done — especially when we cannot, for the life of us, see that He has after all done it.

We may observe that the teaching of Our Lord Himself, in which there is no imperfection, is not given us in that cut-and-dried, foolproof, systematic fashion we might have expected or desired. He wrote no book. We have only reported sayings, most of them uttered in answers to questions, shaped in some degree by their context. And when we have collected them all we cannot reduce them to a system. He preaches but He does not lecture. He used paradox, proverb, exaggeration, parable, irony; even (I mean no irreverence) the 'wisecrack'. He utters maxims which, like popular proverbs, if rigorously taken, may seem to contradict one another. His teaching therefore cannot be grasped by the intellect alone, cannot be 'got up' as if it were a 'subject'. If we try to do that with it, we shall find Him the most elusive of teachers. He hardly ever gave a straight answer to a straight question. He will not be, in the way we want, 'pinned down'. The attempt is (again, I mean no irreverence) like trying to bottle a sunbeam.

The Perfect Penitent OCTOBER 23

God has landed on this enemy-occupied world in human form. And now, what was the purpose of it all? What did He come to do? Well, to teach, of course; but as soon as you look into the New Testament or any other Christian writing you will find they are constantly talking about something different — about His death and His coming to life again. It is obvious that Christians think the chief point of the story lies here. They think the main thing He came to earth to do was to suffer and be killed.

Now before I became a Christian I was under the impression that the first thing Christians had to believe was one particular theory as to what the point of this dying was. According to that theory God wanted to punish men for having deserted and joined the Great Rebel, but Christ volunteered to be punished instead, and so God let us off.... What I came to see later on was that neither this theory nor any other is Christianity. The central Christian belief is that Christ's death has somehow put us right with God and given us a fresh start. Theories as to how it did this are another matter. A good many different theories have been held as to how it works; what all Christians are agreed on is that it does work. I will tell you what I think it is like. All sensible people know that if you are tired and hungry a meal will do you good. But the modern theory of nourishment — about the vitamins and proteins — is a different thing. People ate their dinners and felt better long before the theory of vitamins was ever heard of: and if the theory of vitamins is some day abandoned they will go on eating their dinners just the same. Theories about Christ's death are not Christianity: they are explanations about how it works.

The Perfect Sacrifice   OCTOBER 24

The death of Christ is just that point in history at which something absolutely un-imaginable from outside shows through into our own world. And if we cannot picture even the atoms of which our own world is built, of course we are not going to be able to picture this. Indeed, if we found that we could fully understand it, that very fact would show it was not what it professes to be — the inconceivable, the uncreated, the thing from beyond nature, striking down into nature like lightning. You may ask what good will it be to us if we do not understand it. But that is easily answered. A man can eat his dinner without understanding exactly how food nourishes him. A man can accept what Christ has done without knowing how it works: indeed, he certainly would not know how it works until he has accepted it.

We are told that Christ was killed for us, that His death has washed out our sins, and that by dying He disabled death itself. That is the formula. That is Christianity. That is what has to be believed. Any theories we build up as to how Christ's death did all this are, in my view, quite secondary: mere plans or diagrams to be left alone if they do not help us, and, even if they do help us, not to be confused with the thing itself.

The perfect surrender and humiliation were undergone by Christ: perfect because He was God, surrender and humiliation because He was man. Now the Christian belief is that if we somehow share the humility and suffering of Christ we shall also share in His conquest of death and find a new life after we have died and in it become perfect, and perfectly happy, creatures. This means something much more than our trying to follow His teaching. People often ask when the next step in evolution — the step to something beyond man — will happen. But on the Christian view, it has happened already. In Christ a new kind of man appeared: and the new kind of life which began in Him is to be put into us. How is this to be done? . . .

There are three things that spread the Christ-life to us: baptism, belief, and that mysterious action which different Christians call by different names — Holy Communion, the Mass, the Lord's Supper. At least, those are the three ordinary methods. I am not saying there may not be special cases where it is spread without one or more of these. I have not time to go into special cases, and I do not know enough. If you are trying in a few minutes to tell a man how to get to Edinburgh you will tell him the trains: he can, it is true, get there by boat or by a plane, but you will hardly bring that in. . . . Anyone who professes to teach you Christian doctrine will, in fact, tell you to use all three, and that is enough for our present purpose.

Do not think I am setting up baptism and belief and the Holy Communion as things that will do instead of your own attempts to copy Christ. Your natural life is derived from your parents; that does not mean it will stay there if you do nothing about it. You can lose it by neglect, or you can drive it away by committing suicide. You have to feed it and look after it: but always remember you are not making it, you are only keeping up a life you got from someone else. In the same way a Christian can lose the Christ-life which has been put into him, and he has to make efforts to keep it. But even the best Christian that ever lived is not acting on his own steam — he is only nourishing or protecting a life he could never have acquired by his own efforts. And that has practical consequences. As long as the natural life is in your body, it will do a lot towards repairing that body. Cut it, and up to a point it will heal, as a dead body would not. A live body is not one that never gets hurt, but one that can to some extent repair itself. In the same way a Christian is not a man who never goes wrong, but a man who is enabled to repent and pick himself up and begin over again after each stumble — because the Christ-life is inside him, repairing him all the time, enabling him to repeat (in some degree) the kind of voluntary death which Christ Himself carried out.

Believing on Authority   OCTOBER 27

We have to take reality as it comes to us: there is no good jabbering about what it ought to be like or what we should have expected it to be like. But though I cannot see why it should be so, I can tell you why I believe it is so. I have explained why I have to believe that Jesus was (and is) God. Arid it seems plain as a matter of history that He taught His followers that the new life was communicated in this way. In other words, I believe it on His authority. Do not be scared by the word authority. Believing things on authority only means believing them because you have been told them by someone you think trustworthy. Ninety-nine per cent of the things you believe are believed on authority. I believe there is such a place as New York. I have not seen it myself. I could not prove by abstract reasoning that there must be such a place. I believe it because reliable people have told me so. The ordinary man believes in the Solar System, atoms, evolution, and the circulation of the blood on authority — because the scientists say so. Every historical statement in the world is believed on authority. None of us has seen the Norman Conquest or the defeat of the Armada. None of us could prove them by pure logic as you prove a thing in mathematics. We believe them simply because people who did see them have left writings that tell us about them: in fact, on authority. A man who jibbed at authority in other things as some people do in religion would have to be content to know nothing all his life.

St Simon and St Jude, Apostles   OCTOBER 28

About Lucius' argument that the evangelists would have put the doctrine of the atonement into the Gospel if they had had the slightest excuse, and, since they didn't, therefore Our Lord didn't teach it: surely, since we know from the Epistles that the Apostles (who had actually known Him) did teach this doctrine in His name *immediately* after His death, it is clear that He *did* teach it: or else, that they allowed themselves a very free hand. But if people shortly after His death were so very free in interpreting His doctrine, why should people who wrote much later (when such freedom would be more excusable from lapse of memory in an honest writer, and more likely to escape detection in a dishonest one) become so very much more accurate?

The accounts of a thing don't usually get more and more accurate as time goes on. Anyway, if you take the sacrificial idea out of Christianity you deprive both Judaism and Paganism of all significance.

Christ Acts Through His Church OCTOBER 29

When Christians say the Christ-life is in them, they do not mean simply something mental or moral. When they speak of being "in Christ" or of Christ being 'in them', this is not simply a way of saying that they are thinking about Christ or copying Him. They mean that Christ is actually operating through them; that the whole mass of Christians are the physical organism through which Christ acts — that we are His fingers and muscles, the cells of His Body. And perhaps that explains one or two things. It explains why this new life is spread not only by purely mental acts like belief, but by bodily acts like baptism and Holy Communion. It is not merely the spreading of an idea; it is more like evolution — a biological or superbiological fact. There is no good trying to be more spiritual than God. God never meant man to be a purely spiritual creature. That is why He uses material things like bread and wine to put the new life into us. We may think this rather crude and unspiritual. God does not: He invented eating. He likes matter. He invented it.

The Personality of Jesus OCTOBER 30

If anything whatever is common to all believers, and even to many unbelievers, it is the sense that in the gospels they have met a personality. There are characters whom we know to be historical but of whom we do not feel that we have any personal knowledge — knowledge by acquaintance; such are Alexander, Attila, or William of Orange. There are others who make no claim to historical reality but whom, none the less, we know as we know real people: Falstaff, Uncle Toby, Mr Pickwick. But there are only three characters who, claiming the first sort of reality, also actually have the second. And surely everyone knows who they are: Plato's Socrates, the Jesus of the gospels, and Boswell's Johnson. Our acquaintance with them shows itself in a dozen ways. When we look into the Apocryphal gospels, we find ourselves constantly saying of this or that *logion,* 'No. it's a fine saying, but not His. That wasn't how He talked' — just as we do with all pseudo-Johnsoniana. We are not in the least perturbed by the contrasts within each character: the union in Socrates of silly and scabrous titters about Greek pederasty with the highest mystical fervour and homeliest good

sense; in Johnson, of profound gravity and melancholy with that love of fun and nonsense which Boswell never understood though Fanny Burney did; in Jesus, of peasant
shrewdness, intolerable severity, and irresistible tenderness. So strong is the flavour
of the personality that, even while He says things which, on any other assumption
than that of Divine Incarnation in the fullest sense, would be appallingly arrogant, yet
we – and many unbelievers – accept Him at His own valuation when He says 'I am
meek and lowly of heart'. Even those passages in the New Testament which su-
perficially, and in intention, are most concerned with the Divine, and least with the
Human Nature, bring us face to face with the personality. I am not sure that they don't
do this more than any others. 'We beheld His glory, the glory as of the only begotten of
the Father, full of graciousness and reality...which we have looked upon and our
hands have handled."

We Must Choose   OCTOBER 31

Why is God landing in this enemy-occupied world in disguise and starting a sort of
secret society to undermine the Devil? Why is He not landing in force, invading it? Is
it that He is not strong enough? Well, Christians think He is going to land in force; we
do not know when. But we can guess why He is delaying. He wants to give us the
chance of joining His side freely. I do not suppose you and I would have thought
much of a Frenchman who waited till the Allies were marching into Germany and
then announced he was on our side. God will invade. But I wonder whether people
who ask God to interfere openly and directly in our world quite realize what it will be
like when He does. When that happens, it is the end of the world. When the author
walks on to the stage the play is over. God is going to invade, all right: but what is the
good of saying you are on His side then, when you see the whole natural universe
melting away like a dream and something else – something it never entered your head
to conceive – comes crashing in; something so beautiful to some of us and so terrible
to others that none of us will have any choice left? For this time it will be God without
disguise; something so overwhelming that it will strike either irresistible love or irresistible horror into every creature. It will be too late then to choose your side. There
is no use saying you choose to lie down when it has become impossible to stand up.
That will not be the time for choosing: it will be the time when we discover which
side we really have chosen, whether we realized it before or not. Now, today, this
moment, is our chance to choose the right side. God is holding back to give us that
chance. It will not last for ever. We must take it or leave it.

All Saints   NOVEMBER 1

If you can ask for the prayers of the living, why should you not ask for the prayers of the dead? There is clearly also a great danger. In some popular practice we see it leading off into an infinitely silly picture of Heaven as an earthly court where applicants will be wise to pull the right wires, discover the best 'channels', and attach themselves to the most influential pressure groups. But I have nothing to do with all this. . . . The consoling thing is that while Christendom is divided about the rationality, and even the lawfulness, of praying *to* the saints, we are all agreed about praying *with* them. 'With angels and archangels and all the company of heaven'. . . . One always accepted this *with* theoretically. But it is quite different when one brings it into consciousness at an appropriate moment and wills the association of one's own little twitter with the voice of the great saints and (we hope) of our own dear dead. They may drown some of its uglier qualities and set off any tiny value it has.

Commemoration of All Souls   NOVEMBER 2

Of course I pray for the dead. The action is so spontaneous, so all but inevitable, that only the most compulsive theological case against it would deter me. And I hardly know how the rest of my prayers would survive if those for the dead were forbidden. At our age the majority of those we love best are dead. What sort of intercourse with God could I have if what I love best were unmentionable to Him?

On the traditional Protestant view, all the dead are damned or saved. If they are damned, prayer for them is useless. If they are saved, it is equally useless. God has already done all for them. What more should we ask?

But don't we believe that God has already done and is already doing all that He can for the living? What more should we ask? Yet we are told to ask.

"Yes," it will be answered, "but the living are still on the road. Further trials, developments, possibilities of error, await them. But the saved have been made perfect. They have finished the course. To pray for them presupposes that progress and difficulty are still possible. In fact, you are bringing in something like Purgatory."

Well, I suppose I am. Though even in Heaven some perpetual increase of beatitude, reached by a continually more ecstatic self-surrender, without the possibility of failure but not perhaps without its own ardours and exertions — for delight also has its severities and steep ascents, as lovers know — might be supposed.

Making and Begetting   NOVEMBER 3

The point in Christianity which gives us the greatest shock is the statement that by attaching ourselves to Christ, we can 'become Sons of God'. One asks 'Aren't we Sons of God already? Surely the Fatherhood of God is one of the main Christian ideas?' Well, in a certain sense, no doubt we are sons of God already. I mean, God has brought us into existence and loves us and looks after us, and in that way is like a father. But when the Bible talks of our 'becoming' Sons of God, obviously it must mean something very different. And that brings us up against the very centre of theology.

One of the creeds says that Christ is the Son of God 'begotten, not created'; and it adds 'begotten by his Father before all worlds'. Will you please get it quite clear that this has nothing to do with the fact that when Christ was born on earth as a man, that man was the son of a virgin? We are not now thinking about the Virgin Birth. We are thinking about something that happened before Nature was created at all, before time began. 'Before all worlds,' Christ is begotten, not created. What does it mean? . . .

To beget is to become the father of: to create is to make. And the difference is this. When you beget, you beget something of the same kind as yourself. A man begets human babies, a beaver begets little beavers and a bird begets eggs which turn into little birds. But when you make, you make something of a different kind from yourself. A bird makes a nest, a beaver builds a dam, a man makes a wireless set – or he may make something more like himself than a wireless set: say, a statue. If he is a clever enough carver he may make a statue which is very like a man indeed. But, of course, it is not a real man; it only looks like one. It cannot breathe or think. It is not alive.

Biological Life and Spiritual Life   NOVEMBER 4

What man, in his natural condition, has not got, is spiritual life – the higher and different sort of life that exists in God. We use the same word *life* for both: but if you thought that both must therefore be the same sort of thing, that would be like thinking that the 'greatness' of space and the 'greatness' of God were the same sort of greatness, In reality, the difference between biological life and spiritual life is so important that I am going to give them two distinct names. The biological sort which comes to us through Nature, and which (like everything else in Nature) is always tending to run down and decay so that it can only be kept up by incessant subsidies from Nature in the form of air, water, food, etc. is *Bios*. The spiritual life which is in God from all eternity, and which made the whole natural universe, is *Zoe*. *Bios* has, to be sure, a certain shadowy or symbolic resemblance to *Zoe*: but only the sort of resemblance there is between a photo and a place, or a statue and a man. A man who changed from having *Bios* to having *Zoe* would have gone through as big a change as a statue which changed from being a carved stone to being a real man.

And that is precisely what Christianity is about. This world is a great sculptor's shop. We are the statues and there is a rumour going round the shop that some of us are some day going to come to life.

Beyond Personality   NOVEMBER 5

A good many people nowadays say, 'I believe in a God, but not in a personal God.' They feel that the mysterious something which is behind all other things must be more than a person. Now the Christians quite agree. But the Christians are the only people who offer any idea of what a being that is beyond personality could be like. All the other people, though they say that God is beyond personality, really think of Him as something impersonal: that is, as something less than personal. If you are looking for something super-personal, something more than a person, then it is not a question of choosing between the Christian idea and the other ideas. The Christian idea is the only one on the market.

Again, some people think that after this life, or perhaps after several lives, human souls will be 'absorbed' into God. But when they try to explain what they mean, they seem to be thinking of our being absorbed into God as one material thing is absorbed into another. They say it is like a drop of water slipping into the sea. But of course that is the end of the drop. If that is what happens to us, then being absorbed is the same as ceasing to exist. It is only the Christians who have any idea of how human souls can be taken into the life of God and yet remain themselves — in fact, be very much more themselves than they were before.

The Beginning of the Church   NOVEMBER 6

People already knew about God in a vague way. Then came a man who claimed to be God; and yet he was not the sort of man you could dismiss as a lunatic. He made them believe Him. They met Him again after they had seen Him killed. And then, after they had been formed into a little society or community, they found God somehow inside them as well: directing them, making them able to do things they could not do before. And when they worked it all out they found they had arrived at the Christian definition of the three-personal God. . . .

When you come to knowing God, the initiative lies on His side. If He does not show Himself, nothing you can do will enable you to find Him. And, in fact, He shows much more of Himself to some people than to others—not because He has favourites, but because it is impossible for Him to show Himself to a man whose whole mind and character are in the wrong condition. Just as sunlight, though it has no favourites, cannot be reflected in a dusty mirror as clearly as in a clean one...God can show Himself as He really is only to real men. And that means not simply to men who are individually good, but to men who are united together in a body, loving one another, helping one another, showing Him to one another. For that is what God meant humanity to be like; like players in one band, or organs in one body.

Our 'Unveiling' Before God   NOVEMBER 7

We are always completely, and therefore equally, known to God. That is our destiny whether we like it or not. But though this knowledge never varies, the quality of our being known can. A school of thought holds that 'freedom is willed necessity'. Never mind if they are right or not. I want this idea only as an analogy. Ordinarily, to be known by God is to be, for this purpose, in the category of things. We are like earth-worms, cabbages, and nebulae, objects of divine knowledge. But when we (a) become aware of the fact—the present fact, not the generalization—and (b) assent with all our will to be so known, then we treat ourselves, in relation to God, not as things but as persons. We have unveiled. Not that any veil could have baffled this sight. The change is in us. The passive changes to the active. Instead of merely being known, we show, we tell, we offer ourselves to view.

To put ourselves thus on a personal footing with God could, in itself and without warrant, be nothing but presumption and illusion. But we are taught that it is not; that it is God who gives us that footing. For it is by the Holy Spirit that we cry 'Father'. By unveiling, by confessing our sins and 'making known' our requests, we assume the high rank of persons before Him. And He, descending, becomes a Person to us.

Time and Beyond Time   NOVEMBER 8

Our life comes to us moment by moment. One moment disappears before the next comes along: and there is room for very little in each. That is what time is like. And of course you and I tend to take it for granted that this time series—this arrangement of past, present and future—is not simply the way life comes to us but the way all things really exist. We tend to assume that the whole universe and God Himself are always moving on from past to future just as we do....

Almost certainly God is not in time. His life does not consist of moments following one another. If a million people are praying to Him at ten-thirty tonight, He need not listen to them all in that one little snippet which we call ten-thirty. Ten-thirty — and every other moment from the beginning of the world — is always the Present for Him. If you like to put it that way, He has all eternity in which to listen to the split second of prayer put up by a pilot as his plane crashes in flames.

That is difficult, I know. Let me try to give something, not the same, but a bit like it. Suppose I am writing a novel. I write 'Mary laid down her work; next moment came a knock at the door!' For Mary who has to live in the imaginary time of my story there is no interval between putting down the work and hearing the knock. But I, who am Mary's maker, do not live in that imaginary time at all. Between writing the first half of that sentence and the second, I might sit down for three hours and think steadily about Mary. I could think about Mary as if she were the only character in the book and for as long as I pleased, and the hours I spent in doing so would not appear in Mary's time (the time inside the story) at all.

The Infinite Attention of God NOVEMBER 9

God is not hurried along in the time stream of this universe any more than an author is hurried along in the imaginary time of his own novel. He has infinite attention to spare for each one of us. He does not have to deal with us in the mass. You are as much alone with Him as if you were the only being He had ever created. When Christ died, He died for you individually just as much as if you had been the only man in the world.

The way in which my illustration breaks down is this. In it the author gets out of one time series (that of the novel) only by going into another time series (the real one). But God, I believe, does not live in a time series at all. His life is not dribbled out moment by moment like ours: with Him it is, so to speak, still 1920 and already 1960. For His life is Himself.

If you picture time as a straight line along which we have to travel, then you must picture God as the whole page on which the line is drawn. We come to the parts of the line one by one: we have to leave A behind before we get to B, and cannot reach C until we leave B behind. God, from above or outside or all round, contains the whole line, and sees it all.

We Confuse Ourselves about Time   NOVEMBER 10

Before I became a Christian one of my objections was as follows. The Christians said that the eternal God who is everywhere and keeps the whole universe going, once became a human being. Well then, said I, how did the whole universe keep going while He was a baby, or while He was asleep? How could He at the same time be God who knows everything and also a man asking his disciples 'Who touched me?' You will notice that the sting lay in the *time* words: '*While* He was a baby' — 'How could He *at the same time?*' In other words I was assuming that Christ's life as God was in time, and that His life as the man Jesus in Palestine was a shorter period taken out of that time — just as my service in the army was a shorter period taken out of my total life. And that is how most of us perhaps tend to think about it. We picture God living through a period when His human life was still in the future: then coming to a period when it was present: then going on to a period when He could look back on it as something in the past. But probably these ideas correspond to nothing in the actual facts. You cannot fit Christ's earthly life in Palestine into any time-relations with His life as God beyond all space and time. It is really, I suggest, a timeless truth about God that human nature, and the human experience of weakness and sleep and ignorance, are somehow included in His whole divine life. This human life in God is from our point of view a particular period in the history of our world (from the year A.D. One till the Crucifixion). We therefore imagine it is also a period in the history of God's own existence. But God has no history. He is too completely and utterly real to have one. For, of course, to have a history means losing part of your reality (because it had already slipped away into the past) and not yet having another part (because it is still in the future): in fact having nothing but the tiny little present, which has gone before you can speak about it. God forbid we should think God was like that. Even we may hope not to be always rationed in that way.

The Eternal 'Now'   NOVEMBER 11

Everyone who believes in God at all believes that He knows what you and I are going to do tomorrow. But if He knows I am going to do so-and-so, how can I be free to do otherwise? Well, here once again, the difficulty comes from thinking that God is progressing along the time line like us: the only difference being that He can see ahead and we cannot. Well, if that were true, if God *foresaw* our acts, it would be very hard to understand how we could be free not to do them. But suppose God is outside and above the time line. In that case, what we call 'tomorrow' is visible to Him in just the same way as what we call 'today'. All the days are 'Now' for Him. He does not remember you doing things yesterday; He simply sees you doing them, because, though you have lost yesterday, He has not. He does not 'foresee' you doing things tomorrow; He simply sees you doing them: because, though tomorrow is not yet there for you, it is for Him. You never supposed that your actions at this moment were any less free because God knows what you are doing. Well, He knows your tomorrow's actions in just the same way — because He is already in tomorrow and can simply watch you. In a sense, He does not know your action till you have done it: but then the moment at which you have done it is already 'Now' for Him.

Prayer and 'Predestination'

When we are praying about the result, say, of a battle or a medical consultation the thought will often cross our minds that (if only we knew it) the event is already decided one way or the other. I believe this to be no good reason for ceasing our prayers. The event certainly has been decided — in a sense it was decided 'before all worlds'. But one of the things taken into account in deciding it, and therefore one of the things that really cause it to happen, may be this very prayer that we are now offering. Thus, shocking as it may sound, I conclude that we can at noon become part causes of an event occurring at ten o'clock. (Some scientists would find this easier than popular thought does.) The imagination will, no doubt, try to play all sort of tricks on us at this point. It will ask, 'Then if I stop praying can God go back and alter what has already happened?' No. The event has already happened and one of its causes has been the fact that you are asking such questions instead of praying. It will ask, 'Then if I begin to pray can God go back and alter what has already happened?' No. The event has already happened and one of its causes is your present prayer. Thus something does really depend on my choice. My free act contributes to the cosmic shape. That contribution is made in eternity 'before all worlds'; but my consciousness of contributing reaches me at a particular point in the time series.

The Efficacy of Prayer

Some years ago I got up one morning intending to have my hair cut in preparation for a visit to London, and the first letter I opened made it clear I need not go to London. So I decided to put the haircut off too. But then there began the most unaccountable little nagging in my mind, almost like a voice saying, 'Get it cut all the same. Go and get it cut.' In the end I could stand it no longer. I went. Now my barber at that time was a fellow Christian and a man of many troubles whom my brother and I had sometimes been able to help. The moment I opened his shop door he said, 'Oh, I was praying you might come today.' And in fact if I had come a day or so later I should have been of no use to him.

It awed me; it awes me still. But of course one cannot rigorously prove a causal connection between the barber's prayer and my visit. It might be telepathy. It might be accident. . . .

The question then arises, 'What sort of evidence would prove the efficacy of prayer?' The thing we pray for may happen, but how can you ever know it was not going to happen anyway? Even if the thing were indisputably miraculous it would not follow that the miracle had occurred because of your prayers. The answer surely is that a compulsive empirical proof such as we have in the sciences can never be attained.

Some things are proved by the unbroken uniformity of our experiences. The law of gravitation is established by the fact that, in our experience, all bodies without exception obey it. Now even if all the things that people prayed for happened, which they do not, this would not prove what Christians mean by the efficacy of prayer. For prayer is request. The essence of request, as distinct from compulsion, is that it may or may not be granted. And if an infinitely wise Being listens to the requests of finite and foolish creatures, of course He will sometimes grant and sometimes refuse them.

Prayer is Not a 'Gimmick' NOVEMBER 14

There are, no doubt, passages in the New Testament which may seem at first sight to promise an invariable granting of our prayers. But that cannot be what they really mean. For in the very heart of the story we meet a glaring instance to the contrary. In Gethsemane the holiest of all petitioners prayed three times that a certain cup might pass from Him. It did not. After that the idea that prayer is recommended to us as a sort of infallible gimmick may be dismissed.

Other things are proved not simply by experience but by those artificially contrived experiences which we call experiments. Could this be done about prayer? I will pass over the objection that no Christian could take part in such a project, because he has been forbidden it: 'You must not try experiments on God, your Master.' Forbidden or not, is the thing even possible?

I have seen it suggested that a team of people – the more the better – should agree to pray as hard as they knew how, over a period of six weeks, for all the patients in Hospital A and none of those in Hospital B. Then you would tot up the results and see if A had more cures and fewer deaths. . . .

The trouble is that I do not see how any real prayer could go on under such conditions. 'Words without thoughts never to heaven go', says the King in *Hamlet.* Simply to say prayers is not to pray; otherwise a team of properly trained parrots would serve as well as men for our experiment. You cannot pray for the recovery of the sick unless the end you have in view is their recovery. But you can have no motive for desiring the recovery of all the patients in one hospital and none of those in another. You are not doing it in order that suffering should be relieved; you are doing it to find out what happens. The real purpose and the nominal purpose of your prayers are at variance.

Prayer as Request   NOVEMBER 15

We make requests of our fellow creatures as well as of God: we ask for the salt, we ask for a rise in pay, we ask a friend to feed the cat while we are on our holidays, we ask a woman to marry us. Sometimes we get what we ask for and sometimes not. But when we do, it is not nearly so easy as one might suppose to prove with scientific certainty a causal connection between the asking and the getting.

Your neighbour may be a humane person who would not have let your cat starve even if you had forgotten to make any arrangement. Your employer is never so likely to grant your request for a rise as when he is aware that you could get better money from a rival firm and is quite possibly intending to secure you by a rise in any case. As for the lady who consents to marry you — are you sure she had not decided to do so already? Your proposal, you know, might have been the result, not the cause, of her decision. A certain important conversation might never have taken place unless she had intended that it should.

Thus in some measure the same doubt that hangs about the causal efficacy of our prayers to God hangs also about our prayers to man. Whatever we get we might have been going to get anyway. But only, as I say, in some measure. Our friend, boss, and wife may tell us that they acted because we asked; and we may know them so well as to feel sure, first that they are saying what they believe to be true, and secondly that they understand their own motives well enough to be right. But notice that when this happens our assurance has not been gained by the methods of science. We do not try the control experiment of refusing the rise or breaking off the engagement and then making our request again under fresh conditions. Our assurance is quite different in kind from scientific knowledge. It is born out of our personal relation to the other parties; not from knowing things about them but from knowing *them.*

Does Prayer Work?   NOVEMBER 16

Our assurance – if we reach an assurance – that God always hears and sometimes grants our prayers, and that apparent grantings are not merely fortuitous, can only come in the same sort of way. There can be no question of tabulating successes and failures and trying to decide whether the successes are too numerous to be accounted for by chance. Those who best know a man best know whether, when he did what they asked, he did it because they asked. I think those who best know God will best know whether He sent me to the barber's shop because the barber prayed.

For up till now we have been tackling the whole question in the wrong way and on the wrong level. The very question 'Does prayer work?' puts us in the wrong frame of mind from the outset. 'Work': as if it were magic, or a machine – something that functions automatically. Prayer is either a sheer illusion or a personal contact between embryonic, incomplete persons (ourselves) and the utterly concrete Person. Prayer in the sense of petition, asking for things, is a small part of it; confession and penitence are its threshold, adoration its sanctuary, the presence and vision and enjoyment of God its bread and wine. In it God shows Himself to us. That He answers prayers is a corollary – not necessarily the most important one – from that revelation. What He does is learned from what He is.

Divine Abdication   NOVEMBER 17

'God', said Pascal, 'instituted prayer in order to lend to His creatures the dignity of causality.' But not only prayer; whenever we act at all He lends us that dignity. It is not really stranger, nor less strange, that my prayers should affect the course of events than that my other actions should do so. They have not advised or changed God's mind that is, His over-all purpose. But that purpose will be realized in different ways according to the actions, including the prayers, of His creatures.

For He seems to do nothing of Himself which He can possibly delegate to His creatures. He commands us to do slowly and blunderingly what He could do perfectly and in the twinkling of an eye. He allows us to neglect what He would have us do, or to fail. Perhaps we do not fully realize the problem, so to call it, of enabling finite free wills to co-exist with Omnipotence. It seems to involve at every moment almost a sort of divine abdication. We are not mere recipients or spectators. We are either privileged to share in the game or compelled to collaborate in the work, 'to wield our little tridents'. Is this amazing process simply Creation going on before our eyes? This is how (no light matter) God makes something – indeed, makes gods – out of nothing.

One Continuous Act of God

What I have offered can be, at the very best, only a mental model or symbol. All that we say on such subjects must be merely analogical and parabolic. The reality is doubtless not comprehensible by our faculties. But we can at any rate try to expel bad analogies and bad parables. Prayer is not a machine. It is not magic. It is not advice offered to God. Our act, when we pray, must not, any more than all our other acts, be separated from the continuous act of God Himself, in which alone all finite causes operate.

It would be even worse to think of those who get what they pray for as a sort of court favourites, people who have influence with the throne. The refused prayer of Christ in Gethsemane is answer enough to that. And I dare not leave out the hard saying which I once heard from an experienced Christian: 'I have seen many striking answers to prayer and more than one that I thought miraculous. But they usually come at the beginning: before conversion, or soon after it. As the Christian life proceeds, they tend to be rarer. The refusals, too, are not only more frequent; they become more unmistakable, more emphatic.'

Does God then forsake just those who serve Him best? Well, He who served Him best of all said, near His tortured death, 'Why hast thou forsaken me?' When God becomes man, that Man, of all others, is least comforted by God, at His greatest need. There is a mystery here which, even if I had the power, I might not have the courage to explore. Meanwhile, little people like you and me, if our prayers are sometimes granted, beyond all hope and probability, had better not draw hasty conclusions to our own advantage. If we were stronger, we might be less tenderly treated. If we were braver, we might be sent, with far less help, to defend far more desperate posts in the great battle.

Harking Back

I am beginning to feel that we need a preliminary act of submission not only towards possible future afflictions but also towards possible future blessings. I know it sounds fantastic; but think it over. It seems to me that we often, almost sulkily, reject the good that God offers us because, at that moment, we expected some other good. Do you know what I mean? On every level of our life — in our religious experience, in our gastronomic, erotic, aesthetic, and social experience — we are always harking back to some occasion which seemed to us to reach perfection, setting that up as a norm, and depreciating all other occasions by comparison. But these other occasions, I now suspect, are often full of their own new blessing, if only we would lay ourselves open to it. God shows us a new facet of the glory, and we refuse to look at it because we're still looking for the old one. And of course we don't get that. You can't, at the twentieth reading, get again the experience of reading *Lycidas* for the first time. But what you do get can be in its own way as good.

Encore!   NOVEMBER 20

Many religious people lament that the first fervours of their conversion have died away. They think — sometimes rightly, but not, I believe, always — that their sins account for this. They may even try by pitiful efforts of will to revive what now seem to have been the golden days. But were those fervours — the operative word is *those* — ever intended to last?

It would be rash to say that there is any prayer which God *never* grants. But the strongest candidate is the prayer we might express in the single word *encore*. And how should the Infinite repeat Himself? All space and time are too little for Him to utter Himself in them *once*.

And the joke, or tragedy, of it all is that these golden moments in the past, which are so tormenting if we erect them into a norm, are entirely nourishing, wholesome, and enchanting if we are content to accept them for what they are, for memories. Properly bedded down in a past which we do not miserably try to conjure back, they will send up exquisite growths. Leave the bulbs alone, and the new flowers will come up. Grub them up and hope, by fondling and sniffing, to get last year's blooms, and you will get nothing. 'Unless a seed die...'

The Prayer Preceding All Prayers   NOVEMBER 21

The moment of prayer is for me — or involves for me as its condition — the awareness, the re-awakened awareness, that this 'real world' and 'real self' are very far from being rockbottom realities. I cannot, in the flesh, leave the stage, either to go behind the scenes or to take my seat in the pit; but I can remember that these regions exist. And I also remember that my apparent self — this clown or hero or super — under his greasepaint is a real person with an off-stage life. The dramatic person could not tread the stage unless he concealed a real person: unless the real and unknown I existed, I would not even make mistakes about the imagined me. And in prayer this real I struggles to speak, for once, from his real being, and to address, for once, not the other actors, but — what shall I call Him? The Author, for He invented us all? The

Producer, for He controls all? Or the Audience, for He watches, and will judge, the performance?

The attempt is not to escape from space and time and from my creaturely situation as a subject facing objects. It is more modest: to re-awaken the awareness of that situation. If that can be done, there is no need to go anywhere else. This situation itself is, at every moment, a possible theophany. Here is the holy ground; the Bush is burning now.

Of course this attempt may be attended with almost every degree of success or failure. The prayer preceding all prayers is 'May it be the real I who speaks. May it be the real Thou that I speak to.' Infinitely various are the levels from which we pray. Emotional intensity is in itself no proof of spiritual depth. If we pray in terror we shall pray earnestly; it only proves that terror is an earnest emotion. Only God Himself can let the bucket down to the depths in Us. And, on the other side, He must constantly work as the iconoclast. Every idea of Him we form, He must in mercy shatter. The most blessed result of prayer would be to rise thinking 'But I never knew before. I never dreamed . . .' I suppose it was at such a moment that Thomas Aquinas said of all his own theology, 'It reminds me of straw.'

St Cecilia, Patroness of Church Music   NOVEMBER 22

There are two musical situations on which I think we can be confident that a blessing rests. One is where a priest or an organist, himself a man of trained and delicate taste, humbly and charitably sacrifices his own (aesthetically right) desires and gives the people humbler and coarser fare than he would wish, in a belief (even, as it may be, the erroneous belief) that he can thus bring them to God. The other is where the stupid and unmusical layman humbly and patiently, and above all silently, listens to music which he cannot, or cannot fully, appreciate, in the belief that it somehow glorifies God, and that if it does not edify him this must be his own defect. Neither such a High Brow nor such a Low Brow can be far out of the way. To both, Church Music will have been a means of grace; not the music they have liked, but the music they have disliked. They have both offered, sacrificed, their taste in the fullest sense. But where the opposite situation arises, where the musician is filled with the pride of skill or the virus of emulation and looks with contempt on the unappreciative congregation, or where the unmusical, complacently entrenched in their own ignorance and conservatism, look with the restless and resentful hostility of an inferiority complex on all who would try to improve their taste – there, we may be sure, all that both offer is unblessed and the spirit that moves them is not the Holy Ghost.

Blest Pair of Sirens —Voice and Verse   NOVEMBER 23

It seems to me that we must define rather carefully the way, or ways, in which music can glorify God. There is... a sense in which all natural agents, even inanimate ones, glorify God continually by revealing the powers He has given them. And in that sense we, as natural agents, do the same. On that level our wicked actions, in so far as they exhibit our skill and strength, may be said to glorify God, as well as our good actions. An excellently performed piece of music, as a natural operation which reveals in a very high degree the peculiar powers given to man, will thus always glorify God whatever the intention of the performers may be. But that is a kind of glorifying which we share with 'the dragons and great deeps', with the 'frosts and snows'. What is looked for in us, as men, is another kind of glorifying, which depends on intention. How easy or how hard it may be for a whole choir to preserve that intention through all the discussions and decisions, all the corrections and disappointments, all the temptations to pride, rivalry and ambition, which precede the performance of a great work, I (naturally) do not know. But it is on the intention that all depends. When it succeeds, I think the performers are the most enviable of men; privileged while mortals to honour God like angels and, for a few golden moments, to see spirit and flesh, delight and labour, skill and worship, the natural and the supernatural, all fused into that unity they would have had before the Fall.

Man or Rabbit?   NOVEMBER 24

'Can't you lead a good life without believing in Christianity?' This is the question on which I have been asked to write, and straight away, before I begin trying to answer it, I have a comment to make. The question sounds as if it were asked by a person who said to himself, 'I don't care whether Christianity is in fact true or not. I'm not interested in finding out whether the real universe is more like what the Christians say than what the Materialists say. All I'm interested in is leading a good life. I'm going to choose beliefs not because I think them true but because I find them helpful.' Now frankly, I find it hard to sympathize with this state of mind. One of the things that distinguishes man from the other animals is that he wants to know things, wants to find out what reality is like, simply for the sake of knowing. When that desire is completely quenched in anyone, I think he has become something less than human. As a matter of fact, I don't believe any of you have really lost that desire. More probably, foolish preachers, by always telling you how much Christianity will help you and how good it is for society, have actually led you to forget that Christianity is not a patent medicine. Christianity claims to give an account of *facts* — to tell you what the real universe is like. Its account of the universe may be true, or it may not, and once the question is really before you, then your natural inquisitiveness must make you want to know the answer. If Christianity is untrue, then no honest man will want to believe it, however helpful it might be: if it is true, every honest man will want to believe it, even if it gives him no help at all.

The Christian and the Materialist   NOVEMBER 25

There are quite a lot of things which these two men could agree in doing for their fellow citizens. Both would approve of efficient sewers and hospitals and a healthy diet. But sooner or later the difference of their beliefs would produce differences in their practical proposals. Both, for example, might be very keen about education: but the kinds of education they wanted people to have would obviously be very different. Again, where the Materialist would simply ask about a proposed action, 'Will it increase the happiness of the majority?', the Christian might have to say, 'Even if it does increase the happiness of the majority, we can't do it. It is unjust.' And all the time, one great difference would run through their whole policy. To the Materialist things like nations, classes, civilizations must be more important than individuals, because the individuals live only seventy-odd years each and the group may last for centuries. But to the Christian, individuals are more important, for they live eternally; and races, civilizations and the like, are in comparison the creatures of a day. The Christian and the Materialist hold different beliefs about the universe. They can't both be right. The one who is wrong will act in a way which simply doesn't fit the real universe. Consequently, with the best will in the world, he will be helping his fellow creatures to their destruction.

The Question Before Each of Us   NOVEMBER 26

The question before each of us is not 'Can *someone* lead a good life without Christianity?' The question is, 'Can I?' We all know there have been good men who were not Christians; men like Socrates and Confucius who had never heard of it, or men like J.S. Mill who quite honestly couldn't believe it. Supposing Christianity to be true, these men were in a state of honest ignorance or honest error. If their intentions were as good as I suppose them to have been (for of course I can't read their secret hearts) I hope and believe that the skill and mercy of God will remedy the evils which their ignorance, left to itself, would naturally produce both for them and for those whom they influenced. But the man who asks me, 'Can't I lead a good life without believing in Christianity?' is clearly not in the same position. If he hadn't heard of Christianity he would not be asking this question. If, having heard of it, and having seriously considered it, he had decided that it was untrue, then once more he would not be asking the question. The man who asks this question has heard of Christianity and is by no means certain that it may not be true. He is really asking, 'Need I bother about it? Mayn't I just evade the issue, just let sleeping dogs lie, and get on with being 'good'? Aren't good intentions enough to keep me safe and blameless without knocking at that dreadful door and making sure whether there is, or isn't someone inside?'

To such a man it might be enough to reply that he is really asking to be allowed to get on with being 'good' before he has done his best to discover what *good* means. . . . We need not inquire whether God will punish him for his cowardice and laziness; they will punish themselves. The man is shirking.

The Shirker   NOVEMBER 27

The man who remains an unbeliever for such reasons is not in a state of honest error. He is in a state of dishonest error, and that dishonesty will spread through all his thoughts and actions: a certain shiftiness, a vague worry in the background, a blunting of his whole mental edge, will result. He has lost his intellectual virginity, Honest rejection of Christ, however mistaken, will be forgiven and healed – 'Whosoever shall speak a word against the Son of Man, it shall be forgiven him.' But to *evade* the Son of Man, to look the other way, to pretend you haven't noticed, to become suddenly absorbed in something on the other side of the street, to leave the receiver off the telephone because it might be He who was ringing up, to leave unopened certain letters in a strange handwriting because they might be from Him – this is a different matter. You may not be certain yet whether you ought to be a Christian; but you do know you ought to be a Man, not an ostrich, hiding its head in the sand.

But still – for intellectual honour has sunk very low in our age – I hear someone whimpering on with his question, 'Will it help me? Will it make me happy? Do you really think I'd be better if I became a Christian?' Well, if you must have it, my answer is 'Yes'. But I don't like giving an answer at all at this stage. Here is a door, behind which, according to some people, the secret of the universe is waiting for you. Either that's true, or it isn't. And if it isn't, then what the door really conceals is simply the greatest fraud, the most colossal 'sell' on record. Isn't it obviously the job of every man (that is a man and not a rabbit) to try to find out which, and then to devote his full energies either to serving this tremendous secret or to exposing and destroying this gigantic humbug? Faced with such an issue, can you really remain wholly absorbed in your own blessed 'moral development'?

The Rabbit Must Disappear NOVEMBER 28

All right, Christianity will do you good – a great deal more good than you ever wanted or expected. And the first bit of good it will do you is to hammer into your head (you won't enjoy *that*!) the fact that what you have hitherto called 'good' – all that about 'leading a decent life' and 'being kind' isn't quite the magnificent and all-important affair you supposed. It will teach you that in fact you can't be 'good' (not for twenty-four hours) on your own moral efforts. And then it will teach you that even if you were, you still wouldn't have achieved the purpose for which you were created. Mere *morality* is not the end of life. You were made for something quite different from that. . . . The people who keep on asking if they can't lead a decent life without Christ, don't know what life is about; if they did they would know that 'a decent life' is mere machinery compared with the thing we men are really made for. Morality is indispensable: but the Divine Life, which gives itself to us and which calls us to be gods, intends for us something in which morality will be swallowed up. We are to be re-made. All the rabbit in us is to disappear – the worried, conscientious, ethical rabbit as well as the cowardly and sensual rabbit. We shall bleed and squeal as the handfuls of fur come out; and then, surprisingly, we shall find underneath it all a thing we have never yet imagined: a real Man, an ageless god, a son of God, strong, radiant, wise, beautiful, and drenched in joy.

Morality – Not an End in Itself NOVEMBER 29

I think all Christians would agree with me if I said that though Christianity seems at first to be all about morality, all about duties and rules and guilt and virtue, yet it leads you on, out of all that, into something beyond. One has a glimpse of a country where they do not talk of those things, except perhaps as a joke. Everyone there is filled full with what we should call goodness as a mirror is filled with light. But they do not call it goodness. They do not call it anything. They are not thinking of it. They are too busy looking at the source from which it comes. But this is near the stage where the road passes over the rim of our world. No one's eyes can see very far beyond that: lots of people's eyes can see further than mine.

St Andrew, Apostle   NOVEMBER 30

If you read history you will find that the Christians who did most for the present world were just those who thought most of the next. The Apostles themselves, who set on foot the conversion of the Roman Empire, the great men who built up the Middle Ages, the English Evangelicals who abolished the Slave Trade, all left their mark on earth, precisely because their minds were occupied with Heaven. It is since Christians have largely ceased to think of the other world that they have become so ineffective in this. Aim at Heaven and you will get earth 'thrown in': aim at earth and you will get neither. It seems a strange rule, but something like it can be seen at work in other matters. Health is a great blessing, but the moment you make health one of your main, direct objects you start becoming a crank and imagining there is something wrong with you. You are only likely to get health provided you want other things more – food, games, work, fun, open air. In the same way, we shall never save civilization as long as civilization is our main object. We must learn to want something else even more.

Advent   DECEMBER 1

Imagine yourself as a living house. God comes in to rebuild that house. At first, perhaps, you can understand what He is doing. He is getting the drains right and stopping the leaks in the roof and so on: you knew that those jobs needed doing and so you are not surprised. But presently He starts knocking the house about in a way that hurts abominably and does not seem to make sense. What on earth is He up to? The explanation is that He is building quite a different house from the one you thought of – throwing out a new wing here, putting on an extra floor there, running up towers, making courtyards. You thought you were going to be made into a decent little cottage: but He is building a palace. He intends to come and live in it Himself.

The Way Things Work Now   DECEMBER 2

The Son of God became a man to enable men to become sons of God. We do not know – anyway, I do not know – how things would have worked if the human race had never rebelled against God and joined the enemy. Perhaps every man would have been 'in Christ', would have shared the life of the Son of God, from the moment he was born. Perhaps the *Bios* or natural life would have been drawn up into the *Zoe,* the uncreated life, at once and as a matter of course. But that is guesswork. You and I are concerned with the way things work now.

And the present state of things is this. The two kinds of life are now not only different (they would always have been that) but actually opposed. The natural life in each of us is something self-centred, something that wants to be petted and admired, to take advantage of other lives, to exploit the whole universe. And especially it wants to be left to itself: to keep well away from anything better or stronger or higher than it, anything that might make it feel small. It is afraid of the light and air of the spiritual world, just as people who have been brought up to be dirty are afraid of a bath. And in a sense it is quite right. It knows that if the spiritual life gets hold of it, all its self-centredness and self-will are going to be killed, and it is ready to fight tooth and nail to avoid that.

Obstinate Toy Soldiers   DECEMBER 3

Did you ever think, when you were a child, what fun it would be if your toys could come to life? Well, suppose you could really have brought them to life. Imagine turning a tin soldier into a real little man. It would involve turning the tin into flesh. And suppose the tin soldier did not like it. He is not interested in flesh; all he sees is that the tin is being spoilt. He thinks you are killing him. He will do everything he can to prevent you. He will not be made into a man if he can help it.

What you would have done about that tin soldier I do not know. But what God did about us was this. The Second Person in God, the Son, became human Himself: was born into the world as an actual man — a real man of a particular height, with hair of a particular colour, speaking a particular language, weighing so many stone. The Eternal Being, who knows everything and who created the whole universe, became not only a man but (before that) a baby, and before that a foetus inside a Woman's body. If you want to get the hang of it, think how you would like to become a slug or a crab.

The First Real Man   DECEMBER 4

The result of this was that you now had one man who really was what all men were intended to be: one man in whom the created life, derived from His Mother, allowed itself to be completely and perfectly turned into the begotten life. The natural human creature in Him was taken up fully into the divine Son. Thus in one instance humanity had, so to speak, arrived: had passed into the life of Christ. And because the whole difficulty for us is that the natural life has to be, in a sense, 'killed', He chose an earthly career which involved the killing of His human desires at every turn — poverty, misunderstanding from His own family, betrayal by one of His intimate friends, being jeered at and manhandled by the police, and execution by torture. And then, after being thus killed — killed every day in a sense — the human creature in Him, because it was united to the divine Son, came to life again. The Man in Christ rose again: not only the God. That is the whole point. For the first time we saw a real man. One tin soldier — real tin, just like the rest — had come fully and splendidly alive.

God So Loved the World...   DECEMBER 5

We come to the point where my illustration about the tin soldier breaks down. In the case of real toy soldiers or statues, if one came to life, it would obviously make no difference to the rest. They are all separate. But human beings are not. They look separate because you see them walking about separately. But then, we are so made that we can see only the present moment. If we could see the past, then of course it would look different. For there was a time when every man was part of his mother, and (earlier still) part of his father as well: and when they were part of his grandparents. If you could see humanity spread out in time, as God sees it, it would not look like a lot of separate things dotted about. It would look like one single growing thing — rather like a very complicated tree. Every individual would appear connected with every other. And not only that. Individuals are not really separate from God any more than from one another. Every man, woman, and child all over the world is feeling and breathing at this moment only because God, so to speak, is 'keeping him going'.

Consequently, when Christ becomes man it is not really as if you could become one particular tin soldier. It is as if something which is always affecting the whole human mass begins, at one point, to affect that whole human mass in a new way. From that point the effect spreads through all mankind. It makes a difference to people who lived before Christ as well as to people who lived after Him. It makes a difference to people who have never heard of Him. It is like dropping into a glass of water one drop of something which gives a new taste or a new colour to the whole lot.

Each Must Accept or Reject Salvation

What, then, is the difference which He has made to the whole human mass? It is just this; that the business of becoming a son of God, of being turned from a created thing into a begotten thing, of passing over from the temporary biological life into timeless 'spiritual' life, has been done for us. Humanity is already 'saved' in principle. We individuals have to appropriate that salvation. But the really tough work — the bit we could not have done for ourselves — has been done for us. We have not got to try to climb up into spiritual life by our own efforts; it has already come down into the human race. If we will only lay ourselves open to the one Man in whom it was fully present, and who, in spite of being God, is also a real man, He will do it in us and for us. Remember what I said about 'good infection'. One of our own race has this new life: if we get close to Him we shall catch it from Him.

Of course, you can express this in all sorts of different ways. You can say that Christ died for our sins. You may say that the Father has forgiven us because Christ has done for us what we ought to have done. You may say that we are washed in the blood of the Lamb. You may say that Christ has defeated death. They are all true. If any of them does not appeal to you, leave it alone and get on with the formula that does. And, whatever you do, do not start quarrelling with other people because they use a different formula from yours.

Do Not Dictate to God a 'Formula' for Conversion

Everyone who accepts the teaching of St Paul must have a belief in 'sanctification'. But I should myself be very chary of describing such operations of the Holy Ghost as 'experiences' if by experiences we mean things necessarily discoverable by introspection. And I should be still more chary of mapping out a series of such experiences as an indispensable norm (or syllabus!) for all Christians. I think the ways in which God saves us are probably infinitely various and admit varying degrees of consciousness in the patient. Anything which sets him saying — 'Now Stage II ought soon to be coming along — is this it?' I think bad and likely to lead some to presumption and others to despair. We must leave God to dress the wound and not keep on taking peeps under the bandage for ourselves.

Neither Totalitarians Nor Individualists   DECEMBER 8

Christianity thinks of human individuals not as mere members of a group or items in a list, but as organs in a body-different from one another and each contributing what no other could. When you find yourself wanting to turn your children, or pupils, or even your neighbours, into people exactly like yourself, remember that God probably never meant them to be that. You and they are different organs, intended to do different things. On the other hand, when you are tempted not to bother about someone else's troubles because they are 'no business of yours', remember that though he is different from you he is part of the same organism as you. If you forget that he belongs to the same organism as yourself you will become an Individualist. If you forget that he is a different organ from you, if you want to suppress differences and make people all alike, you will become a Totalitarian. But a Christian must not be either a Totalitarian or an Individualist.

I feel a strong desire to tell you and I expect you feel a strong desire to tell me which of these two errors is the worse. That is the Devil getting at us. He always sends offers into the world in pairs — pairs of opposites. And he always encourages us to spend a lot of time thinking which is the worse. You see why, of course? He relies on your extra dislike of the one error to draw you gradually into the opposite one. But do not let us be fooled. We have to keep our eyes on the goal and go straight through between both errors. We have no other concern than that with either of them.

Dressing Up as Christ   DECEMBER 9

If you are interested enough to have read thus far you are probably interested enough to make a shot at saying your prayers: and, whatever else you say, you will probably say the Lord's Prayer. Its very first words are *Our Father.* Do you now see what those words mean? They mean quite frankly, that you are putting yourself in the place of a son of God. To put it bluntly, you are *dressing up as Christ.* If you like, you are pretending. Because, of course, the moment you realize what the words mean, you realize that you are not a son of God. You are not being like the Son of God, whose will and interests are at one with those of the Father: you are a bundle of self-centred fears, hopes, greeds, jealousies, and self-conceit, all doomed to death. So that, in a way, this dressing up as Christ is a piece of outrageous cheek. But the odd thing is that He has ordered us to do it. . . .

There are two kinds of pretending. There is a bad kind, where the pretence is there instead of the real thing; as when a man pretends he is going to help you instead of really helping you. But there is also a good kind, where the pretence leads up to the real thing. When you are not feeling particularly friendly but know you ought to be, the best thing you can do, very often, is to put on a friendly manner and behave as if you were a nicer person than you actually are. And in a few minutes, as we have all noticed, you will be really feeling friendlier than you were. Very often the only way to get a quality in reality is to start behaving as if you had it already.

Pretence into Reality   DECEMBER 10

The moment you realize 'Here I am, dressing up as Christ', it is extremely likely that you will see at once some way in which at that very moment the pretence could be made less of a pretence and more of a reality. You will find several things going on in your mind which would not be going on there if you were really a son of God. Well, stop them. Or you may realize that, instead of saying your prayers, you ought to be downstairs writing a letter, or helping your wife to wash up. Well, go and do it.

You see what is happening. The Christ Himself, the Son of God who is man (just like you) and God (just like His Father) is actually at your side and is already at that moment beginning to turn your pretence into a reality. This is not merely a fancy way of saying that your conscience is telling you what to do. If you simply ask your conscience, you get one result: if you remember that you are dressing up as Christ, you get a different one. There are lots of things which your conscience might not call definitely wrong (especially things in your mind) but which you will see at once you cannot go on doing if you are seriously trying to be like Christ. For you are no longer thinking simply about right and wrong; you are trying to catch the good infection from a Person. It is more like painting a portrait than like obeying a set of rules. And the odd thing is that while in one way it is much harder than keeping rules, in another way it is far easier.

The real Son of God is at your side. He is beginning to turn you into the same kind of thing as Himself. He is beginning, so to speak, to 'inject' His kind of life and thought, His *Zoe,* into you.

Instruments of Divine Grace   DECEMBER 11

You may say 'I've never had the sense of being helped by an invisible Christ, but I often have been helped by other human beings.' That is rather like the woman in the first war who said that if there were a bread shortage it would not bother her house because they always ate toast. If there is no bread there will be no toast. If there were no help from Christ, there would be no help from other human beings. He works on us in all sorts of ways: not only through what we think our 'religious life'. He works through Nature, through our own bodies, through books, sometimes through experiences which seem (at the time) anti-Christian. When a young man who has been going to church in a routine way honestly realizes that he does not believe in Christianity and stops going – provided he does it for honesty's sake and not just to annoy his parents – the spirit of Christ is probably nearer to him then than it ever was before. But above all, He works on us through each other.

Men are mirrors, or 'carriers' of Christ to other men. Sometimes unconscious carriers. This 'good infection' can be carried by those who have not got it themselves. People who were not Christians themselves helped me to Christianity. But usually it is those who know Him that bring Him to others. That is why the Church, the whole body of Christians showing Him to one another, is so important.

A House Built on Sand

Do not forget this. At first it is natural for a baby to take its mother's milk without knowing its mother. It is equally natural for us to see the man who helps us without seeing Christ behind him. But we must not remain babies. We must go on to recognize the real Giver. It is madness not to. Because, if we do not, we shall be relying on human beings. And that is going to let us down. The best of them will make mistakes; all of them will die. We must be thankful to all the people who have helped us, we must honour them and love them. But never, never pin your whole faith on any human being: not if he is the best and wisest in the whole world. There are lots of nice things you can do with sand; but do not try building a house on it.

The Everlasting Man

And now we begin to see what it is that the New Testament is always talking about. It talks about Christians 'being born again'; it talks about them 'putting on Christ'; about Christ 'being formed in us'; about our coming to 'have the mind of Christ'.

Put right out of your head the idea that these are only fancy ways of saying that Christians are to read what Christ said and try to carry it out – as a man may read what Plato or Marx said and try to carry it out. They mean something much more than that. They mean that a real Person, Christ, here and now, in that very room where you are saying your prayers, is doing things to you. It is not a question of a good man who died two thousand years ago. It is a living Man, still as much a man as you, and still as much God as He was when He created the world, really coming and interfering with your very self; killing the old natural self in you and replacing it with the kind of self He has. At first, only for moments. Then for longer periods. Finally, if all goes well, turning you permanently into a different sort of thing; into a new little Christ, a being which, in its own small way, has the same kind of life as God; which shares in His power, joy, knowledge and eternity.

St John of the Cross

About the higher level — the crags up which the mystics vanish out of my sight — the glaciers and the aiguilles — I have only two things to say. One is that I don't think we are all 'called' to that ascent. 'If it were so, He would have told us.'

The second is this, The following position is gaining ground and is extremely plausible. Mystics (it is said) starting from the most diverse religious premises all find the same things. . . . I am doubtful about the premises. Did Plotinus and Lady Julian and St John of the Cross really find 'the same things'? . . .

I do not at all regard mystical experience as an illusion. I think it shows that there is a way to go, before death, out of what may be called 'this world' — out of the stage set. Out of this; but into what? That's like asking an Englishman, 'Where does the sea lead to?' He will reply, 'To everywhere on earth, including Davy Jones's locker, except England.' The lawfulness, safety, and utility of the mystical voyage depends not at all on its being mystical — that is, on its being a departure — but on the motives, skill, and constancy of the voyager, and on the grace of God. The true religion gives value to its mysticism; mysticism does not validate the religion in which it happens to occur.

I shouldn't be at all disturbed if it could be shown that a diabolical mysticism, or drugs, produced experiences indistinguishable (by introspection) from those of the great Christian mystics. Departures are all alike; it is the landfall that crowns the voyage. The saint, by being a saint, proves that his mysticism (if he was a mystic; not all saints are) led him aright; the fact that he has practised mysticism could never prove his sanctity.

Natural Gifts are Not Enough   DECEMBER 15

If you are a nice person – if Virtue comes easily to you – beware! Much is expected from those to whom much is given. If you mistake for your own merits what are really God's gifts to you through nature, and if you are contented with simply being nice, you are still a rebel: and all those gifts will only make your fall more terrible, your corruption more complicated, your bad example more disastrous. The Devil was an archangel once; his natural gifts were as far above yours as yours are above those of a chimpanzee.

But if you are a poor creature – poisoned by a wretched upbringing in some house full of vulgar jealousies and senseless quarrels – saddled, by no choice of your own, with some loathsome sexual perversion – nagged day in and day out by an inferiority complex that makes you snap at your best friends – do not despair. He knows all about it. You are one of the poor whom He blessed. He knows what a wretched machine you are trying to drive. Keep on. Do what you can. One day (perhaps in another world, but perhaps far sooner than that) He will fling it on the scrap-heap and give you a new one. And then you may astonish us all – not least yourself: for you have learned your driving in a hard school. (Some of the last will be first and some of the first will be last.)

Nice People or New Men   DECEMBER 16

'Niceness' – wholesome, integrated personality – is an excellent thing. We must try by every medical, educational, economic and political means in our power, to produce a world where as many people as possible grow up 'nice'; just as we must try to produce a world where all have plenty to eat. But we must not suppose that even if we succeeded in making everyone nice we should have saved their souls. A world of nice people, content in their own niceness, looking no further, turned away from God, would be just as desperately in need of salvation as a miserable world and might even be more difficult to save.

For mere improvement is not redemption, though redemption always improves people even here and now and will, in the end, improve them to a degree we cannot yet imagine. God became man to turn creatures into sons: not simply to produce better men of the old kind but to produce a new kind of man. It is not like teaching a horse to jump better and better but like turning a horse into a winged creature. Of course, once it has got its wings, it will soar over fences which could never have been jumped and thus beat the natural horse at its own game. But there may be a period, while the wings are just beginning to grow, when it cannot do so: and at that stage the lumps on the shoulders — no one could tell by looking at them that they are going to be wings — may even give it an awkward appearance.

The Presence in Which You Have Always Stood DECEMBER 17

If what you want is an argument against Christianity (and I well remember how eagerly I looked for such arguments when I began to be afraid it was true) you can easily find some stupid and unsatisfactory Christian and say, 'So there's your boasted new man! Give me the old kind.' But if once you have begun to see that Christianity is on other grounds probable, you will know in your heart that this is only evading the issue. What can you ever really know of other people's souls — of their temptations, their opportunities, their struggles? One soul in the whole creation you do know: and it is the only one whose fate is placed in your hands. If there is a God, you are, in a sense, alone with Him. You cannot put Him off with speculations about your next door neighbours or memories of what you have read in books. What will all that chatter and hearsay count (will you ever be able to remember it?) when the anaesthetic fog which we call 'nature' or 'the real world' fades away and the Presence in which you have always stood becomes palpable, immediate, and unavoidable?

The New Men in Christ DECEMBER 18

The thing has happened: the new step has been taken and is being taken. Already the new men are dotted here and there all over the earth. Some . . . are still hardly recognizable: but others can be recognized. Every now and then one meets them. Their voices and faces are different from ours; stronger, quieter, happier, more radiant. They begin where most of us leave off. They are, I say, recognizable; but you must know what to look for. They will not be very like the idea of 'religious people' which you have formed from your general reading. They do not draw attention to themselves. You tend to think that you are being kind to them when they are really being kind to you. They love you more than other men do, but they need you less. (We must get over wanting to be needed: in some goodish people, especially women, that is the hardest of all temptations to resist.) They will usually seem to have a lot of time: you will wonder where it comes from. When you have recognized one of them, you will recognize the next one much more easily. And I strongly suspect (but how should I know?) that they recognize one another immediately and infallibly, across every barrier of colour, sex, class, age, and even of creeds. In that way, to become holy is rather like joining a secret society. To put it at the very lowest, it must be great *fun*.

The Source of All Personalities   DECEMBER 19

The more we get what we now call 'ourselves' out of the way and let Him take us over, the more truly ourselves we become. There is so much of Him that millions and millions of 'little Christs', all different, will still be too few to express Him fully. He made them all. He invented — as an author invents characters in a novel — all the different men that you and I were intended to be. In that sense our real selves are all waiting for us in Him. It is no good trying to 'be myself' without Him. The more I resist Him and try to live on my own, the more I become dominated by my own heredity and upbringing and surroundings and natural desires. In fact what I so proudly call 'Myself' becomes merely the meeting place for trains of events which I never started and which I cannot stop. What I call 'My wishes' become merely the desires thrown up by my physical organism or pumped into me by other men's thoughts or even suggested to me by devils. . . . Most of what I call 'Me' can be very easily explained. It is when I turn to Christ, when I give myself up to His Personality, that I first begin to have a real personality of my own. . . . There are no real personalities anywhere else. Until you have given up your self to Him you will not have a real self. Sameness is to be found most among the most 'natural' men, not among those who surrender to Christ. How monotonously alike all the great tyrants and conquerors have been: how gloriously different are the saints.

Keep Back Nothing   DECEMBER 20

There must be a real giving up of the self. You must throw it away 'blindly' so to speak. Christ will indeed give you a real personality: but you must not go to Him for the sake of that. As long as your own personality is what you are bothering about you are not going to Him at all. The very first step is to try to forget about the self altogether. Your real, new self (which is Christ's and also yours, and yours just because it is His) will not come as long as you are looking for it. It will come when you are looking for Him. Does that sound strange? The same principle holds, you know, for more everyday matters. Even in social life, you will never make a good impression on other people until you stop thinking about what sort of impression you are making.

Even in literature and art, no man who bothers about originality will ever be original: whereas if you simply try to tell the truth (without caring twopence how often it has been told before) you will, nine times out of ten, become original without ever having noticed it. The principle runs through all life from top to bottom. Give up your self and you will find your real self. Lose your life, and you will save it. Submit to death, death of your ambitions and favourite wishes every day and death of your whole body in the end: submit with every fibre of your being and you will find eternal life. Keep back nothing. Nothing that you have not given away will ever be really yours. Nothing in you that has not died will ever be raised from the dead. Look for yourself, and you will find in the long run only hatred, loneliness, despair, rage, ruin, and decay. But look for Christ and you will find Him, and with Him everything else thrown in.

The Coming of the Lord   DECEMBER 21

Just as, on the factual side, a long preparation culminates in God's becoming incarnate as Man, so, on the documentary side, the truth first appears in *mythical* form and then by a long process of condensing or focusing finally becomes incarnate as History. This involves the belief that Myth is...a real though unfocused gleam of divine truth falling on human imagination. The Hebrews, like other peoples, had mythology: but as they were the chosen people so their mythology was the chosen mythology – the mythology chosen by God to be the vehicle of the earliest sacred truths, the first step in that process which ends in the New Testament where truth has become completely historical.

Incarnation Transcends Myth   DECEMBER 22

Now as myth transcends thought, Incarnation transcends myth. The heart of Christianity is a myth which is also a fact. The old myth of the Dying God, *without ceasing to be myth,* comes down from the heaven of legend and imagination to the earth of history. It *happens* – at a particular date, in a particular place, followed by definable historical consequences. We pass from a Balder or an Osiris, dying nobody knows when or where, to a historical Person crucified (it is all in order) *under Pontius Pilate.* ...

Those who do not know that this great myth became Fact when the Virgin conceived are, indeed, to be pitied. But Christians also need to be reminded...that what became Fact was a Myth, that it carries with it into the world of fact all the properties of a myth. God is more than a god, not less; Christ is more than Balder, not less. We must not be ashamed of the mythical radiance resting on our theology. We must not be nervous about 'parallels' and 'Pagan Christs': they *ought* to be there — it would be a stumbling block if they weren't.

Pagan 'Christs' and Christ Himself   DECEMBER 23

Theology, while saying that a special illumination has been vouchsafed to Christians and (earlier) to Jews, also says that there is some divine illumination vouchsafed to all men. The Divine light, we are told, 'lighteneth every man'. We should, therefore, expect to find in the imagination of great Pagan teachers and myth-makers some glimpse of that theme which we believe to be the very plot of the whole cosmic story — the theme of incarnation, death, and rebirth. And the differences between the Pagan Christs (Balder, Osiris, etc.) and the Christ Himself is much what we should expect to find. The Pagan stories are all about someone dying and rising, either every year, or else nobody knows where and nobody knows when. The Christian story is about a historical personage, whose execution can be dated pretty accurately, under a named Roman magistrate, and with whom the society that He founded is in a continuous relation down to the present day. It is not the difference between falsehood and truth. It is the difference between a real event on the one hand and dim dreams or premonitions of that same event on the other. It is like watching something come gradually into focus; first it hangs in the clouds of myth and ritual, vast and vague, then it condenses, grows hard and in a sense small, as a historical event in first-century Palestine.

Myth Became Fact   DECEMBER 24

The essential meaning of all things came down from the 'heaven' of myth to the 'earth' of history. In so doing, it partly emptied itself of its glory, as Christ emptied Himself of His glory to be Man. . . . That is why the New Testament is . . . less poetical than the Old. Have you not often felt in church, if the first lesson is some great passage, that the second lesson is somehow small by comparison — almost, if one might say so, humdrum? So it is and so it must be. That is the humiliation of myth into fact, of God into Man; what is everywhere and always, imageless and ineffable, only to be glimpsed in dream and symbol and the acted poetry of ritual becomes small, solid — no bigger than a man who can lie asleep in a rowing boat on the Lake of Galilee.

Christmas Day

In Pantheism God is all. But the whole point of creation surely is that He was not content to be all. He intends to be *'all in all'.*

One must be careful not to put this in a way which would blur the distinction between the creation of a man and the Incarnation of God. Could one, as a mere model, put it thus? In creation God makes — invents — a person and 'utters' — injects — him into the realm of Nature. In the Incarnation, God the Son takes the body and human soul of Jesus, and, through that, the whole environment of Nature, all the creaturely predicament, into His own being. So that 'He came down from Heaven' can almost be transposed into 'Heaven drew earth up into it', and locality, limitation, sleep, sweat, footsore weariness, frustration, pain, doubt, and death, are, from before all worlds, known by God from within. The pure light walks the earth; the darkness, received into the heart of Deity, is there swallowed up. Where, except in uncreated light, can the darkness be drowned?

Jesus — God Incarnate

God could, had He pleased, have been incarnate in a man of iron nerves, the Stoic sort who lets no sigh escape him. Of His great humility He chose to be incarnate in a man of delicate sensibilities who wept at the grave of Lazarus and sweated blood in Gethsemane. Otherwise we should have missed the great lesson that it is by his *will* alone that a man is good or bad, and that *feelings* are not, in themselves, of any importance. We should also have missed the all-important help of knowing that He has faced all that the weakest of us face, has shared not only the strength of our nature but every weakness of it except sin. If He had been incarnate in a man of immense natural courage, that would have been for many of us almost the same as His not being incarnate at all.

St John, Apostle DECEMBER 27

The fact that God can make complex good out of simple evil does not excuse — though by mercy it may save — those who do the simple evil. And this distinction is central. Offences must come, but woe to those by whom they come; sins *do* cause grace to abound, but we must not make that an excuse for continuing to sin. The crucifixion itself is the best, as well as the worst, of all historical events, but the *role* of Judas remains simply evil. We may apply this first to the problem of other people's suffering. A merciful man aims at his neighbour's good and so does 'God's will', consciously co-operating with 'the simple good'. A cruel man oppresses his neighbour, and so does simple evil. But in doing such evil, he is used by God, without his own knowledge or consent, to produce the complex good — so that the first man serves God as a son, and the second as a tool. For you will certainly carry out God's purpose, however you act, but it makes a difference to you whether you serve like Judas or like John.

The Secret Signature of Each Soul DECEMBER 28

There have been times when I think we do not desire heaven; but more often I find myself wondering whether, in our heart of hearts, we have ever desired anything else. ... Are not all lifelong friendships born at the moment when at last you meet another human being who has some inkling (but faint and uncertain even in the best) of that something which you were born desiring, and which, beneath the flux of other desires and in all the momentary silences between the louder passions, night and day, year by year, from childhood to old age, you are looking for, watching for, listening for? You have never *had* it. All the things that have ever deeply possessed your soul have been but hints of it — tantalizing glimpses, promises never quite fulfilled, echoes that died away just as they caught your ear. But if it should really become manifest — if there ever came an echo that did not die away but swelled into the sound itself — you would know it. Beyond all possibility of doubt you would say 'Here at last is the thing I was made for.' We cannot tell each other about it. It is the secret signature of each soul, the incommunicable and unappeasable want, the thing we desired before we met our wives or made our friends or chose our work, and which we shall still desire on our deathbeds, when the mind no longer knows wife or friend or work. While we are, this is. If we lose this, we lose all.

The House with Many Mansions DECEMBER 29

Be sure that the ins and outs of your individuality are no mystery to Him; and one day they will no longer be a mystery to you. The mould in which a key is made would be a strange thing, if you had never seen a key: and the key itself a strange thing if you had never seen a lock. Your soul has a curious shape because it is a hollow made to fit a particular swelling in the infinite contours of the divine substance, or a key to unlock one of the doors in the house with many mansions. For it is not humanity in the abstract that is to be saved, but you – you, the individual reader, John Stubbs or Janet Smith. Blessed and fortunate creature, your eyes shall behold Him and not another's. All that you are, sins apart, is destined, if you will let God have His good way, to utter satisfaction. The Brocken spectre 'looked to every man like his first love', because she was a cheat. But God will look to every soul like its first love because He is its first love. Your place in heaven will seem to be made for you and you alone, because you were made for it – made for it stitch by stitch as a glove is made for a hand.

Father and Redeemer and Indwelling Comforter DECEMBER 30

The golden apple of selfhood, thrown among the false gods, became an apple of discord because they scrambled for it. They did not know the first rule of the holy game, which is that every player must by all means touch the ball and then immediately pass it on. To be found with it in your hands is a fault: to cling to it, death. But when it flies to and fro among the players too swift for eye to follow, and the great master Himself leads the revelry, giving Himself eternally to His creatures in the generation, and back to Himself in the sacrifice, of the Word, then indeed the eternal dance 'makes heaven drowsy with the harmony'. All pains and pleasures we have known on earth are early initiations in the movements of that dance: but the dance itself is strictly incomparable with the sufferings of this present time. As we draw nearer to its uncreated rhythm, pain and pleasure sink almost out of sight. There is joy in the dance, but it does not exist for the sake of joy. It does not even exist for the sake of good, or of love. It is Love Himself, and Good Himself, and therefore happy. It does not exist for us, but we for it. . . . As our Earth is to all the stars, so doubtless are we men and our concerns to all creation; as all the stars are to space itself, so are all creatures, all thrones and powers and mightiest of the created gods, to the abyss of the self-existing Being, who is to us Father and Redeemer and indwelling Comforter, but of whom no man or angel can say or conceive what He is in and for Himself, or what is the work that He 'maketh from the beginning to the end'. For they are all derived and unsubstantial things. Their vision fails them and they cover their eyes from the intolerable light of utter actuality, which was and is and shall be, which never could have been otherwise, which has no opposite.

Farewell to Shadowlands

Then Aslan turned to them and said: '...you are — as you used to call it in the Shadowlands — dead. The term is over: the holidays have begun, The dream is ended: this is the morning...

And for us this is the end of all the stories, and we can most truly say that they all lived happily ever after. But for them it was only the beginning of the real story. All their life in this world and all their adventures in Narnia had only been the cover and the title page: now at last they were beginning Chapter One of the Great Story which no one on earth has read: which goes on for ever: in which every chapter is better than the one before.

MOVABLE FASTS AND FEASTS

YEAR	ASH WEDNESDAY	MAUNDY THURSDAY	GOOD FRIDAY	HOLY SATURDAY
1984	7 Mar.	19 Apr.	20 Apr.	21 Apr.
1985	20 Feb.	4 Apr.	5 Apr.	6 Apr.
1986	12 Feb.	27 Mar.	28 Mar.	29 Mar.
1987	4 Mar.	16 Apr.	17 Apr.	18 Apr.
1988	17 Feb.	31 Mar.	1 Apr.	2 Apr.
1989	8 Feb.	23 Mar.	24 Mar.	25 Mar.
1990	28 Feb.	12 Apr.	13 Apr.	14 Apr.
1991	13 Feb.	28 Mar.	29 Mar.	30 Mar.
1992	4 Mar.	16 Apr.	17 Apr.	18 Apr.
1993	24 Feb.	8 Apr.	9 Apr.	10 Apr.
1994	16 Feb.	31 Mar.	1 Apr.	2 Apr.
1995	1 Mar.	13 Apr.	14 Apr.	15 Apr.
1996	21 Feb.	4 Apr.	5 Apr.	6 Apr.
1997	12 Feb.	27 Mar.	28 Mar.	29 Mar.
1998	25 Feb.	9 Apr.	10 Apr.	11 Apr.

EASTER	ASCENSION	PENTECOST	HOLY TRINITY	BODY/BLOOD OF CHRIST
22 Apr.	31 May	10 June	17 June	21 June
7 Apr.	16 May	26 May	2 June	6 June
30 Mar.	8 May	18 May	25 May	29 May
19 Apr.	28 May	7 June	14 June	18 June
3 Apr.	12 May	22 May	29 May	2 June
26 Mar.	4 May	14 May	21 May	25 May
15 Apr.	24 May	3 June	10 June	14 June
31 Mar.	9 May	19 May	26 May	30 May
19 Apr.	28 May	7 June	14 June	18 June
11 Apr.	20 May	30 May	6 June	10 June
3 Apr.	12 May	22 May	29 May	2 June
16 Apr.	25 May	4 June	11 June	15 June
7 Apr.	16 May	26 May	2 June	6 June
30 Mar.	8 May	18 May	25 May	29 May
12 Apr.	21 May	31 May	7 June	11 June

Ash Wednesday

What cannot be admitted – what must exist only as an undefeated but daily resisted enemy – is the idea of something that is 'our own', some area in which we are to be 'out of school', on which God has no claim. . . . I do not think any efforts of my own will can end once and for all this craving for limited liabilities, this fatal reservation. Only God can. I have good faith and hope He will. Of course, I don't mean that I can therefore, as they say, 'sit back'. What God does for us, He does in us. The process of doing it will appear to me (and not falsely) to be the daily or hourly repeated exercises of my own will in renouncing this attitude, especially each morning, for it grows all over me like a new shell each night. Failures will be forgiven; it is acquiescence that is fatal, the permitted, regularized presence of an area in ourselves which we still claim for our own. We may never, this side of death, drive the invader out of our territory, but we must be in the Resistance, not in the Vichy government. And this, so far as I can yet see, must be begun again every day. Our morning prayer should be that in the *Imitation: Da hodie pedecte incipere* – grant me to make an unflawed beginning today, for I have done nothing yet.

Maundy Thursday

I do not know and can't imagine what the disciples understood Our Lord to mean when, His body still unbroken and His blood unshed, He handed them the bread and wine, saying *they* were His body and blood. . . . I find 'substance' (in Aristotle's sense), when stripped of its own accidents and endowed with the accidents of some other substance, an object I cannot think. . . . On the other hand, I get on no better with those who tell me that the elements are mere bread and mere wine, used symbolically to remind me of the death of Christ. They are, on the natural level, such a very odd symbol of *that*. . . . And I cannot see why this particular reminder – a hundred other things may, psychologically, remind me of Christ's death, equally, or perhaps more – should be so uniquely important as all Christendom (and my own heart) unhesitatingly declare. . . . Yet I find no difficulty in believing that the veil between the worlds, nowhere else (for me) so opaque to the intellect, is nowhere else so thin and permeable to divine operation. Here a hand from the hidden country touches not only my soul but my body. Here the prig, the don, the modern, in me have no privilege over the savage or the child. Here is big medicine and strong magic. . . . The command, after all, was Take, eat: not Take, understand.

Good Friday

God, who needs nothing, loves into existence wholly superfluous creatures in order that He may love and perfect them. He creates the universe, already foreseeing – or should we say 'seeing'? there are are no tenses in God – the buzzing cloud of flies about the cross, the flayed back pressed against the uneven stake, the nails driven through the mesial nerves, the repeated incipient suffocation as the body droops, the repeated torture of back and arms as it is time after time, for breath's sake, hitched up. If I may dare the biological image, God is a 'host' who deliberately creates His own parasites; causes us to be that we may exploit and 'take advantage of' Him. Here-in is love. This is the diagram of Love Himself, the inventor of all loves.

Holy Saturday

On the one hand Death is the triumph of Satan, the punishment of the Fall, and the last enemy. Christ shed tears at the grave of Lazarus and sweated blood in Geth-semane: the Life of Lives that was in Him detested this penal obscenity not less than we do, but more. On the other hand, only he who loses his life will save it. We are baptized into the *death* of Christ, and it is the remedy for the Fall. Death is, in fact, what some modern people call 'ambivalent'. It is Satan's great weapon and also God's great weapon: it is holy and unholy; our supreme disgrace and our only hope; the thing Christ came to conquer and the means by which He conquered.

Easter Day

I am not referring simply to the first few hours, or the first few weeks of the Resurrec-tion. I am talking of this whole 'huge pattern of descent, down, down, and then up again. What we ordinarily call the Resurrection being just, so to speak, the point at which it turns. Think what that descent is. The coming down, not only into humanity, but into those nine months which precede human birth, in which they tell us we all recapitulate strange pre-human, sub-human forms of life, and going lower still into being a corpse, a thing which, if this ascending movement had not begun, would presently have passed out of the organic altogether, and have gone back into the inor-ganic, as all corpses do. One has a picture of someone going right down and dredging the sea bottom. One has a picture of a strong man trying to lift a very big, complicated burden. He stoops down and gets himself right under it so that he himself disappears; and then he straightens his back and moves off with the whole thing swaying on his shoulders. Or else one has the picture of a diver, stripping off garment after garment, making himself naked, then flashing for a moment in the air, and then down through the green, and warm, and sunlit water into the pitch black, cold, freezing water, down into the mud and slime, then up again, his lungs almost bursting, back again to the green and warm and sunlit water, and then at last out into the sunshine, holding in his hand the dripping thing he went down to get. This thing is human nature; but, associated with it, all nature, the new universe.

The Ascension of the Lord

What really worries us is the conviction that, whatever we say, the New Testament writers meant something quite different. We feel sure that they thought they had seen their Master setting off on a journey for a local 'Heaven' where God sat in a throne and where there was another throne waiting for Him. And I believe that in a sense that is just what they did think. And I believe that, for this reason, whatever they had actually seen . . . they would almost certainly have remembered it as a vertical movement. What we must not say is that they 'mistook' local 'Heavens' and celestial throne-rooms and the like for the 'spiritual' Heaven of union with God and supreme power and beatitude. . . . *Heaven* can mean (1) The unconditioned Divine Life beyond all worlds. (2) Blessed participation in that Life by a created spirit. (3) The whole Nature or system of conditions in which redeemed human spirits, still remaining human, can enjoy such participation fully and forever. This is the Heaven Christ goes to 'prepare' for us. (4) The physical Heaven, the sky, the space in which Earth moves. What enables us to distinguish these senses and hold them clearly apart is not any special spiritual purity but the fact that we are the heirs to centuries of logical analysis: not that we are sons to Abraham but that we are sons to Aristotle. We are not to suppose that the writers of the New Testament mistook Heaven in sense four or three for Heaven in sense two or one. You cannot mistake a half-sovereign for a sixpence until you know the English system of coinage — that is, until you know the difference between them. In their idea of Heaven all these meanings were latent, ready to be brought out by later analysis. They never thought merely of the blue sky or merely of a 'spiritual' Heaven. When they looked up at the blue sky they never doubted that there . . . was the home of God: but on the other hand, when they thought of one ascending to that Heaven they never doubted He was 'ascending' in what we should call a 'spiritual' sense. . . . A man who really believes that 'Heaven' is in the sky may well, in his heart, have a far truer and more spiritual conception of it than many a modern logician who could expose that fallacy with a few strokes of his pen. For he who does the will of the Father shall know the doctrine. Irrelevant material splend-rous in such a man's idea of the vision of God will do no harm, for they are not there for their own sakes.

Pentecost

This third Person is called, in technical language, the Holy Ghost or the 'spirit' of God. Do not be worried or surprised if you find it (or Him) rather vaguer or more shadowy in your mind than the other two. I think there is a reason why that must be so. In the Christian life you are not usually looking *at* Him: He is always acting through you. If you think of the Father as something 'out there', in front of you, and of the Son as something standing at your side, helping you to pray, trying to turn you into another son, then you have to think of the third Person as something inside you, or behind you. Perhaps some people might find it easier to begin with the third Person and work backwards. God is love, and that love works through men — especially through the whole community of Christians. But this spirit of love is, from all eternity, a love going on between the Father and Son.

And now, what does it all matter? It matters more than anything else in the world. The whole dance, or drama, or pattern of this three-Personal life is to be played out in each one of us: or (putting it the other way round) each one of us has got to enter that pattern, take his place in that dance. There is no other way to the happiness for which we were made. Good things as well as bad, you know, are caught by a kind of infection. If you want to get warm you must stand near the fire: if you want to be wet you must get into the water. If you want joy, power, peace, eternal life, you must get close to, or even into, the thing that has them. . . . They are a great fountain of energy and beauty spurting up at the very centre of reality. If you are close to it, the spray will wet you: if you are not, you will remain dry. Once a man is united to God, how could he not live forever? Once a man is separated from God, what can he do but wither and die?

The Most Holy Trinity

A world of one dimension would be a straight line. In a two-dimensional world, you still get straight lines, but many lines make one figure. In a three-dimensional world, you still get figures but many figures make one solid body. In other words, as you advance to more real and more complicated levels, you do not leave behind you the things you found on the simpler levels: you still have them, but combined in new ways – in ways you could not imagine if you knew only the simpler levels.

Now the Christian account of God involves just the same principle. The human level is a simple and rather empty level. On the human level one person is one being, and any two persons are two separate beings – just as, in two dimensions (say on a flat sheet of paper) one square is one figure, and any two squares are two separate figures. On the Divine level you still find personalities; but up there you find them combined in new ways which we, who do not live on that level, cannot imagine. In God's dimension, so to speak, you find a Being who is three Persons while remaining one Being, just as a cube is six squares while remaining one cube. Of course we cannot fully conceive a Being like that: just as, if we were so made that we perceived only two dimensions in space we could never properly imagine a cube. But we can get a sort of faint notion of it. And when we do, we are then, for the first time in our lives, getting some positive idea, however faint, of something super-personal – something more than a person. . . . The thing that matters is being actually drawn into that three-personal life, and that may begin any time tonight, if you like.

What I mean is this. An ordinary simple Christian kneels down to say his prayers. He is trying to get into touch with God. But if he is a Christian he knows that what is prompting him to pray is also God: God, so to speak, inside him. But he also knows that all his real knowledge of God comes through Christ, the Man who was God – that Christ is standing beside him, helping him to pray, praying for him. You see what is happening. God is the thing to which he is praying – the goal he is trying to reach. God is also the thing inside him which is pushing him on the motive power. God is also the road or bridge along which he is being pushed to that goal. So that the three-fold life of the three-personal Being is actually going on in that ordinary little bed-room where an ordinary man is saying his prayers.

The Body and Blood of Christ

Yes, you are always everywhere. But I,
Hunting in such immeasurable forests,
Could never bring the noble Hart to bay.

The scent was too perplexing for my hounds;
Nowhere sometimes, then again everywhere.
Other scents, too, seemed to them almost the same.

Therefore I turn my back on the unapproachable
Stars and horizons and all musical sounds,
Poetry itself, and the winding stair of thought.

Leaving the forests where you are pursued in vain
— Often a mere white gleam — I turn instead
To the appointed place where you pursue.

Not in Nature, not even in Man, but in one
Particular Man, with a date, so tall, weighing
So much, talking Aramaic, having learned a trade;

Not in all food, not in all bread and wine
(Not, I mean, as my littleness requires)
But this wine, this bread . . . no beauty we could desire.

SOURCES

DAILY READINGS

February 6	*Ibid.*
February 7	*Ibid.*
February 8	*Ibid.*
February 9	*Ibid.*
February 10	*Ibid.*
February 11	*Ibid.*
February 12	*Ibid.*
February 13	*Ibid.*
February 14	'The Seeing Eye'
February 15	*Ibid.*
February 16	'Religion and Rocketry'
February 17	*Ibid.*
February 18	*Surprised by Joy,* ch. 13
February 19	*Miracles,* ch. 11
February 20	*Mere Christianity,* Bk 11, ch. 4
February 21	*Ibid.*
February 22	*Ibid.*
February 23	'Miserable Offenders'
February 24	*Ibid.*
February 25	'Dangers of National Repentance'
February 26	'On Forgiveness'
February 27	*Ibid.*
February 28	*Ibid.*
March 1	*Ibid.*
March 2	*Mere Christianity,* Bk III, ch. 1
March 3	*Ibid.*
March 4	*Ibid.*
March 5	*Ibid.,* Bk III, ch. 3
March 6	*Ibid.*
March 7	*Ibid.*
March 8	*Ibid.*
March 9	*Ibid.*
March 10	*Ibid.,* Bk III, ch.4
March 11	*Ibid.*
March 12	*Screwtape Letters,* No. 6
March 13	*Mere Christianity,* Bk III, ch. 2
March 14	*Ibid.*
March 15	*Ibid.*
March 16	*Ibid.,* Bk III, ch. 11
March 17	*Ibid.*
March 18	*Ibid.*
March 19	*Miracles,* ch. 7
March 20	'The Weight of Glory'
March 21	*Mere Christianity,* Bk III, ch. 7
March 22	*Ibid.,* Bk III, ch. 9
March 23	*Ibid.,* Bk III, ch. 12
March 24	*Ibid.*
March 25	'The Psalms'
March 26	*Pilgrim's Regress,* Bk IX ch. 4

March 27	*Mere Christianity*, Bk III ch. 5
March 28	*Ibid.*
March 29	*Screwtape Letters*, No. 9
March 30	*Mere Christianity*, Bk III, ch. 5
March 31	*Ibid.*
April 1	*Ibid.*, Bk III, ch. 8
April 2	*Ibid.*
April 3	*Ibid.*
April 4	*Ibid.*
April 5	*Letters to Malcolm*, ch. 8
April 6	*Ibid.*
April 7	*Ibid.*
April 8	'Miracles'
April 9	'Answers to Questions on Christianity'
April 10	'Miracles'
April 11	*Ibid.*
April 12	*Miracles*, ch. 15
April 13	*Ibid.*
April 14	*Ibid.*
April 15	*Ibid.*
April 16	*Ibid.*, ch. 16
April 17	*Ibid.*
April 18	*Ibid.*
April 19	'Religion Without Dogma?'
April 20	*Miracles*, ch. 16
April 21	*Ibid.*
April 22	*Ibid.*
April 23	'On Three Ways of Writing for Children'
April 24	'The Grand Miracle'
April 25	'The World's Last Night'
April 26	*Miracles*, ch. 16
April 27	*Ibid.*
April 28	'Transposition'
April 29	*Ibid.*
April 30	*Miracles*, ch. 16
May 1	'Good Work and Good Works'
May 2	'On the Reading of Old Books'
May 3	*Reflections on the Psalms*, ch. 11
May 4	*Miracles*, ch. 16
May 5	*Letters to Malcolm*, ch. 22
May 6	*Ibid.*, ch. 20
May 7	'The World's Last Night'
May 8	*Ibid.*
May 9	*Ibid.*
May 10	*Ibid.*
May 11	*Ibid.*
May 12	*Ibid.*
May 13	*Ibid.*
May 14	*Miracles*, ch. 16

May 15	'The World's Last Night'
May 16	'Some Thoughts'
May 17	*Problem of Pain*, ch. 6
May 18	'The World's Last Night'
May 19	*Ibid.*
May 20	*Great Divorce*, Preface
May 21	*Ibid.*
May 22	*Great Divorce*, ch. 5
May 23	*Ibid.*
May 24	*Ibid.*
May 25	*Ibid.*
May 26	*Ibid.*, ch. 9
May 27	*Ibid.*
May 28	*Reflections on the Psalms*, ch. 2
May 29	*Great Divorce*, ch. 8
May 30	*Ibid.*
May 31	*Ibid.*, ch. 9
June 1	*Perelandra*, ch. 9
June 2	'The Weight of Glory'
June 3	*Four Loves*, ch. 6
June 4	*Problem of Pain*, ch. 8
June 5	*Ibid.*
June 6	*Ibid.*
June 7	'The Weight of Glory'
June 8	*Four Loves*, ch. 1
June 9	*Ibid.*
June 10	*Ibid.*
June 11	*Problem of Pain*, ch. 4
June 12	*Four Loves*, ch. 3
June 13	*Ibid.*
June 14	*Ibid.*
June 15	*Ibid.*
June 16	*Ibid.*, ch. 4
June 17	*Ibid.*
June 18	*Ibid.*
June 19	*Ibid.*
June 20	*Ibid*
June 21	*Ibid.*
June 22	*Ibid.*
June 23	*Ibid.*
June 24	Ibid., ch. 5
June 25	*Ibid.*
June 26	*Ibid.*
June 27	*Ibid.*
June 28	*Ibid.*
June 29	'Fern-Seed and Elephants'
	Letters to Malcolm, ch. 2
June 30	*Four Loves*, ch. 5
July 1	*Ibid.*

July 2	*Ibid.*
July 3	'On Obstinacy in Belief'
July 4	*Four Loves*, ch. 5
July 5	*Ibid.*, ch. 6
July 6	*Ibid.*
July 7	*Ibid.*
July 8	*Ibid.*
July 9	*Ibid.*
July 10	*Ibid.*
July 11	*Ibid.*
July 12	'Two Ways with the Self'
July 13	*Ibid.*
July 14	*Ibid.*
July 15	Letter to Walter Hooper (30 November 1954)
July 16	'First and Second Things'
July 17	*Ibid.*
July 18	*Ibid.*
July 19	'Is Progress Possible?'
July 20	'Membership'
July 21	'Equality'
July 22	*Letters to an American Lady* (1 November 1954)
July 23	'Equality'
July 24	'Myth Became Fact'
July 25	*Letters to Malcolm*, ch. 11
July 26	'Screwtape Proposes a Toast'
July 27	*Ibid.*
July 28	*Screwtape Letters*, No. 5
July 29	*Miracles*, ch. 14
July 30	'Horrid Red Things'
July 31	*Letters to Malcolm*, ch. 16
August 1	'Meditation in a Toolshed'
August 2	*Ibid.*
August 3	*Ibid.*
August 4	*Ibid.*
August 5	*Ibid.*
August 6	*Miracles*, ch. 16
August 7	*Experiment in Criticism*, ch. 3
August 8	*Letters to Malcolm*, ch. 16
August 9	'Answers to Questions on Christianity'
August 10	*Letters* (1 April 1952)
August 11	*A Preface to 'Paradise Lost'*, ch. 3
August 12	*Letters to Malcolm*, ch. 1
August 13	*Ibid.*
August 14	'Membership'
August 15	*Ibid.*
August 16	*Ibid.*
August 17	*Ibid.*
August 18	*Ibid.*
August 19	*Ibid.*

August 20	*Ibid.*
August 21	*Ibid.*
August 22	*Ibid.*
August 23	*Ibid.*
August 24	Letter to Stuart Robertson (6 May 1962)
August 25	'Christianity and Literature'
August 26	*Ibid.*
August 27	*Ibid.*
August 28	*Problem of Pain,* ch. 6
August 29	'Christianity and Culture'
August 30	*Ibid.*
August 31	*Ibid.*
September 1	*Ibid.*
September 2	*Ibid.*
September 3	*Ibid.*
September 4	'Learning in War-Time'
September 5	*Ibid.*
September 6	*Mere Christianity,* Bk I, ch. 1
September 7	*Ibid.*
September 8	*Letters to Malcolm,* ch. 14
September 9	*Problem of Pain,* ch. 2
September 10	*Ibid.*
September 11	*Ibid.*
September 12	*Ibid.*
September 13	*Ibid.*
September 14	*Ibid.*
September 15	*Ibid.,* ch. 3
September 16	*Mere Christianity,* Bk II, ch. 3
September 17	*Ibid.*
September 18	*Screwtape Letters,* Preface to 1961 edition
September 19	*Mere Christianity,* Bk II, ch. 2
September 20	*A Preface to 'Paradise Lost',* ch. 13
September 21	*Letters to Malcolm,* ch. 13
September 22	*Problem of Pain,* ch. 5
September 23	*Ibid.*
September 24	*Ibid.,* ch. 6
September 25	*Ibid.*
September 26	*Ibid.*
September 27	*Ibid.*
September 28	*Ibid.*
September 29	*Miracles,* Appendix A
September 30	*Ibid.,* ch. 4
October 1	*Mere Christianity,* Bk I, ch. 1
October 2	*Ibid.*
October 3	*Ibid.,* Bk I, ch. 2
October 4	*Four Loves,* ch. 5
October 5	*Abolition of Man,* ch. I
October 6	*Ibid.,* ch. 2
October 7	'The Poison of Subjectivism'

October 8	*Mere Christianity,* Bk I, ch. 5
October 9	*Ibid.,* Bk II, ch. 1
October 10	'Is Theology Poetry?'
October 11	*Mere Christianity,* Bk I, ch. 4
October 12	*Miracles,* ch. 17
October 13	*Mere Christianity,* Bk II, ch. 2
October 14	*Ibid.*
October 15	*Ibid.*
October 16	*Screwtape Letters,* No. 7
October 17	*Mere Christianity,* Bk II, ch. 3
October 18	*Letters to Malcolm,* ch. 9
October 19	*Mere Christianity,* Bk II, ch. 3
October 20	*Ibid.*
October 21	*Ibid.*
October 22	*Reflections on the Psalms,* ch. 11
October 23	*Mere Christianity,* Bk II, ch. 4
October 24	*Ibid.*
October 25	*Ibid.,* Bk II, ch. 5
October 26	*Ibid.*
October 27	*Ibid.*
October 28	*They Stand Together* (10 January 1932)
October 29	*Mere Christianity,* Bk II, ch. 5
October 30	'Fern-Seed and Elephants'
October 31	*Mere Christianity,* Bk II, ch. 5
November 1	*Letters to Malcolm,* ch. 3
November 2	*Ibid.,* ch. 20
November 3	*Mere Christianity,* Bk IV, ch. I
November 4	*Ibid.*
November 5	*Ibid.,* Bk IV, ch. 2
November 6	*Ibid.*
November 7	*Letters to Malcolm,* ch. 4
November 8	*Mere Christianity, Bk IV, ch. 3*
November 9	*Ibid.*
November 10	*Ibid.*
November 11	*Ibid.*
November 12	*Miracles,* Appendix B
November 13	'The Efficacy of Prayer'
November 14	*Ibid.*
November 15	*Ibid.*
November 16	*Ibid.*
November 17	*Ibid.*
November 18	*Ibid.*
November 19	*Letters to Malcolm,* ch. 5
November 20	*Ibid.*
November 21	*Ibid.,* ch. 15
November 22	'On Church Music'
November 23	*Ibid.*
November 24	'Man or Rabbit?'
November 25	*Ibid.*

November 26   *Ibid.*
November 27   *Ibid.*
November 28   *Ibid.*
November 29   *Mere Christianity,* Bk III, ch. 12
November 30   *Ibid.,* Bk III ch. 10
December 1   *Ibid.,* Bk IV ch. 9
December 2   *Ibid.,* Bk IV ch. 5
December 3   *Ibid.*
December 4   *Ibid.*
December 5   *Ibid.*
December 6   *Ibid.*
December 7   Letter to Edward Dell (4 February 1949).
December 8   *Mere Christianity,* Bk IV, ch. 6
December 9   *Ibid.,* Bk IV, ch. 7
December 10   *Ibid.*
December 11   *Ibid.*
December 12   *Ibid.*
December 13   *Ibid.*
December 14   *Letters to Malcolm,* ch. 12
December 15   *Mere Christianity,* Bk IV, ch. 10
December 16   *Ibid.*
December 17   *Ibid.*
December 18   *Ibid.,* Bk IV, ch. 11
December 19   *Ibid.*
December 20   *Ibid.*
December 21   *Miracles,* ch. 15
December 22   'Myth Became Fact'
December 23   'Is Theology Poetry?'
December 24   *Ibid.*
December 25   *Letters to Malcolm,* ch. 13
December 26   *Letters* (c. October 1947)
December 27   *Problem of Pain,* ch. 7
December 28   *Ibid.,* ch. 10
December 29   *Ibid.*
December 30   *Ibid.*
December 31   *The Last Battle,* ch. 16

MOVABLE FASTS AND FEASTS

Ash Wednesday   'A Slip of the Tongue'
Maundy Thursday   *Letters to Malcolm,* ch. 19
Good Friday   *Four Loves,* ch. 6
Holy Saturday   *Miracles,* ch. 14
Easter Day   'The Grand Miracle'
The Ascension of the Lord *Miracles,* ch. 16
Pentecost   *Mere Christianity,* Bk IV, ch. 4
The Most Holy Trinity   *Ibid.,* Bk IV, ch. 2
The Body and Blood of Christ *Poems,* 'No Beauty We Could Desire

WORKS OF C.S. LEWIS QUOTED IN THIS BOOK

For details of all the published writings of C.S. Lewis, see the bibliography in *C. S. Lewis at the Breakfast Table and Other Reminiscences,* ed. James T. Como (New York: Macmillan 1979. London: Collins, 1980).

Some of the books listed below are collections of essays, but only those essays actually quoted in the book are mentioned here. American editions, except when listed separately (those numbered 10 and 16), are given in brackets. Place of publication is London or New York unless otherwise stated.

Collins Publishers of London now handle the titles originally published by The Centenary Press and Geoffrey Bles Ltd. Fount Paperbacks and Fontana Lions are part of Fontana, the paperback house of Collins.

1. *The Pilgrim's Regress: An Allegorical Apology for Christianity, Reason and Romanticism.* J.M. Dent, 1933; Sheed and Ward, 1935; Geoffrey Bles, 1943, with the author's new Preface on Romanticism, footnotes, and running headlines. [Sheed and Ward, 1944; Eerdmans, Grand Rapids, 1958]
   *Fount Paperbacks, 1977

2. *The Problem of Pain.* The Centenary Press, 1940. [Macmillan 1943]
   *Fount Paperbacks, 1977

3. *The Screwtape Letters.* Geoffrey Bles, 1942. [Macmillan, 1943]; reprinted with 'Screwtape Proposes a Toast' as *The Screwtape Letters and Screwtape Proposes a Toast,* with a new and additional Preface. Geoffrey Bles, 1961. [Macmillan, 1962]
   *Fount Paperbacks, 1977

4. *A Preface to 'Paradise Lost'.* Oxford University Press, 1942.

5. *Perelandra.* John Lane the Bodley Head, 1943. Also published as *Voyage to Venus (Perelandra),* Pan Books, 1953. [First title, Macmillan, 1944]

6. *The Abolition of Man: or Reflections on Education with Special Reference to the Teaching of English in the Upper Forms of Schools.* Oxford University Press, 1943; Geoffrey Bles: The Centenary Press, 1946. [Macmillan, 1947]
   *Fount Paperbacks, 1978

7. 'Equality', *The Spectator,* CLXXI (27 August 1943), p 192.

8. *The Great Divorce: A Dream.* Geoffrey Bles: The Centenary Press, 1945. [Macmillan, 1946]
   *Fount Paperbacks, 1972

9. *Miracles: A Preliminary Study.* Geoffrey Bles: The Centenary Press, 1947. [Macmillan, 1947] With revision of Chapter III, Collins, 1960. [Macmillan, 1978]
   *Fount Paperbacks, 1977

10. *The Weight of Glory and Other Addresses.* New York: Macmillan, 1949. Revised and Expanded Edition, ed. Walter Hooper, 1980. ('The Weight of Glory', 'Learning in War-Time', 'Transposition', 'Is Theology Poetry?', 'Membership ', 'On Forgiveness', 'A Slip of the Tongue')

11. *Mere Christianity: A revised and amplified edition, with a new introduction, of the three books 'Broadcast Talks', 'Christian Behaviour', and 'Beyond Personality'.* Geoffrey Bles, 1952. [Macmillan, 1952]
   *Fount Paperbacks, 1977

12. *Surprised by Joy: The Shape of My Early Life.* Geoffrey Bles, 1952. [Harcourt, Brace & World, 1956]
   *Fount Paperbacks, 1977

13. *The Last Battle.* The Bodley Head, 1956. Fontana Lions paperback, 1980. [Macmillan, 1956]

14. *Reflections on the Psalms.* Geoffrey Bles, 1958. [Harcourt, Brace & World, 1958] *Fount Paperbacks, 1977

15. *The Four Loves.* Geoffrey Bles, 1960. [Harcourt, Brace & World, 1958] *Fount Paperbacks, 1977

16. *The World's Last Night and Other Essays.* New York: Harcourt, Brace & World, 1960. ('The Efficacy of Prayer', 'On Obstinacy in Belief', 'Screwtape Proposes a Toast', 'Good Work and Good Works', 'Religion and Rocketry', 'The World's Last Night')

17. *An Experiment in Criticism.* Cambridge University Press, Cambridge, 1961.

18. *Letters to Malcolm: Chiefly on Prayer.* Geoffrey Bles, 1964. (Harcourt, Brace & World, 1964)

    *Fount Paperbacks, 1977

19. *Poems.* Ed. Walter Hooper. Geoffrey Bles, 1964. [Harcourt, Brace & World, 1965]

20. *Screwtape Proposes a Toast and Other Pieces.* Ed. Jocelyn Gibb. Collins, 1965. ('Screwtape Proposes a Toast', 'On Obstinacy in Belief', 'Good Work and Good Works', 'Is Theology Poetry?', 'Transposition', 'The Weight of Glory', 'A Slip of the Tongue')
    *Fount Paperbacks, 1977

21. *Letters of C.S. Lewis.* Ed. W.H. Lewis. Geoffrey Bles, 1966. [Harcourt, Brace & World, 1966]

22. *Christian Reflections.* Ed. Walter Hooper. Geoffrey Bles, 1967. [Eerdmans, Grand Rapids, 1967] ('Christianity and Literature', 'Christianity and Culture', 'The Poison of Subjectivism', 'On Church Music', 'The Psalms', 'Fern-Seed and Elephants' (As 'Modem Theology and Biblical Criticism' in the USA), 'The Seeing Eye')
    *Fount Paperbacks, 1981

23. *Letters to an American Lady.* Ed. Clyde S. Kilby. Hodder & Stoughton, 1969. [Eerdmans, Grand Rapids, 1967]

24. *Selected Literary Essays.* Ed. Walter Hooper. Cambridge University Press, Cambridge, 1969. ('The Literary Impact of the Authorized Version')

25. *Undeception: Essays on Theology and Ethics.* Ed. Walter Hooper. Geoffrey Bles, 1971. [As *God in the Dock: Essays on Theology and Ethics,* Eerdmans, Grand Rapids, 1970] ('Miracles', 'Dogma and the Universe', 'Answers to Questions on Christianity', 'Myth Became Fact', 'Horrid Red Things', 'The Grand Miracle', 'Christian Apologetics', 'Man or Rabbit?', 'On the Transmission of Christianity', 'Miserable Offenders'. 'Religion Without Dogma?', 'Some Thoughts', 'What Are We to Make of Jesus Christ?', 'Dangers of National Repentance', 'Two Ways with the Self', 'On the Reading of Old Books', 'Meditation in a Toolshed', 'Modern Translations of the Bible', 'First and Second Things', 'Is Progress Possible?')

26. *Fern-Seed and Elephants and Other Essays on Christianity.* Ed. Walter Hooper. Fount Paperbacks, 1975. ('Membership', 'Learning in War-Time', 'On Forgiveness', 'The World's Last Night', 'Religion and Rocketry', 'The Efficacy of Prayer', 'Fern-Seed and Elephants')

27. *God in the Dock: Essays on Theology.* Ed. Walter Hooper. Fount Paperbacks, 1979. ('Miracles', 'Dogma and the Universe', 'Myth Became Fact', 'The Grand Miracle', 'Man or Rabbit?', 'What Are We to Make of Jesus Christ?')

28. *They Stand Together: The Letters of C.S. Lewis to Arthur Greeves* (1914–1963). Ed. Walter Hooper. Collins, 1979. [Macmillan, 1979]

29. *Of This and Other Worlds.* Ed. Walter Hooper. Collins, 1982 and Fount Paperbacks, 1984. [As *On Stories and Other Essays on Literature,* Harcourt Brace Jovanovich, 1982] ('On Three Ways of Writing for Children')